GROWTH IN AGREEMENT

*Reports and Agreed Statements
of Ecumenical Conversations
on a World Level*

edited by
Harding Meyer
and
Lukas Vischer

PAULIST PRESS, New York/Ramsey
WORLD COUNCIL OF CHURCHES, Geneva

Faith and Order Paper no. 108

Library of Congress
Catalog Card Number: 82-61740

ISBN: 0-8091-2497-1 (Paulist)
ISBN: 2-8254-0679-1 (World Council of Churches)
Published by Paulist Press
545 Island Road, Ramsey, N.J. 07446
and
World Council of Churches
1211 Geneva 20, Switzerland

Printed and bound in the United States of America

Contents

GENERAL INTRODUCTION

The decade of the 1970's which lies behind us was a time when churches reached a number of new and pioneering theological agreements. The wealth of documents collected in this volume speaks for itself. One might say these past years have been a decade of steady growth in ecumenical consensus. While the process has not yet come to an end, it is doubtful whether it will continue, or indeed whether it *can* continue, with the same intensity and productivity in the years ahead. Be it as it may, the time has now come to bring together in one volume the many documents published in different places around the world in journals, symposia and church publications or press services in order to give a first general survey and much-needed global view of what has been achieved so far.

The number of such documents to be considered is, of course, so large that only a selection of them could be included in the present volume. Our choice has, therefore, deliberately been restricted to the group of texts relating to *agreements reached in inter-confessional doctrinal dialogues at world level.* Results achieved in local or regional dialogue have not been included here. As far as interconfessional dialogues at world level are concerned, however, this volume can claim to be substantially complete.[1]

At the end of the book an important text of a rather different nature has been included, the three statements on Baptism, Eucharist and Ministry, issued in 1974 by the Commission on Faith and Order. These statements represent an attempt to summarize what all churches can say in common on these subjects. It was, of course, out of the question to include all the texts published by the Commission on Faith and Order relating to the controversies of the past.[2] The three statements referred to here are, however, of special importance because of their closeness in time and content to the interconfessional conversations of recent years.[3]

I. *The New Role of Bilateral Dialogues between the Confessions*

Bilateral interconfessional talks within the ecumenical movement gained in importance during the Sixties. Bilateral dialogues between churches had, of course, taken place before that time; for example, the dialogues between Anglicans and Orthodox, Anglicans and Old Catholics, Old Catholics and Orthodox, all of which had important results. On the whole, however, the ecumenical movement of this century has been guided by a different concept. Its aim has been to bring the churches together into a preliminary communion and to advance together, in that communion, towards the goal of full unity. This was the concept behind the founding of the World Council of Churches, in 1948. In the Sixties, however, bilateral conversations between churches of different traditions began to play a bigger role and today the network of these dialogues is such that it has become very difficult to keep track of developments and results in all of them.[4]

2

What were the reasons and motivations prompting this new emphasis on bilateral dialogue, and what is the special character of such dialogues? The two questions are closely related.

In the first place, it must be stressed that the basis for this new development was laid by the ecumenical endeavours of previous decades. The first thing the ecumenical movement had to do was to create a congenial atmosphere for constructive encounter between the churches. The great conferences between the two world wars and, later, the World Council of Churches made important contributions to this process for they enabled the churches not only to overcome their animosities towards one another, but also to bear common witness on many issues. They deepened the churches' awareness of their universal calling. They helped the churches to see more clearly that their fellowship in Christ transcends barriers of nation, state, race, or culture and reminded them of their duty to make this fellowship visible in their lives. Theological discussions, particularly those conducted in the framework of the Commission on Faith and Order, brought to light important basic theological agreements. The results of the earlier multilateral dialogues on baptism, the relationship of scripture and tradition, and the Eucharist, for instance, are of paramount importance in this respect. In a sense, the growing ecumenical movement formed the framework for new and direct encounter between the churches. The dialogue between the European Lutheran and Reformed Churches, begun in the Fifties, is a striking example of this new kind of encounter.

The intensification of bilateral interconfessional dialogues at world level coincided with the end of the Second Vatican Council. This was no accident. For when the Roman Catholic Church decided to participate actively in the ecumenical movement, this brought into the dialogue a Church which sees itself as a spiritually and structurally united, worldwide communion with a strong conviction of its special identity as the Church of Christ. If one also remembers the numerical size of the Roman Catholic Church, it will be immediately obvious that the ecumenical movement could not fail to be affected by its participation. The Roman Catholic Church entered into close contact with the World Council of Churches and a Joint Working Group was formed as early as 1965. But, at the same time, it sought to establish contacts with individual church Traditions and in the course of the following years several Joint Commissions were set up. The most willing response to this new constellation within the ecumenical movement came in particular from churches which themselves have a fairly strong sense of world-wide unity in doctrine, worship and practice.

II.   *The Principal Features of Bilateral Dialogues*

In addition to being dialogues at world level, that is, between worldwide church communions, these discussions have the following principal features in common:

1.   With the exception of the dialogue between the Lutheran World Federation, the World Alliance of Reformed Churches and the Roman

Catholic Church on 'The Theology of Marriage and the Problem of Mixed Marriages', they are *bilateral,* i.e. they take place between two partners. One of the main reasons for this is the fact that both partners are conscious of their own 'identity' or confessional character which can undoubtedly be given fuller expression in bilateral dialogue than in a multilateral meeting.

2. They are *official* church dialogues in that they are officially authorized by the respective church authorities by whom delegates are appointed and to whom the results must be directly submitted.

3. Most of these dialogues are essentially concerned with *doctrinal* matters, their aim being to overcome the theological and ecclesiological divergences inherited from the past and still existing today, and to elaborate and develop agreements. Even when discussions have dealt with the more practical problems of putting fellowship into practice in the life of the churches, they have been based on previous doctrinal conversations.

The fact that ecumenical dialogues of this kind developed can ultimately be traced to certain convictions. Without denying the value of multilateral ecumenical encounter and endeavour, it was nevertheless felt that a different kind of ecumenical dialogue might offer definite advantages and possibilities

—   The *bilateral* method of dialogue allows for thorough and detailed study of specific issues which separate two traditions and which may at times have led to mutual condemnation. But it also makes it possible to bring out more effectively the elements they have in common and which have been preserved in both traditions, despite their separation.

—   The *official* nature of the discussions helps in reaching results which carry authority in the churches, and thereby contributes to the important process of reception of ecumenical agreements in the life of the churches.

—   The fact that dialogues have hitherto concentrated mostly on questions of faith and order reflects the conviction that the theological differences rooted in the historical heritage of the churches are still operative today. They cannot, therefore, be ignored, but must be taken up and worked through if a strong and lasting fellowship is to be established.

III. *The Need for Interaction between Bilateral and Multilateral Dialogues*

Concern has occasionally been expressed that bilateral dialogues — especially those conducted at world level — might lead to a reinforcement of confessionalism, thus hindering the achievement of unity in local situations, or that they do not concentrate sufficiently on the urgent tasks facing the churches at present in regard to their common witness and service to the world. These are questions which have to be taken seriously, though they do not detract from the value and justification of bilateral dialogues.

It is, however, important to realize that the apparent advantages and opportunities of bilateral as opposed to multilateral dialogues can also, in some ways, constitute certain limits, even dangers.

Most of the bilateral conversations sprang up in response to specific challenges. This was a highly diversified phenomenon, not depending on any over-all strategy which might, for example, have ensured coordination between them. There was, therefore, a danger that the different dialogues would take place in isolation from the wider ecumenical scene and movement, that the results of the various individual talks would bear no relation to one another, indeed might even be conflicting, so that rapprochement between two ecumenical partners could lead to growing estrangement from other ecumenical partners.

In the face of such dangers, it cannot be emphasized enough that the ecumenical endeavour is indivisible, even though encounter may take place in a variety of ways, for instance, in multilateral or bilateral conversations. It is, therefore, of paramount importance to ensure proper communication and interaction both between the various bilateral conversations and between them and multilateral dialogues.

The need for this is now generally recognized so that, as a rule, multilateral and bilateral ecumenical efforts are no longer seen as vying with one another. Rather, the specific opportunities and advantages of each form of dialogue are appreciated and they are considered to be complementary.

There can be no doubt that effective and fruitful interaction already exists between multilateral and bilateral dialogues; this is evident on the personal level, in the participation of individuals in both types of dialogue, in the topics and subject matter discussed and also extends to the study processes and the results achieved.

We have already pointed out the extent to which the earlier multilateral dialogues, especially those conducted within the framework of the Commission on Faith and Order, acted as pacemakers for the subsequent bilateral conversations. They prepared the ground for the more official church bilateral dialogues which might otherwise all too easily have produced 'bilateral confrontation' rather than real encounter. Conversely, for some time now, we have been aware of the increasing input from bilateral conversations in studies and study papers of the Commission on Faith and Order (e.g. on the eucharist and the ministry) so that, today, multilateral efforts are increasingly indebted to bilateral conversations.

This interaction needs to be developed still further, however. An important step in this direction was the founding, in 1978, of the 'Forum on Bilateral Conversations' in which participants in multilaterals are also involved, mainly by way of the Commission and the Secretariat on Faith and Order.

At the first Forum (1978) it was already noted that 'both types of interchurch conversations, the . . . bilaterals and the . . . multilaterals are complementary to one another within the ecumenical movement'.[5] At the second Forum in 1979, which dealt in detail with the results and agreed statements of previous bilateral discussions, this conviction was again endorsed and confirmed. The Report stated, for example: "In the process which led to these statements, the particular bilateral dialogues have, to an increasing degree, taken into account other bilateral as well as multilateral conversations. There has also been an interaction between the international and local, regional and national inter-church conversations. This is often reflected in the texts themselves by explicit references to, or quotations from, other agreed statements (see, for example, the Roman Catholic/Lutheran document 'The Eucharist')".[6]

This shows not only that there are in fact scarcely any 'pure', i.e. isolated bilateral conversations; it also shows how helpful the reference to other bilateral and multilateral dialogues can be. Thus, for example, the Reformed/Roman Catholic conversations ('The Presence of Christ in Church and World') arrived at a valuable understanding of the Eucharist which is bound to have positive repercussions on Lutheran/Reformed conversations and relationships in future. Similarly, if as planned, the Anglican/Roman Catholic conversations take up the problem of justification by faith they may find it helpful to draw upon the findings of the Lutheran/Roman Catholic dialogue.

These efforts towards effective interaction between the many and varied dialogues must at all costs be continued and intensified. With this in mind the Report of the Second Forum on Bilateral Conversations (1979) stresses: "In order to maintain the specific advantages of the bilateral approach and, at the same time, to avoid a lack of coherence between the individual conversations and agreements, bilateral dialogues ought to be carried through with constant attention both to the wider multilateral perspective and to the other bilaterals."[7]

In order to further this "vital interaction between bilateral and multilateral conversations and agreements" the Forum made a series of suggestions which require urgent attention. The process could, for instance, be furthered by:

— receiving and incorporating the findings of other bilateral and multilateral dialogues on the same subject as broadly as possible (cross-references, quotations)

— opening up, as far as suitable and depending on the subject matter, a bilateral dialogue by including further partners (e.g. the participation of the WARC in the dialogue on marriage and mixed marriages originally planned as a conversation between Roman Catholics and Lutherans only)

— by inviting consultants from other bilateral and multilateral conversations to make a specific contribution (lecture, paper) where the subject matter or a particular stage in discussion makes this advisable (e.g.

Anglican or Orthodox contributions could have been useful at a certain stage of the conversation on marriage and mixed marriages between Roman Catholics, Reformed and Lutherans)
— taking up the discussion on a particular subject which has obvious implications for many or all Christian churches in a multilateral conversation (e.g. discussion on the *filioque* clause and the issue of marriage
and mixed marriages)
— joining the efforts of multilateral and bilateral conversations in
developing a common confession of faith (cf. the studies begun by the
Faith and Order Commission)".[8]

IV.   *The Aim of Bilateral Dialogues and the Reception of Their Results*

"However varied the specific definitions of the purposes of bilateral
dialogues may be, they share the general assumption that dialogue is
directed towards reaching a consensus."[9] And this idea of consensus is
more clearly defined by the criterion as to whether "a particular divergence
or conflict is of such a grievous nature that it prevents ecclesial fellowship
or not".[10]

The aim of bilateral conversations is, therefore, to reach a theological
agreement which, although it may not necessarily eliminate all differences,
goes far enough towards overcoming the existing differences to allow ecclesial fellowship to result. Thus the ultimate purpose of all bilateral
dialogues is not theological consensus merely for the sake of theological
consensus or general agreement, but theological consensus for the sake of
church unity. These dialogues thus have an in-built dynamic which does
not stop short with the elaboration of a theological consensus but presses
forward towards the realization of a living ecclesial fellowship. The official character of the dialogues accentuates and strengthens this dynamic
progression. This is apparent in the documents emerging from such
dialogues. Again and again they ask about the consequences of the
agreements they have reached for the living fellowship of the churches, indicating possibilities or even making recommendations concerning, for instance, eucharistic fellowship, mutual recognition of ministries, or the
revision of church regulations relating to the problem of mixed marriages.

In this way, the bilateral dialogues constantly point beyond
themselves to a stage where the principal aim is no longer the reaching of
consensus but translation of these theological agreements into practice in
the living fellowship of the churches.

We are actually speaking here of two phases, distinct from one
another, yet closely interwoven from the very beginning. Clearly, during
the early years, the efforts to overcome theological and ecclesiological
divergences and to reach consensus or convergence had priority. But very
early on, the inherent dynamic of the conversations could be felt, pushing
on towards the conversion of consensus into actual fellowship. The latter
half of the 70's was already clearly a "period of transition" during which

"two phases overlapped: the still on-going quest for theological agreements and convergences on the one hand, and the endeavour to 'convert' these theological agreements into ecclesial fellowship or communion, on the other".[1] There can hardly be any doubt that, if we do not want simply to mark time, our primary task in the years to come must indeed be the implementation of fellowship on the basis of the consensus reached, a process which has come to be known as 'reception' of the results of the dialogues in our churches.

The notion of 'reception' points, however, to a field of work of such scale and diversity that we have scarcely begun to grasp all the problems involved. At all events, the problem of the effective *communication* of the results of the dialogues is only one small, albeit an extremely important, part of the immense task lying ahead of us.

At least as important is that we should attain greater clarity and agreement on our *conception of the kind of unity we are seeking*.[12] It is of the utmost importance for ecumenical motivation whether the ecumenical aim is swathed in a nebulous general desire for unity or whether it is clearly defined, at least in basic outline. The form and direction we give our ecumenical endeavour depend very much on how we ourselves conceive of the unity we are seeking: whether, for example, we see it merely as a 'spiritual unity' or 'fellowship in action', or as a unity based on theological agreement and taking shape according to specific structures: whether it is a fellowship in which the variety of existing traditions is preserved, or a communion in which these traditions are merged in an organic union; whether we place the emphasis on unity 'in each place' or on the realization of a more universal church unity, and so on.

A crucial element in the process of reception will be for the results of the dialogues to be given the *authoritative character* in the churches they have hitherto lacked. So long as this lack of authority persists, it will always be possible for people to ignore the results of the dialogues. But how can these results be given the necessary 'authority' to make them binding on our churches? The very fact that the churches continue to think very differently on what constitutes the 'authority' of teaching and witness and about how it is arrived at, demonstrates the complexity of the problem.[13]

Closely connected with the problem of authority is the task of involving *local congregations and their pastors* in an ecumenical commitment which is not confined to small groups and which goes further than merely a general, reciprocal feeling of tolerance. What this costs in terms of patience, time and effort can be learned from the church union negotiations in which the process of 'education for union' in the individual congregations is always one of the most decisive but also the most protracted phases in the whole process of unification.

It is here, at the local level, that the problem of the close *interrelation between bilateral and multilateral ecumenical efforts* and the need for interaction between them again arises. As a rule, the Christians in a particular region or country are divided into several — not only two — church groups or traditions. In the process of reception of the results of bilateral dialogues and their translation into living fellowship, this largely multilateral ecumenical situation at the local level will have to be taken into account.

Also in the local situation, the significance of the so-called non-theological — or better, perhaps — *non-doctrinal factors* becomes apparent, whether these be historical, cultural, social, psychological or economic in character. While we are generally able to identify and analyse these factors fairly quickly, how do we set about overcoming them when they have a divisive effect and hinder the reception of the agreements? This is another problem to which there is no quick answer.

Effective communication of ecumenical insights, how to remedy the lack of authority of agreements reached, clarification in regard to the conception and models of unity, involvement of the local congregation and intensification of local ecumenical commitment, the comprehension and overcoming of 'non-doctrinal' factors of disunity — all these are questions which have been with us for a long time and which have been, and still are, the subject of numerous studies and investigations. There can hardly be any doubt, however, that the emphasis of future ecumenical endeavour must be in that area of issues which can be placed under the heading of 'reception'. The present volume will, we hope, lead into this task.

* * *

The following documents of dialogues are reproduced in their entirety, mostly with their prefaces as well whenever these have something to add about the course of the discussions or the origin and weight of the subsequent statements of agreement.

For a better understanding of the texts, it is often helpful to see how the dialogue in question originated and developed. This is the purpose of the short "historical introductions" which usually precede the documents and are the responsibility of the editors of this volume. Such "historical introductions" are omitted where the document itself gives a description of the origins and development of the conversations. For a more complete view of the background and the development of the individual dialogues we should like to refer once more to the publication of Nils Ehrenström and to the bibliography edited by the Centro Pro Unione.

The Index was drawn up with the help of Ms. Alice Heyler, of the Strasbourg Institute, and Mr. Stephen Cranford (Louisville, USA), formerly of the Secretariat for Faith and Order, Geneva. The editors wish to express their sincere thanks to them, particularly to Mr. Cranford who also contributed to this volume in many other respects.

Strasbourg — Geneva
October 1983   HARDING MEYER   LUKAS VISCHER

Notes

1. There are two bilateral dialogues on the world level which have only been recently begun: the dialogue between the Disciples of Christ and the Roman Catholic Church, initiated in September 1977 and the dialogue between the Lutheran World Federation and the World Methodist Council, initiated in December 1977. Since they have not yet produced a final report the results of these dialogues could not be included in this volume.

2. A more complete collection of these texts is available in: A Documentary History of the Faith and Order Movement. Ed. Lukas Vischer, St. Louis. Mo., 1963.

3. The texts were sent to the churches for their reactions in 1975 and are now being revised in the light of their comments.

4. See the survey and description of the various interconfessional bilateral dialogues in: N. Ehrenström, 'Confessions in Dialogue', A survey on Bilateral Conversations among World Confessional Families 1959-1974, Third revised and enlarged edition, WCC, Geneva, 1975 (Faith and Order Paper No. 74); also: J. Puglisi: A Workbook of Bibliographies of Interchurch Dialogues, Centro Pro Unione, Rome, 1978; and: A Continuing Bibliography for the Study of Interchurch Dialogues, in: Centro Pro Unione Bi-Annual Bulletin, Spring 1979 & 1980. The Centro Pro Unione plans to edit in 1981 a revised and complete bibliography of international and national interconfessional dialogues with supplements in the spring of each following year. Available at the Centro Pro Unione.

5. Report from the First Forum on Bilateral Conversations, FO/78:5 (April 1978),p. 2.

6. Report from the Second Forum on Bilateral Conversations, Faith and Order Paper No. 96, WCC, Geneva 1979, p. 12

7. Ibid.

8. Ibid., 13

9. N. Ehrenström, Confessions in Dialogue, Geneva 1975, p. 131.

10. Ibid., p. 133

11. H. Meyer, The Future of Bilaterals and the Bilaterals of the Future, in: Lutheran World 1975/3, p. 228.

12. Cf. for example, the reflections of the First Forum on Bilateral Conversations, 1978 (FO/78:5, particularly chapter III: Concepts of Unity). These reflections are closely related to the studies carried on within the Commission on Faith and Order (cf. Sharing in One Hope, Commission on Faith and Order, Bangalore 1978, Faith and Order Paper No. 92, pp. 235-242: Reflections on the Common Goal) and to the discussions among the Christian World Communions or World Confessional Families (cf.: the "Discussion Paper": The Ecumenical Role of the World Confessional Families in the One Ecumenical Movement, December 1974, esp. chapter III: "Confessional Identity and Reconciled Diversity" and chapter IV: "Reconciled Diversity and Church Unity"; and the Report of a Consultation between the World Council of Churches and the World Confessional Families, October 1978, esp. chapter A: "The Unity of the Church").

13. Cf. for example, the study of the Commission on Faith and Order on "How Does the Church Teach Authoritatively Today?" in: The Ecumenical Review, XXXI/I, January 1979, p. 77ff.

ANGLICAN-LUTHERAN CONVERSATION

Pullach Report 1972

1972
Pullach Report

I. INTRODUCTION

(1) In spite of occasional contacts and a common awareness of great areas of affinity of doctrine, worship and church life, Anglican and Lutheran Churches have in the past lived largely in separation and in relative isolation from one another. One painful manifestation of their separate existence has been the absence of *communio in sacris* between Lutheran and Anglican Churches (apart from that enabled by regulations concerning different grades of intercommunion between the Church of England and various Scandinavian Lutheran churches).

(2) A new situation has been created by more frequent encounters in recent times, both between churches and individual members of the two Communions: the recognition of new, converging tendencies in their biblical and theological thinking; the realization of their common task of mission and service in the modern world; more frequent but still responsible acts of intercommunion; and the encounter of Lutheran and Anglican Churches in union negotiations.

(3) This situation demands not only better mutual knowledge and understanding and closer cooperation, it calls at the same time for a reconsideration of the official relationships between Anglican and Lutheran Churches leading to more appropriate expressions of our common faith, witness and service.

(4) This new situation, and in particular the involvement of Lutheran and Anglican Churches in union negotiations, led to the proposal of official conversations between the Lutheran World Federation and the Anglican Communion.

(5) In 1963 the LWF Commission on World Mission passed a resolution requesting the setting up of a study committee for the preparation of worldwide Anglican-Lutheran conversations. This proposal received the endorsement of the LWF Commission on Theology in the same year.

(6) After further deliberations and following a decision of the Executive Committee of the LWF in 1967 contacts with the Archbishop of Canterbury were established which resulted in the appointment of an *ad hoc* Anglican-Lutheran Committee by the Archbishop of Canterbury and the General Secretary of the LWF. This Committee met in Berlin (November, 1967) and elaborated a "Memorandum". This Memorandum proposed that the Lambeth Conference and the Executive Committee of the LWF should authorize "the appointment of a representative 'Anglican-Lutheran Commission' ". This recommendation was accepted by the Lambeth Conference 1968. The Executive Committee of the LWF, meeting shortly after the Lambeth Conference, considered the Memorandum too and arrived at the same decision.

(7) In the Memorandum of 1967 it was stated that the "Anglican-Lutheran Commission" should: "(a) conduct a worldwide Anglican-Lutheran dialog; (b) consider other contacts and areas for practical cooperation; (c) report regularly to their respective appropriate authorities". This was accepted by the Lambeth Conference and by the LWF Executive Committee in 1968.

(8) The Lambeth Conference recommended (taking up a suggestion of the Memorandum) that the "conversations should begin by discussing the general mission of the church in the world and only afterwards proceed to questions of doctrine and order, though major issues should be faced as soon as possible". The Lambeth Conference asked also that these conversations "should be held on four occasions over a two-year period". The LWF Executive Committee concurred in this recommendation. Because of these limitations of time, the conversations had to be concentrated upon some fundamental doctrinal points, but always in the context of the general mission of the church in the world.

(9) After four meetings (at Oxford, September 1970; Légumkloster, Denmark, March-April 1971; Lantana, Florida, January 1972, and Munich, April 1972) our group completed its work insofar as it was possible in the time given to us. We submit our report including its recommendations to our respective authorities. We are aware of its limitations. We have not attempted to say everything that should or could be said in common.

(10) We have attempted to articulate lines of thought which are already accepted in much of the past and present thinking of our Churches. This implies that we tried to be as representative as possible of the traditions and present developments in our Churches. We hope that the articulation of current tendencies may itself advance and extend our ecumenical unity.

(11) We are aware that in every ecumenical conversation the delegates from both sides develop an increasingly friendly relationship; understanding develops, deep spiritual fellowship grows, and with it a strong desire to express the maximum agreement possible. Those they represent are not going through the same experiences, and there is always a danger that both sides, or at least one, will prove to be so far ahead of their constituency, that little good will come of the encounter.

(12) This is particularly true in the matter of language. Phrases have come into currency and have worked their way into the life and thought of Lutheran and Anglican Churches. In some cases the words correspond to those used on the other side and mean much the same thing. Sometimes the words sound similar, but mean something different. Sometimes the words are very strange and foreign in the ears of another tradition in the life of the church.

(13) In conversations like ours each side becomes familiar with the language of the other. Sometimes particular phrases become expressive of

particular points of agreement or disagreement, and thus a special language makes articulate to the participants the spiritual or intellectual processes in which they have been engaged. Their constituencies have not become familiar with this language.

(14)   We therefore think that our report needs a positive effort of understanding on the part of both our Churches and we have tried to initiate this process by adding to the report personal statements written by the two chairmen of the delegations. We believe that all that we are saying and recommending in our report will only be relevant if our Churches make serious attempts to grow closer together at all levels of church life.

(15)   Our conversations were not held in an ecumenical vacuum. Our Churches are involved in conversations and negotiations with other churches. We trust that our work will contribute to the comprehensive movement toward greater unity which is apparent among all Christian churches.

(16)   Our report is now submitted to the authorities which have appointed us and we hope that those authorities will transmit our report to the individual Churches for their consideration and action. We ask all who receive this report to base their decisions not only on the human efforts which we have made but on their trust in the one, living Lord of the church, who wills our unity and who will judge us one day according to our obedience to his will and command.

II.   THEOLOGICAL CONSIDERATIONS

A.   SOURCES OF AUTHORITY

a)   Scripture

(17)   The Anglican and the Lutheran Churches hold that it is Jesus Christ, God and Man, born, crucified, risen and ascended for the salvation of mankind, in whom all Scriptures find their focus and fulfilment. They are at one in accepting the Holy Scriptures of the Old and New Testaments as the sufficient, inspired, and authoritative record and witness, prophetic and apostolic, to God's revelation in Jesus Christ.

(18)   Both Churches hold that through the proclamation of the gospel and the administration of the sacraments, based on the same Scriptures and empowered by the Holy Spirit, Christ is speaking to us and is active amongst us today, calling us to live and serve in his name.

(19)   Both Churches hold that nothing should be preached, taught or ordered in the church which contradicts the word of God as it is proclaimed in Holy Scripture.

(20)   Within both Churches different attitudes exist concerning the nature of inspiration and the ways and means of interpreting the Scriptures, and these attitudes run across the denominational boundaries.

(21)   Both Churches agree in stressing the need and responsibility for a

continuing interpretation of the biblical texts in order to communicate the gospel of salvation to all men in different times and changing circumstances.

(22)   They teach that the whole church, and especially the ministry of the church, has received the responsibility for guarding all proclamation and interpretation from error by guiding, admonishing and judging and by formulating doctrinal statements, the biblical witness always being the final authority and court of appeal.

b)   *Creeds*

(23)   The Anglican and the Lutheran Churches are at one in accepting officially the Apostles' and Nicene Creeds. These Creeds are used regularly in their worship and in their teaching. They recognize the Athanasian Creed as giving a true exposition of the trinitarian faith.

(24)   They believe that these Creeds are authoritative summaries and safeguards of the Christian faith. Their authority is established in the first place by their faithful witness and interpretation of the biblical message, and in the second place by their acceptance and use in the Early Church. They, therefore, hold a unique place among all confessional documents.

(25)   The acceptance of these Creeds implies agreement between both Communions on the fundamental trinitarian and christological dogmas.

c)   *Confessional formularies*

(26)   The Lutheran and the Anglican Churches developed and accepted a number of confessional documents at the time of the Reformation. There are a great number of direct historical and theological connections and similarities between these documents.

(27)   They did not regard these confessions as "foundation documents" of a new church, but rather as means of safeguarding and witnessing to the faith of the church at all times.

(28)   They regarded these confessions as expositions of their final authority, namely Holy Scripture. The confessions were aimed at a renewal and reformation of the church making it as inclusive as possible, but guarding against certain errors and misguided developments in late medieval Roman Catholicism on the one hand, and against "enthusiastic" and extreme reforming movements on the other.

(29)   On the Lutheran side the confessions of the Reformation still occupy officially a prominent place in theological thinking and training, in catechetical teaching, in the constitutions of the individual Lutheran churches and at the ordination of pastors. They serve as a link between the churches of the Lutheran family.

(30)   On the Anglican side the 39 Articles are universally recognized as expressing a significant phase in a formative period of Anglican thought and life. The significance attached to them today in Anglican circles varies between Anglican churches and between groups within Anglican churches. On

the other hand the Book of Common Prayer has for a long time served as a confessional document in a liturgical setting. Though liturgical revisions vary among Anglican churches, the influence of the Prayer Book tradition is still evident.

(31)   Since confessional formularies are not a mark of the church their significance lies in their expression of the living confession to the living Lord. Different approaches to the authority of these formularies are possible between Communions so long as they share a living confession which is a faithful response to the living word of God as proclaimed in Holy Scripture.

d)   Tradition

(32)   The Anglican and the Lutheran Churches are at one in regarding tradition as a normal element in the life of the church.

(33)   By the word "tradition" is meant the way in which the apostolic witness (i.e. "tradition") has been transmitted from one generation to the next, from one culture to the other. By the word "traditions" are meant the ways in which the churches have developed their thinking, worship, common life and attitudes to the world.

(34)   Both Churches agree that all traditions are secondary to tradition and that they, therefore, have to be tested by that tradition. If they are in accordance with and expressions of this ultimate standard they are to be regarded as important means of continuity. In order to serve this purpose they should never become petrified, but remain open for change and renewal.

(35)   The attitude toward the tradition, especially over against the tradition of the Early Church has found within both Churches different expressions at different times and in different schools of thought.

(36)   Anglicans do not make frequent use of the word "tradition" except in a phrase like churches of the Anglican tradition, which is virtually a synonym for the "Anglican Communion". But during the Reformation period (which for Anglicans extended from 1534 to 1662) they called on the teaching of the Early Fathers in their apologies against both Roman Catholics and Puritans.

(37)   A positive appreciation of the patristic tradition, already apparent in the sixteenth century, became more marked in the seventeenth, and made its influence felt in Anglican spirituality, ecclesiology, and liturgy – the Scottish liturgy of 1637 is an example of this. The Oxford Movement of the nineteenth century saw a further phase in the appropriation of both patristic and medieval traditions, and a new sense of the unbroken continuity of the church's history.

(38)   At all times, however, there has been a sharply critical attitude to tradition if this implied an additional source for historical data supplementing the history given in the gospels, or a source for a "secret" doctrine additional to that given in the scriptural witness.

(39)   In modern times there has appeared a desire to sit lightly to "the traditions of men" if they were felt to obscure "the good news for the new age".

(40)   Lutheran theology in the sixteenth century considered ancient church tradition as a kind of contemporary source of Christian truth and as a proof for its own continuity. At the same time the Reformation demand for a scripturally-based critical study of the Fathers was the starting point for a nascent patrology.

(41)   Within Lutheran Church and theology in later centuries early Christianity was not primarily of dogmatic relevance but was studied rather as an important ethical authority witnessing to the practice of the Christian life.

(42)   Lutheran theology always tried to evaluate the patristic tradition in the light of the biblical witness as it was interpreted in different periods and schools of thought.

(43)   In modern times the tradition of the Lutheran churches has become subject to a highly critical examination calling for continuous reformation and renewal.

(44)   Modern scholarship (Exegesis, Patristics) has in many ways served as a means of convergence between different denominations. This also applies to and has consequences for our evaluation of early tradition. But even if there remain a number of different emphases in this field, they are certainly not of fundamental importance but rather expressions of different histories, ways of thinking and life, which should be a source of mutual enrichment and correction.

e) Theology

(45)   Within the Anglican and the Lutheran Churches the position, function and character of theology have developed in a number of different ways.

(46)   Both Communions stress the importance of theological reasoning, and both look back to a rich tradition of theological work.

(47)   The different emphases in Anglican and Lutheran theological studies arise from different historical situations, from different backgrounds in philosophy and general thinking, and from different forms of theological training, church order and church life. The lack of closer contacts between the two Communions in the past may also have contributed to these different developments.

(48)   The stronger lines of communication within the field of theology, which have developed during the last decades, have led to increasing contacts and mutual sharing between theologians all over the world. The result is a convergence of theological thinking which is marked by mutual enrichment as well as by a widespread development of similar new theological schools very often crossing all denominational barriers.

(49)   Both Communions, therefore, are much more closely connected in the field of theology today than ever before. Part of this closer relation grows out of the fact that they face the same problems and tensions within their theological thinking.

(50)   Thus, remaining marked differences in the function and emphasis of theology should be welcomed as an expression and sign of a legitimate variety within the one people of God.

B.   THE CHURCH

(51)   The Anglican and the Lutheran Churches adhere to the traditional Nicene characterization of the church as *one, holy, catholic, and apostolic,* and they believe that they are expressions of this church. This position was reaffirmed by each Church at the Reformation and has been continuously maintained as a specific definition of what the church is called to be in the world.

(52)   Because of different historical circumstances after the Reformation theologians within the two Churches have formulated their teachings about the church differently. Nevertheless, there have been distinctive ecclesiological attitudes in each Church that were present also in the other Church and there have always been areas of agreement or approximation in their ecclesiological thinking.

(53)   Both traditions agree that the *unity* of the church, God's gift and our task, must be manifested in a visible way. This unity can be expressed in different forms depending upon the particular situation. Accordingly there can be various stages in the mutual recognition of churches, in the practice of intercommunion and in the reciprocal acceptance of ministries. The goal should be full "altar and pulpit fellowship" (full communion), including its acceptance by the individual members of the Churches, and structures that will encourage such fellowship and its acceptance.

(54)   The two traditions confess with one accord the *holiness* of the church as a gift of God's grace separating the church to himself as a beloved and forgiven people, which by the power of his Spirit is inspired and called to a life and mission which reflects among men God's own holiness. Within each tradition and between the traditions there have been and are differences of emphasis and interpretation concerning the practical expression of this holiness in the church's life and mission. Such differences are not mutually exclusive and need not prove divisive in the life of the church.

(55)   In maintaining the *catholicity* of the church, Anglicans and Lutherans confess together, that the fullness of the truth of the gospel is committed to the church. Further, they recognize together the universal outreach and inclusiveness of the church, extending to every nation, race and social group. Finally, they seek to comprehend the wholeness of human life in all its aspects under the dominion of Christ. Both Churches, however, are aware of the danger of particularist claims within their denominations. "Catholic fulness" and "the pure doctrine of the gospel"

may be misinterpreted to represent the exclusive privilege of particular groups or parties. Fullness, universality and wholeness belong only to the one body of Christ.

(56)   In the concept of *apostolicity* there is common ground insofar as all teaching, life and ministry of the church have to be in continuity with the fundamental apostolic witness and commission to go out into the world. It is the role which the succession of bishops plays within this wider concept of apostolicity which is one of the main controversial points between the two traditions. Consequently section D. in this report will consider the apostolic nature of the church and its ministry.

(57)   Today, there is a growing agreement about the way we speak of the church. This is based on a renewed interest in biblical theology and ecclesiology and this has coincided with a new awareness on the part of the church of its situation and task in the contemporary world. Particular emphasis has fallen on a dynamic concept of the church as the people of God. This implies that all thinking about the church must start from and find its criteria in the enabling presence and action of the triune God.

(58)   As the people of God growing out of the Old Covenant, the church lives in the New Covenant and is sent by Christ to serve mankind. As the Body of Christ, the church lives in an intimate relationship with him, the head of the Body. Despite its frailty and failures, it is sustained by the faithfulness of its Lord. At the same time, the church is constantly built up, renewed and strengthened by Christ's actual presence and action, through Word and Sacrament, in the Holy Spirit.

(59)   The church, therefore, is the recipient of grace, a community and royal priesthood of the people of God responding to this gift in corporate praise and thanksgiving to God, and responding simultaneously as an instrument for proclaiming and manifesting God's sovereign rule and saving grace. Because the church is sent into the world to continue Christ's service and to witness to his presence among all mankind in liberating men from fear and false idols, in meeting human need, and in fighting against injustice and discrimination, the nature and mission of the church belong inseparably together. Mission and service presuppose an authentic fellowship of the reconciled. A fellowship without mission is disobedient to the commandment of its Lord.

(60)   The fellowship of the church calls for a deep mutual sharing of the spiritual and material gifts of God. Being a fellowship of those who are at once sinful in themselves but made righteous in Christ, the church is, nevertheless, a first fruit of the kingdom and, therefore, it prophetically witnesses to the final joy of mankind which is to lose itself in wonder, love and praise of the Creator, Redeemer and Sanctifier. So the church is a pilgrim people, exposed to God's judgment and nourished on its way by his grace which exceeds both our achievements and our desires or deserts.

C. The Word and the Sacraments

a) *Relation of Word and Sacrament*

(61) Both our Communions affirm in virtually the same words (Conf. Aug. VII; Art. XIX) that the right proclamation of the Word and the proper administration of the sacraments are essential and constitutive to the ongoing life of the church. Where these things happen, there we see the church.

(62) To be obedient to the will of Christ the church must honor both Word and Sacrament and must avoid emphasizing one to the neglect of the other.

(63) While there is some difference in the mode of Christ's action in Word and Sacrament, both Word and Sacrament are occasions of his coming in anamnesis of his first advent and in anticipation of his parousia. The Word imparts significance to the sacrament and the sacrament gives visible embodiment to the Word.

b) *Baptism*

(64) Baptism, administered with water and the threefold name, is the effective means by which God brings a person into the covenant of salvation wrought by Christ and translates him from darkness and bondage into the light and freedom of the kingdom of God. The baptized are grafted into the church, adopted as children of God, brought into a relation with him which means justification, the forgiveness of sins and exposure and the sanctifying power of the Holy Spirit in the believing, witnessing and serving community.

(65) Faith is necessary for the right receiving of the sacrament. Infant baptism, though not certainly attested in the New Testament, is conformable to its doctrine and in particular to the emphasis on the divine initiative in man's redemption. The faith of the parents, sponsors and the whole community, is a pledge that the baptized infant will be brought to respond in faith to what God did for him in baptism.

(66) The practice of infant baptism necessitates the provision of opportunity for personal profession of faith before the congregation. In both our traditions this has been associated with confirmation in which the bishop (in Anglicanism) lays hands upon the candidate or the parish pastor (in Lutheranism) lays hands upon the candidate or otherwise blesses him. We note the debate within each communion about precise aspects of the theology and practice of confirmation, including its relation to admission to communion. Since the points so debated cut across the denominational lines, they ought not to be barriers to communion between us.

c) *The Lord's Supper*

(67) In the Lord's Supper the church obediently performs the acts commanded by Christ in the New Testament, who took bread and wine, gave

thanks, broke the bread and distributed the bread and wine. The church receives in this way the body and blood of Christ, crucified and risen, and in him the forgiveness of sins and all other benefits of his passion.

(68) Both Communions affirm the real presence of Christ in this sacrament, but neither seeks to define precisely how this happens. In the eucharistic action (including consecrations) and reception, the bread and wine, while remaining bread and wine, become the means whereby Christ is truly present and gives himself to the communicants.

(69) Both traditions affirm that Christ's sacrifice was offered once and for all for the sin of the whole world. Yet without denying this fundamental truth both would recognize that the Eucharist in some sense involves sacrifice. In it we offer our praise and thanksgiving, ourselves and all that we are, and make before God the memorial of Christ's sacrifice. Christ's redemptive act becomes present for our participation. Many Anglicans and some Lutherans believe that in the Eucharist the church's offering of itself is caught up into his one offering. Other Anglicans and many Lutherans do not employ the concept of sacrifice in this way.

d) Of the number of the sacraments

(70) Both our traditions recognize the uniqueness of the two gospel sacraments. Of these alone is there in the New Testament a recorded command of Christ to perform specific actions with material things, and to these alone is attached a specific promise of his own action and gift annexed thereto.

(71) In both Communions there are those who would extend the term Sacrament to other rites (e.g., absolution and ordination among Lutherans, and the other five of the traditional "sacraments" by Anglicans). This is largely a matter of nomenclature. Under the stricter definition there can only be two sacraments; under a wider definition there can be others, but when the wider definition is used the preeminence of Baptism and the Lord's Supper is still maintained.

(72) Within both Communions some provision is made for the other "five commonly called sacraments" according to need and local variation. Where unction is practised it is not understood as extreme unction but as a means of healing.

D. Apostolic Ministry

a) Apostolicity and apostolic succession

(73) The apostolicity of the church is God's gift in Christ to the church through the apostles' preaching, their celebration of the gospel sacraments, and their fellowship and oversight. It is also God's sending of the church into all the world to make disciples of all nations in and through the apostolic gospel. Thus apostolicity pertains first to the gospel and then to the ministry of Word and sacraments, all given by the risen Lord to the apostles and through them to the church. Apostolicity requires

obedience to the original and fundamental apostolic witness by reinterpretation to meet the needs of each new situation.

(74)   The succession of apostolicity through time is guarded and given contemporary expression in and through a wide variety of means, activities and institutions: the canon of Scriptures, creeds, confessional writings, liturgies, the activities of preaching, teaching, celebrating the sacraments and ordaining and using a ministry of Word and Sacrament, the exercising of pastoral care and oversight, the common life of the church, and the engagement in mission to and for the world.

b)   The ministry

(75)   In confessing the apostolic faith as a community, all baptized and believing Christians are the apostolic church and stand in the succession of apostolic faith. The apostolic ministry which was instituted by God through Jesus Christ in the sending of the apostles is shared in varying ways by the members of the whole body.

(76)   The ordained ministry of Word and Sacrament is essentially one, though it assumes a diversity of forms which have varied from New Testament times, and which still vary according to local conditions and historic influences down to the present.

(77)   We feel ourselves called to recognize that all who have been called and ordained to the ministry of Word and Sacrament in obedience to the apostolic faith stand together in the apostolic succession of office.

(78)   It is God who calls, ordains and sends the ministers of Word and Sacrament in the church. He does this through the whole people, acting by means of those who have been given authority so to act in the name of God and of the whole church. Ordination to the ministry gives authority to preach the gospel and administer the sacraments according to Christ's command and promise, for the purpose of the continuance of the apostolic life and mission of the church. Ordination includes the prayer of all the people and the laying on of hands of other ministers, especially of those who occupy a ministry of oversight and unity in the church.

c)   Episcopacy

(79)   "Episcope" or oversight concerning the purity of apostolic doctrine, the ordination of ministries, and pastoral care of the church is inherent in the apostolic character of the church's life, mission and ministry. This has been embodied and exercised in the church in a wide variety of forms, episcopal and non-episcopal. Both Communions have continuously held and exercised oversight in accordance with their respective understandings of church order.

(80)   In the Lutheran Communion episcopacy has been preserved in some parts in unbroken succession, in other parts in succession of office, while in other parts oversight has been exercised in non-episcopal forms. In all forms it has experienced the blessings of the ministry in the church.

(81)   In the Anglican Communion episcopacy has been preserved in a succession unbroken at the time of the Reformation and, rightly or wrongly, important deductions have been drawn from this in relation to the organic continuity and unity of the church.

(82)   Both Communions are open to new forms in which episcope may find expressions appropriate to the needs and conditions of the situation and time.

d)   Particular convictions and perspectives of each Communion

Statement of the Anglican participants:

(83)   Anglicans treasure the historic episcopate as part of their own history and because of their belief in the incarnational and sacramental character of God's involvement with the world and his people. As God acts now in and through words spoken, in and through bread and wine, and in and through the reality of human community, so too he acts in the laying on of hands in historic succession, providing for the ministry of Word and Sacrament in the one church.

(84)   They believe that the episcopacy in historic continuity and succession is a gift of God to the church. It is an outward and visible sign of the church's continuing unity and apostolic life, mission and ministry. They hold this belief while recognizing that episcopacy has been and may be abused in the life of the church, as have been the other media of apostolic succession.

(85)   Anglicans do not believe that the episcopate in historic succession alone constitutes the apostolic succession of the church or its ministry. The participants wish to declare that they see in the Lutheran Communion true proclamation of the Word and celebration of the sacraments. How we are able to make this statement while maintaining our adherence to the importance of the historic episcopate we hope the Anglican personal note (see section IV) will make clear. The Anglican Communion has been much influenced and blessed by God through the Lutheran Communion's faithfulness to the apostolic gospel. We, therefore, gladly recognize in the Lutheran churches a true communion of Christ's body, possessing a truly apostolic ministry.

(86)   Such recognition, if reciprocated by the Lutheran churches, implies, according to the mind of the participants, official encouragement of intercommunion in forms appropriate to local conditions.

(87)   The Anglican participants cannot foresee full integration of ministries (full communion) apart from the historic episcopate, but this should in no sense preclude increasing intercommunion between us, which would give fuller and more joyful expression to our unity in Christ, recognize and deepen the similarities which bind us together, and provide the most appropriate context for our common service of the one Lord.

Statement of the Lutheran participants:

(88)   The Lutheran churches have practised full fellowship with each other regardless of the forms of episcope (or even of the episcopate). With ecumenical developments this freedom for fellowship has allowed Lutheran churches to enter into fellowship with non-Lutheran churches with various forms of church government.

(89)   Since full fellowship has been retained between some Lutheran churches which have not preserved the office and name of a bishop and other Lutheran churches which have retained the historic episcopate in a form similar to the Anglican and since the particular form of episcope is not a confessional question for Lutherans, the historic episcopate should not become a necessary condition for interchurch relations or church union. On the other hand, those Lutheran churches which have not retained the historic episcopate are free to accept it where it serves the growing unity of the church in obedience to the gospel.

(90)   The Lutheran participants in these conversations recognize the churches of the Anglican Communion as true apostolic churches and their ministry as an apostolic ministry in unbroken succession, because they see in them true proclamation of the gospel and right administration of the sacraments. As would be true for any church which proclaims the gospel in its purity and administers the sacraments properly the participants regard the historic episcopacy as it has been retained in the Anglican Communion as an important instrument of the unity of the church.

(91)   The Lutheran participants in these conversations recommend to the member churches of the Lutheran World Federation that they work for a still closer fellowship with the churches of the Anglican Communion, including at the present time intercommunion. Where it is expedient for furthering the mission of the church and where it can happen without disturbing already existing relations with other churches, Lutheran churches must be free to manifest a mutual recognition of ministries through the exchange of ministers or through full church union.

E.   WORSHIP

(92)   Our conversations have given the participants renewed opportunities to enter into each other's traditions of worship and spirituality. Both sides have been impressed with the similarity between their respective heritages of liturgical worship and also with the close similarity between the movements for liturgical reform in both Communions. The deep reverence and liturgical care with which their common services of the Eucharist have been conducted remain among the most cherished memories of the experiences which the delegates have gone through together.

(93)   Both traditions emerged after the Reformation from the same matrix of medieval Catholic worship. In both a similar course of events influenced the development of liturgical tradition. In later Lutheran developments the main Sunday service became frequently a purely preaching service while in Anglicanism a separation between eucharistic and non-eucharistic worship services took place.

(94)   Now, in both churches, the Holy Communion is coming back into the center of the picture as the principal worship service of each Sunday. In the Lutheran churches there is a marked re-appropriation of traditional liturgical forms of worship and in Anglicanism there is a noticeable tendency to reintegrate Word and Sacrament, particularly by the use of the sermon in many more celebrations of the Holy Communion. Both traditions use increasingly spontaneous and informal modes of prayer and praise in the setting of traditional liturgical frameworks.

(95)   Is it fanciful to see in these contemporary movements a stirring of the Spirit, whereby our two Communions may more obviously glorify God with one heart and one mouth?

III. RECOMMENDATIONS

A. Intercommunion and Fellowship

a)   *Intercommunion*

(96)   The degree of mutual recognition of the apostolicity and catholicity of our two Churches indicated in the report justifies a greatly increased measure of intercommunion between them. Both Anglican and Lutheran Churches should welcome communicants from the other Church and should encourage their own communicants to receive Holy Communion in churches of the other tradition where appropriate and subject to the claims of individual conscience and respect for the discipline of each Church.

(97)   An anomalous situation exists in Europe. The Church of England should no longer make a distinction in the intercommunion arrangements made for various Lutheran churches, but should extend the arrangements for Sweden and Finland to include all Lutheran churches in Europe. The many years of contact with Sweden and Finland have made a useful introduction to the communion and fellowship which would thus be extended and which should be reciprocal.

b)   *Joint worship*

(98)   In places where local conditions make this desirable, there should be mutual participation from time to time by entire congregations in the worship and eucharistic celebrations of the other Church. Anniversaries and other special occasions provide opportunity for members of the two traditions to share symbolic and ecumenical worship together.

c)   *Integration of ministries*

(99)   In those countries where Anglicans and Lutheran churches are working side by side for the spread of the gospel, or where there are churches with close relationships with our two Communions (we have Africa and Asia especially in mind), there is felt a need for more rapid movement towards organic union. We endorse this. It is our hope that our report, with its encouragement of intercommunion and its recognition of the

apostolicity of both Churches and their ministries, might facilitate progress towards a true integration of ministries. Whatever steps may be taken towards such integration, nothing should call in question the status of existing ministries as true ministries of Word and Sacrament.

B.   ORGANIZATIONAL CONTACTS

a)   Continuation committee

(100)   Our authorizing bodies should appoint a small continuation committee to follow up our conversations by making regular reports to them on reactions to our present report and on implementation of its proposals; by stimulating further developments; and by preparing a full report for the parent bodies after not more than four years on possibilities for further steps toward closer unity.

b)   Staff consultation and observers

(101)   The Lutheran World Federation and the Anglican Consultative Council should encourage regular contacts between their staff members, and arrange attendance of observers at each other's assemblies, liturgical commissions, and conferences where appropriate.

C.   MINISTRIES AND EXCHANGES ABROAD

a)   Chaplains

(102)   Clergy serving their own nationals abroad should realize their importance as ecumenical ambassadors and do their best to make contact with churches and Christians of other traditions among whom they are living. The local churches should welcome such clergy into their fellowship. While the existence of churches for the benefit of ethnic and linguistic groups is fully understood, the development of churches within foreign populations by proselytization should be discouraged.

b)   Tourists and travellers

(103)   The vast increase in tourism and all kinds of international travel, and the probable entry of Great Britain into the European Economic Community, provide an opportunity for greatly increased fellowship between Christians of our two traditions. Special pastoral provision should be made and an educational program embarked upon to prepare church people to avail themselves of opportunities for spiritual fellowship with Christians of other countries. Specialized chaplaincies (e.g., seamen's missions) also provide occasions for international spiritual fellowship.

(104)   More frequent exchanges of theologians and scholars should be much encouraged. Theological students and younger clergy can learn much and give much by spending a period of their early ministry and study in the context of a church other than their own.

D. Joint Local Mission and Social Witness

a) *Shared facilities and ministries*

(105)   In areas where the presence of one or more churches is very small, one ministry might serve more than one communion by incorporating smaller groups into the parish life of larger, although in various ways allowing the smaller groups to remain in touch with their own communions. Isolated clergy of any communion should be welcomed into meetings of clergy of larger churches so that the clergy of many churches might meet as one body. Sharing buildings and pastoral services may provide good opportunities for mutual service and fellowship.

b) *Social witness and evangelism*

(106)   Joint action for mission, social witness, and education is recommended wherever relevant and possible. This might include the interconfessional running of educational institutions such as colleges or schools for the handicapped, and cooperation wherever possible; joint work for the alleviation of illiteracy; joint preparation and publication of Christian literature; and the sharing of facilities on university campuses, for youth centers, and in new industrial areas and housing estates.

c) *Discussion and dialog*

(107)   There should be in all regions some form of continuing interchurch discussions by official joint delegations and local groups on the various ways in which our two traditions may move closer together and on the forms of unity into which God may be calling us. These should include consideration of the theological convictions which may still tend to separate us (e.g., the proclamation of the gospel, the historic episcopate).

(108)   It is our hope that our present discussions will have elucidated many of the issues relevant to our relationships. We submit our report in the hope that it may be made available to all our member churches and contribute to closer fellowship among us in Christ our Lord.

IV. PERSONAL NOTES BY THE TWO CHAIRMEN

A. Personal Note by the Anglican Chairman

However close and intimate has been the fellowship in a joint consultation such as ours — and it has indeed been close — the time comes when the joint report has to be submitted to each constituency separately. In order that its message may be clearly understood and fairly considered the highlights of the report can be pointed out, and in this note I am trying to do that for Anglicans, using the language and idioms to which they have become accustomed.

In the report, an attempt is made to widen the scope of the phrase, and hence of the meaning of "apostolic succession". Anglicans would not, if asked, have imagined the *only* meaning of that phrase was succession of ministers by ordination of bishops in the "succession". They would have wanted to include faith in the apostolic gospel (expressed in the Creeds), acceptance of the Scriptures (which anchored the patristic church to the apostolic church) and the acceptance of the gospel sacraments. But as a fact of history these other forms of continuity (focussed in the Lambeth Quadrilateral) have been taken as marks of "catholicity" rather than of "apostolicity". The adjective "apostolic" happens to have been attached to the continuity of the *ministry*. It can only be widened in its application by a conscious effort to merge apostolicity into catholicity, and *vice versa*.

In Anglican relations with Lutherans special importance has been placed on the presence or absence of episcopal succession in various branches of Lutheranism. Much common ground in other matters has always been recognized. But since 1662 at least the Anglican churches have normally insisted on episcopal ordination as a necessary basis for *communio in sacris*. See, e.g., the Preface to the Ordinal, 1662: "No man shall be accounted or taken to be a lawful Bishop, Priest, or Deacon in the Church of England, or suffered to execute any of the asaid functions, except he be called, tried, examined, and admitted thereunto, according to the form hereafter following, or hath had formerly Episcopal Consecration or Ordination." There have been all kinds of exceptions and variations, but the basic norm has not been in doubt. So it has happened that the Church of England (for instance) gradually entered into full communion with the Church of Sweden in the sense that from 1888 to 1954 successive steps were taken until, in the latter year, communicants of the Swedish Church were given an unqualified right of entry to Anglican communions in England. Members of the Church of Finland received virtually the same permission in 1935 (with some limitations in the decisions of the Lower House of the Canterbury Convocations). Denmark, Norway and Iceland (not having "the succession") were given in 1954 what may be called "hospitality rights"—rather different in kind from rights springing out of the status of the home church concerned.

The theology and ecclesiology underlying Anglican thought and practice in these matters has become the subject of many inevitable questions. A few can be mentioned.

(*a*)   It is seen more and more to be an accident of history (i.e., something that depended upon the availability or otherwise of Reformed bishops in good standing with their monarchs in the sixteenth century) that in modern times Sweden and Finland find themselves on one side in the matter of succession, and the other Lutheran churches on the other. Neither the Churches of Sweden and Finland nor those of the other countries concerned, wish this one matter to be decisive in their relations with us. They rather stress their common obedience to the gospel as they saw it in the sixteenth century, which led to them all having a Reformed ministry, whether episcopal or otherwise.

(*b*) The extent of "the spread" of the succession in Lutheran churches is very difficult to define. It is fairly easy to assert which churches possess it. It is not nearly so easy to assert which churches do not possess it.

(*c*) It is clear that owing to the size and theological self-confidence of the Lutheran churches any kind of "bargaining" on behalf of Anglican views of episcopacy is inappropriate and would certainly be unfruitful. Ecumenical relations have to be settled between the churches *as they are*. This does not preclude either church from observing tendencies already at work in the other, which may indicate a likely growing together and mutual sharing of theological insights and historical benefits.

(*d*) A clearer understanding of the pluralist nature of New Testament Christianity (especially in relation to the ministry) makes all claims to exclusiveness embarrassing to maintain. Hooker's objection to presbyterian exclusiveness in the sixteenth century can easily be turned on Anglicans, if they press their views of episcopacy with the like rigidity.

There is a great difference between setting up "a united church" and setting up new relations with existing churches, which in many parts of the world (not in all) are geographically and nationally separated. The rules for courteous and Christian relationships are not identical with those which must govern organic union. A greater flexibility is possible in the former situation than in the latter.

The acceptance of the possibility of full intercommunion (a phrase which itself is capable of many gradations of meaning) with churches which have varying degrees of attachment to the apostolic succession in the traditional Catholic or Anglican understanding of those words, need not imply the slightest retreat on the Anglican side from a firm attachment to it. Among Anglicans there are, and will be, variations in the theological understanding of "the succession", but as an agreed rule of practice it is still universal in the Anglican world. Anglicans will retain it, in the hope that one day it will be acceptable to all Christians, and as a means of grace which they, for their part, intend, with God's help, never to lose. They need not, however, make it the sole touchstone of ecumenical fellowship with churches holding a different set of priorities. Detailed questions as to the exact implications of intercommunion will demand different answers in different circumstances. Conscience must always be respected, and by both sides. But our delegation was clear that we ought now to greet the Lutheran churches as real sister-churches in the family-life of Christ's universal church. This is the call and challenge of our report.

April, 1972   RONALD LEICESTER

B. PERSONAL NOTE BY THE LUTHERAN CHAIRMAN

In conversations between separated churches statements about points of agreement and points of disagreement have often played an important role.

This comparative method may help the participants in such conversations to a better understanding of the historic background and particular tradition of other churches. But this method is not sufficient in any genuine ecumenical conversation. For in order to be properly evaluated on both sides all points of agreement and disagreement must be examined and judged in the light of a supreme authority accepted by both parties. Only if the points of agreement are examined and judged in the light of such a common, supreme authority will the two Churches be able to decide whether those agreements manifest their common faith in the same Lord or only conceal a basic disunity. And only if the points of disagreement are examined and judged in the light of that same supreme authority may the two Churches decide whether those disagreements are only "adiaphora" which do not preclude a growing unity between them, or whether they are manifestations of an essential disunity which presents a permanent obstacle to any complete unity between the two Churches. Expressed in the traditional Lutheran language; the only necessary condition to full church fellowship is agreement on the truth of the gospel (CA VII).

In this report Lutherans and Anglicans have together stated that both Churches are at one in accepting the Holy Scriptures of the Old and New Testaments as the sufficient, inspired and authoritative record and witness, prophetic and apostolic, to God's revelation in Jesus Christ, and that Jesus Christ, God and man, born, crucified, risen and ascended for the salvation of mankind is the living word of God in whom all Scriptures find their focus and fulfilment. This statement is not to be understood as expressing only one point of agreement among many others, but it describes that basic criterion, accepted by both Churches, which alone makes their conversation possible and meaningful, not only when "agreements" are stated, but also when remaining "disagreements", *e.g.*, concerning the historic episcopate, are expressed.

To Lutherans this fundamental unity about the "sources of authority", expressed in the use of the same Scriptures and Creeds and in the recognition by both sides of the heritage from the sixteenth century Reformation, not only in theology, but above all in worship, is of decisive importance.

The fact that points of disagreement as to the meaning and importance of the historic episcopate still persist cannot diminish the value of that fundamental unity, but it may lead the Lutheran churches to reconsider their traditional conviction that all questions of church order, including the historic episcopate, are "adiaphora", of secondary importance. If this is so, does it necessarily mean that all forms of church order equally serve the church's witness to the truth of the gospel? Is the absence of the historic episcopate in some Lutheran churches only motivated by faithfulness to the gospel, or have other motives been at work? In considering such questions, the Lutheran churches do not abandon their conviction that the true preaching of the gospel and the right administration of the sacraments cannot be linked up with one specific type of church order, but they submit the conviction to a reexamination in the light of the gospel, expecting that the Anglican churches will do the same with regard to their traditional conception of the historic episcopate.

Among various possible ways in which the distinctive doctrines of the two Churches may be reexamined, Lutherans should be committed to continuing conversations with Anglicans as one way. In such conversations the commitment to the gospel also needs further exploration. Although the present conversations affirm the importance of justification and forgiveness of sins, future conversations should say more clearly and fully that the gospel proclaims the unmerited grace, whereby God declares men righteous through faith in Jesus Christ. By elucidating the doctrine of the gospel the authority of the Scriptures will become understood more specifically and differences in teaching will be judged more accurately.

If both Churches maintain their fundamental unity in the recognition of the same supreme authority, then all unsettled disagreements remain only to be overcome through fresh obedience to that supreme authority. By no means should they be allowed to remain, unchallenged and undisputed, as permanent obstacles to that growing unity which both Churches recognize as the will and command of their one Lord.

April, 1972   GUNNAR HULTGREN

PARTICIPANTS

MEMBERS OF THE COMMISSION:

Anglicans:

Bishop R. R. Williams, Leicester, England (co-chairman)
Prof. J. Atkinson, Sheffield, England
Archdeacon J. A. Cable, Itki, Bihar, India
Prof. W. R. Coleman, Downstown, Canada
Bishop R.S.M. Emrich, Detroit, U.S.A.
Prof. R. H. Fuller, New York, U.S.A.
Prof. S. L. Greenslade, Oxford, England
Prof. J. R. Rodgers, Alexandria, U.S.A.
Bishop N. Russell, Roslin/Edinburgh, Scotland

Lutherans:

Archbishop em. G. Hultgren, Uppsala, Sweden (co-chairman)
Bishop H. H. Harms, Oldenburg, Germany
Prof. B. H. Jackayya, Nagercoil, South India

Bishop J. Kibira, Bukoba, Tanzania
Dr. K. Knutson, Minneapolis, U.S.A.
Dr. R. J. Marshall, New York, U.S.A.
Prof. R. Prenter, Aarhus, Denmark
Prof. M. Schmidt, Heidelberg, Germany

SECRETARIES:

Anglicans:

Canon R. M. Jeffery, London, England
Rev. M. Moore, London, England

Lutheran:

Dr. G. Gassmann, Strasbourg, France

WORLD COUNCIL OF CHURCHES OBSERVER:

Prof. N. Robinson, St. Andrews, Scotland

ANGLICAN-OLD CATHOLIC RELATIONS

Bonn Agreement 1931

Historical Introduction:

Shortly after 1870, both the Old Catholics and the Anglicans began to take up contacts with each other. To begin with, such attempts were mainly on the level of personal meetings and endeavours (for example, the participation of Anglicans in the first Old Catholic Congresses and the Union Conferences in Bonn in 1874 and 1875), but towards the end of the 1870's, these efforts began to take on a more official character. In 1878, the Lambeth Conference issued a declaration of sympathy for the Old Catholic Church in the process of formation. This resulted in admissions to Holy Communion on the local level and in occasional acts of intercommunion, mainly between the British and the North American Anglicans and Swiss and German Old Catholics. However, there were still reservations on both sides, particularly on the side of the Dutch Old Catholics.

For a while, this rapprochement seemed to stagnate. The period after the First World War, however, brought decisive change. In 1920, the Lambeth Conference expressed its readiness to once again take up the Union Conferences which had been started in the 1870's. In 1925, the Old Catholic Church in Holland acknowledged the validity of the Anglican Orders so that the Old Catholic Bishops' Conference of that same year was able to endorse this for all Old Catholic churches.

The following Lambeth Conference (1930) recognised this action and declared that reunion with the Old Catholic Church was feasible. In accordance with this resolution, two theological commissions were appointed by the Archbishop of Canterbury and the Archbishop of Utrecht. Their task was to work out an agreement between the two churches. After preliminary clarifications, both commissions met in Bonn on July 2nd, 1931, and formulated the so-called "Bonn Agreement" which was then ratified by the Old Catholic Bishops' Conference and the Convocations of Canterbury and York and subsequently by the other churches of the Anglican Communion.

After the Polish Old Catholic Church in the USA, in 1946, and finally the Anglican Church of Ireland, in 1950, had also ratified the "Bonn Agreement", a comprehensive intercommunion or *"full communion"* (according to the terminology adopted at the 1958 Lambeth Conference) was established between the Old Catholic Church and the Anglican Communion.

STATEMENT

agreed between

the representatives of the Old Catholic Churches and the Churches of the Anglican Communion, 1931

("Bonn Agreement")

Statement agreed between the representatives of
the Old Catholic Churches and
the Churches of the Anglican Communion
at a Conference held at Bonn

JULY 2, 1931

1. Each Communion recognizes the catholicity and independence of the other and maintains its own.
2. Each Communion agrees to admit members of the other Communion to participate in the Sacraments.
3. Intercommunion does not require from either Communion the acceptance of all doctrinal opinion, sacramental devotion, or liturgical practice characteristic of the other, but implies that each believes the other to hold all the essentials of the Christian Faith.

Signed:

A. C. GLOUCESTR:	J. H. DEVENTER.
[A. C. Headlam]	ADOLF KÜRY.
STAUNTON FULHAM.	GEORG MOOG.
[B.S. Batty]	A. RINKEL.
A. S. DUNCAN-JONES.	
N. P. WILLIAMS.	
J. A. DOUGLAS.	
G. F. GRAHAM-BROWN.	
C. B. MOSS.	
C. L. GAGE-BROWN.	

Episcopal Synod of the Old Catholic Churches.
Resolutions.

SEPTEMBER 7, 1931

1. The Synod assembled in Vienna on September 7th, 1931, of the Old
    Catholic Bishops united in the Union of Utrecht, on the basis of the
    recognition of the validity of Anglican Ordinations, agrees to Inter-
    communion with the Anglican Communion.
2. Intercommunion consists in the reciprocal admittance of the members
    of the two Communions to the Sacraments.
3. Intercommunion does not require from either Communion the accept-
    ance of all doctrinal opinions, sacramental devotions, or liturgical
    practices characteristic of the other, but implies that each believes the
    other to hold all the essentials of the Christian Faith.

Convocation of Canterbury.
Resolutions of both Houses

JANUARY 20 AND 22, 1932

UPPER HOUSE

That this House approves of the following statements agreed on between the representatives of the Old Catholic Churches and the Churches
of the Anglican Communion at a Conference held at Bonn on July 2,
1931:

1. Each Communion rcognizes the catholicity and independence of the
    other and maintains its own.
2. Each Communion agrees to admit members of the other Communion
    to participate in the Sacraments.
3. Intercommunion does not require from either Communion the accept-
    ance of all doctrinal opinion, sacramental devotion, or liturgical prac-
    tice characteristic of the other, but implies that each believes the other
    to hold all the essentials of the Christian Faith.

And this House agrees to the establishment of Intercommunion between the Church of England and the Old Catholics on these terms.

LOWER HOUSE

That this House concurs with the establishment of Intercommunion
between the Church of England and the Old Catholics on the terms of the
Resolutions sent down by the Upper House.

ANGLICAN-ORTHODOX CONVERSATIONS

Moscow Statement 1976

Athens Statement 1978

Llandaff Statement 1980

Historical Introduction:

In 1962, the Anglican and Orthodox authorities agreed to resume the series of consultations which had been initiated in 1930.

In order to make a thorough preparation for the forthcoming consultations the Third Pan-Orthodox Conference at Rhodes in 1964 decided to establish an Inter-Orthodox Theological Commission for Dialogue with the Anglicans, composed of delegates representing the various Orthodox Churches. This Commission held four meetings (Belgrade, September 1966; Chambésy/Geneva, October 1970; Helsinki, July 1971; Chambésy/Geneva, September 1972). On the Anglican side a similar Commission — the Commission for Joint Doctrinal Discussions with the Orthodox Church — was established and met twice (Jerusalem, September 1969; Haywards Heath, England, July 1971).

After a meeting of an Anglican and an Orthodox sub-commission (Chambésy/Geneva, September 1972) the first session of the full Commission for Anglican-Orthodox Joint Doctrinal Discussions, sponsored by the Anglican Consultative Council and the Inter-Orthodox Commission for Dialogue with the Anglicans, was held at Oxford, England, July 6-13, 1973. Introductory papers, which had already been considered and revised, as a preparatory stage, and discussions focused on the following subjects: Comprehensiveness and the mission of the Church; the Holy Spirit as interpreter of the Gospel and giver of life in the Church today; the redemptive work of Christ on the cross and the resurrection.

During 1974 and 1975 three Anglican — Orthodox sub-commissions met twice and discussed the following subjects: "Inspiration and revelation in the Holy Scripture"; "The authority of the ecumenical councils"; "The Church as a eucharistic community". The work of the sub-commissions resulted in a number of statements, principles and theses which were submitted to the second meeting of the full Commission in Moscow, July 26-August 2, 1976. The Commission scrutinized and amended the preparatory material and finally came to the agreed "Moscow Statement".

In view of the difficulties caused by the ordination of women to the presbyterate by some provinces of the Anglican Communion, the Commission has since published a Statement on this question, the "Athens Statement" (Athens, 13th-18th July 1978).

Moscow Statement 1976

I. The Knowledge of God

1. God is both immanent and transcendent. By virtue of the divine self-revelation, man experiences personal communion with God. By faith and through obedience he shares truly in the divine life and is united with God the Holy Trinity. By grace he enjoys the pledge and first-fruits of eternal glory. But, however close this union may be, there remains always an all-important distinction between God and man, Creator and creature, infinite and finite.

2. To safeguard both the transcendence of God and the possibility of man's true union with him the Orthodox Church draws a distinction between the divine essence, which remains forever beyond man's comprehension and knowledge, and the divine energies, by participation in which man participates in God. The divine energies are God himself in his self-manifestation. This distinction is not normally used by Anglicans, but in various ways they also seek to express the belief that God is at once incomprehensible, yet truly knowable by man.

3. To describe the fullness of man's sanctification and the way in which he shares in the life of God, the Orthodox Church uses the Patristic term *theosis kata charin* (divinization by grace). Once again such language is not normally used by Anglicans, some of whom regard it as misleading and dangerous. At the same time Anglicans recognize that, when Orthodox speak in this manner, they do so only with the most careful safeguards. Anglicans do not reject the underlying doctrine which this language seeks to express; indeed, such teaching is to be found in their own liturgies and hymnody.

II. The Inspiration and Authority of Holy Scripture

4. The Scriptures constitute a coherent whole. They are at once divinely inspired and humanly expressed. They bear authoritative witness to God's revelation of himself in creation, in the Incarnation of the Word and in the whole history of salvation, and as such express the Word of God in human language.

5. We know, receive, and interpret Scripture through the Church and in the Church. Our approach to the Bible is one of obedience so that we may hear the revelation of himself that God gives through it.

6. The books of Scripture contained in the Canon are authoritative because they truly convey the authentic revelation of God, which the Church recognizes in them. Their authority is not determined by any particular theories concerning the authorship of these books or the historical circumstances in which they were written. The Church gives attention to the results of scholarly research concerning the Bible from whatever quarter they come, but it tests them in the light of its experience and understanding of the faith as a whole.

41

7.   The Church believes in the apostolic origin of the New Testament, as containing the witness of those who had seen the Lord.

8.   Both the Orthodox and the Anglican Churches make a distinction between the canonical books of the Old Testament and the Deutero-canonical books (otherwise called the Anaginoskomena) although the Orthodox Churches have not pronounced officially on the nature of the distinction, as is done in the Anglican Articles. Both Communions are agreed in regarding the Deutero-canonical books as edifying and both, and in particular the Orthodox Church, make liturgical use of them.

III.   *Scripture and Tradition*

9.   Any disjunction between Scripture and Tradition such as would treat them as two separate 'sources of revelation' must be rejected. The two are correlative. We affirm (i) that Scripture is the main criterion whereby the Church tests traditions to determine whether they are truly part of Holy Tradition or not; (ii) that Holy Tradition completes Holy Scripture in the sense that it safeguards the integrity of the biblical message.

10.   (i) By the term Holy Tradition we understand the entire life of the Church in the Holy Spirit. This tradition expresses itself in dogmatic teaching, in liturgical worship, in canonical discipline, and in spiritual life. These elements together manifest the single and indivisible life of the Church.

(ii) Of supreme importance is the dogmatic tradition, which in substance is unchangeable. In seeking to communicate the saving truth to mankind, the Church in every generation makes use of contemporary language and therefore of contemporary modes of thought; but this usage must always be tested by the standard of Scripture and of the dogmatic definitions of the Ecumenical Councils. The mind (phrenoma) of the Fathers, their theological method, their terminology and modes of expression have a lasting importance in both the Orthodox and the Anglican Churches.

(iii) The liturgical and canonical expressions of Tradition can differ, in that they are concerned with varying situations of the people of God in different historical periods and in different places. The liturgical and canonical traditions remain unchangeable to the extent that they embody the unchangeable truth of divine revelation and respond to the unchanging needs of mankind.

11.   The Church cannot define dogmas which are not grounded both in Holy Scripture and in Holy Tradition, but has the power, particularly in Ecumenical Councils, to formulate the truths of the faith more exactly and precisely when the needs of the Church require it.

12.   The understanding of Scripture and Tradition embodied in paragraphs 4 to 11 offers to our Churches a solid basis for closer rapprochement.

IV. *The Authority of the Councils*

13.   We are agreed that the notions of Church and Scripture are inseparable. The Scriptures contain the witness of the prophets and apostles to the revelation of himself which God the Father made to man through his Son in his Holy Spirit. The Councils maintain this witness and provide an authoritative interpretation of it. We recognize the work of the Holy Spirit in the Church, not only in the Scriptures, but also in the Councils, and in the whole process whereby Scriptures and Councils have been received as authoritative. At the same time we confess that the tradition of the Church is a living one in which the Spirit continues his work of maintaining the true witness to the Revelation of God, the faith once delivered to the saints.

14.   We note that Anglican members, while accepting the dogmatic decrees of the fifth, sixth, and seventh Councils, have long been accustomed to lay more emphasis on the first four, and believe that the concept of 'an order or "hierarchy" of truths' can usefully be applied to the decisions of the Councils. The Orthodox members find this concept to be in conflict with the unity of the faith as a whole, though they recognize gradations of importance in matters of practice.

15.   The Orthodox regard the Seventh Council as of equal importance with the other Ecumenical Councils. They understand its positive injunctions about the veneration of icons as an expression of faith in the Incarnation.

The Anglican tradition places a similarly positive value on the created order, and on the place of the body and material things in worship. Like the Orthodox, Anglicans see this as a necessary corollary of the doctrine of the Incarnation. They welcome the decisions of the Seventh Council in so far as they constitute a defence of the doctrine of the Incarnation. They agree that the veneration of icons as practised in the East is not to be rejected, but do not believe that it can be required of all Christians.

It is clear that further discussion of the Seventh Council and of icons is necessary in the dialogue between Orthodox and Anglicans, as also of Western three-dimensional images and religious paintings which we have not adequately discussed.

16.   We are agreed that according to the Scriptures and the Fathers the fullness of saving truth has been given to the Church. She is the Temple of God, in which God's Spirit dwells, the Pillar and the Ground of truth. Christ has promised that he will be with her until the End of the Age and that the Holy Spirit will guide her into all truth (I Cor. 3.16, I Tim. 3.15, Matt. 28. 20, John 16.13).

17.   Both Anglican and Orthodox agree that infallibility is not the property of any particular institution or person in the Church, but that the promises of Christ are made to the whole Church. The ecumenicity of Councils is manifested through their acceptance by the Church. For the

Orthodox, the Ecumenical Council is not an institution but a charismatic event in the life of the Church and is the highest expression of the Church's inerrancy.

18.   It is clear that further exploration and discussion of this and kindred questions will be needed. Among the points to be taken into account are:

(a) The use of the words 'infallible' and 'indefectible' in discussion of ecclesiology is of medieval and modern Western origin.

(b) For Anglicans, the concept of infallibility has acquired unfortunate associations by reason of the definition of the first Vatican Council, and of the manner in which papal authority has been exercised. For the Orthodox, the concept of indefectibility has ambiguous associations on account of the way in which it has been used in modern theology.

(c) A theological evaluation is required of processes whereby the teaching of Councils has been recognized and received.

V.   *The Filioque Clause*

19.   The question of the *Filioque* is in the first instance a question of the content of the Creed, i.e. the summary of the articles of faith which are to be confessed by all. In the Nicaeno-Constantinopolitan Creed (commonly called the Nicene Creed) of 381 the words 'proceeding from the Father' are an assertion of the divine origin and nature of the Son contained in the words 'begotten not made, consubstantial with the Father'. The word *ekporeuomenon* (proceeding), as used in the Creed, denotes the incomprehensible mode of the Spirit's origin from the Father, employing the language of Scripture (John 15.26). It asserts that the Spirit comes from the Father in a manner which is not that of generation.

20.   The question of the origin of the Holy Spirit is to be distinguished from that of his mission to the world. It is with reference to the mission of the Spirit that we are to understand the biblical texts which speak both of the Father (John 14.26) and of the Son (John 15.26) as sending (*pempein*) the Holy Spirit.

21.   The Anglican members therefore agree that:

(a) because the original form of the Creed referred to the origin of the Holy Spirit from the Father,

(b) because the *Filioque* clause was introduced into this Creed without the authority of an Ecumenical Council and without due regard for Catholic consent, and

(c) because this Creed constitutes the public confession of faith by the People of God in the Eucharist,

the *Filioque* clause should not be included in this Creed.

VI. *The Church as the Eucharistic Community*

22. The eucharistic teaching and practice of the Churches, mutually confessed, constitutes an essential factor for the understanding which can lead to reunion between the Orthodox and Anglican Churches. This understanding commits both our Churches to a close relationship which can provide the basis for further steps on the way to reconciliation and union. Already in the past there has been considerable agreement between representatives of our two Churches regarding the doctrine of the Eucharist. We note particularly the six points of the Bucharest Conference of 1935. We now report the following points of agreement:

23. The eucharistic understanding of the Church affirms the presence of Jesus Christ in the Church, which is his Body, and in the Eucharist. Through the action of the Holy Spirit, all faithful communicants share in the one Body of Christ, and become one body in him.

24. The Eucharist actualizes the Church. The Christian community has a basic sacramental character. The Church can be described as a 'synaxis' or an 'ecclesia', which is, in its essence, a worshipping and eucharistic assembly. The Church is not only built up by the Eucharist, but is also a condition for it. Therefore one must be a believing member of the Church in order to receive the Holy Communion.

The Church celebrating the Eucharist becomes fully itself; that is *koinonia,* fellowship — communion. The Church celebrates the Eucharist as the central act of its existence, in which the ecclesial community, as a living reality confessing its faith, receives its realization.

25. Through the consecratory prayer, addressed to the Father, the bread and wine become the Body and Blood of the glorified Christ by the action of the Holy Spirit in such a way that the faithful people of God receiving Christ may feed upon him in the sacrament (I Cor. 10.16). Thus the Church is continually renewed and fulfilled in its members. The Church depends upon the action of the Holy Spirit and is the visible community in which the Spirit is known.

26. The eucharistic action of the Church is the Passover from the old to the new. It anticipates and really shares in the eternal Rule and Glory of God. Following the Apostolic and Patristic teaching, we affirm that the eucharistic elements become, by the grace of the Holy Spirit, the Body and Blood of Christ, the bread of immortality, to give to us the forgiveness of sins, the new creation, and eternal life. The celebration of the Church in liturgy carries with it the sense of the eternal reality which precedes it, abides in it, and is still to come.

27. In the Eucharist the eternal priesthood of Christ is constantly manifested in time. The celebrant, in his liturgical action, has a twofold ministry: as an icon of Christ, acting in the name of Christ, towards the community and also as a representative of the community expressing the priesthood of the faithful. In each local eucharistic celebration the visible

unity and catholicity of the Church is manifested fully. The question of the relationship between the celebrant and his bishop and that among bishops themselves requires further study.

28.   The Eucharist impels the believers to specific action in mission and service to the world. In the eucharistic celebration the Church is a confessing community which witnesses to the cosmic transfiguration. Thus God enters into a personal historic situation as the Lord of creation and of history. In the Eucharist the End breaks into our midst, bringing the judgement and hope of the New Age. The final dismissal or benediction in the liturgy is not an end to worship but a call to prayer and witness so that in the power of the Holy Spirit the believers may announce and convey to the world that which they have seen and received in the Eucharist.

VII.   *The Invocation of the Holy Spirit in the Eucharist*

29.   The Eucharist is the action of the Holy Trinity. The Father gives the Body and the Blood of Christ by the descent of the Holy Spirit to the Church in response to the Church's prayer. The Liturgy is this prayer for the eucharistic gifts to be given. It is in this context that the invocation of the Holy Spirit should be understood. The operation of the Holy Spirit is essential to the Eucharist whether it is explicitly expressed or not. When it is articulated, the *Epiclesis* voices the work of the Spirit with the Father in the consecration of the elements as the Body and the Blood of Christ.

30.   The consecration of the bread and the wine results from the whole sacramental liturgy. The act of consecration includes certain proper and appropriate moments — thanksgiving, *anamnesis, Epiclesis.* The deepest understanding of the hallowing of the elements rejects any theory of consecration by formula — whether by Words of Institution or *Epiclesis.* For the Orthodox the culminating and decisive moment in the consecration is the *Epiclesis.*

31.   The unity of the members of the Church is renewed by the Spirit in the eucharistic act. The Spirit comes not only upon the elements, but upon the community. The *Epiclesis* is a double invocation: by the invocation of the Spirit, the members of Christ are fed by his Body and Blood so that they may grow in holiness and may be strong to manifest Christ to the world and to do his work in the power of the Spirit. 'We hold this treasure in earthen vessels.' The reception of the Holy Gifts calls for repentance and obedience. Christ judges the sinful members of the Church. The time is always at hand when judgement must begin at the household of God (*2 Cor.* 4-7, *I Pet.* 4.17).

32.   Although *Epiclesis* has a special meaning in the Eucharist, we must not restrict the concept to the Eucharist alone. In every sacrament, prayer and blessing the Church invokes the Holy Spirit and in all these various ways calls upon Him to sanctify the whole of creation. The Church is that Community which lives by continually invoking the Holy Spirit.

Participants

Members of the Commission:

Orthodox:

The Most Reverend Stylianos, Greek Orthodox Archbishop of Australia
Oecumenical Patriarchate (co-chairman)

The Most Reverend Basil, Archbishop of Brussels and All Belgium
Russian Orthodox Church

The Most Reverend Basil, Metropolitan of Caesarea
Patriarchate of Jerusalem

The Reverend Ioan Bria
Romanian Orthodox Church

Professor Nicolae Chitescu
Romanian Orthodox Church

The Reverend Professor Nicolai Chivarov
Bulgarian Orthodox Church

The Very Reverend Lucian Gafton
Romanian Orthodox Church

Professor George Galitis
Patriarchate of Jerusalem

Professor Stojan Gosevic
Serbian Orthodox Church

The Right Reverend Gregory, Bishop of Tropaeou
Oecumenical Patriarchate

The Most Reverend John, Metropolitan of Helsinki
Orthodox Church of Finland

The Right Reverend Nikolai, Bishop of Bresov
Orthodox Church of Czechoslovakia

Professor Demetrios Ogitsky
Russian Orthodox Church

The Reverend Professor John Romanides
Patriarchate of Antioch and Orthodox Church of Greece

Dr. Constantine Scouteris
Orthodox Church of Greece

Dr. Andreas Tillyrides
Orthodox Church of Cyprus

Anglicans

The Right Reverend R.A.K.Runcie, Bishop of St. Albans
Church of England (co-chairman)

The Reverend Canon A. M. Allchin
Church of England

Dr. Paul B. Anderson
Episcopal Church in the U.S.A.

The Reverend Roger Beckwith
Church of England

The Reverend Canon M.J.D. Carmichael
Church of the Province of South Africa

The Right Reverend Graham R. Delbridge, Bishop of Gippsland
Anglican Church of Australia

The Reverend Canon Edward Every
Episcopal Church in Jerusalem and the Middle East

The Reverend Professor Eugene R. Fairweather
Anglican Church of Canada

The Right Reverend Richard Hanson
Church of England

The Reverend Dr. Edward Hardy
Episcopal Church in the U.S.A.

The Right Reverend Graham Leonard, Bishop of Truro
Church of England

The Reverend Dr. William Norgren
Episcopal Church in the U.S.A.

The Reverend John Riches
Episcopal Church in Scotland

The Reverend Mark Santer
Church of England

The Right Reverend Jonathan G. Sherman, Bishop of Long Island
Episcopal Church in the U.S.A.

The Right Reverend Dr. Robert E. Terwilliger, Suffragan Bishop of Dallas
Episcopal Church in the U.S.A.

The Reverend Hugh Wybrew
Church of England

MEMBERS UNABLE TO ATTEND THE MOSCOW MEETING:

Orthodox:

The Most Reverend Athenagoras, Archbishop of Thyateira and Great Britain
Oecumenical Patriarchate

The Most Reverend Methodios, Greek Orthodox Metropolitan of Aksum
Patriarchate of Alexandria

The Very Reverend Paul Schneirla
Patriarchate of Antioch

Anglicans:

The Reverend Professor John Mbiti
Church of Uganda

The Reverend Canon Edward West
Episcopal Church in the U.S.A.

SECRETARIES:

Orthodox:

The Very Reverend Archimandrite Kallistos Ware
Oecumenical Patriarchate

Anglican:

The Reverend Colin Davey
Church of England

Athens Statement 1978

I. *Introduction*

(1)   On 13th-18th July 1978 the Anglican/Orthodox Joint Doctrinal Commission held a special meeting at the Inter-Orthodox Centre of the Church of Greece, in Pendeli Monastery, Athens, where they were the guests of His Beatitude Archbishop Seraphim of Athens and All Greece. The Orthodox members represented eleven of the Orthodox Churches, and the Anglican members represented the whole Anglican communion. Two subjects were discussed: the removal of the *Filioque* clause from the text of the Creed used in the Anglican Communion, and the ordination of women. The second of these questions has brought our dialogue to a point of acute crisis. Because of the extreme urgency of the matter, the members of the Commission, meeting at Cambridge in 1977 decided to leave aside, for the time being, the agenda planned at Moscow in 1976, so as to concentrate on this problem.

(2)   The delegates gathered at Pendeli have prepared this present report in order that it may be brought to the attention of the forthcoming Lambeth Conference and be taken into consideration in any recommendations that it makes to the Churches of the Anglican Communion. We note that these issues, together with the general subject of Anglican/Orthodox relations, figure on the agenda of the Conference.

II. *The Filioque*

(3)   The delegates gathered at Pendeli unanimously reaffirm the resolution passed at the Moscow Conference in August 1976:

"(a) Because the original form of the Creed referred to the origin of the Holy Spirit from the Father,

(b) because the *Filioque* clause was introduced into this creed without the authority of an Ecumenical Council and without due regard for Catholic consent, and

(c) because this Creed constitutes the public confession of faith by the People of God in the Eucharist, the *Filioque* clause should not be included in this Creed."

(4)   Both the Orthodox and the Anglican members of the Joint Commission consider this to be a matter of grave importance, and we hope that the Churches of the Anglican Communion will implement the Moscow resolution as soon as is pastorally and constitutionally possible. We ask the bishops of the Lambeth Conference to issue a clear recommendation, that the *Filioque* be omitted from the text of the Creed by all the member Churches of the Anglican Communion.

III.   *The Orthodox position on the ordination of women to the priesthood.*

The Orthodox members of the Commission unanimously affirm the following:

(5)   God created mankind in His image as male and female, establishing a diversity of functions and gifts. These functions and gifts are complementary but, as St. Paul insists (1 Cor. 12), not all are interchangeable. In the life of the Church, as in that of the family, God has assigned certain tasks and forms of ministry specifically to the man, and others — different, yet no less important — to the woman. There is every reason for Christians to oppose current trends which make men and women interchangeable in their functions and roles, and thus lead to the dehumanisation of life.

(6)   The Orthodox Church honours a woman, the Holy Virgin Mary, the Theotokos, as the human person closest to God. In the Orthodox tradition women saints are given such titles as *megalo-martyrs* (great martyr) and *isapostolos* (equal to the apostles). Thus it is clear that in no sense does the Orthodox Church consider women to be intrinsically inferior in God's eyes. Men and women are equal but different, and we need to recognise this diversity of gifts. Both in discussion among themselves and in dialogue with other Christians, the Orthodox recognise the duty of the Church to give women more opportunities to use their specific *charismata* (gifts) for the benefit of the whole people of God. Among the ministries (*diakoniai*) exercised by women in the Church we note the following:

(a)   ministries of a diaconal and philanthropic kind, involving the pastoral care of the sick and needy, of refugees and many others, and issuing in various forms of social responsibility,

(b)   ministries of prayer and intercession, of spiritual help and guidance, particularly but not exclusively in connection with the monastic communities,

(c)   ministries connected with teaching and instruction, particularly in the field of the Church's missionary activity,

(d)   ministries connected with the administration of the Church.

This list is not meant to be exhaustive. It indicates some of the areas where we believe that women and men are called to work together in the service of God's kingdom, and where the many *charismata* of the Holy Spirit may function freely and fruitfully in the building up of the Church and society.

(7)   But, while women exercise this diversity of ministries, it is not possible for them to be admitted to the priesthood. The ordination of women to the priesthood is an innovation, lacking any basis whatever in Holy Tradition. The Orthodox Church takes very seriously the admonition of St. Paul, where the Apostle states with emphasis, repeating himself twice: 'But if we or an angel from heaven preaches to you anything else than what we have preached to you, let him be anathema. As we have already said, so I say to you now once more: if anyone preaches to you anything else than

what you have received, let him be anathema' (Gal. 1.8-9). From the time of Christ and the apostles onwards, the Church has ordained only men to the priesthood. Christians to-day are bound to remain faithful to the example of our Lord, to the testimony of Scripture, and to the constant and unvarying practice of the Church for two thousand years. In this constant and unvarying practice we see revealed the will of God and the testimony of the Holy Spirit, and we know that the Holy Spirit does not contradict Himself.

(8)   Holy Tradition is not static, but living and creative. Tradition is received by each succeeding generation in the same way but in its own situation and thus it is verified and enriched by the renewed experience that the People of God are continually gaining. On the basis of this renewed experience, the Spirit teaches us to be always responsive to the needs of the contemporary world. The Spirit does not bring us a new revelation, but enables us to relive the truth revealed once for all in Jesus Christ, and continuously present in the Church. It is important, therefore, to distinguish between innovations and the creative continuity of Tradition. We Orthodox see the ordination of women, not as part of this creative continuity, but as a violation of the apostolic faith and order of the Church.

(9)   The action of ordaining women to the priesthood involves not simply a canonical point of Church discipline, but the basis of the Christian faith as expressed in the Church's ministries. If the Anglicans continue to ordain women to the priesthood, this will have a decisively negative effect on the issue of the recognition of Anglican Orders. Those Orthodox Churches which have partially or provisionally recognized Anglican Orders did so on the ground that the Anglican Church has preserved the apostolic succession; and the apostolic succession is not merely continuity in the outward laying-on of hands, but signifies continuity in apostolic faith and spiritual life. By ordaining women, Anglicans would sever themselves from this continuity, and so any existing acts of recognition by the Orthodox would have to be reconsidered.

(10)   'If one member of the body suffers, all the other members suffer with it' (1 Cor. 12:26). We Orthodox cannot regard the Anglican proposals to ordain women as a purely internal matter, in which the Orthodox are not concerned. In the name of our common Lord and Saviour Jesus Christ, we entreat our Anglican brothers not to proceed further with this action which is already dividing the Anglican Communion, and which will constitute a disastrous reverse for all our hopes of unity between Anglicanism and Orthodoxy. It is obvious that, if the dialogue continues, its character would be drastically changed.

IV.   *Anglican positions on the ordination of women to the priesthood*

(11)   The Anglican members of the Commission are unanimous in their desire to accept and maintain the tradition of the Gospel, to which the

prophets and apostles bear witness, and to be true to it in the life of the Church. They are divided over the ways in which that tradition should respond to the pressures of the world, over the extent to which the tradition may develop and change, and over the criteria by which to determine what developments within it are legitimate and appropriate. In the case of the ordination of women differences have become particularly acute and divisive within our Communion, now that the convictions of those in favour of it have been translated into action in certain national Churches.

(12)   On this question there is a diversity of views, which was reflected in the two Anglican papers circulated for discussion by the Commission. There are those who believe that the ordination of women to the priesthood and the episcopate is in no way consonant with a true understanding of the Church's catholicity and apostolicity, but rather constitutes a grave deformation of the Church's traditional faith and order. They therefore hope that under the guidance of the Holy Spirit, this practice will come to cease in our Churches. There are others who believe that the actions already taken constitute a proper extension and development of the Church's traditional ministry, and a necessary and prophetic response to the changing circumstances in which some Churches are placed. They hope that in due time, under the guidance of the Spirit, these actions will be universally accepted. There are others who regret the way in which the present action has been taken and believe that the time was not opportune nor the method appropriate for such action, although they see no absolute objection to it. Some of them hope that through the present situation a way forward may be found which will allow for the distinct and complementary contributions of men and women to the Church's ordained ministry.

(13)   The present crisis in our conversations with the Orthodox has forced all of us to reconsider the way in which, in our Communion, decisions are made on matters of such fundamental importance. How far in such questions should consensus precede action; how far may the experience of such actions itself lead to a new consensus? What methods of decision and debate are appropriate in such matters? Should the Synods of particular Church provinces have the freedom to make decisions in matters which affect not only the whole Anglican Communion, but also our relations with all other Churches? Is the traditional Anglican claim to have no specifically Anglican Scriptures, Creeds, Sacraments and Ministry but only those of the universal Church put in jeopardy by actions of this kind? What is the ecclesiological significance of the fact that we now have a ministry not universally recognised within our own Communion? Where does our authority in such matters lie? We do not prejudge the answers to these questions. But we believe that it is vital that they should be faced and answered.

(14)   In our discussions at this Conference we have found a real willingness to listen to one another, to respect one another's view-points and

to hear what those we disagree with are saying. This has brought the discussion on this subject to a welcome level of serious theological exchange which has helped us to find a common language of discourse. It has also given us a new hope that God will show us a way through our present divisions. We believe it to be part of our responsibility to the Gospel, and of our obedience to our Lord Jesus Christ, the only Lord of the Church, to continue together in dialogue with one another, as well as with all our Christian Brethren who are willing to enter into conversation with us. We are grateful to our Orthodox brethren for their contribution to our reflections on this matter, and we look forward to the continuance of our conversations with them. There is no doubt in our minds that there are still large areas to be explored concerning the place of men and women in the ministry (*diakonia*) of the Christian Church and its mission to the world.

V. *Looking to the future*

(15)   We value our dialogue together and we are encouraged that our Churches and their leaders, as well as the members of our Commission, hope that it may continue under conditions acceptable to both sides. For, in spite of all the difficulties of our dialogue, we welcome the opportunities that it provides for us to listen to and learn from each other.

PARTICIPANTS

MEMBERS OF THE COMMISSION:

Orthodox:

The Most Reverend Athenagoras, Archbishop of Thyateira and Great Britain
Oecumenical Patriarchate (co-chairman)

The Most Reverend Stylianos, Greek Orthodox Archbishop of Australia
Oecumenical Patriarchate

The Most Reverend Basil, Archbishop of Brussels and All Belgium
Russian Orthodox Church and Orthodox Church of Poland

The Most Reverend Basil, Metropolitan of Caesarea
Patriarchate of Jerusalem

Professor Nicolae Chitescu
Romanian Orthodox Church

Deacon Dr. Petru David
Romanian Orthodox Church

The Reverend Professor Nicolai Chivarov
Bulgarian Orthodox Church

Professor George Galitis
Patriarchate of Jerusalem

The Right Reverend Gregory, Bishop of Tropaeou
Oecumenical Patriarchate

The Most Reverend John, Metropolitan of Helsinki
Orthodox Church of Finland

The Reverend Professor John Romanides
Patriarchate of Antioch and Orthodox Church of Greece

Dr. Constantine Scouteris
Orthodox Church of Greece

The Most Reverend Methodios, Metropolitan of Aksum
Patriarchate of Alexandria

The Most Reverend Chrysostom, Metropolitan of Kition
Orthodox Church of Cyprus

Dr. Andreas Tillyrides
Orthodox Church of Cyprus

Anglicans:

The Right Reverend R.A.K. Runcie, Bishop of St. Albans
Church of England (co-chairman)

The Reverend Canon A.M. Allchin
Church of England

The Reverend Dr. William Norgren
Episcopal Church in the U.S.A.

The Reverend Roger Beckwith
Church of England

The Reverend Canon M. J. D. Carmichael
Church of the Province of South Africa

The Right Reverend Graham R. Delbridge, Bishop of Gippsland
Anglican Church of Australia

The Right Reverend M. M. Thomas, Bishop of Wangaratta
Anglican Church of Australia

The Reverend Canon Edward Every
Episcopal Church in Jerusalem and the Middle East

The Reverend Dr. Edward Hardy
Episcopal Church in the U.S.A.

The Right Reverend H. G. Hill, Bishop of Ontario
Anglican Church of Canada

The Reverend Professor Eugene R. Fairweather
Anglican Church of Canada

The Right Reverend Graham Leonard, Bishop of Truro
Church of England

The Reverend John Riches
Episcopal Church in Scotland

Mr. John Sentamu
Church of Uganda

The Reverend Mark Santer
Church of England

The Right Reverend Dr. Robert E. Terwilliger, Suffragan Bishop of Dallas
Episcopal Church in the U.S.A.

The Reverend Hugh Wybrew
Church of England

SECRETARIES:

Orthodox:

The Very Reverend Archimandrite Kallistos Ware
Oecumenical Patriarchate

Anglican:

The Reverend Colin Davey
Church of England

Llandaff Statement 1980
The Communion of Saints and the Dead

(1)   All prayer is addressed to the Triune God. We pray to God the Father through our Lord Jesus Christ in the Holy Spirit. The Church on earth is united in a single movement of worship with the Church in heaven, with the Blessed Virgin Mary, 'with angels and archangels, and all the company of heaven'.

(2)   Those who believe and are baptised form one body in Christ, and are members one of another, united by the Holy Spirit. Within the body each member suffers and rejoices with the others, and in each member the Holy Spirit intercedes for the whole. These relationships are changed but not broken by death: 'There is no frontier between two worlds in the Church' (Gwenallt). 'God is not the God of the dead, but of the living' (Mt. 22:32), for all live in and to him. This is the meaning of the Communion of Saints.

(3)   God is 'the God of Abraham, the God of Isaac, and the God of Jacob' (Exod. 3:6), 'the Lord of hosts' (Is. 6:3), 'God the Father of our Lord Jesus Christ' (Rom. 15:6). Our God is not an abstract idea, but the God of persons, revealing himself in and to particular men and women. Union with God therefore involves us in a personal relationship with all who belong to him through the grace of the Holy Spirit who both unites and diversifies: and this personal relationship, which is not broken by death, is precisely the Communion of Saints.

(4)   Our experience of the Communion of Saints finds its fullest expression in the Eucharist, in which the whole Body of Christ realises its unity in the Holy Spirit. We see this in ancient eucharistic prayers of East and West, which commemorate the saints and intercede for the departed as well as for the living.

(5)   'Christ is risen from the dead trampling down death by death . . .'. By virtue of Christ's Cross and Resurrection, death is no longer an impassable barrier. It is this sense of our continuing union in the risen Christ that forms for all Orthodox the basis of prayer for the dead and invocation of the saints. It must be emphasized that, as a result of the abuses of the Medieval West, and the consequent Reformation in the sixteenth century, not all Anglicans practise such prayer and invocation. All, however, agree in affirming our union in the risen Christ.

(6)   God's love is present everywhere. Even those in hell are not deprived of the love of God, but by their own free choice they experience as
torment what the saints experience as joy. The light of God's glory is also
the fire of judgement. God's wrath is not other than his love; how we experience that love, in this life and after death, depends on our attitude.
The Orthodox Church, in the prayers of Pentecost, prays even for those in
hell.

(7)   '. . . from glory to glory' (2 Cor. 3:18): for the righteous there is, in
the view of the Orthodox and also of many Anglicans, endless progress
and growth in the love of God. In its initial stages after death, this progress is to be thought of in terms of purification rather than satisfaction,
healing rather than retribution. As Anglicans and Orthodox we are agreed
in rejecting any doctrine of purgatory which suggests that the departed
through their sufferings are making 'satisfaction' or 'expiation' for their
sins. After death and before the general resurrection the souls of those
who have fallen asleep in the faith are assisted by the prayers of the
Church, through the crucified and risen Christ—through him alone and
nothing else.

(8)   Prayers for the departed are to be seen, not in juridical terms, but
as an expression of mutual love and solidarity in Christ: 'we pray for them
because we still hold them in our love' (Catechism of the Episcopal
Church of the United States of America).

(9)   The prayers of the saints on our behalf are likewise to be understood as an expression of mutual love and shared life in the Holy Spirit.
Such a term as the 'treasury of merits' is foreign to both our traditions.
'There is one God, and one mediator between God and men, the man
Christ Jesus' (1 Tim. 2:5): the intercession of the saints for us is always in
and through this unique mediation of Christ. The saints reign with Christ
(cf. Luke 22:29-30): Christ is the King, and the saints share in his kingly
rule.

(10)   The Blessed Virgin Mary possesses a unique place in the economy
of salvation by virtue of the fact that she was chosen to be Mother of
Christ our God. Her intercession is not autonomous, but presupposes
Christ's intercession and is based upon the saving work of the Incarnate
Word.

(11)   The Orthodox practice of commemorating the saints of the Old
Testament powerfully affirms the way in which the whole history of salvation is made present in the liturgy of the Church.

(12)   Anglicans are accustomed to make a threefold distinction between prayers addressed to God to hear the saints on our behalf, simple requests to the saints to pray for us, and extended prayers addressed to the saints. Only the first kind of prayer has been included in the official prayer book of some Anglican Churches.

(13)   The principle *lex orandi lex credendi* has a particularly clear application in this whole question. The language in which we speak of the saints and the departed is derived from the life of prayer and piety. Many of the Church's affirmations concerning the Communion of Saints are expressed in hymnography and iconography. At the same time there is an appropriate doctrinal reserve which reflects the mystery of our relationship with the departed. It is in God alone that we have communion with them.

ANGLICAN-ROMAN CATHOLIC CONVERSATIONS

Final Report 1981

Malta Report 1968
Common Declaration, 24 March 1966
Common Declaration, 29 April 1977

Final Report 1981

Preface

The Report which follows is the outcome of work begun at Gazzada, Italy, on 9 January 1967. A Joint Preparatory Commission met there, in fulfilment of a joint decision by Pope Paul VI and Archbishop Michael Ramsey, expressed in a Common Declaration during their meeting in Rome in March 1966. Meeting three times in less than a year, that Commission produced a Report which registered considerable areas of Roman Catholic–Anglican agreement, pointed to persisting historical differences and outlined a programme of 'growing together' which should include, though not be exhausted in, serious dialogue on these differences. It proclaimed penitence for the past, thankfulness for the graces of the present, urgency and resolve for a future in which our common aim would be the restoration of full organic unity.

That Report was endorsed in substance by a letter of Cardinal Bea in June 1968 and by the Lambeth Conference a few weeks later. In January 1970 the signatories of the present Report met first as 'The Anglican–Roman Catholic International Commission'. Eight members of the Preparatory Commission continued to serve on the new Commission.

The purpose of this Preface is to explain briefly the aim and methods of ARCIC as these have matured in the light of our own experience, of the developments—in some aspects rapid—within our own Churches in the twelve years of our experience, in response to criticisms we have received and having regard to other ecumenical dialogues.

From the beginning we were determined, in accordance with our mandate, and in the spirit of Phil. 3.13, 'forgetting what lies behind and straining forward to what lies ahead', to discover each other's faith as it is today and to appeal to history only for enlightenment, not as a way of perpetuating past controversy. In putting this resolve into practice we learned as we progressed. As early as 1970 our preliminary papers on our three main topics link each of them with 'the Church', and this perspective was maintained and is reflected in what follows here: our work is introduced with a statement on the Church, building on the concept of *koinonia*. In the Statement *Eucharistic Doctrine* (Windsor 1971) we went so far as to claim 'substantial agreement' which is consistent with 'a variety of theological approaches within both our communions'. The Preface to our Statement *Ministry and Ordination* (Canterbury 1973) expressed the belief 'that in what we have said here both Anglicans and Roman Catholics will recognize their own faith'.

It was in the first of our two Statements on Authority (*Authority in the Church I*, Venice 1976) that we spoke more fully and revealed a more developed awareness of our aims and methods. Because 'it was precisely in the problem of papal primacy that our historical divisions found their unhappy origin', reference was made to the 'distinction between the ideal and the actual which is important for the reading of our document and for the understanding of the method we have used' (Authority I, Preface). Acknowledging the growing convergence of method and outlook of theologians in our two traditions, we emphasized our avoidance of the emotive language of past polemics and our seeking to pursue *together* that restatement of doctrine which new times and conditions are, as we both recognize, regularly calling for (Authority I, para. 25). In concluding we felt already able to invite our authorities to consider whether our Statements expressed a unity at the level of faith sufficient to call for 'closer sharing ... in life, worship, and mission'.

Some provisional response to this was forthcoming a few months later in the *Common Declaration* of Pope Paul VI and Archbishop Donald Coggan, made during the latter's visit to Rome in April 1977. Echoing our original statement of intent, 'the restoration of complete communion in faith and sacramental life', Pope and Archbishop declared, 'Our call to this is one with the sublime Christian vocation itself, which is a call to communion' (cf. 1 John 1.3). This passage (*Common Declaration*, paras. 8–9) provides a striking endorsement of a central theme of our Statements, and insists that though our communion remains imperfect it 'stands at the centre of our witness to the world'. 'Our divisions hinder this witness, but they do not close all roads we may travel together.' In other words, the *koinonia* which is the governing concept of what follows here is not a static concept—it demands movement forward, perfecting. We need to accept its implications.

This official encouragement has been echoed by many of our critics. We have seen all of them, encouraging or not, as reflecting the interest aroused by the dialogue and helping us to make ourselves clearer, as we have tried to do in the *Elucidations* (Salisbury 1979 and Windsor 1981).

Paragraph 24 of our Statement *Authority in the Church I* made it clear that, while we had reached a high degree of agreement on 'authority in the Church and in particular on the basic principles of primacy', differences persisted concerning papal authority. A much closer examination of those differences has been our main task since then. The results of that work are embodied in the Statement *Authority in the Church II* (Windsor 1981) which is here presented for the first time. Though much of the material in this Final Report has been pubished earlier, we are confident that the Report will be read as a whole, and that particular sentences or passages will not be taken out of context.

We believe that growing numbers in both our communions accept that, in the words of the Second Vatican Council's *Decree on Ecumenism,* 'There can be no ecumenism worthy of the name without interior conversion. For it is from newness of attitudes of mind, from self-denial and unstinted love, that desires of unity take their rise and develop in a mature way' (*Unitatis Redintegratio*, para. 7).

It would be wrong, however, to suggest that all the criticisms we have received over the twelve years of our work have been encouraging. We are aware of the limits of our work—that it is a service to the people of God, and needs to find acceptance among them.

But we have as much reason now as ever to echo the concluding lines of the *Common Declaration* of 1977:

> to be baptized into Christ is to be baptized into hope—'and hope does not disappoint us because God's love has been poured into our hearts through the Holy Spirit which has been given us' (Rom. 5.5). Christian hope manifests itself in prayer and action—in prudence but also in courage. We pledge ourselves and exhort the faithful of the Roman Catholic Church and of the Anglican Communion to live and work courageously in this hope of reconciliation and unity in our common Lord.

Introduction

1. Our two communions have been separated for over 400 years. This separation, involving serious doctrinal differences, has been aggravated by theological polemics and mutual intolerance, which have reached into and affected many departments of life. Nevertheless, although our unity has been impaired through separation, it has not been destroyed. Many bonds still unite us: we confess the same faith in the one true God; we have received the same Spirit; we have been baptized with the same baptism; and we preach the same Christ.

2. Controversy between our two communions has centred on the eucharist, on the meaning and function of ordained ministry, and on the nature and exercise of authority in the Church. Although we are not yet in full communion, what the Commission has done has convinced us that substantial agreement on these divisive issues is now possible.

3. In producing these Statements, we have been concerned, not to evade the difficulties, but rather to avoid the controversial language in which they have often been discussed. We have taken seriously the issues that have divided us, and have sought solutions by re-examining our common inheritance, particularly the Scriptures.

4. The subjects which we were required to consider as a result of the Report of the Joint Preparatory Commission all relate to the true nature of the Church. Fundamental to all our Statements is the concept of *koinonia* (communion). In the early Christian tradition, reflection on the experience of *koinonia* opened the way to the understanding of the mystery of the

Church. Although '*koinonia*' is never equated with 'Church' in the New Testament, it is the term that most aptly expresses the mystery underlying the various New Testament images of the Church. When, for example, the Church is called the people of the new covenant or the bride of Christ, the context is primarily that of communion. Although such images as the Temple, the new Jerusalem, or the royal priesthood may carry institutional overtones, their primary purpose is to depict the Church's experience as a partaking in the salvation of Christ. When the Church is described as the body of Christ, the household of God, or the holy nation, the emphasis is upon the relationships among its members as well as upon their relationship with Christ the Head.

5. Union with God in Christ Jesus through the Spirit is the heart of Christian *koinonia*. Among the various ways in which the term *koinonia* is used in different New Testament contexts, we concentrate on that which signifies a relation between persons resulting from their participation in one and the same reality (cf. 1 John 1.3). The Son of God has taken to himself our human nature, and he has sent upon us his Spirit, who makes us so truly members of the body of Christ that we too are able to call God 'Abba, Father' (Rom. 8.15; Gal. 4.6). Moreover, sharing in the same Holy Spirit, whereby we become members of the same body of Christ and adopted children of the same Father, we are also bound to one another in a completely new relationship. *Koinonia* with one another is entailed by our *koinonia* with God in Christ. This is the mystery of the Church.

6. This theme of *koinonia* runs through our Statements. In them we present the eucharist as the effectual sign of *koinonia*, *episcope* as serving the *koinonia*, and primacy as a visible link and focus of *koinonia*.

In the Statement *Eucharistic Doctrine* the eucharist is seen as the sacrament of Christ, by which he builds up and nurtures his people in the *koinonia* of his body. By the eucharist all the baptized are brought into communion with the source of *koinonia*. He is the one who destroyed the walls dividing humanity (Eph. 2.14); he is the one who died to gather into unity all the children of God his Father (cf. John 11.52; 17.20ff).

In the Statement *Ministry and Ordination* it is made clear that *episcope* exists only to serve *koinonia*. The ordained minister presiding at the eucharist is a sign of Christ gathering his people and giving them his body and blood. The Gospel he preaches is the Gospel of unity. Through the ministry of word and sacrament the Holy Spirit is given for the building up of the body of Christ. It is the responsibility of those exercising *episcope* to enable all the people to use the gifts of the Spirit which they have received for the enrichment of the Church's common life. It is also their responsibility to keep the community under the law of Christ in mutual love and in concern for others; for the reconciled community of the Church has been given the ministry of reconciliation (2 Cor. 5.18).

In both Statements on authority the Commission, discussing primacy, sees it as a necessary link between all those exercising *episcope* within the *koinonia*. All ministers of the Gospel need to be in communion with one another, for the one Church is a communion of local churches. They also need to be united in the apostolic faith. Primacy, as a focus within the *koinonia*, is an assurance that what they teach and do is in accord with the faith of the apostles.

7. The Church as *koinonia* requires visible expression because it is intended to be the 'sacrament' of God's saving work. A sacrament is both sign and instrument. The *koinonia* is a sign that God's purpose in Christ is being realized in the world by grace. It is also an instrument for the accomplishment of this purpose, inasmuch as it proclaims the truth of the Gospel and witnesses to it by its life, thus entering more deeply into the mystery of the Kingdom. The community thus announces what it is called to become.

8. The *koinonia* is grounded in the word of God preached, believed and obeyed. Through this word the saving work of God is proclaimed. In the fullness of time this salvation was realized in the person of Jesus, the Word of God incarnate. Jesus prepared his followers to receive through the Holy Spirit the fruit of his death and resurrection, the culmination of his life of obedience, and to become the heralds of salvation. In the New Testament it is clear that the community is established by a baptism inseparable from faith and conversion, that its mission is to proclaim the Gospel of God, and that its common life is sustained by the eucharist. This remains the pattern for the Christian Church. The Church is the community of those reconciled with God and with each other because it is the community of those who believe in Jesus Christ and are justified through God's grace. It is also the reconciling community, because it has been called to bring to all mankind, through the preaching of the Gospel, God's gracious offer of redemption.

9. Christ's will and prayer are that his disciples should be one. Those who have received the same word of God and have been baptized in the same Spirit cannot, without disobedience, acquiesce in a state of separation. Unity is of the essence of the Church, and since the Church is visible its

unity also must be visible. Full visible communion between our two Churches cannot be achieved without mutual recognition of sacraments and ministry, together with the common acceptance of a universal primacy, at one with the episcopal college in the service of the *koinonia*.

EUCHARISTIC DOCTRINE
(Windsor Statement) 1971

Preface

The following Agreed Statement evolved from the thinking and the discussion of the Anglican-Roman Catholic International Commission over the past two years. The result has been a conviction among members of the Commission that we have reached agreement on essential points of eucharistic doctrine. We are equally convinced ourselves that, though no attempt was made to present a fully comprehensive treatment of the subject, nothing essential has been omitted. The document, agreed upon at our third meeting, at Windsor, on 7 September 1971, has been presented to our official authorities, but obviously it cannot be ratified by them until such time as our respective Churches can evaluate its conclusions.

We would want to point out that the members of the Commission who subscribed to this Statement have been officially appointed and come from many countries, representing a wide variety of theological background. Our intention was to reach a consensus at the level of faith, so that all of us might be able to say, within the limits of the Statement: this is the Christian faith of the Eucharist.

H.R. McAdoo
Alan C. Clark
September, 1971

THE STATEMENT

Introduction

1. In the course of the Church's history several traditions have developed in expressing Christian understanding of the eucharist. (For example, various names have become customary as descriptions of the eucharist: Lord's supper, liturgy, holy mysteries, synaxis, mass, holy communion. The eucharist has become the most universally accepted term.) An important stage in progress towards organic unity is a substantial consensus on the purpose and meaning of the eucharist. Our intention has been to seek a deeper understanding of the reality of the eucharist which is consonant with biblical teaching and with the tradition of our common inheritance, and to express in this document the consensus we have reached.

2. Through the life, death and resurrection of Jesus Christ God has reconciled men to himself, and in Christ he offers unity to all mankind. By his word God calls us into a new relationship with himself as our Father and with one another as his children—a relationship inaugurated by baptism into Christ through the Holy Spirit, nurtured and deepened through the eucharist, and expressed in a confession of one faith and a common life of loving service.

I. *The Mystery of the Eucharist*

3. When his people are gathered at the eucharist to commemorate his saving acts for our redemption, Christ makes effective among us the eternal benefits of his victory and elicits and renews our response of faith, thanksgiving and self-surrender. Christ through the Holy Spirit in the eucharist builds up the life of the church, strengthens its fellowship and furthers its mission. The identity of the church as the body of Christ is both expressed and effectively proclaimed by its being centered in, and partaking of, his body and blood. In the whole action of the eucharist, and in and by his sacramental presence given through bread and wine, the crucified and risen Lord, according to his promise, offers himself to his people.

4. In the eucharist we proclaim the Lord's death until he comes. Receiving a foretaste of the kingdom to come, we look back with thanksgiving to what Christ has done for us, we greet him present among us, we look forward to his final appearing in the fulness of his kingdom when "The Son also himself (shall) be subject unto him that put all things under him, that God may be all in all" (1 Cor. 15.28). When we gather around the same table in this communal meal at the invitation of the same Lord and when we "partake of the one loaf", we are one in commitment not only to Christ and to one another, but also to the mission of the church in the world.

II. *The Eucharist and the Sacrifice of Christ*

5.   Christ's redeeming death and resurrection took place once and for all in history. Christ's death on the cross, the culmination of his whole life of obedience, was the one, perfect and sufficient sacrifice for the sins of the world. There can be no repetition of or addition to what was then accomplished once for all by Christ. Any attempt to express a nexus between the sacrifice of Christ and the eucharist must not obscure this fundamental fact of the Christian faith.[1] Yet God has given the eucharist to his church as a means through which the atoning work of Christ on the cross is proclaimed and made effective in the life of the church. The notion of *memorial* as understood in the passover celebration at the time of Christ—i.e. the making effective in the present of an event in the past—has opened the way to a clearer understanding of the relationship between Christ's sacrifice and the eucharist. The eucharistic memorial is no mere calling to mind of a past event or of its significance, but the church's effectual proclamation of God's mighty acts. Christ instituted the eucharist as a memorial (*anamnesis*) of the totality of God's reconciling action in him. In the eucharistic prayer the church continues to make a perpetual memorial of Christ's death, and his members, united with God and one another, give thanks for all his mercies, entreat the benefits of his passion on behalf of the whole church, participate in these benefits and enter into the movement of his self-offering.

III. *The Presence of Christ*

6.   Communion with Christ in the eucharist presupposes his true presence, effectually signified by the bread and wine which, in this mystery, become his body and blood.[2] The real presence of his body and blood can, however, only be understood within the context of the redemptive activity whereby he gives himself, and in himself reconciliation, peace and life, to his own. On the one hand, the eucharistic gift springs out of the paschal mystery of Christ's death and resurrection, in which God's saving purpose has already been definitively realized. On the other hand, its purpose is to transmit the life of the crucified and risen Christ to his body, the church, so that its members may be more fully united with Christ and with one another.

7.   Christ is present and active, in various ways, in the entire eucharistic celebration. It is the same Lord who through the proclaimed word invites his people to his table, who through his minister presides at that table, and who gives himself sacramentally in the body and blood of his paschal sacrifice. It is the Lord present at the right hand of the Father, and therefore transcending the sacramental order, who thus offers to his church, in the eucharistic signs, the special gift of himself.

8.   The sacramental body and blood of the Saviour are present as an offering to the believer awaiting his welcome. When this offering is met by faith, a lifegiving encounter results. Through faith Christ's presence—

which does not depend on the individual's faith in order to be the Lord's real gift of himself to his church — becomes no longer just a presence for the believer, but also a   presence *with* him. Thus, in considering the mystery of the eucharistic presence, we must recognize both the sacramental sign of Christ's presence and the personal relationship between Christ and the faithful which arises from that presence.

9.   The Lord's words at the last supper, "Take and eat; this is my body", do not allow us to dissociate the gift of the presence and the act of sacramental eating. The elements are not mere signs; Christ's body and blood become really present and are really given. But they are really present and given in order that, receiving them, believers may be united in communion with Christ the Lord.

10.   According to the traditional order of the liturgy the consecratory prayer *(anaphora)* leads to the communion of the faithful. Through this prayer of thanksgiving, a word of faith addressed to the Father, the bread and wine become the body and blood of Christ by the action of the Holy Spirit, so that in communion we eat the flesh of Christ and drink his blood.

11.   The Lord who thus comes to his people in the power of the Holy Spirit is the Lord of glory. In the eucharistic celebration we anticipate the joys of the age to come. By the transforming action of the Spirit of God, earthly bread and wine become the heavenly manna and the new wine, the eschatological banquet for the new man: elements of the first creation become pledges and first fruits of the new heaven and the new earth.

Conclusion

12.   We believe that we have reached substantial agreement on the doctrine of the eucharist. Although we are all conditioned by the traditional ways in which we have expressed and practised our eucharistic faith, we are convinced that if there are any remaining points of disagreement they can be resolved on the principles here established. We acknowledge a variety of theological approaches within both our communions. But we have seen it as our task to find a way of advancing together beyond the doctrinal disagreements of the past. It is our hope that, in view of the agreement which we have reached on eucharistic faith, this doctrine will no longer constitute an obstacle to the unity we seek.

Notes

1 The early church in expressing the meaning of Christ's death and resurrection often used the language of sacrifice. For the Hebrew sacrifice was a traditional means of communication with God. The passover, the example, was a communal meal; the day of Atonement was essentially expiatory; and the covenant established communion between God and man.

2 The word *transubstantiation* is commonly used in the Roman Catholic Church

to indicate that God acting in the eucharist effects a change in the inner reality of the elements. The term should be seen as affirming the fact of Christ's presence and of the mysterious and radical change which takes place. In contemporary Roman Catholic theology it is not understood as explaining how the change takes place.

ELUCIDATION (1979)

1. When each of the Agreed Statements was published, the Commission invited and has received comment and criticism. These *Elucidations* are an attempt to expand and explain to those who have responded some points raised in connection with *Eucharistic Doctrine* (Windsor 1971) and *Ministry and Ordination* (Canterbury 1973).

SUBSTANTIAL AGREEMENT

2. The Commission was not asked to produce a comprehensive treatise on the eucharist, but only to examine differences which in the controversies of the past divided our two communions. The aim of the Commission has been to see whether we can today discover substantial agreement in faith on the eucharist. Questions have been asked about the meaning of *substantial* agreement. It means that the document represents not only the judgement of all its members — *i.e.* it is an agreement — but their unanimous agreement 'on essential matters where it considers that doctrine admits no divergence' (*Ministry and Ordination* para. 17) — i.e. it is a substantial agreement. Members of the Commission are united in their conviction 'that if there are any remaining points of disagreement they can be resolved on the principles here established' (*Eucharistic Doctrine* para. 12).

COMMENTS AND CRITICISMS

3. The following comments and criticisms are representative of the many received and are considered by the Commission to be of particular importance.

In spite of the firm assertion made in the Agreed Statement of the 'once for all' nature of Christ's sacrifice, some have still been anxious that the term *anamnesis* may conceal the reintroduction of the theory of a repeated immolation. Others have suspected that the word refers not only to the historical events of salvation but also to an eternal sacrifice in heaven. Others again have doubted whether *anamnesis* sufficiently implies the reality indicated by traditional sacrificial language concerning the eucharist. Moreover, the accuracy and adequacy of the Commissions's exegesis of *anamnesis* have been questioned.

Some critics have been unhappy about the realistic language used in this Agreed Statement, and have questioned such words as *become* and *change*. Others have wondered whether the permanence of Christ's eucharistic presence has been sufficiently acknowledged, with a consequent request for a discussion of the reserved sacrament and devotions associated with it. Similarly there have been requests for clarification of the Commission's attitude to receptionism.

4.   Behind these criticisms there lies a profound but often unarticulated anxiety that the Commission has been using new theological language which evades unresolved differences. Related to this anxiety is the further question as to the nature of the agreement claimed by the Commission. Does the language of the Commission conceal an ambiguity (either intentional or unintentional) in language which enables members of the two churches to see their own faith in the Agreed Statement without having in fact reached a genuine consensus?

ANAMNESIS AND SACRIFICE

5.   The Commission has been criticized for its use of the term *anamnesis*. It chose the word used in New Testament accounts of the institution of the eucharist at the Last Supper:

'Do this as a memorial *(anamnesis)* of me' (1 Cor. 11.24-25; Luke 22.19: JB, NEB).

The word is also to be found in Justin Martyr in the second century.

Recalling the Last Supper he writes:

'Jesus, taking bread and having given thanks, said, "Do this for my memorial *(anamnesin)*: This is my body"; and likewise, taking the cup, and giving thanks, he said, "This is my blood" '*(First Apology* 66; cf. *Dialogue with Trypho* 117).

From this time onwards the term is found at the very heart of the eucharistic prayers of both East and West, not only in the institution narrative but also in the prayer which follows and elsewhere (cf. *e.g.* The Liturgy of St John Chrysostom; Eucharistic Prayer I-The Roman Missal; The Order of the Administration of the Lord's Supper or Holy Communion-The Book of Common Prayer [1662]; and An Order for Holy Communion-Alternative Services Series 3).

The word is also found in patristic and later theology. The Council of Trent in explaining the relation between the sacrifice of the cross and the eucharist uses the words *commemoratio* and *memoria (Session 22, ch. 1)*; and in the Book of Common Prayer (1662) the Catechism states that the sacrament of the Lord's Supper was ordained 'for the continual *remembrance* of the sacrifice of the death of Christ, and of the benefits which we receive thereby'. The frequent use of the term in contemporary theology is illustrated by *One Baptism, One Eucharist and a Mutually Recognised*

Ministry (Faith and Order Commission Paper No. 73), as well as by the *General Instruction on the Roman Missal* (1970).

The Commission believes that the traditional understanding of sacramental reality, in which the once-for-all event of salvation becomes effective in the present through the action of the Holy Spirit, is well expressed by the word *anamnesis*. We accept this use of the word which seems to do full justice to the semitic background. Furthermore it enables us to affirm a strong conviction of sacramental realism and to reject mere symbolism. However the selection of this word by the Commission does not mean that our common eucharistic faith may not be expressed in other terms.

In the exposition of the Christian doctrine of redemption the word *sacrifice* has been used in two intimately associated ways. In the New Testament, sacrificial language refers primarily to the historical events of Christ's saving work for us. The tradition of the Church, as evidenced for example in its liturgies, used similar language to designate in the eucharistic celebration the *anamnesis* of this historical event. Therefore it is possible to say at the same time that there is only one unrepeatable sacrifice in the historical sense, but that the eucharist is a sacrifice in the sacramental sense, provided that it is clear that this is not a repetition of the historical sacrifice.

There is therefore one historical, unrepeatable sacrifice, offered once for all by Christ and accepted once for all by the Father. In the celebration of the memorial, Christ in the Holy Spirit unites his people with himself in a sacramental way so that the Church enters into the movement of his self-offering. In consequence, even though the Church is active in this celebration, this adds nothing to the efficacy of Christ's sacrifice upon the cross, because the action is itself the fruit of this sacrifice. The Church in celebrating the eucharist gives thanks for the gift of Christ's sacrifice and identifies itself with the will of Christ who has offered himself to the Father on behalf of all mankind.

CHRIST'S PRESENCE IN THE EUCHARIST

6.　Criticism has been evoked by the statement that the bread and wine become the body and blood of Christ in the eucharist (*Eucharistic Doctrine* para. 10). The word *become* has been suspected of expressing a materialistic conception of Christ's presence, and this has seemed to some to be confirmed in the footnote on the word *transubstantiation* which also speaks of *change*. It is feared that this suggests that Christ's presence in the eucharist is confined to the elements, and that the Real Presence involves a physical *change* in them.

In order to respond to these comments the Commission recalls that the *Agreed Statement on Eucharistic Doctrine* affirmed that:

(*a*)　It is the glorified Lord himself whom the community of the faithful encounters in the eucharistic celebration through the preaching of the word, in the fellowship of the Lord's supper, in the heart of the believer, and, in a sacramental way, through the gifts of his body and blood, already given on the cross for their salvation.

(*b*) His body and blood are given through the action of the Holy Spirit, appropriating bread and wine so that they become the food of the new creation already inaugurated by the coming of Christ (*cf.* paras. 7. 10. 11).

Becoming does not here imply material change. Nor does the liturgical use of the word imply that the bread and wine become Christ's body and blood in such a way that in the eucharistic celebration his presence is limited to the consecrated elements. It does not imply that Christ becomes present in the eucharist in the same manner that he was present in his earthly life. It does not imply that this *becoming* follows the physical laws of this world. What is here affirmed is a sacramental presence in which God uses realities of this world to convey the realities of the new creation: bread for this life becomes the bread of eternal life. Before the Eucharistic Prayer, to the question: 'What is that?', the believer answers: 'It is bread.' After the Eucharistic Prayer, to the same question he answers: 'It is truly the body of Christ, the Bread of Life.'

In the sacramental order the realities of faith become present in visible and tangible signs, enabling Christians to avail themselves of the fruits of the once-for-all redemption. In the eucharist the human person encounters in faith the person of Christ in his sacramental body and blood. This is the sense in which the community, the Body of Christ, by partaking of the sacramental body of the risen Lord, grows into the unity God intends for his Church. The ultimate change intended by God is the transformation of human beings into the likeness of Christ. The bread and wine *become* the sacramental body and blood of Christ in order that the Christian community may *become* more truly what it already is, the Body of Christ.

GIFT AND RECEPTION

7. This transformation into the likeness of Christ requires that the eucharistic gifts be received in faith. In the mystery of the eucharist we discern not one but two complementary movements within an indissoluble unity: Christ giving his body and blood, and the communicants feeding upon them in their hearts by faith. Some traditions have placed a special emphasis on the association of Christ's presence with the consecrated elements; others have emphasized Christ's presence in the heart of the believer through reception by faith. In the past acute difficulties have arisen when one or other of these emphases has become almost exclusive. In the opinion of the Commission neither emphasis is incompatible with eucharistic faith, provided that the complementary movement emphasized by the other position is not denied. Eucharistic doctrine must hold

together these two movements since in the eucharist, the sacrament of the New Covenant, Christ gives himself to his people so that they may receive him through faith.

RESERVATION

8. The practice of reserving the sacrament for reception after the congregation has dispersed is known to date back to the second century (*cf.* Justin Martyr, *First Apology*, 65 and 67). In so far as it maintains the complementary movements already referred to (as for example, when communion is taken to the sick) this practice clearly accords with the purpose of the institution of the eucharist. But later there developed a tendency to stress the veneration of Christ's presence in the consecrated elements. In some places this tendency became so pronounced that the original purpose of reservation was in danger of becoming totally obscured. If veneration is wholly dissociated from the eucharistic celebration of the community it contradicts the true doctrine of the eucharist.

Consideration of this question requires clarification of the understanding of the eucharist. Adoration in the celebration of the eucharist is first and foremost offered to the Father. It is to lead us to the Father that Christ unites us to himself through our receiving of his body and blood. The Christ whom we adore in the eucharist is Christ glorifying his Father. The movement of all our adoration is to the Father, through, with, and in Christ, in the power of the Spirit.

The whole eucharistic action is a continuous movement in which Christ offers himself in his sacramental body and blood to his people and in which they receive him in faith and thanksgiving. Consequently communion administered from the reserved sacrament to those unable to attend the eucharistic celebration is rightly understood as an extension of that celebration. Differences arise between those who would practise reservation for this reason only, and those who would also regard it as a means of eucharistic devotion. For the latter, adoration of Christ in the reserved sacrament should be regarded as an extension of eucharistic worship, even though it does not include immediate sacramental reception, which remains the primary purpose of reservation (*cf.* the Instruction *Eucharisticum Mysterium* n. 49, of the Sacred Congregation of Rites (ASS 59, 1967). Any dissociation of such devotion from this primary purpose, which is communion in Christ of all his members, is a distortion in eucharistic practice.

9. In spite of this clarification, others still find any kind of adoration of Christ in the reserved sacrament unacceptable. They believe that it is in fact impossible in such a practice truly to hold together the two movements of which we have spoken: and that this devotion can hardly fail to produce such an emphasis upon the association of Christ's sacramental presence with the consecrated bread and wine as to suggest

too static and localized a presence that disrupts the movement as well as the balance of the whole eucharistic action (*cf.* Article 28 of the Articles of Religion).

That there can be a divergence in matters of practice and in theological judgements relating to them, without destroying a common eucharistic faith, illustrates what we mean by *substantial* agreement. Differences of theology and practice may well coexist with a real consensus on the essentials of eucharistic faith — as in fact they do within each of our communions.

OTHER ISSUES

10.   Concern has been expressed that we have said nothing about intercommunion, though claiming to have attained a substantial agreement on eucharistic faith. The reason is that we are agreed that a responsible judgement on this matter cannot be made on the basis of the *Agreed Statement on Eucharistic Doctrine* alone, because intercommunion also involves issues relating to authority and to the mutual recognition of ministry. There are other important issues, such as the eschatological dimension of the eucharist and its relation to contemporary questions of human liberation and social justice, which we have either not fully developed or not explicitly treated. These are matters which call for the common attention of our Churches, but they are not a source of division between us and are therefore outside our mandate.

MINISTRY AND ORDINATION
(Canterbury Statement) 1973

Preface

At Windsor, in 1971, the Anglican-Roman Catholic International Commission was able to achieve an Agreed Statement on Eucharistic Doctrine. In accordance with the programme adopted at Venice in 1970, we have now, at our meeting in Canterbury in 1973, turned our attention to the doctrine of Ministry, specifically to our understanding of the Ordained Ministry and its place in the life of the Church. The present document is the result of the work of this officially appointed Commission and is offered to our authorities for their consideration. At this stage it remains an agreed statement of the Commission and no more.

We acknowledge with gratitude our debt to the many studies and discussions which have treated the same material. While respecting the different forms that Ministry has taken in other traditions, we hope that the clarification of our understanding expressed in the statement will be of service to them also.

We have submitted the statement, therefore, to our authorities and, with their authorization, we publish it as a document of the Commission with a view to its discussion. Even though there may be differences of emphasis within our two traditions, yet we believe that in what we have said here both Anglican and Roman Catholic will recognize their own faith.

H.R. McAdoo
Alan C. Clark
September, 1973

THE STATEMENT

Introduction

1.   Our intention has been to seek a deeper understanding of Ministry which is consonant with biblical teaching and with the traditions of our common inheritance, and to express in this document the consensus we have reached.[1] This statement is not designed to be an exhaustive treatment of Ministry. It seeks to express our basic agreement in the doctrinal areas that have been the source of controversy between us, in the wider context of our common convictions about the ministry.

2.   Within the Roman Catholic Church and the Anglican Communion there exists a diversity of forms of ministerial service. Of more specific ways of service, while some are undertaken without particular initiative from official authority, others may receive a mandate from ecclesiastical authorities. The ordained ministry can only be rightly understood within this broader context of various ministries, all of which are the work of one and the same Spirit.

Ministry in the Life of the Church

3.   The life and self-offering of Christ perfectly express what it is to serve God and man. All Christian ministry, whose purpose is always to build up the community (*koinonia*), flows and takes its shape from this source and model. The communion of men with God (and with each other) requires their reconciliation. This reconciliation, accomplished by the death and resurrection of Jesus Christ, is being realized in the life of the Church through the response of faith. While the Church is still in process of sanctification, its mission is nevertheless to be the instrument by which this reconciliation in Christ is proclaimed, his love manifested, and the means of salvation offered to men.

4.   In the early Church the apostles exercised a ministry which remains of fundamental significance for the Church of all ages. It is difficult to deduce, from the New Testament use of 'apostle' for the Twelve, Paul, and others, a precise portrait of an apostle, but two primary features of the original apostolate are clearly discernible: a special relationship with the historical Christ, and a commission from him to the Church and the world (Matt. 28.19; Mark 3.14). All Christian apostolate originates in the sending of the Son by the Father. The Church is apostolic not only because its faith and life must reflect the witness to Jesus Christ given in the early Church by the apostles, but also because it is charged to continue in the apostles' commission to communicate to the world what it has received. Within the whole history of mankind the Church is to be the community of reconciliation.

5. All ministries are used by the Holy Spirit for the building up of the Church to be this reconciling community for the glory of God and the salvation of men (Eph. 4. 11-13). Within the New Testament ministerial actions are varied and functions not precisely defined. Explicit emphasis is given to the proclamation of the Word and the preservation of apostolic doctrine, the care of the flock, and the example of Christian living. At least by the time of the Pastoral Epistles and 1 Peter, some ministerial functions are discernible in a more exact form. The evidence suggests that with the growth of the Church the importance of certain functions led to their being located in specific officers of the community. Since the Church is built up by the Holy Spirit primarily but not exclusively through these ministerial functions, some form of recognition and authorization is already required in the New Testament period for those who exercise them in the name of Christ. Here we can see elements which will remain at the heart of what today we call ordination.

6. The New Testament shows that ministerial office played an essential part in the life of the Church in the first century, and we believe that the provision of a ministry of this kind is part of God's design for his people. Normative principles governing the purpose and function of the ministry are already present in the New Testament documents (e.g. Mark10.43-45; Acts 20.28; 1 Tim. 4.12-16; 1 Pet. 5.1-4). The early churches may well have had considerable diversity in the structure of pastoral ministry, though it is clear that some churches were headed by ministers who were called *episcopoi* and *presbyteroi*. While the first missionary churches were not a loose aggregation of autonomous communities, we have no evidence that 'bishops' and 'presbyters' were appointed everywhere in the primitive period. The terms 'bishop' and 'presbyter' could be applied to the same man or to men with identical or very similar functions. Just as the formation of the canon of the New Testament was a process incomplete until the second half of the second century, so also the full emergence of the threefold ministry of bishop, presbyter, and deacon required a longer period than the apostolic age. Thereafter this threefold structure became universal in the Church.

The Ordained Ministry

7. The Christian community exists to give glory to God through the fulfilment of the Father's purpose. All Christians are called to serve this purpose by their life of prayer and surrender to divine grace, and by their careful attention to the needs of all human beings. They should witness to God's compassion for all mankind and his concern for justice in the affairs of men. They should offer themselves to God in praise and worship, and devote their energies to bringing men into the fellowship of Christ's people; and so under his rule of love. The goal of the ordained ministry is to serve this priesthood of all the faithful. Like any human community the Church requires a focus of leadership and unity, which the Holy Spirit

provides in the ordained ministry. This ministry assumes various patterns to meet the varying needs of those whom the Church is seeking to serve, and it is the role of the minister to co-ordinate the activities of the Church's fellowship and to promote what is necessary and useful for the Church's life and mission. He is to discern what is of the Spirit in the diversity of the Church's life and promote its unity.

8.　In the New Testament a variety of images is used to describe the functions of this minister. He is servant, both of Christ and of the Church. As herald and ambassador he is an authoritative representative of Christ and proclaims his message of reconciliation. As teacher he explains and applies the word of God to the community. As shepherd he exercises pastoral care and guides the flock. He is a steward who may only provide for the household of God what belongs to Christ. He is to be an example both in holiness and in compassion.

9.　An essential element in the ordained ministry is its responsibility for 'oversight' (*episcope*). This responsibility involves fidelity to the apostolic faith, its embodiment in the life of the Church today, and its transmission to the Church of tomorrow. Presbyters are joined with the bishop in his oversight of the church and in the ministry of the word and the sacraments; they are given authority to preside at the eucharist and to pronounce absolution. Deacons, although not so empowered, are associated with bishops and presbyters in the ministry of word and sacrament, and assist in oversight.

10.　Since the ordained ministers are ministers of the gospel, every facet of their oversight is linked with the word of God. In the original mission and witness recorded in Holy Scripture lies the source and ground of their preaching and authority. By the preaching of the word they seek to bring those who are not Christians into the fellowship of Christ. The Christian message needs also to be unfolded to the faithful, in order to deepen their knowledge of God and their response of grateful faith. But a true faith calls for beliefs that are correct and lives that endorse the gospel. So the ministers have to guide the community and to advise individuals with regard to the implications of commitment to Christ. Because God's concern is not only for the welfare of the Church but also for the whole of creation, they must also lead their communities in the service of humanity. Church and people have continually to be brought under the guidance of the apostolic faith. In all these ways a ministerial vocation implies a responsibility for the word of God supported by constant prayer (cf. Acts 6.4).

11.　The part of the ministers in the celebration of the sacraments is one with their responsibility for ministry of the word. In both word and sacrament Christians meet the living Word of God. The responsibility of the ministers in the Christian community involves them in being not only the persons who normally administer baptism, but also those who admit converts to the communion of the faithful and restore those who have fallen away. Authority to pronounce God's forgiveness of sin, given to bishops and presbyters at their ordination, is exercised by them to bring Christians to a closer communion with God and with their fellow men through Christ and to assure them of God's continuing love and mercy.

12.   To proclaim reconciliation in Christ and to manifest his reconciling love belong to the continuing mission of the Church. The central act of worship, the eucharist, is the memorial of that reconciliation and nourishes the Church's life for the fulfilment of its mission. Hence it is right that he who has oversight in the Church and is the focus of its unity should preside at the celebration of the eucharist. Evidence as early as Ignatius shows that at least in some churches, the man exercising this oversight presided at the eucharist and no other could do so without his consent (*Letter to the Smyrnaeans, 8.1*).

13.   The priestly sacrifice of Jesus was unique, as is also his continuing High Priesthood. Despite the fact that in the New Testament ministers are never called 'priests' (*hiereis*),[2] Christians came to see the priestly role of Christ reflected in these ministers and used priestly terms in describing them. Because the eucharist is the memorial of the sacrifice of Christ, the action of the presiding minister in reciting again the words of Christ at the Last Supper and distributing to the assembly the holy gifts is seen to stand in a sacramental relation to what Christ himself did in offering his own sacrifice. So our two traditions commonly use priestly terms in speaking about the ordained ministry. Such language does not imply any negation of the once-for-all sacrifice of Christ by any addition or repetition. There is in the eucharist a memorial (*anamnesis*)[3] of the totality of God's reconciling action in Christ, who through his minister presides at the Lord's Supper and gives himself sacramentally. So it is because the eucharist is central in the Church's life that the essential nature of the Christian ministry, however this may be expressed, is most clearly seen in its celebration; for, in the eucharist, thanksgiving is offered to God, the gospel of salvation is proclaimed in word and sacrament, and the community is knit together as one body in Christ. Christian ministers are members of this redeemed community. Not only do they share through baptism in the priesthood of the people of God, but they are — particularly in presiding at the eucharist — respresentative of the whole Church in the fulfilment of its priestly vocation of self-offering to God as a living sacrifice (*Rom. 12.1*). Nevertheless their ministry is not an extension of the common Christian priesthood but belongs to another realm of the gifts of the Spirit. It exists to help the Church to be 'a royal priesthood, a holy nation, God's own people, to declare the wonderful deeds of him who called [them] out of darkness into his marvellous light' (1 Pet. 2.9, RSV).

Vocation and Ordination

14.   Ordination denotes entry into this apostolic and God-given ministry, which serves and signifies the unity of the local churches in themselves and with one another. Every individual act of ordination is therefore an ex-

pression of the continuing apostolicity and catholicity of the whole Church. Just as the original apostles did not choose themselves but were chosen and commissioned by Jesus, so those who are ordained are called by Christ in the Church and through the Church. Not only is their vocation from Christ but their qualification for exercising such a ministry is the gift of the Spirit: 'our sufficiency is from God, who has qualified us to be ministers of a new covenant, not in a written code but in the Spirit' (2 Cor. 3.5-6, RSV). This is expressed in ordination, when the bishop prays God to grant the gift of the Holy Spirit and lays hands on the candidate as the outward sign of the gifts bestowed. Because ministry is in and for the community and because ordination is an act in which the whole Church of God is involved, this prayer and laying on of hands takes place within the context of the eucharist.

15.   In this sacramental act,[4] the gift of God is bestowed upon the ministers, with the promise of divine grace for their work and for their sanctification; the ministry of Christ is presented to them as a model for their own; and the Spirit seals those whom he has chosen and consecrated. Just as Christ has united the Church inseparably with himself, and as God calls all the faithful to lifelong discipleship, so the gifts and calling of God to the ministers are irrevocable. For this reason, ordination is unrepeatable in both our churches.

16.   Both presbyters and deacons are ordained by the bishop. In the ordination of a presbyter the presbyters present join the bishop in the laying on of hands, thus signifying the shared nature of the commission entrusted to them. In the ordination of a new bishop, other bishops lay hands on him, as they request the gift of the Spirit for his ministry and receive him into their ministerial fellowship. Because they are entrusted with the oversight of other churches, this participation in his ordination signifies that this new bishop and his church are within the communion of churches. Moreover, because they are representative of their churches in fidelity to the teaching and mission of the apostles and are members of the episcopal college, their participation also ensures the historical continuity of this church with the apostolic church and of its bishop with the original apostolic ministry. The communion of the churches in mission, faith, and holiness, through time and space, is thus symbolized and maintained in the bishop. Here are comprised the essential features of what is meant in our two traditions by ordination in the apostolic succession.

Conclusion

17.   We are fully aware of the issues raised by the judgement of the Roman Catholic Church on Anglican Orders. The development of the thinking in our two Communions regarding the nature of the Church and of the Ordained Ministry, as represented in our Statement, has, we consider, put these issues in a new context. Agreement on the nature of Ministry is prior to the consideration of the mutual recognition of ministries. What we have to say represents the consensus of the Commis-

sion on essential matters where it considers that doctrine admits no divergence. It will be clear that we have not yet broached the wide-ranging problems of authority which may arise in any discussion of Ministry, nor the question of primacy. We are aware that present understanding of such matters remains an obstacle to the reconciliation of our churches in the one Communion we desire, and the Commission is now turning to the examination of the issues involved. Nevertheless we consider that our consensus, on questions where agreement is indispensable for unity, offers a positive contribution to the reconciliation of our churches and of their ministries.

Notes

1 An Agreed Statement on Eucharistic Doctrine, para. 1 which similarly speaks of a consensus reached with regard to the Eucharist.

2 In the English language the word 'priest' is used to translate two distinct Greek words, *hiereus* which belongs to the cultic order and *presbyteros* which designates an elder in the community.

3 Cf. *An Agreed Statement on Eucharistic Doctrine,* para. 5.

4 Anglican use of the word 'sacrament' with reference to ordination is limited by the distinction drawn in the Thirty-nine Articles (Article 25) between the two 'sacraments of the Gospel' and the 'five commonly called sacraments'. Article 25 does not deny these latter the name 'sacrament', but differentiates between them and the 'two sacraments ordained by Christ' described in the Catechism as 'necessary to salvation' for all men.

ELUCIDATION (1979)

COMMENTS AND CRITICISMS

1. After the publication of the Canterbury Statement on *Ministry and Ordination* the Commission received comments and criticisms, among which it judged the following to be of special concern.

It has been suggested that in the discussion of *ministry* insufficient attention was given to the *priesthood* of the whole people of God, so that the document seemed to have too clerical an emphasis. In this connection it has also been said that the distinction between this *priesthood* of all the faithful and the *priesthood of the ordained ministry* was not clearly enough explained. Questions have also been raised about the Commission's treatment of the origins and historical development of the *ordained ministry* and its threefold form; about its comparison of that development with the emergence of the canon of *scripture*; and about its views on the place of *episcopacy* within *episcope* as it is outlined in the Statement (para.9).

Some have wondered whether the Statement adequately expressed the sacramental nature of the rite of *ordination*, others whether this aspect has been overemphasized. The Commission has been asked to consider the implications of the Statement for the question of the *ordination of women*. There have also been inquiries about the bearing of the *Agreed Statement* upon the problem of recognizing the validity of Anglican Orders.

PRIESTHOOD

2.   In common Christian usage the term *priesthood* is employed in three distinct ways: the priesthood of Christ, the priesthood of the people of God, the priesthood of the ordained ministry.

The priesthood of Christ is unique. He is our High Priest who has reconciled mankind with the Father. All other priesthood derives from his and is wholly dependent upon it.

The priesthood of the whole people of God (1 Peter 2.5) is the consequence of incorporation by baptism into Christ. This priesthood of all the faithful, dealt with in *Ministry and Ordination* (para. 7), is not a matter of disagreement between us. In a document primarily concerned with the ordained ministry, the Commission did not consider it necessary to develop the subject further than it has already done in the Statement. Here the ordained ministry is firmly placed in the context of the ministry of the whole Church and exists for the service of all the faithful.

The Agreed Statement (para. 13) explains that the ordained ministry is called priestly principally because it has a particular sacramental relationship with Christ as High Priest. At the eucharist Christ's people do what he commanded in memory of himself and Christ unites them sacramentally with himself in his self-offering. But in his action it is only the ordained minister who presides at the eucharist, in which, in the name of Christ and on behalf of his Church, he recites the narrative of the institution of the Last Supper, and invokes the Holy Spirit upon the gifts.

The word *priesthood* is used by way of analogy when it is applied to the people of God and to the ordained ministry. These are two distinct realities which relate, each in its own way, to the high priesthood of Christ, the unique priesthood of the new covenant, which is their source and model. These considerations should be borne in mind throughout para. 13, and in particular they indicate the significance of the statement that the ordained ministry 'is not an extension of the common Christian priesthood but belongs to another realm of the gifts of the Spirit'.

In this as in other cases the early Church found it necessary for its understanding and exposition of the faith to employ terminology in ways in which it was not used in the New Testament. Today in seeking to give an account of our faith both our communions in the interpretation of the Scriptures, take cognisance of the Church's growing understanding of Christian truth (*cf. Authority in the Church* paras. 2, 3, and 15).

SACRAMENTALITY OF ORDINATION

3. The phrase *in this sacramental act* in para. 15 has caused anxiety on two different counts: that this phrase seems to give the sacrament of ordination the same status as the two 'sacraments of the Gospel'; and that it does not adequately express the full sacramentality of ordination.

Both traditions agree that a sacramental rite is a visible sign through which the grace of God is given by the Holy Spirit in the Church. The rite of ordination is one of these sacramental rites. Those who are ordained by prayer and the laying on of hands receive their ministry from Christ through those designated in the Church to hand it on; together with the office they are given the grace needed for its fulfilment (*cf. Ministry and Ordination* para. 14). Since New Testament times the Church has required such recognition and authorization for those who are to exercise the principal functions of *episcope* in the name of Christ. This is what both traditions mean by the sacramental rite of ordination.

Both traditions affirm the pre-eminence of baptism and the eucharist as sacraments 'necessary to salvation'. This does not diminish their understanding of the sacramental nature of ordination, as to which there is no significant disagreement between them.

ORIGINS AND DEVELOPMENT OF
THE ORDAINED MINISTRY

4. Our treatment of the origins of the ordained ministry has been criticized. While the evidence leaves ground for differences of interpretation, it is enough for our purpose to recall that, from the beginning of the Christian Church, there existed *episcope* in the community, however its various responsibilities were distributed and described, and whatever the names given to those who exercised it (*cf.* paras. 8, 9, and especially 6). It is generally agreed that, within the first century, evidence of ordination such as we have described above is provided by the *First Epistle of Clement,* chapters 40-44, commonly dated 95 A.D. Some New Testament passages appear to imply the same conclusion, e.g. Acts 14.23. Early in the second century, the pattern of a threefold ministry centered on episcopacy was already discernible, and probably widely found (*cf.* the Epistles of Ignatius to the *Ephesians,* 4; *Magnesians,* 13; *Trallians,* 2; *Philadelphians,* 2; *Smyrnaeans, 8).* It was recognized that such ministry must be in continuity not only with the apostolic faith but also with the commission given to the apostles (*cf.* the *First Epistle of Clement,* 42).

Our intention in drawing a parallel between this emergence of the threefold ministry and the formation of the New Testament canon was to point to comparable processes of gradual development without determining whether the comparison could be carried further (*cf. Ministry and Ordination* para. 6). The threefold ministry remained universal until the divisions of western Christianity in the sixteenth century. However, both our communions have retained it.

We both maintain that *episcope* must be exercised by ministers ordained in the apostolic succession (*cf*. para. 16). Both our communions have retained and remained faithful to the threefold ministry centred on episcopacy as the form in which this *episcope* is to be exercised. Because our task was limited to examining relations between our two communions, we did not enter into the question whether there is any other form in which this *episcope* can be realized.

ORDINATION OF WOMEN

5. Since the publication of the *Agreed Statement on Ministry and Ordination* there have been rapid developments with regard to the ordination of women. In those churches of the Anglican Communion where canonical ordinations of women have taken place, the bishops concerned believe that their action implies no departure from the traditional doctrine of the ordained ministry (as expounded, for instance, in the Agreed Statement). While the Commission realizes that the ordination of women has created for the Roman Catholic Church a new and grave obstacle to the reconciliation of our communions (*cf*. Letter of Pope Paul VI to the Archbishop of Canterbury, 23 March 1976), it believes that the principles upon which its doctrinal agreement rests are not affected by such ordinations; for it was concerned with the origin and nature of the ordained ministry and not with the question who can or cannot be ordained. Objections, however substantial, to the ordination of women are of a different kind from objections raised in the past against the validity of Anglican Orders in general.

ANGLICAN ORDERS

6. In answer to the questions concerning the significance of the Agreed Statements for the mutual recognition of ministry, the Commission has affirmed that a consensus has been reached that places the questions in a new context (*cf. Ministry and Ordination* para. 17). It believes that our agreement on the essentials of eucharistic faith with regard to the sacramental presence of Christ and the sacrificial dimension of the eucharist, and on the nature and purpose of priesthood, ordination, and apostolic succession, is the new context in which the questions should now be discussed. This calls for a reappraisal of the verdict on Anglican Orders in *Apostolicae Curae* (1896).

Mutual recognition presupposes acceptance of the apostolicity of each other's ministry. The Commission believes that its Agreements have demonstrated a consensus in faith on eucharist and ministry which has brought closer the possibility of such acceptance. It hopes that its own conviction will be shared by the members of both our communions; but mutual recognition can only be achieved by the decision of our authorities. It has been our mandate to offer to them the basis upon which they may make this decision.

AUTHORITY IN THE CHURCH   I
(Venice Statement) 1976

Preface

The Malta Report of the Anglican-Roman Catholic Joint Preparatory Commission (1968) outlined the large measure of agreement in faith which exists between the Roman Catholic Church and the churches of the Anglican Communion (para. 7). It then went on to note three specific areas of doctrinal disagreement. These were listed in the Report as matters for joint investigation. Accordingly the Anglican-Roman Catholic International Commission, proposed by the Report, was recommended to examine jointly 'the question of intercommunion, and the related matters of Church and Ministry', and 'the question of authority, its nature, exercise, and implications'.

To our previous Agreed Statement on the Eucharist (Windsor 1971) and Ministry (Canterbury 1973) we now add an Agreed Statement on Authority in the Church (Venice 1976). The Commission thus submits its work to the authorities who appointed it and, with their permission, offers it to our churches.

The question of authority in the Church has long been recognized as crucial to the growth in unity of the Roman Catholic Church and the churches of the Anglican Communion. It was precisely in the problem of papal primacy that our historical divisions found their unhappy origin. Hence, however significant our consensus on the doctrine of the Eucharist and of the Ministry, unresolved questions on the nature and exercise of Authority in the Church would hinder the growing experience of unity which is the pattern of our present relations.

The present Statement has, we believe, made a significant contribution to the resolution of these questions. Our consensus covers a very wide area; though we have not been able to resolve some of the difficulties of Anglicans concerning Roman Catholic belief relating to the office of the bishop of Rome, we hope and trust that our analysis has placed these problems in a proper perspective.

There is much in the document, as in our other documents, which presents the ideal of the Church as willed by Christ. History shows how the Church has often failed to achieve this ideal. An awareness of this distinction between the ideal and the actual is important both for the reading of the document and for the understanding of the method we have pursued.

The consensus we have reached, if it is to be accepted by our two communities, would have, we insist, important consequences. Common recognition of Roman primacy would bring changes not only to the Anglican Communion but also to the Roman Catholic Church. On both sides the readiness to learn, necessary to the achievement of such a wider *koinonia*, would demand humility and charity. The prospect should be met with faith, not fear. Communion with the see of Rome would bring to the churches of the Anglican Communion not only a wider *koinonia* but also a strengthening of the power to realize its traditional ideal of diversity in unity. Roman Catholics, on their side, would be enriched by the presence of a particular tradition of spirituality and scholarship, the lack of which has deprived the Roman Catholic Church of a precious element in the Christian heritage. The Roman Catholic Church has much to learn from the Anglican synodical tradition of involving the laity in the life and mission of the Church. We are convinced, therefore, that our degree of agreement, which argues for greater communion between our churches, can make a profound contribution to the witness of Christianity in our contemporary society.

It is in this light that we would wish to submit our conclusions to our respective authorities, believing that our work, indebted, as it is, to many sources outside the Commission as well as to its own labours, will be of service not only to ourselves but to Christians of other traditions in our common quest for the unity of Christ's Church.

H.R. McAdoo
Alan C. Clark
September, 1976

THE STATEMENT

Introduction

1.   The confession of Christ as Lord is the heart of the Christian faith. To him God has given all authority in heaven and on earth. As Lord of the Church he bestows the Holy Spirit to create a communion of men with God and with one another. To bring this *koinonia* to perfection is God's eternal purpose. The Church exists to serve the fulfilment of this purpose when God will be all in all.

I.   Christian Authority

2.   Through the gift of the Spirit the apostolic community came to recognize in the words and deeds of Jesus the saving activity of God and their mission to proclaim to all men the good news of salvation. Therefore they preached Jesus through whom God has spoken finally to men. Assisted by the Holy Spirit they transmitted what they had heard and seen of the life and words of Jesus and their interpretation of his redemptive work. Consequently the inspired documents in which this is related came to be accepted by the Church as a normative record of the authentic foundation of the faith. To these the Church has recourse for the inspiration of its life and mission; to these the Church refers its teaching and practice. Through these written words the authority of the Word of God is conveyed. Entrusted with these documents, the Christian community is enabled by the Holy Spirit to live out the gospel and so to be led into all truth. It is therefore given the capacity to assess its faith and life and to speak to the world in the name of Christ. Shared commitment and belief create a common mind in determining how the gospel should be interpreted and obeyed. By reference to this common faith each person tests the truth of his own belief.

3.   The Spirit of the risen Lord, who indwells the Christian community, continues to maintain the people of God in obedience to the Father's will. He safeguards their faithfulness to the revelation of Jesus Christ and equips them for their mission in the world. By this action of the Holy Spirit the authority of the Lord is active in the Church. Through incorporation into Christ and obedience to him Christians are made open to one another and assume mutual obligations. Since the Lordship of Christ is universal, the community also bears a responsibility towards all mankind, which demands participation in all that promotes the good of society and responsiveness to every form of human need. The common life in the body of Christ equips the community and each of its members with what they need to fulfil this responsibility: they are enabled so to live that the authority of Christ will be mediated through them. This is Chris-

tian authority: when Christians so act and speak, men perceive the authoritative word of Christ.

II.   Authority in the Church

4.   The Church is a community which consciously seeks to submit to Jesus Christ. By sharing in the life of the Spirit all find within the *koinonia* the means to be faithful to the revelation of their Lord. Some respond more fully to his call; by the inner quality of their life they win a respect which allows them to speak in Christ's name with authority.

5.   The Holy Spirit also gives to some individuals and communities special gifts for the benefit of the Church, which entitle them to speak and be heeded (e.g. Eph. 4.11, 12; 1 Cor. 12.4-11).

Among these gifts of the Spirit for the edification of the Church is the *episcope* of the ordained ministry. There are some whom the Holy Spirit commissions through ordination for service to the whole community. They exercise their authority in fulfilling ministerial functions related to 'the apostles' teaching and fellowship, to the breaking of bread and the prayers' (Acts 2.42). This pastoral authority belongs primarily to the bishop, who is responsible for preserving and promoting the integrity of the *koinonia* in order to further the Church's response to the Lordship of Christ and its commitment to mission. Since the bishop has general oversight of the community, he can require the compliance necessary to maintain faith and charity in its daily life. He does not, however, act alone. All those who have ministerial authority must recognize their mutual responsibility and interdependence. This service of the Church, officially entrusted only to ordained ministers, is intrinsic to the Church's structure according to the mandate given by Christ and recognized by the community. This is yet another form of authority.

6.   The perception of God's will for his Church does not belong only to the ordained ministry but is shared by all its members. All who live faithfully with the *koinonia* may become sensitive to the leading of the Spirit and be brought towards a deeper understanding of the gospel and of its implications in diverse cultures and changing situations. Ordained ministers commissioned to discern these insights and give authoritative expression to them, are part of the community, sharing its quest for understanding the gospel in obedience to Christ and receptive to the needs and concerns of all.

The community, for its part, must respond to and assess the insights and teaching of the ordained ministers. Through this continuing process of discernment and response, in which the faith is expressed and the gospel is pastorally applied, the Holy Spirit declares the authority of the Lord Jesus Christ, and the faithful may live freely under the discipline of the gospel.

7.   It is by such means as these that the Holy Spirit keeps the church under the Lordship of Christ, who, taking full account of human weak-

ness, has promised never to abandon his people. The authorities in the Church cannot adequately reflect Christ's authority because they are still subject to the limitations and sinfulness of human nature. Awareness of this inadequacy is a continual summons to reform.

III. Authority in the Communion of the Churches

8.   The *koinonia* is realized not only in the local Christian communities, but also in the communion of these communities with one another. The unity of local communities under one bishop constitutes what is commonly meant in our two communions by a 'local church', though the expression is sometimes used in other ways. Each local church is rooted in the witness of the apostles and entrusted with the apostolic mission. Faithful to the gospel, celebrating the one eucharist and dedicated to the service of the same Lord, it is the Church of Christ. In spite of diversities each local church recognizes its own essential features in the others and its true identity with them. The authoritative action and proclamation of the people of God to the world therefore are not simply the responsibilities of each church acting separately, but of all the local churches together. The spiritual gifts of one may be an inspiration to the others. Since each bishop must ensure that the local community is distinctively Christian he has to make it aware of the universal communion of which it is part. The bishop expresses this unity of his church with the others: this is symbolized by the participation of several bishops in his ordination.

9.   Ever since the Council of Jerusalem (Acts 15) the churches have realized the need to express and strengthen the *koinonia* by coming together to discuss matters of mutual concern and to meet contemporary challenges. Such gatherings may be either regional or world-wide. Through such meetings the Church, determined to be obedient to Christ and faithful to its vocation, formulates its rule of faith and orders its life. In all these councils, whether of bishops only, or of bishops, clergy, and laity, decisions are authoritative when they express the common faith and mind of the Church. The decisions of what has traditionally been called an 'ecumenical council' are binding upon the whole Church; those of a regional council or synod bind only the churches it represents. Such decrees are to be received by the local churches as expressing the mind of the Church. This exercise of authority, far from being an imposition, is designed to strengthen the life and mission of the local churches and their members.

10.   Early in the history of the Church a function of oversight of the other bishops of their regions was assigned to bishops of prominent sees. Concern to keep the churches faithful to the will of Christ was among the considerations which contributed to this development. This practice has continued to the present day. This form of *episcope* is a service to the Church carried out in co-responsibility with all the bishops of the region;

for every bishop receives at ordination both responsibility for his local church and the obligation to maintain it in living awareness and practical service of the other churches. The Church of God is found in each of them and in their *koinonia*.

11.   The purpose of *koinonia* is the realization of the will of Christ: 'Father, keep them in thy name, which thou hast given me, that they may be one, even as we are one . . . so that the world may believe that thou hast sent me' (John 17.11, 21, RSV). The bishop of a principal see should seek the fulfilment of this will of Christ in the churches of his region. It is his duty to assist the bishops to promote in their churches right teaching, holiness of life, brotherly unity, and the Church's mission to the world. When he perceives a serious deficiency in the life or mission of one of the churches he is bound, if necessary, to call the local bishop's attention to it and to offer assistance. There will also be occasions when he has to assist other bishops to reach a common mind with regard to their shared needs and difficulties. Sharing together and active mutual concern are indispensable to the churches' effective witness to Christ.

12.   It is within the context of this historical development that the see of Rome, whose prominence was associated with the death there of Peter and Paul, eventually became the principal centre in matters concerning the Church universal.

The importance of the bishop of Rome among his brother bishops, as explained by analogy with the position of Peter among the apostles, was interpreted as Christ's will for his Church.

On the basis of this analogy the First Vatican Council affirmed that this service was necessary to the unity of the whole Church. Far from overriding the authority of the bishops in their own dioceses, this service was explicitly intended to support them in their ministry of oversight. The Second Vatican Council placed this service in the wider context of the shared responsibility of all the bishops. The teaching of these councils shows that communion with the bishop of Rome does not imply submission to an authority which would stifle the distinctive features of the local churches. The purpose of the episcopal function of the bishop of Rome is to promote Christian fellowship in faithfulness to the teaching of the apostles.

The theological interpretation of this primacy and the administrative structures through which it has been exercised have varied considerably through the centuries. Neither theory nor practice, however, has ever fully reflected these ideals. Sometimes functions assumed by the see of Rome were not necessarily linked to the primacy: sometimes the conduct of the occupant of this see has been unworthy of his office: sometimes the image of this office has been obscured by interpretations placed upon it: and sometimes external pressures have made its proper excercise almost impossible. Yet the primacy, rightly understood, implies that the bishop of Rome exercises his oversight in order to guard and promote the faithfulness of all the churches to Christ and one another. Communion with him is intended as a safeguard of the catholicity of each local church, and as a sign of the communion of all the churches.

13.   A local church cannot be truly faithful to Christ if it does not desire to foster universal communion, the embodiment of that unity for which Christ prayed. This communion is founded on faith in Jesus Christ, the incarnate Son of God, crucified, risen, ascended, and now living through his Spirit in the Church. Every local church must therefore ever seek a deeper understanding and clearer expression of this common faith, both of which are threatened when churches are isolated by division.

14.   The Church's purpose in its proclamation is to lead mankind to accept God's saving work in Christ, an acceptance which not only requires intellectual assent but also demands the response of the whole person. In order to clarify and transmit what is believed and to build up and safeguard the Christian life, the Church has found the formulation of creeds, conciliar definitions, and other statements of belief indispensable. But these are always instrumental to the truth which they are intended to convey.

15.   The Church's life and word are shaped by its historical origins, by its subsequent experience, and by its endeavour to make the relevance of the gospel plain to every generation. Through reflection upon the word, through the proclamation of the gospel, through baptism, through worship, especially the eucharist, the people of God are moved to the living remembrance of Jesus Christ and of the experience and witness of the apostolic community. This remembrance supports and guides them in their search for language which will effectively communicate the meaning of the gospel.

All generations and cultures must be helped to understand that the good news of salvation is also for them. It is not enough for the Church simply to repeat the original apostolic words. It has also prophetically to translate them in order that the hearers in their situation may understand and respond to them. All such restatement must be consonant with the apostolic witness recorded in the Scriptures; for in this witness the preaching and teaching of ministers, and statements of local and universal councils, have to find their ground and consistency. Although these clarifications are conditioned by the circumstances which prompted them, some of their perceptions may be of lasting value. In this process the Church itself may come to see more clearly the implications of the gospel. This is why the Church has endorsed certain formulas as authentic expressions of its witness, whose significance transcends the setting in which they were first formulated. This is not to claim that these formulas are the only possible, or even the most exact, way of expressing the faith, or that they can never be improved. Even when a doctrinal definition is regarded by the Christian community as part of its permanent teaching, this does not exclude subsequent restatement. Although the categories of thought and the mode of expression may be superseded, restatement always builds upon, and does not contradict, the truth intended by the original definition.

16. Local councils held from the second century determined the limits of the New Testament, and gave to the Church a canon which has remained normative. The action of a council in making such a decision on so momentous a matter implies an assurance that the Lord himself is present when his people assemble in his name (Matt. 18.20), and that a council may say, 'it has seemed good to the Holy Spirit and to us' (Acts 15.28). The conciliar mode of authority exercised in the matter of the canon has also been applied to questions of discipline and of fundamental doctrine. When decisions (as at Nicea in 325) affect the entire Church and deal with controverted matters which have been widely and seriously debated, it is important to establish criteria for the recognition and reception of conciliar definitions and disciplinary decisions. A substantial part in the process of reception is played by the subject matter of the definitions and by the response of the faithful. This process is often gradual, as the decisions come to be seen in perspective through the Spirit's continuing guidance of the whole Church.

17. Among the complex historical factors which contributed to the recognition of conciliar decisions considerable weight attached to their confirmation by the principal sees, and in particular by the see of Rome. At an early period other local churches actively sought the support and approbation of the church in Rome; and in course of time the agreement of the Roman see was regarded as necessary to the general acceptance of synodal decisions in major matters of more than regional concern, and also, eventually, to their canonical validity. By their agreement or disagreement the local church of Rome and its bishop fulfilled their responsibility towards other local churches and their bishops for maintaining the whole Church in the truth. In addition the bishop of Rome was also led to intervene in controversies relating to matters of faith — in most cases in response to appeals made to him, but sometimes on his own initiative.

18. In its mission to proclaim and safeguard the gospel the Church has the obligation and the competence to make declarations in matters of faith. This mission involves the whole people of God, among whom some may rediscover or perceive more clearly than others certain aspects of the saving truth. At times there result conflict and debate. Customs, accepted positions, beliefs, formulations, and practices, as well as innovations and re-interpretations, may be shown to be inadequate, mistaken, or even inconsistent with the gospel. When conflict endangers unity or threatens to distort the gospel the Church must have effective means for resolving it.

In both our traditions the appeal to Scripture, to the creeds, to the Fathers, and to the definitions of the councils of the early Church is regarded as basic and normative.[1] But the bishops have a special responsibility for promoting the truth and discerning error, and the interaction of bishop and people in its exercise is a safeguard of Christian life and fidelity. The teaching of the faith and the ordering of life in the Christian community require a daily exercise of this responsibility; but there is no guarantee that those who have an everyday responsibility will — any more than other members — invariably be free from errors of judgement, will never tolerate abuses, and will never distort the truth. Yet, in Christian hope, we are confident that such failures cannot destroy the Church's ability to proclaim the gospel and to show forth the Christian life; for we believe that Christ will not desert his Church and the Holy Spirit will lead it into all truth. That is why the Church, in spite of its failures, can be described as indefectible.

V.   Conciliar and Primatial Authority

19.   In times of crisis or when fundamental matters of faith are in question, the Church can make judgements, consonant with Scripture, which are authoritative. When the Church meets in ecumenical council its decisions on fundamental matters of faith exclude what is erroneous. Through the Holy Spirit the Church commits itself to these judgements, recognizing that, being faithful to Scripture and consistent with Tradition, they are by the same Spirit protected from error. They do not add to the truth but, although not exhaustive, they clarify the Church's understanding of it. In discharging this responsibility bishops share in a special gift of Christ to his Church. Whatever further clarification or interpretation may be propounded by the Church, the truth expressed will always be confessed. This binding authority does not belong to every conciliar decree, but only to those which formulate the central truths of salvation. This authority is ascribed in both our traditions to decisions of the ecumenical councils of the first centuries.[2]

20.   The bishops are collectively responsible for defending and interpreting the apostolic faith. The primacy accorded to a bishop implies that, after consulting his fellow bishops, he may speak in their name and express their mind. The recognition of his position by the faithful creates an expectation that on occasion he will take an initiative in speaking for the Church. Primatial statements are only one way by which the Holy Spirit keeps the people of God faithful to the truth of the gospel.

21.   If primacy is to be a genuine expression of *episcope* it will foster the *koinonia* by helping the bishops in their task of apostolic leadership both in their local church and in the Church universal. Primacy fulfils its purpose by helping the churches to listen to one another, to grow in love and unity, and to strive together towards the fullness of Christian life and witness; it respects and promotes Christian freedom and spontaneity; it does not seek uniformity where diversity is legitimate, or centralize administration to the detriment of local churches.

A primate exercises his ministry not in isolation but in collegial association with his brother bishops. His intervention in the affairs of a local church should not be made in such a way as to usurp the responsibility of its bishop.

22. Although primacy and conciliarity are complementary elements of *episcope* it has often happened that one has been emphasized at the expense of the other, even to the point of serious imbalance. When churches have been separated from one another, this danger has been increased. The *koinonia* of the churches requires that a proper balance be preserved between the two with the responsible participation of the whole people of God.

23. If God's will for the unity in love and truth of the whole Christian community is to be fulfilled, this general pattern of the complementary primatial and conciliar aspects of *episcope* serving the *koinonia* of the churches needs to be realized at the universal level. The only see which makes any claim to universal primacy and which has exercised and still exercises such *episcope* is the see of Rome, the city where Peter and Paul died.

It seems appropriate that in any future union a universal primacy such as has been described should be held by that see.

VI. Problems and Prospects

24. What we have written here amounts to a consensus on authority in the Church and, in particular, on the basic principles of primacy. This consensus is of fundamental importance. While it does not wholly resolve all the problems associated with papal primacy, it provides us with a solid basis for confronting them. It is when we move from these basic principles to particular claims of papal primacy and to its exercise that problems arise, the gravity of which will be variously judged:

(*a*) Claims on behalf of the Roman see as commonly presented in the past have put a greater weight on the Petrine texts (Matt. 16.18, 19; Luke 22.31, 32; John 21.15-17) than they are generally thought to be able to bear. However, many Roman Catholic scholars do not feel it necessary to stand by former exegesis of these texts in every respect.

(*b*) The First Vatican Council of 1870 uses the language of 'divine right' of the successors of Peter. This language has no clear interpretation in modern Roman Catholic theology. If it is understood as affirming that the universal primacy of the bishop of Rome is part of God's design for the universal *koinonia* then it need not be a matter of disagreement. But if it were further implied that as long as a church is not in communion with the bishop of Rome, it is regarded by the Roman Catholic Church as less than fully a church, a difficulty would remain: for some this difficulty would be removed by simply restoring communion, but to others the implication would itself be an obstacle to entering into communion with Rome.

(*c*) Anglicans find grave difficulty in the affirmation that the pope can be infallible in his teaching. It must, however, be borne in mind that the doctrine of infallibility[3] is hedged round by very rigorous conditions laid down at the First Vatican Council. These conditions preclude the idea that the pope is an inspired oracle communicating fresh revelation, or that he can speak independently of his fellow bishops and the Church, or on matters not concerning faith or morals. For the Roman Catholic Church the pope's dogmatic definitions, which, fulfilling the criteria of infallibility, are preserved from error, do no more but no less than express the mind of the Church on issues concerning the divine revelation. Even so, special difficulties are created by the recent Marian dogmas, because Anglicans doubt the appropriateness, or even the possibility, of defining them as essential to the faith of the believers.

(d)　The claim that the pope possesses universal immediate jurisdiction, the limits of which are not clearly specified, is a source of anxiety to Anglicans who fear that the way is thus open to its illegitimate or uncontrolled use. Nevertheless, the First Vatican Council intended that the papal primacy should be exercised only to maintain and never to erode the structures of the local churches. The Roman Catholic Church is today seeking to replace the juridical outlook of the nineteenth century by a more pastoral understanding of authority in the Church.

25.　In spite of the difficulties just mentioned, we believe that this Statement of Authority in the Church represents a *significant convergence* with far-reaching consequences. For a considerable period theologians in our two traditions, without compromising their respective allegiances, have worked on common problems with the same methods. In the process they have come to see old problems in new horizons and have experienced a *theological convergence* which has often taken them by surprise.

In our three Agreed Statements we have endeavoured to get behind the opposed and entrenched positions of past controversies. We have tried to reassess what are the real issues to be resolved. We have often deliberately avoided the vocabulary of past polemics, not with any intention of evading the real difficulties that provoked them, but because the emotive associations of such language have often obscured the truth. For the future relations between our churches the *doctrinal convergence* which we have experienced offers hope that remaining difficulties can be resolved.

CONCLUSION

26.　The Malta Report of 1968 envisaged the coming together of the Roman Catholic Church and the churches of the Anglican Communion in terms of 'unity by stages'. We have reached agreements on the doctrines of the Eucharist, Ministry, and, apart from the qualifications of para. 24, Authority. Doctrinal agreements reached by theological commissions cannot, however, by themselves achieve the goal of Christian unity. Accordingly, we submit our Statements to our respective authorities to consider whether or not they are judged to express on these central subjects a unity at the level of faith which not only justifies but requires action to bring about a closer sharing between our two communions in life, worship, and mission.

Notes

1 This is emphasized in the Anglican tradition. Cf. the Lambeth Conferences of 1948 and 1968.
2 Since our historical divisions, the Roman Catholic Church has continued the practice of holding general councils of its bishops, some of which it has designated as ecumenical. The churches of the Anglican Communion have developed other forms of conciliarity.
3 'Infallibility' is a technical term which does not bear precisely the same meaning as the word does in common usage. Its theological sense is seen in paras. 15 and 19 above.
4 Cf. supra para. 39, infra para. 49.

ELUCIDATION (1981)

COMMENTS AND CRITICISMS

1. After the publication of the first Statement on Authority the Commission received comments and criticisms. Some of the questions raised, such as the request for a clarification of the relation between infallibility and indefectibility, find an answer in the second Statement on Authority. Another question, concerning our understanding of *koinonia*, is answered in the Introduction to this Final Report, where we show how the concept underlies all our Statements.

Behind many reactions to the Statement is a degree of uneasiness as to whether sufficient attention is paid to the primary authority of Scripture, with the result that certain developments are given an authority comparable to that of Scripture. Serious questions have also been asked about councils and reception, and some commentators have claimed that what the Statement says about the protection of an ecumenical council from error is in conflict with Article 21 of the Anglican Articles of Religion. It has been suggested that the treatment of the place and authority of the laity in the Church is inadequate. There have also been requests for a clarification of the nature of ministerial authority and of jurisdiction. Some questions have been asked about the status of regional primacies—for example, the patriarchal office as exercised in the Eastern churches. Finally, a recurring question has been whether the Commission is suggesting that a universal primacy is a theological necessity simply because one has existed or been claimed.

In what follows the Commission attempts to address itself to these problems and to elucidate the Statement as it bears on each of them. In seeking to answer the criticisms that have been received we have sometimes thought it necessary to go further and to elucidate the basic issues that underlie them. In all that we say we take for granted two fundamental principles—that Christian faith depends on divine revelation and that the Holy Spirit guides the Church in the understanding and transmission of revealed truth.

THE PLACE OF SCRIPTURE

2. Our documents have been criticized for failing to give an adequate account of the primary authority of Scripture in the Church, thereby making it possible for us to treat certain developments as possessing an authority comparable to that of Scripture itself. Our description of 'the inspired documents . . . as a normative record of the authentic foundation of the faith' (para. 2) has been felt to be an inadequate statement of the truth.

The basis of our approach to Scripture is the affirmation that Christ is God's final word to man—his eternal Word made flesh. He is the culmination of the diverse ways in which God has spoken since the beginning (Heb. 1. 1–3). In him God's saving and revealing purpose is fully and definitively realized.

The patriarchs and the prophets received and spoke the word of God in the Spirit. By the power of the same Spirit the Word of God became flesh and accomplished his ministry. At Pentecost the same Spirit was given to the disciples to enable them to recall and interpret what Jesus did and taught, and so to proclaim the Gospel in truth and power.

The person and work of Jesus Christ, preached by the apostles and set forth and interpreted in the New Testament writings, through the inspiration of the Holy Spirit, are the primary norm for Christian faith and life. Jesus, as the Word of God, sums up in himself the whole of God's self-disclosure. The Church's essential task, therefore, in the exercise of its teaching office, is to unfold the full extent and implications of the mystery of Christ, under the guidance of the Spirit of the risen Lord.

No endeavour of the Church to express the truth can add to the revelation already given. Moreover, since the Scriptures are the uniquely inspired witness to divine revelation, the Church's expression of that revelation must be tested by its consonance with Scripture. This does not mean simply repeating the words of Scripture, but also both delving into their deeper significance and unravelling their implications for Christian belief and practice. It is impossible to do this without resorting to current language and thought. Consequently the teaching of the Church will often be expressed in words that are different from the original text of Scripture without being alien to its meaning. For instance, at the First Ecumenical Council the Church felt constrained to speak of the Son of God as 'of one substance with the Father' in order to expound the mystery of Christ. What was understood by the term 'of one substance' at this time was believed to express the content of Christian faith concerning Christ, even though the actual term is never used in the apostolic writings. This combination of permanence in the revealed truth and continuous exploration of its meaning is what is meant by Christian tradition. Some of the results of this reflection, which bear upon essential matters of faith, have come to be recognized as the authentic expression of Christian doctrine and therefore part of the 'deposit of faith'.

Tradition has been viewed in different ways. One approach is primarily concerned never to go beyond the bounds of Scripture. Under the guidance of the Spirit undiscovered riches and truths are sought in the Scriptures in order to illuminate the faith according to the needs of each generation. This is not slavery to the text of Scripture. It is an unfolding of the riches of the original revelation. Another approach, while different, does not necessarily contradict the former. In the conviction that the Holy Spirit is seeking to guide the Church into the fullness of truth, it draws upon everything in human experience and thought which will give to the content of the revelation its fullest expression and widest application. It is primarily concerned with the growth of the seed of God's word from age to age. This does not imply any denial of the uniqueness of the revelation. Because these two attitudes contain differing emphases, conflict may arise, even though in both cases the Church is seeking the fullness of revelation. The seal upon the truthfulness of the conclusions that result from this search will be the reception by the whole Church, since neither approach is immune from the possibility of error.

COUNCILS AND RECEPTION

3. The Commission has been said to contradict Article 21 of the Articles of Religion in its affirmation that the decisions of what have traditionally been called ecumenical councils 'exclude what is erroneous'. The Commission is very far from implying that general councils cannot err and is well aware that they 'sometimes have erred'; for example the Councils of Ariminum and of Seleucia of 359 AD. Article 21 in fact affirms that general councils have authority only when their judgements 'may be declared that they be taken out of Holy Scripture'. According to the argument of the Statement also, only those judgements of general councils are guaranteed to 'exclude what is erroneous' or are 'protected from error' which have as their content 'fundamental matters of faith', which 'formulate the central truths of salvation' and which are 'faithful to Scripture and consistent with Tradition'. 'They do not add to the truth but, although not exhaustive, they clarify the Church's understanding of it' (para. 19).

The Commission has also been asked to say whether reception by the whole people of God is part of the process which gives authority to the decisions of ecumenical councils.

By 'reception' we mean the fact that the people of God acknowledge such a decision or statement because they recognize in it the apostolic faith. They accept it because they discern a harmony between what is proposed to them and the *sensus fidelium* of the whole Church. As an example, the creed which we call Nicene has been received by the Church because in it the Church has recognized the apostolic faith. Reception does not create truth nor legitimize the decision: it is the final indication that such a decision has fulfilled the necessary conditions for it to be a true expression of the faith. In this acceptance the whole Church is involved in a continuous process of discernment and response (cf. para. 6).

The Commission therefore avoids two extreme positions. On the one hand it rejects the view that a definition has no authority until it is accepted by the whole Church or even derives its authority solely from that acceptance. Equally, the Commission denies that a council is so evidently self-sufficient that its definitions owe nothing to reception.

THE PLACE OF THE LAITY

4. The Commission has been accused of an over-emphasis upon the ordained ministry to the neglect of the laity.

In guarding and developing communion, every member has a part to play. Baptism gives everyone in the Church the right, and consequently the ability, to carry out his particular function in the body. The recognition of this fundamental right is of great importance. In different ways, even if sometimes hesitantly, our two Churches have sought to integrate in decision-making those who are not ordained.

The reason why the Statement spoke at length about the structure and the exercise of the authority of the ordained ministry was that this was the area where most difficulties appeared to exist. There was no devaluing of the proper and active role of the laity. For instance, we said that the Holy Spirit gives to some individuals and communities special gifts for the benefit of the Church (para. 5), that all the members of the Church share in the discovery of God's will (para. 6), that the *sensus fidelium* is a vital element in the comprehension of God's truth (para. 18), and that all bear witness to God's compassion for mankind and his concern for justice in the world (Ministry, para. 7).

THE AUTHORITY OF THE ORDAINED MINISTRY

5. We have been asked to clarify the meaning of what some of our critics call 'hierarchical authority'—an expression we did not use. Here we are dealing with a form of authority which is inherent in the visible structure of the Church. By this we mean the authority attached to those ordained to exercise *episcope* in the Church. The Holy Spirit gives to each person

power to fulfil his particular function within the body of Christ. Accordingly, those exercising *episcope* receive the grace appropriate to their calling and those for whom it is exercised must recognize and accept their God-given authority.

Both Anglicans and Roman Catholics, however, have criticized the emphasis we placed on a bishop's authority in certain circumstances to require compliance.

The specific oversight of the ordained ministry is exercised and acknowledged when a minister preaches the Gospel, presides at the eucharist, and seeks as pastor to lead the community truly to discern God's word and its relevance to their lives. When this responsibility laid upon a bishop (or other ordained minister under the direction of a bishop) requires him to declare a person to be in error in respect of doctrine or conduct, even to the point of exclusion from eucharistic communion, he is acting for the sake of the integrity of the community's faith and life. Both our communions have always recognized this need for disciplinary action on exceptional occasions as part of the authority given by Christ to his ministers, however difficult it may be in practice to take such action. This is what we meant by saying that the bishop 'can require the compliance necessary to maintain faith and charity in its daily life' (para. 5). At the same time the authority of the ordained minister is not held in isolation, but is shared with other ministers and the rest of the community. All the ministers, whatever their role in the body of Christ, are involved in responsibility for preserving the integrity of the community.

JURISDICTION

6. Critics have asked for clarification on two matters.

First, what do we mean by jurisdiction? We understand jurisdiction as the authority or power (*potestas*) necessary for the effective fulfilment of an office. Its exercise and limits are determined by what that office involves (cf. Authority II, paras. 16–22).

In both our communions we find dioceses comprising a number of parishes, and groups of dioceses at the provincial, national or international level. All of these are under the oversight of a special *episcope* exercised by ministers with a shared responsibility for the overall care of the Church. Every form of jurisdiction given to those exercising such an *episcope* is to serve and strengthen both the *koinonia* in the community and that between different Christian communities.

Secondly, it has been questioned whether we imply that jurisdiction attached to different levels of *episcope*—even within the same order of ministry—is always to be exercised in an identical way. Critics give the example of the relation and possible conflict between metropolitans and local bishops. We believe that the problem is not basically that of jurisdiction but of the complementarity and harmonious working of these differing forms of *episcope* in the one body of Christ. Jurisdiction, being the power necessary for the fulfilment of an office, varies according to the specific functions of each form of *episcope*. That is why the use of this juridical vocabulary does not mean that we attribute to all those exercising *episcope* at different levels exactly the same canonical power (cf. Authority II, para. 16).

REGIONAL PRIMACY

7. Concern has been voiced that the Commission's treatment of regional primacy is inadequate. In particular, reference has been made to the ancient tradition of patriarchates.

The Commission did not ignore this tradition in its treatment of the origins of primacy (cf. para. 10). It avoided specific terms such as 'metropolitan' and 'patriarch', but in speaking of bishops with a special responsibility of oversight in their regions, the Commission intended to point to the reality behind the historical terms used for this form of episcopal coresponsibility in both east and west. It also pointed to the contemporary development and importance of new forms of regional primacy in both our traditions, e.g. the elective presidencies of Roman Catholic episcopal conferences and certain elective primacies in the Anglican Communion.

PRIMACY AND HISTORY

8. It has been alleged that the Commission commends the primacy of the Roman see solely on the basis of history. But the Commission's argument is more than historical (cf. para. 23).

According to Christian doctrine the unity in truth of the Christian community demands visible expression. We agree that such visible expression is the will of God and that the maintenance of visible unity at the universal level includes the *episcope* of a universal primate. This is a doctrinal statement. But the way *episcope* is realized concretely in ecclesial life (the balance fluctuating between conciliarity and primacy) will depend upon contingent historical factors and upon development under the guidance of the Holy Spirit.

Though it is possible to conceive a universal primacy located elsewhere than in the city of Rome, the original witness of Peter and Paul and the continuing exercise of a universal *episcope* by the see of Rome present a unique presumption in its favour (cf. Authority II, paras. 6–9). Therefore, while to locate a universal primacy in the see of Rome is an affirmation at a different level from the assertion of the necessity for a universal primacy, it cannot be dissociated from the providential action of the Holy Spirit.

The design of God through the Holy Spirit has, we believe, been to preserve at once the fruitful diversity within the *koinonia* of local churches and the unity in essentials which must mark the universal *koinonia*. The history of our separation has underlined and continues to underline the necessity for this proper theological balance, which has often been distorted or destroyed by human failings or other historical factors (cf. para. 22).

The Commission does not therefore say that what has evolved historically or what is currently practiced by the Roman see is necessarily normative: it maintains only that visible unity requires the realization of a 'general pattern of the complementary primatial and conciliar aspects of *episcope*' in the service of the universal '*koinonia* of the churches' (para. 23). Indeed much Anglican objection has been directed against the manner of the exercise and particular claims of the Roman primacy rather than against universal primacy as such.

Anglicanism has never rejected the principle and practice of primacy. New reflection upon it has been stimulated by the evolving role of the archbishop of Canterbury within the Anglican Communion. The development of this form of primacy arose precisely from the need for a service of unity in the faith in an expanding communion of Churches. It finds expression in the Lambeth Conferences convoked by successive archbishops of Canterbury which originated with requests from overseas provinces for guidance in matters of faith. This illustrates a particular relationship between conciliarity and primacy in the Anglican Communion.

The Commission has already pointed to the possibilities of mutual benefit and reform which should arise from a shared recognition of one universal primacy which does not inhibit conciliarity—a 'prospect (which) should be met with faith, not fear' (Co-Chairmen's Preface). Anglicans sometimes fear the prospect of over-centralization, Roman Catholics the prospect of doctrinal incoherence. Faith, banishing fear, might see simply the prospect of the right balance between a primacy serving the unity and a conciliarity maintaining the just diversity of the *koinonia* of all the churches.

AUTHORITY IN THE CHURCH   II
(Windsor Statement) 1981

THE STATEMENT

Introduction

1. In our conclusion to our first Statement on Authority in the Church we affirmed that we had reached 'a consensus on authority in the Church and, in particular, on the basic principles of primacy', which we asserted to be of 'fundamental importance' (para. 24). Nevertheless we showed that four outstanding problems related to this subject required further study since, if they remained unresolved, they would appear to constitute serious obstacles to our growing together towards full communion. The four difficulties were the interpretation of the Petrine texts, the meaning of the language of 'divine right', the affirmation of papal infallibility, and the nature of the jurisdiction ascribed to the bishop of Rome as universal primate. After five years of further study we are able to present a fresh appraisal of their weight and implications.

Petrine Texts

2. The position of Peter among the apostles has often been discussed in relation to the importance of the bishop of Rome among the bishops. This requires that we look at the data of the New Testament and what are commonly called the Petrine texts.
3. While explicitly stressing Christ's will to root the Church in the apostolic witness and mandate, the New Testament attributes to Peter a special position among the Twelve. Whether the Petrine texts contain the authentic words of Jesus or not, they witness to an early tradition that Peter already held this place during Jesus' ministry. Individually the indications may seem to be inconclusive, but taken together they provide a general picture of his prominence. The most important are: the bestowal on Simon of the name Cephas, his being mentioned first among the Twelve and in the smaller circle of the three (Peter, James and John), the faith which enabled him to confess Jesus' Messiahship (Matt. 16.16; Mark 8.29; Luke 9.20; and John 6.69), and the answer of Jesus (Matt. 16.18) in which he is called rock, the charge to strengthen his brethren (Luke 22.31–32) and to feed the sheep (John 21.16–17) and the special appearance to him of the risen Lord (e.g. Luke 24.34; 1 Cor. 15.5). Although the author of Acts underlined the apostolic authority of Paul in the latter part of his book, he focused in the first part on Peter's leadership. For instance, it is Peter who

frequently speaks in the name of the apostolic community (Acts 3.15, 10.41), he is the first to proclaim the Gospel to the Jews and the first to open the Christian community to the Gentiles. Paul seems to have recognized this prominence of Peter among the apostles as well as the importance of James (Gal. 1.18–19). He appears also to have accepted the lead given by Peter at the Council of Jerusalem (Acts 15), even though he was prepared to oppose Peter when he held Peter to be at fault (Gal. 2.11).

4. Responsibility for pastoral leadership was not restricted to Peter. The expression 'binding and loosing', which is used for the explicit commission to Peter in Matt. 16.19, appears again in Matt. 18.18 in the promise made by Christ directly to all the disciples. Similarly the foundation upon which the Church is built is related to Peter in Matt. 16.18 and to the whole apostolic body elsewhere in the New Testament (e.g. Eph. 2.20). Even though Peter was the spokesman at Pentecost, the charge to proclam the Gospel to all the world had previously been given by the risen Christ to the Eleven (Acts 1.2–8). Although Paul was not among the Twelve, he too was conspicuous for the leadership which he exercised with an authority received from the Lord himself, claiming to share with Peter and others parallel responsibility and apostolic authority (Gal. 2.7–8; 1 Cor. 9.1).

5. In spite of being strongly rebuked by Christ and his dramatic failure in denying him, in the eyes of the New Testament writers Peter holds a position of special importance. This was not due to his own gifts and character although he had been the first to confess Christ's Messiahship. It was because of his particular calling by Christ (Luke 6.14; John 21.15–17). Yet while the distinctive features of Peter's ministry are stressed, this ministry is that of an apostle and does not isolate him from the ministry of the other apostles. In accordance with the teaching of Jesus that truly to lead is to serve and not to dominate others (Luke 22.24ff), Peter's role in strengthening the brethren (Luke 22.32) is a leadership of service. Peter, then, serves the Church by helping it to overcome threats to its unity (e.g. Acts 11.1–18), even if his weakness may require help or correction, as is clear from his rebuke by Paul (Gal. 2.11–14). These considerations help clarify the analogy that has been drawn between the role of Peter among the apostles and that of the bishop of Rome among his fellow bishops.

6. The New Testament contains no explicit record of a transmission of Peter's leadership; nor is the transmission of apostolic authority in general very clear. Furthermore, the Petrine texts were subjected to differing interpretations as early as the time of the Church Fathers. Yet the church at Rome, the city in which Peter and Paul taught and were martyred, came to be recognized as possessing a unique responsibility among the churches: its bishop was seen to perform a special service in relation to the unity of the churches, and in relation to fidelity to the apostolic inheritance, thus exercising among his fellow bishops functions analogous to those ascribed to Peter, whose successor the bishop of Rome was claimed to be (cf. para. 12).

7. Fathers and doctors of the Church gradually came to interpret the New Testament data as pointing in the same direction. This interpretation has been questioned, and it has been argued that it arose from an attempt to legitimize a development which had already occurred. Yet it is possible to think that a primacy of the bishop of Rome is not contrary to the New Testament and is part of God's purpose regarding the Church's unity and catholicity, while admitting that the New Testament texts offer no sufficient basis for this.

8. Our two traditions agree that not everything said of the apostles as the witnesses to the resurrection and saving work of Christ (Acts 1.21–22) is transmitted to those chosen to continue their mission. The apostles are the foundations precisely because they are the unique, commissioned witnesses to the once-for-all saving work of Christ. Peter's role is never isolated from that of the apostolic group; what is true of the transmissibility of the mission of the apostolic group is true of Peter as a member of it. Consequently though the sentence, 'On this rock I will build my church', is spoken to Peter, this does not imply that the same words can be applied to the bishop of Rome with an identical meaning. Even if Peter's role cannot be transmitted in its totality, however, this does not exclude the continuation of a ministry of unity guided by the Spirit among those who continue the apostolic mission.

9. If the leadership of the bishop of Rome has been rejected by those who thought it was not faithful to the truth of the Gospel and hence not a true focus of unity, we nevertheless agree that a universal primacy will be needed in a reunited Church and should appropriately be the primacy of the bishop of Rome, as we have specified it (Authority I, para. 23). While the New Testament taken as a whole shows Peter playing a clear role of leadership it does not portray the Church's unity and universality exclusively in terms of Peter. The universal communion of the churches is a company of believers, united by faith in Christ, by the preaching of the word, and by participation in the sacraments assured to them by a pastoral ministry of apostolic order. In a reunited Church a ministry modelled on the role of Peter will be a sign and safeguard of such unity.

Jus Divinum

10. The first Statement on Authority poses two questions with respect to the language of 'divine right' applied by the First Vatican Council to the Roman primacy: What does the language actually mean? What implications does it have for the ecclesial status of non-Roman Catholic communions (Authority I, para. 24*b*)? Our purpose is to clarify the Roman Catholic position on these questions; to suggest a possible Anglican reaction to the Roman Catholic position; and to attempt a statement of consensus.

11. The Roman Catholic conviction concerning the place of the Roman

primacy in God's plan for his Church has traditionally been expressed in the language of *jus divinum* (divine law or divine right). This term was used by the First Vatican Council to describe the primacy of the 'successor in the chair of Peter' whom the Council recognized in the bishop of Rome. The First Vatican Council used the term *jure divino* to say that this primacy derives from Christ.[1] While there is no universally accepted interpretation of this language, all affirm that it means at least that this primacy expresses God's purpose for his Church. *Jus divinum* in this context need not be taken to imply that the universal primacy as a permanent institution was directly founded by Jesus during his life on earth. Neither does the term mean that the universal primate is a 'source of the Church' as if Christ's salvation had to be channelled through him. Rather, he is to be the sign of the visible *koinonia* God wills for the Church and an instrument through which unity in diversity is realized. It is to a universal primate thus envisaged within the collegiality of the bishops and the *koinonia* of the whole Church that the qualification *jure divino* can be applied.

12. The doctrine that a universal primacy expresses the will of God does not entail the consequence that a Christian community out of communion with the see of Rome does not belong to the Church of God. Being in canonical communion with the bishop of Rome is not among the necessary elements by which a Christian community is recognized as a church. For example, the Roman Catholic Church has continued to recognize the Orthodox churches as churches in spite of division concerning the primacy (Vatican II, *Unitatis Redintegratio,* para. 14). The Second Vatican Council, while teaching that the Church of God subsists in the Roman Catholic Church, rejected the position that the Church of God is co-extensive with the Roman Catholic Church and is exclusively embodied in that Church. The Second Vatican Council allows it to be said that a church out of communion with the Roman see may lack nothing from the viewpoint of the Roman Catholic Church except that it does not belong to the visible manifestation of full Christian communion which is maintained in the Roman Catholic Church (*Lumen Gentium,* para. 8; *Unitatis Redintegratio,* para. 13).

13. Relations between our two communions in the past have not encouraged reflection by Anglicans on the positive significance of the Roman primacy in the life of the universal Church. Nonetheless, from time to time Anglican theologians have affirmed that, in changed circumstances, it might be possible for the churches of the Anglican Communion to recognize the development of the Roman primacy as a gift of divine providence—in other words, as an effect of the guidance of the Holy Spirit in the Church. Given the above interpretation of the language of divine right in the First Vatican Council, it is reasonable to ask whether a gap really exists between the assertion of a primacy by divine right (*jure divino*) and the acknowledgement of its emergence by divine providence (*divina providentia*).

14. Anglicans have commonly supposed that the claim to divine right for the Roman primacy implied a denial that the churches of the Anglican Communion are churches. Consequently, they have concluded that any reconciliation with Rome would require a repudiation of their past history, life and experience—which in effect would be a betrayal of their own integrity. However, given recent developments in the Roman Catholic understanding of the status of other Christian churches, this particular difficulty may no longer be an obstacle to Anglican acceptance, as God's will for his Church, of a universal primacy of the bishop of Rome such as has been described in the first Statement on Authority (para. 23).

15. In the past, Roman Catholic teaching that the bishop of Rome is universal primate by divine right or law has been regarded by Anglicans as unacceptable. However, we believe that the primacy of the bishop of Rome can be affirmed as part of God's design for the universal *koinonia* in terms which are compatible with both our traditions. Given such a consensus, the language of divine right used by the First Vatican Council need no longer be seen as a matter of disagreement between us.

Jurisdiction

16. Jurisdiction in the Church may be defined as the authority or power (*potestas*) necessary for the exercise of an office. In both our communions it is given for the effective fulfilment of office and this fact determines its exercise and limits. It varies according to the specific functions of the *episcope* concerned. The jurisdictions associated with different levels of *episcope* (e.g. of primates, metropolitans and diocesan bishops) are not in all respects identical.

The use of the same juridical terms does not mean that exactly the same authority is attributed to all those exercising *episcope* at different levels. Where a metropolitan has jurisdiction in his province this jurisdiction is not merely the exercise in a broader context of that exercised by a bishop in his diocese: it is determined by the specific functions which he is required to discharge in relation to his fellow bishops.

17. Each bishop is entrusted with the pastoral authority needed for the exercise of his *episcope*. This authority is both required and limited by the bishop's task of teaching the faith through the proclamation and explanation of the word of God, of providing for the administration of the sacraments in his diocese and of maintaining his church in holiness and truth (cf. Authority I, para. 5). Hence decisions taken by the bishop in performing his task have an authority which the faithful in his diocese have a duty to accept. This authority of the bishop, usually called jurisdiction, involves the responsibility for making and implementing the decisions that are required by his office for the sake of the *koinonia*. It is not the arbitrary power of one man over the freedom of others, but a necessity if the bishop

is to serve his flock as its shepherd (cf. Authority Elucidation, para. 5). So too, within the universal *koinonia* and the collegiality of the bishops, the universal primate exercises the jurisdiction necessary for the fulfilment of his functions, the chief of which is to serve the faith and unity of the whole Church.

18. Difficulties have arisen from the attribution of universal, ordinary and immediate jurisdiction to the bishop of Rome by the First Vatican Council. Misunderstanding of these technical terms has aggravated the difficulties. The jurisdiction of the bishop of Rome as universal primate is called ordinary and immediate (i.e. not mediated) because it is inherent in his office; it is called universal simply because it must enable him to serve the unity and harmony of the *koinonia* as a whole and in each of its parts.

The attribution of such jurisdiction to the bishop of Rome is a source of anxiety to Anglicans (Authority I, para. 24*d*) who fear, for example, that he could usurp the rights of a metropolitan in his province or of a bishop in his diocese; that a centralized authority might not always understand local conditions or respect legitimate cultural diversity; that rightful freedom of conscience, thought and action could be imperilled.

19. The universal primate should exercise, and be seen to exercise, his ministry not in isolation but in collegial association with his brother bishops (Authority I, paras. 21 and 23). This in no way reduces his own responsibility on occasion to speak and act for the whole Church. Concern for the universal Church is intrinsic to all episcopal office; a diocesan bishop is helped to make this concern a reality by the universal jurisdiction of the universal primate. But the universal primate is not the source from which diocesan bishops derive their authority, nor does his authority undermine that of the metropolitan or diocesan bishop. Primacy is not an autocratic power over the Church but a service in and to the Church which is a communion in faith and charity of local churches.

20. Although the scope of universal jurisdiction cannot be precisely defined canonically, there are moral limits to its exercise: they derive from the nature of the Church and of the universal primate's pastoral office. By virtue of his jurisdiction, given for the building up of the Church, the universal primate has the right in special cases to intervene in the affairs of a diocese and to receive appeals from the decision of a diocesan bishop. It is because the universal primate, in collegial association with his fellow bishops, has the task of safeguarding the faith and unity of the universal Church that the diocesan bishop is subject to his authority.

21. The purpose of the universal primate's jurisdiction is to enable him to further catholicity as well as unity and to foster and draw together the riches of the diverse traditions of the churches. Collegial and primatial responsibility for preserving the distinctive life of the local churches involves a proper respect for their customs and traditions, provided these do not contradict the faith or disrupt communion. The search for unity and concern for catholicity must not be divorced.

22. Even though these principles concerning the nature of jurisdiction be accepted as in line with the understanding which Anglicans and Roman Catholics share with regard to the Church's structure, there remain specific questions about their practical application in a united Church. Anglicans are entitled to assurance that acknowledgement of the universal primacy of the bishop of Rome would not involve the suppression of theological, liturgical and other traditions which they value or the imposition of wholly alien traditions. We believe that what has been said above provides grounds for such assurance. In this connection we recall the words of Paul VI in 1970: 'There will be no seeking to lessen the legitimate prestige and the worthy patrimony of piety and usage proper to the Anglican Church . . .'[2]

Infallibility

23. It is Christ himself, the Way, the Truth and the Life, who entrusts the Gospel to us and gives to his Church teaching authority which claims our obedience. The Church as a whole, indwelt by the Spirit according to Christ's promise and looking to the testimony of the prophets, saints and martyrs of every generation, is witness, teacher and guardian of the truth (cf. Authority I, para. 18). The Church is confident that the Holy Spirit will effectually enable it to fulfil its mission so that it will neither lose its essential character nor fail to reach its goal.[3] We are agreed that doctrinal decisions made by legitimate authority must be consonant with the community's faith as grounded in Scripture and interpreted by the mind of the Church, and that no teaching authority can add new revelation to the original apostolic faith (cf. Authority I, paras. 2 and 18). We must then ask whether there is a special ministerial gift of discerning the truth and of teaching bestowed at crucial times on one person to enable him to speak authoritatively in the name of the Church in order to preserve the people of God in the truth.

24. Maintenance in the truth requires that at certain moments the Church can in a matter of essential doctrine make a decisive judgement which becomes part of its permanent witness.[4] Such a judgement makes it clear what the truth is, and strengthens the Church's confidence in proclaiming the Gospel. Obvious examples of such judgements are occasions when general councils define the faith. These judgements, by virtue of their foundation in revelation and their appropriateness to the need of the time, express a renewed unity in the truth to which they summon the whole Church.

25. The Church in all its members is involved in such a definition which clarifies and enriches their grasp of the truth. Their active reflection upon the definition in its turn clarifies its significance. Moreover, although it is not through reception by the people of God that a definition first acquires authority, the assent of the faithful is the ultimate indication that the Church's authoritative decision in a matter of faith has been truly pre-

served from error by the Holy Spirit. The Holy Spirit who maintains the Church in the truth will bring its members to receive the definition as true and to assimilate it if what has been declared genuinely expounds the revelation.

26. The Church exercises teaching authority through various instruments and agencies at various levels (cf. Authority I, paras. 9 and 18–22). When matters of faith are at stake decisions may be made by the Church in universal councils; we are agreed that these are authoritative (cf. Authority I, para. 19). We have also recognized the need in a united Church for a universal primate who, presiding over the *koinonia,* can speak with authority in the name of the Church (cf. Authority I, para. 23). Through both these agencies the Church can make a decisive judgement in matters of faith, and so exclude error.

27. The purpose of this service cannot be to add to the content of revelation, but is to recall and emphasize some important truth; to expound the faith more lucidly; to expose error; to draw out implications not sufficiently recognized; and to show how Christian truth applies to contemporary issues. These statements would be intended to articulate, elucidate or define matters of faith which the community believes at least implicitly. The welfare of the *koinonia* does not require that all the statements of those who speak authoritatively on behalf of the Church should be considered permanent expressions of the truth. But situations may occur where serious divisions of opinion on crucial issues of pastoral urgency call for a more definitive judgement. Any such statement would be intended as an expression of the mind of the Church, understood not only in the context of its time and place but also in the light of the Church's whole experience and tradition. All such definitions are provoked by specific historical situations and are always made in terms of the understanding and framework of their age (cf. Authority I, para. 15). But in the continuing life of the Church they retain a lasting significance if they are safeguarding the substance of the faith.

The Church's teaching authority is a service to which the faithful look for guidance especially in times of uncertainty; but the assurance of the truthfulness of its teaching rests ultimately rather upon its fidelity to the Gospel than upon the character or office of the person by whom it is expressed. The Church's teaching is proclaimed because it is true; it is not true simply because it has been proclaimed. The value of such authoritative proclamation lies in the guidance that it gives to the faithful. However, neither general councils nor universal primates are invariably preserved from error even in official declarations (cf. Authority Elucidation, para. 3).

28. The Church's judgement is normally given through synodal decision, but at times a primate acting in communion with his fellow bishops may articulate the decision even apart from a synod. Although responsibility for preserving the Church from fundamental error belongs to the whole Church, it may be exercised on its behalf by a universal primate. The ex-

ercise of authority in the Church need not have the effect of stifling the freedom of the Spirit to inspire other agencies and individuals. In fact, there have been times in the history of the Church when both councils and universal primates have protected legitimate positions which have been under attack.

29. A service of preserving the Church from error has been performed by the bishop of Rome as universal primate both within and outside the synodal process. The judgement of Leo I, for example, in his letter received by the Council of Chalcedon, helped to maintain a balanced view of the two natures in Christ. This does not mean that other bishops are restricted to a merely consultative role, nor that every statement of the bishop of Rome instantly solves the immediate problem or decides the matter at issue for ever. To be a decisive discernment of the truth, the judgement of the bishop of Rome must satisfy rigorous conditions. He must speak explicitly as the focus within the *koinonia*; without being under duress from external pressures; having sought to discover the mind of his fellow bishops and of the Church as a whole; and with a clear intention to issue a binding decision upon a matter of faith or morals. Some of these conditions were laid down by the First Vatican Council.[5] When it is plain that all these conditions have been fulfilled, Roman Catholics conclude that the judgement is preserved from error and the proposition true. If the definition proposed for assent were not manifestly a legitimate interpretation of biblical faith and in line with orthodox tradition, Anglicans would think it a duty to reserve the reception of the definition for study and discussion.

30. This approach is illustrated by the reaction of many Anglicans to the Marian definitions, which are the only examples of such dogmas promulgated by the bishop of Rome apart from a synod since the separation of our two communions. Anglicans and Roman Catholics can agree in much of the truth that these two dogmas are designed to affirm. We agree that there can be but one mediator between God and man, Jesus Christ, and reject any interpretation of the role of Mary which obscures this affirmation. We agree in recognizing that Christian understanding of Mary is inseparably linked with the doctrines of Christ and of the Church. We agree in recognizing the grace and unique vocation of Mary, Mother of God Incarnate (*Theotokos*), in observing her festivals, and in according her honour in the communion of saints. We agree that she was prepared by divine grace to be the mother of our Redeemer, by whom she herself was redeemed and received into glory. We further agree in recognizing in Mary a model of holiness, obedience and faith for all Christians. We accept that it is possible to regard her as a prophetic figure of the Church of God before as well as after the Incarnation.[6] Nevertheless the dogmas of the Immaculate Conception and the Assumption raise a special problem for those Anglicans who do not consider that the precise definitions given by these dogmas are sufficiently supported by Scripture. For many Anglicans the teaching authority of the bishop of Rome, independent of a council, is

not recommended by the fact that through it these Marian doctrines were proclaimed as dogmas binding on all the faithful. Anglicans would also ask whether, in any future union between our two Churches, they would be required to subscribe to such dogmatic statements. One consequence of our separation has been a tendency for Anglicans and Roman Catholics alike to exaggerate the importance of the Marian dogmas in themselves at the expense of other truths more closely related to the foundation of the Christian faith.

31. In spite of our agreement over the need of a universal primacy in a united Church, Anglicans do not accept the guaranteed possession of such a gift of divine assistance in judgement necessarily attached to the office of the bishop of Rome by virtue of which his formal decisions can be known to be wholly assured before their reception by the faithful. Nevertheless the problem about reception is inherently difficult. It would be incorrect to suggest that in controversies of faith no conciliar or papal definition possesses a right to attentive sympathy and acceptance until it has been examined by every individual Christian and subjected to the scrutiny of his private judgement. We agree that, without a special charism guarding the judgement of the universal primate, the Church would still possess means of receiving and ascertaining the truth of revelation. This is evident in the acknowledged gifts of grace and truth in churches not in full communion with the Roman see.

32. Roman Catholic tradition has used the term infallibility to describe guaranteed freedom from fundamental error in judgement.[7] We agree that this is a term applicable unconditionally only to God, and that to use it of a human being, even in highly restricted circumstances, can produce many misunderstandings. That is why in stating our belief in the preservation of the Church from error we have avoided using the term. We also recognize that the ascription to the bishop of Rome of infallibility under certain conditions has tended to lend exaggerated importance to all his statements.

33. We have already been able to agree that conciliarity and primacy are complementary (Authority I, paras. 22–23). We can now together affirm that the Church needs both a multiple, dispersed authority, with which all God's people are actively involved, and also a universal primate as servant and focus of visible unity in truth and love. This does not mean that all differences have been eliminated; but if any Petrine function and office are exercised in the living Church of which a universal primate is called to serve as a visible focus, then it inheres in his office that he should have both a defined teaching responsibility and appropriate gifts of the Spirit to enable him to discharge it.

Contemporary discussions of conciliarity and primacy in both communions indicate that we are not dealing with positions destined to remain static. We suggest that some difficulties will not be wholly resolved until a practical initiative has been taken and our two Churches have lived together more visibly in the one *koinonia*.

CONCLUSION

This Final Report of the Anglican—Roman Catholic International Commission represents a significant stage in relations between the Anglican Communion and the Roman Catholic Church. The decision by our respective authorities, made as long ago as 1966, to enter into serious dialogue in order to resolve long-standing issues which have been at the origin of our separation, resulted in our concentration on three main areas of controversy: the doctrine of the eucharist, ministry and ordination, and the nature and exercise of authority in the Church.

This dialogue, however, has been directed not merely to the achievement of doctrinal agreement, which is central to our reconciliation, but to the far greater goal of organic unity. The convergence reflected in our Final Report would appear to call for the establishing of a new relationship between our Churches as a next stage in the journey towards Christian unity.

We understand but do not share the fears of those who think that such Statements constitute a threat to all that is distinctive and true in their own traditions. It is our hope to carry with us in the substance of our agreement not only Roman Catholics and Anglicans but all Christians, and that what we have done may contribute to the visible unity of all the people of God as well as to the reconciliation of our two Churches.

We are well aware of how much we owe to others and of how much we have left others still to do. Our agreement still needs to be tested, but in 1981 it has become abundantly clear that, under the Holy Spirit, our Churches have grown closer together in faith and charity. There are high expectations that significant initiatives will be boldly undertaken to deepen our reconciliation and lead us forward in the quest for the full communion to which we have been committed, in obedience to God, from the beginning of our dialogue.

Notes

1. 'ex ipsius Christi Domini institutione seu iure divino' (*Pastor Aeternus,* ch. 2).
2. There will be no seeking to lessen the legitimate prestige and the worthy patrimony of piety and usage proper to the Anglican Church when the Roman Catholic Church—this humble "Servant of the servants of God"—is able to embrace her ever beloved Sister in the one authentic communion of the family of Christ . . .' (AAS 62 (1970), p. 753).
3. This is the meaning of *indefectibility,* a term which does not speak of the Church's lack of defects but confesses that, despite all its many weaknesses and failures, Christ is faithful to his promise that the gates of hell shall not prevail against it.
4. That this is in line with Anglican belief is clear from the Thirty-nine Articles (Article 20): 'The Church hath . . . authority in Controversies of Faith'.
5. The phrase 'eiusmodi . . . definitiones ex sese, non autem ex consensu ecclesiae

irreformabiles esse': 'such definitions are irreformable by themselves and not by reason of the agreement of the Church' (*Pastor Aeternus,* ch. 4) does not deny the importance of reception of doctrinal statements in the Roman Catholic Church. The phrase was used by the Council to rule out the opinion of those who maintained that such a statement becomes 'irreformable' only subsequently when it is approved by the bishops. The term 'irreformable' means that the truth expressed in the definition can no longer be questioned. 'Irreformable' does not mean that the definition is the Church's last word on the matter and that the definition cannot be restated in other terms.

6. The affirmation of the Roman Catholic Church that Mary was conceived without original sin is based on recognition of her unique role within the mystery of the Incarnation. By being thus prepared to be the mother of our Redeemer, she also becomes a sign that the salvation won by Christ was operative among all mankind before his birth. The affirmation that her glory in heaven involves full participation in the fruits of salvation expresses and reinforces our faith that the life of the world to come has already broken into the life of our world. It is the conviction of Roman Catholics that the Marian dogmas formulate a faith consonant with Scripture.

7. In Roman Catholic doctrine, *infallibility* means only the preservation of the judgement from error for the maintenance of the Church in the truth, not positive inspiration or revelation. Moreover the infallibility ascribed to the bishop of Rome is a gift to be, in certain circumstances and under precise conditions, an organ of the infallibility of the Church.

PARTICIPANTS

Anglican Delegates

The Most Revd. Henry McAdoo, Archbishop of Dublin (Co-Chairman)

The Rt. Revd. Felix Arnott, formerly Archbishop of Brisbane, now Anglican Chaplain in Venice

The Rt. Revd. John Moorman, formerly Bishop of Ripon

The Rt. Revd. Edward Knapp-Fisher, Archdeacon of Westminster

The Rt. Revd. Arthur A. Vogel, Bishop of West Missouri

The Revd. Professor Henry Chadwick, Regius Professor of Divinity, University of Cambridge

The Revd. Julian Charley, Rector, St Peter's, Everton, and Warden of Shrewsbury House

The Revd. Canon Eugene R. Fairweather, Keble Professor of Divinity, Trinity College, University of Toronto

The Revd. Canon Howard Root, Director of the Anglican Centre in Rome

Consultants

The Revd. Canon John Halliburton, Principal, Chichester Theological College

The Revd. Dr Harry Smythe, formerly Director of the Anglican Centre, Rome

Secretaries
The Revd. Colin Davey, Assistant Chaplain, Archbishop of Canterbury's Counsellors on Foreign Relations (*until July 1974*)
The Revd. Christopher Hill, Assistant Chaplain, Archbishop of Canterbury's Counsellors on Foreign Relations (*from August 1974*)

Roman Catholic Delegates
The Rt. Revd. Alan Clark, Bishop of East Anglia (Co-Chairman)
The Rt. Revd. Christopher Butler, OSB, Auxiliary Bishop of Westminster
The Revd. Fr Barnabas Ahern, CP, Professor of Sacred Scripture, Rome
The Revd. Fr Pierre Duprey, WF, Under Secretary, Vatican Secretariat for Promoting Christian Unity
The Revd. Dr Herbert Ryan, SJ, Professor of Theology, Loyola Marymount University, Los Angeles
Professor John Scarisbrick, Professor of History, University of Warwick
The Revd. Fr George H. Tavard, AA, Professor of Theology, Methodist Theological School, Delaware, Ohio
The Revd. Fr Jean Tillard, OP, Professor of Dogmatic Theology, Dominican Faculty of Theology, Ottawa
The Revd. Dr Edward Yarnold, SJ, Tutor in Theology, Campion Hall, Oxford

Secretary
The Rt. Revd. Mgr William Purdy, Staff Member, Vatican Secretariat for Promoting Christian Unity

World Council of Churches Observer
The Revd. Dr Günther Gassmann, President, Lutherisches Kirchenamt, Hannover

APPENDICES

THE MALTA REPORT

Report of the Anglican-Roman Catholic Preparatory Commission, 1968

I.

1. The visit of the Archbishop of Canterbury to Pope Paul VI in March 1966, and their decision to constitute an Anglican/Roman Catholic Joint Preparatory Commission, marked a new stage in relations between our two Churches. The three meetings of the Commission, held during 1967 at Gazzada, Huntercombe, and in Matla, were characterized not only by a spirit of charity and frankness, but also by a growing sense of urgency, penitence, thankfulness, and purpose: of urgency, in response to the pressure of God's will, apprehended as well in the processes of history and the aspirations and achievements of men in his world as in the life, worship, witness, and service of his Church; of penitence, in the conviction of our shared responsibility for cherishing animosities and prejudices which for four hundred years have kept us apart, and prevented our attempting to understand or resolve our differences; of thankfulness for the measure of unity which through baptism into Christ we already share, and for our recent growth towards greater unity and mutual understanding; of purpose, in our determination that the work begun in us by God shall be brought by his grace, to fulfilment in the restoration of his peace to his Church and his world.

2. The members of the Commission have completed the preparatory work committed to them by compiling this report which they submit for their consideration to His Holiness the Pope and His Grace the Archbishop. The Decree on Ecumenism recognizes that among the Western Communions separated from the Roman See the Churches of the Anglican Communion 'hold a special place'. We hope in humility that our work may so help to further reconciliation between Anglicans and Roman Catholics as also to promote the wider unity of all Christians in their common Lord. We share the hope and prayer expressed in the common declaration issued by the Pope and the Archbishop after their meeting that 'a serious dialogue founded on the Gospels and on the ancient common traditions may lead to that unity in truth for which Christ prayed'.

3. We record with great thankfulness our common faith in God our Father, in our Lord Jesus Christ, and in the Holy Spirit; our common baptism in the one Church of God; our sharing of the holy Scriptures, of the Apostles' and Nicene Creeds, the Chalcedonian definition, and the

teaching of the Fathers; our common Christian inheritance for many centuries with its living traditions of liturgy, theology, spirituality, Church order, and mission.

4.   Divergences since the sixteenth century have arisen not so much from the substance of this inheritance as from our separate ways of receiving it. They derive from our experience of its value and power, from our interpretation of its meaning and authority, from our formulation of its content, from our theological elaboration of what it implies, and from our understanding of the manner in which the Church should keep and teach the Faith. Further study is needed to distinguish between those differences which are merely apparent, and those which are real and require serious examination.

5.   We agree that revealed Truth is given in holy Scripture and formulated in dogmatic definitions through thought-forms and language which are historically conditioned. We are encouraged by the growing agreement of theologians in our two Communions on methods of interpreting this historical transmission of revelation. We should examine further and together both the way in which we assent to apprehend dogmatic truths and the legitimate means of understanding and interpreting them theologically. Although we agree that doctrinal comprehensiveness must have its limits, we believe that diversity has an intrinsic value when used creatively rather than destructively.

6.   In considering these questions within the context of the present situation of our two Communions, we propose particularly as matter for dialogue the following possible convergences of lines of thought: first, between the traditional Anglican distinction of internal and external communion and the distinction drawn by the Vatican Council between full and partical communion; secondly, between the Anglican distinction of fundamentals from non-fundamentals and the distinction implied by the Vatican Council's references to a 'hierarchy of truths' (Decree on Ecumenism, 11), to the difference between 'revealed truths' and 'the manner in which they are formulated' (Pastoral Constitution on the Church in the Modern World, 62), and to diversities in theological tradition being often 'complementary rather than conflicting' (Decree on Ecumenism, 17).

II.

7.   We recommend that the second stage in our growing together begin with an official and explicit affirmation of mutual recognition from the highest authorities of each Communion. It would acknowledge that both Communions are at one in the faith that the Church is founded upon the revelation of God the Father, made known to us in the Person and work of Jesus Christ, who is present through the Holy Spirit in the Scriptures and his Church, and is the only Mediator between God and Man, the ultimate Authority for all our doctrine. Each accepts the basic truths set forth in

the ecumenical Creeds and the common tradition of the ancient Church, although neither Communion is tied to a positive acceptance of all the beliefs and devotional practices of the other.

8. In every region where each Communion has a hierarchy, we propose an annual joint meeting of either the whole or some considerable representation of the two hierarchies.

9. In the same circumstances we further recommend:

(*a*) Constant consultation between committees concerned with pastoral and evangelistic problems including, where appropriate, the appointment of joint committees.

(*b*) Agreements for joint use of churches and other ecclesiastical buildings, both existing and to be built, wherever such use is helpful for one or other of the two Communions.

(*c*) Agreements to share facilities for theological education, with the hope that all future priests of each Communion should have attended some course taught by a professor of the other Communion. Arrangements should also be made where possible for temporary exchange of students.

(*d*) Collaboration in projects and institutions of theological scholarship to be warmly encouraged.

10. Prayer in common has been recommended by the Decree on Ecumenism and provisions for this common worship are to be found in the *Directory* (para. 56). We urge that they be implemented.

11. Our similar liturgical and spiritual traditions make extensive sharing possible and desirable; for example, in noneucharistic services, the exploration of new forms of worship, and retreats in common. Religious orders of similar inspiration in the two Communions are urged to develop a special relationship.

12. Our closeness in the field of sacramental belief leads us further to recommend that on occasion the exchange of preachers for the homily during the celebration of the Eucharist be also permitted, without prejudice to the more general regulations contained in the *Directory*.

13. Since our liturgies are closely related by reason of their common source, the ferment of liturgical renewal and reform now engaging both our Communions provides an unprecedented opportunity for collaboration. We should co-operate, and not take unilateral action, in any significant changes in the seasons and major holy days of the Christian Year; and we should experiment together in the development of a common eucharistic lectionary. A matter of special urgency in view of the advanced stage of liturgical revision in both Communions is that we reach agreement on the vernacular forms of those prayers, hymns, and responses which our people share in common in their respective liturgies. (A list of these texts is appended.) We recommend that this be taken up without delay.

    We are gratified that collaboration in this work has been initiated by the exchange of observers and consultants in many of our respective liturgical commissions. Especially in matters concerning the vernacular, we recommend that representatives of our two Communions (not excluding other Christian bodies with similar liturgical concerns) be associated on a basis of equality both in international and in national and regional committees assigned this responsibility.

14.   We believe that joint or parallel statements from our Church leaders at international, national, and local level on urgent human issues can provide a valuable form of Christian witness.

15.   In the field of missionary strategy and activity ecumenical understanding is both uniquely valuable and particularly difficult. Very little has hitherto been attempted in this field between our two Communions and, while our other recommendations of course apply to the young Churches and mission areas, we propose further the institution at international level of an official joint consultation to consider the difficulties involved and the co-operation which should be undertaken.

16.   The increasing number of mixed marriages points to the need for a thorough investigation of the doctrine of marriage in its sacramental dimension, its ethical demands, its canonical status, and its pastoral implications. It is hoped that the work of the Joint Commission on Marriage will be promptly initiated and vigorously pursued, and that its recommendations will help to alleviate some of the difficulties caused by mixed marriages, to indicate acceptable changes in Church regulations, and to provide safeguards against the dangers which threaten to undermine family life in our time.

III.

17.   We cannot envisage in detail what may be the issues and demands of the final stage in our quest for the full, organic unity of our two Communions. We know only that we must be constant in prayer for the grace of the Holy Spirit in order that we may be open to his guidance and judgement, and receptive to each other's faith and understanding. There remain fundamental theological and moral questions between us where we need immediately to seek together for reconciling answers. In this search we cannot escape the witness of our history; but we cannot resolve our differences by mere reconsideration of, and judgement upon, the past. We must press on in confident faith that new light will be given us to lead us to our goal.

18.   The fulfilment of our aim is far from imminent. In these circumstances the question of accepting some measure of sacramental intercommunion apart from full visible unity is being raised on every side. In the minds of many Christians no issue is today more urgent. We cannot ignore this, but equally we cannot sanction changes touching the very heart

of Church life, eucharistic communion, without being certain that such changes would be truly Christian. Such certainty cannot be reached without more and careful study of the theology implied.

19. We are agreed that among the conditions required for intercommunion are both a true sharing in faith and the mutual recognition of ministry. The latter presents a particular difficulty in regard to Anglican Orders according to the traditional judgement of the Roman Church. We believe that the present growing together of our two Communions and the needs of the future require of us a very serious consideration of this question in the light of modern theology. The theology of the ministry forms part of the theology of the Church and must be considered as such. It is only when sufficient agreement has been reached as to the nature of the priesthood and the meaning to be attached in this context to the word 'validity' that we could proceed, working always jointly, to the application of this doctrine to the Anglican ministry of today. We would wish to re-examine historical events and past documents only to the extent that they can throw light upon the facts of the present situation.

20. In addition, a serious theological examination should be jointly undertaken on the nature of authority with particular reference to its bearing on the interpretation of the historic faith to which both our Communions are committed. Real or apparent differences between us come to the surface in such matters as the unity and indefectibility of the Church and its teaching authority, the Petrine primacy, infallibility, and Mariological definitions.

21. In continuation of the work done by our Commission, we recommend that it be replaced by a Permanent Joint Commission responsible (in co-operation with the Secretariat for Promoting Christian Unity and the Church of England Council on Foreign Relations in association with the Anglican Executive Officer) for the oversight of Roman Catholic/Anglican relations, and the co-ordination of future work undertaken together by our two Communions.

22. We also recommend the constitution of two joint subcommissions, responsible to the Permanent Commission, to undertake two urgent and important tasks:

> ONE to examine the question of intercommunion, and the related matters of Church and Ministry;
> THE OTHER to examine the question of authority, its nature, exercise, and implications.

We consider it important that adequate money, secretarial assistance, and research facilities should be given to the Commission and its subcommissions in order that their members may do their work with thoroughness and efficiency.

23. We also recommend joint study of moral theology to determine similarities and differences in our teaching and practice in this field.

24. In concluding our Report we cannot do better than quote the words of those by whom we were commissioned, and to whom, with respect, we now submit it:

In willing obedience to the command of Christ Who bade His disciples love one another, they declare that, with His help, they wish to leave in the hands of the God of mercy all that in the past has been opposed to this precept of charity, and that they make their own the mind of the Apostle which he expressed in these words: 'Forgetting those things which are behind, and reaching forth unto those things which are before, I press towards the mark for the prize of the high calling of God in Christ Jesus' (Phil. 3.13-14).

The Common Declaration by Pope Paul VI and the Archbishop of Canterbury 24 March 1966

Malta, 2 January 1968

The Common Declaration by Pope Paul VI and the Archbishop of Canterbury

Rome, Saint Paul Without-the-Walls, 24 March 1966

In this city of Rome, from which Saint Augustine was sent by Saint Gregory to England and there founded the cathedral see of Canterbury, towards which the eyes of all Anglicans now turn as the centre of their Christian Communion, His Holiness Pope Paul VI and His Grace Michael Ramsey, Archbishop of Canterbury, representing the Anglican Communion, have met to exchange fraternal greetings.

At the conclusion of their meeting they give thanks to Almighty God Who by the action of the Holy Spirit has in these latter years created a new atmosphere of Christian fellowship between the Roman Catholic Church and the Churches of the Anglican Communion.

This encounter of the 23 March 1966 marks a new stage in the development of fraternal relations, based upon Christian charity, and of sincere efforts to remove the causes of conflict and to re-establish unity.

In willing obedience to the command of Christ who bade His disciples love one another, they declare that, with His help, they wish to leave in the hands of the God of mercy all that in the past has been opposed to this precept of charity, and that they make their own the mind of the Apostle which he expressed in these words: 'Forgetting those things which are behind, and reaching forth unto those things which are before, I press towards the mark for the prize of the high calling of God in Christ Jesus' (Phil. 3. 13–14).

They affirm their desire that all those Christians who belong to these two Communions may be animated by these same sentiments of respect, esteem and fraternal love, and in order to help these develop to the full, they intend to inaugurate between the Roman Catholic Church and the Anglican Communion a serious dialogue which, founded on the Gospels and on the ancient common traditions, may lead to that unity in truth, for which Christ prayed.

The dialogue should include not only theological matters such as Scripture, Tradition and Liturgy, but also matters of practical difficulty felt on either side. His Holiness the Pope and His Grace the Archbishop of Canterbury are, indeed, aware that serious obstacles stand in the way of a restoration of complete communion of faith and sacramental life; nevertheless, they are of one mind in their determination to promote responsible contacts between their Communions in all those spheres of Church life where collaboration is likely to lead to a greater understanding and a deeper charity, and to strive in common to find solutions for all the great problems that face those who believe in Christ in the world of today.

Through such collaboration, by the Grace of God the Father and in the light of the Holy Spirit, may the prayer of Our Lord Jesus Christ for unity among His disciples be brought nearer to fulfilment, and with progress towards unity may there be a strengthening of peace in the world, the peace that only He can grant who gives 'the peace that passeth all understanding', together with the blessing of Almighty God, Father, Son and Holy Spirit, that it may abide with all men for ever.

MICHAEL CANTUAR   PAULUS PP. VI

The Common Declaration
by Pope Paul VI and the
Archbishop of Canterbury

From the Vatican 29 April 1977

1. After four hundred years of estrangement, it is now the third time in seventeen years that an Archbishop of Canterbury and the Pope embrace in Christian friendship in the city of Rome. Since the visit of Archbishop Ramsey eleven years have passed, and much has happened in that time to fulfil the hopes then expressed and to cause us to thank God.

2. As the Roman Catholic Church and the constituent Churches of the Anglican Communion have sought to grow in mutual understanding and Christian love, they have come to recognize, to value and to give thanks for a common faith in God our Father, in our Lord Jesus Christ, and in the Holy Spirit; our common baptism into Christ; our sharing of the Holy Scriptures, of the Apostles' and Nicene Creeds, the Chalcedonian definition, and the teaching of the Fathers; our common Christian inheritance for many centuries with its living traditions of liturgy, theology, spirituality and mission.

3. At the same time in fulfilment of the pledge of eleven years ago to 'a serious dialogue which, founded on the Gospels and on the ancient common traditions, may lead to that unity in truth, for which Christ prayed' (*Common Declaration* 1966) Anglican and Roman Catholic theologians have faced calmly and objectively the historical and doctrinal differences which have divided us. Without compromising their respective allegiances, they have addressed these problems together, and in the process they have discovered theological convergences often as unexpected as they were happy.

4. The Anglican—Roman Catholic International Commission has produced three documents: on the Eucharist, on Ministry and Ordination and on Church and Authority. We now recommend that the work it has begun be pursued, through the procedures appropriate to our respective Communions, so that both of them may be led along the path towards unity.

   The moment will shortly come when the respective Authorities must evaluate the conclusions.

5. The response of both Communions to the work and fruits of theological dialogue will be measured by the practical response of the faithful to

the task of restoring unity, which as the Second Vatican Council says 'involves the whole Church, faithful and clergy alike' and 'extends to everyone according to the talents of each' (*Unitatis Redintegratio,* para. 5). We rejoice that this practical response has manifested itself in so many forms of pastoral cooperation in many parts of the world; in meetings of bishops, clergy and faithful.

6. In mixed marriages between Anglicans and Roman Catholics, where the tragedy of our separation at the sacrament of union is seen most starkly, cooperation in pastoral care (*Matrimonia Mixta,* para. 14) in many places has borne fruit in increased understanding. Serious dialogue has cleared away many misconceptions and shown that we still share much that is deep-rooted in the Christian tradition and ideal of marriage, though important differences persist, particularly regarding remarriage after divorce. We are following attentively the work thus far accomplished in this dialogue by the Joint Commission on the Theology of Marriage and its Application to Mixed Marriages. It has stressed the need for fidelity and witness to the ideal of marriage, set forth in the New Testament and constantly taught in Christian tradition. We have a common duty to defend this tradition and ideal and the moral values which derive from it.

7. All such cooperation, which must continue to grow and spread, is the true setting for continued dialogue and for the general extension and appreciation of its fruits, and so for progress towards that goal which is Christ's will—the restoration of complete communion in faith and sacramental life.

8. Our call to this is one with the sublime Christian vocation itself, which is a call to communion; as St John says, 'that which we have seen and heard we proclaim also to you, so that you may have fellowship with us; and our fellowship is with the Father and his Son Jesus Christ' (1 John 1.3). If we are to maintain progress in doctrinal convergence and move forward resolutely to the communion of mind and heart for which Christ prayed we must ponder still further his intentions in founding the Church and face courageously their requirements.

9. It is this communion with God in Christ through faith and through baptism and self-giving to Him that stands at the centre of our witness to the world, even while between us communion remains imperfect. Our divisions hinder this witness, hinder the work of Christ (*Evangelii Nuntiandi,* para. 77) but they do not close all roads we may travel together. In a spirit of prayer and of submission to God's will we must collaborate more earnestly in a 'greater common witness to Christ before the world in the very work of evangelization' (*Evangelii Nuntiandi,* ibid.). It is our desire that the means of this collaboration be sought: the increasing spiritual hunger in all parts of God's world invites us to such a common pilgrimage.

This collaboration, pursued to the limit allowed by truth and loyalty, will create the climate in which dialogue and doctrinal convergence can bear fruit. While this fruit is ripening, serious obstacles remain both of the past and of recent origin. Many in both communions are asking themselves whether they have a common faith sufficient to be translated into communion of life, worship and mission. Only the communions themselves through their pastoral authorities can give that answer. When the moment comes to do so, may the answer shine through in spirit and in truth, not obscured by the enmities, the prejudices and the suspicions of the past.

10. To this we are bound to look forward and to spare no effort to bring it closer: to be baptized into Christ is to be baptized into hope—'and hope does not disappoint us because God's love has been poured into our hearts through the Holy Spirit which has been given us' (Rom. 5.5).

11. Christian hope manifests itself in prayer and action—in prudence but also in courage. We pledge ourselves and exhort the faithful of the Roman Catholic Church and of the Anglican Communion to live and work courageously in this hope of reconciliation and unity in our common Lord.

DONALD CANTUAR   PAULUS PP. VI

BAPTIST-REFORMED
CONVERSATION

Report 1977

REPORT

of Theological Conversations sponsored by the World Alliance of Reformed Churches and the Baptist World Alliance, 1977

INTRODUCTION

Between 1969 and 1973 a variety of contacts at various levels between the World Alliance of Reformed Churches and the Baptist World Alliance led to a mutually agreed proposal that the two world families of churches should engage in theological conversations. At an official planning consultation held in Rūschlikon, Switzerland, February 3, 1973, a documented plan of work was approved by representatives appointed by the WARC and the BWA.

The motivation of the conversations was agreed:
"Both Baptist and Reformed traditions recognize a common root in their history, which runs back through the Reformation period, the early Fathers of the church, to the New Testament. It is interesting to observe that historically the theology of Calvin and Zwingli has had a very great influence on the development of Baptist thinking since the Reformation. It can also be noted that both traditions share a common emphasis on the normative source of Holy Scripture, the central place of the Word of God, the witness to Jesus Christ as Saviour and Lord, the sovereignty of grace. Further both traditions have a common concern to live out today a witness and service in the obedience of the faith. At the same time obvious theological and historical differences come to mind. Because of the deepgoing divergence in theology and practice between Baptist and Reformed traditions and because of our close kinship it would seem very important that we explore together the nature of our disagreement and how best we may overcome our differences."

"Further relevant aspects may be noted as the widespread concern in many Reformed churches about the doctrine and practice of baptism (infant baptism, believer's baptism); the emergence of church union consultations and indeed one union now consummated in North India in which Baptist churches are fully involved; and further to all this there is the basic importance of investigating a theological problem which is central to the ecclesiological question, confronting the whole ecumenical movement, on the nature and understanding of the church. Both traditions are fully aware that this bilateral conversation should be properly carried out in the awareness of our responsibility within the one Family of the People of God."

Possible subjects were recommended:
"*a*)   The identification of possible areas of agreement:
        The centrality of Scripture as witnessing to Jesus Christ as Saviour

and Lord, the trinitarian basis of theology, the emphasis on the Headship of Christ in the Church. The interrelationship of justification and sanctification; the meaning and implications of conversion; Christian witness in church, state and culture. Again the responsibility of the Christian church in the field of social ethics and the witness of the Christian at every level, in his life, in the world, etc."

"*b*) Specific Topics:
   1. Baptism and its context
      Gospel
      Christology, person and work of Christ
      Atonement
      Holy Spirit
      Conversion and faith
      Church membership
   2. The doctrine and structures of the Church
      Community
      Ministries
      Order
      Church and State."

(Reformed/Baptist Planning Consultation, February 3, 1973)

At a subsequent planning session, held in Rüschlikon, June 20, 1974, it was reported that the recommendations of the 1973 meeting had been approved by the Executive Committees of the WARC and the BWA. Agreement was also reached that the conversations proper should begin in December, 1974. Concerning the structure of the discussion, it was felt that the group appointed for the conversations should as a whole have the freedom to determine the particular subjects and the approach within the terms of their mandate.

This controlled the general nature of the papers presented at the first full session, December 14-18, 1974, held in the Baptist Theological Seminary, Rüschlikon, Switzerland: The Distinctive Elements of the Baptist and Reformed Heritages Today, authors respectively, Dr. Ernest Payne (Baptist), England, and Dr. Sandor Czegledy (Reformed), Hungary; The Baptist and Reformed Perspectives in Understanding the Gospel, authors respectively, Dr. Günter Wagner (Baptist), Switzerland, and Dr. Karel Blei (Reformed), Netherlands. Detailed discussion of these papers provided both direction and specificity for the ensuing three years of work: "Our discussions have been most stimulating and illuminating when we have seen these traditional 'loci' of theological reflection in the context of wider questions about the world and God's purpose in it through our Lord Jesus Christ that confront all the churches in our time." (Interim report, 1974).

The same meeting articulated clearly the agreed aim of the projected discussions: "We have noted in our mandate that the Executive Committees of the BWA and WARC recognize it as 'very important that we explore together the nature of our disagreement and how best we may overcome our differences'. The mandate speaks also of baptism as presenting 'a theological problem which is central to the ecclesiological question, confronting the whole ecumenical movement, on the nature and understanding of the Church'. A programme of the above nature and methodology will have the threefold aim (a) to provide our member churches with information on our present theological positions, (b) to do this in a way which helps to overcome the differences which still exist along with so much that we have in common, and (c) to treat our particular convictions about baptism in a way which illuminates their relation to, and consequential nature within, a total understanding of theology and of the Church's task today."

The second session, September 7-11, 1975, Cartigny, Switzerland, had as its theme and work plan the following scheme: *The Christian Understanding of God's Purpose for the World in Our Lord Jesus Christ: Doctrine of God and Man.* General issues:

Context:
(i): The Sovereignty of God, the Lordship of Christ, Creation and Redemption, Covenant, Relation between community and individual, Personal responsibility before God.

Context:
(ii): The way in which divergent views on these matters are derived from the same Scriptures, the way in which views on these matters both determine and are influenced by basic understandings of man and history.

Particular issues:
The relation of baptism to covenant: the 'newness' of the new covenant as expressed in baptism and the Lord's Supper.

Theme papers:
(i) The understanding of covenant in the Old and New Testaments (Paper by Dr. Jannes Reiling, reaction by Dr. Sandor Czegledy).
(ii) Changing understandings of man and their bearing on theology (Paper by the Rev. Prof. Martin H. Cressey, reaction by Dr. Rudolf Thaut).

The third session, March 26-30, 1976, Rüschlikon, centred on two distinct presentations:
A. The church in the world but not of it
(The church as a holy community in relation to justification; world affirming and world denying forms of Christian thought and life; the church in its local fellowship; the church in its universal dimension and mission. Paper by the Rev. Prof. Martin H. Cressey, reaction by Dr. Penrose St. Amant).

B. A detailed survey and analysis of recent statements on baptism and church membership from a selection of Baptist and Reformed sources, prepared jointly by Dr. Karel Blei and Dr. Günter Wagner.

The fourth session, December 10-14, 1976, Rüschlikon, dealt with Baptist and Reformed thinking in the light of their understanding of the work and gift of the Holy Spirit.

Specific theses were presented on the following issues:

A. The church: with special emphasis on the local and universal church, Dr. Karel Blei and Dr. Jannes Reiling.
B. The ministry: with special emphasis on charism and office, the Reverend Professor Martin H. Cressey and Dr. Rudolf Thaut.
C. Baptism: with special emphasis on Spirit and baptism in the complex of initiation, Dr. Sandor Czegledy and Dr. Günter Wagner.

At this fourth session, the various reports of previous sessions were further examined and within the scope of the original mandate the ensuing final report was worked out and agreed for submission to the WARC and the BWA.

Readers of the report will be aware of the developing processes of the discussion which inevitably emerged from a debate centred in a relatively small intimate group and spread over a four-year time-span. In the final editorial work on the report as a whole it was agreed that such obvious signs of theological growth should be allowed to stand. In this way the report has to be read not as it were in 'the flat' but with the dimension of 'depth', taking note of those elements of seeming repetition which are never in themselves mere repetition but signposts marking our common pilgrimage in learning together.

THE CENTRALITY OF SCRIPTURE

(1) Both the Reformed and the Baptist traditions share a common emphasis on Holy Scripture as the normative source for faith and practice. We have therefore attempted to subject our respective convictions and tenets to the biblical scrutiny in order to test their foundations in Scripture. In the course of our discussion, however, we have noticed again and again that biblical interpretation is more than just finding out "what the Bible says" and that we have to take into account various factors on the part of the interpreters.

The biblical revelation as the normative source (norma normans)

(2) We have registered considerable agreement on what has been pointed out in one of the theme papers; that the Scriptures are always read through "spectacles", and that every theological opinion has not only "theological grounds", but also different (psychological, sociological, cultural, etc.) "causes", of which we have to be (and are more and more) aware. There was also agreement on the necessity to discriminate between what is read into the Scripture and what is objectively given in it. "The text has its own

weight". Yet on this last point there is some difference of emphasis within each of our traditions. Some underline the difficulty of making that distinction, more than its necessity. Is not everyone ready to find his own opinion in the Scripture? Therefore, it is said, we must keep in close contact with Christians of other traditions; it is in the living interplay with them that we are mutually corrected. Others underline the necessity (despite the difficulty) of going back to the normative significance of the Scripture, the Scripture as itself "norma normans".

The interpretation of the Bible and of history in grappling with today's problems

(3)   In all ecumenical conversations the problem of biblical interpretation and of the lessons of history arises. Ours is no exception to this rule and much time has been spent on the subject. There is much common understanding in biblical and historical scholarship across the lines of traditions and denominations. But the great question is always how the results of biblical and historical scholarship can be put to a good use in the situation of today. The problem of hermeneutics is universal and not even a specific Christian one. Yet for the Christian Church which lives on the Word it is a very crucial issue.

The discussion of the concept of covenant led to the following consideration: in order to determine the relevance of a concept like 'covenant' for today we should begin to investigate what meaning it had for Israel in understanding its own place in the purpose of God and then address the same question to the history of Christian thought and practice. We should then proceed and see what help and guidance this would give us in grappling with the problems of our own day with regard to God's purpose for the world and the role of the Church in that purpose.

A similar process was followed in our preliminary discussion of baptism. After some consideration of specific New Testament passages, e.g., Col. 2:11, Romans 4:11, 6:1-6, we discussed the meaning and practice of baptism in the concrete pastoral and missionary situations of our churches today. We found many common problems confronting our churches. All of them are set in an environment where they must present the gospel to secularized men and women or to those of other faiths. No longer can any church assume an identity between itself and its surrounding society.

We recognized further that this changed situation produces many perplexing pastoral issues in dealing with those who have some superficial link with the Church or have been separated from a church with which they were related in childhood. The movement of individuals from one Christian group to another also poses questions which cannot easily be answered from our traditional theological positions.

These practical considerations enabled us to reconsider the classical Baptist and Reformed approaches to (A) ecclesiology, (B) baptism and (C) to reflect upon the relationships between mission, church and baptism.

RECONSIDERATION OF CLASSICAL REFORMED AND BAPTIST APPROACHES

(4)   A.   *Mutual questioning of our ecclesiologies*

Our probing of ecclesiological questions included such issues as: people of God (cf. I Peter); the new covenant; the status of children in the church; the "holiness" of children according to I Cor. 7:14 ff.; the understanding of the church as mission; the boundaries of the church.

(5)   1.   *The people of God*

It cannot be overlooked that "people of God" is one of the names or images characterizing the church in the New Testament. It underlines the continuity of God's purpose in the discontinuity of history and thus raises the question not only of the connection between the Old Testament and the New Testament but also of the relationship between church and Israel. Where the designation occurs in I Peter, a diaspora situation and the mission of the church to proclaim the acts of God, who has brought his people to a new birth through the resurrection of Christ (I Peter 1:1, 2:9, 1:3), are envisaged. While the concept "people of God" as such does not contribute to the solution of the question "Volkskirche" versus "believers" or "gathered" church, it underlines the fact that also the believer under the new covenant belongs to a community of faith which is more than the sum-total of individual believers.

(6)   2.   *The new covenant*

We agree in seeing the "newness" of the new covenant in Jesus Christ himself, in the eschatological significance of his person and work and in the eschatological gift of the Spirit (cf. Heb. 3:10, I Cor. 11:23-25, Acts 2:33-39). This "newness" in Christ is expressed in forgiveness, "law written in the heart" (Jer. 31:33) and is a kainè ktísis (new creature/creation, II Cor. 5:17).

We were not agreed whether kainè ktísis means primarily the "new individuals" or the "new mankind". Our different understandings of a text like this result in the Reformed emphasis on the community aspect of the church and the Baptist emphasis on "personalism".

(7)   3.   *The status of children of believing parents*

While the Reformed tradition, with its practice of infant baptism, includes children as members of the church, Baptists emphasize that a person is not "born into a church", i.e., cannot be brought into membership by the role of the parents; rather he/she becomes a member by personally appropriating the gift of God's grace in faith.

We have gained greater understanding and appreciation of our different positions; Reformed Christians face the fact that the best care of the church and the family for the child by no means guarantees the growth of the child into a committed Christian. Baptists need to consider more seriously the blessings of a Christian family for a child and the child's faith before baptism as well as the continued challenge to and growth in faith after baptism. Both traditions have to face the problems arising for Christian nurture from a general weakening of family-life in many parts of the world.

(8) 4. *The church as community of salvation (Heilsgemeinde) and as mission*

Both Baptists and Reformed regard the church as community of salvation *and* as mission.

The Reformed tradition emphasizes the aspect of community of salvation and thus the thought of the church as also a mixed body (*corpus permixtum,* cf. Mt. 13:24-30, 47-50). It understands mission as an activity pervading all realms of life and society by the gospel.

The Baptist tradition emphasizes the aspect of mission (cf. "every Baptist a missionary" — Johann Gerhard Oncken) and the thought of the church as "gathered believers" committed to the task of proclaiming the gospel to each individual (cf. Mt. 28:16-20). We also need to explore the relationship within each tradition between the concepts of church, of mission, and of baptism.

We are agreed that these emphases are not mutually exclusive but need to be seen as complementary and that we need mutual correction.

(9) B. *Mutual questioning of our baptismal teachings: baptism, grace and faith.*

Baptists and Reformed are in agreement as to the universal scope of the purpose of God and his gifts, the priority of God's grace and the nature of faith as a gift of his Spirit.

However, while we agree that grace is prevenient, we differ in our understanding of its consequences for the practice of baptism: Baptists see the manifestation of prevenient grace in the cross and resurrection of Christ while the rite of baptism belongs to the process of the appropriation of God's gift through faith.

The Reformed tradition emphasizes prevenient grace as manifested in infant baptism. Of course, this infant baptism implies the challenge to Christian education (Eph. 6:4) and Christian living (Rom. 6). The acceptance of this challenge to Christian living in many Reformed churches is expressed in a special act of confession of faith and confirmation.

We realize that the relationship of baptism and faith is a question of great importance for our dialogue. We agree that baptism and faith are related, but disagree as to the prerequisite of personal faith on the part of the baptized at the moment of baptism.

Reformed churches see infant baptism as a sacramental expression of the grace of God, and therefore, if rightly practised, as a firm foundation for a growth to personal faith.

Baptists underline that the offer of God's grace in the gospel requires the response of personal faith and its confession in baptism (Acts 2:37

ff.), and are thus constrained by their understanding of the New Testament to set the challenge of the gospel before those who are able in response to seek baptism of their own volition, though this decision of faith may be greatly helped by Christian nurture of children within the family of the church.

From these positions we can arrive at a mutual respect for the intentions of our varied practices, even though we cannot yet reach a common mind as to the right way of fulfilling our discipleship together in today's situation of mission. We shall need to explore further the implications of such mutual respect for church fellowship and cooperation.

(10)　C.　*The relationships between mission, church and baptism*

God's purpose for the world in Jesus Christ is his eternal will for the salvation of mankind. Therefore, from the perspective of Christian faith, it is possible to see this purpose at work in all the history and witness of the Old Testament. However difficult it is to determine the relation to Christ of specific aspects of the covenants, law or the priestly and prophetic ministries, we are agreed in tracing a continuing succession of faith from Abraham to Christ.

We see a preparation for Christ in all aspects of the vocation of Israel as the nation of priests, the people of God. When Christ came, he too in his teaching and ministry related God's purposes to every aspect of human life.

The New Testament writers are able to apply to the new community gathered from all nations titles originally given to Israel as the covenant nation. Nevertheless, the New Testament emphasized the "newness" of what God has done in Christ and faith as the mode of reception for this new act of grace.

In the light of this New Testament witness we are agreed that the life of the church and its practice and ordinances should be directed to the bringing of men and women to the response of faith as a mature and fully human reception of God's grace.

MISSION, CHURCH AND BAPTISM

(11)　I.　*The church in the world today*

Throughout the centuries the church has had the obligation to fulfil its mission under Christ. We agree that the situation we face in the world today provides a new context for agreement concerning this mission. Large numbers of our contemporaries in every country, and on all continents, are alienated from Christian faith or have not been adequately confronted with its claims, or, more likely, are indifferent to it.

In this specific missionary situation we find different — sometimes extreme — approaches to, and visions of, mission. There are those who conceive of mission almost exclusively in terms of saving individual souls and of church growth, with little interest in seeking to pervade all realms of life and society with the gospel. There are also those who understand mission almost exclusively in terms of social involvement. There are, thirdly, those whom the relativism of our time has affected so deeply that, though they have not rejected the Christian faith totally, they see their task only in terms of maintaining ethical values within a general religious context, at the expense of the uniqueness of the gospel.

But the churches today are struggling to find together a concept of mission which includes the individual, churchly and societal dimensions and proclaims the gospel in its uniqueness in a way properly responsive to the experience and convictions of our fellow men and women.

One of our chief difficulties is that it has become harder to distinguish between "believers" and "unbelievers". There are indeed those who declare their unbelief. There are also people who have not yet come to a point of full commitment in faith and yet may be called believers because of their relation to Jesus Christ through their traditional knowledge of him and the thought-patterns of their society. Such situations give us all, Reformed and Baptists, a special pastoral task.

(12)   II.   *Mission and baptism*

Both our Reformed and Baptist traditions show a variety of attitudes and approaches to the problems referred to in the last two paragraphs. It has become clear in our conversations that we must seek ways for our churches to work together in the common mission of Christ. That is why we have placed our study of baptism in the wider context of the work of Christ and the mission and nature of the church. It is in the light of conclusions about the wider context that we can best approach our distinctive baptismal doctrines and practices; for we are agreed that they must not be treated in isolation and that our distinctive attitudes and approaches are not derived only from them.

(13)   III.   *Christ and his church*

Christ is the head of the church, his body. The concept of the body of Christ implies an understanding of the church as the community of those who are included in Christ, i.e., those whose existence is determined by what has happened in and to the body of Jesus in the event of his cross and resurrection. It expresses the intimate unity of Christ and his church without obscuring the distinction of the church from Christ, and its subordination under him (cf. *One Lord One Baptism*, Faith and Order, 1960, p. 25). It is Christ who in his mercy takes the initiative, an initiative, however, which calls for the human response of faith. An objectivism which does not pay due attention to this human response is as objectionable as a subjectivism for which it is the only important factor.

Neither individually nor together are the existing denominations simply identical with the body of Christ. Nevertheless, there is a connection: it is in the empirical church bodies that the body of Christ becomes manifest.

(14)   IV.   *Baptism: act of God and act of man*

God's gift of grace in Jesus Christ evokes the human response of faith. In baptism the merciful God and the believing and confessing man meet. God acts in baptism by laying hold of man, and man acts by responding to the claims and promises of God's grace: in baptism man suffers death with Christ and is raised to a new life under the power of the living God, who liberates from sin and constantly renews by the Spirit. In this sense we agree that baptism is a powerful sign and an effective means of grace: in baptism administered with water, God himself, by his Spirit, is acting. As we look at baptism as being both act of God *and* act of man, we affirm the unity of the rite and the spiritual reality which it signifies.

(15)   V.   *Church and baptism*

As the body of Christ, the church embodies the community of salvation-in-Christ (cf. Acts 2:47). Baptism is the sacrament of incorporation into Christ and therefore into his body, the church. It is more than admission into the membership of a concrete church organisation. On the other hand, this incorporation into Christ cannot take place without admission into such a membership. In baptism man is united with both Christ and his body. Hence, rather than emphasizing in a negative, exclusive sense the proposition "extra ecclesiam nulla salus" (outside the church no salvation), we should affirm the positive content: "in the church salvation!" We can set no limits to the power of Christ: he is leading men to salvation in his own way. Yet this does not at all entitle us to hold baptism in contempt. It is not that Christ is bound to baptism as a means of grace, but we in our faith are. The Word became flesh (John 1:14); it is to proclaim and underline this fact, and as a consequence of it, arising from the life, death and resurrection of Jesus our Lord, that the church celebrates baptism as an outward, visible action. "God became man in Christ. God's revelation took place in history in a particular yet universally relevant event. The outward sign reflects this particularity" (*Faith and Order*, Louvain, 1971, p. 42).

(16)   VI.   *Baptism and faith*

As to the dilemma of believer's baptism versus infant baptism, the Scriptures do not address themselves directly to that question. Furthermore, they are not a "code of law" but a book of proclamation. In fact and directly the New Testamant only speaks about those who come to baptism out of their own volition, confessing their personal faith (e.g., Acts 2:38, 41; 8:38). This is to be seen in the light of the missionary situation in which men hear the gospel for the first time and assent to it.

Those who reject infant baptism feel compelled to do so out of the conviction that the act of God in baptism is such (cf. IV) that it must be met, at the time of baptism, by an undoubtedly personal response of faith from the one baptized (cf. Rom. 10:9 ff.).

On the other hand, the New Testament makes it equally clear that the believing individual is not detached from the environment of faith. The "household" references (e.g., Acts 10:46, cf. v. 2; 16:15, 33; 18:8; I Cor. 1:16) neither prove nor disprove that children were involved in the so-called "household baptisms"; however, like other texts, they do show that an individual believer is always part of a believing community, and is supported in faith by fellow believers (cf. Mk. 2:5; I Peter 2:9).

It is this consideration that brings defenders of infant baptism to their point: they are convinced that the act of God in baptism (cf. IV) finds its response of faith not only from the one baptized but also from the community of faith, which includes a child's family; it is in this community, the church, that a child develops as a person to the point where, later in time, he or she personally appropriates the response of faith.

Modern patterns of life have weakened and often destroyed traditional family ties, with the result that sometimes the community of faith as a context of infant baptism is missing, thus making it in many cases problematic. The number of children brought to baptism has decreased, especially in urbanized areas. However, infant baptism, if rightly practised, does not intend to "sanctify" or "crown" natural ties, rather it puts them into another perspective, upon another basis. Where parents sincerely and faithfully wish their children to be baptized, a new sense of family solidarity and responsibility is established and grows.

The churches which are convinced that they are entitled only to practise believer's baptism should keep in mind that their practice should not result from a disregard for the priority of God's grace and of the receptive, and not creative, character of human faith, which has to be expressed and confessed, not once for all, but again and again. The churches which are convinced that they are entitled to practise infant baptism should keep in mind that their practice should not result from a disregard of the call for personal faith, which call is involved in God's prevenient grace.

(17)   VII.   *Baptismal practice in the future*

We find ourselves led, by our agreements so far, to confront the difficult question whether Christians of Reformed and Baptist convictions who are members in good standing of their churches could recognize one another as both occupying the position of those who have received and responded to the grace of God in baptism as this grace is understood in the New Testament. Such a mutual recognition could only arise from:

(i)   an agreed understanding that a complex of elements, including baptism with water in the name of the Trinity, public profession of faith and admission to the Lord's Supper, are all parts of the reception of and response to this grace of God;

(ii) the acceptance (still problematic) that this complex of elements could find place in the life of any individual either contemporaneously in the act of believer's baptism, where profession of faith, water baptism and communion come together in time, or over a period of time, short or long, in which (infant) baptism, profession of faith (at "confirmation" as it is often called), and admission to communion follow one another as separable stages in a process.

We do not yet know how to answer fully this question that we are led to face. Furthermore, such a mutual recognition would still leave unresolved many questions, such as: whether the division in the stages in time is, or is not, entirely in harmony with the New Testament; whether infant baptism in itself admits to membership in Christ; whether delay of baptism for the child of a Christian parent is in some way a failure to minister God's grace as he intends it for children of Christian families, and so on. Despite this agenda of questions, we consider that our own dialogue and the changing situation in some of our churches are leading us forward in a positive manner.

In this context Baptists consider it as a hopeful development that in several Reformed churches a so-called "double practice" of baptism (according to which believer's baptism is as legitimate as infant baptism) is being discussed or (e.g., in the French Reformed Church) even has been introduced.

Where in consequence of this "double practice" parents do not ask for the baptism of their newborn child, an act of thanksgiving and intercession on behalf of this child and its parents has a place in the context of Christian worship. It is important that such an act should not be so ordered as to give the impression of being a substitute for baptism. Where in a church of "double practice" infant baptism is chosen, the question arises why baptized children should not be admitted to the Lord's Supper, and this is actually the tendency in several Reformed churches. In the case of this admittance, however, the meaning and functions of "confirmation" need reconsideration, within the unity of the several stages of "initiation".

In the same context Reformed consider it as an important fact that many Baptist churches admit other Christians, baptized as infants, to the Lord's Supper on the basis of their personal faith in Christ and when they are in good standing with their own churches, a practice which is a *de facto* recognition of their Christian status. Cooperation in mission frequently involves a similar *de facto* recognition. Likewise, Reformed see it as a hopeful development that a few Baptist Unions have expressed and even consummated membership in a larger church fellowship which has adopted the "double practise" of infant and believer's baptism for a united church without imposing it upon the local congregation (e.g., Church of North India).

We see the question posed at the beginning of this section and the changing situations described in it as part of the continual challenge confronting our Reformed and Baptist traditions, which we believe, under God, demands of us that we seek ways of overcoming those differences which are still church-divisive between us. In the following concluding sections in thesis form we make our suggestions for this search and emphasize certain areas of concern in which further theological work is required.

THESES

THE HOLY SPIRIT, BAPTISM
AND MEMBERSHIP IN THE CHURCH OF CHRIST

(18)   1. *Both in the Reformed and in the Baptist tradition, there has been emphasis on the work of the Holy Spirit in bringing men and women to salvation and on baptism as the sign of this regenerating activity of God himself.* Many questions have arisen concerning the work of the Spirit and the sign of baptism and their interrelation. Some, in both traditions, would say that baptism has, in the words of R. E. Neighbour, "utility simply as a beautiful and expressive symbol of certain basal facts in the redemptive mission of our Lord Jesus Christ" (quoted by Dr. Beasley-Murray in *Baptism Today and Tomorrow*, 1966, p. 14). Others speak rather of baptism as sign and seal or effective sign.

(19)   2. *In our discussions we have made progress in relating these two viewpoints by considering that a sign exists for the purpose of communication.* We therefore asked ourselves to whom the sign of baptism is addressed. Our answer is twofold. On the one hand, it is addressed to man with good news from God, of incorporation into Christ and the benefits of his death and resurrection. On the other hand, it is addressed from man to God with a confession of faith, by the church in all cases and also by the baptizand in the case of believer's baptism. It is precisely this dual sign-character of baptism which leads us to affirm its character as action of God by his Holy Spirit: for it is only by the Spirit that Jesus can be confessed as Lord (1 Cor. 12:3) and it is only by the Spirit that man is enabled to perceive the meaning of Jesus Christ for him (Jn. 16:13-14). This, we believe, is the reason why in the New Testament baptism is not presented as a "bare" or "mere" sign, a beautiful and expressive symbol and no more, but is intimately associated with such realities as the forgiveness of sins, union with Christ, and the reception of the Spirit (cf. Acts 2:38; 19:2; 22:16; Col. 2:12; Rom. 6:1-11). The sign is not to be separated from the thing signified.

(20)   3. *Hence, Christian baptism is to be understood in relation to the work of the Holy Spirit.* In baptism, administered with water, the Holy Spirit himself is acting, who, as the supreme agent of the baptismal event, imparts to man the benefits of Christ's atonement. Baptism is a door to the treasure house of all the gifts of the Spirit prepared for God's people. But the act of entering through this door is also made possible by the Spirit who gives faith and unites with Christ. If a man does not possess the spirit

of Christ he does not belong to him. Hence baptism in the name of Christ cannot be other than baptism through the Spirit.

(21) 4. *Baptism is a powerful sign of God's saving grace and, by virtue of the action of the Holy Spirit in it, an effective instrument of grace, actually imparting what it promises*: the forgiveness of sins, union with Christ in his death and resurrection, regeneration, elevation to the status of sonship, membership in the church, the body of Christ, new life in the Spirit, the earnest of the resurrection of the body. The New Testament looks upon the operation of the Spirit in baptism as the application of the fulness of saving grace.

(22) 5. *Because of the Spirit's action, baptism is effective through personal response.* While affirming the priority of the Holy Spirit as the ultimate agent of baptism, we also affirm man's response, that is, his faith, his confession, his obedience, which, too, are works of the Spirit. We refrain from defining the interaction between the Spirit and man's spirit in terms that go beyond Romans 8:16 ("the Spirit of God joins with our spirit in testifying that we are God's children", NEB), but we affirm that it is precisely because it is the Holy Spirit that is at work in baptism, that man's decision, his faith and confession, his submission to God's claim upon his whole being is indispensable. Baptism is not an automatic vehicle of salvation nor does the Holy Spirit act as a physical force. "An objectivism which does not pay due attention to this human response is as objectionable as a subjectivism for which it is the only important factor" (see above).

(23) 6. Our conversations about the work of the Holy Spirit in baptism have impressed us anew with the need for mutually understanding our specific traditions and for refraining from imputing unspiritual motives to each other. The Reformed praise of God's prevenient grace is quite other than a concern for perpetuating the crumbling "Volkskirche" structures, while the Baptist insistence on personal decision is quite other than mere individualism, or the zeal of the servants in the parable to separate, before the harvest, the wheat from the tares. *The Reformed emphasis on the priority of God's grace in baptism and the Baptist accent on man's active participation in the baptismal event are, in a sense, complementary and as such contribute to ecumenical rapprochement.*

(24) 7. *Our conversations have made us realize again that the ecclesiological and sociological context of baptismal practice must always be carefully considered.* Where Christianity is a tiny minority, Christian identity is easier to define, and the dividing line between the church and the world, believers and unbelievers, is sharply drawn. Hence initiation into the Christian community is less complex in that situation than it is where traditions carry the rich heritage and also the ballast of two millennia, or where the process of secularization poses a challenge not only to the Reformed practice of baptism but also to the realization of the Baptist concept of a "gathered community" of believers. Baptismal practice is also

affected by the fact that family life today has in many places been deeply changed by modern individualism and technological civilization.

(25) 8. *While we affirm the New Testament view of baptism as a once-for-all incorporation into the church, the body of Christ, we propose to view baptism in the context of the Spirit's total action upon the total life of the individual and the Christian community.* Baptism, at whatever age administered, requires Christian nurture in the spiritual fellowship of the Christian family and of the congregation. This Christian nurture is as much the work of the Spirit as is baptism. To the question how the work of the Spirit in baptism is related to the work of the Spirit in Christian nurture our respective answers are different.

The Baptists hold that the work of the Spirit in Christian nurture begins before baptism and that baptism should only take place when the Spirit has engendered the beginnings of an answer of faith, however immature that answer may be.

The Reformed recognize this as an appropriate order of events in the case of adult converts, but also believe that the Spirit's work of nurture can appropriately take place after his work in baptism for those who are brought to receive baptism within the community of faith.

It thus becomes clear that the remaining disagreement between Baptists and Reformed should be discussed not primarily in terms of the meaning of baptism and its relation to the work of the Spirit, but rather around the question of how and where it may, in faithfulness to the Scriptural witness, be affirmed that the Holy Spirit is at work.

(26) 9. In this same context of the Spirit's total work, while the Baptists also envisage the Christian community of faith, including the family of the baptizand, as the appropriate climate for the growth of faith, the Reformed churches attach special importance to the new covenant which, they hold, encompasses believers as well as their children. With regard to baptism, there is no vicarious faith, and yet the faith of the church, which precedes that of the individual, is the soil in which the faith of the individual is rooted, because the work of the Holy Spirit pervades the whole life of the church. *We propose to regard the children of believers — Baptist and Reformed — as being involved in a process of preparation for the full privileges and responsibilities of membership in the church of Christ: they are already within the operational sphere of the Holy Spirit.* This statement is in no way intended to obscure the general offer of the gospel but rather to emphasize the blessings of a Christian family.

(27) 10. Those who hold that this process of preparation is consummated in a composite rite of confession, baptism with water, admission to the Lord's Supper at one specific point of time and those who embody the significant elements of this process by way of a temporal differentiation between its successive acts and phases may jointly recognize that, *in either case, the Spirit willing, the result is actual membership in the church in the full New Testament sense of the word "member"* (cf. above).

(28)   11. *We are thankful to God for this mutual recognition of each other's good standing as Christians* and for the fact that many Baptist and Reformed churches practise mutual admission to the communion of the Lord's Supper. On the basis of such mutual recognition, including in many cases open communion, Baptists and Reformed are being led to take much more seriously each other's convictions concerning baptism. We have already noted on the one hand the discussion or introduction of a so-called "double practice" in several Reformed churches (see p. 147 above). On the Baptist side, while recognition and admission to communion is generally grounded not on the fact of (infant) baptism but on the profession of faith of the Reformed believer, we note statements by some Baptist theologians, arguing that baptism is not an appropriate way of receiving into membership of a Baptist church those Christians who have already made a public confession of faith in Christ and have entered into the privileges and responsibilities of membership in some other Christian community.

(29)   12. *Our conversations have not produced any arguments or excuses for indiscriminate baptism or for the relaxation of baptismal dicipline.* Reformed churches in particular should do their utmost to extricate baptism from the maze of unbiblical notions, misconceptions and false expectations which, in our secularized societies, often tend to distort and obscure the meaning of the sacrament. The majestic meaning of baptism — dying and rising with Christ, transference and assignment to his Lordship, the duty of discipleship, and commitment to service — should be brought with uncompromising clarity before the candidates for baptism or the parents. It must also be made clear that the baptism of infants without careful Christian nurture in the family and in the Christian community is not only meaningless but also against the will of God. At the same time, the Reformed churches should make pastoral provision for the growing frequency of adult baptism — the natural practice in a missionary situation.

In matters of baptism, as in all the other tasks of Christian life, both Baptists and Reformed must seek to obey the guidance of the Holy Spirit who, in the midst of the upheavals of this era, may employ the means of grace in new and unaccustomed ways. With this thought in mind we now turn to consider the ministry of the church of Jesus Christ and the ministries in the church, local and universal.

THE MINISTRY OF THE CHURCH OF JESUS CHRIST AND THE MINISTRIES IN THE CHURCH

(30)   1. Along with many other churches Reformed and Baptists agree that "the church as the communion of the Holy Spirit is called to proclaim and prefigure the Kingdom of God by announcing the gospel to the world and by being built up as the body of Christ". This requires "a variety of activities, both permanent and provisional, spontaneous and institutional.

To fulfil these needs the Holy Spirit gives diverse and complementary gifts to the church. These gifts are given by God to individuals for the common good of his people and their service . . . " (Faith and Order Paper No. 73, World Council of Churches, *One Baptism, One Eucharist and a Mutually Recognized Ministry,* p. 32, paras. 11 and 12).

The particular ministry of preaching the Word and administering the sacraments is thus seen in relation to the apostolate, the furtherance of which is committed by Jesus Christ our Lord to the people of God as a whole.

(31)   2. Agreement between Reformed and Baptists likewise exists on the point that already in the New Testament out of the multiplicity of gifts and ministries particular ministries become prominent, whose function it is to gather the Christian fellowship together through the preaching and teaching of the word, to build up the church, to lead and train for service. Also related to this function is the presidency at the celebration of the Lord's Supper and at the observance of baptism (administration of the sacraments).

According to biblical interpretation today, no one structure of the ministry of the church can claim to be the one New Testament pattern of ministry. But from the New Testament the general principles may be derived for the ordering of the life of the people of God according to the gospel for the furthering of the service of the Christian community in the world.

Both Baptists and Reformed are averse to the sacramental concept of a ministerial priesthood and rather put the emphasis on the functional nature of the pastoral office and of the particular ministries. Together they reject the doctrine that a particular understanding of spiritual office and succession in office, bound with the historic form of the episcopate, belongs to the being of the church and is therefore essential to it.

(32)   3. In both Reformed and Baptist traditions the preaching of the Word and the administration of the sacraments belong usually to the ministry of the pastor. Neither family of churches however ties these acts of service exclusively to the ordained ministry.

In the majority of Reformed churches, when an exception is admitted to the usage stated in the first sentence of paragraph 3, such a decision is juridically affirmed in the relevant council or court of the church in which the ministers and elders participate. Among Baptists and Congregationalists what is required is delegation by the local congregation since the congregation has and exercises in principle responsibility for all ministries. Usually it entrusts its pastor with the discharge of these particular tasks, but they are also frequently entrusted to lay people.

(33)   4. The function of presiding over the affairs of the congregation is in Reformed churches usually linked with the office of the pastor. Among Baptists it may be entrusted to the pastor, and there are places where this system is customary. But in principle among both Reformed and Baptists

the various ministries on which responsibility rests for the building up of the congregation are so distinct that they can be entrusted to different persons, according to the gifts of the Spirit.

A distribution of ministries is not only grounded in the pragmatic concern for the division of labour (Acts 6:1 ff.) but above all in the understanding of the nature of the whole church as the body of Christ, in which the work of the Holy Spirit and the service of the church cannot be separated one from the other. All ministries in the church are charismatic in nature, and all spiritual gifts are given for the common good (I Cor. 12:7), "to equip God's people for work in his service, to the building up of the body of Christ" (Eph. 4:12, N.E.B.).

(34) 5. While the doctrine concerning episcopal succession is rejected by Reformed and Baptists, there exists among both Baptists and Reformed in particular areas a type of ministry which superintends a number of individual congregations; among Baptists this ministry is never designated by the title "bishop", nor does it have juridical authority.

For both Reformed and Baptists, encounter with episcopally ordered churches can usefully raise the question as to the beneficial role of the "pastor pastorum" (pastor of the pastors) in the life of the church for the encouragement of the ministry.

THE CHURCH – LOCAL AND UNIVERSAL

(35) 1. The one church belongs to the one Lord. It is built, assembled and sustained by him. The "ekklesia" is the one holy universal Christian church. It is not an idea which floats invisibly over earthly reality; for the Word which sustains it became flesh (John 1:14).

(36) 2. *The church is first and foremost an event,* rather than an institution; the church "exists" in that it continually "happens", namely where the Lord effectively exercises his rule and where it is recognized and accepted; i.e., where the Word is proclaimed and believed, where the sacraments are administered and received, where the communion with the Lord and with each other is celebrated and upheld, and where the church in the name and in the power of the Lord goes out in witness and service. The purpose of the institutional elements of the life of the church is to give form and continuity to the events of the Spirit.

(37) 3. *The one holy universal Christian church becomes concrete in the local congregation.* The local congregation is not a sub-department of the one church of Christ, but manifests and represents it. This is generally recognized today, as e.g., by the Roman Catholic Church at its Second Vatican Council: "The church of Christ is truly present in all local gatherings of believers" (Dogmatic Constitution on the Church *Lumen Gentium*, No. 26). The local congregation cannot be bypassed by those who want to belong to the church of Christ, for this is where the church "happens". In the New Testament "ekklesia" frequently is the designation of the local

congregation and as such it occurs in the plural as well (e.g., Acts 16:5; Rom. 16:4, 16; I Cor. 7:18; Rev. 1:4).

(38)   4. *At the same time the local congregation is necessarily related to other local congregations.* In itself, it is not the universal church of Christ. The local congregation which isolates itself from its sister congregations impairs the character of the true church, and becomes sectarian. The local congregation cannot monopolize the Lord for itself. Such isolation, moreover, would cloud its vision with regard to the world as the one great field of mission. This call for mission unites the local churches and makes them interdependent. The New Testament makes clear how congregations were in contact with each other. The collection, for instance, which Paul organized for the church of Jerusalem, expressed the common ties which united the churches in Macedonia with the one in Jerusalem (I Cor. 16:1-4; II Cor. 8:1-9; Gal. 2:9 ff.).

(39)   5. *Thus the wider church relationships* (area, national, regional, world-wide) *have ecclesiological significance.* Church "happens" not only where Christians gather as a congregation, but also where congregations meet as such or through their appointed representatives. There also the one Lord builds his one church. It is obvious that, if the local congregation needs an institutional form, this also goes for the wider gatherings of congregations. Just as the local congregation is not simply a sub-department, the wider church relationships are not simply a sum of their parts. The local congregation may be the specific manifestation of the one holy universal Christian church, but it is not the only one. Local church life should be receptive not only of encouragement through the wider church relationships but also of criticism from their side, as in their turn local churches can bring encouragement and criticism to the wider church relationships.

(40)   6. Baptists have always emphasized the church as the local congregation. The *Reformed*, without disregarding the special significance of the local congregation, attribute to the "wider councils" (presbytery, synod) which represent the church on the regional and national levels, their own specific value. If the latter is stressed too much, there is the danger of centralism: general rules and arrangements might dominate local church life and stifle it. Encounter with Baptists can help them to recognize this danger and to avoid it.

(41)   7. The Baptists too know the wider relationships on various levels: the national union/convention, the world alliance, for the purpose of common service and witness. Common service and witness as such have ecclesiological significance, and yet Baptists tend to attach to the wider relationships only pragmatic importance. They fear ecclesial superstructures above the local level. This could cause a failure in the understanding and appreciation of the fulness of the body of Christ in the world and thus result in missionary colonialism and ghetto-like existence; there is the danger of isolation and thus of spiritual poverty and myopia: the danger

of exchanging the Holy Spirit for a club-mentality. Encounter with the Reformed can help them to recognize this danger and to avoid it.

We do not wish to end on a note of such mutual warnings of danger! We rejoice together in our membership of the one church of Jesus Christ and we close our report and our fourth and final meeting with praise and thanks to him for bringing us together and for showing us more of his gospel and his grace.

PARTICIPANTS

Reformed:

Martin H. Cressey, Cambridge, England (co-chairman)
Reverend Dr. Karel Blei, Haarlem, Netherlands
Reverend Dr. Sandor Czegledy, Debrecen, Hungary
Reverend Richmond Smith, Geneva, Switzerland

Baptists:

Reverend Dr. Rudolf Thaut, Hamburg, F.R.G. (co-chairman)
Dr. Jannes Reiling, Bilthoven, Netherlands
Dr. Penrose St. Amant, Rüschlikon, Switzerland
Dr. Günter Wagner, Rüschlikon, Switzerland
Reverend Dr. C. Ronald Goulding, Washington, D.C., U.S.A.

DISCIPLES-
ROMAN CATHOLIC
CONVERSATIONS

Report 1981

I. INTRODUCTION

In September, 1977 a five year international dialogue between the Disciples of Christ and the Roman Catholic Church was launched on the theme: "Apostolicity and Catholicity in the Visible Unity of the Church." The eighteen-member Commission had been appointed jointly by the Secretariat for Promoting Christian Unity in collaboration with the U.S. Bishops' Committee for Ecumenical and Interreligious Affairs, and the Disciples Ecumenical Consultative Council and the Council on Christian Unity of the Christian Church (Disciples of Christ) in the U.S. and Canada. Its membership included Roman Catholic theologians and pastors from Canada, France, Ireland, the United States, and the Vatican, and Disciples theologians and pastors from Canada, England, Puerto Rico, the United States, and Zaire. Dr. Paul A. Crow, Jr. and the Most Reverend Stanley J. Ott were named as co-chairmen for the Commission.

In developing the main theme of its work, the Commission selected four sub-themes to focus discussion at each annual meeting: "The Nature of the Church and Elements of its Unity" (Indianapolis, 1977); "Baptism: Gift and Call in the Search for Unity" (Rome, 1978); "Faith and Tradition in the Life of the Church" (Annapolis, 1979); "The Dynamics of Unity and of Division" (New Orleans, 1980). At its fifth session (Ardfert, Ireland, 1981), the Commission prepared a final report to be submitted to its authorizing bodies.

Each annual meeting lasted five days and followed a regular pattern of work, of sharing in worship and prayer, and of worshipping with Disciples and Roman Catholics in local congregations and parishes. Four papers, two from each team, were presented and discussed with the tasks of identifying present agreements, convergences, new insights and continuing tensions or problems for further consideration. An "agreed account" of each meeting was prepared to serve as a common memory for the Commission's work. The papers and agreed accounts were published in *Mid-Stream: An Ecumenical Journal* (Vol. XVIII, No. 4, October, 1979; Vol. XX, No. 3, July, 1981).

This final report does not summarize the papers and the agreed accounts from our previous meetings. Rather, it is a statement of shared insights and findings which the Commission identified out of its work, its discussion and debate, and its life together in fellowship and prayer during these five years.

II. OUR LIFE TOGETHER

These five years of the dialogue between Disciples of Christ and Roman Catholics have been the occasion of joy as we have grown together in theological understanding, in fellowship, and in the way we approach the problems of doctrine. We have been led to a better understanding of the nature of the one Church of God, the situation of our divided traditions, and also of the pressure of our common calling to visible unity in Christ.

We are aware that we come from two very different Christian backgrounds. Our histories, our cultural journeys, our theological traditions and methods have, in some often important respects, been different. Some of the problems between us spring from these differences. Yet, the very diversity of our histories and Christian experiences frees us for a new kind of ecumenical dialogue. The Disciples movement was born out of the churches of the Reformation but has developed its own unique position among them. In particular, there was no deliberate, formal break in communion between the Disciples of Christ and the Roman Catholic Church, although our histories have included the general bias which in the past reflected uncharitable attitudes between Protestants and Roman Catholics. This fact has allowed us to move beyond any initial apprehensions or presumed distance into cordial relationships and to discover that we have more in common than we expected.

A significant amount of what we thought initially to be division cannot be so defined. We have begun to discover that when we go beneath the current theological descriptions of our traditions, a convergence becomes evident. As we understand our traditions and our ecclesiologies more clearly, we discover a common source has fed them. The customary vocabulary of division does not exactly describe our situation, even though there are still some important things we cannot do together or on which we cannot yet be at one.

This dialogue has been liberating because both Disciples and Roman Catholics set the fullness of communion at the heart of their understanding of the Church. Barton Warren Stone claimed for Disciples: "Let Christian unity be our polar star." Alexander Campbell proclaimed that "The union of Christians is essential to the conversion of the world." The same vocation, inherent in the Catholic tradition, was also claimed for Roman Catholics by the Second Vatican Council: "The restoration of unity among all Christians is one of the principal concerns of the Second Vatican Council . . . The concern for restoring unity involves the whole Church, faithful and clergy alike" (*Decree on Ecumenism*, nn. 1,5).

Paradoxically, some of our differences spring from the ways we have understood and pursued Christian unity. For example, the Disciples of Christ, called into being as an instrument of unity among divided Christians, have refused to make creeds the definitive faith in order to promote unity and communion among Christians. The Roman Catholic Church, on the other hand, holds to the creeds and the Petrine ministry for the same purpose. Our dialogue has helped us see this and other contrasts in the context of the fundamental commitment of Disciples and Roman Catholics to serve the visible unity of the whole People of God. In this perspective, some issues that seem to divide us can be traced to the same roots and certain of our differences appear complementary.

The nature of our ecumenical dialogue requires us to listen to each other's theological words while searching for the language of convergence, always in faithfulness to the truth of the Gospel. Our report gives substantial commentary on the issues which have been at the heart of the first phase of our dialogue and gives our churches hope for the future.

III. SPIRITUAL ECUMENISM

In Christ God has shown his supreme love for the world (Jn. 3:16), destroying the power of sin, reconciling us to himself (II Cor. 5:18–19) and breaking down the barriers of division in the human family. The Spirit of God is in the Church to bring this reconciling work of Christ to completion and continues to gather into it all who are ready to accept the saving Gospel. As human history unfolds, the Spirit of God prepares the coming of the final Kingdom. Already in the Church, the future unity of the Kingdom is anticipated as the Spirit brings together in faith and love those who acknowledge the Lordship of Christ.

The Spirit of God draws the Church towards full unity. God's Spirit also works in the world for a new humanity through the liberation of human beings from the oppression and alienation that comes from sin. Both realms of the work of the Spirit are integral parts of one plan of salvation.

The unity God has given and continues to give the Church has its origins in God's own life. The spirit of God is the author of the Church's unity. Through the Spirit, all who are one in the Church are drawn into the loving communion of the Father and Son and in that communion are united to one another. Thus, they are being made one in mind and understanding, since through faith they adhere to the one eternal Word in whom the wisdom of God is fully expressed. In this unity, the divine plan of salvation accomplished in Christ is expressed in the world and is being ever more fully revealed.

This theological awareness permits us to affirm that visible unity will come from the one grace of the Spirit of God dynamically present among Christians even in their divided condition. The Spirit calls all Christians to assume responsibility for giving authentic expressions to their unity in life, in worship and in mission. The Spirit enables them to overcome obstacles and empowers them to grow together towards full visible unity.

The work of Christian unity, then, is profoundly and radically a spiritual one, i.e., it comes from and is a response to the Holy Spirit. We are encouraged that both our churches share a will for unity but acknowledge that, for this unity to be made fully manifest, our will and our commitments must be sustained by what has been called *"spiritual ecumenism"* (*Decree on Ecumenism, paragraph 8*).

Spiritual ecumenism does not permit us to avoid the pain of our separated existence, being content to remain as we are. Indeed, the Spirit gives us the courage to confront our divided state.

Spiritual ecumenism does not allow us to leave aside the need to deal with the visible manifestation of the unity of the Church. Indeed, we understand that just as the Word of God became flesh in Jesus, so in a similar way, the power of the Spirit of God is manifested in the Church as a visible communion.

Nor does spiritual ecumenism relieve us of the Gospel concern for the poor, the alienated and the oppressed. Indeed, Christians often become truly aware of the bonds that unite them and hear the call to conversion of heart as they meet the challenge to promote a society of justice, freedom and charity serving the dignity of every human being.

Spiritual ecumenism arises from the realization that the one Spirit of God has already brought us into Christ and continues to move us towards full visible unity. Spiritual ecumenism gives us hope that the Spirit will lead us from the imperfect unity we know painfully in our divided condition to a wholeness we shall experience in joy.

Spiritual ecumenism implies a clear consciousness of the sinfulness of division among Christians. Through spiritual ecumenism we are set free as communities and as individuals from seeking to justify our divisions and we are moved to seek a shared life in a reconciled community. Spiritual ecumenism impels us to a quality of evangelical life marked by the will to be faithful to Christ and open to one another. It also implies repentance and renunciation of egoism, as well as newness of mind, humility and gentleness in the service of others, that is conversion of heart. This *metanoia* thus provides what might be called an "evangelical space"—an arena for the operation of the Gospel—in which we find God's grace newly available to bind us together in praising, blessing, beseeching the God who makes us one. In this evangelical space, we discover new possibilities for genuine exchange and sharing and for seeing in a new light these affirmations that find historical expression in our still separated communities.

Thus, spiritual ecumenism allows us to be open to the grace of God. The Holy Spirit is freeing us to experience together his unifying power in the many ways open to us in the ongoing life of the Church, that is, accepting and proclaiming together the Word of God in the Scriptures, confessing together the same Lord, praying together, attending one another's celebration of the Lord's Supper and having a common mission as the priestly people of God in the whole human community. Although we do not yet fully share these experiences owing to our desire to be authentic and faithful to the Church as we have known it heretofore in our communions, we nevertheless realize that God makes the power of his unifying love felt even now. He speaks to us about the contradictions of our divisions when together we open ourselves to Him in prayer and worship, in our joint efforts at articulating a common theological language in ecumenical dialogue, and in the common struggle for justice and peace in the world.

In this evangelical space we are empowered both to grow together and at the same time to pay the price of suffering caused by our present divisions and by the efforts to overcome them. Here we discern a reflection of the present growth in painful struggle that marks the whole ecumenical movement. But we take hope, knowing that "the whole creation has been groaning in travail together until now and not only the creation but we ourselves, who have the first fruits of the Spirit, groan inwardly as we await . . . . redemption." So "we wait for it with patience", confident that "the Spirit helps us in our weakness" and trusting that "the Spirit intercedes for the saints according to the will of God" (cf. Rom. 8:22–27).

IV. BAPTISM

By its very nature, baptism impels Christians toward oneness. In baptism a person is incorporated into Christ Jesus and into his Body, the Church. The fundamental unity which God has given us is rooted in the sacrament and cannot be destroyed. We are called to the one baptism by the Gospel that is the way of salvation for all humanity. Baptism is, therefore, the fundamental source of our oneness in Christ's life, death and resurrection.

Yet, we came to the subject of baptism with an awareness of differences in baptismal practice which could not be treated lightly. At first sight, these differences might seem to represent divergent understandings which could threaten our fundamental unity through baptism.

In fact, we have discovered important areas in which our understanding and practice of baptism encourage us to speak truly of one baptism. These areas were found to have varying degrees of significance.

(a) We share a common attribution of the origins of baptismal observance to the example of Jesus, the command of the risen Christ, and the practice of the primitive Church.

(b) For both Disciples of Christ and Roman Catholics baptism is with water and "in the name of the Father, and of the Son, and of the Holy Spirit".

(c) In both our traditions, baptism is ordinarily administered by a duly authorized minister.

(d) In both our traditions, it is affirmed that we enter into a new relationship with God as his children and as brothers and sisters, one of another in Christ, for in baptism our sins are forgiven and we become a new creation.

(e) Since God never revokes the new relationship brought about in baptism, rebaptism is contrary to the Gospel and should never be practiced. Nevertheless, we are aware of the need for continued repentance after baptism and we experience forgiveness in the ongoing life of the Church.

(f) Both our traditions maintain the necessity for the role of faith in baptism. For both Roman Catholics and Disciples, incorporation into the Body of Christ and forgiveness of sins are primarily acts of God that presuppose faith and call for a continuing active response of faith for their full development and fruitfulness.

This fundamental agreement must be kept in mind as we seek to interpret anew certain differences in regard to baptism. These differences fall under two headings:

The Relation of Personal Faith to Baptism

Since believers' baptism is the form of baptism explicitly attested in the New Testament, the conviction of Disciples is that the rite of baptism should be preceded by a personal confession of faith and repentance.

For historical, theological and pastoral reasons, Roman Catholics baptize infants. They see this as the first sacrament in the process of Christian . initiation, followed by Christian nurture and instruction, and culminating in the sacraments of Confirmation and Eucharist, accompanied by a life of continual repentance and conversion.

However, Catholics see the fundamental belief of their church regarding baptism as expressed with new clarity in the revised rite for adult baptism, which includes personal confession of faith.

At the same time, Disciples have an increasing appreciation for the place of infant baptism in the history of the Church. In part, this involves understanding infant baptism in relation to Christian nurture in both the family and the Christian community. Also, Disciples have seen that infant baptism has been a pastoral response in a situation where members are no longer predominantly first-generation Christians.

The Mode of Baptism

Disciples practice immersion, believing it to be the practice of New Testament times and the clearest symbolic representation of our participation in the death and resurrection of Christ. Roman Catholics, on the basis of early Christian tradition, regard pouring as an acceptable mode while acknowledging the symbolic value of descent into the baptismal waters. They have always recognized and sometimes practice baptism by immersion. Disciples are coming to recognize the other modes, while retaining a preference for immersion.

Although God's saving power in the world is unlimited, baptism is fundamental in Christian life. By it, we become members of Christ's Body and participate in the life he gives. Participation in Christ's life calls us to enter his ministry, suffering, death and resurrection, as is prefigured in our baptism, for the salvation of the whole world.

Because both baptism and the eucharist involve participation in the Body of Christ and since the grace of God received in baptism is nurtured and strengthened by participation in the eucharist meal, the oneness achieved by grace in baptism should find manifestation and completion in the *anamnesis* (memorial/remembrance) of the sacrifice of Christ for all humanity at the table of the one Lord.

Baptism is, paradoxically, a sign of unity and a reminder of disunity. It is a sign of unity inasmuch as it incorporates all Christians into Christ. It is a reminder of disunity in that, as administered, it also initiates Christians into separated ecclesial communities with their special traditions and doctrines.

We have been helped in our further consideration of this paradox by distinguishing two affirmations of faith. The one is the fundamental assent of the person to God's gift of grace in Jesus Christ, a gift that is, in itself, life-transforming and that is signified in baptism. This affirmation brings our lives under the determination of God's grace, thereby turning us outward from ourselves and making us one in Christ. The other is the acceptance of the elaboration of the faith as that has come to expression in our separated ecclesial communities. Baptism is also the induction into a particular ecclesial community with its own explication of the one faith. Making this distinction, therefore, has helped us to understand our fundamental unity and to locate the source of our separation.

However, in conclusion, we affirm the mutual recognition of baptism administered by Roman Catholics and Disciples, convinced that the oneness we received by the grace of God in baptism must find its completion in visible ecclesial unity, so that the world may believe that Jesus is the Christ, the Son of the living God, as we together confess him to be. We are determined, therefore, by the same grace to discover more fully the truth that shall set us all free.

V. FAITH AND TRADITION

Our two traditions are called to proclaim to the world the fundamental truth of God's reconciliation in Christ, to which both have given assent. This common assent is sealed through baptism in separated ecclesial bodies;

nevertheless, in our baptism we are given radical unity. This realization impels us as the Church, the Body of Christ, to witness to the Apostolic faith in our life, teaching, liturgy, and service.

The Church, under the guidance of the Holy Spirit, has developed the means for proclaiming the Apostolic faith from age to age, as it has sought to defend the faith and communicate it faithfully in different times and circumstances. Scripture and Tradition embody these responses to the faith that God gives.

Faith is God's gift, both to the individual and to the community. In both cases, it is through the power of the Holy Spirit that we believe, grow in faith and live by faith. Our faith is that Christ is the Risen Lord who is the reason for the existence of the Church. This faith begets a new relationship among all who believe. The faith which commits a person to Christ commits that person to the Church which is his Body; because faith is given by the one Spirit of Christ, it is the one basic faith that binds Roman Catholics, Disciples and other Christians in one fellowship in that Spirit. However, in spite of this radical unity in the Body of Christ, we recognize that we have not yet fully achieved the visible ecclesial unity which he willed. While gratefully recognizing the measure of agreement reached on this topic, we also became acutely aware at this point, of some serious unresolved issues that need further discussion in our dialogue; these, we believe, should be a major part of our future agenda.

The conversion process by which one commits oneself in faith to Christ and to Discipleship is a gradual, continuous and difficult one. Christ promised that his Spirit would be present to the individual in and through the community of believers. The Christian community, therefore, calls forth, nurtures, illumines, and sustains the faith of the individual in its liturgy and prayer, and its example of Christlike love and service.

Christian life is life in community, a community which recognizes the dignity and freedom of human conscience, while also acknowledging the need for the individual conscience to develop in greater obedience to the Gospel. The Church is called to guide and enable this process.

Each Christian's faith is inseparable from the faith of the community. Personal faith is an appropriation of the Church's faith and depends on it for authenticity as well as for nurture. At the same time, bearing witness to personal faith builds up the life of the Church and quickens and strengthens the faith of all.

Insofar as the Church as a community of faith and love is the sign of Christ in the world, believers are called to offer a common witness of faith, so that the world might believe that Jesus is Lord. Thus the life of faith, both of the individual and of the community, is expected to manifest a certain quality by which it becomes a "light in the world," "salt of the earth." Both the individual believer and the pilgrim Church are ever called to a deeper conversion to Christ, a more authentic faith. Scripture, mediating the Word of God, has a central, normative, and irreplaceable role in this process of personal and ecclesial conversion.

Together the Disciples of Christ and the Roman Catholic Church acknowledge the important role of Tradition in the life of the Church. The relationship between faith and Tradition has to do with the question of how Christians from age to age come to the knowledge that Jesus Christ is the Lord of life and the way of salvation for the whole world.

The Apostles were called by Christ and commissioned to a unique position in the life of the Church. They attest the presence of the risen Lord and hold a special place in the communication of faith to subsequent generations. In that communication, the Holy Spirit is always present in the life of the Church, guaranteeing that the Church shall not fail to bring about the fulfillment of the divine plan.

Under the inspiration of the Spirit, the New Testament expresses the response in faith of the Apostolic Church to the risen Lord. This response was itself conditioned by God's revelation and promises to Israel.

The New Testament Scriptures, resting on the authority of the Apostles and interpreted with the aid of the Holy Spirit, constitute the inspired record of the Tradition which stems from the Apostolic Era. This Tradition reflects the *sensus fidelium* (the shared awareness of the faithful) of the primitive church as a whole. However, the *sensus fidelium* is not fixed in the past, but is ever dynamic and living through the dialectical interaction of Scripture and Tradition in the ongoing life of the Church from age to age.

Each generation must come to faith anew through the power of the Holy Spirit and hand on this faith to succeeding generations. At the same time, the Church in every age inherits the successes and failures of the past.

In the process of making explicit the implications of revelation, various traditions arise. This resultant diversity is to be expected and is frequently itself an expression of the catholicity of the Church. Problems arise when the ecclesial context in which a baptismal assent is made exercises an influence of such a kind that the communion in faith is compromised. Roman Catholic and Disciples both recognize that they move beyond the fundamental reality of faith in God revealed in Jesus Christ to understandings that have grown out of a diversity of Christian traditions.

Roman Catholics hold that the living transmission of the Gospel in and by the Church is necessary for a more complete articulation, manifestation and application of the truths that are in Scripture than Scripture alone affords. They look to the affirmations of faith and interpretations expressed in the Church's official liturgical texts, creedal statements, teachings of the episcopal college, especially in councils, and papal teachings which they believe to be formulated with the guidance of the Spirit. While the Scriptures are normative and the soul of all subsequent theological investigation, their adequate understanding is possible only within the life of the believing community.

Disciples believe that the New Testament is a sufficient expression of the essential faith, doctrine, and practice of the individual Christian and the Christian community. Thus while being conscious of standing in the Tradition of the Church, they have not given a normative position to later expressions of the faith of the Church, and in particular have not used creeds and confessions as tests of eucharistic fellowship. Disciples believe their history shows that a church can develop and sustain its own distinctive character without a formal creed, and that the exercise of freedom and diversity in expressions of belief and worship need not threaten its unity. However, where affirmations of faith, both ancient and modern, have been used as a basis for the expression of the essential unity of the whole Church (for example, in united churches), Disciples have gladly accepted them.

Both Disciples and Roman Catholics are committed to the appropriation in their own lives of all that is good from the traditions of others, both in the past and today.

VI. AFFIRMATIONS ABOUT THE UNITY WE SEEK

Through a convergence of doctrinal understanding and in the experience of the reality of our oneness in the fundamental assent to God, we are able to accept as a basic principle of ecumenism that there can be only one Church of God (*unica Ecclesia*) and that this Church already exists. It is the accomplishment of salvation, both individually and corporately, for all humanity. This salvation to which Scripture bears witness expresses God's purpose for the entire creation.

The new humanity in Jesus Christ which God wills comes to exist in the one Church of God. The coming definitive form of the Church as God's eschatological people can be fully known only to God. Both Roman Catholics and Disciples believe that the Church takes visible shape in history and that one sign of this visibility is the common profession of the Gospel with reception of baptism. This visible community belongs to the very *esse* of the Church.

Through their common life and fellowship (*koinonia*) the members of this community which is the Church witness to salvation as they pray and worship together, forgive, accept, and love one another, and stand together in time of trial. Such communion is made possible by a deeper communion, a communion in the good things that come from God who makes the people of the Church his own as a new creation in Christ.

We become this new creation through the means of grace which God has given to his Church. Thus the Church is the visible form of God's grace. It opens the way to salvation through preaching, sacraments, and other institutions derived from apostolic authority. Participation in these means of grace constitutes the deeper communion that unites us together in true fellowship in the Spirit.

To this one Church belong all those who are baptized in water and the Spirit with the authentic confession of faith in Jesus as the Son of God. These persons become members of the Body of Christ and receive the seal of the Holy Spirit, which cannot be removed even by schism. Divisions among Christians cannot destroy the one Church of God.

As we look at differences between Roman Catholics and Disciples we often discover in them elements of complementarity. We see ourselves as having a communion *in via*. The unique unity of the one Church of God is the goal. We are already on the way; we have taken the first step in faith through baptism which is also the call to that final unity. Now we have the task of giving external expression to the communion *in via*. In the very process of our mutual discovery of certain ecclesial elements in each other, we are called in a renewed fidelity to actions that will make our relationship more intense and more profound.

VII. LOOKING TO THE FUTURE

Our situation as Disciples of Christ and Roman Catholics, discovering each other in this dialogue, is a reflection of what is happening everywhere among Christians as they yield themselves in obedience to what God is doing through the ecumenical movement. We are not yet at the point where we can ask the churches to which we belong to make a definitive judgment on our work or to commit themselves to some decision which could have structural consequences.

Yet our experience tells us and we must declare, that the relation between the Roman Catholic Church and the Disciples of Christ is in the process of a growth which is deeply important for both partners. This process calls for loyalty and courage as we pursue it towards maturity and, here and now, it challenges and makes demands on us both in a practical and costly way. The Lord is confronting us with these demands. We believe several of them especially require us to give a faithful response and to draw certain conclusions in practice:

(a) Catholics and Disciples along with many other Christians are discovering that, in essence, their commitment to Christ and their fellowship in the Gospel are the same. There is already a unity of grace which in some measure is present, bearing fruit, and which is disposing us for visible unity and urging us to move ahead to it. One of the most striking insights we have received in our dialogue is the awareness that the interior communion between Christians across divisions is an essential element of unity and a necessary part of achieving the goal of full visible unity. This is something we have experienced as we have learned to take each other seriously in our theological awareness and in our commitment to the mission of Jesus Christ. Above all, we have experienced it together in our prayer, our reading of the Scriptures, and the meditation which has seasoned all our work and given a special flavor and substance to this dialogue. We have come to appreciate more deeply also the importance in our two traditions of the renewal of the liturgy and the centrality of the Eucharist. It is our immediate task to reflect seriously on what all of this means for the relationship between Roman Catholics and Disciples of Christ in each parish and congregation.

(b) Spiritual ecumenism leads to more than the sum of doctrinal agreements. It requires us to "do the truth" of unity by acting together in the name of the Gospel. Our obedience to Christ, the Lord of history, has to be made incarnate as we carry our own responsibility of enabling the Kingdom to penetrate the world, its life, and its institutions. In its own way, it can be as full an expression of the common faith as doctrinal agreement, for action in harmony with the demands of the Gospel makes known Christian truth and reveals its riches. Communion expressed through practices is an important element of the emerging *koinonia* among churches. Joint action, both of individuals and of separated churches, is a factor in unity which reaches to the roots of the ecumenical task. This, too, has implications now for Disciples of Christ and Roman Catholics in each place.

(c) Preparation for visible unity is taking place already through discussion of important doctrinal issues. This is clear from the work which has been done in our dialogue commission over the past five years. That is a significant beginning. We have now the framework in which it becomes possible and necessary to do further work on unresolved issues, particularly the nature and mission of the Church, the Eucharist, and the ministry.

The dialogue commission gives thanks to God that certain doctrinal convergences on some key issues begin to be discernible in our work already. This encourages us to work for no less than visible unity—not a limping compromise achieved by paring away divergences, but nothing less than common witness to the one apostolic faith.

The dialogue between Disciples of Christ and the Roman Catholic Church has begun and already we must live in the logic of what is happening. It demands that we begin now, as far as possible, to proclaim together the same Lord Jesus Christ, giving common witness to "the hope that is in us" (I Pet. 2:13). It demands, even now, that we enter to fullest extent possible into that process of mutual recognition which is ultimately a worshipful acknowledgment of the one Lord in whom we are baptized, whose gifts we enjoy, to whose service we are called.

PARTICIPANTS

Disciples of Christ:

Dr. Paul A. Crow, Jr., Indianapolis, Indiana, U.S.A. (Co-Chairman)
Dr. Jorge L. Bardeguez, Hato Rey, Puerto Rico (1977–1978)
Dr. William D. Carpe, Lexington, Kentucky, U.S.A.
Dr. Efefe Elonda, Mbandaka, Zaire
The Rev. Faye Feltner, Cleveland, Ohio, U.S.A.
Dr. H. Jackson Forstman, Nashville, Tennessee, U.S.A. (1979–1981)
Dr. Russel D. Legge, Waterloo, Ontario, Canada
Dr. Paul S. Stauffer, Indianapolis, Indiana, U.S.A.
Dr. M. Jack Suggs, Fort Worth, Texas, U.S.A.
Dr. David M. Thompson, Cambridge, England (1980–1981)
Dr. Robert K. Welsh, Indianapolis, Indiana, U.S.A. (Staff)

Roman Catholic:

Most Rev. Stanley J. Ott, STD, DD, New Orleans, Louisiana, U.S.A. (Co-Chairman)
The Rev. Schuyler Brown, SJ, London, England
Sister Agnes Cunningham, Mundelein, Illinois, U.S.A.
Rt. Rev. Kevin McNamara, Killarney, Ireland
Msgr. Basil Meeking, Vatican City, Europe
The Rev. Philip D. Morris, South Orange, New Jersey, U.S.A.
Dr. James Patrick, Irving, Texas, U.S.A.
The Rev. Jean M. Tillard, Ottawa, Canada
The Rev. John F. Hotchkin, Washington, D.C., U.S.A. (Staff)

World Council of Churches Observers:

Dr. Klaus-Martin Beckmann, Darmstadt, Germany (1978–1980)
The Rev. Robin H. S. Boyd, Dublin, Ireland (1981)

LUTHERAN-ROMAN CATHOLIC CONVERSATIONS

Malta Report 1972
The Eucharist 1978
Ways to Community 1980
All Under One Christ 1980
The Ministry in the Church 1981

REPORT

of the Joint Lutheran - Roman Catholic Study Commission on "The Gospel and the Church", 1972 ("Malta Report")

PREFACE

The text which follows is the report of the Lutheran/Roman Catholic Study Commission appointed by the Secretariat for Promoting Christian Unity and the Executive Committee of the Lutheran World Federation. Under the general theme of "The Gospel and the Church" this commission discussed the theological questions which are of essential significance for the relationship between the Roman Catholic Church and the Lutheran churches. The Study Commission formulated and accepted this report as a summary of its work. The general theme was formulated in so broad a way as to make it impossible for certain problems to be treated in detail. The appended *Special Statements* are to be considered as part of the report. They indicate where members of the commission felt they had to abstain or to modify the positions taken.

The report has been submitted to the appropriate church authorities as the outcome of the commission's work. Now it is being offered to the churches with a recommendation for thorough study. It is hoped that the work of the Study Commission will contribute to further clarification and improvement of relationships between the Lutheran churches and the Roman Catholic Church. This report has no binding character for the churches.

ANDRÉ APPEL
*General Secretary,
Lutheran World
Federation*

JAN WILLEBRANDS
*President, Secretariat for
Promoting Christian Unity*

Rome and Geneva,
February 9, 1972.

INTRODUCTION

(1)   Contact established between the LWF and the Roman Catholic Church on the occasion of the Second Vatican Council led to the formation of a "Lutheran/Roman Catholic Working Group" which met in Strasbourg in August 1965 and April 1966. It was officially authorized by both parties and discussed the question of possible contacts, conversations and forms of cooperation.[1]

(2)   Both delegations were convinced that the traditionally disputed theological issues between Catholics and Lutherans are still of importance but that these appear in a different light "through the emergence of the modern world" and because of new insights in the natural, social and historical sciences and in biblical theology. In view of these new insights the delegations, therefore, agreed to "engage in serious discussions on theological issues" and thus to "identify and eliminate misunderstandings and causes of irritation".[2] They agreed that it is not of primary importance to look for quick solutions to practical problems but rather to enter into a comprehensive dialog about the basic problems which both separate and unite the two churches.

(3)   For this purpose the appropriate church authorities appointed a study commission of international composition and assigned to it the topic, "The Gospel and the Church". In addition to the regular members, special participants were invited to individual sessions as theological experts on particular themes.

(4)   The first session, held November 26-30, 1967 in Zurich, Switzerland, dealt with "Gospel and Tradition". The reason for choosing to start with this biblical-theological question of the gospel and its transmission in the New Testament was that it could be anticipated, on the basis of general experience in interconfessional encounters, especially between Protestant and Catholic theologians, that the chances of agreement would be particularly great in biblical-exegetical discussions. Further, the report of the joint working group had pointed out that the "development of modern biblical scholarship has modified the traditional formulations of the respective positions and opened a new approach to the confessional differences".[3] For its second session held September 15-19, 1968 in Båstad, Sweden, the study commission decided on the theme of "World and Church under the Gospel". In doing so the commission built on the recognition in the first session that in order for the gospel, as saving event, to remain the same in every historical situation, it must always be proclaimed anew. Gospel and church cannot therefore be adequately defined apart from reference to the world. In addition, the study commission hoped that both churches could find a new unity in common service to the world.

(5)   After having thus traced and clarified the broad outlines of its assigned topic, the study commission was able to turn to more specifically ecclesiological problems in its next two sessions. Here the outstanding questions between the two confessions are particularly urgent. Under the theme "The Structures of the Church", the third session, meeting May 4-8, 1969 in Nemi, Italy, focused especially on the problem of ecclesiastical office. The fourth session met February 22-26, 1970 in Cartigny, Switzerland and, under the theme "Gospel and Law — Gospel and Christian Freedom" carried further the discussion of the themes raised at Nemi, adverting in this connection also to the questions of papal primacy and intercommunion.

(6)   The fifth session held February 21-26, 1971 in San Anton, Malta was chiefly devoted to composing a comprehensive final report. A small subcommittee had met October 27-30, 1970 in Hamburg to prepare a preliminary draft. After a thorough reworking of this draft, the final report was adopted unanimously by the study commission on February 25, 1971. The study commission appointed a small editorial committee which held a meeting in Tübingen, May 28-30, 1971. Its assignment was simply to make necessary editorial changes taking into consideration individual suggestions by members of the study commission.

(7)   In evaluating the present report it is important to recognize that it was not the task of the study commission to deal with the theological controversies of the 16th century as such; rather the commission was to examine once again the confessional differences in the light of contemporary biblical theology and church history as well as of perspectives opened up by the Second Vatican Council. For such purposes the concept "gospel" has become a key concept in ecumenical dialog. This fact has also affected the choice of theme. The theme "The Gospel and the Church" was intentionally kept general in order to make possible the discussion of a variety of controversial points.

(8)   By and large, the members of the study commission are convinced that within the framework of their theme they have achieved a noteworthy and far-reaching consensus. This consensus extends not only to the theological understanding of the gospel of its basic and normative importance for the church and of its christological and soteriological center but also to closely related and highly important points of doctrine which until now have been controversial. Undoubtedly some questions require further clarification. Yet we ask ourselves whether the still remaining differences must be viewed as hindrances to church fellowship. Are not the differences cutting across church lines, arising from diverse response to contemporary challenges at least as great as the traditional differences between the Lutheran churches and the Roman Catholic Church? These questions concern all of us together even if we approach them from different starting points and they can be answered only through a common effort.

(9)   The study commission however is also conscious of the limitations of its work. As the theme assigned to it imposed restrictions on its approach, some of the problems under consideration could not be discussed in a theologically comprehensive way. Other questions, as for example the problem of papal infallibility, were discussed to some extent, but were not included in this report. In part this was due to a lack of time. Among the theologically disputed points which were not expressly considered by the study commission we would like to mention the following: the relationship of church and gospel to the sacraments; the relationship of nature and grace and of law and gospel; the question of the teaching office; the question of Mariology. Our experience, however, has shown that the common discussion of such questions can lead to solutions which previously could not have been automatically anticipated.

(10)   Some themes discussed by us should be treated more comprehensively than was possible for the study commission. That is true above all of the theme "The Gospel and the World". Comprehensive treatment of this problem would have called for a type of expertise not represented in our commission. For an adequate theological consideration of these questions, such disciplines as ethics, sociology and psychology among others have a more than auxiliary function for theology. Further, a full understanding of the concept of gospel requires greater attention to the Old Testament. To be sure, in the present report this concept is in no way limited to the New Testament gospels nor identified with them. Yet a more intensive study of the witness of the Old Testament would lead to further insight.

(11)   Interconfessional conversations have their own peculiar problems. This became apparent in our conversations also. Often the problems were stated in a way derived from the manner of inquiry characteristic of the tradition of only one of the two churches. To be sure, this can be challenging and fruitful to the other partner and lead him to a deeper understanding of his own tradition. Here, however, there often arises the difficulty of finding a verbal formulation acceptable to both sides. Often the dogmatic conceptualizations customary to a tradition must be avoided, even when treating those matters with which these conceptualizations were intended to deal. There is a special difficulty for Lutherans in that it is often hard to give an authoritative characterization of the present Lutheran understanding of the faith. While Catholics can point to recent magisterial statements, especially those of the Second Vatican Council, Lutherans must always refer back to the 16th century confessions. This makes it difficult to present authoritatively the diversity, freedom and strengths of the actual life and witness to the faith in today's Lutheran churches.

(12)   The limitations of the work of the study commission can be partially off-set by submitting the present report to as broad as possible a discussion among the churches. The work of international ecumenical commissions should be supplemented by work on regional levels. The results of

such work could then be submitted to similar groups in other lands and cultural areas and finally evaluated by an international commission.

(13)   The present report presents the convictions and insights of the study commission. These were gradually formed over the course of a four-year dialog. Although the commission had an official assignment, it is nevertheless aware that the result of its work has no binding character for the churches. It submits this report to the appropriate church authorities with the hope that it will contribute to the clarification and improvement of the relations between Lutheran churches and the Roman Catholic Church.

I.   THE GOSPEL AND TRADITION

A)   *The question of the gospel*

(14)   The break between Lutherans and Catholics had numerous causes rooted in the peculiar historical situations of the 16th century. Yet ultimately Lutherans and Catholics separated over the issue of the right understanding of the gospel. Although the historical situation has changed extensively, they are even today convinced that their respective traditions contain elements which cannot be abandoned. The unity of the church can be a unity only in the truth of the gospel. Therefore we ask, how can we understand and actualize the gospel today?

(15)   In dealing with this decisive question, it became apparent from the very beginning that it is impossible for us to simply repeat the traditional controversial theological positions. Not only have there been changes in the historical situation in which these arose, but also theological methods and ways of stating questions have been profoundly altered by modern biblical and historical research. A new view of the confessional differences has developed. Therefore the question of the gospel must be raised anew from the perspective of contemporary theology and ecclesiology.

B)   *Jesus' proclamation and the primitive Christian kerygma*

(16)   The point of departure for our deliberations was the question of the relationship of the primitive kerygma to Jesus' proclamation. Here there was agreement that the life and proclamation of Jesus are accessible only through the primitive Christian tradition. Yet the participants differed in their evaluation of the possibility of reconstructing the life and proclamation of Jesus as well as on the question of continuity in the preaching of the gospel. However, there was consensus that the gospel rests fundamentally on the witness to the Easter event. What God has done for the salvation of the world in Jesus Christ is transmitted in the gospel and made present in the Holy Spirit. The gospel as proclamation of God's saving action is therefore itself a salvation event.

(17)   From the very beginning, the gospel of Jesus Christ was the subject matter of the tradition.[4] Out of and in the service of the proclamation of the gospel, certain writings were composed which were later designated as the New Testament. This poses the old controversial question regarding

the relationship of Scripture and tradition in a new way. The Scripture can no longer be exclusively contrasted with tradition, because the New Testament itself is the product of primitive tradition. Yet as the witness to the fundamental tradition, Scripture has a normative role for the entire later tradition of the church.[5]

C) *Criteria for the church's proclamation*

(18) Since testimony must be given to the gospel in constantly new historical situations, there arises the question of the criteria by means of which one may distinguish between legitimate and illegitimate later developments. This question cannot be answered in a purely theoretical manner. Neither the *sola scriptura* nor formal references to the authoritativeness of the magisterial office are sufficient. The primary criterion is the Holy Spirit making the Christ event into a saving action. To be sure, this raises the question of how the power of the Holy Spirit can be concretely identified as criterion. If the continuity of tradition with its original source is to be concretely manifest, then obviously secondary criteria are necessary.

(19) In the Lutheran view the living word of preaching is the normal form of authoritative interpretation of the gospel. The Confessions of the church possess authority as a correct interpretation of Scripture. In special situations (cf. the *Kirchenkampf*) the church as the people of God may be led to confess the gospel afresh and with authority in reference to new questions.

(20) In the Catholic view, the Lord authenticates his word through the reciprocal interaction of official and unofficial charisma, both of which remain under Scripture.[6] Since the gospel is constantly interpreted in faith and life, the living faith-experiences of Christians constitute a secondary criterion. In this way, the church is kept in fundamental faithfulness to Christ and his truth and is brought to renewal again and again. It receives the liberty to free itself from forms and formulations which are no longer timely, in order that the gospel might be preached in ways appropriate to current situations.

(21) Participants on both sides agreed that the authority of the church can only be service of the word and that it is not master of the word of the Lord. Therefore the church's tradition must remain open to the word and must transmit it in such a way that the word constantly bestows the understanding which comes from faith and freedom for Christian action.

(22) In spite of this historical variability of proclamation, Lutherans and Catholics are convinced that the Holy Spirit unceasingly leads and keeps the church in the truth. It is in this context that one must understand the concepts of indefectibility and infallibility which are current in the Catholic tradition. These two predominantly negative concepts are subject to misunderstanding. Although they are of late origin, that to which they refer was known in the ancient church and they are based on an interpretation of New Testament texts.[7]

(23) Infallibility must, first of all, be understood as a gift to the entire church as the people of God. The church's abiding in the truth should not be understood in a static way but as a dynamic event which takes place with the aid of the Holy Spirit in ceaseless battle against error and sin in the church as well as in the world.

D) *The center of the gospel and the hierarchy of truths*

(24) Concern for an abiding truth within the diversity of traditions leads to the question of what is that foundation and center of the gospel in relation to which the manifold witness of the church in various historical situations can be conceived as testimony and development. This foundation and this center cannot be reduced to a theological formula, but rather is constituted by the eschatological saving act of God in Jesus' cross and resurrection. It is this which all proclamation seeks to explicate.

(25) The discussion made evident a certain convergence of the Catholic idea of the hierarchy of truths and the Lutheran understanding of the gospel in terms of the central events to which it witnesses. The concept of the hierarchy of truths[8] enables Catholic theology instead of viewing all truths of faith as on the same plane, to introduce a consideration of their actual content, and thus makes evident the different levels or degrees of importance of individual truths of faith. At the same time, all truths of faith, whatever the level to which they are assigned, are given a common reference point in the foundation of the Christian faith. This brings the idea of the hierarchy of truths very close to that of the center of the gospel. To be sure, the obvious closeness does not eliminate differing emphases. While in the case of the idea of the hierarchy of truths, the aspect of completeness and fullness emerges more strongly, there is a stronger critical stress implied by the idea of the center, especially when one considers its use in the history of theology. On the basis of this it suggests that church traditions must ask themselves whether they rightly testify to the gospel.

E) *The problem of the doctrine of justification*

(26) Out of the question about the center of the gospel, arises the question of how the two sides understand justification. At this point the traditional polemical disagreements were especially sharply defined. Today, however, a far-reaching consensus is developing in the interpretation of justification. Catholic theologians also emphasize in reference to justification that God's gift of salvation for the believer is unconditional as far as human accomplishments are concerned. Lutheran theologians emphasize that the event of justification is not limited to individual forgiveness of sins, and they do not see in it a purely external declaration of the justification of the sinner.[9] Rather the righteousness of God actualized in the Christ event is conveyed to the sinner through the message of justification as an encompassing reality basic to the new life of the believer.[10]

(27) In this sense justification can be understood as expressing the totality of the event of salvation. One should, however, not fail to recognize

that in Paul's writings the comprehensive witness to God's righteousness is sharpened by his concrete dispute with Jewish legalism. As the message of justification is the foundation of Christian freedom in opposition to legalistic conditions for the reception of salvation, it must be articulated ever anew as an important interpretation of the center of the gospel. But it was also pointed out that the event of salvation to which the gospel testifies can also be expressed comprehensively in other representations derived from the New Testament, such as reconciliation, freedom, redemption, new life and new creation.

(28) Although a far-reaching agreement in the understanding of the doctrine of justification appears possible, other questions arise here. What is the theological importance of this doctrine? Do both sides similarly evaluate its implications for the life and teaching of the church?

(29) According to Lutheran understanding, and on the basis of the confession of justification, all traditions and institutions of the church are subject to the criterion which asks whether they are enablers of the proper proclamation of the gospel and do not obscure the unconditional character of the gift of salvation. It follows that the rites and orders of the church are not to be imposed as conditions for salvation, but are valid only as the free unfolding of the obedience of faith.[11]

(30) Lutherans and Catholics alike are convinced that the gospel is the foundation of Christian freedom. In the New Testament this freedom is described as freedom from sin, freedom from the power of the law, freedom from death and freedom for service toward God and neighbor. Since, however, Christian freedom is linked to the witness of the gospel, it needs institutional forms for its mediation. The church must therefore understand and actualize itself as institution of freedom. Structures which violate this freedom cannot be legitimate in the church of Christ.

F) *The gospel and church law*

(31) Church orders arise, above all, from that ministry of word and sacrament which is constitutive for the church. That which belongs to the proper proclamation of the gospel and proper administration of the sacraments is indispensable. The concrete shape of orders is presented in the New Testament in various forms. In subsequent history it has undergone many further changes. Greater awareness of the historicity of the church in conjunction with a new understanding of its eschatological nature, requires that in our day the concepts of *ius divinum* and *ius humanum* be thought through anew. In both concepts the word *ius* is employed in a merely analogical sense. *Ius divinum* can never be adequately distinguished from *ius humanum*. We have the *ius divinum* always only as mediated through particular historical forms. These mediating forms must be understood not only as the product of a sociological process of growth but, because of the pneumatic nature of the church, they can be experienced also as fruit of the spirit.

(32)   Church law is not a mere juridical system. The final decisive viewpoint must be that of the salvation of the individual believer. Church law must serve the free development of the religious life of the believer. Church norms can be of help for the formation of conscience. No law, however, may release a member of the church from his direct responsibility to God.[12] Church norms, therefore, can become binding only through the personal conscience. The area of freedom for the work of the Lord must remain open.

(33)   The church is permanently bound in its ordering to the gospel which is irrevocably prior to it. It is in respect to this that Catholic tradition speaks of the *ius divinum*. The gospel, however, can be the criterion for a concrete church order only in living relationship with contemporary social realities. Just as there is a legitimate explication of the gospel in dogmas and confessions, so there also exists a historical actualization of law in the church. Therefore, the church must discern the signs of the Holy Spirit in history and in the present, and in faithfulness to the apostolic proclamation must consider the restructuring of its orders.[13]

(34)   The Catholic participants, therefore, expect the reform of church law to proceed in such a way that the function of laws and institutions in the church will be to serve the religious life of the believers, protect Christian freedom and the rights of the person and prevent laws and institutions from ever becoming ends in themselves. For the Lutheran participants, it is a hopeful sign that the revision of the *Codex Iuris Canonici* is being carried out at a time of ecumenical rapprochement. They further hope that it will be remembered in making this revision that, although the codification of Catholic church law is of binding character only for the members of the Catholic church, it nevertheless has an indirect effect on all of Christendom. In addition they acknowledge that in many respects the structures of their own Lutheran churches are in need of radical reordering so that freedom may be further protected and promoted.

II.   THE GOSPEL AND THE WORLD

A)   *The importance of the world for the understanding of the gospel*

(35)   It is in the world and for the sake of the world that Christ lived, died and rose again. Likewise, it is in the world and for the sake of the world that the church witnesses to these saving acts of God. The world is both the *locus* and the goal of the proclamation of the gospel. These realities are so intimately interrelated that what the world is and how we understand it, inevitably influences the formulation of the gospel and the life and structures of the church.

(36)   In discussing this theme we realize anew that many doctrinal disagreements, which in the past have separated our churches, are beginning to disappear. Those controversies arose in a world very different from the present. Consequently it has become to a large extent impossible to make use of a past understanding of the world in the context of our pres-

ent proclamation. Thus many of our traditional doctrinal disagreements are losing importance.

(37) This does not mean, however, that we now possess a new and uniform "theology of earthly realities". There are far too many new problems. It is very difficult to even arrive at a clear-cut definition of the concept "world". Special attention needs to be called to such meanings of the concept of world as cosmos, as the network of social and cultural relationships, as *locus* and object of human activity—individually and corporately—and, finally, as the created, fallen and divinely-redeemed order.

(38) The similarities and differences of opinion in this area, perhaps more than anywhere else, cut across confessional lines. Roman Catholics and Lutherans are here confronted with the same fundamental questions and have similar difficulties in trying to answer them.

B) *The importance of the gospel for the world*

(39) We came to the agreement that the world must be viewed from the center of the gospel, that is, from the perspective of God's eschatological, saving act in the crucifixion and resurrection of Christ. The gospel aims for the reconciliation of all men. Two important conclusions can be drawn from this.

(40) First, God's redemptive act in Christ takes place on and through the cross. There is here no room for the triumphalism and theocratic tendencies to which Christians have so often fallen victim. The church must ever remember that Christ's victory in and over the world continues to be a hidden one and that it must witness to Christ's work of reconciliation in such a way as to share in his sufferings by struggling against the powers of evil in this age which is passing away. It must witness to God's saving acts not only through word and sacrament, not only through the verbal proclamation of the forgiveness of sins, but also by following Christ in bearing the weaknesses of the weak and identifying with the needy and oppressed. For the gospel is more than a message. It reveals the power of the eschaton already at work in our world under the form of the cross.[14]

(41) Secondly, the gospel applies to all domains of being and to all aspects of human life. Christ's victory through his death and resurrection encourages believers to live by his promise and to perform works of love. We are thereby warned against all dualistic patterns of piety and thought. The gospel cannot be confined to a purely spiritual, private or inward sphere which has no consequences for bodily or public life. Contrary to a certain Catholic tradition, "nature" cannot be conceived as the self-sufficient presupposition for supernatural grace. At the same time we must reject the notion, corresponding to a widespread Lutheran way of thinking, of a "worldly kingdom" which has no relationship to the gospel.

C) *The historicity of the gospel*

(42) In our day all reality is seen as an open-ended process and, in reference to mankind, as history. Here is our confession of faith: in his

love for the world God enters into history and makes it part of his saving act. This has always been part of the belief in the incarnation. Today, however, it becomes necessary to conceive of this historicity of the gospel more clearly.

(43) Although the gospel cannot be derived from the world, it must nevertheless be recognized that it is concretized only in specific and ever-changing circumstances. It becomes the *viva vox evangelii* only when it is formulated and expressed through the power of the Holy Spirit in reference to the ever new questions raised by men of today.[15] Only when the gospel is proclaimed for such specific situations do we grasp its saving character. Thus the world not only provides opportunities for the communication of the gospel, but it also has a hermeneutical function. It is this very world which to a certain extent enriches us with a deeper understanding of the fullness of the gospel.

(44) From this it also follows that the structures and formulations in which the gospel is concretized share in the historical conditionedness of the world in its social and cultural transformations. Since the gospel is directed toward the eschatological fulfilment, these structures and formulations are simultaneously transitory and anticipatory. Their role is to open up the future and not be closed to it. Thus the continuity of the gospel — a gift of the Holy Spirit — is to be seen, not only in fixed structures and formulations, but also in its ability to make itself known in ever new forms by constant reflections on Holy Scripture and on its interpretation in the church's history. This insight also freed ecumenical dialog from an unquestioning attachment to the fixed positions and dominant problems of the past.

(45) There is a further reason why special attention must be given to the relationship of the world to the gospel. We view this world as a global environment in which all factors influence each other. The church stands in the midst of this complex of reciprocal interrelations which, albeit unconsciously, often shape the communication of the gospel, just as this communication of the gospel also shapes and influences the world. This also frequently happens in ways of which neither the world nor the church is aware. At times the church's indirect communication through its style of life and organization is more powerful than its direct witness through word, sacrament and social action. At other times, this indirect message contradicts the gospel which the church intends to proclaim. Conversely, however, it can also happen that certain aspects of the gospel may be conveyed even where there is no awareness or intention of doing so. When reflecting on the proclamation of the gospel it is, therefore, imperative also to consider the actual social, psychological and political function of the churches in our society. In a secularized world the churches have been increasingly forced into the private sphere of things. Consequently they play an increasingly less effective, less central role in public life, whereas the gospel they proclaim concerns itself with life in its totality. At least one

of the reasons for this failure is that the churches are burdened with life styles and organizational patterns which may have been appropriate in the 'folk church' era, but which in our increasingly dechristianized society have become useless, if not harmful. A vast transformation is needed for our churches to become communities which provide the appropriate institutional and spiritual conditions for the concrete actualization of true freedom, human dignity and unity among their members. In divesting all ideologies and forms of political, social and economic life of their claims to absoluteness, the church is enabled to contribute more effectively toward an opening of the world to the future. The entire life of the church, and not only its pronouncements and programs, must become a protest against the inhuman aspects of society.

(46)   The ecumenical importance of these considerations is evident. The relationship of the world to the gospel points to the necessity of new structures for our churches. Given the charismatic total structure of the church, it was asked whether the function of the office holders could not be understood and organized in new ways and thereby enhance the importance of the priesthood of all believers. The task over against the world requires opportunities for freedom and public opinion within the church. Such new structures provide possibilities for the removal of major barriers to unity. For with the progressive overcoming of doctrinal disputes, it is now precisely structural problems which are largely responsible for continuing to keep our churches divided. With this comment concerning the relationship of the world to the gospel we now turn our attention to the problem of the office of ministry in the church.

III.   THE GOSPEL AND THE OFFICE OF THE MINISTRY IN THE CHURCH[16]

A)   *The common point of departure*

(47)   The question of the office of the ministry in the church, its origin, its position and correct understanding represents one of the most important open questions between Lutherans and Catholics. It is here that the question of the position of the gospel in and over the church becomes concrete. What, in other words, are the consequences of the doctrine of justification for the understanding of the ministerial office?

(48)   Lutherans and Catholics share the conviction that we owe our salvation exclusively to the saving act of God accomplished once for all in Jesus Christ according to the witness of the gospel. Yet the ministry of reconciliation belongs to the work of reconciliation.[17] In other words the witness of the gospel requires that there be witnesses to the gospel.[18] The church as a whole bears witness to Christ; the church as a whole is the priestly people of God.[19] As *creatura et ministra verbi*, however, it stands under the gospel and has the gospel as its superordinate criterion. Its gospel ministry is to be carried out through the proclamation of the word, through the administration of the sacraments, and, indeed, through its total life.

(49)   Since the church as the pilgrim people of God has not yet reached its eschatological goal, it depends during the present interval of time — between the "already" and the "not-yet" on ministries, structures and orders which should serve the realization of the saving act of God in Christ.

(50)   The correct determination of the relationship between this ministry assigned to the entire church and a special office in the church is a problem for Lutherans and Catholics alike. Both agree that the office of the ministry stands over against the community as well as within the community. Further they agree that the ministerial office represents Christ and his over-againstness to the community only insofar as it gives expression to the gospel. Both must examine themselves as to how effectively the critical superiority of the gospel is maintained in practice.

B)   *The normative position of its origin*

(51)   The New Testament testifies to these points in many ways. Especially important and helpful for our present problem is the concept of the apostolic as well as the charismatic structure of the congregations as portrayed especially in Paul's letters.[20]

(52)   According to the New Testament witnesses the apostles were sent by the Lord himself as witnesses of his resurrection.[21] The apostolate in the strict sense is not transferable. The apostles belong to the time of the original establishment of the church,[22] are of fundamental importance for the church,[23] and — together with the Christian prophets — can be designated as the foundation of the church.[24] The church is apostolic insofar as it stands on this foundation and abides in the apostolic faith. The church's ministry, doctrine and order are apostolic insofar as they pass on and actualize the apostolic witness.

(53)   The commission of the whole church, going back to the apostles, is carried out through a variety of charisms. These are manifestations of the Holy Spirit and make us participants in the mission and ministry of Jesus Christ.[25] Therefore the charisms are not given to only a particular group in the church nor are they limited only to its offices.[26] They exhibit their authenticity in that they testify to Christ[27] and are for others, thus serving the unity and building-up of the body of Christ.[28] Therefore the charisms are of constitutive importance for the order and structure of the church. The gospel can be maintained only in the cooperative and at times also tension-filled interaction of the various charisms and ministries.[29]

(54)   We are told quite early in the New Testament period of special ministries and offices.[30] To some extent at least they were viewed as charisms.[31] The New Testament writings testify to the great differences in congregational functions, ministries and orders in the various areas and periods of the church. These were only partially retained in later church history and they were partially interpreted in new ways (cf. the offices of presbyter, bishop and deacon). Further, these ministries and orders were imbedded in earlier historical (Jewish, Hellenistic, etc.) structures. Thus,

although there is a continuity of basic structure, it can be seen that historicity is part of the essential nature of the church's ministerial office and of its congregational ordering. The gospel as witnessed to by Scripture can be criterion for church order only when it stands in living relationship to the current social realities. Orders in the New Testament are, therefore, to be seen largely as models which are open to ever new actualizations.

C) *Historical development of church structures*

(55)   During the course of the church's history, the understanding and shaping of the ministerial office has undergone considerable change and development. Only in recent years have we become fully aware of this in our study of history. It was not until the second century that the three-fold division of the ministerial office into bishop, presbyter and deacon finally came about. The relationship of the local to the universal church, of episcopal collegiality to primacy, shifted significantly between the first and second millennia. To some extent the various churches are differentiated by their development of differing New Testament models.

(56)   These insights into the historicity of the church, combined with a new understanding of the eschatological nature of the church, have led also to changes in the theological understanding of the office of the ministry in the church. Although the ministerial office belongs constitutively to the church and has a continuing basic structure, still it is possible for concrete forms of office, which were necessary and important at a specific time for the proper carrying out of the church's mission, to be of no or little value in other situations. This enables us today also to undertake restructuring in order to adapt to new situations. In so doing, old structures, as for example, the office of deacon, can be renewed and new structures can emerge. Especially is there great need today to consider the prophetic function of the church towards the world and the structural consequences of this for the church. The exercise of the prophetic function demands an area of freedom and of public opinion within the church.

D)   *The understanding of apostolic succession*

(57)   The basic intention of the doctrine of apostolic succession is to indicate that, throughout all historical changes in its proclamation and structures, the church is at all times referred back to its apostolic origin. The details of this doctrine seem to us today to be more complicated than before. In the New Testament and the early fathers, the emphasis was obviously placed more on the substance of apostolicity, i.e., on succession in apostolic teaching. In this sense the entire church as the *ecclesia apostolica* stands in the apostolic succession. Within this general sense of succession, there is a more specific meaning: the succession of the uninterrupted line of the transmission of office. In the early church, primarily in connection with defence against heresies, it was a sign of the unimpaired transmission of the gospel and a sign of unity in the faith. It is in these terms that

Catholics today are trying once again to develop a deeper understanding of apostolic succession in the ministerial office. Lutherans on their side can grant the importance of a special succession if the preeminence of succession in teaching is recognized and if the uninterrupted line of transmission of office is not viewed as an *ipso facto* certain guarantee of the continuity of the right proclamation of the gospel.

(58)   It can also be of ecumenical importance to indicate that the Catholic tradition knows of individual instances of the ordination of priests by priests which were recognized as valid. It still needs to be clarified to what extent this leaves open the possibility of a presbyterial succession.[32]

E)   *Toward a new interpretation of the traditional teaching on the ministerial office*

(59)   Today it is possible for us to have a better understanding of various traditional elements in the doctrine of the office of the ministry as this has developed on both sides. We see more clearly than before that the question of whether ordination is a sacrament is chiefly a matter of terminology. Catholics view ordination as a sacrament which graciously equips the office bearer for ministry to others. Lutherans customarily limit usage of the word "sacrament" to baptism and the Lord's Supper (at times also absolution).[33]   In practice, however, transmission of office proceeds in both churches in a similar manner, that is, through the laying on of hands and the invocation of the Holy Spirit for his gifts for the proper exercise of ministry. In spite of all still remaining differences, there is here a substantial convergence.

(60)   A certain rapprochement can be noticed also because of a change in the Catholic understanding of "priestly character". According to the original Augustinian understanding, this had to do with the outward call and ordination to public office in the church. Later, however, there was a shift to understanding this "character" as an inner qualification of the person, and it was in this sense that it was rejected by the Reformers. In defence against a onesided metaphysical understanding, many Catholic theologians today emphasize a more strongly functional conception which is more acceptable to Lutherans. Furthermore, Lutherans in practice have the equivalent of the Catholic doctrine of the "priestly character" to the extent that they do not repeat ordination. In both churches, to be sure, there is also the problem of how the preeminence of the gospel can be made effective within the historically developed official structures.

(61)   The Second Vatican Council has emphasized in a new way that the basic task of priests is the proclamation of the gospel. Further, it is stressed in the administration of the sacraments that these are sacraments of the faith which are born from the word and nourished by the word.[34] According to the Lutheran Confessions, it is the task of the ministerial office to proclaim the gospel and administer the sacraments in accordance with the gospel, so that in this way faith is awakened and strengthened.[35] Over against an earlier onesided emphasis on proclamation, the sacraments in

the Lutheran churches are currently coming to have a more important place in the spiritual life of the congregations.

(62)   On the basis of these findings it seems necessary to examine whether the still remaining differences on these and related questions must necessarily be viewed as church-dividing differences in faith, or whether they can be understood as the expression of different ways of thinking. While Lutherans emphasize more the "event" character of God's saving acts, Catholic tradition is more concerned about the metaphysical implications of statements about salvation. These two ways of thinking are not mutually exclusive insofar as they do not become self-contained and orientate themselves in terms of the critical norm of the gospel.

F)   *The possibility of a mutual recognition of the ministerial office*

(63)   The Catholic participants are convinced in view of recent biblical and historical insights as well as on the basis of the ecumenical experience of the working of the Holy Spirit in other churches, that the traditional rejection of the validity of the Lutheran ministerial office must be rethought. The recognition of the ecclesial character of other church communities, as expressed by Vatican II,[36] can be, theologically speaking, interpreted as a first step toward the recognition of the ministerial offices of these churches. Also worthy of note is the point that the ministerial office arose in Lutheran churches through a spiritual break-through in an emergency situation. Reconsideration of the doctrine of apostolic succession and reflection on ministries of charismatic origin as well as on presbyterial succession seem to permit a correction of the traditional point of view. Therefore, the Catholic members request the appropriate authorities in the Roman Catholic Church to consider whether the ecumenical urgency flowing from Christ's will for unity does not demand that the Roman Catholic Church examine seriously the question of recognition of the Lutheran ministerial office.

(64)   The question of recognition of the ministry is viewed differently by Lutherans because they never denied the existence of the office of the ministry in the Roman Catholic Church. According to the Lutheran confessional position, the church exists wherever the gospel is preached in its purity and the sacraments are rightly administered.[37] Lutheran confessional writings leave no doubt that the one church has never ceased to exist, and they also emphasize the churchly character of the Roman Catholic communion. Also, changes in the understanding and practice of the Roman Catholic ministerial office, especially the stronger emphasis on the *ministerium verbi*, have largely removed the reasons for the reformers' criticism. The awareness of a common responsibility for the proclamation of the gospel in the world should impel the Lutheran churches also to examine seriously the question of the explicit recognition of the Roman Catholic ministerial office. Because of the already noted similarities in the understanding of the gospel, which has decisive effects on proclamation, administration of the sacraments and liturgical practice, the Lutherans

feel that even now exchange of pulpits and common eucharistic celebrations can on occasion be recommended.[38]

IV. THE GOSPEL AND THE UNITY OF THE CHURCH

(65) The commission was unable to deal with the problem of the unity of the church in a comprehensive way. It limited itself to a few aspects which appeared important in the context of its theme.

A) *The question of papal primacy*

(66) In this connection the question of papal primacy emerges as a special problem for the relationship between Lutherans and Catholics. Catholics pointed to the beginning of this doctrine in the biblical witness concerning the special position of Peter and also to the differences in the understanding of primacy in the first and second millennia. By its doctrine of episcopal collegiality, the Second Vatican Council placed the primacy in a new interpretive framework and thereby avoided a widespread onesided and isolated way of understanding it. The primacy of jurisdiction must be understood as ministerial service to the community and as bond of the unity of the church. This service of unity is, above all, a service of unity in faith. The office of the papacy also includes the task of caring for legitimate diversity among local churches. The concrete shape of this office may vary greatly in accordance with changing historical conditions. It was recognized on the Lutheran side that no local church should exist in isolation since it is a manifestation of the universal church. In this sense the importance of a ministerial service of the communion of churches was acknowledged and at the same time reference was made to the problem raised for Lutherans by their lack of such an effective service of unity. The office of the papacy as a visible sign of the unity of the churches was therefore not excluded insofar as it is subordinated to the primacy of the gospel by theological reinterpretation and practical restructuring.[39]

(67) The question, however, which remains controversial between Catholics and Lutherans is whether the primacy of the pope is necessary for the church, or whether it represents only a fundamentally possible function. It was nevertheless agreed that the question of altar fellowship and of mutual recognition of ministerial offices should not be unconditionally dependent on a consensus on the question of primacy.[40]

B) *Intercommunion*

(68) Fellowship in eucharistic celebration is an essential sign of church unity.[41] Therefore, striving for altar fellowship is central for all those who seek the unity of the church.

(69) In our day the problem of altar fellowship or intercommunion presents itself in a new way. Mutual recognition has progressed among the churches and they have become much more strongly aware of their com-

mon mission in the world. In some places members of our churches have met together at the Lord's table and are convinced that they have thereby rediscovered fellowship in the Lord. It is clear to us that at times unthinking and spiritually irresponsible actions are a hindrance to a final solution. On the other hand, the various experiments in common celebration of the Lord's Supper are also signs of the seriousness of the question and make urgent additional theological and canonical clarification. In this situation church leaders have a manifold responsibility. They must consider that the celebration of the Lord's Supper cannot be separated from confessing Christ and his eucharistic presence nor from the fellowship of the church; but they must also take care lest they hinder the work of the Spirit. They should by their helpful instructions lead the community of believers in hope for the reunion of all separated Christians.

(70) It is apparent to us that the questions raised here and the attempts at solution which have been offered call for still more thorough investigation. Nevertheless, at least some directions which lead to answers to these questions can be indicated. There was agreement that our common baptism is an important starting point in this matter of eucharistic fellowship.[42] To be sure, this is not the only prerequisite for complete altar fellowship, but it should force us to examine the question of whether the former exclusion of certain communities of baptized Christians can be rightfully continued today.

(71) Although there are considerable differences of opinion on this matter in the Catholic Church it is pointed out on the Catholic side that there is no exclusive identity between the one church of Christ and the Roman Catholic Church.[43] This one church of Christ is actualized in an analogous manner also in other churches. That also means that the unity of the Roman Catholic Church is not perfect but that it strives toward the perfect unity of the church. In this sense the eucharistic celebration in the Catholic church also suffers from imperfection. It will become the perfect sign of the unity of the church only when all those who through baptism have been invited in principle to the table of the Lord and are able in reality to partake.

(72) The Lutherans emphasized that the communion practices of the separated churches must receive their orientation from that which is demanded of the church by the ministry of reconciliation among men. For the Lord's Supper is given to men by the crucified and risen Lord so that they might be received into his fellowship and saved through it. A celebration of the Lord's Supper in which baptized believers may not participate suffers from an inner contradiction and from the start, therefore, does not fulfil the purpose for which the Lord established it. For the Lord's Supper is the reconciling acceptance of men through the redemptive work of Jesus Christ.

(73) Practical consequences emerge from these considerations for Lutherans and for Roman Catholics. All steps taken by the churches must

be shaped by serious efforts to further the unity of the churches. Because of the anomalies of present church divisions, this unity will not be suddenly established. A process of gradual rapprochement is necessary in which various stages are possible. At present it should already be recommended that the church authorities, on the basis of what is already shared in faith and sacrament and as sign and anticipation of the promised and hoped for unity, make possible occasional acts of intercommunion as, for example, during ecumenical events or in the pastoral care of those involved in mixed marriages. Unclarity concerning a common doctrine of the ministerial office still makes for difficulties in reciprocal intercommunion agreements. However, the realization of eucharistic fellowship should not depend exclusively on full recognition of the offices of the ministry.

(74)   In this connection it should be considered that the pastoral responsibility of the church leadership can obligate it to proceed in such a way on this question of intercommunion as not to confuse the faithful. But pastoral responsibility also demands taking into account the situation of those faithful who suffer in special ways under the necessities of separation or who because of their convictions think that they must seek fellowship in Christ in joint celebrations of the Lord's Supper. Both sides point out that a solution to the question of intercommunion between Catholics and Lutherans must not neglect concern for fellowship with other churches.

(75)   At the conclusion of their work the members of the commission look back in joyful gratitude on the experience of this truly brotherly encounter. Even the discussion of opposing convictions and opinions led us to sense even more deeply our profound community and joint responsibility for our common Christian heritage. Of course, the participants also became aware of the difficulties on the road towards complete church unity. This road will be discovered only if both churches pursue in all humility and honesty the question of the truth of the one gospel of Jesus Christ. The encounter with the Lord who encourages us ever anew by his gospel is more than a rational process. Joint theological efforts, therefore, will have to become part of a spiritual life process. This process of spiritual encounter should, so far as possible, become an increasingly united one. For the Lord strengthens us with his word in the spirit and makes it effective wherever "two or three" are "gathered in [his] name"[44] and "agree about anything they ask".[45]

Special Statement by Bishop H. L. Martensen and subscribed to by Professor A. Vögtle

According to the Catholic understanding of the faith, eucharist and ministry can simply not be separated. Even in exceptional cases it is not possible to celebrate the eucharist without the office of the ministry. Similarly there can be no eucharist without it being community-related.

Although the realization of eucharistic fellowship, as it is called in no. 73, can *not exclusively* be made dependent of the recognition of the ministerial office, such a recognition is essential and necessary for the eucharistic celebration and should never be lacking if it is to be recognized by the Catholic Church.

Catholic authorities, therefore, would be well advised, independent of the question of recognition of the office of the ministry, not to permit Catholics to receive the Lord's Supper on special occasions at non-Catholic worship services.

Special Statement by Professor H. Schürmann

I did not attend the third session of the study commission, May 4-8 in Nemi, concerning the "Structures of the Church" (cf. no. 5), nor the fifth session, February 21-26, 1971 in San Anton, Malta and the consultations at that meeting as well as the voting on the final report (cf. no. 6). Therefore I wish to explain my understanding of the "request" in no. 63 and the "recommendation" in no. 73 so as to give specific meaning to my signature.

In view of the realities of the Lutheran churches today or of the Lutheran World Federation, it hardly seems possible to speak of a uniform understanding and assessment of "the Lutheran ministry" (cf. final sentence no. 11). Therefore the "request . . . (to) examine seriously the question of recognition of the Lutheran ministerial office" (no. 68) seems to include the desire to achieve a more binding common understanding within the Lutheran churches on the doctrine of the ministry as for instance is expressed in this report.

In view of the "unclarity concerning a common doctrine of the ministerial office" in no. 73 and the emphasis on "the pastoral responsibility of the church leadership" in no. 74, I can only conceive of the "recommendation" in no. 73 addressed to the church authorities in the sense of limited admission to the respective eucharistic celebrations in the cases specified.

Special Statement by Professor J. L. Witte, S.H.

I agree with the report of the Joint Lutheran/Roman Catholic Study Commission on "The Gospel and the Church". However, I have the following reservations concerning no. 73, concerns already expressed by me at the final session at Malta.

In view of the "unclarity concerning a common doctrine of the ministerial office", the recommendation that "church authorities . . . make possible occasional acts of intercommunion" (in the sense of "reciprocal admission"), seems to me to be, theologically and pastorally, a premature recommendation from the Catholic point of view (citations are from no. 73). From the Catholic perspective I am convinced that in the present situation the commission should not have done more than recommend that church authorities, on the basis of what is already shared in faith and sacrament and as sign and anticipation of the promised and hoped for unity, make possible *occasional acts of limited admission to the respective eucharistic celebrations,* as for example at ecumenical occasions and in the case of mixed marriages.

Special Statement by Professor D. H. Conzelmann

When after thorough reflection I sign my name to the report of the Commission, I do so because I consider its work to be good, useful and worthy of continuation. My signature does not imply that I identify myself with the theological views which appear in the "Lutheran parts" of the report.

1.   At several points a unified Lutheran position is lacking, as for example on the nature and importance of church law, of the apostolic office and, beyond that, of the ministry in general, or ordination, etc.

2.   Contemporary movements both among church people and also particularly among the younger generation of theologians should in my view receive more consideration, as for example, the demand for making infant baptism optional or even abolishing it.

3.   For theological reasons I am forced to take direct issue with several statements, as for example the historical relativization of the question of truth (no. 24; no. 27, no. 63) and the statements in the second sentence of no. 29.

I consider it my duty to inform the commission of these reservations. For in the debates which will follow the publication of this report I can and shall stand solidly behind the work of the commission, but for purposes of theological argumentation, I must retain my freedom in relation to the Lutheran theses as well as in reference to the criticism of the Catholic positions. It would be very helpful for these discussions if also the documentation on which the report is based were made available to the public.

PARTICIPANTS

Members of the Commission:

Roman Catholics:

Professor W. Kasper, FRG (co-chairman)
Professor J. A. Fitzmyer, U.S.A.
Bishop H. L. Martensen, Denmark
Professor E. Schillebeeckx, OP, Netherlands
Professor E. Schürmann, GDR
Professor A. Vögtle, FRG
Professor J. L. Witte, Rome

Lutherans:

Professor E. Molland, Norway (co-chairman)
Professor H. Conzelmann, FRG
Professor G. Lindbeck, U.S.A.
Professor W. Lohff, FRG
Professor P. E. Persson, Sweden
Professor K. Stendahl, U.S.A.
Professor G. Strecker, FRG

CONSULTANT:

Lutheran:

Professor V. Vajta, France

SECRETARIES:

Roman Catholic:

Dr. August Hasler, Rome

Lutheran:

Dr. Harding Meyer, Geneva

THE EUCHARIST
Final Report of the Joint Roman Catholic - Lutheran Commission, 1978

Historical Introduction:

After publication of the report "The Gospel and the Church" ("Malta Report", 1973), a new Joint Roman Catholic — Lutheran Commission was set up. Its membership is even more international than that of the preceding Joint Lutheran — Roman Catholic Study Commission. Church authorities and congregational pastors are also more strongly represented than before. The commission members, as was the case with the preceding Study Commission, were nominated by the Executive Committee of the Lutheran World Federation and the Secretariat for Promoting Christian Unity.

The first two sessions of the Commission (Geneva, March 1973; Rome, January 1974) attempted an analysis of the contemporary relations between the Roman Catholic Church and Lutheran Churches in different countries and continents. At the same time, the reactions of the churches to the "Malta Report" were evaluated, and the aim of the new dialogue determined. It became apparent that three thematic areas which had still not been sufficiently discussed in the "Malta Report" would have to be dealt with above all else: 1) Eucharist 2) Episcopal Office 3) Ways to Community.

One sub-commission was set up for each of the three themes, in which, as well as commission members, other participants were present as consultants. The results of the work carried out within the sub-commissions were laid before the full Commission at its sessions and discussed, then handed back to the sub-commissions for revision.

"The Eucharist" is the first concrete result of the newly undertaken dialogue. On the basis of a preparatory and then a revised draft of the sub-commission dealing with this theme, which made substantial use of the findings of other bilateral and multilateral dialogues on the Eucharist, the document was worked over in two sessions of the full commission (Strasbourg, March 1976, Paderborn/FRG, March 1977). After some smaller revision it was published in 1978.

"The Eucharist", in its complete German edition, contains two appendices; on the one hand, eucharistic liturgies of both churches (four Roman Catholic eucharistic prayers and six Lutheran schemes for eucharistic worship from different countries and traditions) in order to show how the celebration of the Eucharist is actually experienced by each side of the dialogue; on the other hand, six brief essays by a Catholic and Lutheran theologian respectively, in which at several significant points (presence of Christ; eucharist as sacrifice, and others) it is assessed how far the historical points of controversy and division can now be resolved as a result of theological and historical research and developments within the churches. Due to lack of space these appendice are not included here.*

PREFACE

The Lutheran/Roman Catholic Joint Commission established by the Secretariat for Promoting Christian Unity and the Lutheran World Federation has completed its work on a document concerning the Lord's Supper. Following its unanimous passage by commission members, the document is now presented for discussion. Agreement has been reached on significant points. In large measure it has been possible to make a common witness. Thus we are confident that those questions which remain open will be clarified mutually. We hope that the following document will further full community in faith and, thus, that community at the Lord's Table for which we yearn.

HANS L. MARTENSEN......................................GEORGE A. LINDBECK
Bishop of Copenhagen.............................*Professor, Yale University*
Denmark..New Haven, USA

Chairpersons

---

* They can be found in the complete edition of the document: "Das Herrenmahl", Paderborn/Frankfurt, 1978.

INTRODUCTION

1. Since 1965 — after more than 400 years of separation — discussions have been taking place at a world level between officially appointed representatives of the Lutheran World Federation and the Roman Catholic Church. The competent church authorities set up an international study commission to consider the theme "The Gospel and the Church" and, in this connection, to re-examine in the light of more recent insights certain theological problems, particularly the traditional theological controversies. A report on the results reached by the commission was published in 1972.[1] This document gave expression to important convergences and a certain consensus. But as was expressly pointed out in the preface, the theme put before the commission was so broad that certain important questions could either not be considered at all or at least not extensively. These included problems connected with the Eucharist and the Ministry. The need for a thorough clarification of these questions is not only underscored by the commission itself, and also by the reactions to the Malta Report, but one is made painfully aware of the urgency of this matter by our continuing separation in the Supper of unity: the full unity of Christians, presupposing unity in faith, includes eucharistic communion. In continuing the official dialogue, therefore, the Lutheran/Roman Catholic Joint Commission has paid special attention to the Eucharist and now presents the results of its efforts.[2] This is to be followed by a study of the ministry of the church in which special consideration will be given to the ministry of the bishop; many of the questions connected with the Eucharist can only find an answer in this subsequent document.

2. In working out the present text, the Lutheran/Catholic commission sought to give a joint witness whenever possible and, at the same time, to define the open questions as well as bringing them nearer a solution. What Lutheran and Catholic Christians can jointly confess will thus be able to find a place in the life of the church and the congregations.

3. The text of the document took shape through reflection on the witness of Holy Scripture and on ecclesial traditions. The concrete shape of the liturgy had a special place in our considerations, because the eucharistic reality embraces doctrine and life, confession and liturgical form, piety and practice. In gratitude for what others have already done, and with a view to achieving the widest possible ecumenical impact, we have freely drawn on statements in already existing ecumenical documents in so far as these conform to the Lutheran and Catholic understanding.[3]

4. The statement is subdivided as follows:

– The first part, on "joint witness", expresses what Lutheran and Catholic Christians are able to confess jointly.

– The second part turns to "joint tasks". It identifies and discusses points of disagreement, and indicates the consequences and imperatives for the life, teaching and especially liturgy of the church which emerge from the document.

– The exposition is followed by some examples of eucharistic liturgy which exemplify the liturgical traditions and practices of the two churches.

– In the attached appendices, a Lutheran and a Catholic member of the commission consider the degree to which historical research and ecclesial developments can now overcome on certain essential points the controverted issues which have in the past caused division. The commission has agreed to receive these texts, which were prepared by the authors on their own responsibility.

5. This document is addressed to all Catholic and Lutheran Christians, to church authorities, theologians, pastors, local communities, and especially to all groups now engaged in the ecumenical dialogue. But it is addressed not only to Lutheran and Catholic Christians. Just as the commission gratefully accepted and utilized the suggestions of other Christian groups, it now hopes that the Lutheran/Catholic consideration of the Eucharist will be of help to others. To this end an attempt was made in this document to testify to a truth which is for all people, Christian and non-Christian alike.

Part I

JOINT WITNESS

I. THE LEGACY OF CHRIST ACCORDING TO THE SCRIPTURE

6. Before Jesus went to his death in order to bestow on human beings peace and communion with God and with one another, he prepared the last Supper for his disciples: "In the night in which he was betrayed and gave himself up to suffer, he took bread and gave thanks, broke it and gave it to his disciples with the words 'Take and eat, all of you, this is my body which is given for you'. Likewise he took the cup after supper, gave thanks and gave it to his disciples saying, 'Take and drink from it, all of you: this is the cup of the new and eternal covenant, my blood, shed for you and for all people for the forgiveness of sins. Do this for the remembrance of me.'"[4] In this new passover meal the Lord gave himself as nourishment to his disciples and thus, in anticipation of his coming glory, made them partakers in his work, life and suffering (cf. Matthew 26:26-29; Mark 14:22-25; Luke 22:16-20; 1 Corinthians 11:23-26).

Whenever Christians celebrate the Lord's Supper according to his will in remembrance of him, he grants anew this communion and with it "forgiveness of sins, life and salvation".[5]

II. MYSTERY OF FAITH

7.   The Lord's Supper is a mystery of faith in the fullest sense of the word. It belongs to the all-encompassing and incomprehensible mystery of salvation and participates in its character as mystery. God himself must communicate himself if human beings are to recognize the mystery, and it enters the range of our vision only to the extent that the Lord wills and effects. The Eucharist is thus only accessible to us through the divine gift of faith.

8.   Even the attitudes and actions required of those who participate in the celebration are a matter of faith, not of their own power. The eucharistic community of life and action can grow only out of the community of faith created by the Holy Spirit (see 23 below).

9.   Since Christian faith is essentially something shared with all fellow believers, the Eucharist is primarily an affair of the community and through this of individuals. Like the "new covenant", the "blood of the covenant" given in the Eucharist (Matthew 26:28; Mark 14:24; Luke 22:20; 1 Corinthians 11:25) is granted to the new people of God and thus to its members.

10.   All "grace and truth" (John 1:14) are now in our midst, in our Lord present in the Eucharist, which is thus also a mystery of faith in the sense of including the essential dimensions of the truth of faith.

The eucharistic celebration reflects the phases of salvation history: we are reminded of God's good creation, for which we give praise and thanks; the reality of sin becomes apparent and demands recollection and confession;

> the consolation and promise of God's word are addressed to us anew and are received in hearing, obedience and response;
> bread and wine, things of the world, are drawn into the process of salvation and healing, as are also basic features of human life: eating and drinking and communal celebration and action;
> the union of Christians with their Lord and with each other is both the proclamation and the beginning of God's kingdom in our midst and a promise of the coming fulfilment.

11.   Finally, the mystery of the Eucharist unites us to the ultimate mystery from, through, and towards which all things exist: the mystery of the triune God.

Our heavenly Father is the first source and final goal of the eucharistic event.

The incarnate Son of God is the living centre of the eucharistic event: the one in, with and through whom it unfolds.

The Holy Spirit is the immeasurable power of love which gives the Eucharist life and lasting effect.

12.   This most profound mystery of the Lord's Supper and of our life is celebrated at the end of many eucharistic prayers in the doxology. In view of the presence of our Lord Jesus Christ, it says:

"Through him, with him, in him
in the unity of the Holy Spirit
all honour and glory is yours, almighty Father
now and forever. Amen".

Joining in this song of praise, which together we make our own, we can unite in the following common testimony:

III. THROUGH, WITH AND IN CHRIST

Through Christ

13.   Only *through Christ Jesus* does the Eucharist exist. He was the first to celebrate it in the circle of the disciples. From him comes the commission to celebrate it ever anew for his remembrance until he comes again. It is he who prepares the Supper and extends the invitation. Through him the full, conscious and active participation of all believers in the eucharistic event is made possible and actual.[6] Through him those who preside over the eucharistic celebration in his name are called and commissioned. Their service is a clear indication that "the congregation is not proprietor of the action it is performing; that it is not the master of the eucharist but receives it from Another, Christ living in his Church"[7] (see below 65-68).

With Christ

14.   Through him we can celebrate the Eucharist *with him*. The wonder of his presence occurs, not from human merit nor through human ability, but in the power of his grace alone. The meaning and consequences of this can be discerned only if we are open to the different ways in which the Lord is present.

15.   Jesus Christ fulfils his promise, "I am with you always, to the close of age" (Matthew 28:20) in manifold ways. "We confess a manifold presence of Christ, the Word of God and Lord of the world. The crucified and risen Lord is present in his body, the people of God, for he is present 'where two or three are gathered' in his name (Matthew 18:20). He is present in baptism, for it is Christ himself who baptizes. He is present in the reading of the scriptures and the proclamation of the gospel."[8] The Lord is present in the poor and distressed since he said: "As you did it to one of the least of my brethren, you did it to me" (Matthew 25:40).

16.   The eucharistic presence is continuous with all these modes of presence and is, at the same time, of a special character. "Christ is present and active, in various ways, in the entire eucharistic celebration. It is the same Lord who through the proclaimed word invites his people to his

table, who through his minister presides at that table, and who gives himself sacramentally in the Body and Blood of his paschal sacrifice."[9]

In the sacrament of the Lord's Supper Jesus Christ, true God and true man, is present wholly and entirely, in his body and blood, under the signs of bread and wine.

"Through the centuries Christians have attempted various formulations to describe this presence. Our confessional documents have in common affirmed that Jesus Christ is 'really', 'truly' and 'substantially' present in this sacrament. This manner of presence 'we can scarcely express in words', but we affirm his presence because we believe in the power of God and the promise of Jesus Christ, 'This is my body . . . This is my blood . . . '. Our traditions have spoken of this presence as 'sacramental', 'supernatural' and 'spiritual'. These terms have different connotations in the two traditions, but they have in common a rejection of a spatial or natural manner of presence, and a rejection of an understanding of the sacrament as only commemorative or figurative."[10]

17. "Christ instituted the eucharist, sacrament of his body and blood with its focus upon the cross and resurrection, as the *anamnesis* of the whole of God's reconciling action in him. Christ himself with all that He has accomplished for us and for all creation (in his incarnation, servanthood, ministry, teaching, suffering, sacrifice, resurrection, ascension and Pentecost) is present in this *anamnesis* as is also the foretaste of his *Parousia* and the fulfilment of the Kingdom"[11] (see below 36).

18. The Lord present among us wants to draw us into the movement of his life. He, who in his love gave himself up to death, lives in us (Gal. 2:20). With him and through his grace we have "passed from death to life" (John 5:24). Participating in the eucharistic sacrament, we are on pilgrimage with him from this world to the world to come (*pascha, transitus*). Endowed and quickened by his Spirit we may hand on his love and so glorify the Father. The more powerless we are to offer to God a worthy sacrifice so much more shall we be taken up by the power of Christ into his offering. "When, in the Lord's Supper, we come to God in self-surrender, we do so only 'through Christ', that is in union with his own surrender of himself . . . To surrender oneself means ultimately 'to open oneself in order to receive him'."[12]

"Thus, united to our Lord, who offers himself to his Father, and in communion with the universal Church in heaven and on earth, we are renewed in the covenant sealed with the blood of Christ and we offer ourselves as a living and holy sacrifice which must be expressed in the whole of our daily life."[13]

In this way the perpetual meaning of the Christian faith is ever to be realized anew; a basic link with the Lord as he is in the whole range of actual destiny. Anyone united with him is summoned to die and rise with him (see below 34-36).

In Christ

19. This being-with-Christ has its basis and climax in *being-in-Christ*. Under the signs of bread and wine the Lord offers as nourishment his body and blood, that is himself, which he has given for all. He thus shows himself to be the "living bread which came down from heaven" (John 6:51). When a believer receives this food in faith, he will be taken into a communion with Christ which is akin to the communion of the Son with the Father: "As the living Father sent me, and I live because of the Father, so he who eats me will live because of me" (John 6:57). Christ wills to be in us, and we are enabled to be in Christ: "He who eats my flesh and drinks my blood abides in me, and I in him" (John 6:56). This communion is rooted in eternity and reaches out again beyond time into eternity. "He who eats this bread will live for ever" (John 6:58).

20. In giving himself Christ unites all who partake at his table: the many become "one body" (1 Corinthians 10:17). In the power of the Holy Spirit, they are built up as the one people of God. "It is the spirit that gives life" (John 6:63). The eucharistic meal is thus the source of the daily new life of the people of God who through it are gathered together and kept in one faith.

IV. IN THE UNITY OF THE HOLY SPIRIT

The Holy Spirit and the Eucharist

21. During his life on earth, Jesus Christ did all things in the Holy Spirit (cf. Luke 4:1, 14, 17-21). It was in the power of the Spirit that he offered himself as sacrifice (Hebr. 9:14) and conquered sin and death and rose from the tomb, and lives in the midst of his Pentecost community. Through and in the Spirit Christians are to remain bound to Christ and continue his work.

It is also through the Holy Spirit that Christ is at work in the Eucharist. All that the Lord gives us and all that enables us to make it our own is given to us through the Holy Spirit. In the liturgy this becomes particularly clear in the invocation of the Holy Spirit (*epiklesis*).[14]

22. In remembrance of the intercession of Christ, its high priest, the church asks with confidence for his Spirit, in order to be renewed and sanctified through the eucharistic gifts and so strengthened to accomplish its mission in the world. In the power of the Holy Spirit the bread and wine become the body and blood of Christ through the creative word. The spirit of love causes the sacrament of love to become real in that the divine love seeks us in our earthly reality in order to bring us home again.

23. Only in the Holy Spirit does the congregation come to the faith without which it cannot celebrate the Eucharist. Thus the *epiklesis* is also the prayer for a living faith which prepares us to celebrate the remembrance of the suffering and resurrection of Christ. The Eucharist is not an automatic means for the salvation of the world; it presupposes the presence of the Holy Spirit within the believers (see above 7-9).

24. In the *fruits* of the Holy Spirit—the love, joy and peace which believers receive in the Eucharist in a special way—the ultimate fulfilment of all things is anticipated. The Eucharist is the meal celebrated in expectation of his coming in glory for the strengthening of the faithful. The invocation of the Holy Spirit is (accordingly) a plea for the future world to break into our present one (see below 42-45).

Eucharist and Church

25. Baptized by the one Spirit into the one body (cf. 1 Corinthians 12:13) believers—nourished by the body of Christ—become ever more one body through the Holy Spirit (cf. 1 Corinthians 10:17). The Eucharist and the Church are thus, in manifold ways, linked together in a living bond.

26. As Christ gives himself to his people in the Eucharist his life becomes their life, his Spirit their spirit. The enduring form of life of the ecclesial communion with Christ arises from the event of the sacramental communion with Christ. "Nought else follows the partaking in the body and blood of Christ than that we become what we receive"[15] . . . "truly, we too are drawn and transformed into that spiritual body which is the communion of Christ and all the Saints, we are established through this sacrament in the virtues and graces of Christ and His Saints."[16] The Eucharist is thus at once the source and climax of the church's life. Without the eucharistic community there is no full ecclesial community, and without the ecclesial community there is no real eucharistic community.

27. This is true, first for the actual congregation wherever it gathers to celebrate the Lord's Supper, but equally it concerns the whole of Christianity. "The sharing of the common loaf and the common cup in a given place demonstrates the oneness of the sharers with the whole Christ and with their fellow sharers in all times and places. By sharing the common loaf they show their unity with the Church catholic."[17]

Even the limits of earthly reality are transcended in that the Holy Spirit also unites us to those who have gone before in faith and been called to eternal communion in God.

28. In view of this unity bestowed by Christ, the fact that Christians again and again sin against this unity is all the more serious. This occurs when they fail in faith and hope, but also when they tolerate or even cause deep divisions between human beings both in personal and social spheres.

Whoever has entered into communion with God must with him attack the walls of enmity which human beings erect against each other: walls of enmity between families, nations, races, classes, sexes, generations, confessions and religions.[18]

V. GLORIFICATION OF THE FATHER

29. The union with Christ into which we are drawn in the Eucharist through the power of the Holy Spirit ultimately leads to the eternal Father. This occurs at different levels and in varying, yet internally related ways.

Proclamation

30. The Eucharist as a whole—that is, not simply through reading and preaching—proclaims the greatness and mercy of God. Each of the elements in the service receives, appropriate to its nature, a particular significance.

The confession of sins by the assembled congregation always implies a public assent to God's act of reconciliation.

Through the reading and exposition of the Scriptures God's word penetrates and becomes effective in ever-new situations. The witness of the Scriptures and the preaching of the mighty acts of God not only call forth the confession of faith but are themselves a function of this confession.

The praying of the early Christian creeds proclaims the bond both with the early church and with all those who also adhere to them.

Bread and wine, "fruit of the earth and of human labour"[19] are first and foremost gifts of the Father and epitomize his good creation. Their inclusion in the eucharistic action is a striking witness to the sustaining creative power which upholds all things at each moment and leads toward their fulfilment.

Above all, each eucharistic meal testifies to that love for the whole world made manifest on the cross by God who gave his Son for the world (cf. John 3:16): "For as often as you eat this bread and drink this cup, you proclaim the Lord's death until he comes" (1 Corinthians 11:26).

Thanksgiving

31. Their very nature links proclamation and thanksgiving closely together. Accordingly the Eucharist "is the great thanksgiving to the Father for everything which He accomplished in creation, redemption and sanctification, for everything which He accomplishes now in the Church and in the world in spite of the sins of men, for everything that He will accomplish in bringing his Kingdom to fulfilment. Thus the Eucharist is the benediction (*berakah*) by which the Church expresses its thankfulness to God for all his benefits."[20]

Thanksgiving to God the Father and Creator of all good gifts is expressed materially as well as verbally in the congregation's celebration. The self-giving of Christ and the promise of the coming kingdom relativises all the riches of this world and makes us aware of God as the giver and ourselves as the stewards of these gifts. In the offering of bread and wine we praise God who through our work provides us with the earthly gifts necessary for our life. We offer ourselves (cf. Romans 12:1) and share one with the other what has been given us.

Intercession

32. Strengthened through faith in God's mercies the congregation intercedes in the same eucharistic celebration for all men, for the needs of the world, for the concerns of the faithful and of those who have special

responsibilities in church and society. The church is thus united with the intercession its Lord is making in the presence of the Father (cf. Hebrews 7:25) and pleads through him for that promised salvation of the world of which the congregation has received a foretaste through its faith and hope through the Holy Spirit. We rejoice that this trust in God's saving action in the world is being more clearly expressed in the celebrations of our congregations, but this also involves obligations of active solidarity with all who suffer.[21]

Praise

33.   "The eucharist is the great sacrifice of praise by which the Church speaks on behalf of the whole creation."[22]Through the fall of man the sacrifice of praise due to God from mankind was silenced. In Christ it is brought to life again. Renewed in Christ the creation sings its praise in the eucharistic congregation, above all in the Preface and the Sanctus. It is enabled to worship the Father in spirit and truth (cf. John 4:23f).

Self-giving

34.   In his body given for his own (Luke 22:19, 1 Corinthians 11:24) and in his blood poured out for them (Matthew 26:28; Mark 14:24; Luke 22:20), the Lord in his still-giving is present. He is amongst us as the one given by the Father in the Holy Spirit and as the one giving himself for the Father and mankind in the Holy Spirit. It is thus that he imparts himself and wills to continue to be effective. The more the celebrating community is drawn into this act of self-offering, the more it lives to the greater glory of God. The church which proclaims the Lord's death is summoned to unite itself with this death. It should not only know and talk about sacrifice, it should allow itself to be seized by it. In dying with its Lord, the church will be prepared for rising with him.

35.   The union with himself which Christ offers also affects the desires and acts of his people. "That is the fruit of the Lord's Supper, that you give yourself with all your life just as Christ in these words gave himself for you together with all that he is"[23] (see above 18).

36.   When the church actually follows the command of the Lord: "Do this in remembrance of me" (Luke 22:19; 1 Corinthians 11:24), it comes in contact with the sacrifice of Christ anew: it receives new life from him and the power to die with him.

"The notion of *memorial* as understood in the passover celebration at the time of Christ—i.e., the making effective in the present of an event in the past—has opened the way to a clearer understanding of the relationship between Christ's sacrifice and the Eucharist"[24] (see above 17).

In the *memorial celebration of the people of God* more happens than that past events are brought to mind by this power of recall and imagination. The decisive point is not that what is past is called to mind, but that the Lord calls his people into his presence and confronts them with his salvation. In this creative act of God, the salvation event from the past becomes the offer of salvation for the present and the promise of salvation for the future.

All those who celebrate the Eucharist in remembrance of him are incorporated in Christ's life, passion, death and resurrection. They receive the fruit of Christ's offering his life and thereby of the entire reconciling saving act of God. In the passover meal of the new covenant, they are freed and united with God and one another. So they give thanks "for all his mercies, entreat the benefits of his passion on behalf of the whole church, participate in these benefits and enter into the movement of his self-offering."²⁶

In receiving in faith, they are taken as his body into the reconciling sacrifice which equips them for self-giving (Romans 12:1) and enables them "through Jesus Christ" to offer "spiritual sacrifices" in service to the world (1 Peter 2:5). Thus is rehearsed in the Lord's Supper what is practised in the whole Christian life. "With contrite hearts we offer ourselves as a living and holy sacrifice, a sacrifice which must be expressed in the whole of our daily lives."²⁶

37. Our two traditions agree in understanding the Eucharist as a *sacrifice of praise*. This is neither simple verbal praise of God, nor is it a supplement or a complement which people from their own power add to the offering of praise and thanksgiving which Christ has made to the Father. The eucharistic sacrifice of praise has only become possible through the sacrifice of Christ on the cross: therefore this remains the main content of the church's sacrifice of praise. Only "by him, with him, and in him who is our great High Priest and Intercessor we offer to the Father, in the power of the Holy Spirit, our praise, thanksgiving and intercession"²⁷ (see below 56-61).

VI. For the Life of the World

38. The movement of Jesus' life towards the Father into which he leads his people, is meant for all. The bread that Christ himself is and gives is intended "for the life of the world" (John 6:51).

The Eucharist's Relation to the World

39. "For the world which God in Christ reconciled with Himself is present at each Eucharist: in the bread and the wine, in the persons of the faithful and in the prayers they offer for all humankind. Thus the Eucharist opens up to the world the way to its transfiguration."²⁸ It reveals to the world what it is and what it is to become.²⁹ Rooted in the past, translated into reality in the present, and directed to the future, the Eucharist concentrates in itself all dimensions of historical growth. That indicates its deep bond with our changing world, and contributes to a deeper understanding and more responsible action in it.

In the eucharistic unity, the new unity of mankind begins to emerge. Christ as head of the church is head of the whole of saved humanity. He gives the church his life so that in this way all may receive it. "When we gather around the same table in this communal meal at the invitation of the same Lord and when we 'partake of one loaf', we are one in commitment not only to Christ and to one another, but also to the mission of the Church in the world."[30]

The Responsibility of the Christians for the World

40.   The Eucharist as a whole — and not just in one part or another — is directed towards the salvation of the world. Therefore, Christians who celebrate the Eucharist are called to service to the world. Communion with Christ enables and obliges us to help all men.

41.   "Reconciled in the Eucharist, the members of the body of Christ become the servants of reconciliation among men and witnesses of the joy of the resurrection. Their presence in the world implies fellowship in suffering and hope with all men, among whom they are called upon to bear witness to the love of Christ in service and in combat. The celebration of the Eucharist, the breaking of a bread that is necessary to life, is an incitement not to accept conditions in which men are deprived of bread, justice, and peace."[31]

Such actions are particularly necessary when social, national or racial divisions develop within the church (cf. 1 *Corinthians* 11:18-30). Evils of this kind can have as disastrous effects as schisms in faith. They contradict the nature of the church and render its witness ineffective and its sacramental celebrations unworthy. The words of the Lord: "First be reconciled to your brother, and then come and offer your gift" (Matthew 5:24) apply to the Eucharist also.

VII.   WITH A VIEW TO THE FUTURE GLORY

42.   In the Eucharist we proclaim "the Lord's death until he comes" (1 Corinthians 11:26). In it the future glory is promised, as well as, in an initial way, revealed and mediated.

Promise

43.   The form and effect of the Eucharist are a promise of the eternal glory to which we are destined, and a sign pointing to the new heaven and new earth towards which we are moving: "that is why the Eucharist directs our thoughts to the Lord's coming and brings it near to us. It is a joyful anticipation of the heavenly banquet, when redemption shall be fully accomplished and all creation shall be delivered from bondage".[32] "Blessed are those who are invited to the marriage supper of the Lamb" (Rev. 19:9).

Initial Revelation

44.   The Lord's Supper enables us to understand the future glory as the boundless and eternal wedding feast to which we are invited by the Lord. As a fraternal meal in which Christ frees and unites, it turns our gaze to the promised eternal kingdom of unlimited freedom and righteousness.

Those who celebrate together are called to join personal commitment and communal service, and thereby to point to that fulfilment of personal and social life which belongs to the glory of God, the glory in which by his grace we may share.

Mediation

45. The promised future begins in a mysterious way here and now in the Lord's Supper. He who receives the bread of life has eternal life (John 6:54). He is without waiting taken straight away into the great future opened to us by the Lord. Everlasting life does not begin in the future, but is already present in anyone who is united with the Lord. The future world breaks into our present one even now.

"Thus, by giving the Eucharist to his Church, which, in its weakness, will live to the last in the midst of suffering and strife, our Lord enables it to take new heart and to persevere;"[33] he gives it the power to work untiringly for the renewal of the life and structures of the world. The life of the world to come, promised, disclosed and mediated to believers, shall and must become effective already in this world.

Part II.

COMMON TASKS

46. The common witness to the Lord's Supper confronts us with tasks which we ought to face together as far as possible.

(I) We must give an account of how far we have been able to clarify and overcome the problems which once broke up the communion of faith and Eucharist, and to what degree they still prevent a complete fellowship.

(II) The concrete liturgical form of the eucharistic celebration in our congregations must be in accordance with what we confess in faith.

(III) The witness of faith must not be confined either to the theoretical or individual realm; as many members as possible of the people of God should accept and vitally transmit it (reception).

I. Overcoming Controverted Positions

47. Common statements and convictions fill us with hope: much of what earlier divided us has on both sides been removed and the remaining differences exist within a common framework. Controverted positions which hinder complete fellowship of faith and Eucharist must be recognized, described and faced with the purpose of recognizing and overcoming what is divisive.

Eucharistic Presence

48. Roman Catholic and Lutheran Christians together confess the real

and true presence of the Lord in the Eucharist. There are differences, however, in theological statements on the mode and therefore duration of the real presence.

49.   In order to confess the *reality* of the eucharistic presence without reserve the Roman Catholic Church teaches that "Christ whole and entire"[34] becomes present through the transformation of the whole substance of the bread and the wine into the substance of the body and blood of Christ while the empirically accessible appearances of bread and wine (*accidentia*) continue to exist unchanged. This "wonderful and singular change is most aptly called transubstantiation by the Catholic Church"[35]. This terminology has widely been considered by Lutherans as an attempt rationalistically to explain the mystery of Christ's presence in the sacrament: further, many suppose also that in this approach the present Lord is not seen as a person and that naturalistic misunderstandings are suggested.

50.   The Lutherans have given expression to the reality of the eucharistic presence by speaking of a presence of Christ's body and blood in, with and under bread and wine — but not of transubstantiation. Here one sees the real analogy to the Lord's incarnation: as God and man are united in Jesus Christ, so Christ's body and blood, on the one hand, and the bread and wine, on the other, become a sacramental unity. Catholics, on this point, find that this does not do sufficient justice to this very unity and to the force of Christ's word "This *is* my body".

51.   The ecumenical discussion has shown that these two positions must no longer be regarded as opposed in a way that leads to separation. The Lutheran tradition affirms the Catholic tradition that the consecrated elements do not simply remain bread and wine but rather by the power of the creative word are given as the body and blood of Christ. In this sense Lutherans also could occasionally speak, as does the Greek tradition, of a "change".[36] The concept of transubstantiation for its part is intended as a confession and preservation of the mystery character of the eucharistic presence; it is not intended as an explanation of *how* this change occurs.[37] (See appendix "The Presence of Christ in the Eucharist".)

52.   Differences related to the *duration* of the eucharistic presence appear also in liturgical practice.

Catholic and Lutheran Christians together confess that the eucharistic presence of the Lord Jesus Christ is directed toward believing reception, that it nevertheless is not confined only to the moment of reception, and that it does not depend on the faith of the receiver however closely related to this it might be.

53.   According to Catholic doctrine the Lord grants his eucharistic presence even beyond the sacramental celebration for as long as the species of bread and wine remain. The faithful are accordingly invited to "give to this holy sacrament in veneration the worship of *latria*, which is due to the true God"[38].

54.   Lutherans have not infrequently taken exception to certain of the forms of eucharistic piety connected with this conviction. They are regarded as inadmissibly separated from the eucharistic meal. On the other hand, Catholic sensibilities are offended by the casual way in which the elements remaining after communion are treated sometimes on the Lutheran side, and this indicates a discrepancy which is not yet overcome (cf. appendix "The Presence of Christ in the Eucharist", 2).

55.   In order to remedy this situation, it would be good "for Catholics to remember, particularly in catechism and preaching, that the original intention in preserving the eucharistic gifts was to distribute them to the sick and those not present", and for Lutherans "the best means should be adopted of showing respect due to the elements that have served for the celebration of the Eucharist, which is to consume them subsequently, without precluding their use for communion of the sick"[39].

Regarding eucharistic adoration, Catholics should be watchful that their practice does not contradict the common conviction of the fact that in the Orthodox churches, for example, other forms of eucharistic piety exist without their eucharistic faith being questioned (by Rome). Lutherans for their part should consider "that adoration of the reserved sacrament" not only "has been very much a part of Catholic life and a meaningful form of devotion to Catholics for many centuries"[40], but that also for them "as long as Christ remains sacramentally present, worship, reverence and adoration are appropriate"[41].

Eucharistic Sacrifice

56.   Catholic and Lutheran Christians together recognize that in the Lord's Supper Jesus Christ "is present as the Crucified who died for our sins and who rose again for our justification, as the once-for-all sacrifice for the sins of the world"[42]. This sacrifice can be neither continued, nor repeated, nor replaced, nor complemented; but rather it can and should become effective ever anew in the midst of the congregation. There are different interpretations among us regarding the nature and extent of this effectiveness.

57.   According to *Catholic teaching*, in each Eucharist "a true and proper sacrifice is offered" through Christ.[43] "This sacrifice is truly propitiatory and has this effect that we 'obtain mercy and find grace to help in time of need' (Hebrews 4:16) . . . For the victim is one and the same, the same now offering by the ministry of the priests who then offered Himself on the cross, the manner of offering alone being different . . . Wherefore, according to the tradition of the Apostles, it is rightly offered not only for the sins, punishments, satisfactions and other necessities of the faithful who are living, but also for those departed in Christ but not yet fully purified."[44]

58.   As members of his body the believers are included in the offering of Christ. This happens in different ways: none of them is added externally to

the offering of Christ, but each derives from him and points to him:

The liturgical preparation of the Lord's Supper with the offering of bread and wine is part of the eucharistic sacrifice. Above all, inner participation is necessary: acknowledgement and confession of one's own powerlessness and total dependence on God's help, obedience to his commission, faith in his word and his promise.

It is in the eucharistic presence of the offered and offering Lord that those who are redeemed by him can, in the best sense, make an offering. They bring to the heavenly Father a gift which allows no sort of self-complacency and self-righteousness to arise. It is wholly and completely a free, unmerited gift of the love of God which is in no way merited by man; at the same time it is intimately joined with human beings, more than can be the case with anything else which could otherwise be offered: Christ has become completely ours, he is our head. Of ourselves we have nothing and are unable to do anything. Therefore we do not point to ourselves but to him. Of ourselves we cannot offer to God praise, glory and honour, but we offer Christ: he is praise, glory and honour. It is this act of testifying to one's own powerlessness, of complete reliance on Christ and of offering and presenting him to the Father which is intended when the Catholic Church dares to say that not only Christ offers himself for humanity, but that the church also "offers" him. "The members of the body of Christ are united through Christ with God and with one another in such a way that they become participants in his worship, his self-offering, his sacrifice to the Father. Through this union between Christ and Christians, the eucharistic assembly 'offers Christ' by consenting in the power of the Holy Spirit to be offered by him to the Father. Apart from Christ, we have no gifts, no worship, no sacrifice of our own to offer to God. All we can plead is Christ, the sacrificial lamb and victim whom the Father himself has given us."[45]

59.   *The Lutherans* have feared that the understanding of the Eucharist as propitiatory sacrifice is contrary to the uniqueness and complete sufficiency of the sacrifice of the cross and calls in question Christ's exclusive mediation of salvation (cf. the appendix "The Mass as Sacrifice for Atonement"). According to the interpretation of the Lutheran Reformation, the celebration of the Eucharist is wholly directed to imparting to the gathered community the gift of the sacrifice of the cross made present as the effective means of salvation, and this in such a way that the community may receive it in faith. The diminution in practice of congregational communion was regarded as scandalous, and the primary blame for this was placed on the idea of the Mass as a propitiatory sacrifice. It was thought that this idea allowed for a view which made unnecessary the reception in faith of eucharistic grace and attributed an autonomous sacrificial power to the priest (cf. the Reformation polemic against the Mass as *opus operatum*). Therefore the Lutheran tradition avoids even today any mention of "sacrifice of the Mass".

60. On the other hand the Lutheran Reformation affirmed the understanding of the Lord's Supper as a sacrifice of thanksgiving in return for the sacrifice of the cross present in the sacrament. This sacrifice is an expression of faith and happens in such a way "that we offer with Christ, that is, that we cast ourselves upon Christ with unwavering faith in his testament and we do not appear otherwise before God with our prayer, praise and sacrifice than through Him and His means (of salvation) and that we do not doubt that He is our own Pastor and Priest before God's face in heaven"[46]. The "eucharistic sacrifice"[47] thus understood is performed by those reconciled in faith, and is expressed in thanks and praise, in invoking and confessing God, in suffering and in all the good works of believers. These are the offerings which are particularly emphasized in the Reformation teaching in connection with 1 Peter 2:5 and Romans 12:1.[48]

61. In ecumenical discussion we have learned better to understand each other's interpretations. Research into the historical background of the Reformation polemic as well as the consideration of new developments in both churches has proved especially helpful. Increasingly we recognize the interpretations of the other as a challenge to our own position and as a help in improving, deepening and enlivening it.

We can thankfully record a growing convergence on many questions which have until now been difficulties in our discussions:

a) according to Catholic doctrine the sacrifice of the Mass is the making present of the sacrifice of the cross. It is not a repetition of this sacrifice and adds nothing to its saving significance. When thus understood, the sacrifice of the Mass is an affirmation and not a questioning of the uniqueness and full value of Christ's sacrifice on the cross;

b) according to Catholic doctrine the *ex opere operato* should witness in the context of the sacramentology to the priority of God's action. To stress this priority is likewise the concern of the Lutherans.

c) Such an understanding of *opus operatum* does not exclude the believing participation of the whole worshipping community: God's action calls for this and makes it possible;

d) the conviction that the fruits of the Eucharist extend beyond the circle of those present at a celebration does not diminish the importance of active believing participation. Christ's gift of his flesh and blood to those who receive the Eucharist in faith cannot be transferred to others. Yet we may hope, however, that he allows others to share in his help. Whether and how this happens is entirely dependent on the sovereign love of the Lord. Intercessions and intentions at the Mass for specific persons — living as well as dead — do not limit his freedom.

These insights give us the confidence to be able to clarify the questions which are still outstanding.

Eucharistic Communion

62.   Lutheran and Catholic Christians confess together that in the Eucharist the body and blood of the Lord are really received, either for salvation or for condemnation (cf. 1 Corinthians 11:27-29). They confess that the believing reception of the eucharistic bread and wine gives us personal union with Jesus Christ, our Lord and Saviour. They also agree that the efficacy of believers' reception of the Lord cannot be measured by human standards but belongs in the sphere of the free and humanly uncontrollable action of God.

63.   Lutherans and Catholics confess together the conviction that by its very essence the Eucharist is a communal meal. For Lutherans the participation of the congregation is an indispensable part of the celebration of the Eucharist according to its institution by the Lord. They regard Masses in which the people do not participate as a custom that corresponds neither to the practice of the ancient church nor to the institution of the Lord. (Such Masses have been given the misleading and theologically unsatisfactory label of "private Masses".) Since the Second Vatican Council a significant change has taken place in the liturgical practice of the Roman Catholic Church which underlines the superiority of the "communal celebration involving the presence and active participation of the faithful . . . even though every Mass has of itself a public and social nature"[49]. This priority of communal celebration signifies an important *rapprochement* in our eucharistic practice (cf. the appendix "The Eucharist as a Communal Meal").

64.   Catholics and Lutherans are at one in the conviction that bread and wine belong to the complete form of the Eucharist. In the Catholic celebration of the Eucharist the faithful are for the most part given only the species of the bread. This occurs chiefly for practical reasons and is based on the conviction that Christ is fully present under both species so that reception in one kind constitutes no diminution in effect. In contrast the Reformers see the completeness and wholeness of the sacramental sign in accordance to Christ's words of institution as preserved only where all drink from the cup. Nevertheless the Lutheran Church does not deny the doctrine that Christ is completely present in both species, and Lutheran practice recognizes urgent cases of pastoral necessity in which the Eucharist can also be received in one species (cf. the appendix "The Eucharist as a Communal Meal").

The possibilities of receiving the Eucharist in both kinds have been considerably extended by the Second Vatican Council in regard to both the occasions and the communicants. If differences in doctrine and practice continue also to persist in this area, they no longer have a church-dividing character.

Eucharistic Ministry

65.   Catholic and Lutheran Christians are of the conviction that the

celebration of the Eucharist involves the leadership of a minister appointed by the church.

66.   According to Catholic doctrine every licit eucharistic celebration is "regulated by the bishop, to whom is committed the office of offering the worship of Catholic religion to the divine Majesty and of administering it in accordance with the Lord's commandments and with the Church's laws"[50]. "Only those Eucharists are lawful which are performed by the bishop or a person charged by him."[51] The ordination of a bishop or priest is accordingly the essential prerequisite to his presiding at the Lord's Supper: even in exceptional cases there can be no eucharistic celebration without an ordained priest. In so far as the sacrament of ordination is lacking, the Roman Catholic Church sees even separated Christians as not having "preserved the genuine and total reality (*substantia*) of the Eucharistic mystery"[52].

67.   According to Lutheran doctrine as well, the eucharistic service is led by ordained ministers.[53] It is "the task of the ministerial office to proclaim the gospel and administer the sacraments in accordance with the gospel, so that in this way faith is awakened and strengthened"[54]. For Lutherans the ecclesial office is a divine institution, although ordination is not usually characterized as a sacrament.[55]

68.   The dialogue between our two traditions has already been able to ascertain significant convergences on the question of the ministry. These convergences have to do with the understanding of the basis and function of the ministry as well as the manner of transmission through the laying on of hands and the invocation of the Holy Spirit;[56] and they have led to the suggestion that the possibility of mutual recognition of ecclesial ministries be submitted for serious examination.[57] In carrying out this recommendation, it must be asked, among other things, how the Lutheran Churches regard a Eucharist celebrated without an ordained minister. It must also be asked, in view of the Lutheran interpretation and practice of ordination, how the Roman Catholic Church evaluates the Eucharist celebrated in the Lutheran Church. What needs to be clarified, then, is the importance and ecclesiological ordering of the ministry, and what consequences it has for the structure of the Church.

Eucharistic Fellowship

69.   Catholic and Lutheran Christians confess together that Jesus Christ joins together all those who are joined to him.

70.   According to Catholic conviction this holds also for the eucharistic communion with Christ. In this are included those who have passed away in the peace of the Lord. Intercessions for the dead are therefore a part of the Catholic eucharistic celebration. The Roman Catholic Church also remembers those departed from this life who have gone into heavenly joy. It thanks God for the grace granted them and commends itself to their intercession and protection.

71. The Lutheran celebration of the Eucharist also gives expression in thanksgiving and in intercession to the communion of the heavenly and earthly congregation. The Reformation rejected the invocation of the saints, but did not deny the intercession of the saints in heaven.[58] A doctrinal reticence regarding the fate of the dead also restrains Lutherans from interceding for them.

72. The eucharistic fellowship calls for and fosters actual community of faith within the Church according to Catholic doctrine. Its nature comprises:

— "the ministerial power which Christ gave to his apostles and to their successors, the bishops, along with the priests, to make effective sacramentally his own priestly act — that act by which once and forever he offered himself to the Father in the Holy Spirit, and gave himself to his faithful that they might be one in him;

— the unity of the ministry, which is to be exercised in the name of Christ, Head of the Church, and hence in the hierarchial communion of ministers;

— the faith of the Church, which is expressed in the eucharistic action itself — the faith by which she responds to Christ's gift in its true meaning".[59]

Therefore the Second Vatican Council stated: "As for common worship (*communicatio in sacris*), however, it may not be regarded as a means to be used indiscriminately for the restoration of unity among Christians"[60]. Therefore, though a joint celebration by Catholics and Lutherans is forbidden, admission to the Catholic celebration of the Eucharist is possible, "given sufficient reasons" (*propter rationes sufficientes*)[61].

73. The Lutheran Church is also aware of the link between eucharistic communion and communion between churches. Nevertheless, it recognizes, even in the present state of church division, a number of possibilities of eucharistic fellowship. The criteria it employs enables it to acknowledge the validity of the eucharistic celebration of others more freely than does the Roman Catholic Church. "Because of the already noted similarities in the understanding of the gospel, which has decisive effects on proclamation, administration of the sacraments and liturgical practice, the Lutherans feel that even now exchange of pulpits and common eucharistic celebrations [with the Catholic Church] can on occasion be recommended . . . The Lutherans emphasized that the communion practices of the separated churches must receive their orientation from that which is demanded of the church by the ministry of reconciliation among men . . . A celebration of the Lord's Supper in which baptized believers may not participate, suffers from an inner contradiction and from the start, therefore, does not fulfil the purpose for which the Lord established it."[62]

II. LITURGICAL FORM

74.   The truth affirmed in faith about the Eucharist must shape the content and form of the liturgy. This involves a common duty which in large measure can and must be cooperatively discharged. At the same time, tasks and approaches vary because of the different types of churches, historical periods and traditions.

75.   "The best way toward unity in eucharistic celebration and communion is the renewal of the eucharist itself in the different churches in regard to teaching and liturgy."[63] In the Eucharist, too, it is progress towards the centre which brings us nearer to each other. This means that "the faithful come to it with proper dispositions, that their thoughts match their words, and that they cooperate with divine grace lest they receive it in vain"[64].

The call for renewal must always point in two directions: first to the Lord, his word and his will, and then to the people around us with all their difficulties and potentialities: the "small flock" of fellow Christians, as well as the innumerable multitude of fellow human beings for whose salvation the Eucharist is intended.

The common witness of eucharistic faith and the common attempt to do justice to this life have nothing to do with uniformity. Just as in theology and piety there is also a variety of possibilities in liturgical forms. These can and indeed should illuminate and complement each other. "Thus in their diversity all bear witness to the admirable unity of the Body of Christ. This very diversity of graces, ministries, and works gathers the children of God into one, because 'all these things are the work of one and the same spirit' (1 Cor. 12:11)."[65]

76.   Without impairing this diversity, greater *agreement in certain basic patterns* needs to be sought.

According to common conviction, the eucharistic celebration forms a whole which includes a number of constitutive elements. Among these are: proclamation of the word of God, thanksgiving for the acts of God in creation and redemption together with the remembering of the death and resurrection of Christ, the words of institution in accordance with the witness of the New Testament, the invocation of the Holy Spirit on bread and wine and on the congregation, intercession for the church and the world, the Lord's prayer and eating and drinking in communion with Christ and every member of the church.[66]

Liturgical practice should correspond to this jointly affirmed fundamental pattern. In addition to the common tasks which this agreement implies, there are others which involve special challenges to our churches. Lutherans are convinced that Catholics should seek:

1.   the avoidance of celebrations of the Mass without participation of the people;

2.   better use of the possibilities for proclamation within each celebration of the Eucharist;

3. the administration of Holy Communion under both species.

Catholics are convinced that Lutherans should seek:

1. more frequent celebrations of Holy Communion ("As the Eucharist is the new liturgical service Christ has given to the Church, it seems normal that it should be celebrated not less frequently than every Sunday, or once a week"[67]);
2. a greater participation by the congregation as a whole (particularly by children);
3. a closer link between liturgy of the word and liturgy of the sacrament.

It should be acknowledged that the differences in practice reflected in these diverse requests are connected with continuing differences in the understanding of faith. We must join together in clarifying and overcoming them.

III. RECEPTION

77. A theological teaching remains a theory of individuals as long as it is not affirmed and adopted by the whole people of God. Even conciliar declarations only come fully into effect when they take shape in the life and thought of the faithful. It is therefore essential that our common witness to the Lord's Supper evoke response and co-responsibility from our fellow Christians. We thus turn to them with the request that they examine and consider our reflections in order to improve them where needed and make them their own in so far as possible.

PARTICIPANTS

MEMBERS OF THE COMMISSION:

Roman Catholics:

Bishop H. L. Martensen, Denmark (co-chairman)
Professor J. Hoffmann, France
Reverend J. F. Hotchkin, U.S.A.
Professor Dr. St. Napiorkowski, Poland
Professor Dr. Vinzenz Pfnür, FRG
Bishop Professor Dr. P. W. Scheele, FRG

Lutherans:

Professor G. Lindbeck, U.S.A. (co-chairman)
Bishop D. H. Dietzfelbinder, FRG
Reverend Dr. K. Hafenscher, Hungary
Dr. P. Nasution, Indonesia
Professor Dr. L. Thunberg, Sweden
Professor Dr. Bertoldo Weber, Brazil

CONSULTANT:
Lutheran:
Professor Dr. Harding Meyer, France

SECRETARIES:
Roman-Catholic:
Professor Dr. H. Schütte, FRG

Lutheran:
Professor V. Vajta, France

WORLD COUNCIL OF CHURCHES OBSERVER:
Professor Dr. A. Bronkhorst, Netherlands

Notes

1 See "Joint Report of the Roman Catholic/Lutheran Working Group" in *Lutheran World,* Vol. 13, No. 4, 1966, p. 436 ff.
2 *ibid.,* p. 437.
3 ibid., p. 437.
4 Cf. 1 Cor. 15:3; also 1 Cor. 11:2 & 23; Luke 1:2.
5 Cf. Vatican II, Dogmatic Constitution on Divine Revelation, 10 and 24.
6 Cf. Vatican II, Dogmatic Constitution on the Church, 12.
7 John 16:13, *inter alia.*
8 See Vatican II, Decree on Ecumenism, II.
9 Rom. 1:16; 3:26; 5:17.
10 Rom. 1:16f; 3:21f; 5:17; 6:7; 1 Cor. 6:11.
11 Augsburg Confession, VII.
12 Cf. Vatican II, Declaration on Religious Freedom, 2:10-12.
13 Cf. Vatican II, Pastoral Constitution on the Church in the Modern World, 43.
14 Cf. Vatican II, Pastoral Constitution on the Church in the Modern World, 37 & 38.
15 Cf. Vatican II, Pastoral Constitution on the Church in the Modern World, 44.
16 The most complete treatment of this theme so far within the context of Catholic-Lutheran conversations has taken place in North America. See *Eucharist and Ministry, Lutherans and Catholics in Dialogue* IV (New York: USA National Committee of the LWF; Washington: US Catholic Conference, 1971).
17 2 Cor. 5:18.
18 Rom 10:14:14-17.
19 Cf. Vatican II, Dogmatic Constitution on the Church, 10-12; Decree on the Apostolate of the Laity, 2-3; also *Luther's Works* (Philadelphia Edition), "An Open Letter to the Christian Nobility", p. 52 (WA 6, 407); cf. further WA 38, 247.
20 1 Cor. 12:7-11; 28-30; Rom. 12:6-8; cf. Eph. 4:7-12.
21 1 Cor. 9:1; Acts 1:22.
22 1 Cor. 15:7.
23 1 Cor. 3:10 ff.
24 Eph. 2:20; cf. Rev. 21:14.
25 Cf. 1 Cor. 12:4-6.

26   Cf. 2 Cor. 12:7-11; Rom. 12:3.
27   Cf. 1 Cor. 12:3.
28   Cf. Rom. 12:3-8; Eph. 4:11-16.
29   Cf. Vatican II. Dogmatic Constitution on the Church. 12.
30   Cf. 1 Thess. 5:12; Phil. I:1.
31   Cf. 1 Cor. 12:28.
32   Cf. C. Baisi, *Il Ministro straordinario degli ordini sacramentali* Rome: 1935);
     Y. Congar, *Heilige Kirche* (Stuttgart: Schwabenverlag, 1966), pp. 285-316;
     P. Fransen, in *Sacramentum Mundi,* IV, 1969, col. 1270f; W. Kasper, "Zur Frage
     der Anerkennung der Ämter in den lutherischen Kirchen", in *Theol. Quar-
     talschrift* (Tübingen), Vo.. 151, 1971, pp. 97-109.
33   Cf. Augsburg Confession, XIII, and Apology of the Augsburg Confession,
     XIII.
34   See Vatican II, Decree on the Ministry and Life of Priests, 4.
35   Cf. Augsburg Confession V; VII.
36   Cf. Decree on Ecumenism, 3f; 19.
37   Cf. Augsburg Confession, VII.
38   Cf. nos. 68-74 of this report.
39   See the signatures to the Smalcald Articles, Melanchthon's intervention.
40   Cf. Vatican II, Decree on Ecumenism, 3.
41   See 1 Cor. 10:17.
42   Cf. Vatican II, Decree on Ecumenism 3.
43   See Vatican II, Dogmatic Constitution on the Church, 8.
44   Cf. Matt. 18:20.
45   Cf. Matt. 18:19.

WAYS TO COMMUNITY, 1980

INTRODUCTION

1. The disunity of Christians causes offence and distress to both church and world. It quite "openly contradicts the will of Christ, provides a stumbling block to the world, and inflicts damage on the most holy cause of proclaiming the good news to every creature"[1]. Moreover, it impairs the ever-urgent call for Christian service to the world (cf. Is 61:1f. and Lk 4:18f.).

2. We are therefore obligated to do all we can to help overcome the division. We must strive, among other things, for a maximum "common vision of the unity of the Church at every level in obedience to the faith"[2]. We need a "common vision" because we shall grow further apart if we do not aim towards a common goal. If we have conflicting views of this goal, we shall, if we are consistent, move in opposite directions. We need unity "at every level" because it affects all areas of our life. Whatever the circumstances in which Christians find themselves, they must be concerned about their unity in Christ and each is called upon to make a contribution. This demands "obedience to the faith". Only what the Lord wills, what he gives and commissions is decisive. He discloses what this is only to believers, and calls them in turn to witness in word and deed, personally and communally to what they have received in faith.

3. This is the spirit in which we want to say together in "obedience to the faith" how we as Roman Catholic and Lutheran Christians see (I) the *goal of unity* and (II) the *steps toward unity* which seem necessary to us.

Part I

UNITY AS GOAL

INTRODUCTION

4. The goal of unity is *given* to us *beforehand*. It is not constructed or manipulated, but is received. It is not a totally new reality reserved for a distant future, but is in its fundamental elements already present and active among us.

215

5. The goal of unity is discernible in the word and work of the Lord, in the testimony of Holy Scripture, and in the teaching and life of the church.

6. The unity we seek has *already begun to be realized.* Despite our sins, the Lord has not ceased his unifying activity. Just as he went to his death "to gather into one the children of God who are scattered abroad" (Jn 11:52), so he continues to live and work "that they may all be one" (Jn 17:21). Against all powers threatening Christian unity from within and without, he is bringing his work to its goal through the might of his resurrection and ascension in the Holy Spirit. He is completing what he has begun.

7. By the *gifts* he has entrusted to his church, he leads the scattered flock towards full unity. Without active loyalty to these gifts, the goal of unity remains unrecognized and unattained.

8. Regarding the concretization of the unity already given and yet also awaited and worked for in the future, it must be said:
Christian unity is (a) a blessing of the Triune God, a work which he accomplishes, (b) by means he chooses, (c) in ways he determines, (d) shaped by basic structures he has established, and (e) directed towards a unique, truly all-encompassing community.

a. Community Through Grace

9. Like every good gift, unity also comes from the Father through the Son in the Holy Spirit.
The will and work of the Father is "in Christ as a plan for the fullness of time, to unite all things in him" (Eph 1:10). In the Father is the origin of all the Son does for unity. "And he has put all things under his feet and has made him the head over all things for the church, which is his body, the fullness of him who fills all in all" (Eph 1:22-23).

10. The basic work of unification occurs in the *incarnation* of the Son of God, in whom divinity and humanity are inseparably united in one person. Everything *Jesus Christ* says, does and suffers lives from this unity and has its aim "that they may all be one" (Jn 17:21). He suffered death on the cross for the sake of unity. Unity is integral to his gift of redemption and reconciliation, and to participation in his glory: "The glory which thou hast given me I have given to them, that they may be one even as we are one" (Jn 17:22).

11. Through his blood the wall of partition is torn down which separates human beings from each other and from God (Eph 2:11-22). His crucifixion is judgment on all sins, including sins against unity, and yet is the acquittal of all sinners. The peace which unifies is established "by the blood

of his cross" (Col 1:20). Thus unity always stands *under the sign of the cross.* In the midst of contradiction and opposition, misunderstanding and abuse, it lives from Jesus Christ's Lord. "It is by entering into His passion for the redemption of a sinful and divided world that the Church finds its unity in its crucified and risen Lord."[3]

12. Jesus Christ accomplishes his work on the cross and all other works of unification *in the Holy Spirit.* Since he wants his own to be one as the Father and he himself are one, he promises them that same Spirit which is the bond of unity between Father and Son. Pentecost is the great sign to the church that the Lord fulfils this promise.

13. Incorporation into living unity takes place only through the Holy Spirit. "For by one Spirit we were all baptized into one body—Jews or Greeks, slaves or free—and all were made to drink of one Spirit" (1 Cor 12:13; cf. 1 Cor 12:1-11). "For any achievement of a fuller unity than that now manifest, we are wholly dependent upon the Spirit's presence and governance."[4] The Spirit revives what is dead and unites what is separated into an all-encompassing community. Christian unity exists in the power of the Holy Spirit. It is the community of the Holy Spirit.

b. MEDIATION OF COMMUNITY

14. Since we cannot find, much less construct, life and unity in Christ on our own, we must rely on their mediation through the Holy Spirit. As the Bible testifies, this occurs through (1) the Lord's word and (2) his sacraments, (3) with the help of the diversified ministries of the whole people of God. "The Church as the body of Christ lives by its Lord's gifts in Word and Sacrament; it knows it is called, gathered and sanctified to faith by the Holy Spirit and it exists as God's people in the world as a human fellowship."[5]

1. Word

15. In his high-priestly prayer for unity, Jesus says, "I have given them thy word . . . Sanctify them in the truth; thy word is truth" (Jn 17:14,17). "He calls his own sheep by name and leads them out" (Jn 10:3), "so there shall be one flock, one shepherd" (Jn 10:16). Whenever and wherever we hear and trust his voice, and allow ourselves to be called again and again to the shepherd and to the flock despite disintegrating forces, there unity becomes reality. Thus we must listen together to the word of God and faithfully cling to the one gospel (cf. Gal 1:6-10) as indispensable steps along the road to full unity.
"Christ Himself builds the Church and in doing so creates its unity"[6] in his word. This is bound up with his sacramental action.

2. Sacrament

16. The same letter to the Galatians which emphasizes that from one gospel comes one faith also stresses one baptism as source of unity. It is written, "for in Christ Jesus you are all sons of God, through faith. For as many of you as were baptized into Christ have put on Christ. There is neither Jew nor Greek, there is neither slave nor free, there is neither male nor female; for you are all one in Christ Jesus" (Gal 3:26-28). Christ forms his church "by the washing of water with the word" (Eph 5:26).

17. Furthermore, he nourishes it with his flesh and blood. Not only is the individual recipient thereby benefited, but the whole church is built up. The believers become one body by receiving the one *body of the Lord.* "Because there is one bread, we who are many are one body, for we all partake of the one bread" (1 Cor 10:17).[7] Where "baptism and the Lord's Supper are dispensed in accordance to the New Testament charge, there Christ is truly present, grants reconciliation and gathers his community"[8].

18. *According to Catholic conviction,* there are, together with the chief basic sacraments of baptism and eucharist,[9] five further sacraments: confirmation, penance, extreme unction, ordination and marriage. In each of these, Catholic faith sees the Lord at work bestowing grace and creating unity. In each, not only the individual recipient, but the whole church is involved[10] which sees itself as "sacrament of unity"[11], as sign and instrument "of intimate union with God, and of the unity of all mankind"[12].

19. *The Lutheran conviction* also is that the Lord does not bestow his grace exclusively through the preached word and the administration of baptism and the Lord's Supper. Confession and pastoral care, as well as ordination, confirmation and marriage between believers are understood as actions in which human beings are promised and granted grace, even though it is generally held that these acts should not be seen as sacraments in the full sense.[13]

3. Ministry

20. The church, which lives by word and sacrament, is at the same time called to their service. The Lord entrusts each *member* with specific gifts and tasks. "From whom [Christ] the whole body, joined and knit together by every joint with which it is supplied, when each part is working properly, makes bodily growth and upbuilds itself in love" (Eph 4:16; cf. Col 2:19).

21. Within this context, the service of the *special ministry* is indispensable. "With the Word to be proclaimed and the sacraments to be administered,

the church's ministry is also divinely instituted and it is conferred through ordination. It is Christ himself who acts through this office and its functions."[14] "The essential and specific function of the special ministry is: to assemble and build up the Christian community, by proclaiming and teaching the Word of God, and presiding over the liturgical and sacramental life of the eucharistic community."[15]

22. Yet though Lutherans and Catholics both affirm the special ministry, they differ in their views of its *concrete shape(s)*. According to *Catholic conviction,* Jesus Christ established the church "by sending forth the apostles as He Himself had been sent by the Father (cf. Jn 20:21). He willed that their successors, namely the bishops, should be shepherds in His Church even to the consummation of the world. In order that the episcopate itself might be one and undivided, He placed blessed Peter over the other apostles, and instituted in him a permanent and visible source and foundation of unity of faith and fellowship"[16].

23. Also according to *Lutheran understanding,* the individual congregation is essentially related to the church as a whole. There is a need beyond the local congregation for leadership services (*episcopē*) with pastoral responsibility for proclamation, sacraments and church unity. Thus in addition to the office of parish pastor, there is a place for supracongregational ministries in the church. Although Lutherans do not regard the historic episcopacy as based on an explicit irrevocable command from the Lord valid for all times and situations, yet this polity arose through the work of the Holy Spirit, and there are historical and ecumenical reasons for seriously considering its restoration in Lutheran churches. Further, a ministry serving the unity of the church as a whole is, for Lutherans, in accord with the will of the Lord, but without its concrete form having been fixed once for all.

c. REALIZATION OF COMMUNITY

24. If community in Christ is to be realized, we must accept the unifying gifts of the Lord despite all temptations to do otherwise. Only where there is (1) common faith, (2) hope and (3) love does unity live, grow and bear fruit.

1. Unity of Faith

25. *Only in faith* is a human being able to recognize the gift of God and who it is who speaks to him (cf. Jn 4:10). When Christians believe, the promise is fulfilled: "They will heed my voice" and "there shall be one flock, one shepherd" (Jn 10:16). On the one hand, individuals are "added" (Acts 2:41) to the one church, and, on the other hand, unity itself is

thus constantly realized anew and grows to its fullness until we all come "to the unity of the faith" (Eph 4:13).[17]

26. The yes of faith must affect *all areas of life*. That is why witnessing, confessing and teaching are an essential part of it.[18] Everything which fosters common witness, common confession and common teaching not only leads towards unity, but is already lived unity—unity in faith, unity in truth. There are, it should be remembered, different ways of expressing or articulating the community given or achieved in witness, confession and teaching. "A fundamental unity in faith exists wherever church and church communities confess Jesus Christ as true God and true man and as only mediator of salvation according to the scriptures to the glory of God, Father, Son, and Holy Spirit."[19]

2. Unity of Hope

27. "Unity requires companionship in struggle and hope."[20] The *call "to the one hope"* belongs to "one body and one Spirit" (Eph 4:4). "The unity of the Church will be achieved as Christians are united in the anticipation and expectation of God's future."[21]

28. Whoever thinks that the present state of ecumenical relations is either so bad that no decisive improvement is possible, or so good that no decisive improvement is necessary, is acting *in opposition to hope*. In both cases, unity is impaired along with hope.

29. The service to unity demanded of all Christians must be the expression of an unswerving, unwearied and *unabridged Christian hope*. "Ecumenical endeavours therefore have their deepest basis in the knowledge of the kingdom of God or the new world, which has already come in Jesus Christ but whose fulfilment remains an object of Christian hope."[22]

3. Unity of Love

30. The community grows in Christ to the degree in which faith and hope become *effective in love*. In love, the human being becomes fully receptive to the gifts of the giving Lord; in love, the person learns to follow and "gather" with God (cf. Mt 12:30; Lk 11:23). "Love . . . binds everything together in perfect harmony" (Col 3:14). It unites the individual members "into one fully committed fellowship"[23], and simultaneously leads to communion with the Triune God. Thus the high-priestly prayer (Jn 17:26) concludes with the petition "that the love with which thou hast loved me may be in them, and I in them". Through love, we can "grow up in every way into him who is the head, into Christ, from whom the whole body, . . . makes bodily growth and upbuilds itself in love" (Eph 4:15f.).

31. The *eucharist* is an essential part of the acceptance of God's unifying gifts. In its communal celebration, we confess our common faith, witness to our common hope, give a sign of our common love in terms of "one fully committed fellowship".

d. THE FORM OF COMMUNITY

32. There is a basic pattern of unity through which all its aspects are interrelated. Unity in Christ is unity in (1) visibility, (2) diversity, and (3) dynamism.

1. Visibility

33. Both "one body and one Spirit" (Eph 4:4) belong to the common life in Christ. "We want to stress the fact that the unity we seek should be an outward, visible unity which is becoming historically manifest in the life of the churches."[24] We believe "that we live under the obligation to make this unity historically manifest, visible and recognizable to the world, that it may believe"[25].
This by no means, however, signifies a rigid uniformity: living unity in Christ is essentially manifold and dynamic.

2. Diversity

34. Unity in Christ does not exist despite and in opposition to diversity, but is given *with and in diversity*. The work of the one unifying Spirit of God does not begin with the uniting of the already separated, but rather creates and maintains diverse realities precisely in order to lead them into the unity of love.

35. The one body is composed of *many members* (1 Cor 12:4-30; Rom 12:4-8; Eph 4:7-16. "A lively variety marks corporate life in the one Body of one Spirit."[26]

36. The different members have become part of a larger whole in a *reconciled diversity* in which differences have not been dimmed, but highlighted and thus made beneficial. "Thus in their diversity all bear witness to the admirable unity of the Body of Christ. This very diversity of graces, ministries, and works gathers the children of God into one, because 'all these things are the work of one and the same Spirit' (1 Cor 12:11)"[27].

37. The Pentecostal Spirit addresses everyone "in his own native language" (Acts 2:8). It testifies to *the one gospel in many tongues*. It allows

many forms of proclamation, reception and response. It renews and unites the most diverse forms of teaching and piety, life-style and law, tradition and rite, and thus guides more deeply into "all the truth" (Jn 16:13) and into full unity. Thus life together in Christ requires individuals as well as communities gratefully to recognize their own talents, to husband them faithfully and to place them willingly at the disposal of the whole. At the same time, they must be open to the special gifts which others have received. "While preserving unity in essentials, let all members of the Church, according to the office entrusted to each, preserve a proper freedom in the various forms of spiritual life and discipline, in the variety of liturgical rites and even in the theological elaborations of revealed truth. In all things let charity be exercised."[28]

3. Dynamism

38. As *historical reality*, the unity in Christ exists in a process of becoming; as living reality, it is directed towards growing and bearing fruit even though decay constantly threatens.

39. *In a world afflicted by sin*, unity is forever involved in the struggle between "Spirit and flesh", "light and darkness", good and evil, between Christ and all God's adversaries. It is inevitably affected by the dramatic dynamism of this struggle which lasts until the end of the world. Threatened from within and without, the church is called to strive for unity and salvation "with fear and trembling" (Phil 2:12) and to trust fully in the Lord.

40. To the extent that this happens, Christian unity is drawn into the *dynamism of grace*. As unity in *faith*, it grows and works, just as faith does. Like faith, life together in Christ is "being-on-the-way". As unity in *hope*, it must, like hope itself, reach out for what is to come. Like hope, unity lives more on what is to come than on what is. It is never satisfied with what has been attained and never despairs because of the unattained. As unity in *love*, it never reaches its final consummation on earth. Like love, life together in Christ always strives for more than what has been achieved.

41. Like all Christian life in this world, unity stands under the sign of the *"already"* and the *"not yet"*. Because a gift has been received which cannot be comprehended, there is the assurance of an ineffably greater grace yet to come. "It does not yet appear what we shall be, but we know that when he appears we shall be like him" (1 Jn 3:2). "The Lord who is bringing all things into full unity at the last is he who constrains us to seek the unity which he wills for his Church on earth here and now."[29]

e. ALL-ENCOMPASSING COMMUNITY

42. Life together in Christ is lived in *manifold personal and social relationships.* (1) They are rooted and flow into the Triune God, (2) they encompass all believers and (3) finally all human beings.

1. Unity of the One Triune God

43. "The love of the Father and the Son in the unity of the Holy Spirit is the souce and goal of the unity which the Triune God wills for all men and creation."[30]

44. Christian unity is created in the *image and likeness of* the Triune God. "The highest exemplar and source of this mystery is the unity, in the Trinity of Persons, of one God, the Father and the Son in the Holy Spirit."[31] Thus the plea in the high-priestly prayer is, "even as thou, Father, art in me, and I in thee, that they also may be in us" (Jn 17:21).

45. Christian unity is lived in *personal fellowship* with the Triune God. Inasmuch as human beings are enabled to live, through the Holy Spirit, as sons and daughters of the Father with and in Christ, they become truly one. "And our fellowship is with the Father and with his Son Jesus Christ" (1 Jn 1:3). "I in them and thou in me, that they may become perfectly one" (Jn 17:23). This takes place through the Holy Spirit, "For by one Spirit we were all baptized into one body" (1 Cor 12:13), "one spirit with him" (1 Cor 6:17). The more intensive the believer's personal nearness to the Triune God, the stronger is the bond uniting him to the neighbour. "For they can achieve depth and ease in strengthening mutual brotherhood to the degree that they enjoy profound communion with the Father, the World, and the Spirit."[32]

2. Unity of All Believers in Christ

46. Unity in Christ is both *personal and social.* It consists not of an external bond but of personal ties. These ties are actualized ever anew where human beings obey the call of grace. They *transcend the limits of space and time* and encompass all believers. "All in each place who are baptized into Jesus Christ and confess him as Lord and Saviour are brought by the Holy Spirit into one fully committed fellowship . . . all . . . at the same time are united with the whole Christian fellowship in all places and all ages."[33]

47. "Such a fellowship means for those who participate in it nothing less than a renewed mind and spirit, a full participation in common praise and prayer, the shared realities of penitence and forgiveness, mutuality in suffering and joy, listening together to the same Gospel, responding in faith,

obedience and service, joining in the one mission of Christ in the world, a self-forgetting love for all for whom Christ died."[34]

3. Unity for the World

48. Like Christ, his church exists *"for the life of the world"* (Jn 6:51). Its members are to be one "so that the world may believe" (Jn 17:21). Their corporate witness together with their common life is to lead the world to the faith on which its salvation depends.

49. Just as *mission and unity* are intimately connected in Jesus' high-priestly prayer, so they belong together in the life of the church. The church can fulfil its mission only to the extent it is one. It will be one only in so far as it obeys the call of its Lord and proclaims the gospel to all creation (cf. Mk 16:15). Its *missionary* activity has a twofold goal: "evangelization and the planting of the Church among those peoples and groups where she has not yet taken root"[35]. Neither is fully attainable without unity. The good news of reconciling love appears incredible when the messengers are unreconciled or even in conflict with each other. Similarly, the planting of the church is gravely endangered when it suffers from schism at its roots. "Hence, by the same mandate which makes missions necessary, all the baptized are called to be gathered into one flock, and thus to be able to bear unanimous witness before the nations to Christ their Lord."[36]

50. Moreover, Christian unity is of decisive help in promoting yet other forms of *service in the world*. The corporate life in Christ is to be "the sign of the coming unity of humankind"[37] and an aid to its free and just development. "The surrender of confessional complacency, and the respect for the convictions of others, helps to diminish the explosiveness of human and social conflicts. The struggle for fellowship among all Christians, in which social and cultural differences, race membership and national ties have lost their divisive power, is part of the great battle for the healing of a world lacerated by tension and enmity."[38]

51. On the other hand, the one church *receives* and *learns from all* fellow human beings. Christian striving for unity is influenced for good and ill by secular events. Social, political and cultural activity cannot produce Christian unity, but may greatly contribute to its realization. Much in the modern ecumenical movement has undoubtedly first become possible through general historical developments. Even hostile actions can serve the corporate life in Christ, for many who had not sufficiently heeded the Lord's call to unity have been drawn closer together by persecution and need. On the other hand, secular factors can jeopardize Christian unity both from within and without. False ideals, for example, can block insight into what is essential to unity and set ideologies in place of faith. Similarly, efforts

towards unification confined to single nations, races or classes can lead to erroneous ways of seeing and practising Christian unity.

52. Both church and world in their manifold interrelationships are constantly in need of the creative love of God. They are always *in every way* dependent on "the God . . . who gives life to the dead and calls into existence the things that do not exist" (Rom 4:17). The Lord who calls the dead to fruitful life can overcome all threats and obstacles to Christian unity and turn that unity into an effective instrument for the salvation of the world. He who creates that which is truly new can transform our wasted opportunities into reality. He can create new forms of unity beyond what we have yet glimpsed or conceived. We cannot speak of them adequately, but we can together remain open for them. If we keep our eyes fixed on the unity and mission of the church and the redemption and consummation of the world, there is nothing which we cannot expect from the Lord who says, "Behold, I make all things new" (Rev 21:5).

Part II

STEPS TOWARDS UNITY

Introduction

53. We have spoken with one voice in "obedience to the faith" about the "goal of unity" in the sense of a full spiritual and ecclesial fellowship. Our comon testimony on this point impels us to address the question of what concrete "steps towards unity" can be taken by Roman Catholic and Lutheran Christians and churches now and in the immediate future. Only by means of such concrete steps shall we draw nearer to "the goal of visible unity in one faith and in one eucharistic fellowship expressed in worship and in common life in Christ . . . in order that the world may believe"[39].

54. Our search is for steps in "a process of gradual rapprochement . . . in which various stages are possible"[40]. In such an open process of growing together we can and should set our eyes on *intermediate goals* and keep on re-examining the methods of advance. By moving in this way from an incomplete to a more and more complete communion, we shall be able to take account of a wide variety of different historical, theological and regional situations. In being willing to enter into such an open process, we are well aware that God the Holy Spirit himself will show us steps and lead us in paths which for the most part we cannot at present envisage.

55. In accordance with our reflections on "unity as goal", we now propose to ask what "steps toward units" are implied by (a) the grace of ec-

clesial communion, (b) the "means" which constitute it, (c) the spiritual
manner of its realization, (d) its structural form and (e) its universality.

a. COMMUNITY THROUGH GRACE

56. What "steps towards unity" are implied by the nature of ecclesial fellowship (*communio*) as a gift of God's grace which precedes all our efforts?

57. We are first reminded that, because ecclesial communion is a gift of
God's grace, we must give priority to *spiritual ecumenism* in our striving
for church unity. "There can be no ecumenism worthy of the name without a change of heart. For it is from newness of attitudes, from self-denial
and unstinted love, that yearnings for unity take their rise and grow towards maturity. We should therefore pray to the divine Spirit for the
grace to be genuinely self-denying, humble, gentle in the service of others,
and to have an attitude of brotherly generosity towards them."[41] The Reformation also understood itself as a call to repentance and renewal in the
one church; indeed, it demanded that the life of Christians be a daily penitence.

58. In the relationship of our churches, as well as in that of Roman Catholic and Lutheran Christians to each other, such a basic attitude will be
concretized in these *spiritual steps towards unity:*

— We shall note with deep remorse that, in light of the history of our separation, we cannot one-sidedly shift the blame to our partners, but must
instead confess our own fault for the separation.

— We must become open to discovering great spiritual treasures in the
past and the present of other churches and to receiving in our encounters
with them all the gifts, stimulation and guidance which these treasures offer.

— We discover that, despite the divisions caused by our sin, the Spirit has
maintained through its work in our churches a fundamental fellowship
which constitutes the primary precondition for all our striving for the visible unity of the church.

59. Spiritual ecumenism has been furthered through general historical
studies as well as special *research* in the history of theology and doctrine.
During the past decades these have already helped to *reduce prejudice, improve knowledge and provide a fairer evaluation of the past and the present*

of both churches, particularly the history of the schism since the 16th century. But we deem it essential:

— to continue this process of removing confessionally conditioned prejudices and misjudgments of other churches from the entirety of theological research and consciousness as well as from textbooks of church history and systematic theology, and to develop an ecumenical view of church history and history of doctrine since the 16th century. The joint Roman Catholic/Lutheran study on the Augsburg Confession is a promising example;[42]

— beyond the area of specialized theological literature, to eliminate tendentious school-book accounts of the 16th century breach and of the churches involved in it and, more generally, to arrive at a wider and more critical view of the past and the present of one's own church;

— to strive for an ever more intensive and direct knowledge of the other church (its worship, piety, artistic and cultural achievements, and service to society) and thereby gain a more vivid impression of its spiritual wealth and greater openness to closer fellowship.

60. Such steps can be signs of conversion by which both churches show that they are united by the joint resolve, not to conform to the world, but rather to overcome every form of self righteousness.

b. MEDIATION OF COMMUNITY

61. What then, are the "steps towards unity" which should be taken in the separate as well as joint practice of our churches in the light of the bestowal of the spirit of fellowship through word, sacrament and diaconal service.

1. Word

62. It is the conviction of both our churches that spiritual fellowship in Christ is imparted through the word. This word of salvation is basic to the church and is normatively given in *Holy Scripture.* It is therefore an ever-necessary step towards unity for both churches to live and be guided in their spiritual life by the testimony of Holy Scripture. This makes it essential to utilize the full range of scriptural utterances—rather than simply a selection—in theology, preaching and in group and personal Bible study. This certainly does not exclude the quest for a centre of Scripture, for central and less central statements, and for rules of interpretation which derive therefrom. Yet the failure on both sides to hear and accept the full range of scriptural testimonies has contributed in no small measure to the estrangement of the churches.

63. Both churches must increasingly *adopt a common orientation* towards Holy Scripture. This includes jointly sponsored translations of the Bible, common commentaries on biblical books, and the kind of joint ministerial and congregational Bible studies which are already being carried out in many places. The coordination of the scriptural readings in the worship services (*pericopes*) of both churches should also be considered.

64. It is the conviction of both churches that God's word is also transmitted through *church traditions* even though they differ in their theological evaluations. The canon of Holy Scripture is certainly itself a weighty and fundamental part of church tradition.[43] Further, the creeds and official dogmatic decisions of the undivided church have special importance. Greater consideration of the early church and medieval pre-Reformation tradition shared by both churches could function as a decisive step towards unity. Strenuous efforts to understand the diverging traditions since the 16th century are also important as steps on the way to unity. Here, too, the ecumenical treatment of the Augsburg Confession provides an important example.

65. Cooperative concern for Scripture and tradition includes critical *hermeneutical reflection*. It is an important theological task to seek for common principles of interpretation of Scripture and of the differing church traditions. Such principles could help significantly in dealing with controversial issues such as the development of the office of the ministry. These principles must acknowledge the impossibility of simply ignoring our traditions or surrendering our historical identities on the way to unity. On the other hand, however, it must be remembered that our identities are themselves involved in a process which leads us to relate our traditions in new ways to Holy Scripture and to interpret them critically in terms of our contemporary understanding of reality for the sake of today's witness to the world. By noting the converging elements in this process, we are enabled to arrive at a newly conscious and determined identity.

2. Sacraments

66. Spiritual communion in Christ is also imparted through the sacraments. It would thus be a decisive step on the way to unity if in each of the two churches the sacraments were to assume a *central significance* through the dedicated and active participation of believers in their celebration.

67. Consciousness of the basic importance of *baptism* for both salvation and fellowship must be promoted in both churches. A renewal of baptismal practice can above all contribute to this end. Both children and adults should be increasingly baptized in the worship service of the whole congregation; water should be used in such a way that its symbolic signifi-

cance is unmistakable; and the correct baptismal formula shoud never be omitted; remembrance of baptism should be fostered, and particular stress should be laid on a Christian education as deriving from or leading to baptism. If these conditions are fulfilled, as many churches have discovered, all doubts regarding the mutual recognition of baptism become superfluous.

68. "In the Eucharist, too, it is progress towards the centre which brings us nearer to each other."[44] Despite the legitimate variety of existing possibilities, the liturgical form of the *Lord's Supper* in both churches should have the basic features and elements summarized in the document on the Lord's Supper.[45] Both churches must promote knowledge and understanding of the different but not church-dividing customs in the celebration of the eucharist (*e.g.* as regards liturgical vestments, sign of the cross, kneeling), and the differences which exist even within the two churches must be respected. In any case, the festive character of the eucharist should be emphasized enough to endear this celebration to the congregations. There should also be more eucharistic services designed especially for children and adolescents. At present, after periods of neglect, there is a renewal of eucharistic practice in Lutheran churches. It is urgently necessary to integrate the celebration of the eucharist fully into the main Sunday service and to urge congregations to commune more frequently. Care should be taken to deal reverently with the consecrated elements after the eucharistic celebration. Both churches should together endeavour to define the conditions for admission to the Lord's Supper—both with regard to age and to the various pastoral needs.

69. In reference to the other rites which the Roman Catholic Church regards as sacraments, theological endeavours have led to a better mutual understanding. Confession and penance, which the Augsburg Confession treats in conjunction with the sacaments of baptism and the Lord's Supper, have become a particular pastoral task for both churches in which it is necessary to rethink the understanding of sin. The Lutheran tradition does not fundamentally reject the application of the concept of sacrament to the office of the ministry and ordination, and both churches hold that through the act of ordination the Holy Spirit with his gracious gifts takes the ordinand into service.[46] According to Lutheran understanding and practice, weddings and confirmation are also acts of grace to be celebrated amidst the prayers of the congregation.[47]

3. Service

70. Both churches hold that the imparting of spiritual fellowship through word and sacrament needs the ministry of *ordained office-holders*. The ministry of these office-holders is for both churches inseparably connected with the ministry carried on by the whole congregation through the mani-

fold gifts of its members in proclamation, prayer and action. Yet we must move beyond this common starting point. The ministry is at present under discussion both within and between our churches, and further theological and canonical clarifications of the conepts of the ministerial office and of ordination are essential steps towards unity. Such clarifications must constantly keep in mind the views and discussions in the other church. The way ministry is exercised must be marked by the spirit of brotherhood and partnership, by readiness to serve and by deep piety. When practice becomes credible, it will be easier to eliminate distorted views of the ministry and to achieve ecumenical agreement in this area.

71. Since both the success and failure of ecumenical rapprochement depend heavily on the church's ministers, stress must be laid on their acquiring *ecumenical awareness and experience.* Ecumenical awareness needs to be developed by permeating *theological education* with ecumenism. This is not merely a matter of providing basic information regarding the state and progress of the ecumenical and theological dialogue. Moreover, there are already examples of cooperation between theologians of both churches in a single educational institution and also cases of integrated theological education for which other churches are jointly responsible. It would be desirable to expand these initiatives and develop new ones in other places. The existence of such ecumenical institutions can help insure that theologians of the future will contribute even more than in the past to the ecumenical dialogue.

72. The growth of ecumenical consciousness should also lead to regular *ecumenical retreats and courses of study* for ministers. Joint academic study of pastoral concerns and of the gospel entrusted to us would thus be combined with the spiritual experience of common prayer and worship and with exchanges on the personal dimensions of faith. It is necessary for theological reflection and spiritual experience to interact in order to avoid intellectualizing the dialogue or engaging in unreflective pastoral practice. Indeed, all aspects of the inter-church dialogue should be characterized by the interaction of doctrinal discussions and spirituality.

c. REALIZATION OF COMMUNITY

73. What "steps towards unity" are suggested by looking at the realization of spiritual community in faith, hope and love?

1. Community of Faith

74. Encounters between Roman Catholics and Lutherans on matters of faith have shifted increasingly in the last decades from confrontation and polemics towards a *dialogue* committed to the joint search for the *fullness of truth.* Dialogue requires openness towards the testimony of others re-

garding the faith and serves to test one's own understanding of faith and of the doctrinal tradition in which one stands. The purpose of mutual questioning in fraternal encounters is to manifest and recognize the truth in all its diversity or else to correct and formulate anew previous views. Unanswered questions are also bearable given the presence of a sincere desire for "fraternal rivalry"[48], and providing they stimulate growth together into the fullness of the Holy Spirit (Eph 4:15; 1 Cor 13:9-11).

75. The dialogue between our churches has led in the last few years to the production of documents in which it has been possible to make joint statements on questions of faith where church-dividing contradictions previously prevented unity.[49] The reception of these results of the dialogue by our churches is an urgent task and step towards unity. Such a reception can occur in many ways: ministers may study these documents and make them fruitful in their preaching and practice, or the documents can be used in the education of church workers, or congregational groups can get to know them. In each of these cases, it makes good sense to involve the members of both churches in the process of reception, for in this way they can themselves experience the dialogical activity which has produced the results. It is particularly important, however, for the leaders of both churches to engage officially in the reception process and to decide on the ecclesiastical and ecumenical status of these documents.

76. Another necessary step towards unity occurs when that fellowship in faith which has been given to us is actually practised by means of a common *witness to Christian faith* for which both sides assume responsibility. Joint services of the word are already being held in many places. There should be closer cooperation than before on the mission field. Wherever possible, joint radio and television broadcasts on behalf of the Christian message should be arranged. In many countries, it appears extremely urgent to arrive at close Catholic-Lutheran cooperation in the school systems, and in any case, the churches have a joint responsibility for the Christian education of children and young people. There are also responsibilities for working together in the field of both theological and non-theological Christian literature, as has been shown by cooperation between Roman Catholic and Protestant publishers and by the collaborative production and translation of Roman Catholic-Protestant writings. Extensive opportunities also exist in the fields of church music and fine arts.

77. What can be said in general regarding the *pastoral responsibilities* of the churches is that no one church can single-handedly carry on the work of evangelization in a secularized or traditionally non-Christian society. Moreover, the very credibility of the Christian witness is here at stake. In so far as varied circumstances in the different countries allow, there should be joint planning of pastoral care in new housing developments, in hospitals, at universities and colleges, and in work with children or youth.

"Ecumenical bridgehead communities" could result, which might provide examples and stimuli for pastoral care in traditional congregations. Pastoral care for confessionally mixed marriages presents a particular area of Christian responsibility. It is of decisive importance for Christian witness whether such families develop into nuclei of ecumenical understanding or into battlefields of separated traditions which, in the end, lead to alienation from the faith.

2. Community of Hope

78. Christian faith lives in an attitude of hope. Spiritual fellowship in faith necessarily becomes fellowship in hope. The hope, which "does not disappoint us" (Rom. 5:5), is our support on our way towards each other. All the "steps towards unity" mentioned above, and all those still to be considered, are possible only if we are carried forward by our common hope. Sin is not only the deepest cause of our separation, but it also leads us again and again to setbacks and manifestations of discouragement on the way to each other. Our hope is in the faithfulness of the Lord who continually triumphs within our sinful hearts and desires to lead us to final and complete communion. In spite of everything, therefore, he gives us courage anew to take new steps towards each other.

79. Our hope, however, is not solely concerned with our own road towards Christian unity, but is also focused on the *salvation and redemption of the world as a whole*. We are empowered in this all-embracing perspective to give an "accounting of hope" against both resignation and Promethean self-assertion, and are encouraged to take together those concrete steps of hope which are at the same time "steps towards the unity" of our churches. Such steps of hope are taken in the knowledge that all the scientific, technological and humanitarian progress of the world cannot bring redemption. Instead, Christ will return to judge and to establish a new world. Yet in light of that coming, signs of the future can already be raised aloft in the world as it now is.

80. Steps taken in hope are such signs of Christ's future. They occur where Christians and churches offer themselves in *service* to suffering people, in service to changing those social conditions which in part cause human suffering, and in service to overcoming the worldwide dangers arising from the ecological crisis. They occur where Christians accept hope as an invitation to risk.[50] This service, based on common hope, should be jointly carried out by Christians and churches in their diaconal and charitable activities. Appropriate joint initiatives should be developed or newly started on all levels. The churches should also jointly support, as much as possible, the studies necessary to carry out these initiatives as well as the liaison work with non-church authorities. Such steps of hope, which lead us both towards Christian unity and common prayer, can become signs of

the presence of Christ among us as the one who bears and overcomes our maladies.

3. Community of Love

81. Christian faith proves itself in love (1 Cor 13:13; Gal 5:6), and thus our spiritual fellowship must be a fellowship of love. Such love arises from the ever new *encounter with Christ in the word and eucharist,* for "greater love has no man than this, that a man lay down his life for his friends" (Jn 15:13). Thus when the community of faith takes shape as a community of love it is represented in a particularly important form in the joint celebration of the eucharist. We are saddened that the present relationships of our churches do not yet allow full eucharistic fellowship. We confess anew our longing for "the goal of visible unity in one faith and in one eucharistic fellowship"[51]. The credibility of our witness to the world and of our very celebrations of the eucharist is menaced by our divisions at these celebrations. This suggests that the work of the Holy Spirit is not absent from the great pressure for eucharistic fellowship we are now experiencing. We shall not cease to search for possible ways to allow mutual admission to communion in special cases.

82. In place of the as yet impossible full eucharistic fellowship, we must create opportunities in which our still separated churches can unite in common *praise, prayer* and *supplication* for each other, for all churches and for the world, and in the preaching of the word of God and confession of his glorious deeds. This was the reason for the establishment of the week of prayer for Christian unity. This week of prayer should pose a challenge to prayer life of all of Christendom. It would lose its spiritual significance if it were demoted to an isolated annual manifestation of an otherwise non-existent ecumenical practice. It is our hope that such joint services of prayer will lead our church congregations towards a more and more perfect community of love.

83. Despite remaining difficulties, efforts should be made to promote *mutual participation* in Sunday worship, at baptisms, weddings, and funerals, and at ministerial ordinations and installations, otherwise our expressions of brotherliness will be limited to secular occasions such as receptions or other social events. In any case, quite apart from joint worship, greater *ecumenical exchange of visits,* encounters and conversations will contribute, by means of better mutual acquaintance and involvement in a common spirituality, to a deepening of a spiritual sharing perfected in love. Wherever such encounters result in unusual forms of ecumenical fellowship, even when they may seem to have gone too far, the church authorities should not pass judgment until they have had first-hand contact with those immediately involved. If they thus at least indirectly participate in ecumenical learning processes, they will be more ready to grant in love the

necessary trust to those who are engaged in continuing brotherly ecumenical conversations.

84. The unity for which we hope and towards which we move as brothers on the road will not spare us conflicts. For "the Church . . . is at the same time holy and always in need of being purified"[52]. It "goes on its way in sin and weakness"[53]. The conflicts require consultations between representatives of the church leadership which should be carried on in a spirit of love and forgiveness. In addition, it is possible to form *"groups of reconciliation"*, made up of representatives from both churches. These could function as independent ecumenical courts of appeal. Over and over again our congregations discover that problems of pastoral care (such as those of religious liberty, changes in church membership, use of church buildings and mixed marriages) serve as fuel for hostile actions and occasions for anti-ecumenical prejudice. Groups such as those just mentioned could provide a forum for the open discussion and resolution of minor or even major conflicts. As expressions of readiness for reconciliation and examples and signs of love and peace, they could have significance far beyond the boundaries of the church.

85. The love which tests our common faith cannot in any case remain confined to our fellowship with each other. We are rather called to undertake joint responsibilities in following the Lord in his *loving devotion* to the whole world. We must make clear in our life and in our teaching what the "new commandment" (Jn 13:34-35; 1 Jn 2:7-11) gives and demands. That is why one indispensable step is the striving for as united a witness as possible in ethical and social-ethical questions. Only when we together dedicate ourselves to the love and charity which also serves the social needs of human beings throughout the world—loved by God yet suffering in many ways—will the love which unites us be placed in the proper perspective.

d. THE FORM OF COMMUNITY

86. What are the "steps towards unity" suggested by the visible shape of our spiritual fellowship in its diversity and dynamism?

1. Recognition of Ministries

87. The relations between our churches continue to be troubled by the non-recognition of ministries. As is well known, Catholics and Lutherans consider this question from different viewpoints. Whereas Lutherans have "never denied the existence of the office of the ministry in the Roman Catholic Church"[54] (although, at the time of the Reformation, they made obedience to Roman Catholic bishops dependent on their permitting the Reformation proclamation), Vatican II speaks of a *defectus* ("lack") of the

sacrament of orders in the transmission of the ministry in the Reformation churches.[55] Meanwhile, the conviction has been growing that it is not a matter of a total absence, but instead as a "lack of the fullness of ministry", and it is not denied that the ministry in Lutheran churches exercises essential functions of the office which, according to Roman Catholic conviction, Jesus Christ instituted for his church.[56] It is especially urgent that on the basis of the present state of ecumenical understanding the responsible church authorities take whatever steps are possible towards full recognition of ministries in the context of mutual reception by the churches as a whole. This includes the broadest possible *reception for the results* of the ecumenical dialogue on the ministry, during the course of which church leaders should rethink prior positions. *Ordination liturgies,* for example, should be examined to see whether they accord with positions arrived at in ecumenical discussions.

2. Credible Practice

88. Just as the pastoral practice of ordained parish clergy is of great importance on the local level, so that *actualization of ministries of church leadership beyond the congregational level* is of decisive significance for possible mutual readiness to enter the fellowship of the historic episcopacy or of the Petrine office. Thus, a credible practice of church government must avoid the dangers of bureaucracy and anonymous administration. Policies must be understandable and concern for cooperation with all who serve in the church unmistakable. A certain quality of spiritual power— and not mere juridical competence—must be present. In these ways the directives and decisions of those who exercise oversight (or *episcopē*) will be visibly related to what actually is needed and their words will possess an intrinsic authority.

3. Collaboration

89. Mutual respect and collaboration of ministers *on all levels* should be practised more extensively than heretofore. One especially important step on the way to a common episcopacy could take place through a more intensive and thoroughly institutionalized cooperation between the leaders of both churches than that which is at present customary. Consideration should be given to forming liaison groups (which might have either a more episcopal or more synodical structure) with authority to make decisions in particular matters. In any case, greater cooperation should be sought, not only on a regional basis, but also on the world-wide level.

90. Naturally *discrimination* must cease if ministers are to cooperate on all levels. Partners cannot cast aspersions on each other and must renounce every form of proselytism (though not mutual criticism or requests for change). Such cooperation, moreover, in which the partners become to

some extent co-responsible for each other, provides initiation into the experience of real and legitimate diversity in the church. It is against the nature of the search for Christian unity to level down all differences in the realm of church life or to make unfair demands on one side or the other. The operative principle must here be that the changes reciprocally risked by increased cooperation should be balanced by a legitimate concern to preserve the identities and special characteristics which each side derives from its tradition.

e. ALL-ENCOMPASSING COMMUNITY

91. Lastly what are the "steps towards unity" suggested by the all-encompassing character of the community towards which we move?

1. Fellowship of All Christians

92. The goal of full communion towards which Catholic and Lutheran Christians and churches are now moving together points far beyond itself. It points to that perfect communion which we shall have with the Triune God at the end of all time. But it also points beyond itself in the sense that Roman Catholic-Lutheran fellowship is not yet the fellowship of all Christians. We must see our rapprochement in the *context of the whole ecumenical movement,* and not least in relationship to the notable institutional expression of that movement in the World Council of Churches. A community limited to Catholics and Lutherans would not be all-encompassing, because substantial parts of Christendom (such as the Orthodox, Anglicans, Reformed, Methodists and Baptists, but also, for example, the independent churches of Africa) would be missing from this fellowship. This would not only be a numerical loss, but also a substantive deficiency because of the absence of insights of spiritual and theological importance and the resultant lack of full catholicity. The road to Catholic and Lutheran unity must therefore be unmistakably open to the wider and greater fellowship of Christians.

93. This means we must always be alert in the Roman Catholic-Lutheran dialogue to what others in other traditions and churches and other bilateral and multilateral ecumenical dialogues are saying and thinking on the questions with which we deal. The results of the Roman Catholic-Lutheran dialogues can prove fruitful to other bilateral and multilateral theological discussions, but they must also be critically examined in the light of the conclusions which others reach. Our various levels of encounter with each other in worship and action must be continually open to other *ecumenical partners.* Especially significant examples of this wider cooperation are provided by national Christian or church councils as well as by various joint church working groups. These may serve as starting points for more and more intensive ecumenical fellowship. It is therefore important

that the various bilateral dialogues should have the possibility of meeting together regularly in common forums. The membership of Roman Catholic theologians in the Commission on Faith and Order together with other forms of collaboration between the Roman Catholic Church and the World Council of Churches suggests possibilities of even more intensive collaboration which should be realized.

2. Unity of Humankind

94. There is also another and more far-reaching sense in which Catholic-Lutheran fellowship points beyond itself. God "desires *all men* to be saved" (1 Tim 2:4) and to gather before his throne in perfect fellowship. The unity of the church is directed to the unity of humankind. We Christians have a shared responsibility throughout history for the sowing of hate and discord instead of love and reconciliation. Power, egotism and a misconceived orthodoxy have played a calamitous role in the church and through the church in the world. So also the present state of Christianity with its many divisions and impotence damages the effectiveness of its witness. Yet however modestly and reticently Christians must speak of themselves at this point, we nevertheless know that God wills to work continuously in Christianity by his saving and reconciling power and through Christianity in the world. When Christians and churches re-unite, their way of reconciliation and love could become a sign and ferment in the midst of a world rent asunder by conflicts and enmity. Yet we must remember that God, on the contrary, also calls the church to its senses through the world and through his dealings with it. The world, in other words, challenges the church in manifold ways.

95. "Steps towards unity" will be taken in this universal sense (which embraces the whole of divided humanity) whenever our ecumenical efforts lead Christians of different nationality, race, colour, culture, social and political conviction, and class background to unite in mutual understanding and join hands in mutual reconciliation. "Steps towards unity" in this wider sense, therefore, include all the efforts jointly undertaken for peace, justice and reconciliation in the world and serving to eliminate political as well as confessional images of enmity and all the self-righteousness associated with them. We need increasingly to transform the still prevalent parallel existence of the churches into an ecumenical fellowship of planning, speaking and acting on the congregational level, on the level of regional study and action groups, as well as on the level of responsibility for church government. This would greatly enhance the credibility and effectiveness of Christian commitment for *a reconciled and peaceful humanity,* and would draw all people closer together by allowing the light which comes from Christ to shine more brightly.

96. When we think of the steps that bring us closer to the all-embracing fellowship of human beings in Christ, we also know that these steps of ours will never themselves attain the hoped-for community. They are at best *Spirit-worked signs* of what Christ alone can bring to perfection when he returns after having prepared the ground for the new age through his first coming. This confidence for the future, however, should not become an excuse for the constant failures of imagination, commitment and openness which we must ever confess anew. It should rather console and uphold us in the certainty of hope even when our efforts are repeatedly frustrated by factors inside and outside the churches. It leads us finally to the adoration of him who alone is the beginning, the midst and the end of all our steps and ways.

PARTICIPANTS

Roman Catholic Members:
The Rt. Rev. H. L. Martensen (chairperson)
Prof. Dr. J. Hoffmann
The Rev. J. F. Hotchkin
The Rev. Chr. Mhagama
Prof. Dr. St. Napiorkowski
Dr. V. Pfnür
The Rt. Rev. Dr. P.-W. Scheele

Lutheran Members:
Prof. Dr. G. A. Lindbeck (chairperson)
The Rt. Rev. D. H. Dietzfelbinger
The Rev. Dr. K. Hafenscher
Dr. P. Nasution
The Rev. I. K. Nsibu
Dr. L. Thunberg
Prof. Dr. Bertoldo Weber

Consultants:
Prof. Dr. G. Forell (Lutheran)
Dr. U. Kühn (Lutheran)
The Rev. H. Legrand, OP (Roman Catholic)
Prof. Dr. H. Meyer (Lutheran)
Prof. Dr. H. Schütte (Roman Catholic)

Staff Members:
Mgr. Dr. A. Klein (Secretariat for Promoting Christian Unity)
The Rev. Dr. Carl H. Mau, Jr. (Lutheran World Federation)
The Rev. Dr. Daniel F. Martensen (Lutheran World Federation)
Mgr. Dr. C. Moeller (Secretariat for Promoting Christian Unity)
Prof. Dr. V. Vajta (Lutheran World Federation)

23 February 1980

Notes

1. Vatican II, Decree on Ecumenism, No. 1.
2. Discussion Paper on the Ecumenical Role of the World Confessional Families in the One Ecumenical Movement, 1974, No. 53.
3. *The Evanston Report.* The Second Assembly of the World Council of Churches in Evanston 1954 (London: SCM Press, 1955), Report of Section I, No. 9, p. 85.
4. *The New Delhi Report.* The Third Assembly of the World Council of Churches 1961 (New York: Association Press, 1962), Report of the Section on Unity, No. 9, p. 119 (hereafter: New Delhi).
5. *Ecumenical Relations of the Lutheran World Federation.* Report of the Working Group on the Interrelations Between the Various Bilateral Dialogues (Geneva, 1977), No. 171. See also *Lutheran Identity* (Strasbourg: Institute for Ecumenical Research, 1977), No. 7.
6. *Ecumenical Relations,* No. 181.
7. Cf. *The Eucharist,* Lutheran/Roman Catholic Joint Commission (Geneva: Lutheran World Federation, 1980), Nos. 25-28.
8. *Lutheran Identity,* No. 26.
9. Cf. Vatican II, Dogmatic Constitution on the Church, No. 7.
10. Cf. ibid., No. 11.
11. Ibid., Constitution on the Sacred Liturgy, No. 26.
12. Ibid., Dogmatic Constitution on the Church, No. 1.
13. Cf. Apology of the Augsburg Confession, XIII, 3-17, The Book of Concord, pp. 211ff.; The Smalcald Articles, III, IV, The Book of Concord, p. 310. See also Report of the Joint Lutheran/Roman Catholic Study Commission on "The Gospel and the Church". *Lutheran World,* Vol. XIX, No. 3, 1972, pp. 268f., No. 59 (hereafter: Malta).
14. *Lutheran Identity,* No. 28.
15. *One Baptism, One Eucharist And a Mutually Recognized Ministry.* Three agreed statements (Geneva: World Council of Churches, 1978[5], Faith and Order Paper No. 73) (hereafter: Accra), The Ministry, No. 15; see also on the understanding of the ministry, Malta, Nos. 47-67.
16. Vatican II, Dogmatic Constitution on the Church, No. 18.
17. Cf. *Ecumenical Relations,* No. 37.
18. Cf. ibid., No. 161.
19. Gemeinsame Synode der Bistümer in der Bundesrepublik Deutschland, Pasto-

240 Growth In Agreement

rale Zusammenarbeit der Kirchen im Dienst an der christlichen Einheit (Würzburg, 1974), 3.21.

20. *Breaking Barriers—Nairobi 1975*, The Official Report of the Fifth Assembly of the World Council of Churches (London: SPCK and Grand Rapids: Wm. B. Eerdmans, 1976), Report of Section II, No. IV, 13–18, p. 64 (hereafter: Nairobi).

21. *What Kind of Unity?* (Geneva: World Council of Churches, 1974, Faith and Order Paper 69), p. 120, A. II.

22. *Ecumenical Relations*, No. 39.

23. New Delhi, No. 2, p. 116.

24. *Ecumenical Relations*, No. 205.

25. *In Christ—A New Community*, The Proceedings of the Sixth Assembly of the Lutheran World Federation, Dar-es-Salaam, Tanzania, June 13-25, 1977 (Geneva: Lutheran World Federation, 1977), Models of Unity, No. 13, p. 173.

26. New Delhi, No. 10, p. 120.

27. Vatican II, Dogmatic Constitution on the Church, No. 32.

28. Ibid., Decree on Ecumenism, No. 4.

29. New Delhi, No. 1, p. 116.

30. Ibid.

31. Vatican II, Decree on Ecumenism, No. 2.

32. Ibid., No. 7.

33. New Delhi, No. 2, p. 116.

34. Ibid., No. 10, p. 119.

35. Vatican II, Decree on the Church's Missionary Activity, No. 6.

36. Ibid.

37. Nairobi, No. 7, p. 61.

38. "More than Church Unity". Study Document for the Fifth Assembly. *Lutheran World*, Vol. XVII, No. 1, 1970, pp. 49f.

39. Constitution of the World Council of Churches, III.

40. Malta, No. 73.

41. Vatican II, Decree on Ecumenism, No. 7.

42. *Confessio Augustana—Bekenntnis des einen Glaubens*. Gemeinsame Untersuchung katholischer and lutherischer Theologen. Edited by H. Meyer and H. Schütte, together with E. Iserloh, W. Kasper, G. Kretzschmar, W. Lohff, G. W. Forell, J McCue (Frankfurt/M.—Paderborn, 1980).

43. Cf. Malta, No. 17.

44. *The Eucharist*, No. 75.

45. Cf. ibid., No. 76: and Accra, The Eucharist, No. 28.

46. Cf. Malta, No. 59.

47. See above, No. 19.

48. Vatican II, Decree on Ecumenism, No. 11.

49. Cf. especially Malta and *The Eucharist*

50. *Sharing in One Hope*, Commission on Faith and Order, Bangalore, 1978 (Geneva: World Council of Churches, 1979, Faith and Order Paper No. 92), VII.

51. Constitution of the World Council of Churches, III.

52. Vatican II, Dogmatic Constitution on the Church, No. 8.

53. Gemeinsame Synode der Bistümer, No. 4.3.3.

54. Malta, No. 64.

55. Vatican II, Decree on Ecumenism, No. 22.

56. Cf. Groupe des Dombes, *Pour une réconciliation des ministères* (Taizé: Les Presses de Taizé, 1973).

ALL UNDER ONE CHRIST, 1980

Statement on the Augsburg Confession
by the Roman Catholic/Lutheran Joint Commission

PREFACE

The Roman Catholic/Lutheran Joint Commission of the Vatican Secretariat for Promoting Christian Unity and the Lutheran World Federation has produced a statement on the Confessio Augustana. This statement was unanimously approved by the members of the Commission. It is our hope that the unanimity expressed in it may hasten the hoped-for unity of our churches.

I

1. When Catholics and Lutherans look back to the Augsburg Confession today, we do so from a situation which differs considerably from that in 1530.

2. Though seriously threatened at that time, the unity of the Western Church had not yet been shattered. In spite of conflict and differences of conviction between them, the "religious parties" at that time still felt themselves to be "under one Christ" and committed to that church unity.[1]

3. But with the subsequent course of events not only did an increasingly bitter note creep into their dealings with one another but the differences between them sharpened in doctrine, in religious practices, in church structures, and in the ways in which they sought to obey the mandate of the crucified and risen Lord and to testify to his gospel among humankind. Non-church factors also helped to bring about this growing estrangement and to accentuate the differences. In the centuries since, these tensions and differences have been carried to other countries and other continents by the missionary work of our churches.

4. We recognize our own responsibility for the fact that these differences have divided our churches from one another and that this division has weakened our witness to Christ and brought suffering to individuals and nations.

5. It is with thankfulness, then, that we see how the Holy Spirit is leading

241

242 Growth In Agreement

us ever more deeply today into the unity of the Son with the Father (Jn 17:21ff.) and helping us to achieve a new community with one another.

6. Since the Second Vatican Council especially, our churches have been in dialogue in many countries and in many places. Striking convergences have been achieved and agreements reached on important controversial questions. The mutual bonds between congregations and members of our churches have led to cooperation and practical fellowship in a variety of forms. There are several differences between us which are also beginning to lose their divisive edge. Even when we must wrestle with each other for the truth, we recognize and experience many of the remaining differences as a source of mutual enrichment and correction. After centuries of deepening estrangement, there is a new sense among us that we are "all under one Christ".

7. The dialogue of recent years, the theological common understanding reached as a result of this dialogue, and the climate of real fellowship lead us back to Augsburg and to the Augsburg Confession. For, in content and structure, this confession, which is the basis and point of reference for the other Lutheran confessional documents, reflects as no other confession does the ecumenical purpose and catholic intention of the Reformation.

8. Very important, too, is the fact that this ecumenical purpose and catholic intent find expression in a confessional document which, subject to and together with Holy Scripture, is still the doctrinal basis of the Lutheran churches and still has binding authority for them even today. In the stage now reached in the understanding and convergence between our churches, this is a particularly important factor. For the character of the post-conciliar dialogue, as conducted for example in our Roman Catholic/Lutheran Joint Commission since 1967, is no longer that of private and unofficial meetings. On the contrary, it is conducted on the official instructions of our churches. Inasmuch as this dialogue has succeeded in arriving at convergences and agreements on fundamental issues,[2] it urges our churches to accept its findings officially and poses the question of the realization of church community.

9. It is in profound accord with this dynamic of a dialogue officially sponsored by our churches which now presses us in the direction of the realization of church fellowship that the confession which is binding for the life, doctrine and community of the church should become the special focus of our common attention and study.

II

10. The express purpose of the Augsburg Confession is to bear witness to the faith of the one, holy, catholic and apostolic church. Its concern is not

with peculiar doctrines nor indeed with the establishment of a new church (CA VII,1), but with the preservation and renewal of the Christian faith in its purity—in harmony with the ancient church, and "the church of Rome", and in agreement with the witness of Holy Scripture.[3] This explicit intention of the Confessio Augustana is also still important for our understanding of the later Lutheran confessional documents.

11. Joint studies by Catholic and Lutheran theologians[4] have shown that the contents of the statements of the Augsburg Confession in large measure fulfil this intention and to this extent can be regarded as an expression of the common faith.

12. This conclusion is reinforced by a whole series of recent studies and research efforts in a wide variety of disciplines, including a number of joint studies:

— Biblical and patristic studies have made us aware of the richness of our common Christian heritage; we are now better placed to judge the extent to which the arguments adduced from Scripture and tradition in the controversies of the 16th century were valid or are now in need of correction.
— Historical studies have thrown new light on conditions in church, society and economics at the time of the Reformation, showing us the extent to which political and economic factors also contributed to estrangement and division.
— Research into doctrinal history in the Middle Ages, the Reformation and, above all, the Confutatio—a refutation of the Confessio Augustana, composed at the Emperor's request—and the Augsburg union negotiations of 1530, has produced insights favourable to a more objective view of earlier controversies, to a defusing of mutual condemnations, and to a new evaluation of unions already achieved at that time.

13. Against this background of study and research, we are able to appeal to the Augsburg Confession when we say:

— Together we confess the faith in the Triune God and the saving work of God through Jesus Christ in the Holy Spirit, which binds all Christendom together (CA I and III). Through all the disputes and differences of the 16th century, Lutheran and Catholic Christians remained one in this central and most important truth of the Christian faith.

14. A broad consensus emerges in the doctrine of justification, which was decisively important for the Reformation (CA IV): it is solely by grace and by faith in Christ's saving work and not because of any merit in us that we are accepted by God and receive the Holy Spirit who renews our hearts and equips us for and calls us to good works.[5]

15. Together we testify that the salvation accomplished by Christ in his death and resurrection is bestowed on and effectively appropriated by humanity in the proclamation of the gospel and in the holy sacraments through the Holy Spirit (CA V).

16. A basic if still incomplete accord is also registered today even in our understanding of the church, where there were serious controversies between us in the past. By church we mean the communion of those whom God gathers together through Christ in the Holy Spirit, by the proclamation of the gospel and the administration of the sacraments, and the ministry instituted by him for this purpose. Though it always includes sinners, yet in virtue of the promise and fidelity of God it is the one, holy, catholic and apostolic church which is to continue forever (CA VII and VIII).

17. Reflecting on the Augsburg Confession, therefore, Catholics and Lutherans have discovered that they have a common mind on basic doctrinal truths which points to Jesus Christ, the living centre of our faith.

18. This basic consensus also comes out in and is confirmed by the documents of the official Roman Catholic/Lutheran dialogue today:

— the joint statements on the relation between gospel and church;[6]
— a broad common understanding of the eucharist;[7]
— the agreement that a special ministerial office conferred by ordination is constitutive for the church and does not belong to those elements which the Augsburg Confession denotes as "not necessary"[8].

19. Of the second part of the Augsburg Confession in which a sometimes severe polemical position was adopted in opposition to contemporary abuses in the church, it must be said that changes have come about in the life and judgment of our churches that substantially remove the grounds for the sharp criticism expressed in the Augsburg Confession. Important doctrinal questions are also touched on in this second part. Although certain problems still require to be clarified, a broad consensus has also been achieved even in doctrines broached in this second part.

20. In respect of the Mass (CA XXII and XXIV), this transformation in doctrine and practice has been demonstrated above all by our dialogue on the Lord's Supper. We still have different emphases, questions to put to one another and common tasks.[9] But all these are encompassed by a profound accord in our witness to the Lord's Supper and to a large extent also in respect to its liturgical celebrations.[10]

21. As far as monasticism and the life of the religious orders are concerned, in view of the now prevailing understanding and practice of the

monastic life in the Roman Catholic Church, it is impossible to continue to maintain the severe condemnation of them in the Augsburg Confession.[11] Both theologically and practically,[12] monastic forms of common life are a legitimate option for Catholics and Lutherans wishing to commit themselves to practising the gospel in this dedicated form, even though, at the present stage in the dialogue, certain details of interpretation still remain open, even within Lutheranism.

22. As far as the question of the episcopal office is concerned, here again it has to be noted that, in accord with the historic church, the Confessio Augustana specifically affirms its desire to maintain the episcopal structure. The assumption here was that the true proclamation of the gospel is helped and not hindered by this office. The Confessio Augustana affirms a ministry of unity and leadership set over the local ministers (CA XXVIII) as essential for the church, therefore, even if the actual form to be given to this ministerial office remains open.

23. Honesty in our dialogue on the Augsburg Confession also compels us to admit that there are still open questions and unresolved problems, among them the following:

— The Confessio Augustana does not adopt a position on the number of the sacraments, the papacy, or on certain aspects of the episcopal order and the church's teaching office.
— The Confessio Augustana naturally makes no mention of dogmas which have only been promulgated since 1530: the primacy of jurisdiction and the infallibility of the Pope (1870); the gracious preservation of the Virgin Mary from original sin (1854) and her bodily assumption into heaven (1950).

24. These questions will have to be considered in the future dialogue. We shall also have to examine the question of the weight to be given to the differences and open questions which still remain even as our churches move closer to one another, as well as the further question of the significance of the fact that some of these differences only acquired their sharpened contemporary form in recent centuries.

25. Our newly discovered agreement in central Christian truths gives good ground for the hope that in the light of this basic consensus answers will also be forthcoming to the still unsettled questions and problems, answers which will achieve the degree of unanimity required if our churches are to make a decisive advance from their present state of division to that of sister churches.

26. The Second Vatican Council summoned Catholics to "joyfully acknowledge and esteem the truly Christian endowments from our common

heritage"[13] which are found among Christians of other churches. That both Catholics and Lutherans have made a considerable advance along this road by their joint study of the Augsburg Confession is ground for joy and thanksgiving.

III

27. The common faith which we have discovered in the Augsburg Confession can also help us to confess this faith anew in our own times. This is the commission laid upon our churches by the ascended Lord and it is what we owe to the world and to humanity. This is also in harmony with the intention of the Augsburg Confession, concerned as it was in its time not only to maintain the unity of the church but also at the same time to witness to the truth of the gospel in its own time and its own world.

28. Faced as we are with new questions, challenges and opportunities in our world today, we cannot rest content with simply repeating and referring back to the confession of 1530. What we have rediscovered as an expression of our common faith cries out for fresh articulation. It points the way to a confession of our faith here and now, with Catholics and Lutherans no longer divided and in opposition to each other but bearing witness together to the message of the world's salvation in Jesus Christ and proclaiming this message as a renewed offer of the divine grace today.

CHAIRPERSONS

Hans L. Martensen   George A. Lindbeck
Bishop of Copenhagen   Professor, Yale University
Denmark   New Haven, USA

Augsburg, 23 February 1980

Notes

1. This is stressed in the Emperor's invitation to the Diet of Augsburg (1530) and taken up in the Preface to the Augsburg Confession, The Book of Concord, pp. 24f.
2. Reports of the official dialogue of Roman Catholics and Lutherans in the United States:
   Lutherans and Catholics in Dialogue I–III, edited by P. C. Empie and T. A. Murphy (Minneapolis: Augsburg Publishing House, 1965).
   "Eucharist and Ministry", *Lutherans and Catholics in Dialogue IV* (Washington, D. C. and New York, N.Y., 1970).
   "Papal Primacy and the Universal Church", *Lutherans and Catholics in Dia-*

Lutheran-Roman Catholic Conversations

logue V, edited by P. C. Empie and T. A. Murphy (Minneapolis: Augsburg Publishing House, 1974).
"Teaching Authority and Infallibility in the Church", *Lutherans and Catholics in Dialogue VI*, edited by P. C. Empie, T. A. Murphy, and J. A. Burgess (Minneapolis: Augsburg Publishing House, 1978, 1980).
The official world level Lutheran/Roman Catholic dialogue: Report of the Joint Lutheran/Roman Catholic Study Commission "The Gospel and the Church". *Lutheran World*, Vol. XIX, No. 3, 1972 (hereafter: Malta); Lutheran/Roman Catholic Joint Commission: *The Eucharist* (Geneva: Lutheran World Federation, 1980).
3. Cf. The Augsburg Confession (CA), XXI, The Book of Concord, p. 47.
4. Cf. *Confessio Augustana—Bekenntnis des einen Glaubens.* Gemeinsame Untersuchung katholischer und lutherischer Theologen. Edited by H. Meyer and H. Schütte, together with E. Iserloh, W. Kasper, G. Kretschmar, W. Lohff, G. W. Forell, J. McCue (Frankfurt/M.—Paderborn, 1980).
5. Cf. CA IV, VI and XX. The Book of Concord, pp. 30ff., 41ff.; Malta, Nos. 26 and 48.
6. Cf. Malta, Nos. 18ff. and 47ff.
7. Cf. *The Eucharist*
8. CA VII, 3, The Book of Concord, p. 32; cf. Malta, Nos. 47ff.
9. Cf. *The Eucharist*, Nos. 46-76.
10. Cf. ibid., Nos. 1-45, and The Liturgical Celebration of the Eucharist, pp. 29ff.
11. Cf. Vatican II, Decree on the Appropriate Renewal of the Religious Life.
12. Cf. the phenomenon of Protestant communes and communities resembling monastic orders.
13. Vatican II, Decree on Ecumenism, No. 4.

THE MINISTRY IN THE CHURCH, 1981

I. INTRODUCTION

1. The task of the Roman Catholic/Lutheran Joint Commission appointed by the Secretariat for Promoting Christian Unity and the Executive Committee of the Lutheran World Federation is to seek solutions to problems which the 1972 report on *The Gospel and the Church* (Malta Report) could not deal with or dealt with in insufficient detail and which have been noted as in need of further examination in evaluations of that report from both the Lutheran and the Catholic side.

2. As a first result of this task a document on the Lord's Supper, *The Eucharist,* was published in 1980. It expressed a joint witness and dealt with common problems that need further clarification.[1] Now, as promised in the document on the eucharist, the statement on *The Ministry in the Church,* with special reference to the episcopate, is presented. Greater agreement on the understanding of the eucharist requires the overcoming of hitherto existing differences concerning the ordained ministry; and this makes necessary joint consideration of episcopal ministry in order to remove the obstacles in this area to a Lutheran-Catholic *communio.*

3. The discussion of these problems needed to be focused and set within limits. It was possible to deal with fundamental christological and pneumatological questions quickly as here there are no major controversies between the two churches.[2] The same is not the case with respect to the theme of the papal office, which represents a serious problem between our churches. In view of the complexity of the exegetical and historical problems connected with this theme, a separate study needs to be devoted to it.[3] Reference will be made in the present document only to the place, the significance, and the problem of the Petrine office. This is possible because the Catholic attitude to the ministry of other churches, as illustrated by the Catholic position vis-à-vis the ministry of the Orthodox churches, is not directly dependent on the question of the primacy. So, too, the Lutheran understanding of ministry can be discussed without reference to the question of the papacy.

4. We have tried in our reflections not to lose sight of the ecumenical implications—the relationship to other churches—even if the problems we

---

[1] Lutheran/Roman Catholic Joint Commission, *The Eucharist,* Geneva, 1980.
[2] Cf. B. "Documentation of Ordination Liturgies."
[3] Cf. the various reports on the official theological conversations between representatives of the Lutheran and the Roman Catholic traditions in the USA:
— "Differing Attitudes Toward Papal Primacy", *Papal Primacy and the Universal Church,* edited by Paul C. Empie and T. Austin Murphy, Minneapolis, 1974, pp. 9–42.
— *Teaching Authority and Infallibility in the Church,* edited by Paul C. Empie, T. Austin Murphy, and Joseph A. Burgess, Minneapolis, 1978.

have touched upon are presented rather differently in other churches, as for example in the tradition of the Eastern churches.[4]

5. The matters we have dealt with must be seen not only in the context of Europe and North America. Urgent problems are arising in all parts of the world which are important for understanding the nature and tasks of the church's ministry. Social justice, racial equality, the dignity of the individual, improvement of basic living conditions (especially in the countries of the Third World), the creation of new forms of society—all these and many others are questions related to the proclamation of the gospel. Also the discussion of the longstanding differences between our churches must be viewed against the horizon of the challenges of today and must help to accomplish the missionary tasks that arise from them. Every step we are able to take in clearing away obstacles to the achievement of community between our churches will help us better to fulfil our Christian responsibilities toward the world.[5]

1. THE SAVING ACT OF GOD ACCOMPLISHED THROUGH JESUS CHRIST IN THE HOLY SPIRIT

1.1 Salvation Once for All

6. The saving act of God accomplished through Jesus Christ in the Holy Spirit is the common centre of our Christian faith. "Lutherans and Catholics share the conviction that we owe our salvation exclusively to the saving act of God accomplished once for all in Jesus Christ according to the witness of the gospel."[6] Christ's death on the cross and his resurrection is

---

[4]Cf. B. "Documentation of Ordination Liturgies," especially "Notes on the Character of the Ordination Liturgies."

[5]We are referring to the following ecumenical documents:
Agreed Statement of the Commission on Faith and Order of the World Council of Churches: "The Ministry", *One Baptism, One Eucharist and a Mutually Recognized Ministry*, Faith and Order Paper No. 73, Geneva, 1978[5], pp. 29–56; quoted: Accra. Reports on official Roman Catholic/Lutheran dialogues:
— Report on the Joint Lutheran/Roman Catholic Study Commission "The Gospel and the Church" (the so-called Malta Report), *Lutheran World*, Vol. XIX, No. 3, 1972, pp. 259–273; quoted: Malta.
— "Eucharist and Ministry", *Lutherans and Catholics in Dialogue*, Washington, D.C. and New York, N.Y., 1970, Vol. IV, pp. 7–33; quoted: USA IV.
— "Differing Attitudes Toward Papal Primacy", *Papal Primacy and the Universal Church*, op. cit.; quoted: USA V.
Texts of agreement issued by the Group of Les Dombes, France, consisting of French-speaking Roman Catholic, Lutheran and Reformed theologians:
— "Pour une réconciliation des ministères", Group des Dombes, Les Presses de Taizé, 1973; quoted: Dombes III.
— "Le ministère épiscopal", ibid., 1976; quoted: Dombes IV.
[6]Malta No. 48.

the climax of God's saving act for the redemption of the whole world. By his death Christ offered himself once for all in obedience to the Father for the sins of the world (Heb 9:26–28; 10:11f.). Jesus Christ is the only mediator between God and human beings (1 Tim 2:5). Through Jesus Christ "the world is reconciled to the Father in the communion of the Holy Spirit"[7].

7. As a result of Christ's exaltation, his saving act is valid and effective for the whole of humankind. Jesus Christ is therefore the high priest not just once, but once for all, who intercedes for his flock before the Father for all time (Heb 7:25). He is always the shepherd who gathers and guides his people; he is for ever the teacher of truth. As the glorified one, he remains present and active in history.

8. Jesus Christ is always present in his church through the outpouring of the Holy Spirit. It is the Holy Spirit who leads us ever deeper into the word and the work of Christ (Jn 14:20; 16:13). Through the Holy Spirit Christ grants us salvation, freedom, peace, reconciliation, justification and new life. Through the Holy Spirit we become a "new creation" in Christ (2 Cor 5:17; Gal 6:15). The Spirit himself is the gift of salvation.

9. The doctrine of the justification of sinners was the central point of controversy in the sixteenth century. "Today, however, a far-reaching consensus is developing in the interpretation of justification."[8] This consensus also helps us to see the earlier attempts to achieve unity in the doctrine of justification in a new light. Consequently, we now have a *joint starting point* for the question of the communication of salvation in history.

1.2 The Communication of Salvation in History

10. Just as Christ, in the Holy Spirit, was sent into the world by the Father, he now sends his disciples into the world so that in his name they bring the gospel to all humankind (Mt 28:19, Mk 16:15).[9] The promise and the outpouring of the Holy Spirit assures the apostles that they act in behalf of the risen Christ and not by their own strength.

11. "The witness of the gospel requires that there be witnesses to the gospel."[10] The ministry of reconciliation belongs also to the act of reconciliation. Through this "ministry of reconciliation" (2 Cor 5:18) the risen Lord makes us participate in his saving work accomplished once for all. In the Holy Spirit and by his messengers, Christ gathers his community on earth. The church is the community in which by faith the new life, reconciliation, justification and peace are received, lived, attested and thus communicated

---

[7]Accra No. 5.
[8]Malta No. 26.
[9]Cf. Accra No. 18; and the reading from Mt 28 in the ordination liturgies.
[10]Malta No. 48.

to humanity. The Holy Spirit enables and obliges the church to be an effective sign in the world of the salvation obtained through Christ.

12. The people of God called in this way is a people with a special mission in the world: "a holy priesthood, to offer spiritual sacrifices" and to "declare the wonderful deeds of him" (1 Pet 2:5–9). Under the one shepherd this people is held together in the unity of the Holy Spirit. Thus the church, as God's temple, is built with "living stones"; it is one body with many members and a diversity of gifts. "Membership in the community of the Church involves fellowship with God the Father through Jesus Christ, in the Holy Spirit."[11] The church is the recipient of salvation in Christ, and is at the same time sent with the authority of Christ to pass on the received salvation to the world. The community bears witness to the Lord "who was put to death for our trespasses and raised for our justification" (Rom 4:25); it offers to God the praise which humankind owes him as his due and it serves humankind in loving self-sacrifice.

13. *Martyria, leiturgia* and *diakonia* (witness, worship and service to the neighbour) are tasks entrusted to the whole people of God. All Christians have their own charismata for service to God and to the world as well as for building up of the one body of Christ (Rom 12:4–8; 1 Cor 12:4–31). Through baptism all constitute the one priestly people of God (1 Pet 2:5, 9; Rev 1:6; 5:10). All are called and sent to bear prophetic witness to the gospel of Jesus Christ, to celebrate the liturgy together and to serve humankind. This doctrine of the common priesthood of all the baptized is amply attested in the church fathers and the theologians of the High Middle Ages.[12] The Reformation was against emphasizing a special clerical class within the people of God and stressed the universal priesthood of the baptized.[13] In both our churches, consciousness of this calling of the whole people of God diminished greatly in recent centuries. In contemporary Protestant teaching regarding the church, the universal priesthood of all the

---

[11]Accra No. 4.

[12]Among others Thomas Aquinas, *Summa Theologica*, III q. 63 a. 1–3; Bonaventura, *Commentarium in Sententias*, IV, d. 6, p. 2, a. 3, q. 2, concl. 13.

[13]Note that "clergy" is not identical with "ordination". Cf. Decretum Gratiani C.XII, qu. 1 c. 7: "Duo sunt genera Christianorum. Est autem genus unum, quod mancipatum diuino offitio, et deditum contemplationi et orationi, ab omni strepitu temporalium cessare conuenit, ut sunt clerici, et Deo deuoti, uidelicet conuersi . . .
Aliud uero est genus Christianorum, ut sunt laici . . .
His licet temporalia possidere . . ." (E. A. Friedberg, Textkritische Ausgabe des Corpus Iuris Canonici, Leipzig 1879–81, Vol. I, 678).
"The acceptance into the clergy, which had become a privileged class, is not conferred by an ordination, but by the tonsure . . . All members of an order participate also in the rights of the clergy, even if they are no clergy or can never become clergy, as for example the nuns" (Wetzer-Welte, Kirchenlexikon, Freiburg[2] 1884, III 544f.). Cf. Works of Martin Luther, Philadelphia Edition, II, 66 (. . . priests and monks).

baptized is once again stressed. The Second Vatican Council expressly emphasized the common priesthood of the faithful.[14]

14. Within this priestly people of God, Christ—acting through the Holy Spirit—confers manifold ministries: apostles, prophets, evangelists, pastors and teachers "to equip the saints for the work of ministry, for building up the body of Christ" (Eph 4:11f.). Called into the ministry of reconciliation, and as those being entrusted the word of reconciliation, they are "ambassadors in Christ's stead" (cf. 2 Cor 5:18–20);[15] yet they are not lords over the faith but ministers of joy (2 Cor 1:24). They render their service in the midst of the whole people and for the people of God which, as a whole, is the "one, holy, catholic and apostolic Church".

15. The doctrine of the common priesthood of all the baptized and of the serving character of the ministries in the church and for the church represents in our day a *joint starting point* for Lutherans and Catholics in their attempt to clarify as yet open problems regarding the understanding of the ordained ministry in the church.

2. THE ORDAINED MINISTRY IN THE CHURCH

2.1 Apostolic Origin and Missionary Openness

16. The church stands once for all on the foundation of the apostles.[16] It was the exalted Lord himself who sent the apostles into the world to proclaim the gospel. This special mission of theirs is therefore unique and cannot be transferred. The post-apostolic church must forever maintain its relation to its apostolic beginning. The doctrine of the apostolic succession[17] underscores the permanently normative character of the apostolic origin while at the same time intending to insist on the continuance of the missionary task.

17. In addition to their unique function in founding the church, the apostles also had a responsibility for building up and leading the first communities, a ministry that later had to be continued.[18] The New Testament shows how there emerged from among the ministries a special ministry which was understood as standing in the succession of the apostles sent by Christ. Such a special ministry proved to be necessary for the sake of leadership in the communities. One can, therefore, say that according to the New Testament

---

[14]Vatican II, Dogmatic Constitution on the Church, Nos. 10–12; Decree on the Apostolate of the Laity, Nos. 2–4.
[15]Cf. the readings from 2 Cor 5 and Eph 4 foreseen in several ordination liturgies.
[16]Cf. Malta No. 52.
[17]Cf. chapter 3.4 below.
[18]Accra No. 13.

the "special ministry" established by Jesus Christ through the calling and sending of the apostles "was essential then—it is essential in all times and circumstances"[19]. For Lutherans and Catholics it is an open theological problem as to how one theologically defines more exactly the relationship of the one special ministry to the various other ministries and services in the church, and whether, therefore, and to what extent some of the characteristics attributed to the special ministry in what follows also belong analogously to other ministries and services. Yet Lutherans and Catholics start from the common conviction that the trend towards the emergence of the special ministry which finds expression in the New Testament is of normative significance for the post-apostolic church.

18. The special ministry and the other manifold ministries in the church take shape according to existing historical structures and thus respond to the respective missionary needs of the church. Thus while the existence of a special ministry is abidingly constitutive for the church, its concrete form must always remain open to new actualizations.[20]

2.2 The Christological and Pneumatological Dimension

19. In the New Covenant Jesus Christ is the one Lord, the one priest, the one shepherd and the one mediator between God and human beings. In the Holy Spirit he is ever present in the church to realize his word and his work. He is present through the church as a whole and through all its members. Through baptism all the members jointly constitute the one priestly people of God (1 Pet 2:5, 9; Rev 1:6).

20. Within the church, there is a diversity of services and charismata of the Holy Spirit which jointly bear witness to Jesus Christ, and all together serve to build up the one body of Christ (1 Cor 12:4–31). Paul testifies that God has given the first place in the church to the apostles; but at the same time he indicates that within the manifold structure of charismata the gift of leadership also has its place (1 Cor 12:28). In the pastoral epistles, a ministry of leadership is already clearly identifiable (1 Tim 3:1; 4:14; 2 Tim 1:6; Tit 1:6f.). The ministry in the early church developed on the basis of such a variety of New Testament starting points.[21] In continuous relation to the normative apostolic tradition, it makes present the mission of Jesus Christ. The presence of this ministry in the community "signifies the priority of divine initiative and authority in the Church's existence"[22].

---

[19]Ibid.
[20]Cf. Malta Nos. 54–56.
[21]As regards the participation of the manifold ministries in the service of Christ, see Nos. 14 and 17 above.
[22]Accra No. 14.

Consequently, this ministry is not simply a delegation "from below", but is instituted by Jesus Christ.[23]

21. The ministry in the church is, therefore, subordinated to the one ministry of Jesus Christ. It is Jesus Christ who, in the Holy Spirit, is acting in the preaching of the Word of God, in the administration of the sacraments, and in the pastoral service. Jesus Christ, acting in the present, takes the minister into his service; the minister is only his tool and instrument. Jesus Christ is the one and only high priest of the New Covenant. When ministers are described as priests in the Catholic tradition, this is to be understood only in the sense that in the Holy Spirit they share in and manifest the one priesthood of Jesus Christ.[24] In the Lutheran church, the minister has not ordinarily been termed a priest, but the purpose has been to avoid obscuring the distinction between the priesthood of Christ by which God has reconciled the world to himself and the service of the minister. According to the understanding of both traditions, the minister does not have "power" over Christ during the consecration when celebrating the eucharist, but he speaks on behalf of and in the name of Jesus Christ: "this is my body"—"this is my blood". Jesus Christ himself speaks and acts through him.[25] This ministry is therefore performed in the communion of the Holy Spirit through Jesus Christ to the honour of the Father.

22. The christologically based authority (*exousia*) of the ministry must be exercised in the Holy Spirit. The minister must bring Christ's cross into the present not only through his words and the administration of the sacraments, but through his whole life and his service (2 Cor 4:8–18; 11:22–33). The church's ministers must constantly look afresh to Jesus Christ and be renewed by him. They must also heed the Spirit which acts in the other members of the church. The ministers as well as the other church members are dependent day by day on the renewed forgiveness of their sins. Following the example of Jesus Christ, the ministry in the church cannot claim any worldly advantages, but must rather be characterized by radical obedience and service.[26]

---

[23]When Vatican II affirms that the ordained ministry differs from the common priesthood of all the baptized in essence and not only in degree (Dogmatic Constitution on the Church, No. 10), this formulation wants to say the following: the church ministry cannot be derived from the congregation, but it is also not an enhancement of the common priesthood, and the minister as such is not a Christian to a greater degree. The ministry is rather situated on a different level; it includes the ministerial priesthood which is interrelated with the common priesthood.
[24]See Yves Congar, "One Mediator."
[25]Apology of the Augsburg Confession VII, 28 and 47f., The Book of Concord, pp. 173 and 177; Formula of Concord, Solid Declaration VII, 75ff., The Book of Concord, pp. 583f; Vatican II, Constitution on the Sacred Liturgy, No. 7; Decree on the Ministry and Life of Priests, No. 5; cf. also the relation of the celebration of the Lord's Supper to the ordination in the ordination liturgies.
[26]As a sign of this availability for Christ and for the congregation the Latin Church considers in general the celibacy of priests as a condition for ordination. However, it does not understand

2.3 Ministry and Community

23. For Lutherans and Catholics it is fundamental to a proper understanding of the ministerial office that "the office of the ministry stands over against the community as well as within the community"[27]. Inasmuch as the ministry is exercised on behalf of Jesus Christ and makes him present, it has authority over against the community. "He who hears you hears me" (Lk 10:16).[28] The authority of the ministry must therefore not be understood as delegated by the community.

24. This authority of the ministry is however not to be understood as an individual possession of the minister, but it is rather an authority with the commission to serve in the community and for the community. Therefore, the exercise of the authority of the ministry should involve the participation of the whole community. This applies also to the appointment of the ministers.[29] The ordained minister "manifests and exercises the authority of Christ in the way Christ himself revealed God's authority to the world: in and through *communion*"[30]. For this reason the ministry must not suppress Christian freedom and fraternity, but should rather promote them.[31] The Christian freedom, fraternity and responsibility of the whole church and of all its members must find its expression in the conciliar, collegial and synodical structures of the church.

25. The church is called to present the image of a society molded by God's recreating Spirit. This must also be evident in the form of the community of men and women in the church. Both men and women can make a specific contribution within the ministry of the people of God. The church needs the special form of ministry which can be exercised by women just as it needs that exercised by men. "Since in our times women have an ever more active share in the whole life of society, it is very important that they participate more widely also in the various fields of the Church's apostolate."[32] In this context the question of the entrance of women into the ordained ministry arises. Different answers are given to this question in our respective churches and it poses a problem that is not yet solved. In all efforts to reach a common understanding, the significance of theological hermeneutics be-

---

it as demanded by the nature of the priesthood (cf. Vatican II, Decree on the Ministry and Life of Priests, No. 16). The Reformation has opposed this order in the name of Christian freedom (cf. Confessio Augustana [quoted: CA] XXIII and XXVIII, The Book of Concord, pp. 51ff. and 81ff.). This does not exclude that the Lutheran church knows celibacy as a personal call.
[27]Malta No. 50.
[28]As regards the interpretation, cf. CA XXVIII, 22, The Book of Concord, p. 84; Apology of the Augsburg Confession VII, 28 and 47f., The Book of Concord, pp. 173 and 177.
[29]Cf. No. 34 below.
[30]Accra No. 18.
[31]Cf. also Vatican II, Dogmatic Constitution on the Church, Nos. 18, 30, 32.
[32]Vatican II, "Decree on the Apostolate of the Laity, No. 9; cf. Congregation for the Doctrine of the Faith, "Declaration on the Admission of Women to the Ministerial Priesthood", 13 October 1976, introduction (Acta Apostolicae Sedis 1977, 99).

comes obvious. The question of the ordination of women cannot be regarded as simply a special point in the theology of the ministry, but is related indissolubly to a number of other prior theological decisions. The divergence of opinions in the churches with regard to this question does not coincide completely with the confessional boundaries.

It can be said that in general the *Lutheran* churches which have introduced the ordination of women do not intend a change of either the dogmatic understanding or the exercise of the ministerial office. Since the new practice of ordination of women is spreading in the Lutheran churches, it is becoming more and more necessary to intensify the dialogue both between conflicting views within Lutheranism and with the Catholic church.

The *Catholic* church according to its practice and doctrine does not see itself in a position to admit women to ordination. Nevertheless it is able to strive for a consensus on the nature and significance of the ministry without the different conceptions of the persons to be ordained fundamentally endangering such a consensus and its practical consequences for the growing unity of the church.[33]

2.4 The Function of the Ministry

26. In the past Catholics and Lutherans had different starting points when defining the ordained ministry. The Reformers protested against tendencies in the Middle Ages to emphasize almost exclusively the sacramental functions of the ministry of the priest, particularly the offering of the sacrifice of the mass.[34] They emphasized as task of the ministry the proclamation of the gospel in which word and sacrament are closely connected with each other.

---

[33]Cf. H. Legrand/J. Vikström: "The Admission of Women to the Ministry." This article is recommended for thorough study as a helpful theological orientation and introduction to the entire question of the ordination of women.

[34]In the Middle Ages since the 12th century there has been a change in the emphasis of the understanding of the ministry because of an exchange of the content of *corpus Christi mysticum* (mystical body of the church instead of sacramental body) and *corpus Christi verum* (real presence of Christ's body in the eucharist instead of church as body of Christ). The function of the ministry is directed primarily (*principaliter*) to the presence of the real body of Christ in the sacrament of the eucharist and no longer primarily to the church as body of Christ, so that now the offering of the sacrifice of the mass is understood as central function of the priest. J. Altenstaig, Vocabularius theologiae, Hagenau 1517, Sacerdos: "Sacerdos Evangelicus est, qui ex traditione Episcopi acceptit in sua ordinatione potestatem super corpus Christi verum in altaris sacrificio conficiendum, offerendum et populo dispensandum. Et super corpus Christi mysticum ad membra huius corporis incorporandum . . ."; Thomas Aquinas, Sent. 1. IV/ dist. 24, qu. 1, art. 3, sol. II ad 1; ibid. qu. 3, art. 2, sol. I. Cf. H. de Lubac, Corpus mysticum, Paris[2] 1949. J. Ratzinger, *Das neue Volk Gottes,* Düsseldorf, 1969, 98f. Against the background of a certain doctrine of the sacrifice of the mass which was opposed by Luther, the Reformation rejects the definition of the priest as sacrificer (cf. Apology XIII, 7f., The Book of Concord, p. 212).

27. The *medieval understanding of the ministry* remained influential in the *Council of Trent* which placed the emphasis primarily on the administration of the sacraments. Yet the Tridentine decrees are meant positively and not exclusively: according to the Council of Trent the proclamation of the gospel is included in the task of the ministry.[35] The Second Vatican Council highlighted three basic functions: the proclamation of the word, the administration of the sacraments, and pastoral ministry.[36] The pastoral ministry includes service of unity in the congregation and between congregations. In contemporary Catholic theology this service often constitutes the starting point for understanding the ministry of the church as a whole; for through the word and sacrament the church is built up as the one body of Christ in the Holy Spirit.[37]

28. The Catholic teaching that the ordained ministry is of constitutive importance for the celebration of the eucharist can also be understood in terms of the service of unity.[38] The eucharist is the sacrament of unity; it is the source and climax of the whole life of the church.[39] Therefore the ministerial service of unity belongs to the full reality of the eucharistic mystery.[40]

29. The *Reformation* was critical of an understanding of the ministry as a sacrificial priesthood because this seemed to endanger the once-and-for-all validity of the high priestly ministry of Christ.[41] "According to the Lutheran Confessions, it is the task of the ministerial office to proclaim the gospel and administer the sacraments in accordance with the gospel, so that in this way faith is awakened"[42], and the community of Christ is built up. The unity of the church is thereby based on the right proclamation of the gospel and the right administration of the sacraments.[43] Included in this commission is the

---

[35]Council of Trent, Sessio XXIII, De reformatione, Canones I, XIV (Conciliorum Oecumenicorum Decreta, Ed. G. Alberigo et alii, Freiburg, Br., 1962, 720, 725); H. Denzinger/A. Schönmetzer, Enchiridion Symbolorum definitionum et declarationum de rebus fidei et morum, Freiburg, Br.,³⁴ 1965 (quoted: DS) 1764, 1771, 1777.

[36]Vatican II, Decree on the Ministry and Life of Priests, Nos. 4 and 6.

[37]Synod of Bishops, Rome 1971, Acta Apostolicae Sedis, Vol. LXIII, 1971, 898–922. Letter of the German bishops about the priestly ministry. Herder-Korrespondenz, Trier, 1969, No. 45. Joint Synod of the Dioceses in the Federal Republic of Germany, *Die pastoralen Dienste in der Gemeinde,* Nos. 2.51; 5.11 (Offizielle Gesamtausgabe I, Freiburg, Basel, Wien, 1976).

[38]Lateran Council IV, DS 802; Council of Trent, DS 1764, 1771; Vatican II, Dogmatic Constitution on the Church, No. 17; Decree on the Ministry and Life of Priests, No. 5.

[39]Lateran Council IV, ibid.; Vatican II, Dogmatic Constitution on the Church, No. 11.

[40]Vatican II, Decree on Ecumenism, No. 22.

[41]In the document *The Eucharist* the Lutheran/Roman Catholic Joint Commission has dealt extensively with the controversial question of the mass as sacrifice and has reached considerable convergence. Cf. *The Eucharist,* Nos. 56–62 and Supplementary Studies, 4, pp. 76ff. Consequently it is possible to see in a new light the Catholic understanding of the ministry in its relationship to the mass as sacrifice.

[42]Cf. Malta No. 61; cf. also the Lutheran ordination formulae II, III, VII, XI, XII.

[43]CA VII, The Book of Concord, p. 32.

authority to forgive sins and to retain sins. For this a special ministry was instituted by God.[44] To that extent the ministry, also in the Lutheran understanding of it, serves the unity of the church and is one of its fundamental marks.

30. From this derives the importance of the ministry for the celebration of the Lord's Supper. It is true that in the doctrine of the Lord's Supper only the performance of the action according to the Lord's institution is mentioned as essential for validity and as a presupposition for Christ's real presence. The ministry itself is not mentioned. According to the Confessio Augustana V, however, the ministry is presupposed for the administration of the sacraments. According to the Confessio Augustana XIV this ministry of public proclamation and administration of the sacraments is exercised only by those who have been duly called, i.e., as would be said today, by ordained ministers. "Wherever the ministry of the church is to be exercised, ordination is essential."[45] This affirmation does not only reflect disciplinary considerations, but rather has substantive significance for the public manifestation of unity of the church.

31. Our churches are thus able today to declare _in common_ that the essential and specific function of the ordained minister is to assemble and build up the Christian community by proclaiming the word of God, celebrating the sacraments and presiding over the liturgical, missionary and diaconal life of the community.[46]

2.5 Sacramental Nature of Ordination

32. Since apostolic times the calling to special ministry in the church has taken place through the laying on of hands and through prayer in the midst of the congregation assembled for worship.[47] In this way the ordained person is received into the apostolic ministry of the church and into the community of ordained ministers. At the same time, through the laying on of hands and through prayer (_epiklesis_), the gift of the Holy Spirit is offered and conveyed for the exercise of ministry. On the basis of such an understanding of and practice of ordination the possibility of substantial convergence between the two churches is open.[48]

33. The _Catholic_ tradition speaks of this act of the church, in which the Holy Spirit works through word and signs, as a sacrament. In the Catholic

---

[44]CA V, The Book of Concord, p. 31.
[45]Statement by the Theological Committee of the United Evangelical Lutheran Church in Germany (VELKD) on the question of the church ministry and ordination, 13 October 1970, _Amt und Ordination im Verständnis evangelischer Kirchen und ökumenischer Gespräche_, A. Burgmüller and R. Frieling (ed.), Gütersloh, 1974, 73 (B 3 b).
[46]Cf. Accra No. 15.
[47]Cf. Ordination liturgies, imposition of hands during the prayer for the Holy Spirit (_epiklesis_).
[48]Cf. Malta No. 59.

church this sacramental understanding of ordination is binding.[49] The *Lutheran* tradition uses a more restricted concept of sacrament and therefore does not speak of the sacrament of ordination. Yet in principle a sacramental understanding of the ministry is not rejected.[50] Wherever it is taught that through the act of ordination the Holy Spirit gives grace strengthening the ordained person for the life-time ministry of word and sacrament, it must be asked whether differences which previously divided the churches on this question have not been overcome. For both Catholics and Lutherans it is incompatible with this understanding of ordination to see ordination merely as a mode or manner of ecclesiastical appointment or installation in office.[51]

34. This *fundamental mutual understanding* also leads Catholics and Lutherans to common statements about the minister of ordination. Ordination is primarily the act of the exalted Lord who moves, strengthens and blesses the ordained person through the Holy Spirit.[52] Since the ministry expresses the priority of the divine initiative, and since in the service of unity it stands in and between the local churches, its transmission takes place through those who are already ordained. Thus the fact that ministers can perform the service of unity only in community with other ordained ministers is expressed in this way.[53] It is also important, however, that the congregation be involved in the calling and appointment of ministers because the ministry is for the congregation and must carry out its mission in concert with the whole congregation.

35. In the *Lutheran* tradition the view is held that a congregation in situations of extreme need can entrust one of its members with the ministry. This outlook is connected with the sixteenth-century experience.[54] Yet, without prejudice to this view, in practice ordination according to the constitutional regulations of the Lutheran churches takes place in conformity with the above mentioned principles.

2.6 Uniqueness of Ordination

36. By means of ordination Christ calls the ordained person once and for all into the ministry in his church. Both in the Catholic and in the Lutheran understanding, therefore, ordination can be received only once and cannot be repeated. Ordination must be distinguished from commissioning to service in a particular congregation. Commissioning can be repeated and, in certain circumstances, can be withdrawn. This distinction between ordination given once for all and a commissioning, which is repeatable, to ministry

---

[49]DS 1766; 1773.
[50]Apology of the Augsburg Confession XIII, 11, The Book of Concord, p. 212.
[51]Statement by the Theological Committee of the VELKD (manuscript of the Lutheran church office of the VELKD, Hanover, 1976), Nos. 3 and 4.
[52]Accra No. 14.
[53]See chapter 3.1 below.
[54]Cf. Nos. 42f. below.

in a specific congregation is a distinction in many ways comparable to that between *ordo* and *iurisdictio.*[55]

37. Both distinctions, to be sure, raise problems that have not yet been satisfactorily resolved on either side. In the *Catholic* tradition, the mission transmitted once for all was expressed in ontological categories in the doctrine of the *character indelebilis.*[56] The relation with baptism and confirmation, which also impresses a spiritual sign which cannot be destroyed and taken away, is thereby emphasized. This means that God's calling and commissioning subjects the ordained person for all time to the promise and the claims of God. This doctrine was sometimes mistakenly materialized. Moreover, there was often the danger of seeing the ordination of priests as primarily a means for personal sanctification. In contemporary Catholic doctrinal statements, the *character indelebilis* is again understood more in terms of the promise and mission which permanently mark the ordained and claim them for the service of Christ.[57]

38. In the *Lutheran* tradition, polemical reaction against the idea of a so to speak "free-floating" ministry, completely separated from the people of God, has partly contributed towards ignoring the distinction between ordination and installation into a concrete ministry. Thus the conviction has been expressed that in principle ministry and congregation cannot be separated, but must be related to each other. Yet in the area of the Lutheran Reformation general ordination, not limited to a particular congregation, has usually been practised. In the Lutheran view, the renewed distinction between ordination and installation expresses the conviction that the ministry of proclaiming the gospel is not in principle restricted in time and space, but is for the whole church. In the same way, the individual local congregation cannot be thought of as isolated and autonomous when it comes to the conferring of the ministerial office. The call to the ministry of preaching and administering the sacraments, which takes place in the name of Christ, can only occur in the context of the ministry as instituted for the whole church. For the same reason, the repetition of ordination is opposed. In the Lutheran understanding also, ordination to the ministry of the church on behalf of Christ, conferred in the power of the Holy Spirit, is for life and is not subject to temporal limitations. Thus even if one avoids the use of the concept of the *character indelebilis* because of its ontological implications, the act of

---

[55]The complex problem of *ordo* and *iurisdictio* cannot be dealt with in detail here.

[56]DS 1313, 1609, 1767, 1774; Vatican II, Dogmatic Constitution on the Church, No. 21.

[57]Cf. the letter of the German bishops about the priestly ministry, op. cit., No. 33; cf. also Malta No. 60. The "character *indelebilis*" shows that the three sacraments of baptism, confirmation and ordination cannot be repeated. Cf. Conc. Trid. Sess. VII, Can. 9: "In tribus sacramentis, baptismo, confirmatione et ordinatione . . . characterem in anima, hoc est signum quoddam spirituale et indelebile, unde ea iteri non possunt" (DS 1609). The "character *indelebilis*" is also a gift of the Spirit (DS 1774).

ordination is characterized by a uniqueness which cannot be given up. It remains valid even if the service of a specific congregation is abandoned.

39. Wherever there exists this understanding of an ordination that is imparted once and for all and where one-sidedness and distortions have been overcome, it is possible to speak of a *consensus* on the reality.

3. The Various Forms of Ministry

3.1 *Historical Development*

40. Both churches distinguish various ministries. However, they theologically evaluate these distinctions in different ways.

41. *Catholic* teaching starts from the development in the ancient church. While there are differences in the ways in which the New Testament speaks about the episcopal and presbyteral ministry, it was not until the second century that the threefold division of the ministry into episcopate, presbyterate and diaconate emerged.[58]

When the area of the episcopate later on became larger, the structure of the local congregation of the bishop became internally differentiated. The presbyters, on behalf of the bishop, acquired functions in congregations within the episcopal diocese which were originally exercised by the bishop (especially celebrating the eucharist and baptizing). Through this internal differentiation of the episcopal local congregation, the local episcopal ministry also became in practice a ministry of regional government.

In the late Middle Ages the distinction between bishop and presbyter was seen almost exclusively from the point of view of jurisdiction.[59] In addition it was of far-reaching practical importance that spiritual and secular power were generally intermingled in the episcopal office in the Middle Ages. For all these reasons, the relationship between episcopate and presbyterate long remained unclarified. Jerome's opinion that bishops and priests were originally one and the same also played a role and was later referred to by the Lutheran Confessional Writings.[60]

The Second Vatican Council for the first time introduced greater clarity on this point in the Roman Catholic Church. The Council tried to do justice to the development of the ancient church by calling the diocese over which the

---

[58]Cf. Malta No. 55.

[59]Cf. Huguccio, Summa d. 95 c. 1; Petrus Aureoli, Sent. IV d. 24 q. un. a. 2 prop. 2 (fol. 163 a–b). See also Thomas Aquinas, S. Th. Suppl. q. 40 a. 4 Respondeo; Super IV lib. Sententiarum 4, d 17, q. 3, a 3, q. 5 Solutio.

[60]Articles of Christian doctrine, The Smalcald Articles, Part II, IV, The Book of Concord, pp. 298 ff.; Treatise on the Power and Primacy of the Pope, 59–73, The Book of Concord, pp. 330 ff.

bishop presides a "local congregation".[61] Accordingly, the fullness of the ministry belongs to the bishop alone; the sacramental character of the episcopal consecration is expressly affirmed by the Council.[62] According to the teaching of the Council the presbyters in exercising their ministry depend on the bishop; they are co-workers, helpers and instruments of the bishop and form in community with their bishop a single presbyterate.[63] Yet even after the Second Vatican Council, questions regarding the more precise determination of the relationship of episcopate and presbyterate still remain open.

42. The *Lutheran Confessions* wanted to retain the episcopal polity of the church and with it the differentiation of the ministerial office[64] on the condition that the bishops grant freedom and opportunity for the right proclamation of the gospel and the right administration of the sacraments and not prevent these by the formal requirement of obedience. The fact that it was impossible at this time to arrive at an agreement in doctrine and to persuade the bishops to ordain Reformation ministers led perforce to forsaking continuity with previous order. In this emergency situation the installation of ministers by non-episcopal ministers or even by the congregation appeared legitimate provided it took place *rite,* i.e., publicly and in the name of the whole church.[65] Moreover, the appointment of inspectors was equivalent to a recognition of the need for a ministry of leadership and of pastoral supervision (*episcopé*).[66] It was provided for in the German area through the function of the territorial princes as "emergency bishops"[67] and by the appointment of inspectors under various titles (superintendent, *propst,* etc.)[68].

43. In view of the emergency situation, the Lutheran Confessions avoided prescribing any specific form of *episcopé* in the sense of regional church leadership. Episcopacy, to be sure, was normal at least for the Confessio Augustana. The loss of this office in its historic character has nevertheless had certain consequences for the Lutheran understanding of the church's ministerial structure. The Lutheran office of pastor, comparable to that of presbyter, has really taken over the spiritual functions of the bishop's office[69]

---

[61]Vatican II, Dogmatic Constitution on the Church, No. 26; Decree on the Bishops' Pastoral Office in the Church, No. 11.
[62]Ibid., Dogmatic Constitution on the Church, Nos. 21 and 26.
[63]Ibid., No. 28.
[64]Apology of the Augsburg Confession XIV, 1, The Book of Concord, p. 214; CA XXVIII, 69, The Book of Concord, p. 93.
[65]CA XIV, The Book of Concord, p. 36.
[66]Cf. Dombes IV, No. 2.
[67]The princes, of course, never exercised the religious supervisory function in the strict sense but delegated it to visitors.
[68]I. Asheim and Victor R. Gold (ed.), *Episcopacy in the Lutheran Church?* Philadelphia, 1970.
[69]USA IV, No. 21.

and was even at times theologically interpreted as identical with it. This was seen as a return to an earlier ministerial structure in church history in which the bishop's office was a local one. Within this context the function of *episcopé* was retained as necessary for the church; but its concrete ordering was taken to be a human and historical matter.[70] The holders of this superordinated office are at present given a variety of titles; bishop, church president, superintendent. In some Lutheran areas, where this was possible, the historical continuity of the episcopal office has been maintained.

44. We are, therefore, confronted with the empirical fact that in both churches there are local congregational ministries (priest, pastor) as well as also superordinated regional ministries. These regional ministries have the function of pastoral supervision and of service of unity within a larger area. These functions are connected with the commission to preach, administer the sacraments and lead the congregation, and involve teaching and doctrinal discipline, ordination, supervision, church order and in western Catholic practice (which in this respect, however, is clearly different from that of the Eastern as well as Lutheran churches) also confirmation. These tasks are entrusted to local ministries only in exceptional circumstances. In the two churches there thus exists a significant convergence as regards the actual character of ecclesical practice.

3.2 The Theological Distinction between Episcopate and Presbyterate, i.e., between Bishop and Pastor

45. The existence of local congregational ministries and superordinated regional ministries on both sides is for both churches more than the result of purely historical and human developments or a matter of sociological necessity. Rather, they recognize here the action of the Spirit as this has been experienced and attested from the very beginnings of the church. The development of the one ministry of the church into different ministries can be understood as having an intimate connection with the nature of the church. The church is actualized at different levels: as the local church (congregation), as the church of a larger region or country, and as the universal church. At each of these levels, albeit in different forms, it is essential that the ministry be both "in and over against" the ecclesial community.[71] There is thus a noteworthy structural parallelism between the two churches.

---

[70]"According to divine right, therefore, it is the office of the bishop to preach the Gospel, forgive sins, judge doctrine and condemn doctrine that is contrary to the Gospel, and exclude from the Christian community the ungodly whose wicked conduct is manifest. On this account parish ministers and churches are bound to be obedient to the bishops according to the saying of Christ in Luke 10:16. On the other hand, if they teach, introduce or institute anything contrary to the Gospel, we have God's command not to be obedient in such cases" (CA XXVIII, 21ff.) The Book of Concord, p. 84.

[71]At the level of the universal church, moreover, there also arise some special problems; cf. chapter 3.5 below.

46. The Catholic and Lutheran traditions nevertheless give different descriptions and theological evaluations of the development of the one ministry.

47. In respect to the one apostolic office, the *Lutheran* tradition does make a distinction between bishop and pastor so far as the geographical area of ministry is concerned. Traditionally this distinction has been described as one of human law. At the same time it recognizes that the *episcopé* is indispensable for historical unity and continuity. It was for this reason that after the loss of the link with the historic episcopate, a new structuring of *episcopé* was needed.

48. The *Catholic* tradition makes a theological distinction between bishop and priest (episcopate and presbyterate). The Council of Trent held that this distinction exists *divina ordinatione,*[72] and thereby deliberately avoided the term *de iure divino.* All that the Second Vatican Council says is that this distinction has existed from antiquity (*ab antiquo*).[73] Nevertheless, the Catholic tradition also speaks of only one single sacrament of orders in which bishop, priest and deacon share in different ways.

49. *If* both churches acknowledge that for faith this historical development of the one apostolic ministry into a more local and a more regional ministry has taken place with the help of the Holy Spirit and to this degree constitutes something essential for the church, then a *high degree of agreement* has been reached.

3.3 *Teaching Ministry and Teaching Authority*

50. In the *Catholic* teaching the most eminent task of the bishops consists of the preaching of the gospel.[74] In this the bishops are both preachers of the faith and authentic teachers of the faith.[75] They do not stand above the Word of God, but serve it; they have to listen to it devoutly, guard it scrupulously, and interpret it faithfully.[76] They should bear witness to the glad tidings in a manner adapted to the needs of the times, i.e., to speak to the difficulties and questions by which people are burdened and troubled. But they should also protect the Good News and defend it against omissions and falsifications. They should show how closely the church's teaching is connected with the dignity of human persons, their freedom and their rights, with the questions of peace and of the just distribution of earthly goods among all peoples.[77]

---

[72]DS 1776.
[73]Vatican II, Dogmatic Constitution on the Church, No. 28. As regards the problem and the meaning of the term *ius divinum,* cf. Malta Nos. 31–34.
[74]Council of Trent, op. cit., Sessio XXIV, Can. IV, 739.
[75]Vatican II, Dogmatic Constitution on the Church, No. 25.
[76]Ibid., Dogmatic Constitution on Divine Revelation, No. 10.
[77]Ibid., Decree on the Bishops' Pastoral Office in the Church, No. 12.

51. The bishops can discharge this task only in community with the whole church. For the entire people of God participates in the prophetic office of Christ; the entire people of God receives the supernatural sense of the faith from the Holy Spirit.[78] Priests share Christ's prophetic office in a special manner; they are co-workers in the preaching and teaching ministry of the bishops.[79] If the bishops are to perform their functions, especially today, they also need the collaboration of theologians. The theologians must intellectually investigate the faith by interpreting it on the basis of the witness of Holy Scripture and of the church tradition and by making it accessible to contemporary minds. For this they need adequate freedom within the church. The teaching ministry of the bishops, therefore, takes place in a many-sided exchange regarding faith with believers, priests, and theologians.

52. When controversies endanger the unity of faith in the church, the bishops have both the right and the duty to make binding decisions. On those matters where the bishops interpret the revealed faith in universal agreement with each other and in communion with the Bishop of Rome, their witness has final authority and infallibility.[80] Such infallible decisions, however, in order to be juridically valid, do not need a special formal consent by the totality of the local congregations of the faithful, but they depend on extensive reception in order to have living power and spiritual fruitfulness in the church.

53. In the *Lutheran* view the office of the bishop is "to preach the Gospel, forgive sins, judge doctrine and condemn doctrine that is contrary to the Gospel". The holders of the episcopal office are therefore entrusted in a special manner with the task of watching over the purity of the gospel, and this involves a teaching ministry which should be carried out "not by human power but by God's Word alone"[81].

54. Given the situation created by the Reformation, it was in actual fact the theologians who fulfilled this teaching function, above all in the formulation of the Confessions. Thus the theological faculties and with them the officials charged with supervising church affairs became the authorities in formulating doctrine, even though doctrinal decisions acquired legal status through the action of the territorial princes as "emergency bishops". Always, however, the binding character of doctrine became manifest through the process of reception in which each adult Christian, as receiver of the Spirit, was accorded, at least in dogmatic principle, full power of authority to judge teaching.

---

[78]Ibid., Dogmatic Constitution on the Church, No. 12.
[79]Ibid., Decree on the Ministry and Life of Priests, No. 4
[80]Ibid., Dogmatic Constitution on the Church, No. 25.
[81]CA XXVIII, 21ff., The Book of Concord, p. 84.

55. Also in our day there is interpretation and development of church doctrine in Lutheran churches through the decisions of the appropriate ecclesial authorities (synods, church authorities, etc.) A decisive part in these is played by teachers of theology together with non-ordained church members and ordained ministers. Such decisions have the purpose of serving the contemporary proclamation and unity of the church. Yet here there appear a number of difficult problems. University theology has sometimes become remote from the life of the church. In other cases there have been doubts that there is any need for a further binding development. Even where such further development is considered necessary, appropriate means are often lacking, or there is not enough clarity about the teaching competence of existing agencies.

56. The Lutheran churches are therefore confronted with the need to rethink the problem of the teaching office and the teaching authority. The question of the function of the episcopal ministry arises especially in this connection. On the other hand, the significance of the reception of doctrinal statements by the community and the competence of the community to judge in questions of faith must be considered.

57. *In both churches* there thus exists a teaching responsibility at a supra-congregational level, which, of course, is performed in different ways. But one can recognize a certain parallelism between the two churches. In both churches, teaching responsibility is tied to the whole church's witness to the faith. Both churches know that their norm is the gospel. Both churches are faced by the question of the nature and the binding character of doctrinal decisions. The treatment of this problem constitutes a common task, in which particular attention will have to be paid to the question of infallibility.

58. Already today Catholics and Lutherans can *join* in saying "that the Holy Spirit unceasingly leads and keeps the church in the truth". "The church's abiding in the truth should not be understood in a static way, but as a dynamic event which takes place with the aid of the Holy Spirit in ceaseless battle against error and sin in the church as well as in the world."[82]

3.4 The Problem of Apostolic Succession

59. The most important question regarding the theology of the episcopal office and regarding the mutual recognition of ministries is the problem of the apostolic succession. This is normally taken to mean the unbroken ministerial succession of bishops in a church. But apostolic succession is also often understood to refer in the substantive sense to the apostolicity of the church in faith.

---

[82]Malta Nos. 22 and 23.

60. The starting point must be the apostolicity of the church in the substantive sense. "The basic intention of the doctrine of apostolic succession is to indicate that, throughout all historical changes in its proclamation and structures, the church is at all times referred back to its apostolic origin."[83] In the New Testament and in the period of the early fathers, the emphasis was placed more on the substantive understanding of the apostolic succession in faith and life. The Lutheran tradition speaks in this connection of a *successio verbi.* In present-day Catholic theology, more and more often the view is adopted that the substantive understanding of apostolicity is primary. Far-reaching agreement on this understanding of apostolic succession is therefore developing.

61. As regards the succession of the ministers, the joint starting point for both Catholics and Lutherans is that there is an integral relation between the witness of the gospel and witnesses to the gospel.[84] The witness to the gospel has been entrusted to the church as a whole. Therefore, the whole church as the *ecclesia apostolica* stands in the apostolic succession. Succession in the sense of the succession of ministers must be seen within the succession of the whole church in the apostolic faith.[85]

62. The *Catholic* church sees this succession of ministers as realized in the succession in the episcopal office.[86] In Catholic teaching the fullness of the ordained ministry exists only in the episcopal office.[87] Nevertheless, the apostolic succession in the episcopal office does not consist primarily in an unbroken chain of those ordaining to those ordained, but in a succession in the presiding ministry of a church, which stands in the continuity of apostolic faith and which is overseen by the bishop in order to keep it in the communion of the Catholic and apostolic church. Thus originates the college of those who maintain the communion of the church. The episcopal college serves on its level and on the foundation of the apostles to continue the function of the college of the apostles.

The episcopate which stands in the apostolic succession is bound to the canon of Scripture and the apostolic doctrinal tradition and must bear living witness to them. While it is possible for the individual bishop to fall away from the continuity of the apostolic faith, he loses *eo ipso,* according to Catholic tradition, the right to exercise his ministry. Catholic tradition holds that the episcopate as a whole is nevertheless kept firm in the truth of the gospel. In this sense, Catholic doctrine regards the apostolic succession in the episcopal office as a sign and ministry of the apostolicity of the church.

---

[83] Ibid., No. 57.
[84] Cf. ibid., No. 48.
[85] Cf. ibid., No. 57.
[86] Vatican II, Dogmatic Constitution on the Church, No. 20
[87] Ibid., Nos. 21 and 26.

63. For the *Lutheran* tradition also the apostolic succession is necessary and constitutive for both the church and for its ministry. Its confessional writings claim to stand in the authentic Catholic tradition,[88] and emphasize the historical continuity of the church which has never ceased to exist.[89]

64. For the Lutherans in the sixteenth century, the authenticity of apostolic succession in the form of historic succession in the episcopal office was called in question because it failed to witness to agreement in the proclamation of the gospel, and because the episcopate refused fellowship with them, especially by denying them the service of ordaining their preachers, and thus deprived them of the historic succession in office. For them, therefore, apostolic succession came to focus on the right preaching of the gospel, which always included the ministry, and on faith and the testimony of a Christian life. Yet they were convinced that the gospel had been given to the church as a whole and that, with the right preaching of the Word and the celebration of the sacraments according to the gospel, apostolic succession in the substantive sense continued within the congregations. Based on this, the ordination of ministers by ministers continued to be performed in the Lutheran church. This ordination remained oriented towards the entire church and towards recognition by its ministers.

65. Thus, despite diverse historical developments, the Lutheran Reformation affirmed and intended to preserve the historical continuity of church order as an expression of the unity of the apostolic church among all peoples and throughout all centuries, presupposing, of course, that the gospel is rightly proclaimed. This intention must be maintained even in the face of contrary historical developments for the sake of the faith that the church abides.[90] This point is expressly stressed in the fundamental articles of the Augsburg Confession,[91] and also by the references made in the confessional writings to church teachers of all times.[92]

66. These considerations provide the basis for a Lutheran evaluation of the historic succession as a sign of such unity. The Lutheran conviction is that acceptance of communion with the episcopal office in the historic succession is meaningful not as an isolated act,[93] but only as it contributes to the unity of the church in faith and witnesses to the universality of the gospel of reconciliation.

---

[88]CA XXI, Epilogue, The Book of Concord, pp. 47f.; CA XXII, Preface, The Book of Concord, pp. 48f.; CA XXVIII, Conclusion, The Book of Concord, p. 95; cf. USA IV, No. 23.
[89]CA VII, The Book of Concord, p. 32; Apology of the Augsburg Confession IV, 211, The Book of Concord, p. 136; Catalogus Testimoniorum, BSLK 1101–1135; cf. USA IV, No. 26.
[90]CA VII, 1, The Book of Concord, p. 32.
[91]Cf. ibid.; CA XXI, Epilogue, The Book of Concord, pp. 47f.; CA XXI conclusion of part I and introduction to part II, The Book of Concord, pp. 48f.
[92]Cf. especially Catalogus Testimoniorum, op. cit.
[93]Cf. No. 82 below.

3.5 The Episcopal Ministry and Service for the Universal Unity of the Church

67. Along with reflection on episcopacy, there naturally also arises the question of ministry to the universal unity of the church. This question can be mentioned here only as a problem. It calls for further and more detailed treatment.

68. According to *Catholic* teaching, it is primarily by preaching and teaching that the bishops minister to unity within their local churches and between the local churches. Each local church is a realization and representation of the one church of Jesus Christ[94] only in community (*communio*) with the other local churches. This is why the individual bishop with his office forms a part of the community of all the bishops (collegiality). Each individual bishop and all the bishops together are entrusted with the care of the entire church, which exists in and arises from the many local churches.[95]

69. This *communio* between the local churches and their bishops has its point of reference in communion with the Church of Rome and the Bishop of Rome as the holder of the Chair of Peter. In this capacity he presides over the *communio (Agape)*.[96] Rome is the place of the martyrdom of the apostles Peter and Paul; the Church of Rome was preserved amid the storms of persecution and in the confrontation with heresies, and played a leading role in the establishment of the canon of Scripture and the apostolic creed. From the fourth century onward, the promise given to Peter "on this rock I will build my church" (Mt 16:18) and the commission assigned to him "strengthen your brethren" (Lk 22:32) was applied to the Church of Rome and to the Bishop of the *cathedra Petri*. According to Catholic teaching, the Lord has transmitted to the Bishop of Rome, as the successor of Peter, the supreme pastoral office in the church. The ministry of the Bishop of Rome is to serve the unity of the universal church and legitimate diversity in the church.[97] His ministry of unity is "the perpetual and visible source and foundation of the unity of the bishops and of the multitude of the faithful"[98].

70. Since the unity of the church is primarily unity in the one faith, the ministry of the Bishop of Rome within the episcopal college includes a special ministry to the unity of the faith of the church. He serves the unity of the whole church in faith and mission. It is promised to him that through the power of the Holy Spirit he is preserved from error in teaching when he solemnly declares the faith of the church (infallibility).[99] In his succession to the chair of Peter he is a witness of faith in the Jesus Christ to whom Peter

---

[94]Vatican II, Decree on the Bishops' Pastoral Office in the Church, No. 11.
[95]Ibid., Dogmatic Constitution on the Church, No. 23.
[96]Cf. Ignatius of Antioch, *Epistula ad Romanos* (Inscr.).
[97]Vatican II, Dogmatic Constitution on the Church, Nos. 22f.
[98]First Vatican Council, DS 3050f.; Vatican II, Dogmatic Constitution on the Church, No. 23.
[99]First Vatican Council, DS 3074; Vatican II, Dogmatic Constitution on the Church, No. 25.

was the first to bear witness in an abiding and authoritative way. This is the witness to which the church must always refer (Mt 16:16; Lk 24:34; 1 Cor 15:5).[100]

71. There were differences in detail in the ways the ministry of unity of the Bishop of Rome was understood and exercised in the first and second millennia. With its two dogmas of the universal primacy of the papal jurisdiction and the infallibility of particular papal doctrinal decisions, the First Vatican Council highlighted the service to unity of the Bishop of Rome, though without, to be sure, making sufficiently clear the degree to which this service is embedded in the total church. The Second Vatican Council confirmed this teaching of the First Vatican Council, but at the same time firmly anchored it once again in an all-embracing ecclesial context by its statements on the significance of the local churches and the collegiality of the episcopate. The frequent talk of the "Petrine office" in the post-conciliar period reflects the effort to interpret the papacy in terms of the Peter typology of the New Testament. This shows that "the concrete shape of this office may vary greatly in accordance with changing historical conditions"[101]. Aware as the Catholic church is that the papacy remains to this day for many Christians one of the greatest obstacles on the road to unity of the churches, it nevertheless hopes that as it is structurally renewed in the light of Holy Scripture and the tradition, it may more and more in the future provide an important service to unity.

72. For the *Lutheran* churches, likewise, it is essential to be aware of the interrelationship of the individual local and regional churches. Increasingly questions arise regarding the visible forms of church fellowship which represent a world-wide bond of faith. The churches have learned to collaborate in practical and theological matters in various ecumenical organizations. They have come to know each other better and have established concrete contacts with each other and thus have come into a deeper community. In recent years, the ecumenical dialogue among other things has led to the discussion of various models for the unity of the universal church, including first and foremost the model of conciliar fellowship of the churches. According to this model, the local churches form part of a world-wide and binding fellowship without having to give up their legitimate individual characteristics.

73. Also in this connection the question arises for Lutherans of service to the unity of the church at the universal level. The Reformers never surrendered the view that the council is the locus for the expression of the consensus of all Christendom, and, therefore, of universal church unity, even when they doubted whether a genuinely universal and free council could still be assembled. It seemed to Lutherans that the papacy suppressed

---

[100]Cf. Vatican II, Dogmatic Constitution on Divine Revelation, No. 10.
[101]Malta No. 66.

the gospel and was to this extent an obstacle to true Christian unity. The doctrinal decision of the First Vatican Council confirmed this conviction in the minds of many. While the traditional controversies have not yet been completely settled, it can nevertheless be said that Lutheran theologians today are among those who look not only to a future council or to the reponsibility of theology, but also to a special Petrine office, when it is a question of service to the unity of the church at the universal level.—Much remains theologically open here, especially the question as to how this universal ministry in the service of truth and unity can be exercised, whether by a general council, or by a group, or by an individual bishop respected by all Christians. But in various dialogues, the *possibility* begins to emerge that the Petrine office of the Bishop of Rome also need not be excluded by Lutherans as a visible sign of the unity of the church as a whole, "insofar as [this office] is subordinated to the primacy of the gospel by theological reinterpretation and practical restructuring"[102].

4. MUTUAL RECOGNITION OF MINISTRIES

4.1 Present Situation

74. The convergences in the understanding and the structuring of the church's ministry presented in chapters two and three give great urgency to the question of the mutual recognition of ministries. This is true especially because eucharistic fellowship between our two churches depends essentially on the answer to this question. The question arises for both sides in a different way.

75. Before the Second Vatican Council there were no official pronouncements in *Catholic* teaching on the question of the validity or invalidity of the ministries in the Lutheran church. It was traditionally assumed that they were invalid. The Second Vatican Council speaks of a *defectus* in the sacrament of orders in the churches stemming from the Reformation.[103] It did not explain in what sense this applies to the individual churches and ecclesial communities who "differ . . . among themselves to a considerable degree"[104]. Its intention, in any case, was not to take a final position, but rather to highlight a number of considerations that "can and ought to serve as a basis and motivaton for such [ecumenical] dialogue"[105].

76. The ecumenical dialogue that has been going on since that time has increasingly given rise to the question whether *defectus* refers to a partial lack rather than a complete absence. In considering this problem, the ecumenical experience of the action of the Holy Spirit in the other

---

[102]Malta No. 66; cf. USA V.
[103]Vatican II, Decree on Ecumenism, No. 22.
[104]Ibid., No. 19.
[105]Ibid.

churches[106] and of the spiritual fruitfulness of their ministries plays an important role. In addition, recent insights in the fields of biblical theology and of the history of theology and of dogma are of importance, especially the recognition of the diversity both of the ecclesial ministries in the New Testament and of their relationships to the community and to changing historical situations. In this connection it may also be worthy of mention that in the history of the Catholic church there have been cases of the ordination of priests by priests.[107]

77. In the light of post-conciliar ecumenical discussion—as also reflected in the preceding chapters—it seems possible to speak of a *defectus ordinis* in the sense of a lack of the fullness of the church's ministry. In fact it is the Catholic conviction that standing in the historic succession belongs to the fullness of the episcopal ministry. But this fact does not, according to the Catholic view, preclude that the ministry in the Lutheran churches exercises essential functions of the ministry that Jesus Christ instituted in his church.[108]

78. The Catholic attitude to the ministry of other churches, as its view of the ministry in the Orthodox churches shows, does not depend directly on the question of the primacy. Yet for a full recognition of ministries in a reconciliation of churches, according to Catholic understanding, the Petrine office must also be taken into consideration.

79. For *Lutherans* the question presents itself differently. According to the Lutheran Confessions, the church exists wherever the gospel is preached in its purity and the sacraments are rightly administered.[109] Thus, Lutherans do not claim that the office of the ministry is found only in their own churches' ministry, i.e., they do not deny that it exists in the Catholic church.

80. If, as Augsburg Confession VII declares, agreement in the above two marks (in which the ministry is included)[110] is sufficient for the true unity of the church, then these marks are fundamental conditions for identifying church unity. The *satis* must not be understood, however, as if it somehow denied the legitimacy of further agreements. When such further agreements are described as "not necessary", this does not oppose the growth of unity in Christ even in the sense of structural unification, but rather promotes the

---

[106]Cf. ibid., No. 3.
[107]Papal bulls of Pope Bonifatius IV, DS 1145–46; Martin V, DS 1290; Malta Nos. 58, 63; USA IV, No. 20.
[108]Dombes III, No. 40.
[109]CA VII, The Book of Concord, p. 32; Malta No. 64.
[110]CA V, The Book of Concord, p. 31; CA XXVIII, 20, The Book of Concord, p. 84. The *satis* is not intended to suggest that the church ministry is superfluous for unity, because it has been instituted by God with the task of preaching and administering the sacraments.

right kind of freedom for such growth. Unification should take place as an expression of Spirit-worked faith in the gospel which—like the works of the justified sinner—follows this faith. Understood in this manner, the Lutheran *satis est* is, therefore, not contrary to the desire for the "fullness" of church life, but actually opens up the way to this fullness. One must ask, in other words, what form of church structure most effectively helps the proclamation of the gospel and the life and mission of the church. The *satis est* understood in this sense frees Lutherans to face up to the call for communion with the historic episcopal office.

4.2 Future Possibilities

81. The rapprochement between the divided churches which has been reached, the advances in ecumenical discussion, increasingly close practical cooperation between the ministers and congregations of both churches and, not least, the urgent pastoral problems which can only be solved in common, particularly the hope for joint celebration of the Lord's Supper, suggest the desirability of the mutual recognition by the two churches of their ministries in the not too distant future. This would be a decisive step towards eliminating the scandal of our separation at the Lord's Supper. Christians of both churches could then bear more credible testimony before the world of their fellowship in the love of Christ. Even before the mutual recognition of the ministries has been achieved, each church should by all means take into consideration developments in the other church when further developing its own ministries.

82. On what conditions and in what way would such a mutual recognition of ministries be possible? There is as yet no generally agreed upon answer to this question. Proposals for such procedures as a supplementary ordination, a juridical declaration or a mutual laying on of hands, any of which could be interpreted as either an act of ordination or as an act of reconciliation, are not completely satisfactory if they are understood as isolated acts. Nor can the question be answered exclusively in terms of canonical criteria of validity. Mutual recognition must not be regarded as an isolated act or carried out as such. It must occur in the confession of the one faith in the context of the unity of the church and in the celebration of the Lord's Supper, the sacrament of unity. Lutherans and Catholics, therefore, share the conviction that ordination by bishops, apart from reference to specific church communities, does not represent a solution. The only theologically meaningful way of solving this question is through a process in which the churches reciprocally accept each other. From this standpoint, the acceptance of full church communion would signify also the mutual recognition of ministries. The precondition for such acceptance of full church communion is agreement in the confession of faith—which must also include a common understanding of the church's ministry—a common understanding of the sacraments, and fraternal fellowship in Christian and church life.

83. Such a recognition can only come about gradually. The various stages lead from a mutual respect of ministries through practical cooperation to full recognition of the ministry of the other church which is identical to the acceptance of eucharistic fellowship. We are grateful that today mutual respect of ministries and practical cooperation already take place to a large extent, and that in the meantime a considerable degree of common understanding of the faith, including a common understanding of the church's ministry, has been reached. For this reason it seems to us that further steps in the direction of a full mutual recognition of ministries are now indicated.[111]

84. A primary desideratum is as broad as possible a process of reception of the findings of previous ecumenical dialogues on the ministry of the church. We therefore request church leaders to distribute the present document to their churches for study. In addition, we ask the churches to continue to seek and to promote the cooperation of congregations and of ministers. Each church must make sure that its practice in the ordination and installation of ministers corresponds to the consensus that has already been achieved. Liturgical ordination formulae that do not correspond to the present state of the ecumenical discussion need revision.

85. If all this is done, the next step could consist of a mutual recognition that the ministry in the other church exercises essential functions of the ministry that Jesus Christ instituted in his church and, which one believes, is fully realized in one's own church. This as yet incomplete mutual recognition would include the affirmation that the Holy Spirit also operates in the other church through its ministries and makes use of these as means of salvation in the proclamation of the gospel, the administration of the sacraments, and the leadership of congregations. Such a statement is possible on the basis of what has been said up to now. It would be an important step in helping us through further reciprocal reception to arrive eventually at full mutual recognition of ministries by the acceptance of full church and eucharistic fellowship.

86. The hope of achieving full church and eucharistic fellowship is not based on our human possibilities, but is rather founded on the promise of the Lord who through his Spirit is effectively manifest in the growing unity of our churches. Such hopes will also patiently withstand difficulties and disappointments, trusting in the prayer of our Lord "that they may all be one" (Jn 17:21).

---

[111]Cf. Accra Nos. 93–100.

PARTICIPANTS

Roman Catholic Members:

The Rt. Rev. H. L. Martensen (chairperson)
The Rt. Rev. Dr. P. W. Scheele
Prof. Dr. J. Hoffmann
The Rev. Dr. J. F. Hotchkin
The Rev. Chr. Mhagama
Prof. Dr. St. Napiorkowski
Dr. V. Pfnür

Lutheran Members:

Prof. Dr. G. A. Lindbeck (chairperson)
The Rt. Rev. D. H. Dietzfelbinger
The Rev. Dr. K. Hafenscher
Dr. P. Nasution
The Rev. I. K. Nsibu
Prof. Dr. L. Thunberg
Prof. Dr. Bertoldo Weber

Consultants:

Prof. Dr. P. Bläser MSC (Roman Catholic)
Prof. Dr. W. Kasper (Roman Catholic)
Prof. Dr. U. Kühn (Lutheran)
Prof. Dr. H. Legrand OP (Roman Catholic)
Prof. D. Dr. W. Lohff (Lutheran)
Prof. Dr. H. Meyer (Lutheran)
Prof. Dr. H. Schütte (Roman Catholic)
The Rt. Rev. Dr. J. Vikström (Lutheran)

Staff Members:

P. Dr. P. Duprey PA (Secretariat for Promoting Christian Unity)
Msgr. Dr. A. Klein (Secretariat for Promoting Christian Unity)
The Rev. Dr. C. H. Mau, Jr. (Lutheran World Federation)
The Rev. Dr. D. F. Martensen (Lutheran World Federation)
Prof. Dr. V. Vajta (Lutheran World Federation)

LUTHERAN-REFORMED-ROMAN CATHOLIC CONVERSATIONS

*The Theology of Marriage
and the Problem
of Mixed Marriages
1976*

Historical Introduction:

During the post-conciliar preparation for a Roman Catholic-Luthern dialogue (consultations held in Strasbourg, August 1965 and April 1966), it was suggested that, alongside the more strictly doctrinal conversation, a dialogue be entered into on the subject of "The Theology of Marriage and the Problem of Mixed Marriages". While the doctrinal conversation was already initiated in 1967 (see above; "Malta Report" and "The Lord's Supper") the establishment of the Marriage—Mixed Marriage-Commission was held up as the result of inner-Catholic developments — primarily the expectation of a revision of the existing canonical regulations concerning mixed marriages.

In the meantime, the Reformed World Alliance had also decided to enter into conversation with the Roman Catholic Church. Moreover, during this time, the dialogue between Lutherans and Reformed had become more involved and intense, such that the two World Confessional Families considered it not only possible but relevant and desirable to enter jointly into conversation — as one partner — with the Roman Catholic Church concerning the questions of marriage and interconfessional marriage. In two preparatory consultations between representatives of the Lutheran and Reformed churches (Cartigny/Geneva, November 1969 and March 1970) preparations were made for the dialogue with the Catholic Church, which thus, in a formal sense, represented a kind of "trilateral" dialogue.

It was already apparent during the Lutheran/Reformed preparatory consultations, and especially so at a consultation in Rome (December 1970) held for joint planning of the dialogue, that the problem of interconfessional marriages "is today affected and aggravated by a general crisis with regard to the understanding and the function of marriage" in general. The forthcoming dialogue was therefore to deal with this further aspect, having as its starting-point "marriage as a reality to all humanity" and then to continue with an examination of the more controversial questions concerning the theology of marriage and the problems of church regulations with respect to mixed marriages.

The Commission's work was originally planned to cover four sessions. The question of the indissolubility of marriage proved to be so difficult to deal with, however, that a more thorough examination of the problem seemed necessary and so five sessions were called for (Strasbourg, November 1971, Madrid, December 1972, Basel, October 1973, Strasbourg, December 1974, Venice, April-May 1976).

The members of the Commission were delegated respectively by the Lutheran World Federation, the Reformed World Alliance and the Secretariat for Promoting Christian Unity. It should be mentioned that the Vatican was represented not only by the Secretariat for Promoting Christian Unity but also by the Congregation for the Doctrine of the Faith and the Laity Council.

278

The Report of the Commission is preceded by a covering letter from the three Chairpersons to the authorities of the churches involved, in which, among other things, reference is made to the "theological divergencies" still existing, which make it necessary for the church authorities to pay "most careful attention" to the report. It is suggested that an evaluation of the reactions received from the churches with regard to the report should be undertaken in due time.

The Theology of Marriage and the Problem of Mixed Marriages

Final Report of the Roman Catholic — Lutheran — Reformed Study Commission on "The Theology of Marriage and the Problem of Mixed Marriages" 1976

I. CRISIS AND CHALLENGE

(1) In its discussion of the problems of marriage the Commission has been acutely aware of the contemporary crisis affecting marriage. While acknowledging the magnitude of the present challenge, however, we would wish to keep it in perspective by bearing in mind that there has always been an element of crisis or of tension in marriage, in so far as what marriage is has often fallen short of what it ought to be, and that this has not seldom been accepted through corruptions of the ideal, such as the double moral standard for husband and wife. Moreover, we are deeply convinced that the Churches should not disguise whatever responsibility they may have for contributing to the crisis, partly by their own divisions and divided witness, partly by caring too much for the institution and too little for those involved in it.

(2) None the less, the crisis exists at present, although once again it should not be too rigidly separated from other contemporary movements

and trends which call in question accepted standards and authorities, for it is probably not mistaken to see at the root of these the search for a reality and meaning which have been lost by many traditional forms of life and behaviour; and this search commands a degree of sympathetic and appreciative understanding. On the other hand, this search for reality is probably not the only factor in the present situation: and there is no doubt that the emancipation of women has brought great changes to the marital situation, as have technological discoveries affecting this area of human existence. Another factor, operating at a deeper level, is an attitude of the human spirit which has readily emerged at a stage of modern civilisation which owes much to scientific achievements and scientific ways of thinking. Perhaps this attitude of the human spirit reflects the detachment of a scientific age, and it is certainly tentative and sceptical, uncommitted and prone to experiment. It fits in well with a period of pluralism and secularism; but it lacks the criteria for gauging the success of the adventure of human life and history. Moreover, in reaction against this emptiness of the human spirit, many in our time have sought participation in reality in a wide diversity of ways. Some of these ways have carried with them peculiar dangers to the human person. Others have had an essentially religious character and have been attempts to recover that existential sense of God the lack of which lies at the deepest root of our present problems.
(3)   Yet whatever place there is for experiment here and there in the course of human life, there is no place for it at the very roots of life, in connection with life itself. When we allow ourselves to consider the matter, we experience life both as a gift to us and as something we are enabled to pass on to future generations — as if God had not only called us into existence but has even made us partners with Himself in the promotion and enhancement of human life. With life itself we are given the promise of more life, and the possibility of its development in our children for good or for ill. Moreover, each marriage, with the children who may be given to it, must work itself out, again for good or ill, through a succession of situations in circumstances of sickness and health, of good fortune and bad, of prosperity and adversity, of life and death. It seems impossible to be existentially aware of this basic experience which has something of the character of a mystery and a challenge, without feeling the need for some interpretative vision; and certainly for its part the Christian Church has always assigned and must continue to assign, a very great importance and significance to the coming together of the sexes in marriage, which is, as it were, a focus of this basic situation.
(4)   In articulating this vision one may fall into all sorts of reductionist errors, and the Churches themselves have not always been free of these. They have sometimes treated sexuality as a merely biological means for the sole purpose of procreation: but others may likewise treat it as a merely anthropological language of communication and self-expression to the total exclusion of procreation. Both views, however, are partial and onesided. Others again may treat sexuality as a sphere merely for self-

satisfaction and the obsessive pursuit of pleasure; but this is a double mistake. It reduces the human personality to nothing more than instinct and sentiment, and it isolates the individual from his or her partner, from children, from society, from future generations, and from God.

(5)   There are clearly questions at issue here concerning potentiality and genuinely human reality which it would be tragic to allow to go by default; and certainly even if our Churches have sometimes seemed unduly legalistic and inward-looking, their present concern in these conversations is to recover the reality and values in their traditions and under the Gospel of Jesus Christ, to serve humanity in its needs and responsibilities in a rapidly changing world, which finds it easier to despair than to believe. Believing in the values of our traditions, we must help our people to grasp them afresh, in terms of their contemporary existence, lest they be lost in the confusion of change.

II.   General Aspects of Marriage

(6)   The starting point for our analysis of marriage is the fact that marriage is subject to constant change. The historicity of man comes to the fore also in this matter. Particular changes have been brought about in modern times, and among these changes one must include the transition from the pre-industrial form of life to the complex industrial society of the present time. This transition does not occur simultaneously in all places, and all stages of the process may therefore exist side by side with each other. Examples of this are provided by comparing the characteristic forms of marriage in different cultures and also by the influence that in one way or another is being continuously exerted on individuals in modern society, i.e., in political, moral, economic and other respects. History and ethnology, as well as psychology and sociology, give striking accounts of these factors of transformation, influence and change. In the most recent past this transformation has been considerably influenced by the technological development that has made man independent of nature to an extent hitherto unknown. Other developments therefore occurred in the wake of this technological process, the "sexual revolution" being a case in point.

(7)   It is quite astonishing that even a radical change in marriage uses and customs could not destroy the basic character of marriage. The transformation of marriage uses and customs is a consequence of the historicity of man. Culture is not something static or invariable, but is in a constant process of development. The nature of many of these developments is not alien to the Church, and indeed many aspects of the transformation only bring her face to face with the effects of her own preaching. Examples of this are provided by the idea of man as a person, the importance of personal freedom, and the preeminence of love. These themes have always stood in the foreground of church teaching. But even in the secularized world they have become dominant concepts governing the general way of life.

(8)   A description of the exterior reality of marriage leads to a catalogue of complementary characteristics that are common everywhere:

— Marriage, especially in Western tradition, means a free union based on reciprocity.
— It means cohabitation that involves the life, the work and the interests of the partners.
— It is based on a community of life that embraces and gives security to the persons and becomes enlarged into a community for the begetting and raising of children.
— The description of marriage as a "spiritual community" expresses the fact that in marriage the fundamental and all-embracing questions of life have to be answered jointly by the partners. Since the community regards the binding and all-of-life-embracing nature of such questions, marriage has a religious character which is essential to its nature.

In the case of an individual marriage, these characteristics never constitute an invariable and fixed inventory. Neither the spouses nor the marriage itself remain stationary at their starting point. The decision of the partners to share their entire existence forms part of a development that permits maturation and growth in all fields.

(9)   The lived marriage of the present day cannot therefore by any means be understood as a mere multiplicity of forms of life that have nothing in common and are of quite different stamp. Everywhere in the world marriage is the institution that responds to the fundamental experience of humanity, according to which the human person exists as a sexual being. Notwithstanding all the historical, cultural and psycho-sociological differences, marriage contains a number of common and important elements. One of these lies in the fact that a man and a woman enter into a community both with respect to themselves and with respect to society. The fact that marriage as a primary institution confers a social form upon the relationship between the sexes, excludes the arbitrary treatment of the relationship. A man and a woman who enter into a marriage therefore know that—in this marriage—they are accepted, sheltered and protected by society and all social authorities. On the other hand, especially in modern times, it is precisely in the sexual relationship that people seek personal happiness. This emphasis placed on the sexual relationship for personal love and private happiness clearly stands in a state of tension with marriage as an institution: Marriage cannot be founded exclusively on the loving sentiments of the spouses and have its fate depend on these sentiments, but it is just as obvious that it cannot be said to be nothing more than a social institution. This polarity may harbour dangers that—in individual cases—lead to the destruction of a marriage. In a successful marriage, on the other hand, the unity of this tension filled polarity is experienced as an enhancement of the quality of life. A lived marriage is the place where such genuinely human life is attained, where the opposition

between institution and person and between self-love and conjugal love becomes cancelled. It is the framework in which one partner accepts the other with all his limitations, but also has the good fortune of being accepted by the other, again with all his limitations. The partners free each other of the fear that this acceptance may be withdrawn and they do so by seeking "institutional support", i.e., by making a public promise of constancy and, consequently, being taken at their word by society.

(10) We can therefore speak of three aspects or dimensions of marriage. These are three aspects of its significance or its function. The first aspect shows the married couple in its own life, its history, and its fate. The second aspect brings the family as such into sharper focus: Children are an expression of both the nature of the institution and of personal love, they add nothing alien to the marriage but rather enlarge it to the other dimensions. Lastly, the third aspect throws the limelight on the importance of marriage for society. Marriage represents the living cell, the fundamental element of both civil society and of the religious community. These three dimensions mark the living expression of marriage, and also its significance as going far beyond mere individual interest. But at the same time they also indicate aspects of menace for each individual marriage. In each of these three dimensions, indeed, a lived marriage is liable to failure or lack of success: It is menaced to an equal extent by a failure of the conjugal partnership, by a breakdown of the family relationship and by a destruction of its social integration. A marriage is already threatened when one of these dimensions is neglected as compared with the others or is considered to be less relevant. One of the best means of preventing marriage failure is to help individual married people to gain insight into these aspects and to accept responsibility for all dimensions. In this way they become in the full sense fit for marriage.

(11) The third of these aspects merits some additional remarks. The relationship between a marriage and the culture or the society in which that marriage is lived is the result of interaction. On the one hand, marriage represents the formative and effective element out of which society and community are constructed. On the other hand, the values, the yardsticks and the criteria for the orientation of married life are derived from society. And it is precisely within this interaction that both the life of society and the history of each lived marriage unfold. But this makes marriage depend in an altogether particular manner on the things that a given society considers to be valid: Society must be open to the vital needs of marriage in all its dimensions. Marriage proves to be vulnerable and sensitive not only to limitation of and interference with its living space ("Lebensraum") but even to shortcomings in the public support and sustenance that it needs. Although the religious community is able to provide essential foundations for marriage, it can also become a threat in a similar way. Indeed, it is just the religious community that must allow marriage the space and the support to develop its life in all dimensions. A religious community that

recognizes only one of these dimensions—the family aspect say—and neglects or undervalues the others represents a menace to the vitality of marriage. In this sense the religious community too must be open to all the vital needs of marriage. In married life, of course, none of these aspects is in practice separated from the others. Together, rather, they form a complex and irrevocable unity.

III. THE RELATION OF CHRIST TO MARRIAGE

(12)   In treating of the relation of Christ to marriage we touch also on the paradoxical source of our divisions as Christians. What divides us here is not, evidently, Christ himself, but the different conceptions our Churches have of his action on us through grace; or at any rate the way these different conceptions are spoken of. According to Catholics the Reformation was particularly radical in its approach to the question of marriage. In the name of a doctrine of grace that was often reduced solely to the act, in itself essential, of justification, the Reformation Churches contested the doctrine of the Catholic Church on marriage, founded mainly on a doctrine of sanctification. The Catholic Church on her part developed a sacramental doctrine of marriage which seemed unacceptable to the Reformation Churches. To them it appears that the Catholic Church in this way introduced in marriage an—as it were—automatic efficaciousness of grace which is theologically unacceptable and spiritually unverified. It seems to them that in this connection the Catholic Church does not respect the natural ("weltlich") character of marriage which belongs to it by virtue of creation itself and of the civil institutions of man. She also appeared to them to give too much weight in this domain of marriage to the role of the Church as opposed to that of the State. Catholic doctrine seems to them, too, to overlook the fact that such a human institution as marriage is itself in need of salvation. In the view of Lutherans and the Reformed Churches, the Catholic Church, in holding that marriage is a sacrament, seems to forget that marriage does not of itself give grace but needs to receive it. Lastly, to the Reformation Churches it seems at least doubtful whether Christ himself instituted this sacrament.

(13)   Our intention here is not to try to solve all these problems. We simply wish to indicate the direction we may need to take if we are to discover together a Christian view of marriage which might truly become the object of a common teaching of faith.

(14)   Revelation teaches us first of all that God, the living and true God, is not only not a stranger to the human greatness of love, but that He personally is its principle and source. In reality only love can explain that God is truly the Creator and that it is His plan that there should exist the human family, which is founded on, and lives by, love. God, who desires that humanity should become, at all costs, a community of freedom and love, does not want to accomplish His plan without the conjugal ministry of man and woman. As a project for total communion which has as its conse-

quence the bearing and upbringing of human beings in a human way, conjugal love manifests, therefore, the creative plan of God for a world where human creatures are made according to, and live in, His image.

(15)   However, God is not merely at the creative source of the world and of humanity. He has Himself given within history an unequalled, an unsurpassable, example of love. The People of the Covenant loomed up through the centuries as the unique beneficiary and as the prophetic witness for all men of a Love without limits which nothing can exhaust or destroy. In fact, this Love led God to share wholly in our condition through the Incarnation of His Son. In uniting Himself for ever in the flesh of Christ to our humanity, God reveals that His Covenant love is comparable to conjugal love. As Spouse, totally faithful to the People of Israel, God reveals Himself in Christ as the Spouse par excellence, He who gives proof of His absolute love for the Church and for humanity by offering Himself up for them on the cross.

(16)   We are convinced that such a mystery as this is not, cannot, be unconnected with the conjugal relationship. In fact, the Covenant that is projected forward from the world's creation, manifested through Israel, realized in Jesus Christ, announced by the Church of the Apostles, and communicated by the Holy Spirit, reveals that God commits Himself in Jesus Christ to lead every form of love to its complete truth. If we are asked who is this Christ who plays such a prominent role in conjugal love, we may answer unhesitatingly: he is the Lord of the Promise, the Lord of the Covenant and of grace. This is why, without ever forgetting the action of the Spirit present in the core of all conjugal love, the fact that Christians belong to the Lord by virtue of being incorporated into his Life through baptism, also has a bearing on their conjugal existence.

(17)   If we are ready to step out of our conventional formulations of one form or another, we shall see that this relationship of Christ to the conjugal life of Christians is nothing other than what we all of us refer to as grace. In reality grace is the presence of Christ given to men in the Spirit according to the promise. Thus, without being contained in the state of marriage as if it constituted a reality independent of Jesus Christ, or as if marriage were sufficient of itself to produce it, grace is wholly a gift of Christ to the married couple. This grace, which is granted above all as a lasting promise, is as durable as marriage itself is called to be.

(18)   This relationship of grace between the mystery of Christ and the conjugal state requires a name. We all of us believe that the biblical term "Covenant" truly characterizes the mystery of marriage. It is this Covenant that the Catholic Church calls a sacrament. The Reformation Churches prefer not to employ this term chiefly because of their definition of what a sacrament is, because of the special character of marriage in relation to the sacraments of baptism and Eucharist, and finally because of the controversies and misunderstandings of the past. We believe, however, that in the light of our different mentalities and historical situations, we

can have a view of marriage which is in a profound sense a common one. (19) In fact we are all equally convinced that marriage is closely connected with God's promise. This promise is nothing other than Christ himself turning to look upon the spouses so that their love too should become a real and lasting union. This promise is not simply an idea, but the reality itself of Jesus Christ. Because it is the face of Christ himself turned toward married life, this promise is never under the power of those who are called to benefit from it. It is given to them without their ever being able to become its masters. Therefore it presupposes an explicit and ever-renewed annunciation of the word which is no more the prerogative of the minister than it is of the beneficiaries of the grace of marriage.

(20) This promise, then, holds the initiative from the beginning and maintains it throughout. It has a kind of autonomy in regard to the spouses. It summons them ceaselessly to allow themselves to be formed by it, without the spouses ever being able to take for granted that they have finally succeeded in wholly identifying themselves with the full measure of its demands and its grace.

(21) To bring together in this way the initiative of the promise in regard to the spouses and the re-creative experience which the spouses are called to have of its power over them, is to speak of the sacramental power of marriage considered in the light of the Covenant. It also means that marriage is a sign of the Covenant.

(22) Understood in this manner, marriage confers on Christians a responsibility both as beneficiaries and as witnesses. The spouses accept more particularly to live their love according to this promise of grace which they know makes it possible for them to put their deep longing for each other in concrete form through the unreserved gift of self, as well as to surmount its ambiguities.

(23) In this way Catholics should envisage grace, not as a kind of purely objective gift which acts unconditionally on the spouses, but as an experience of fidelity and life that Christ stimulates in their hearts through the gift of the Spirit. As for Lutherans and members of the Reformed Churches, they accept that the promise sealed with the death and resurrection of Christ is active in the hearts and lives of married Christians who live the mystery of Christ, in this way becoming its beneficiaries and witnesses. Both are well aware that in expressing in this manner the "sacramental" aspect of marriage in the light of the promise and the Covenant, we have not resolved all the differences that exist between us. We are merely attempting to get beyond the theological ambiguities which can be, and must be, overcome. We also know that we don't exhaust the wealth of meaning inherent in this mystery of grace, a mystery that goes beyond the frontiers of the Christian life. That is why we should not exclude from the beneficial effects of the Covenant couples who are not believers. In trying to describe the relationship between Christ's grace and Christian marriage, we simply wish to point out what a wealth of grace the mystery of Christ

contains that may be put at the service of conjugal love which in this way acquires its true greatness. But this greatness can never be separated from our weakness. The message of our Churches, especially at such a time of crisis as ours, should point at one and the same time to the values which Christ himself proclaimed, and to the weakness which He denounced and from which He wishes to save us. Christ hands us over the grace which both judges and saves us.

IV.   MARRIAGE FOR LIFE

(24)   It is our common conviction that in the conjugal union a man and a woman commit themselves for their whole lives, and that the couple is destined through marriage to remain united "as long as life lasts", as is said in our liturgies. Being a reciprocal gift that makes the spouses "one flesh", it must be total, without reserve and unconditional. This is required by the dynamism inherent in any authentic love which by its very nature tends to be life-long. It is a matter of the deep respect for each other of those who mutually commit themselves, and of the good of their children, as well as of the common good of the human community. That is why, in our efforts to be in our Churches constant witnesses in this conjugal love, we feel we can render a service to humanity and to the individual couples concerned.

(25)   Although we have this common conviction, the fact remains that we also have divisions, clear divisions just as we have with regard to the "sacramental" aspect of marriage. In this latter case our divisions are rather of a theological nature. In the recent matter our divisions concern, in great measure, pastoral work. They are so important that it is necessary at this point to give a brief exposition of the motives underlying those differences.

(26)   The Catholic Church acknowledges it is powerless over a marriage that has been validly contracted and truly agreed upon between two Christians (what is called by the Church a marriage *ratum et consummatum*). In fact, in the Church's view such a marriage is the sacrament or sign of the union of Christ with the Church, and thus it is as indissoluble as this union.

(27)   Confronted by the difficulties that such a marriage can encounter, one may ask oneself—from the Catholic Church's viewpoint—whether these may not derive from a certain shortcoming inherent in this marriage, and which in effect renders such a union inexistent or null. If the marriage appears to be truly valid and effected in the normal manner, one tries by every possible means to save the union by having recourse to the grace that the relationship of marriage to the mystery of grace puts at the disposal of the spouses. If in the end the continuation of conjugal life seems impossible, separation is then considered legitimate. But if the spouses decide to obtain a divorce, then the Catholic Church considers that it has not the right to view the second marriage which might follow as a Christian mar-

riage or even as a valid one. That is, it denies that this second marriage, following upon a divorce, can represent the union of Christ with the Church, a union which lasts for ever.

(28)   The Catholic Church does not, therefore, consider that the passages in Matthew 5 and 19 imply tolerance of divorce. The purpose of the Church's severe exclusion from the the sacraments of such spouses, is to manifest here disagreement with their behaviour, and to point out how they are acting against the mystery of Christ by contracting a second marriage. But this exclusion from the sacraments should not mean withholding the spiritual support which such spouses have the right to find, in any event, within the Church.

(29)   Even though they hold that marriage is a sign of the Covenant, the Reformation Churches do not consider Christian marriage to be a sacrament in the full sense of the word. Undoubtedly they see in the union of Christ with his Church the model of Christian marriage. Therefore they too, in accordance with Ephesians 5, endeavour in every possible way that marriage should possess the quality of fidelity which Christ expects of it. But this relationship with Christ does not mean that the spouses who are mutually committed consider incompatible with the mystery of Christ the fact that they might possibly in the case of a complete failure, seek a divorce.

(30)   That is why, when it seems that the marriage cannot continue any longer, the Reformation Churches consider that the bond of marriage has been destroyed, a fact which is ascertainable, like death. Nothing remains of the first marriage, therefore, that could prevent re-marriage. This does not mean that in this way the Reformation Churches resign themselves to divorce; but once divorce exists, they would not consider themselves bound to hold that a new Christian marriage is always impossible. The second marriage might perhaps achieve what was not possible in the first one, that is, a greater conformity with the love of Christ for the Church.

(31)   The difference between this and the Catholic position is clear. In the Catholic Church marriage exists as a Christian marriage only in so far as it represents — must and can represent — in its fidelity the love of Christ for the Church. The Reformation Churches, on the other hand, consider that, since marriage needs to conform to the unity of Christ with the Church, the unity that the first marriage has not been able to realize, may possibly be realized in a second marriage after a divorce. They do not therefore view divorce as a radical obstacle to a second marriage.

(32)   The presuppositions of such an attitude are numerous. Without entering here into the relation between creation and sin, we shall refer to the following points: 1) the doctrine of the justification of the sinner; 2) a view of the Gospel which, over and above all its requirements, sees the need for a spirit of mercy and forgiveness; 3) an interpretation of the passage in Matthew as indicating a Christian tolerance of divorce. As regards these last two points, the Reformation Churches adopt a position

that is close to the Orthodox practice of 'oikonomia', since they too in their own manner wish to give witness to the Gospel by showing mercy toward those who are divorced. And lastly, 4) there is some support for this doctrine in certain facts in the history of the Catholic Church. Moreover, attention is called to the fact that although the Catholic Church reaffirmed the indissolubility of marriage at the Councils of Florence and Trent, she has never formally condemned the position of the Orthodox.

(33)   The differences between our various Churches, therefore, are considerable. None of us dreams of denying this, and none imagines that such problems can be resolved by us in an artificial way. But one thing is certain, a thing we all share in common: that we all desire, each in his own way, to be submissive to Christ who indicates for marriage a fidelity which before his time was too often sacrificed. It is therefore in his presence that we must together place ourselves.

(34)   When confronted with the problem that divorce presents to the conjugal union, Christ, taking up again the teaching of Genesis, proclaims formally: "What therefore God has joined together, let no man put asunder" (Mt 19:6). The weakness and "hardness of heart" of men had obscured the plan laid down "from the beginning" by God himself, and the Lord Christ opposes with all His authority the tolerance introduced by the mosaic law. He calls spouses to an irrevocable fidelity with such great force that His disciples take fright, forgetting that what is impossible for men is possible for God.

(35)   In reality, just as God goes to meet His people in a Covenant of love and fidelity, one that is described by Hosea and other prophets with symbolism derived from conjugal life, so too Christ, the Saviour of men and the Spouse of the Church, goes toward the love of Christian spouses, whose model He is through His union with the Church. If He spoke, therefore, about the indefectible union of man and woman, this was not just in virtue of the lucidity of a legislator, but principally because He is in His person the very source of this requirement of married love. Or better, this requirement flows directly from His way of being in regard to men. In His saving power, in effect, He remains ever-present with them so that, as He himself has loved the Church and given Himself for her, so too the spouses may be able to love each other faithfully as long as life lasts.

(36)   This fidelity to God, which was fully revealed by Christ through the crucifixion and resurrection, renders possible and supports the fidelity of the spouses to the love which they have promised and owe one another. The sexual impulse is assuredly an essential component of this love; but notwithstanding its great importance, it does not suffice by itself to ensure the perennial quality of love. As long as sin exists in the world, conjugal love will remain vulnerable, just as marriage itself is vulnerable. But since the promise made by Christ to the spouses is a promise of fidelity, it is able to make their love durable. This promise which is both a gift and an expression of God's will, a vocation and an exigence, can also become a judgement when it is refused.

(37)   The mark of the Christian couple, therefore, consists in this promise which precedes and accompanies them. It is also the fact that this promise is received with faith, is lived out and verified, as it were, every single day. By means of it the conjugal union is enabled to persevere, to grow through joys, as well as perils and sufferings, and even to last throughout life.

(38)   The indissolubility of conjugal love is manifested to us from then on as a fruit of the fidelity of God which demands and makes possible a similar fidelity in the spouses. And so, before being a law, indissolubility is a vital requirement of the love which the spouses have for each other and which they also owe to their children.

(39)   It is true that we live in a society that tends to question the validity of institutions and of marriage in particular. The aim of a protest of this kind against marriage is to protect couples from what used to be, or seems to be, a mere formality. This is why many young couples refuse to give their relationship any official character, whether civil or religious. Sociology and psychology have contributed to the fact that today perhaps more than in the past marriage is seen as a means to success, personal fulfilment and happiness, a view which tends to make marriage more vulnerable. Also, life together is envisaged as an experience the duration of which one cannot, and does not wish to, guarantee. However difficult it may be to evaluate all the consequences of this calling in question of marriage — consequences which are not all negative and which go beyond the boundaries of marriage itself — our common concern is to see that nothing should damage marriage as a call of life and of love.

(40)   This concern is for Christians and indeed for all men. The problem is such a profound one that it goes beyond our doctrinal and practical differences. Therefore, with one heart and one faith we proclaim once more our common conviction that God wishes marriage to be a bond for the whole of life, in both depth and duration; and this is for the good of humanity. The doctrine and behaviour of our Churches should therefore proclaim this message unceasingly, just as it is proclaimed in our liturgies in such a strikingly similar way and with a conviction born of faith.

(41)   And yet, however deep this accord, the fact remains that, as we have pointed out, our views and our practical pastoral approaches are opposed to each other in regard to the relation of Christian marriage to divorce. While Christian marriage and divorce remain incompatible in the Catholic Church, this is not always the case for the Reformation Churches and for the Orthodox. But each of us is convinced to be faithful to the Gospel, even if this does not exclude serious differences between us.

(42)   Lutherans and the Reformed Churches ask Catholics whether in their approach to the indissolubility of Christian marriage they forget the quality of mercy for the sake of a "mystery" which to their brothers of the Lutheran and Reformed Churches seems to have become a "law" that has not much to do with the Gospel. Catholics ask Lutherans and members of the Reformed Churches whether the way they reconcile divorce and Chris-

tian marriage does not contradict the mystery of Christ, and also whether the practice of re-marriage after a divorce does not blur the principle itself of indissolubility.

(43) To these questions there are no ready-made answers which could satisfy all concerned. On the one hand it is true that an attitude of mercy should never favour solutions that are destructive of marriage and of love. On the other hand, there is the Orthodox usage of 'oikonomia', and the passage of Matthew is a fact which remains a problem. It is clear, therefore, that we cannot overcome these difficulties by employing any short-cuts which might, mistakenly, be considered ecumenical. It is better to face the fact that our pastoral differences on this matter for the time being remain unreconciled, if not, perhaps, unreconcilable.

(44) However, since we all wish to be faithful to the mystery of Christ, our main concern is with this mystery, and not just with our mutual relations. Consequently, we all need to answer a question which should exclude the possibility of any complacency: how are we serving, and do we truly serve, or do we serve as much as we should, the truth of Christian marriage through our different practical approaches to this matter, above all at a time when this spiritual service, both in regard to marriage and to love, is more than ever necessary in society?

(45) And so we are led to Him whom we have never ceased to discover at the heart and source of Christian marriage: the Christ whose mystery of life and salvation we want to make shine out among us: something we are never completely certain that we are doing, but also never give up hope of doing. It is in any case this desire which should inspire the attitude we have to adopt toward mixed marriages, without minimising or over-stating either our points of agreement or our points of dissent.

V. PASTORAL CARE

(46) The problems the Commission has been given to deal with are theological problems and have been dealt with theologically; but the concern of the Commission is also a practical, that is, a pastoral one. The Commission has dealt with the question of the sacramental aspects and the life-long character of the marriage of one man and one woman of whatever Church, and with what our Churches can say and do in the immediate situation in which we live to enable that man and woman to live together in marriage under the Lordship of Christ.

(47) The Church has always been acutely aware that it does not live in an ideal world, and over the years the different communions have developed their own ways of preparing people for marriage. Generally these provisions for pastoral care have been worked out by the Churches in isolation from each other, and even in opposition to each other. However, the crisis the Churches face today in a world that has to a considerable extent rejected the Christian faith lays upon all Churches the common task of exercising a stronger prophetic and pastoral mission. Needless to say, the

pastoral mission should not be concerned exclusively with the casualties of marriage but should aim to play a constructive role in building up individual marriages and in the realization and fulfilment of our human potentialities. Moreover, the mission could be more effectively carried out, it is believed, if it could be regarded as a common task to be dealt with by the Churches working together in concrete situations, such as a common approach to mixed marriages and even common celebrations of the marriage rite through the use of common liturgical elements.

(48)   Although it is aware that it is working in a constantly changing situation and that the need for pastoral care in relation to marriage can never be precisely anticipated, the Commission has identified a number of areas where special attention must be given to the nature of the pastoral care likely to be required.

1.   The nature of pastoral care

(49)   In the first place the Church must give attention to what it will mean by pastoral care, assisting both pastor and people to come to a deeper understanding. The Commission recognizes the broad dimensions of this pastoral task. It is persuaded that marriage counseling as generally conceived is only a part of the pastoral responsibilities of the Church and, in fact, cannot be done apart from the larger job. It is persuaded also that the care for the needs of individuals and families is not the task of the pastor alone but is the responsibility of the whole Church. Members of the Church have by virtue of their vocation, an obligation of mutual care for one another, of providing insofar as they are able a community of grace in which everyone may find comfort and strength and in which everyone may extend comfort and support to his neighbour. Some Churches have come to regard pastoral care as including social and political action in the community, thinking of it as whatever the organized Church as individuals and groups may do in the name of the Church to improve the conditions in which people live.

(50)   It will be the pastor's task to assist members of his congregation in understanding their calling and in equipping themselves to enter into it faithfully. Obviously he will do this through a wide variety of activities — in his preaching from the pulpit, in the teaching in the school of the Church, in his special classes for parents, in his own relationship with the children and young people of the congregation, in vocational groups, and in other groups organized to meet particular needs of the larger community. In effect, the Church provides pastoral care for its members and equips them for marriage by drawing them into a worshipping, studying, witnessing community where they may know themselves to be a part of the ongoing people of God who have been called to live together under the Lordship of Christ and to minister to the needs of the world.

2. The preparation of the pastor for pastoral care

(51) The second task of the Church in its work of pastoral care will be the preparation of the pastor for his responsibility of equipping individuals and families for life and therefore for marriage. This will include but will not be limited to couples who will enter mixed marriages or who have already done so, and will thus require of them a new way of looking at Church regulations. Time is running out to save Christian marriages of the future and it is urgent that the Church interpret its rules as an expression of God's love and concern for human nature as he made it and therefore as written for our good and for our happiness.

(52) It will be no easy task to overcome the limitations of the traditional approaches to marriage. But fortunately seminaries are awakening to the need for providing a broader course of study for their ministerial students, going beyond the traditional biblical, theological and historical studies and including pastoral studies and even apprenticeships in pastorates under capable and experienced pastors. The recent Apostolic Letter issued by Pope Paul VI in 1970 on Mixed Marriages opens new possibilities of understanding the nature of the regulations of the Roman Catholic Church. This letter shows Canon Law, as is no doubt intended, as an expression of Christ's loving care for his people, and the Church's attempt to carry out the love in the daily circumstances of life. Students who hope to enter the pastoral ministry should be encouraged to interpret Canon Law from this point of view, and to work with pastors of other Churches to enable the couple to overcome the difficulties inherent in a mixed marriage.

(53) The nature of pastoral care of mixed marriages presents the Churches with an urgent challenge to provide joint pastoral preparation and continuing pastoral care. It presupposes the training of our pastors on the special nature of mixed marriages (Norm 14 of *Matrimonia Mixta*), as to the new approach to presenting rules, in a manner to which married people can relate, and taking into account the vast growth of knowledge and understanding which was not available when many church norms were formulated.

3. The pastoral care of the congregation as a whole

(54) A third situation which calls for pastoral care on the part of the Church is the crucial need of all its people in relation to marriage and family life in this period of stress and change. It is clear to the Committee that in marriage as in all areas of life Christ creates a crisis. His presence at one and the same time brings to the world forgiveness and new life and calls into question all accepted values. The Churches, then, have with regard to marriage, and especially mixed marriages, a twofold responsibility. The first is to teach all of its people a strongly theological view of marriage as rooted in the covenant of God with his people and of the Christian family as a community of love and a fellowship of faith. The sec-

ond is to mediate the liberating grace which will assist the members of the Church not only to live their own marriage under the Lordship of Christ but to become a supporting, sustaining community for the mutual strengthening of one another.

4. *The pastoral care of individuals*

(55) In addition to the provisions it makes for the congregation as a whole the Church through pastor and congregation must provide pastoral care for individuals as they move through life.

a) *Pastoral care of children*

(56) Preparation for marriage like preparation for all of life should begin at an early stage. The child of a Christian marriage comes into the world as an expression of the couple's love for one another, and knows himself to be the beloved creature of God through the full creative love of his parents. Thus the child's preparation for life and for marriage will not begin with verbal admonitions but he will know the love of God from the experience of living in a community of love and grace from the moment of birth. To assist parents in receiving the grace of God so that their household may become a community of grace is the Church's first task in the pastoral care of the child. Knowing from the beginning the meaning of God's grace by living with parents who have themselves experienced God's grace, who have dealt with their own sin and its attendant problems and deficiencies and are able to assist the child in dealing with his/hers, the person may approach marriage with confidence and clear intent, having been set free to enter into a covenant with his marriage partner and having the assurance that in this covenant Christ already awaits them.

(57) Should persons, whose development has occurred in a family and community of grace, love and security, contract a mixed marriage, they will be prepared to enter into it in the love of Christ, the foundation of the grace and faith they know they share. Such a marriage, like any other marriage between Christians will bear witness to the grace of God in Christ.

b) *Pastoral care of adolescents*

(58) Present-day adolescents, who increasingly reject the institutional Churches and their rules, in which they claim not to find Christ, will nonetheless rise to a challenge and an ideal, and it is in this context that the Churches must strive to present the theology of marriage and their regulations, in relation to God's plan for those he has created and loves. Marriage must also be presented in relation to the Church and secular community.

c) *Pre-marriage counselling*

(59) This will lead naturally to actual pre-marriage training. Sex education should from the beginning be linked to love, which, in marriage, God has made the symbol of the Covenant, seen in the Bible. Training must in-

clude factors common to all marriages, but which assume even greater importance in the context of mixed marriages. The pastor must be able to give information about the different Churches, particularly the Churches of the two partners. The couple will need to know, for example, not only the differences in doctrinal belief in the two Churches, but also their different regulations regarding the marriage ceremony. They must be clear about the expectations the Churches may have with regard to children. These regulations and expectations are set forth in Chapter VI of this report. A major concern of such intending couples will be to decide on the best way to bring up their children, in the knowledge, love and service of God in the light of these regulations and expectations. This demands mutual understanding of the possible consequences of different theological and practical interpretations of the faith they share, not only in the chosen form of religious instruction, but also on such basic matters as family planning and abortion.

(60)   The Commission lays great emphasis on the need for joint pastoral support for the partners of broken marriages, including cases where there has been a civil divorce, and on a permanent concern for those whose marriages are performed and lived outside the Church.

(61)   We would refer to the valuable guidelines on joint pastoral care, contained in paras. 73-76 of the final report of the Anglican/Roman Catholic Commission on the same subject as that of the present commission. Examples include the side diversities between national temperaments and socio-cultural patterns, to which pastoral care must be related and the various experiments in this connection which have been made in different parts of the world. It is stressed that the clergy have a duty to exercise a high degree of mutual understanding and trust, which will help better joint pastoral preparations and support for mixed marriages. Furthermore, there is the need to realize that the solution of delicate personal problems involved in mixed marriages, of which no two are alike, is to be found in the maturing and sensitive growing together of the family itself. This sensitiveness must be matched by any source of outside assistance from which, if joint pastoral care is assumed, all hints of competitiveness, suspicion or possessiveness must be banished, since these would inhibit the necessary sensitiveness from the start.

(62)   The Commission has been heartened by the new insights which have come to it through its work together and which hold out to it the hope of even greater understanding of the nature of marriage under the Lordship of Christ. It is the hope of the Commission that through its work this gift of understanding may be reflected day by day in the Churches' pastoral care of the People of God. The Commission also hopes that through the common work of the pastors of the various Churches, the Churches themselves may be brought into a closer fellowship with one another. As the Churches make joint provision for training their pastors, as pastors work together across denominational lines in the case of particular couples

and particular families who are involved in mixed marriages, it may be that these instances can point us towards oneness which is God's will for his Church. Already little ecumenical groups are emerging in places where pastors are discovering that they are already one in understanding the sacramental and life-long character of marriage and one in the call they have from God to minister to his people as they attempt to live out their lives under his Lordship. It may be that the consequences of our work as a commission may bring healing to individuals and families but may also seem in some measure to bring our Churches into a unity that is visible to the world.

VI.   STATEMENT AND DISCUSSION OF THE NORMS OF THE CATHOLIC
      CHURCH REGARDING MIXED MARRIAGES

(63)   The Commission was able to note in many matters a great deal of agreement between the views of the Churches. These agreements exist, above all, in dogmatic matters and in the practical and theological aspects of pastoral care of spouses and families in mixed marriages.

(64)   In other matters, however, differences have come to the fore and appear to be rather complex. The Catholic Church sees certain matters against a different horizon, or on a completely different plane from the Lutheran and Reformed Churches. This is particularly true in the field of canon law relating to marriage. This is not only a matter of the function and the weight that the Catholic Church on the one hand and the Lutheran and Reformed Churches on the other attribute to such a juridical system. Each of the two sides, quite obviously, sees the juridical system in a different dimension, as belonging to an altogether different plane. The two sides therefore treat canon law in completely different contexts, assess it in different ways, and assign altogether different tasks and functions to it.

(65)   But the subject of canon law on marriage is of great importance for ecumenical dialogue about the theology of marriage and, above all, of mixed marriages. The Lutheran and Reformed members of the Commission therefore deem it desirable for the present report to include a detailed statement about the present state of legislation regarding mixed marriages in the Catholic Church. This provides occasion for illustrating the different ideas of the Churches in this matter and thus of beginning a dialogue between them.

A.   NORMS OF THE CATHOLIC CHURCH ON MIXED MARRIAGES

(66)   Like all ecclesiastical laws and rules, the norms on mixed marriages have a pastoral function whose primary and fundamental goal is the salvation of souls. The principle "salus animarum suprema lex" expresses the final end of all the normative activity of the Church. On the other hand the regulations on mixed marriages, like other ecclesiastical laws, are an expression of theology, which makes it necessary to examine their motives and their deep roots in relation to the Gospel message and its theological explanation. .

(67)   The Catholic regulations at present in force may be found in Paul VI's Motu Proprio "Matrimonia Mixta", of 31 March, 1970. This document contains a synthesis of the resolutions passed, after prolonged discussion, at the first Synod of Bishops in 1967. It is generally known that the Fathers of Vatican II, unable to treat the question of mixed marriages in a definitive manner, requested the Pope to reform canonical discipline in this regard. This is what the Pope in effect did, after meeting once again with the Bishops and in answer to their wishes.

(68)   The Pope's document is a kind of general law for the whole Catholic Church which leaves to the episcopal conferences the power of filling in the details in regard to certain aspects such as the concrete form of the promises to be made by the Catholic party, the reason for which a dispensation may be obtained from the canonical form of the marriage ceremony, the way of registering mixed marriages, and the different forms of pastoral care to be adopted in this matter. To learn about these aspects it is essential to have recourse to the complementary norms issued by the various episcopal conferences.

(69)   Paul VI's Motu Proprio is in two parts, one doctrinal, the other normative. The first underlines certain general principles of primary importance for the understanding of the Catholic Church's position on mixed marriages.

(70)   1.   The Catholic Church, like other Churches for that matter advises against mixed marriages in so far as they can easily cause difficulties in families, since in such cases living together can endanger the faith, and divisions in the faith can create problems in married life.

(71)   2.   The Catholic Church reaffirms as fundamental and primordial the right of all men to marry and to have children. Respect for this right leads the Catholic Church to take into special consideration the difficulties encountered by Catholics in finding a Catholic partner in countries where Catholics are a small minority.

(72)   3.   "The Church does not place on the same level, either from a doctrinal or from a canonical viewpoint, a marriage contracted between a Catholic and a non-Catholic who is baptised, and a marriage between a Catholic and a non-baptised person. In fact, as was affirmed at Vatican II, those who, among non-Catholics, 'believe in Christ and are validly baptised, may be said to be in communion, even if an imperfect one, with the Catholic Church'. There exists therefore in a marriage between two baptised persons — which is a true sacrament — a certain communion of spiritual goods which is lacking in a union where one partner is baptised but not the other" (MM, para. 5).

(73)   With regard to the communion of spiritual goods, the Catholic Church distinguishes in theology and in canon law between three kinds of mixed marriages among its members: 1) with members of the Oriental Orthodox Churches; 2) with other baptised persons; 3) with the non-baptised.

(74)   Baptism is a fundamental and precious bond of union. It forms the basis of the sacramental character of marriage. The identity between the bond of marriage and the sacrament and sacramental reality of Christian marriage is the reason for the (Church's) pastoral concern for the marriage of Catholics as regards its essential presuppositions, its conditions, its preparation and celebration, and for the development of married life.

(75)   This sacramental character is also one of the reasons for the different attitude adopted by the Catholic Church in connection with different kinds of mixed marriages. Those of Catholics with *baptised* persons cannot be *licitly* contracted without first obtaining a dispensation from the diocesan authority. For marriage of Catholics with *un-baptised* persons the dispensation is required for *validity*.

(76)   Ecclesiastical regulations touch on the following aspects of mixed marriages:

1) The promises made by the Catholic partner.
2) The canonical form of the celebration.
3) The liturgical form of the celebration.
4) Regulations concerning pastoral care of mixed marriages.

1. *Promises*

(77)   Catholic regulations underline the responsibility in conscience of the Catholic partner to profess his (or her) faith and to transmit it to the children as a requirement inherent in the faith itself.

From this there follow these rules:

(78)   *a)* "The Catholic partner should declare himself ready to remove any danger to the loss of his faith", even dangers that may result from a mixed marriage.

(79)   *b)* The Catholic partner "has a grave obligation to promise sincerely to do everything he can so that his children are baptised and educated as Catholics".

(80)   To provide a religious education for the children is viewed as a requirement that derives from the nature of the faith. This obligation, however, is conditioned by circumstances which may escape the control of the Catholic parent. That is why it is stated that he is obliged to do all that lies within his power, all that is possible.

(81)   *c)* Abiding by the principles laid down at Vatican II, the Catholic Church does not wish to impose on the non-Catholic partner anything contrary to his conscience. But the Church has the duty to support and enlighten the conscience of the Catholic partner (and so also his freedom of conscience), since it is directly responsible for his salvation. Consequently, the Church requires that the non-Catholic partner be *informed* of the moral obligations of the Catholic spouse, without, however, asking him to make any promises.

2. *The canonical form of the celebration of marriage*

(82)   If a marriage, even a mixed marriage, is to be recognized as valid by the Catholic Church, the Church requires its own faithful to celebrate it according to the canonical form. The canonical form consists in the celebration of the wedding in the presence of a Catholic priest or deacon empowered to do so, and in the presence of two witnesses. This law applies to all marriages of Catholics. It was introduced at the Council of Trent, but not with any polemical intention or any wish to defend the Catholic faith against the Reformers.

(83)   At the Synod of Bishops of 1967, a large majority of the world's episcopate delegates agreed that this law was still necessary for mixed marriages also, since it offered a greater safeguard of the sacred and sacramental character of marriage, a greater guarantee of the indissolubility of marriage, a greater certitude of the validity of marriage and the respect for its essential qualities, and finally, greater possibilities for the pastoral care of married life. These are reasons which in the course of time have become more important than the original aim of the avoidance of clandestine marriages.

(84)   Whenever, in the case of mixed marriages, serious difficulties arise in the implementation of the canonical form, local Ordinaries have the right to grant dispensation from it. But it is the task of each episcopal conference to establish the rules according to which this dispensation may be granted in a licit and uniform manner throughout their region or territory, with due attention to the fact that the celebration should possess a certain public character.

(85)   It is evident that dispensation from the canonical form does not mean that the Catholic partner is dispensed from the other obligations concerning the faith and mentioned above.

3. *The liturgical form*

(86)   The canonical form normally coincides with the liturgical form of the celebration of marriage. In the case of a marriage of a Catholic with a baptised person, two possibilities are envisaged:

a) A celebration without a Mass, according to the rite of the "Ordo celebrandi matrimonium" of 1969, nos. 39-54, in the framework of a liturgy of the word, followed by the exchange of promises and the blessing of the spouses;

b) alternatively, with the consent of the local Ordinary, a celebration during Mass, according to the same "Ordo" nos. 19-38; but in this case for the distribution of Communion the rules concerning intercommunion must be observed.

(87)   Paragraph 13 of MM is intended to prevent a form of celebration which might be to the detriment of sound ecumenism instead of promoting it; or else one that might cause doctrinal confusion. This paragraph forbids a simultaneous celebration in two different rites, or a non-Catholic

celebration preceding or following the Catholic one, if this includes a fresh expression or renewing of the marriage vows. In fact, since the Church considers as valid the exchange of vows of the spouses in the presence of a Catholic priest, or deacon, another exchange of vows, either before or after, would be like performing a second marriage, for a marriage is made effective through a single act.

4. *Regulations concerning the pastoral care of mixed marriages*

(88)   Paragraph 14 of MM lays down that diocesan authorities and parish priests should give special attention to mixed marriages, since this pastoral care in the course of the preparation, celebration and the entire development of such marriages, can help to prevent and to resolve numerous problems. More particularly, those who have the care of souls should:

— offer the Catholic partner and the children born of the mixed marriage the spiritual support they need to accomplish their duties in conscience;
— offer this support especially to help him to give witness to his faith;
— offer such help so that the unity of the couple and of the family should grow above all on the basis of their common baptism in Jesus Christ;
— finally, this paragraph supports the wish of the 1967 Synod of Bishops that in mixed marriage ceremonies there should be a loyal and sincere collaboration with the ministers of other religious communities.

(89)   Local Ordinaries and parish priests should take care that the Catholic partner and the children born of a mixed marriage should not lack the spiritual help they need to perform the duties they have in conscience. They should also encourage the Catholic partner to always take care of the divine gift of the Catholic faith and to give witness "with gentleness and reverence and with a clear conscience" (1 Pt 3:16); and they should help the spouses to strengthen the unity of their conjugal and family life which, since they are Christians, is founded also on their baptism. For this reason it is desirable that those responsible for souls should establish with ministers of other religious communities relations of sincere loyalty and enlightened confidence. This regulation has encouraged fruitful collaboration at various levels.

(90)   The norms in the Apostolic Letter "Matrimonia Mixta" are general laws for the Catholic Church. In different countries these laws are embodied in regulations laid down by the appropriate episcopal conference. From an ecumenical viewpoint these regulations may often be of more interest since they go into detail, facing diverse situations and suggesting possible solutions in particular cases. But particular regulations laid down for a given territory cannot go beyond the limits stated in the general law.

B   LUTHERAN-REFORMED COMMENT

(91)   In the Lutheran and Reformed Churches we are accustomed to marriages between spouses who belong to different ecclesiastical traditions

such as our own and the Anglican, Methodist and Baptist communions and although at one time these presented problems, and although even yet it is impossible to make unqualified universal judgements, by and large the problem has disappeared, and conventions have arisen to govern situations of this kind. One such convention, for example, which operates in some areas, is that whereby the wedding takes place according to the form of the bride's Church and the married couple thereafter attach themselves to the husband's Church. There is no doubt that a major factor in bringing about this state of affairs is the growth of mutual understanding and recognition within the ecumenical movement and the family of Churches it has produced.

(92) In the past there has been, however, a serious and a difficult problem where one of the intending partners was a Catholic; and it can hardly be disputed that the difficulties stemmed from the legal norms imposed on the situation by the Canon Law of the Catholic Church. This idea of legal norms in this connection is foreign to the spirituality of the Lutheran and Reformed Churches. From their point of view these norms seemed to place the first importance upon the fulfilment of the Catholic spouse's obligations to the Catholic Church and, hopefully, upon the fulfilment of similar obligations on the part of the children; whereas it has been possible for Lutheran and Reformed ministers and Churches to give the first priority to the Christian good and growth in grace of husband and wife together as a married couple and so of the whole family.

(93) Against this historical background the Lutheran and Reformed Churches welcome the changes in the legal norms which have taken place in recent years and which are expressed in *Matrimonia Mixta*; and they appreciate the intention of the Catholic Church to seek the Christian good of the whole family. The Lutheran and Reformed Churches recognize further that the legal norms seek to express a pastoral concern and that they have their roots in underlying theological convictions regarding such topics as the nature of the Church and of divine revelation.

(94) It is necessary, however, to affirm that the legal norms continue to create problems especially in connection with the provisions concerning the promises and the canonical form. We must raise the question whether especially at these two points the legal norms do not hinder a fully ecumenical solution to the problem of mixed marriages. In other words, in view of the undoubted intention of the Catholic Church to seek the Christian good of the whole marriage and in view of the pastoral concern behind the Canon Law we should ask whether that pastoral concern is fully and adequately expressed by the legal norms. It is significant to note that the conversations on marriage between Anglicans and Catholics found difficulties at the same points and we venture to suggest that the question may be raised whether the degree of consensus which our own dialogue has achieved does not justify some modification of the legal norms.

C. A CATHOLIC REPLY

(95)   The difficulties of the Lutheran and Reformed Churches mentioned above seem to derive from the fact that the theological roots and the eminently pastoral function of the Catholic regulations have not been studied deeply enough. This could lead to two forms of distortion:

— that of thinking that the various Churches are united in faith and doctrine concerning mixed marriages and of regarding ecclesiastical regulations as the sole source of differences in this matter;

— that of viewing ecclesiastical laws themselves as "the law" in the formalistic and legalistic Old Testament sense, and of pushing divergent ideas of law to the point of giving the impression that one wishes to reduce the radical character of the Gospel to a mere invitation by Christ which is not binding and which vanishes when confronted with the failure of man's weakness.

(96)   In the Catholic view, on the contrary, the laws of the Church are a function of theology and an expression of pastoral concern. They express in a practical manner the requirements of the doctrine of faith, and are intended to introduce Christian values into the life of the faithful. It is therefore true that theological convictions about the nature and obligatory character of the faith, as well as about the nature of the Church, influence the characteristic spirit of Catholic regulations: the conception of the Church as both visible and invisible, the role of Bishops as doctors and guides of the faithful, what in the faith binds believers, the very conception of the Incarnation of Christ and the sacramental nature of His Church (as institution and mystery, sign and instrument, of the grace of Christ) . . . all this implies a fuller embodiment of theological insights in ordinary practical life, even by means of numerous and detailed rules of behaviour.

(97)   The pastoral concern of the Catholic Church is expressed in various ways: through the liturgy, through a great variety of means of evangelization, through the personal contacts of bishops and parish priests with the faithful, as well as through juridical rules. These regulations then do not exhaust the pastoral activity of the Church; but their purpose is still profoundly pastoral.

(98)   Therefore it may be true that pastoral concern is not totally and fully expressed in juridical rules. Yet it remains true that they have a pastoral function, that of guiding bishops and parish priests and the faithful toward a conduct which introduces into the daily Christian life of married couples values brought by Christ and communicated to us by the Church. These regulations, moreover, can at times help to give direction to other pastoral activities (of a non-juridical kind), and in this sense they serve a doubly pastoral purpose.

(99)   Apart from the differences in doctrinal and theological convictions on the nature and authority of the Church, on the obligatory nature of the faith, and on the sacramental and indissoluble character of marriage,

there are certain other differences which create difficulties with regard to mixed marriages. These concern chiefly moral principles.

(100) The Catholic Church possesses a single general law for mixed marriages, which can be applied in a highly flexible manner in different situations in accordance with the directions of national episcopal conferences. But the Church is now in relation with the numerous Churches that came from the Reformation, Churches with diverse theological convictions and sometimes also different legal principles regarding mixed marriages. Hence agreements arrived at by a commission need to be very closely studied, while at the same time seeking their practical expression at various levels.

(101) In spite of difficulties that persist, the present dialogue and the partial progress already made by this Commission would seem to indicate, not that dialogue should be brought to a close, but that it should be continued and made more effective at various levels.

CONCLUSION: *Further Outlook and Tasks*

(102) 1) Looking back over the course of our discussions as reflected in the present document, one may summarize matters as follows: starting from an examination of marriage as a human reality, we immediately encountered two questions that are fundamental for the theology of marriage, two questions whose importance became more and more apparent to us as we went along and to which we therefore felt bound to dedicate particular attention, i.e., the problems of the "sacramentality" and the "indissolubility" of marriage. The result of our work is therefore primarily of a theological nature, and we are convinced that it is fundamental for all further dialogue between our Churches in matters of marriage and mixed marriages. Even though it did not prove possible to obtain a complete consensus on all points, we did discover or work out agreements that have brought us decisively closer to a common understanding of marriage and also have a positive effect on the problem of mixed marriages. Undoubtedly, however, it is not the aim of an interconfessional dialogue like our own to heap up a mere series of theological agreements. It will be just as important for our Churches to translate on a broad basis theological convergences into the practical life of the Churches. In this sense we should like to place particular emphasis on the following points:

(103) — The particular nature of Christian marriage should be clearly stressed in the doctrine and the preaching of our Churches and an appropriate liturgical form of contracting marriage should be preserved. The Lutheran and Reformed Churches must use the possibility of remarrying divorcees in such a manner that this will not obscure their basic conviction and their witness that marriage is of lifelong duration.

(104) — Given the prospect of a theological rapprochement, our Churches should endeavour, especially in the field of the problems of mixed

marriages, to abandon the mutual mistrust which still often prevails; as far as the Catholic Church is concerned, moreover, every attempt should be made—albeit without interfering with the pastoral responsibility of the competent authorities—to ensure that the possibilities opened by the Apostolic Letter *Matrimonia Mixta* in connection with mixed marriages between Catholics and Lutherans or Reformed will be fully utilized in all countries and not merely applied in a restrictive manner.

(105)   2) The Lutheran and Reformed members of our Commission felt that there were two questions that they had specially to formulate for their Catholic partners:

a) Given the theological agreements that have already been obtained, would it not be desirable to examine very seriously in each country whether a mixed marriage celebrated by a Lutheran or Reformed pastor could not be recognized as valid by the Catholic Church even in the absence of dispensation from canonical form, especially since this would correspond to the practice of the Lutheran and Reformed Churches? When examining this question, the non-Catholic members stressed it should be borne in mind that the Catholic Church in its relationship with the Orthodox Church does not make the dispensation from canonical form necessary for validity in the event of a mixed marriage, and this notwithstanding the fact that there are still serious differences between the way in which the two Churches understand marriage.

b) Moreover, would it not be desirable to examine whether the obligation of the Catholic partner of a mixed marriage to baptize and educate his children in the Catholic faith could not be safeguarded in a more pastoral and also more ecumenical manner than by exacting a formal promise? In this connection the non-Catholic members drew particular attention to the suggestion for an alternative made in the report of the Anglican/Roman Catholic Commission on the theology of marriage with special reference to mixed marriages (cf. No. 71).[1]

(106) The Catholic members of the Commission showed great understanding for these requests, and stressed their hope that such steps would eventually be taken. But they did feel that the present state of the dialogue could not yet justify these steps, which both sides desire.[2] Quite apart from the ethical questions closely connected with marriage, insufficient consideration had yet been given, above all, to the nature and the intention of the canonical form of contracting marriage. But both sides were convinced that the theological agreements attained in the course of the dialogue were of decisive importance for the treatment of these questions, and, indeed, formed a fundamental condition for tackling them.

(107)   Over and above this, the results of our dialogue make it possible to tackle jointly a number of questions that our Commission encountered in the course of its work and which should therefore become the subject of further discussions between our Churches; they include:

(108) — The religious function of Canon Law
— The problem of Christian ethics (justification and sanctification; law and grace)
— The concept of man underlying marriage
— The understanding of revelation and the role of Holy Scripture as a binding witness
— The relationship between sociological facts and Christian norms.

PARTICIPANTS

MEMBERS OF THE COMMISSION:

Roman Catholics:

Mrs. Jacqueline Stuyt, London, England (co-chairperson)
Reverend Franz Beffart, Cologne, FRG
Mr. Michael Dousse, Rome
Reverend Jérôme Hamer, OP,Rome (meetings 1971 and 1972)
Reverend Gustave Martelet, SJ,Lyon, France
Msgr. Charles Moeller, Rome (meetings 1973 — 1976)
Msgr. Jozef Tomko, Rome

Lutherans:

Prof. Dr. Dietrich Rössler, Tübingen, FRG (co-chairperson)
Reverend Maurice Sweeting, Valentigney, France
Mrs. Sophia Tung, Taipei, Taiwan

Reformed:

Reverend Dr. Rudolf Ehrlich, Edinburgh, Scotland (co-chairperson, deceased 1974)
Reverend Prof. Rachel Henderlite, Austin, U.S.A. (co-chairperson)
Prof. Frank Nichol, Dunedin, New Zealand (meeting 1974)
Prof. N.H.G. Robinson, St. Andrews, Scotland (meeting 1975 and 1976)
Reverend Prof. Daniel Vidal, Madrid, Spain

SECRETARIES:

Roman Catholics:

Reverend Olaf Wand, AA(meeting 1971)
Dr. Wolfdieter Theurer, Rome (meeting 1972; deceased 1973)
Reverend Pierre-M. de Contenson, OP, Rome (meetings 1973 — 1976)

Lutheran:

Prof. Dr. Harding Meyer, Strasbourg, France

Reformed:

Reverend Richmond Smith, Geneva

WORLD COUNCIL OF CHURCHES OBSERVERS:
Reverend Dr. Leslie Clements, Geneva (meetings 1972, 1973 and 1976)
Reverend Rex Davies, Geneva (meeting 1971)

OBSERVER FROM THE ANGLICAN COMMUNION:
Reverend Prebendary Henry Cooper, London (meetings 1972 and 1973)

METHODIST-ROMAN CATHOLIC CONVERSATIONS

Denver Report 1971
Dublin Report 1976
Honolulu Report 1981

DENVER REPORT, 1971

I. GENERAL RETROSPECT

1.   As a result of initiatives taken after Vatican Council II and of decisions made at the World Methodist Council in London, August, 1966, a dialogue was inaugurated between groups representing the Roman Catholic Church and the World Methodist Council. This Joint Commission held its first meetings at Ariccia, near Rome, in 1967.

2.   Opening papers at Ariccia were given by the co-chairmen, both pastors, on the question "Why are we here?" and one striking answer was "In expression of the 'one ecumenism' of the Holy Spirit seizing the kairos, the Lord's moment, for full and frank discussion".

3.   All present were conscious in general of the spectacular change in atmosphere between the two Churches in the past six or seven years, but this was underlined with some hard facts. John Wesley's "Letter to a Roman Catholic" of July 18, 1749, stood out, we were reminded, as an almost isolated overture in a general picture of aloofness and suspicion which could be illustrated, e. g. from a Methodist text book as late as 1953, while changes in Roman Catholic ecumenical attitudes and policy were even more recent.

4.   It is against such a background that our present mood and opportunity must be seen in perspective. Catholics recognize how perceptive and generous many Methodists were in seeing and responding to the spirit at work in Vatican II, and acknowledging hitherto unsuspected affinities with their own tradition in some of the great acts of the Council.

5.   At the same time we both recognize that for our people the experience of the past decade is new and not yet fully assimilated. It is an experience which, to remain fruitful, must be deepened, built on and more widely shared. Further ecumenical progress becomes harder, not easier, because it cannot be a mere linear progress in the negotiating of differences.

6.   From the outset we recognized that Roman Catholic/Methodist dialogue had a singular advantage—there is no history of formal separating between the two Churches, none of the historical, emotional problems consequent on a history of schism. When speakers reflected at Ariccia on "how a Roman Catholic looks at Methodism" and "how a Methodist looks at Roman Catholicism" (each theme was treated twice, once by an American and once by an Englishman) it was made clear, without any glossing over difficulties, that there were yet more solid grounds for affinity.

7.   First among these was the central place held in both traditions by the ideal of personal sanctification, growth in holiness through daily life in Christ. Speakers from either side bore witness independently to this. For both, holiness is rooted in theology and in disciplined life. Conversion for

the Methodist is but the beginning of a vital process, the ideal which is equally familiar to the Roman Catholic. If the cultivation of "Scriptural holiness" and its spread has always been seen by the Methodist as a common task, making the Church a fellowship rather than a hierarchy, Methodists gratefully recognize new emphasis present in "Lumen Gentium" 9-10 and in its chapter V on "The Universal Call to Holiness" while Roman Catholics can strengthen their own new insights by study of Methodist experience (the pursuit of this theme later gave rise to some of the commission's most satisfying work, which is reported on and its further prospects discussed below, Section III).

8. The disciplined life of the early Methodist, aimed at renewing a lax Church, set standards for the whole of Methodism which have found Roman Catholic parallels more often in the early life of religious foundations such as the Jesuits.

9. If a Methodist ideal was expressed in the phrase "a theology that can be sung", it was appreciated on the Roman Catholic side that the hymns of Charles Wesley, a rich source of Methodist spirituality, find echoes and recognition in the Catholic only. This is not least true of the eucharistic hymns, which we saw as giving a basis and hope for discussion of doctrinal differences about the nature of the Real Presence and the sense of the 'sacrificial' character of the Eucharist. Methodists on their side were candid in considering Roman Catholic questions on how far the Wesleys remain a decisive influence in contemporary Methodism.

10. One Methodist speaker stressed as early as Ariccia that "we need to keep before us the vision of our common mission", and this was the governing idea behind seven *practical proposals* elaborated there:

1. That everything possible be done by the Churches in cooperation to promote ecumenical instruction, discussion and action at all levels.

2. That ways be explored of cooperating in the training of ministers so far as local authorities see prudent.

3. That cooperation be sought with other Christian Churches with a view to securing as far as possible uniform wording for prayers which are in frequent use in common prayer. The common use of hymns should also be fostered without prejudice to existing tradition.

4. That in all ecumenical encounters there should be effort to begin dialogue towards common Christian moral standards.

5. That Methodists and Roman Catholics in their dialogue should be constantly aware of the challenge of secularism.

6. That the Roman Catholic and Methodist Churches explore with others further possibilities of social cooperation at various levels. This should include not only joint statements on social issues but also joint effort in fields such as world peace, world development, family life, poverty, race and immigration.

7. That ways of sharing facilities of all kinds be thoroughly explored, though with prudence and realism.

11.   While we recognize that a great deal of incidental Roman Catholic/Methodist collaboration reflects these proposals and even goes beyond them, we are disappointed at how little they have been considered and taken up in official ways. We realise of course that some of the purposes in question may be as well or even better achieved in a multilateral cooperation, but in the growing together of two Churches there can be no substitute in this or any age for the basic task of joint witness to fundamental Christian values. (This theme is taken up more fully later in Nos. 34–50.)

12.   So far this report has no more than alluded to the great doctrinal issues between our Churches; but in fact the friendship and mutual confidence we were able to establish so quickly at Ariccia ensured a welcome for the candour of the chief speakers on doctrine. If the passages in *Lumen Gentium* about the People of God were welcomed by Methodists, it was asked equally how they were to be related to the dogmas, found unacceptable, concerning the papacy. Equally Roman Catholics who speak warmly of Charles Wesley's eucharistic hymns said that "few Methodists would hold the doctrine of the Real Presence in any sense akin to the Catholic meaning". In either case the effect was not to inhibit dialogue but to stimulate it, though progress differed considerably in the two cases (cf. below Section V and VII).

13.   Methodists, like others who had followed the progress of Vatican II, showed great interest in the references to non-Roman Christians in *Unitatis Redintegratio,* Nos. 31-33 and in *Lumen Gentium,* 15. The crucial question here is, how far are Roman Catholics committed to the developments of which these apparently tentative passages seem capable? A related interest was shown in recent Roman Catholic writings on *ministry,* in which reflection on ordinary and extraordinary ministries seems to have many points of contact with the original Methodist situation (cf. No. 97).

14.   All these interests assume a purpose in our dialogue which goes far beyond dialogue for its own sake; a Methodist speaker invited the Commission to face squarely from the start the final prospect, if not of full organic union, at least of sharing at Holy Communion and there was no dissent voiced to this approach.

15.   The problems of *mixed marriages* were discussed at some length and the need for a thorough common study of the theology of marriage and its relation to mixed marriages and other contemporary problems was accepted. The nearest to an implementation of this has been the study on Christian Home and Family undertaken for and completed at our last (Lake Junaluska) meeting (See below Section IV). There seems no reason why our dialogue should not benefit here from work being done in other bilateral and multilateral dialogue.

16.   The problem of organizing adequate work between sessions is one that faces every series of annual ecumenical discussions. The most useful results are often yielded by small joint consultations out of which papers to

be presented grow. Two such groups met in Cambridge, England during 1968 in preparation for our second meeting in London, and another in 1970 in preparation for our last meeting at Lake Junaluska. Such meetings possibly suggest a fruitful method of future collaboration. It was found to be helpful to meet in a university where two foundations, one Methodist and one Roman Catholic, could cooperate and where Methodist and Roman Catholic scholars were within call. The method of beginning with short memoranda, sets of questions posed by one side to the other, might well serve in the future (see below Nos. 68 and 124-6.)

17.   With material from the first Cambridge meeting to hand, on the subjects Eucharist and Authority in the Church (the latter with particular reference to the papacy) the full joint commission met for the second time in London from August 31 to September 4, 1968.

18.   Great themes of Eucharist theology such as transubstantiation, relations of Word and Sacrament, and the place of sacrifice were found to have emerged at Cambridge, but the conditions and time limits of the London meeting as well as the Joint Commission's terms of reference, prevented anything more than the opening of these issues.

19.   There was clarification of what is meant by describing the Eucharist as a memorial. It was agreed that while traditional Methodist reverence for the preaching of the Gospel finds an echo in recent Roman Catholic theological and liturgical thinking, there are signs that Methodists on their part are re-capturing through the liturgical movement an appreciation of the sacraments such as is enshrined for example in Charles Wesley's eucharistic hymns.

20.   Turning to the theme of authority, discussion centred on the following problems of authority:

a)   What are the implications of the incarnation for any doctrine of authority in the Church? (Cf. Nos. 102 et sqq.)

b)   How to discern the *sensus fidelium* in contemporary conditions.

c)   The nature of obedience ("internal" and "external").

d)   The relation of conscience to informed reasoning (Cf. Nos. 113-6).

e)   How far can the authority of conclusions be divorced from the arguments supporting them?

21.   In preparation for its next meeting, the Joint Commission resolved that a small group should survey the ground covered by the first two meetings and submit practical suggestions for the way ahead. The hope was also expressed that the next meeting of the Joint Commission in autumn, 1969, might result in an interim report.

In accordance with this decision, it was at Oxford in July, 1969, that a group endeavoured to discharge this task by preparing a report for the third meeting of the Joint Commission at Rabat, Malta, September 15 to 19, 1969.

22.   The two main themes under discussion at Rabat, apart from the

review just referred to, were Ministry in the Methodist and Roman Catholic traditions, and Methodist and Roman Catholic reflection on the Church in the contemporary world.

23.   A first paper outlined how the original Methodist societies with their extraordinary preaching ministry developed into the Methodist Church with its ordinary ministry of the Sacraments as well as of Word. A Roman Catholic paper took as its starting principle the primacy of the Church's memory of what Jesus had said and done and tried summarily to trace the developments of the theology of the Ministry from earliest times to Vatican II. The discussion centred on the sacramental nature of the ordination rite in Methodism and also on the distinction between the ordained ministry and the common priesthood of all the faithful; here it was suggested and widely agreed that the difference in kind was a difference of functions in the Body. We feel that there is a great deal of room for further joint reflection here especially with regard to the prophetic, charismatic aspects of ministry which could be fruitful not only for our own dialogue but in other ecumenical fields as well (Cf. No. IV).

24.   Papers on Secularization given at Rabat will be referred to in section II of the report (No. 28).

25.   The wider vision of the possibilities of Roman Catholic/Methodist dialogue, which this four years' experience and other parallel experiences have opened up, convinced both the Roman Catholic and the Methodists concerned that the time is ripe for a reorganization of the dialogue. The commission at Rabat decided that proposals for such a reorganization should be discussed at Junaluska in 1970 and presented to the World Methodist Conference in 1971 and to the Plenary of the Secretariat for Promoting Christian Unity in the same year (Section VIII).

Meanwhile four themes were chosen as continuation of the dialogue — themes which had already emerged as crucial and which it was hoped might be well prepared by working (with cooperation of experts from outside the commission) in the intervening months (details and assessment of this work will be found in Sections III, IV, V and VII).

The commission has reason to be grateful to all who collaborated in this work.

II. CHRISTIANITY AND THE CONTEMPORARY WORLD

I.   SUMMARY OF COMMISSION'S WORK ON THIS THEME

26.   The Joint Commission has reflected seriously on the problems and challenges which Catholics and Methodists alike confront in the world today. We have found unity in thought and feeling in understanding and interpreting the contemporary situation.

27.   The papers and discussions bearing on Christianity in the contemporary world primarily invited more or less intellectual reflection without

making much effort to speak to the masses of Christians who are living and struggling in these times. The interests of these latter are of the first importance and communication with them needs to be a chief object of future discussion if we are to carry out our common mission in the world.

28.   One paper on secularization was presented and discussed at the sessions in Rabat, developing the idea that all of the humanitarian efforts of the secular world today actually express the spirit of Jesus. Consequently, those who act outside the Church toward this end may be called anonymous Christians. This paper was tempered by some warnings against facile tendencies to identify Christianity with the secular world. For, in addition to the humanitarian advances made possible by science and technology, we agreed that there are demonic factors which warn against any naive identification of Christianity with secularity. Some preliminary efforts were made to define "secularization", but no searching analysis was forthcoming. The members of the Commission were in agreement that the extensive processses of secularization need to be taken seriously even though they did not have time to develop their own reflections fully and clearly.

29.   An English group from both sides prepared a booklet entitled *Christian Belief: A Catholic-Methodist Statement,* which was made available and discussed briefly at the Junaluska meeting. This addresses itself to the contemporary situation. Parts I and II identify, on the one hand, some of the major characteristics of the world in which Christians are called upon to live, and, on the other hand, the ways by which men may move towards a living faith in these times. This seems to us an excellent beginning of the kind of work we might be doing together (Cf. No. 125).

30.   A paper, entitled, "Trends in Spirituality: The Contemporary Situation", also reflected this desire to understand and assess what is going on in the modern world. Here a serious attempt was made to bring into full view some of the major factors which threaten and challenge Catholics and Methodists in their concern for spirituality. This paper suggested that Christians need to be aware of a new mentality which has been emerging over a long period. This mentality, which has been produced in large measure by the extensive and rapid developments in science and technology, goes deeper than and is the primary source of the phenomenon of secularism (the belief that if God is he does not matter). There seemed to be agreement that one of the obstacles to spirituality is an antimetaphysical spirit in the contemporary world though not all current tendencies here are discouraging. Along with this there is the loss of confidence in man's reason, a loss reflected in the various antirational moods and fads of this era. It was noted in discussion that one of the tragedies on the contemporary scene is the emergence of revolutionary idealism based on emotional and ideological rather than rational and moral foundations. We felt that joint efforts in the recovery and nurture of a basic theistic world-view are essential to spirituality. For when men doubt and deny God, it is obvious that they will doubt and deny the reality and relevance of revelation, the moral order, the redemptive process through Jesus

Christ, the work of the Holy Spirit in the community of faith, the life everlasting, etc. Modern doubt and denial is pervasive, and its influence, recognised or unconscious, is difficult to exaggerate.

31.   The Commission shared, however, in the conviction that the present situation is full of promise for spirituality. For in man's very experience of failure without God—that is, in his rootlessness, distraction, despair, disillusionment, frustration, loneliness, in obvious moral disasters on the national and international scenes—God is calling men to new and authentic life in the community of faith. On the positive side, the current desire for human dignity and compassion present a special opportunity for Catholics and Methodists to unite in giving new voice to the ancient verities of the faith. Men in danger of dehumanization need more urgently than ever the life of Christian truth.

32.   Again, on the positive side, it was observed that there is an emerging concern among men for community. There are signs of inferior expressions of community which require the corrective and elevating guidance of the historic community of faith. Besides this, the thought was registered that men today, amid all their distraction, pressures, hurry and bias towards mediocrity, require the kind of contemplation made possible through the higher expressions of the devotional life among Catholics and Methodists. In short, life today is complex, dynamic—life in which God calls us to acknowledge the real problems, but also to seize boldly the opportunity of renewing genuine spiritual life.

33.   A further concern of the Commission needs to be noted before considering those common resources which are available for appealing to men who are looking toward the twenty-first century. In the discussions there was the recurring sense of unity concerning the moral values with which Catholics and Methodists assess what is going on in the world today. Here it was observed that even among highly sophisticated people there are often subhuman standards of thought and life. Among the masses everywhere there are signs of moral deterioration which make new life in Christ a desperate need. This was noted particularly in some of the discussions on marriage and family life (See Section IV).

II. AREAS OF AGREEMENT WHICH MAY SERVE AS AIDS TO JOINT EFFORTS TO ENCOUNTER THE CONTEMPORARY WORLD.

34.   As we look toward the future, we are immensely encouraged by the areas of profound agreement which, if properly explored and actively shared, can enable us both to strengthen ourselves and engage in effective dialogue with the nonbelieving world. In particular, seven such regions of substantial agreement in thought, feeling and concern have become increasingly visible.

35.   *First,* we agree that Jesus Christ alone is the supreme and final authority. It has been commonly supposed that our differences on

authority are so deep-seated and conflicting that there is not likely to be any real consensus. We have discovered, however, that when we start with Jesus Christ as the supreme and final authority both Catholics and Methodists find themselves sharing in a common conviction, whatever other and secondary authorities may be officially recognized. Christ is the last word and the final authority in relation to whom everything else pertaining to salvation is to be understood, interpreted and judged. Both Catholics and Methodists can build unhesitatingly on this foundation, and can move into the world to carry out the mission which Christ commanded (Cf. Section VII).

36.   *Second,* closely related to this is our essential agreement on the Bible as God's living Word.

Some of the statements of Vatican II on this subject open the way to important advances both for Catholics and Methodists, on the one hand, and for the contemporary secular world, on the other. One of the basic contributions of the Council is its interpretation of the Biblical vision as a massive sweep of God's revelation of his purpose for mankind. In an age which tends to deny the reality of ultimate purpose, the stress on the category of purpose becomes essential in understanding and using the Bible. (See for example *Lumen Gentium,* Pars 2-3; and see also "The Constitution on Revelation", Pars 2-6). There are points to be discussed here, but the vision of God's revealed purpose as set forth in bold outline would seem to be central for both Churches, something indispensable unless we are prepared to abandon the Christian religion itself. One of the tasks with which Catholics and Methodists are jointly charged is that of identifying certain basic principles for interpreting the Bible, which aim to recover the sense of the authority and finality of the Bible without lapsing into obscurantism. The essentials would appear to be precisely those stressed by Vatican II.

37.   *Third,* we share in affirming a total theistic world-view. This world-view, so gravely needed in our age, is not developed philosophically by the Biblical writers, but it is there in bold outline and can therefore be used as a basis for communicating with the modern mentality. In fact one of the beauties of the Bible at this point is that it presents a total vision concerning ultimate reality and the purpose of God which can be comprehended by the generality of mankind.

38.   There are philosophical systems that move in the right direction, but they cannot be made available to the general public. Very few men have either the interest or the ability to philosophize in any authentic way. Besides, even among philosophers only a limited number will be convinced by any particular system of thought. Again, philosophical systems, while serving their own important ends, appeal chiefly to the intellect. This restricts their usefulness still further. More important still, philosophy is one thing, religion is another. Men need both a responsible world-view and a vital faith. This combination alone furnishes an intellectual at-

mosphere in which the soul of a man can thrive. It alone opens the way to a living encounter with God that nurtures love and hope.

39. The genius of the Biblical revelation, in part at least, is that it affirms a world-view that is both intellectually plausible and open to confirmation by experience. It appeals to the best thinking of men and at the same time calls them to commitment and faith. But unless this can be made credible to modern man, with his inevitable doubts, the message of the Bible cannot pierce through.

40. Briefly stated, the range of theistic world-view embraces the following convictions we share. God's creation has a purpose; He created man that man might perfect himself morally and spiritually in community under the lordship of Jesus Christ; there is a real moral order grounded in God; human dignity and freedom are real and crucial; men are called to responsible living in community as well as individually; there is a life after death wherein the pilgrimage begun on earth is consummated in God's eternal love.

41. There are Catholic and Methodist theologians grappling with theoretical issues touching metaphysics and the nature of ultimate reality. We should promote collaboration here, for we have much to share and to offer each other in a field where guidance and leadership are wanted.

42. *Fourth,* we are in essential agreement in seeking to diagnose the human situation in the world today. We need to work together in interpreting the theological and spiritual meaning of modern man's despair and disillusionment. We need to talk about his quest for identity and what that implies both negatively and positively. We have a common ground on which to move in interpreting modern man's quest for meaning in his secular experience. We have a wealth of ideas to share on modern man's quest for community, contemplation, compassion, and dignity (Cf. the important paper on this theme, referred to in §30).

43. In "The Constitution on the Church in the Modern World", Methodists recognize very important statements on the situation which all Christians today face. Consider this:

> . . . growing numbers of people are abandoning religion in practice. Unlike former days the denial of God or of religion, or the abandonment of them, are no longer unusual and individual occurrences. For today it is not rare for such decisions to be presented as requirements of scientific progress or of a certain new humanism. In numerous places these views are voiced not only in the teachings of philosophers, but on every side they influence literature, the arts, the interpretation of the humanities and of history, and civil laws themselves. As a consequence, many people are shaken (Para. 7).

44. There is also an excellent statement on "the forms and roots of atheism" which "must be accounted among the most serious problems of this age, and is deserving of closer examination":

> Yet believers themselves frequently bear some responsibility for this

situation. For, taken as a whole, atheism is not a spontaneous development but stems from a variety of causes, including a critical reaction against religious belief, and in some places against the Christian religion in particular (Para. 19).

45. We have now reached a point in history when the stark realities of doubt and massive abandonment of God and the things of God are a present reality. The end is not yet in sight. We believe that Catholics and Methodists, tackling this general theme together, can analyze and interpret the human situation so as to indicate how the Holy Spirit Himself is working on the contemporary scene for the purpose of drawing people into the orbit of God's Kingdom. We can confront the world with an alternative interpretation of the meaning of contemporary experience, including experience felt by many of the absence of God. We need to think more seriously on the ways in which the Holy Spirit functions in our negative as well as in our positive experiences: to identify more clearly how the Holy Spirit acts on the human spirit at each stage of man's earthly life.

46. *Fifth,* Methodists find in the statements of Vatican II on human dignity and autonomy many echoes of their own tradition (Cf. *Gaudium et Spes*, Ch. 1). Combining objectivity with a steady relation of human activity to God, these statements offer opportunities for development and application which Catholics and Methodists should exploit together, recognising that amid the threat of dehumanization here is an approach to man's secular achievements which promises better fruit. If the genuine autonomy of the secular is recognised the Christian will be more open and sympathetic towards the artist, the scientist and other creative workers; he will be more willing to learn from them and to hear the voice of God speaking through them, and they in their turn will feel less alienated, more encouraged and stimulated. There is no more eloquent witness the Church can give to the dignity of man than intelligent support of and scope to his highest activities, and she has a remarkable history in this.

47. *Sixth,* though we recognize in the Christian heritage a recurring tendency towards passivity and withdrawal, Catholic and Methodist thought and practice call for responsible living in community within the Church and alongside it. Joint efforts in thinking and practice are possible here, and call for careful study.

48. *Seventh,* perhaps the agreement we have most strongly felt has been in our sense of the importance of Christian spirituality, greater than ever in today's situation. This is treated fully in the next section of the report (See §§57-61).

49. By way of summary we may say that Catholics and Methodists can unite and share at many points in a vast programme of interrelated activities in behalf of the conversion of the world and the elevation of mankind throughout the world. This includes an adventurous quest for peace, for justice, for ministry to the needs of men in ignorance and poverty and for the entire benefit of the human world both physical and

spiritual. In and through all this there is the glorious shared vision of the life after death when Jesus Christ shall be all in all.

50. We would recall here Chapter V of *Lumen Gentium.* This is entitled "The Call of the Whole Church to Holiness". There is no part of that document more congenial to the Methodist heritage, properly understood, than this. Here there is a universal call to holiness which erases the false distinction between higher and lower levels of Christian faithfulness. And we share in the concern that holiness be affirmed as both a possibility and an imperative for all Christians. Whatever definition we give to the term, the idea of sanctity — that is, the idea that God has called men to enter into new life dominated by the love of Christ and motivated by the example of Christ — this gives a vast area of agreement. And in the practical sphere it has the most far reaching possible promise. For on both sides we are eager to emphasize the mysterious dynamic interaction between the Holy Spirit and the human spirit. This divine-human interaction, rightly understood, seems to be God's chosen way for the recreation of men and the conversion of the world.

III. SPIRITUALITY

I. INTRODUCTION

51. Our sub-committee on Prayer and Spirituality took its beginning from a recommendation in the interim report made at Rabat in September, 1969. Two themes for further study were suggested because of their "particular scope" for making the dialogue an occasion for "common witness to great Christian values". One of these themes was, "Christian Life and Spirituality - Holiness of Heart and Life". The report expanded this theme in the following words:

> This would examine the genesis of Methodism as a movement of personal, spiritual renewal, and its emphasis on the social implications of perfect love. Development of the theme might include consideration of the priesthood of all believers, the universal call to holiness, the Holy Spirit and grace, the meaning of prayer, the relation of liturgical prayer to personal piety, the spiritual life, devotion to the Sacred Heart, Marian devotion, devotion to the Saints, monasticism, the Pentecostalist phenomenon among Catholics and Methodists, attention to the Word as a constitutive element of the spiritual life, the complementary relation of the interior life and the life of good works. The treatment should reflect the current practice of Methodists and Roman Catholics, as well as providing a historical and theological development.

52. The first meeting of the sub-committee was held at Raleigh in December, 1969. Results of the study of this sub-committee were available for the final meeting of the Joint Commission at Lake Junaluska in August, 1970. The subject might well have been broached earlier, since its importance was early realised. In one of the opening papers at Ariccia, in

1967, it had been pointed out that, "Catholics and Methodists have always had one very important thing in common, though they have not fully realized it: . . . the conviction of John Wesley that each man has a duty to seek holiness and Christian perfection". Personal sanctification and growth in holiness through daily life were seen as prominent in both traditions. The Methodist view of "entire sanctification", that is, sanctification of everything in daily life and work, met the Catholic view of the continuous growth in perfection which makes up the whole progress of the spiritual life. The disciplined life of the early Methodists recalled the ascetism of the early Jesuits.

53.   Both Methodists and Roman Catholics found common ground from agreement in the universal call to holiness which helped to confirm what one of the speakers at Ariccia saw as, "the discovery of meaningful harmony between Wesley's 'evangelical catholicism' and the spirit of Vatican II". Following the recommendations made at Malta, the discussion on spirituality was taken up in terms of both the historical background of the two traditions and their contemporary situation.

II.   HISTORICAL BACKGROUND

54.   Investigation of the historical dimension gave special emphasis to the nineteenth century in both Methodist and Roman Catholic spirituality. Here, again, in spite of some differences, it could be seen that Catholics and Methodists shared a wider, deeper, richer heritage of Christian spirituality than might have been suspected. This heritage is rightly called, "Life in the Spirit". In it, we find common roots in mutual reverence for Scripture, in mutual stress on conversion and renewal, in mutual insistence that "heart religion" shall find expression in social action, in mutual concern for the Christian home and family as the 'domestic Church'.

55.   Out of their separate traditions, both Methodists and Roman Catholics come together as they recognize God's gracious prevenience, and as they express belief in Jesus Christ as God's Love Incarnate and the Holy Spirit as God with us. Both traditions hold man's cooperation with God in the mystery of salvation as necessary; both look upon life itself as liturgy. Both traditions converge in

> "compatible definitions of goals for the Christian life (however disparate the means and uneven the results), a dynamic process of growth in grace, from the threshold of faith (justification) toward the fullness of faith (sanctification) — by means of affective patterns of moral and spiritual discipline (ascesis), charismatic gifts and outpourings, sacrificial love and service as 'effective signs' of faith's professions and of pious feeling".

56.   A study of the historical background of Methodist and Roman Catholic spirituality leads to the conclusion that what has mattered most in both traditions has been the reality of religion as it brings about the transformation of man's heart and mind in everyday living. In our conversations, we saw that here was the meaning of the *theologia cordis,* by

which we come to know the crucified and risen Christ as Lord and Saviour and the Spirit present in us and in the Church.

III. THE CONTEMPORARY SITUATION

57.   It is not enough in ecumenical dialogue to look to the past for the comfort of a common heritage of spirituality. For this reason, a further study was made of current trends in both Methodist and Roman Catholic prayer and spirituality. This was found to be necessary since Christians, too, are in a sense, "men of our time". As such, they are faced with both the threat and the challenge which the contemporary situation offers to Christian spirituality.

58.   The negative aspects of the contemporary situation have been considered separately in this report (Cf. §30). The conversations on prayer and spirituality also brought to light a number of positive factors which exist in the world today. Some of these touch on personal relations and contribute to the development of spirituality through their worth for human existence. Others reveal a call to spirituality in the frustrations, the emptiness and the boredom which man experiences in many phases of daily life and culture.

> The void in the world he has constructed is, itself, a plea for fulfilment that must come from beyond man. The contemporary situation betrays man's thirst for the God whom he strives to find, often unknowingly — at times, even while rejecting him.

59.   At least three trends in spirituality have been discerned recently, suggesting that there are possibilities for a creative response on the part of the Church and the Christian in facing the contemporary world. In the first place, there is a search for prayer as *contemplation*. This search reveals our deep need of God, our longing for salvation, our eagerness to know and to do God's will as revealed in Jesus Christ. Secondly, there is a call for *compassion*. This call is addressed to the Church which is dedicated to the primary mission of guiding persons in corporate action and in the works of justice, truth and love. Finally, there is a desire for *community*. This desire gives witness to the fact that we are to be saved as a people. It recognizes also that the Churches must pray and work together toward the true unity, wherever and whenever this is possible.

60.   Such a creative response as that suggested above can be assured only if the Church and all members of the Church realize the importance of inner renewal. Through constant renewal, the Church will become truly catholic, evangelical and reformed. The Church will be *catholic* in knowing how to express what is universal in the Christian message of God's love for all men. It will be *evangelical* in reaching out effectively to share this good news by word and by responsible living in community. It will be *reformed* in willing to engage in self-criticism and to weed out the inauthentic in thought and practice.

61.   The discussion on spirituality led us to agree that the Churches must proclaim community by showing the way through compassion and contemplation in Christian living to communion-in-unity. Spirituality in the Church must be a witness to the capacity of men to live as human beings and as Christians in the institutions and structures of contemporary society and under all the conditions which go to make up the contemporary situation.

IV.   CRITIQUE

62.   We acknowledge with gratitude and joy the discovery of a vision shared by Methodists and Roman Catholics in our understanding of prayer and spirituality in the Christian life. The study which led to this discovery, however, did not treat every facet of this topic in the same manner.

63.   For example, to countless Roman Catholics, devotion to Mary is an integral and important part of their Christian experience and of the "Life in the Spirit". For Methodists, on the other hand, the dogmatic status of Roman Catholic doctrines concerning the Mother of our Lord was identified at Ariccia as one of three "hard-core issues of *radical* disagreement" between the two traditions. Neither the positive nor the negative side of Mariology was treated in the study of spirituality covered by this report. No special attention was given to the restatement of the Marian question effected by Vatican II.

64.   The Junaluska report referred to common Methodist — Roman Catholic reverence for Scripture and to the eucharistic foundation of both traditions of spirituality. Both of these marks were accepted without question as implicitly basic to the study. This acceptance, however, did not take up the questions or state the real ambiguities which rise out of certain attitudes toward Scripture and Eucharist, at times, in the two traditions (Cf. Sections V and VII).

65.   At the end of the discussions on spirituality, Methodists found that inadequate treatment had been given to two strong traditions in their devotional history: That of *hymnody*—particularly as seen in the eucharistic hymns of Charles Wesley—and that of the *koinonia*—as carried on in the class meetings. Roman Catholics were quick to admit that they had much to gain from a better knowledge of these two facets of Methodist spirituality.

66.   There was general agreement too that the question of communion *in sacris* and the possibility of sharing in the Lord's Supper ought properly to have been raised in relation to the discussion of spirituality, as much as in any other areas of ecumenical concern.

67.   The great wealth found in the common heritage and shared vision discovered by both Methodists and Roman Catholics during our conversations on prayer and spirituality led the members of the commission to see

the need for a continued education along this line. They strongly recommend that programmes be begun to assure mutual enrichment at every level on this topic.

68. We add some *practical suggestions* which are addressed especially to the concerns expressed by the commission elsewhere in this report regarding communication:

1. Informal colloquies, such as those held at Cambridge ought to be devoted to the study of spirituality.

2. We need continued opportunities for discussion together on the different sacramental and non-sacramental ways of fostering spirituality in both traditions.

3. There is a need for devotional material which can be shared by both traditions to help the general body of the faithful in their use of the Bible and prayer in everyday life.

4. Means must be taken to make it possible to share such practices as lay missions.

5. We need to study the problem of wide-spread communication in view of promoting a fuller understanding of our common heritage of "Scriptural holiness".

6. We must learn how to deal with the old suspicions and gradually do away with them — for example, the Catholic rejection of what seems to be a life-refusing attitude in certain disciplinary practices in Methodism.

7. We must learn how to develop common devotion, such as the Methodist devotion to the five wounds of the crucified and risen Lord alongside the Roman Catholic devotion to the Sacred Heart of Jesus and, in this matter, be mutually enriched.

8. Practical means must be found to help both Methodists and Roman Catholics move into a growth in their devotional life with balance and vitality. Such means might include shared retreats, small prayer or Bible study groups, groups of Christian response to all areas of human experience, shared devotional and instructional material, shared facilities for Christian and spiritual education at all levels.

IV. CHRISTIAN HOME AND FAMILY

69. Our two Churches welcome the recent dialogue between them at theological and sociological levels on various aspects of the Christian home and family and recommend that arrangements should be made for this work to be continued.

70. Both Churches find much ground for agreement on Christian marriage and family life in the Decree of Vatican II, "The Church in the Modern World", Part III, Chapter I, Section 47-52 and commend this document as a basis for future study and dialogue on these issues.

71. We agree that the well-being of the individual person and of society as a whole is intimately linked with marriage and family life. We are agreed that married life is a holy and honourable estate instituted by God for the mutual love and sanctification of men and women, as well as the rearing and education of children. We agree that a marriage between two baptised Christians is a voluntary union for life, of one man to one woman to the exclusion of all others so that they become one flesh (*Matthew* 19:6) and as such a sign of God's fidelity to His people and symbol of the unity between Christ and His Church (*Eph.* V). A married couple render mutual help to each other through the intimate union of their persons and of their actions. The permanent nature of Christian marriage provides a suitable environment in which children can develop into mature and responsible citizens. Christian marriage also calls us to and produces mutual fidelity, unity and love which are themselves great God-given blessings. Pre- and extra-marital intimate sexual relationships are incompatible with the teachings of Christ and with the standard of personal holiness both Churches expect their members to attain. Holy Scripture directs and inspires married couples and their families to live in love and friendship with God. To this end Christian parents should encourage family prayers, Bible study and the perfect fulfillment of their duties and obligations as a means for the personal sanctification of themselves and their children.

72. *Inter-Church Marriages.* God has made man and woman in His own image but in such a way that each sex is complementary to the other. We are agreed that there are great advantages if husband and wife have much in common especially in matters of religious faith and practice. We are agreed that marriage in which one spouse is Methodist and one Roman Catholic presents a special opportunity and responsibility for joint pastoral concern by both our Churches. The basic unity in faith through baptism and attendance to the Word should make it possible for couples in such marriages to help one another in spiritual growth, and to share with their children that rich Christian heritage which they hold in common.

73. We are not unmindful of the difficulties which can occur when the Church allegiance and doctrine of two parties differ, and both are deeply committed to their different Christian traditions. This conflict must be seen in the context of the right to marry, the inviolability of conscience, the joint obligation of the parents for the care and education of their children, other mutual rights and obligations in marriage and the teaching and self understanding of the Churches involved.

74. While recent changes in the legislation of the Roman Catholic Church on inter-Church marriages are seen as an ecumenical advance, we are nevertheless conscious of the fact that the conflict and agony in such marriages have not been created by positive law, nor will they resolve by positive law. The difficulties inherent in inter-Church marriages should compel us not only to work with greater zeal for fuller ecclesial unity, but also to do everything possible to help the partners of such marriages to use

them as means of grace and of ecumenical growth. We urge a special World Methodist Council/Roman Catholic working party be set up to deal with the theology of marriage and problems of inter-Church marriages or that the World Methodist Council consider the possibility of joining in dialogue in progress on this subject between the Roman Catholic Church and the World Federation of the Reformed Churches.

75. *Divorce.* The Roman Catholic Church does not allow the divorce of baptised partners of a consummated marriage with a view of re-marriage, nor has she allowed the re-marriage of divorced persons. The Methodist Church has taken a different point of view on these matters. Nevertheless, we are well aware that special problems are created by the breakdown of marriages and that these cause great suffering, not least to the children of that marriage. We are aware that theological reflection is at present active in this whole field, and recommend that further joint study and dialogue be given to this important problem. We are greatly concerned with the increasing incidence of divorce and the disintegration of family life and jointly urge both Churches to make common effort to reduce their occurrence.

76. *Contraception.* We agree that human sexual intercourse has two equal and inter-related functions, namely fostering love, affection, unity and fidelity between husband and wife as well as that of reproduction. Under the stress and strain of modern social and economic conditions, parents have a right and duty before God to decide the number of children they may bear, support, rear and educate. How this decision is to be implemented is a moral matter, a matter of conscience which should be the subject of prayerful consideration by the parents who are to seek help and guidance from the Church. We recognize, however, that at present there exist differences between the official positions of our respective Churches on the application of contraceptive methods by responsible parents. As we take cognizance of existing movements within our two Churches and of the sociological, ecological and demographic conditions of mankind, we would encourage further dialogue on this matter.

77. *Abortion.* We agree that the Holy Scripture affirms the sacredness and dignity of human life and that we have, therefore, a duty and obligation to defend, protect and preserve it. Our two Churches are at present confronted with complex moral issues relative to abortion and with wide differences between them in their teaching and interpretations. We have a responsibility to explore, clarify and emphasise the moral and ethical issues involved in abortion and confront our people with them as the ultimate basis for decision. We recommend that this be the subject of special dialogue between experts from our respective Churches.

78. *Care of the Aged.* At the other end of life the problems of geriatrics are formidable and increasing. Now that people are living longer, special housing and other facilities are needed for those whose natural powers have atrophied or are declining. We recognize this to be a family, Church

and society responsibility to make possible the maintenance of family life for the aged. We recommend that both Churches should cooperate in caring for the needs of the elderly by providing preparation courses for retirement and giving the aged and infirm a sense of being loved, wanted and cared for. This assurance which is needed as we enter the world and develop into adult life is needed no less as we prepare to depart from this life to eternity.

78a. *Moves towards Unity.* We believe that our present desires for greater unity between the Roman Catholic and Methodist Churches can be greatly helped and accelerated if means are available for local Churches to be kept informed of the results of dialogue between theologians on matters which at present concern us. To this end we recommend that Catholic dioceses and Methodist districts or conferences establish local, joint committees to foster and encourage better mutual understanding between members of the clergy, local Churches, and lay organisations (Cf. §§ 121-122).

V. EUCHARIST

79.   The subject of the Eucharist, Mass, Lord's Supper is one to which the commission has devoted a good deal of attention, and not only in its main meetings and in its sub-committees: this theme took up a good deal of time at the colloquia at Cambridge. This was not because of any undue preoccupations with sacramentalism, but because there was an obvious place of common agreement and appreciation with which to begin, i.e. the emphasis on frequent Communion of the Wesleys which led to a eucharistic revival in the first part of the Methodist story, and of which the eucharistic hymns of Charles Wesley are a permanent legacy. So our first conversations included an appraisal of those hymns from a Catholic view.

80.   It should be stressed that at no point of our conversations has there been more friendly honesty and candour. It was not disguised, for example, that the eucharistic devotion of the Wesleys and the hymns of Charles Wesley are no index at all to the place of Holy Communion in the life, thought and devotion of modern Methodists. The conversations ranged from the great recurring theological themes to such practices as the Methodist custom of using unfermented wine, and to Roman practices of extra-liturgical devotions to the Sacrament. In our discussions, it has been a little like ascending a spiral staircase, coming back again and again to the same points, but at another level and with a wider horizon.

81.   Obviously two of these points were, first, the sense in which Christ is *present,* the mode of his presence and how our awareness of his presence is realized in the sacrament; second, the question of how far we may speak of a *sacrifice.* Other questions, the nature of our memorial (as the Protestant Reformers themselves stressed, much more than a bare act of intellectual remembrance of a past event) and the whole eschatological and for-

ward looking element in the Eucharist, with its implications in the life of the believer, of the whole body of Christ and of the Body of Christ in relation to the world—were dealt with in less detail. The whole problem of the relation of Christ's presence to the elements of bread and wine demanded and received the full treatment of a massive paper on the problem of transubstantiation in relation to modern ways of thought.

82.　　Here are continuing problems and neither in this case nor in that of the idea of sacrifice could our commission hope to come up with solutions of questions which still exercise the scholars in the learned world. Nonetheless we can register an astonishing, helpful and hopeful measure of agreement, which we have thought fit to summarize and record:

83.　POINTS OF AGREEMENT:

I.　*The real presence*

1.　Both Methodists and Roman Catholics affirm as the primary fact the presence of Christ in the Eucharist, the Mass, or the Lord's Supper.

2.　This is a reality that does not depend on the experience of the communicant.

3.　It is only by faith that we become aware of the presence of Christ in the Eucharist.

4.　Within the worship of the Church, this is a distinctive mode or manifestation of the presence of Christ.

5.　Christ in the fullness of His being, human and divine, crucified and risen, is present in this sacrament.

6.　The presence of Christ is mediated through the sacred elements of bread and wine over which the words of institution have been pronounced.

7.　Bread and wine do not mean the same outside the context of the Eucharistic celebration as they do within that context. Within the eucharistic celebration they become the sign par excellence of Christ's redeeming presence to His people. To the eyes of faith, they now signify the Body and Blood of Jesus, given and shed for the world; as we take, eat and drink, and share the bread and wine, we are transformed into Him. The eucharistic bread and wine are therefore efficacious signs of the Body and Blood of Christ.

II.　*The sacrifice*

1.　The Eucharist is the celebration of Christ's full, perfect and sufficient sacrifice, offered once and for all, for the whole world.

2.　It is a memorial which is more than a recollection of a past event. It is a re-enactment of Christ's triumphant sacrifice and makes available for us its benefits.

3.　For this reason Roman Catholics call the Eucharist a sacrifice, though this terminology is not used by Methodists.

4. In this celebration we share in Christ's offering to Himself in obedience to the Father's will.

III. *Communion*

1. The perfect participation in the celebration of the Eucharist is the communion of the faithful.
2. By partaking of the Body and Blood we become one with Christ, our Saviour, and one with one another in a common dedication to the redemption of the world.

84. POINTS OF DIFFERENCE:

I. *The presence*

1. The presence in the Eucharist for the Methodists is not fundamentally different from the presence of Christ in other means of grace, i.e. preaching.
2. For some Methodists the preaching of the Word provides a more effective means of grace than the Eucharist.
3. To the faith of the Roman Catholic, the bread and wine within the context of the Eucharistic celebration are transformed into another reality, i.e. the Body and Blood of the glorified Jesus. The external of the bread and wine remain unchanged. For the Roman Catholic this transformation takes place through the words of institution pronounced by a validly ordained priest.
4. The worship of the Blessed Sacrament is linked with the Roman Catholic doctrine of the transformation of the elements, and does not obtain in Methodism.

II. *Intercommunion*

1. In Methodism any Christian who can conscientiously accept the invitation is welcomed to the Lord's table. Except in cases of urgent necessity, eucharistic communion is extended by Roman Catholics only to those who share the same faith.

   We welcome the ongoing study of this problem in actual dialogue, and look forward to the day when we can partake of the Eucharist together. We rejoice in the increasing agreements in doctrine between the two communions which are working to bring this about.

85. POINTS FOR FURTHER STUDY:

   In addition to the problem already raised these further issues *relating* to the Eucharist need further study:

1. The ministry and the apostolic succession (Cf. Section VI).
2. Our common faith.
3. The relation between eucharistic union and ecclesiastical fellowship.

86.   It might be felt that in the light of this concentrated common study and conversation this is a theme which might be left for a time while attention is turned to other subjects. If so, it would be important to return to it at convenient points — in the light for example of further understanding about the nature of the Church, or of our common experience of worship — not only in theoretical discussion but even more in the light of our experience of worshipping with one another. In any case there remains before us the task of getting across our agreements to the Churches at large and to bodies of Christians who have perhaps hardly begun to consider some of our problems, let alone our solutions. Nor can we ignore the agreement already registered between Catholics and Orthodox and Catholics and Anglicans in which we recognize an overall growth in ecumenical understanding.

VI. MINISTRY

87.   Two illuminating papers on the ministry, one from the Catholic side, the other from the Methodist, were presented for study at Rabat. From these, though no concrete conclusions were drawn by the Commission, it was recognised that this is one of the primary areas for more extensive sharing and exploration, particularly in view of the renewed emphasis by both Catholics and Methodists on the ministry in relation to the cultivation of spirituality in local Churches. The possibilities for mutual benefits from further dialogue are evident also because of the new emphasis on the Bible and preaching among Catholics since Vatican II and because of the growing appreciation of the sacraments among Methodists.

88.   On the basis of the two papers presented at Rabat and in the light of certain general presuppositions among Catholics and Methodists concerning the ministry, there are *areas of agreement* which await further reflection and action. The following may be singled out for special mention:

89.   1) The primary authority and finality of Jesus Christ as the One through whom the ministry, whether sacramental or otherwise, is both identified and ultimately authorized. The minister participates in Christ's ministry, acts in Christ's name.

90.   2) The importance of the work of the Holy Spirit in calling people into the ministry (we recognize, of course, that the call comes in various ways — sometimes suddenly, usually gradually — and no effort needs to be made here to say what it means to be called).

91.   3) The understanding of the ministry primarily in terms of a) the *full-time* dedication to Christ for *life,* for studying and communicating the Gospel, and *b)* the functions of the minister (both of these concern the work of administering the Sacraments, preaching the Word, teaching Christian truth, defending the faith, nurturing souls in spirituality, and, by teaching and example, showing leadership through acts of reconciliation and of service to people in need).

92. 4) The understanding of the ministry as, in some mysterious way, an extension of the incarnational and sacramental principle whereby human beings (as ministers), through their souls and bodies, become, by the power of the Holy Spirit, agents of Christ for bringing God into the lives and conditions of men (this means also, of course, that they are agents for enabling men to find their way toward God).

93. 5) The shared recognition of prophetic and special ministries with their distinctive moral and charismatic qualities.

94. 6) The "connectional" character of the ministry (the term is a Methodist usage but the general meaning corresponds to the Catholic conception) whereby everyone who is authentically called by the Holy Spirit is both authorized by that same Spirit through duly recognized persons (for Catholics, bishops) in the community of faith and assigned a place of service in that community. Each is bound to the other through the varied connectional systems to form a "ministry" in the corporate sense. For example, in the Methodist Churches there are ways of recognizing a person as a minister, namely, ordination and conference membership wherein he subjects himself to appointment for service.

95. 7) The need for high standards of education and spiritual training for ministry. For this the basic theological and pastoral studies are as necessary as ever, but we would agree that they need to be supplemented by a sensitive and open attitude to the arts and sciences, especially those concerned seriously with human behaviour. Readiness to gain from the advances and achievements of human knowledge, and receptiveness to those spiritual elements deriving from the common Christian inheritance, often latent in literature and the arts, are needed in ministry today. In this regard, much in Part II of the Roman Directorium Ecumenicum leads us to hope that much more serious efforts at joint study of common problems and at practical collaboration in preparing for ministry may prudently develop between us.

96. 8) Encouraging experiments are already there to point to an awareness of problems and ambiguities arising in an age of rapid change concerning the meaning and function of ministry.

97. In the immediate future there are certain problems facing us, certain questions that Methodists especially would wish to ask which may be clearly and briefly stated:

1. How are we to understand the relationship of the ordained ministry to the laity? What does it mean to speak of "a difference in kind (*essentia*) and not merely in degree" (*Lumen Gentium,* 10, ii). In what sense is there a difference in kind?

2. What specifically stands in the way of Roman Catholic recognition of Methodist *ministry* as *authentic*? Do the changes of emphasis in thinking about ministry manifested in Vatican II offer promise of progress here? What can be expected of new thinking and research on the concept of apostolic succession?

3. What is the bearing on the question of ministry of prophetic and special ministries?

4. In what specific functions may and should Catholic priests and Methodist ministers *share*? If they can share in these (whatever the list), are they not alike ministers in those functions?

5. In view of the lack of clarity in both the New Testament and the early history of the Church on the nature and authorization of the ministry (except for the Master's selection and authorization of the disciples), what guiding principles are indicated for understanding the meaning of orders? How important have pragmatic factors been and how much influence should they continue to have in defining orders? Why should there be three orders instead of two or one?

98.   We do not of course suggest that these questions are either original or exclusive to us. For instance, they have, together with important related questions, concerning e.g. episcopacy and primacy, been the object of expert study within the "Catholicity and Apostolicity" commission of the Joint Working Group between the Roman Catholic Church and the World Council of Churches, an interim account of whose work has recently been published. Our two Churches in the next phase of their dialogue should welcome the latter commission's proposal to "study in depth and examine critically" these themes and should welcome equally the commission's compilation as "a tool in the service of Joint research".

VII.   AUTHORITY

99.   Problems connected with authority have exercised the commission from the beginning of our conversations, and have cropped up during our discussions of other themes, e.g. ministry, Eucharist. We do not feel that our direct discussions on this theme have been more than exploratory, opening up rather than exploring the question deeply. We believe that discussions on this subject will be a necessary item on any future agenda of Roman Catholic/Methodist conversations.

100.   From the beginning of our discussions it was recognized that problems of authority were implicit in some of the deep "crevasses" between us, and notably the Mariological dogmas and the doctrines of the Infallibility or Indefectibility of the Church on the one hand; while on the other hand the whole question of the origin and development of Methodism as a work of the Spirit, of an extraordinary and prophetic character, has at some point to be related to the Catholic view of church order and of its understanding of the authority of Christ in His Church. We agreed to postpone these important questions because it seemed to us fundamentally important to begin, not with our differences and disagreements, but with our agreements and with that fundamental unity without which all our conversations would cease to be conversations between Christians.

101.   Yet we realize that those questions do bear on the problem of authority, and have to be faced in our hope of approaching our goal of genuine communion between our Churches *in sacris*. Thus one of the most hopeful conceptions in recent discussion has been the concept of a hierarchy of truths: the possibility that because we might hold and affirm truths which are central and which concern the heart of the Christian gospel, we might live together on this basis, while differing in many lesser things, and while we still search for agreement and understanding in others. But the question then arises — is our agreement in obedience to Christ, our acceptance of the authority of the Scripture, our acknowledgement of the apostolic faith as witnessed to in the creeds of the Ecumenical Councils — are these the hierarchy of truth at its indispensable, top level? Or must, say, the dogmas laid down in 1856 and 1870 be included among the indispensables? It will be remembered that Newman stressed the importance of the word "irreformable" in relation to 1870 and interpreted this to mean that once the Church has made up its mind, and declared itself, then, however much the meaning of this pronouncement might be modified in a later context, such doctrine must be accepted by the faithful. If this is so and the Mariological dogmas and infallibility are regarded as necessary to any communion *in sacris,* the way ahead is obviously going to be long, precarious and uncertain. We mention this not because we have studied this issue but to show why further discussions on the nature of authority cannot finally ignore these problems.

102.   We began therefore by our common acceptance of the paramount authority of Christ in His Church (Cf. § 35) and asked what kind of authority was consonant with the Incarnation, that is with the condescension of God to become man, to enter history, and so to put himself, it seems "at risk", suffering the consequences of living among sinners in a sinful world, and indeed doing this to the very limit (*Phil.* 2:1-11) — and in the Cross seeming to put Himself at the mercy of history. To this question asked by Methodists at the first Cambridge colloquium, a paper was read from the Catholic point of view which further defined the authority of Christ as the authority of the Gospel. Thus if the gospel partakes of the authority of Christ, Christ who lives with His people and is present with them, ruling and guiding them, it becomes clear that this simple acceptance of the authority of Christ is bound to lead to the consideration of subsidiary "authorities" and even perhaps to a hierarchy of authorities recalling what has been said earlier about a hierarchy of truths.

103.   Thus the distinguished Methodist historian, Sir Herbert Butterfield, at the end of his study of Christianity in history, sums up the whole matter with the words "Hold to Christ, and for the rest be uncommitted" intimating not only that commitment to Christ is the heart of the matter but that such commitment leads to whole areas of Christian freedom. This is entirely in harmony with Catholic teaching that authority is not absolute but God-directed and that it is a service aimed at the unfolding of the free, human, Christ-directed personality. But when the implications of this ap-

parently simple commitment to Christ are examined they are seen to involve consideration not only of the apostolic kerygma and the Scriptural witness to it, but also the continuing investigation of the mystery of salvation, and the connection with it of the mystery of His own person, which occupied so massively the thought of the Church in the first centuries and of which the great Christological treatises of the Fathers and the creeds and confessions of the great Councils bear witness. It is similar with another apparently simple statement—the famous toast of Newman—"The Pope and Conscience—but Conscience First".

104.   That Christians have a duty to obey the voice of conscience at all costs, that it is one of the ways in which God speaks directly to men, and that all Christians have the duty to respect the consciences of others, are matters on which we might easily agree. But again investigation shows that the matter is not as simple as this, though historical polemical oppositions of "authority" and "conscience" have often induced the simplification. We know what crimes have been committed in the name of conscience, including some of the more terrible war crimes of the People of God. We understand the meaning of Philip Melanchthon's saying "a good conscience is the invention of the Devil". In other words, the conscience itself needs to be enlightened, instructed, corrected, informed, by the Holy Spirit indeed, but a Holy Spirit showing himself in many ways, and using the Holy Scriptures on the one hand, and the discipline of the Church on the other; nor can the individual conscience be isolated from the mind of the whole Church, from the "consensus fidelium" insofar as it exists and can be ascertained in matters of faith and morals. An informed Christian conscience makes a responsible decision in the light of the example, the principles, the life of Christ; of the experience of the Christian community from Christ to the present; of the guidance and authoritative teaching of the Church; while the consciences of societies outside the Church, and the insights and compelling perceptions of all men may have their importance for the individual. No doubt in the end each man must have this freedom to obey his conscience against the whole world, and certainly against the decisions and commands of any "Establishment". But just as certainly no man's conscience is an island, entire of itself.

105.   Our acceptance of the authority of Christ, of the gospel, and of the witness to the gospel in the Scripture and in the creeds poses a whole series of questions concerning the relation of Scripture and tradition which we have noted, but which we have not explored. An important paper pointed us to the Fourth Gospel and to Christ's claim to bear witness to the truth—and this might well be further explored in relation to two other Johannine utterances, that "the truth shall make you free"—that is the authority of Christ in his witness to truth is always a liberating one, and comes to deliver men from legalism, not to entangle them further in commandments of men.

106.   Again in the light of Christ's washing the feet of his disciples, his "I have called you friends" speaks of authority in terms of service and

discipleship from which all thought of triumphalism is removed. Christ's disciples are his friends because they are to know and understand what the Lord has done and be able to imitate him. In Pauline terms which come close to the heart of John Wesley and the original Methodist testimony (but no less close to, say, the rule of St. Benedict) Christ's authority is manifestation in the faith not of servants but of sons—sons who share in the glorious liberty of God's children. Only an authority given in love and received in love expresses the deepest meaning of the word for Christians. By comparison all uses of the word in terms of the rule of the Gentiles, of juridical and political usage, are beside the point. Here Methodists would say that half-a-dozen more John XXIIIs and Paul VIs in the next century would do more than anything to dispose of a thousand years of conflict and misunderstanding.

107.   Thus, an important paper read at Lake Junaluska set our questions amid a general crisis about the nature of authority in our modern world, and we might add the fact that in two important fields, in education and in the home, it is authoritarian and "paternalistic" view of authority which are being most sharply challenged. Nonetheless (however much the historic expression of the authority of Christ in his Church throughout the centuries may need to be re-appraised in terms of the new insights of recent times) for us the problem of Christian authority must be sought and expressed within the Christian dimension.

108.   This paramount authority of Christ in the Church has in fact been regarded by both our Churches as exercised in varying and diverse modes, and it is perhaps an omission that in our conversations, though the attempt was made, tardily and with insufficient time for success, at Lake Junaluska, we never listed side by side our hierarchies of authorities and studied the place of the varying elements in them in our list of priorities. Both Churches, e.g., acknowledge an authority of conscience, also an authority of discipline exercised by the proper courts of the Church; all accept the authority of Scripture, but within this authority there are many questions some of which have not been and some of which may never be finally resolved. The various elements in the holy tradition, which we all accept and on which our continuing life as Churches also depends— theologies, liturgies, devotion, the sacraments, preaching of the Word and study of the Bible, the authority of the ministry and of Pope and bishop or of the Methodist Conferences and ministry—it is likely that the two lists of authorities might not turn out to be as dissimilar as we might expect. But almost certainly we should place them in a differing order and lay more stress here on one element and there on another. Indeed until we have done this, the problem of authority remains an abstract one, perhaps an obsessive one in which we spend too much time talking about the problem of the problem, certainly one unrelated to the enduring purpose of our conversations, which is to bring us into living relation and communion with one another.

109.   Another possible field of useful discussion would be those "prin-

ciples of the Reformation" to which the Deed of Union of the Methodist Church in Great Britain explicitly refers, but which it does not further define. Without wishing to revive what was bitter controversy, not so much—at this point—in the 16th as in the 19th century (when on an Ultramontanist view private judgment was regarded as an individualist arrogance which was the root of all schisms while Protestants saw it as the great bulwark against a blind and irrational acceptance of priestcraft) there are one or two important matters on which agreement can be registered and about which affirmations should be made.

110.   Thus, many Protestants would have seen the heart of the doctrine of private judgment in the affirmation (the priesthood of all believers meant the same thing at this point) that no priests can intervene between a man's soul and God. And yet this view has never been more unreservedly stated than in a great passage in Newman's Apologia:

"From a boy I had been led to consider that my Maker and I, His creature, were the two beings luminously such . . . I know full well now, and did not know then that the Catholic Church allows no image of any sort, material or immaterial, no dogmatic symbol, no rite, no sacrament, no saint, not even the Blessed Virgin herself to come between the soul and his creator. It is face to face 'solus cum solo' in all matters between man and his God. He alone created: He alone has redeemed: before His awful eyes we go in death: in the vision is our eternal beatitude" (§ 177.1. 5-14).

The "Dream of Gerontius" is a commentary on this. Later in the same work Newman observes:

"It is the custom with Protestant writers to consider that whereas there are two great principles in acting on the history of religion, authority and private judgment, they have all the private judgment to themselves and we have . . . authority . . . but this is not so . . . Catholic Christendom is no simple exhibition of religious absolutism but presents a continuous picture of authority and private judgment alternately advancing and retreating as the ebb and flow of the tide" (§ 237 1.7).

111.   Also in the Apologia and again in his famous essay on the function of the laity in matters of doctrine he points out how again and again in Church history the breakthrough in creative thought has come from an individual or small group of Christians. Methodists, on the other hand, also recognize that private judgment alone is not enough. The very recognition of doctrinal standards—Scripture, the principles of the creeds and Reformation, and in a narrower sense Wesley's sermons, as preaching standards; the whole discipline of the Church as exercised by the Conference over ministers and laity; the Conference's whole process in ordaining those who believe themselves to be inwardly called of God, by confirming and accepting this in the name of the Church—all these are ways in which private judgment and authority are seen to belong together and to safeguard one another.

112. Discussion therefore of the relation of private judgment to authority might fruitfully lead to consideration of two other related problems. The first is the place of reason in the hierarchy of authorities. John Wesley's "appeal to men of reason and religion" shows that for him a renewal of inward religion could not safely be left to emotion without the critical safeguard of reason. He thought in terms of his own century and we as the heirs of so many recent genuine advances in philosophy and psychology could (perhaps) no longer think of reason exactly as did the men of his age. Nor can we revert to any kind of scholasticism, Catholic or Protestant. Yet in a world which at the moment is being swept along (and much of the Church with it) by vast tides of irrationalism, ought not our two Churches from their own tradition to be speaking words of sane and moderate common sense, and eschewing the current violence of the tongue and an emotive romanticism which seems to drag us to the edge of dire danger? (Cf. § 30).

113. The other question concerning private judgment is one which from the time of John Oman has been regarded as important among Protestants — the view that truth has not simply to be accepted but seen to be true. Methodists might ask, did even Our Lord expect to be believed on his own "say so" or because he was bearing witness to a truth which men might understand and prove by trying it out for themselves — and so discovering that they were building not on sand but on a rock? Is not here part of the meaning of being "friends" of Christ and "sons of God"? Does not God will all his children to see and understand and know to the fullest and uttermost of their capacity? Does not then the saying of a great Evangelical Temple Gairdner "let us believe the maximum" become intelligible, since new beliefs are not so many fetters on the mind but magic casements opening on ever new enthralling vistas of truth?

114. Catholics, while by no means rejecting all of this might in turn ask whether faith is not primarily a relation to persons, not propositions. Though it necessarily implies also a faith in assertions (in truths; in propositions) this is not something isolated, but encompassed and sustained by the *person* who is believed, Christ. Any statement of the kind "I believe that . . . " is based upon the authority of the person at the centre of the belief, Christ, and upon the assurance derived from thence.

115. Yet we might agree that Catholic as well as Protestant history shows the importance of the "Ulysses factor" in the Christian way — the creative importance of men who explore truth for its own sake; at all costs and wherever it may lead. On the other hand there are implications for the problem of authority and private judgment in the fact that the wholeness of the Christian faith is so many-sided that no individual can wholly comprehend it for himself.

116. The Catholic would recall here that, if creation is already a kind of revelation and self-disclosure of God (*Rom.* 1:18), there is an essential difference between the inadequate knowledge of God attainable through creation and the self-disclosure of his mystery through revelation. God is

not only the object and goal of faith, but through his self-revelation is its principle and ground. Faith is a preeminent way in which the biblical word is manifested, "It is no longer I who live but Christ who lives in me". There is much for further discussion here, if only to dispel misunderstandings, surviving suspicions that Catholics demand some blind submission of the intellect while Protestants cherish a wilful and arrogant individualism.

117.   Of the ways in which authority both safeguards and limits freedom we have had little discussion, yet it is evident that here too there lies before us an important task. It has been said that Vatican II while having nobler statements about liberty has added little to a Christian rationale of toleration based not on indifferentism but on a sense of the truth of Christianity and its final efficacy for all men, combined with a reverence for the dignity and liberty of the consciences of others. Protestants have not lived up to what they have said about this but at least such documents as Milton's "Areopagitica" put forward a view of truth in freedom which has unexhausted implications for our two Churches in relation to other Christians and to the modern world.

118.   We have tried to indicate that a fruitful beginning has been made with a subject so important that it must surely be continued, if not on these then on other lines, in any continuing conversations.

VIII.   THE WAY AHEAD

119.   Our instructions were to devote the last section of this report to developing and setting out the commission's ideas on how Roman Catholic-Methodist dialogue might profitably go forward following the first phase of which the report marks the conclusion.

120.   In the field of theological dialogue what has been said above in sections II to VII will not suggest any lack of material for future programmes, whether they be programmes of further thinking and acting together in areas where we feel we have much to share and to offer each other, or programmes which boldly tackle the chief difficulties which keep us apart. In none of the areas covered by this report do we feel that the possibilities of dialogue have been exhausted. In some of them it has hardly begun, and we are concerned chiefly to suggest what we hope might be improvements in organization and method.

121.   In working these out we have borne in mind one of two main considerations already aired in the progress report drafted at Rabat, e.g. §§ 22-5: "We would hope that those responsible for the deeper (theological) inquiry . . . would bear continually in mind the responsibility we feel for serious planning of the education of our Churches at lay, ministerial and local levels, for the overcoming of prejudices and misunderstandings and for offering guidance toward cooperation between local Churches. If this responsibility should remain unfulfilled, the work of our Joint Commission will be to that extent unfruitful.

This in turn raises the vital question of communication. Given the nature and mandate of the Joint Commission, it cannot be expected that the general public will share fully in all phases of the consultation. On the other hand, it is *not* easy to see how the serious planning of the education of our Churches at lay, ministerial and local level is to begin, or how our Churches are to be convinced that their spokesmen are doing anything, if there is no better communication than in the conventional press release.

It is therefore suggested that provided the status of papers be clearly established (working papers, e.g.) they might be circulated among responsible and qualified people, and summaries of them might be incorporated in reports. This last could be done even if the papers did not command general acceptance, since dissent could be recorded as part of an account of the substance of discussion.

It might be that certain of the papers prepared for these consultations would prove suitable for publication in one form or another.

122. It is the judgment of the commission that the dialogue would be most efficiently continued under a central committee with a maximum of six members from each side, and with more precisely defined functions. It should be responsible in general for relations between the World Methodist Council and the Secretariat for Promoting Christian Unity; and an important part of this responsibility should be the stimulating of good relations, of dialogue and cooperation at national and local level. This should include collecting information about activity and experiments wherever they are shared by Methodists and Roman Catholics and in whatever context, and facilitating its circulation and exchange. Thus useful comparative judgments can be made and clearer ideas may emerge of how we can best achieve our shared purposes in Christian life and witness and in the search for unity. The dialogue in the fullest and liveliest sense can hardly be thought of as something merely to be kept ticking from one annual central committee meeting to another.

123. The task of the committee in regard to serious theological dialogue should be mainly one of organization, coordination and review.

124. *Organization* should be as flexible as possible, regulated only by the principle that the best work is done only by adequately equipped people giving adequate time, energy and interest to it. This entails regular cooperation, usually possible only to people who have regular access to each other in the right kind of circumstances. An example of such circumstances has been briefly considered above (§ 16). Another joint work the commission might stimulate and to some extent organize is written work for publishing, of various scope, whether aimed at involving larger numbers from the learned world in the dialogue and bringing it into useful relationship with other dialogues, or whether aimed at making our people (and others) at large aware that progress is being made and familiarizing them with a situation of friendship and joint activity.

125. Favourable reference has already been made (§ 29) to the English

joint publication *Christian Belief*. As well as further examples of this type, we think that other types, such as formal symposia on given themes, books in the form of exchange of letters, sympathetic commented editions of the works of one side by members of the other *e.g.* of C. Wesley's hymns from the Roman Catholic side or of some Catholic classic from the other.

126.   But in an age when less and less reading can be relied on to be done this literary activity would need to be supplemented, especially below the specialized level, by joint effort in the other communications media, and by stimulating well-directed discussion among our people in order to create constructive Christian criticism towards the vast impact of the mass media in general.

127.   The committee's *coordinating* and *reviewing* function would include taking account of the total ecumenical picture, including both other dialogue and such schemes as either Church might be involved in — e.g. the Consultation on Church Union in U.S.A. The commission should also feel the need to see the dialogue in the context of human unity in general and of the many problems involving religion and culture in the conditions of our age. This might sometimes involve encouraging certain types of expert enterprise more than others.

128.   Finally the committee should have the task of seeing that the authorities in the two Churches are adequately aware of what is being done, give it adequate attention and make adequate response.

129.   We would have no illusions, however, about the fruitfulness of all these activities if they were divorced from the spiritual renewal and the spiritual sharing which are at the heart of ecumenical progress. It is because (as this report has so insisted) we have become aware of exceptional affinities between Roman Catholics and Methodists in that religion of the heart which is the heart of religion, that we believe in the future of Roman Catholic-Methodist relations.

130.   Roman Catholics would not consider this complete without grateful reference to the noble Resolution of Intent, unanimously adopted by the General Conference of the United Methodist Church in U.S.A. on April 23, 1970. Disavowing the traditional polemical understanding of those among its "articles of religion" which were part of an anti-Catholic inheritance from a less happy age, the resolution gives courageous practical and public expression of that "change of heart" which the Second Vatican Council saw as the soul of the ecumenical movement, and a solemn responsibility of all in every Church. It has been our privilege in the commission to be spurred to such change of heart by the heart-warming experience of our work together. We are profoundly thankful to God for the koinonia, the shared spiritual experience of prayer and self-scrutiny together.

131.   Measured against our age-old estrangements, our progress in ecumenical experience in the past three years has been swift and surely led by the Spirit. For this we give heartfelt thanks to God and from it we take

hope and courage. But measured against the exigencies of our Churches and the challenge of our times, it leaves us aware of the distance that still lies between us now and our professed goals. We know too well that the latter stages of the ecumenical dialogue are more formidable than the early ones, requiring of us redoubled efforts and devotion, not merely to the work we have to do together, the joint witness to great Christian values that we must give and widely promote in our Churches, but to the tasks of educating our people and communicating to them something of the joys and inspiration that have been vouchsafed to us. As we look to the future, therefore, we renew our commitments and reaffirm our confidence in God's providential leading, in which we have already been so richly blessed.

PARTICIPANTS

MEMBERS OF THE COMMISSION:

Catholics:

Archbishop J. Murphy, Cardiff, Wales, U.K.
Bishop Joseph Brunini, Jackson, Miss., U.S.A.
Bishop James W. Malone, Youngstown, Ohio, U.S.A.
Msgr. Bernard F. Law, Washington, D.C., U.S.A.
Msgr. Francis Davis, Birmingham, England
Mr. Daniel D. Meaney, Corpus Christi, Texas, U.S.A.
Dr. Edward J. Popham, Mellor, Blackburn, England
Reverend Michael Hurley, SJ, Dublin, Ireland
Reverend Robert Murray, SJ, Heythrop College, England
Reverend Jerome Hamer, OP, Rome
Canon W. A. Purdy, Rome

Methodists:

Bishop William R. Cannon, Atlanta, Georgia, U.S.A.
Bishop Fred Pierce Corson, Philadelphia, Penn., U.S.A.
Bishop F. Gerald Ensley, Columbus, Ohio, U.S.A.
Dr. E. Bolaji Idowu, Ibadan, Nigeria
Dr. Harold Roberts, Cambridge, England
Dr. Albert Outler, Dallas, Texas, U.S.A.
Dr. Eric Baker, London, England
Dr. E. Gordon Rupp, Cambridge, England
Dr. Lee F. Tuttle, Lake Junaluska, North Carolina, U.S.A.
Reverend Max Woodward, London, England (meetings 1967 and 1968)

DUBLIN REPORT, 1976

Historical Introduction:

After the first series of conversations (1967 – 1970) which resulted in the so-called "Denver Report" (see above), a new stage of Methodist – Roman Catholic dialogue was entered into. The task and composition of the new Joint Commission, smaller than the first, was determined according to the recommendations contained in chapter VIII (No. 119ff) of the "Denver Report".

The Joint Commission met four times. The first meeting (Rome, December 1972) was mainly concerned with the reorganisation and planning of the new dialogue. The second meeting (Reuti/Switzerland, October 1973) focused on the topic "Salvation Today" with special reference to the Bangkok Conference of the World Council of Churches/Commission on World Mission and Evangelism (December 1972 – January 1973) on the same subject. The next meeting (Venice/September – October 1974) dealt with a variety of questions such as evangelisation, prevenient grace, conversation, spirituality, eucharist, mixed marriages, Methodist involvement in church union negotiations. This was continued at the fourth and last meeting in Bristol/England (September 1975). In pursuing these inquiries, the Commission collaborated with national Methodist – Roman Catholic groups in various countries.

The final report written with constant references to the preceding "Denver Report" was presented to the Thirteenth World Methodist Conference in Dublin (1976) and therefore called "Dublin Report".

I

INTRODUCTION

1. The volume recording the *Proceedings of the Twelfth World Methodist Conference* at Denver, Colorado, August 18-26, 1971 (ed. Lee F. Tuttle, Nashville & New York: Abingdon Press), was doubtless unique in the history of such reports in devoting a considerable number of its pages to Roman Catholic/Methodist matters. In addition to a personal report by Bishop William R. Cannon on the conversations which had taken place since 1967, and the text of a lengthy address given to the Conference by Cardinal J. G. M. Willebrands, President of the Vatican Secretariat for Promoting Christian Unity, the book contained the full-scale "Report of the Joint Commission between the Roman Catholic Church and the World Methodist Council, 1967-70" (pp. 39-68).

2. It is the nature of such a report both to reveal progress and achievement and to point to further areas of study and discussion which have been opened up and defined. The Denver Report, as it has come to be known familiarly among us, did this under six heads:

Christianity and the Contemporary World
Spirituality
Christian Home and Family
Eucharist
Ministry
Authority

3. A final section entitled "The Way Ahead" embodied precise recommendations to the respective authorities about the next stage of the dialogue. A smaller joint Commission was proposed which should have a stimulating and facilitating function over the whole field of Roman Catholic/Methodist relations while its task "in regard to serious theological dialogue should be mainly one of organization, coordination and review".

4. These recommendations were accepted in principle by the authorities and the new Commission met for the first time in Rome in December 1972. Two position papers were read, one from each side, which attempted to set out with some frankness our tasks, our problems and our awareness of our defects. The new style in which the reduced Commission set out to work involved some trial and error. It presupposed also an act of faith — of confidence in a response from Roman Catholics and Methodists in cooperation in many places at national and local levels. In this spirit "A Call to Action" was published at the end of our first meeting. This act of faith has proved only partly justified, but in some instances at least the response looked for has been generous enough to enable the Commission to tackle with varying degrees of thoroughness a good proportion of the list of desirable projects it drew up at its first meeting.

5. The present report, taking the Denver Report as its point of departure, aims to show how this collaboration and the work the Commission has been able itself to do at its four meetings since 1972 have advanced our joint search and mutual understanding. To those whose help has made this advance possible — their names will appear in the course of the report — we are deeply grateful.

II

COMMON WITNESS AND SALVATION TODAY

6. One of the common concerns of Roman Catholics and Methodists, which emerged in our first series of conversations and was registered in the Denver Report, was for a just analysis of the contemporary situation from the point of view of those who wish to live the gospel of Jesus Christ and announce it to others. What obstacles and what opportunities are offered them in today's world?

7. The second part of section II of the Report was able to set out eight "Areas of Agreement Which May Serve as Aids to Joint Efforts to Encounter the Contemporary World." These are well worth considering

again.[1] The emphasis here, it will be noted, was on agreement not for its own sake but looking toward joint action, and the second series of talks was launched with a "Call to Joint Action" addressed to our respective churches.

8. Since the Denver Report was written, parallel concern has been manifested widely over the religious field and several other important discussions of it helped to induce us to give it the central place in our second series of conversations. The Denver Conference itself, at which our report was received, issued a call to Methodist churches to join in intensified mission to the world, and passed appropriate concrete resolutions, one of which was that "every effort shall be made to work in concert and in cooperation with other communions and churches."[2]

9. The renewed Roman Catholic/World Methodist Commission first met (December 1972) a few weeks before the World Council of Churches' Bangkok Conference on Salvation Today, and since some of its members could look forward to being in Bangkok, the Commission decided to appropriate to its own direct study the theme "Common Witness and Salvation Today". Hence papers and reports were prepared for our second meeting which were largely developed out of reflections on Bangkok, and discussion of them represented the first stage of our work on the theme.[3]

10. At this same time it was known that the Synod of Bishops of the Catholic Church, meeting in Rome in October 1974, would be choosing the theme of Evangelisation. In fact, our Commission met for the third time in Venice just after the Synod had begun its sessions. Hence the position papers for the meeting, which had been commissioned at Reuti,[4] were supplemented by a critique of the Synod's programme as set out in its preliminary document. Therefore, in drawing up the present joint statement we have been able to reflect not only on our own papers and discussions but also on the proceedings of the Synod as so far known, and on the work of the World Methodist Council at its Mexico and Jerusalem consultations. These have been referred to directly where it seemed appropriate.

11. We begin by stating briefly five general themes which appear to run through the documents and reports we have examined and which command our joint acceptance:

(*a*) The Church's calling to witness in word and life to God's saving work in Christ is fundamental to her being;

(*b*) This witness can be fully effective only when the churches witness together, not out of expediency or for practical convenience but for the sake of the truth being proclaimed and lived;

(*c*) Salvation has individual and social dimensions that must not be separated, involving as it does relationship to God and to fellow-man, and transformation in Christ of both the person and the society which he helps to make up and which shapes him in turn;

(*d*) God's saving work in Christ is not restricted to Christians but extends also to non-Christian communities and the whole created order;

(*e*) Witness today calls for a re-interpretation of salvation that goes beyond translation into contemporary language and takes account of the many ways in which people now hope and seek for salvation.

(*f*) The Church is still commissioned to preach the gospel to all men, in the hope that all may come to know God revealed in Christ.

12.   Common usage of the word "salvation" implies that the existence of somebody or something is threatened, that there is a menace or danger from which somebody or something is being saved. In theological terms this menace was long summed up in the phrase "the wrath to come," but in mature Christian thought this "negative" was inseparable from a positive vision of what God's salvific will, manifest in the reality of Christ's saving work, meant for man, namely a transformation in the living Christ, begun already in baptism and kindling a hope[5] of eternal transformation for those who held to Christ.

13.   If "salvation from" in its more starkly eschatological form has faded in contemporary consciousness, the conditions of contemporary life in which every sort of insecurity looms have thrust it forward again in other forms, just as acutely felt. Today we can distinguish concern for salvation:

(*a*) On the elemental level, where fully one-third of human beings live, salvation means deliverance from the day-to-day threat of failure of the means of survival;

(*b*) On a higher level, salvation means deliverance from the wretchedness of mere subsistence and entry into a fuller human life—work for the unemployed, learning for the illiterate, dignity and power for the despised and downtrodden.

(*c*) On the highest level, salvation means deliverance from those anxieties, that discontent and even despair to which material comfort offers no answer. Indeed we should have to go further and say that man seems so made that obsession with or complacency about the "primary" forms of salvation is self-defeating and likely to threaten that very social and political order in which primary needs are met. Man's glory is a "divine discontent" which distances these needs by a sense of the transcendent. The point was superbly expressed by the Anglican poet George Herbert:

> Yet let him keep the rest
> But keep them with repining restlessnesse
> Let him be rich and wearie, that at least
> If goodness lead him not, yet wearinesse
> May tosse him to My breast.

14.   The Judeo-Christian message of salvation has never artificially separated these three levels, although its ultimate concern is with the last. The Old Testament shows God's salvation as concerned, whether for the

individual or the nation, with concrete experiences, dangers, afflictions, deprivations, injustices, but culminating with the prophetic emphasis on "salvation for" the kingdom, the peace of God.

15. The Christian message of salvation has always been vulnerable to an interpretation involving rejection of matter, escape from "the world"; but in fact it embraces every human need while transcending it. It affirms eternal life which encompasses yet goes beyond our mortal condition. It finds its ground and hope in the life and death and resurrection of Jesus Christ.

16. Given a longing for salvation which is as wide as humanity, and the concern of all churches to witness to its true meaning, what in particular can Roman Catholics and Methodists say and do?

17. More than once since 1966, when these conversations began, we have been called to recognise our shared heritage; not just to put an ecumenical veneer on the otherwise unaltered furniture of our separation but to discover the underlying realities on which our churches are founded and to which the common features of our heritage point. Now we must go further and see that, arising out of that shared heritage, there are things that we are impelled to insist on and to do that will contribute to the current debate on Common Witness and Salvation, but more, that will involve us together in the common witness itself:

18. (*i*) The affirmation of the *reality of sin* which Roman Catholics and Methodists have traditionally made has never seemed more relevant than today. The weight of sin needs to be seen in all its gravity, against either naive Pelagianism or Promethean humanism, but also without overstressing the trivial. The total picture of human injustice, venality, selfishness, not least where the churches have seemed to condone it, needs to be seen and denounced in the prophetic spirit of the great preachers of history.

19. (*ii*) But in the same spirit of sober realism the reality and glory of the *grace of God,* equally central in our traditions, needs to be proclaimed, as answering in truth to all needs of man. There will be liberation only as God's grace transforms the will of those who exercise power. There will be love only as God's grace evokes in us response to his initiative of love in Christ. With all our technical resources there will be food enough for all only as God's grace leads us to responsible parenthood and finally changes our wills so that we are more ready to produce and to share. In the words of the 1974 Synod of Catholic Bishops, union with Christ is the only thing which raises the individual "lost in the ocean of history and the incalculable multitude of humanity" to the challenge of today.

20. (*iii*) *Social concern* has been characteristic of the Roman Catholic and Methodist traditions. Today, when care for salvation often manifests itself on only one of the levels mentioned earlier, we need to witness that our social concern is a fruit of faith, and that we test whether salvation at any level is the work of the Holy Spirit by relating it to the teaching of Jesus Christ, God's saving work made manifest. Such a test must be a moral test of the means employed to achieve the desired end, e.g. in the search for

liberation. When unjust power is overwhelming and deaf to persuasion, force may not simply be ruled out, but the *spirit* of faction and violence remains alien to the Christian's concern for the poor and oppressed.

21. (*iv*) A strong *missionary impulse* is common to us, and recently our churches have publicly recognised both that it must continue and that it must develop new forms of expression. The gospel may well by now have been preached to every corner of the earth, but there have never been so many people living who have never heard of the saving grace of God in Christ. All over the world people are growing up in communities that have not heard, or who have heard and no longer listen, or who follow other voices that speak of salvation.

22. (*v*) Our traditional shared concern for *sanctification* has been a source of strength, but we have sometimes (especially where we have been an extra-establishment minority) shared also a tendency, contrary to our true traditions, to understand regeneration largely as the new birth of the *individual*.[6] Thus sanctification has been thought of as limited to the work of the Holy Spirit in the individual life. While maintaining the fundamental importance of personal spirituality, we need to explore the fullest implications of the biblical view of salvation as new creation, so that sanctification will be seen to include the fulfilment of God's purpose for the whole created order and we shall hear the call to witness together to the responsibility of mankind for the earth which is God's good creation.

23. Looking outward in this way we must be sensitive to the riches in other living faiths. Even unbelief challenges us to purify our faith. Especially we must be sensitive to the possibilities of *preparatio evangelica* in the searchings and aspirations of our contemporaries, while recognising the essential ambiguity of many social, cultural and ideological movements. A *real* sensitivity to the gospel and to the world will enable us to be true to our aim as Christians: to help people towards a living faith in Christ *within* their own society and culture, and not to offer a way of thinking and living as Christians belonging only to our own society. It is essential that above all, our own way of life must reflect faithfully the gospel which we preach. Where it does not, our credibility as Christians is seriously challenged.

24. (*vi*) If we are to be taken seriously, we must ourselves take seriously the *call to unity*. Our present series of conversations began with a Call to Joint Action — "What can Roman Catholics and Methodists do together?" The discernment of common traditions and concerns by a few does not of itself produce joint action on any significant scale. Our people must share the discernment as part of their own Christian commitment which they must see as pointing to unity not division. Catholics might well reflect that Methodism has had from the beginning structural possibilities for healthy and expanding lay participation in evangelism, and be prepared to learn much from this tradition. Methodists, on the other hand, might well feel that concern for lay involvement has most recently been more manifest

among Catholics, and this could well be a matter for consultation and further cooperation between us.

25.   The tests of the seriousness of our joint concern about salvation and evangelisation must be of the practical order pointed to in section VIII of the Denver Report[7] and in the Call to Action of December 1972. These pointed to the need for "serious planning of the education of our churches" and the connected "vital question of communication". Since the Denver assembly we can point gratefully to growth in collaboration at national, regional and local levels, some of which have produced valuable contributions to the present report: there is room for wider and more generous response. We cannot repeat too often the last words of the "Call to Action" we made at our meeting in 1972: "We do not want merely to accumulate paper for our files, but we want to stimulate one another to common action, so that the world which is starving for lack of good news may not through our unnecessary divisions be prevented from receiving the food of the Gospel".

III

SPIRITUALITY

26.   It has been recognized from the beginning of our dialogue that among the "more solid grounds for affinity" between our two traditions the first was "the central place held in both traditions by the ideal of personal sanctification, growth in holiness through daily life in Christ".[8] This recognition was not voiced in any exclusive or pharisaical spirit, but simply as a fruit of our emergence from a long period of comparative estrangement. Hence section III of the Denver Report[9] was based in the first place on the work of a sub-commission done in accordance with a careful brief given by the joint Commission as a whole.[10]

27.   Two or three points may be re-emphasised about this, perhaps the most mature section of the Denver Report:

(a) It recognised the need for both an historical and a contemporary treatment, the one complementing the other.

(b) It was not seen as unconnected with the preceding section on "Christianity and the Contemporary World," or even as merely complementing it, but as being interwoven with it.

It frankly recognised certain lacunae and certain obstacles in our discovered affinity.[11]

(d) It offered its own set of practical suggestions.[12]

28.   It might be argued that the very first fruit of this practical-minded section was the address given by Cardinal Willebrands at Denver and so generously received there.[13]It was a development of the theme of our shared tradition of concern for holiness which must find a leading place in any bibliography of this dialogue, and its influence on the second phase of our conversations is undoubted.

29. It may at first sight seem disappointing that in the present report we have no substantial addition of our own to offer to what was presented and said at Denver, but must rather point to several examples of work in progress. But the aim of Denver's words was not simply to provoke more words, nor to boil down everything to committee language; the programme offered at Denver — and it was offered not simply to the renewed Commission but to the two world-wide communities — was an exploratory programme aimed at mutual enrichment. Spiritual richness like any other, lies partly in variety, and we were reminded at our Venice meeting that in the Catholic Church, however "monolithic" it may have seemed from some points of view, there is a long tradition of rich variety in spirituality — sometimes given institutional form in the various religious congregations, but as often manifesting itself in Christian living at the heart of "the world". Nor did Methodists repudiate the idea of such fruitful variety in their own tradition.

30. Hence it is not surprising that, among the examples we have to report of work in progress in this joint exploration there should be interesting contrasts. Taking them in chronological order we begin with the work of the Ecumenical Institute of Spirituality in America which, based in Evanston, Illinois, brings Catholics (of various spiritual families) into collaboration with Methodists and with some of other traditions in spiritual dialogue and exploration.

31. The Institute organized in 1974 the "Wingspread" conference whose specific aim was to examine the implications of section III of the Denver Report, and the Commission was able to benefit directly from the Institute's work when the Institute's Director of Protestant Spirituality, the Methodist Dr. E. W. Gerdes, gave a paper at our Venice meeting and did much to enliven our discussions. Here is one form of collaboration, a continuing one.

32. Another form, and an important one, is represented by the paper, "The Ordained Ministry," which deals with the question of holiness and spirituality. Unfortunately the final draft arrived too late to be considered by the Commission; it is published in *Origins,* January 22, 1976, and we hope it will be widely read. It is the joint work of the U.S. team appointed by the Catholic Bishops' Conference and the United Methodist Church, a work which has been going on since 1971. As the authors stress, their limiting of their theme aims at a deepening, not a "clericalist" narrowing of our joint concern with spirituality. The aim is achieved and it is to be hoped that the title will not mislead anyone as to the scope and importance of this very wise joint reflection, which not only contributes to our study of growth in holiness but also enriches our shared ideal of Ministry.[14] The paper seems to the Commission an outstanding example of the kind of work it was charged by the Denver Report to promote.

33. A third form of collaboration, that of an individual and wide-ranging mind from either side, in which a mutual sympathy clearly develops and finds expression, is represented by a paper "Towards a

Spirituality for Today," which was commissioned from the Rev. Gordon Wakefield and Fr. Emmanuel Sullivan, S.A. They describe their approach thus: "We propose to take seriously the insistence of the Denver Report that the contemporary situation be regarded and assessed and we would like to lift the discussion out of the old entrenchments and try to discover the essential characteristics of ecumenical spirituality for our time. The questions are not so much 'what have we in common—where do we differ and what may we learn from each other?' as 'what kind of Christian does God want us to be?' " Their discussion of contemporary trends takes place against a background of theology.

34. This paper would have suffered especially from being drained of blood by the clumsy surgery characteristic of committees. It is due to be published in *The Epworth Review,* January, 1977, and we hope that it also may be widely read. More perhaps than any others, the papers discussed in this section suggest that justice to our dialogue and to our collaborators demands re-addressing our attention to the suggestion made in the Denver Report, Para. 121, "provided the status of papers be clearly established (working papers e.g.) they might be circulated among responsible and qualified people, and summaries made of them might be incorporated in reports."

IV

CHRISTIAN HOME AND FAMILY:
INTER-CHURCH MARRIAGES

35. The consultation returned to one aspect of this topic at its Venice meeting in 1974, when it discussed a survey it had commissioned from Msgr. Purdy of "Discussions between the Roman Catholic Church and other Christian Churches on Marriage and the Problems of Mixed Marriages" since 1967. This dealt most fully with the Roman Catholic/Anglican dialogue but also surveyed discussions with the World Council of Churches, Lutherans, Reformed, Methodists, Old Catholics and Orthodox. It also described "changes in legislation and discipline and other official pronouncements which have occurred within the field, and their repercussions on dialogue".

36. The drafters of the fourth section of the Denver Report, which dealt with the theme of Christian Home and Family, thought it relevant to their particular task to conclude by laying stress on the need for greater Roman Catholic/Methodist collaboration and for better exchange of information among local churches. In matters which come home so closely to the faithful in everyday life this emphasis is clearly right.

37. Australian Roman Catholic/Methodist dialogue, having produced as its first fruit a joint statement on baptism 1972–73, turned its attention immediately to the theme of Christian marriage: its meaning and pastoral implications. A statement of 1973–74 dealt

(*a*) with marriage in general, starting from a firm basis in scripture;

(*b*) with mixed marriages;

(*c*) with some practical recommendations.

The Australian statement thus took very seriously the practical implications of that joint pastoral care which was recommended by *Matrimonia Mixta* and is coming to be seen more and more widely as the most fruitful approach to a problem for which, in a divided church, no perfect solution exists.

38.   Since the Denver Report on Christian Home and Family, nothing has occurred that would lead us to qualify the statement that our churches find "much ground for agreement" about marriage and family life, nor to amend in any significant way the terms in which this agreement is spelled out.[15]

39.   It has, however, become increasingly clear that this view that we have in common concerning the sanctity of marriage and its place as the God-given context for sexual relationships, development of family life and basis for stable human society, is being severely challenged and widely disregarded. This widespread rejection of the Christian understanding and practice of marriage serves to emphasize that what differences remain between us (e.g. on the possibility of divorce and re-marriage and on ways of regulating conception) are far outweighed by what we hold in common, and to remind us that however important it may be to try to settle our differences it is imperative that we witness together to the centrality of marriage in God's purpose for human community. Such common witness must be seen not as an attempt to hide our disagreements for the sake of ecumenical goodwill but as an urgent necessity if the world at large is to be influenced at all by the ideal and practice of Christian marriage.

40.   This same realistic assessment of the widespread disregard of the meaning of marriage must be brought to bear on any consideration of interchurch marriages. These are often spoken of as posing a "problem" in terms of doctrine, ecclesiastical polity and pastoral care. They are in fact a problem to those marrying only if they belong to the small minority within a minority, that is those who are not only church members but also take the responsibilities of membership seriously. Consequently those who do belong to different churches and who seek guidance concerning interchurch marriage should be welcomed for their faithful concern and not chided for posing a problem, especially since they can hardly be held responsible for the division between our churches which is the underlying cause of the problem. Again, this is not to advocate a disregarding of the difficulties nor a weakening of discipline concerning marriage. It is to urge that what we already hold in common should be used as a basis for marriage and family life that reflects the will of God in Christ for human society.

41.   As we have noted earlier, the problem of mixed marriages has been treated, always simultaneously with a joint exploration of the theology of

marriage, at various levels in dialogue between the Catholic Church and other confessional families — notably at international level with the Anglican Communion and in a tripartite consultation with the Lutheran World Federation and the World Reformed Alliance. In the former instance a report has been completed and in the latter it is nearing completion.

42. The Denver Report made alternative recommendations either for a special working party to perform this same task for Roman Catholics and Methodists or "that the World Methodist Council consider the possibility of joining in dialogue in progress on this subject between the Roman Catholic Church and the World Federation of the Reformed Churches."[16]

43. It is now too late for the second alternative, and it seems likely that much treading of the same ground would be avoided if, when the two reports referred to become available, our consultation were to turn its attention to a comparative study of them. This could be of value not simply to our own growth in understanding but to the ecumenical dialogue at large: our discussions in this field have generally revealed a calm approach and a positive emphasis which is not always easily achieved.

V

MORAL QUESTIONS — EUTHANASIA

44. While there are differences between Methodists and Roman Catholics on certain moral issues, there is, of course, much that could be affirmed jointly. We all agreed that this subject should be given priority in our future studies together. Unfortunately, an original plan to include moral theology in the present series of talks came to nothing.[17]

45. We were, however, able to consider a statement on euthanasia prepared by the Methodist Division of Social Responsibility and endorsed by the British Methodist Conference of 1974. It seems to provide a good example of a moral question on which we can all agree. After examining the arguments, the statement rejects voluntary euthanasia but recognises that doctors attempting the adequate control of pain have occasionally to use treatment which has the side effect of shortening life. Examples are given when medical interference to prolong life is inappropriate in the light of the patient's total situation. Withholding such interference is not euthanasia, which essentially consists of an action aimed at precipitating death.

46. The Catholic members of our joint Commission felt they, too, could wholeheartedly endorse this Methodist statement, especially the positive section on the Christian attitude to death and the pastoral care of the chronic sick and the dying. It is here that the ultimate answer to the problem of euthanasia lies.

VI

THE EUCHARIST

47.   Although the subject of the eucharist was treated somewhat briefly
and schematically in the Denver Report, the section (V) did in fact sum-
marise the results of a good deal of discussion both in our annual main
meetings of the first series and in colloquia held in between. It was a few
weeks after the Denver Conference that the Anglican/Roman Catholic
Agreed Statement on Eucharistic Doctrine was completed at Windsor, and
this was published at the end of the same year, 1971. This attracted much
sympathetic attention from Methodists, and at our own first meeting in
Rome in December 1972, we were quickly able to agree on inviting the
English Roman Catholic/Methodist Commission[18] to arrange for a study
of the Windsor Statement together with section V of the Denver Report
with a view to producing a more complete Roman Catholic/Methodist
statement for the present report. We are glad to record our deep gratitude
to the English Commission for their acceptance and very thorough carrying out of this task. The first draft we received from them stimulated us to
a long discussion at our Venice meeting, in the light of which the English
Commission revised their draft. At Bristol we adopted this revision with
some changes and it is here set out.

Roman Catholic/Methodist Statement on the Eucharist

48.   Roman Catholics and Methodists approach the eucharist without a
history of explicit disagreement. Our traditions have indeed developed in
separation from each other but not in direct historical conflict. Our
churches did not engage in debate on this issue, as in the sixteenth century
Catholic and Protestant theologians did both in Britain and in continental
Europe.

49.   In our conversations we have discovered significant agreement on
much that is central in our understanding of the eucharist. This was
foreshadowed in the section on the eucharist in the Report of the Joint
Commission between the Roman Catholic Church and the World
Methodist Council, 1967-70 (the Denver Report). It is seen also in the large
measure of assent that we, both Methodists and Catholics, can give to the
Agreed Statement on Eucharistic Doctrine presented by the Anglican-
Roman Catholic International Commission, 1971 (the Windsor Statement). There remain, of course, matters of varying importance where we
do not agree or where we express ourselves differently.

50.   Our churches have used different language about the eucharist, even
in their words for the service itself. A Roman Catholic naturally refers to
the Mass, a Methodist to the Lord's Supper or Holy Communion. We use
the word eucharist here as the one that has widest acceptance in the church
as a whole, both in the past and in the present.

51.   One major difficulty in comparing the Roman Catholic and Method-

ist eucharistic teaching lies in the fact that in the Methodist Church there has not been any historical reason for issuing a comprehensive doctrinal statement on the eucharist. The nearest equivalent to such a statement lies in the hymns and sermons of the Wesleys. Methodist practice and theology often fall short of those of the Wesleys but that does not alter their unique importance for Methodists. In recent years moreover there has been a notable recovery of eucharistic faith and practice among Methodists, with a growing sense that the fullness of Christian worship includes both word and sacrament. Similarly among Roman Catholics there has been a renewal in the theology and practice of the ministry of the word. These developments have resulted in a remarkable convergence, so that at no other time has the worshipping life of Methodists and Roman Catholics had so much in common.

52.   In a full statement we should want to place the eucharist in a broad theological context, for it relates to the whole of Christian doctrine, and focuses Christian faith and life. The following affirmations, however, express our common mind:

(a) The eucharist as a sacrament of the gospel is the fullest presentation of God's love in Jesus Christ by the power of the Holy Spirit; through it God meets us here and now in his forgiving and self-giving love.

(b) It is the commemoration of the sacrificial death and resurrection of Christ, which is the climax of the whole action of God in creation and salvation;

(c) It expresses our response — both personal and corporate — to God's initiative in a sacrifice not only of praise and thanksgiving, but also of the glad surrender of our lives to God and to his service. Thus we are united with Christ in his joyful and obedient self-offering to the Father and his victory over death;

(d) It is our response of faith and love whereby we receive his gift of himself and are renewed as members of his body, that we may be the focus of his presence and the agents of his mission to the world;

(e) It is the pointing to and the anticipation of his final triumph and it is our vision of that hope and our sharing in that victory.

53.   Eucharistic debate has often centered in the sacrifice of Christ and the presence of Christ. Both the Denver Report and the Windsor Statement give their attention chiefly to these two matters. We do the same.

The Presence of Christ

54.   We gladly re-affirm the points of agreement in the Denver Report about the real presence.[19] They may be summarised in this way:

Christ, in the fullness of his being, human and divine, is present in the eucharist; this presence does not depend on the experience of the communicant, but it is only by faith that we become aware of it. This is a distinctive mode of the presence of Christ; it is mediated through the sacred elements of bread and wine, which within the eucharist are efficacious signs of the body and blood of Christ.

55.   We rejoice also in the similar affirmations of the Windsor Statement, such as:

(*a*)   "Christ is present and active, in various ways, in the entire eucharistic celebration."[20]

(*b*)   "Communion with Christ in the eucharist presupposes his true presence, effectually signified by the bread and wine . . ."[21]

56.   The Denver Report raises the question of the contrast often made between Christ's presence in the eucharist and his presence in other means of grace. This contrast, however, is somewhat misleading. We would not wish to set word and sacrament over against one another. While there are different emphases, we both affirm that wherever Christ is present he is present in his fullness.

57.   Methodists, like Roman Catholics, believe that when they receive the elements at the eucharist they do indeed partake by faith of Christ's body and blood, and in this sense Methodists affirm the real presence of Christ thus mediated to them. Roman Catholics, like Methodists, affirm the presence of Christ in the proclamation of the gospel and in the other sacraments.

58.   The Constitution on the Sacred Liturgy of Vatican II, says " . . . Christ is always present in His Church, especially in her liturgical celebrations." Then after speaking of his presence in the eucharist and in baptism, it continues, "He is present in His word, since it is He Himself who speaks when the holy Scriptures are read in the church. He is present finally when the church prays and sings, for He promised: 'Where two or three are gathered together for my sake, there am I in the midst of them' (Mt. 18:20)."[22] This setting of the eucharistic presence in a wider context finds an echo in the Windsor Statement, which speaks of the Lord "who through the proclaimed word invites his people to his table . . . "[23]

59.   The chief point of difference concerns the question of the transformation of the bread and wine into the body and blood of Christ. Roman Catholics affirm that the physical and chemical composition of the bread and wine remain unchanged, but that their inner reality is that of the body and blood of Christ. Methodists could use such expressions from the Windsor Statement as "mysterious and radical change" "in the inner reality of the elements"[24] or "become his body and blood"[25] only in the sense that the bread and wine acquire an additional significance as effectual signs of the body and blood of Christ. They do not, however, consider this change to be of such a nature that the bread and wine cease to be bread and wine.

60.   Hence the question arises whether the Methodist way of understanding the change sufficiently resembles the Roman Catholic way of understanding it, and in particular whether the "significance" of the elements can be equated with their "inner reality".

61.   The Roman Catholic practice of reservation has the bringing of communion to the sick as its primary and original purpose. Adoration of Christ present in the elements is a secondary end. Both ends have their foundation in belief in the real presence. Methodists do not reserve the elements but reverently dispose of them.

The Sacrifice of Christ

62.   The Denver Report records four points of agreement on the eucharist as sacrifice and no points of disagreement. Our conversations have revealed certain differences in language and emphasis, although we have a clear measure of agreement.

63.   We are one in affirming that "The Eucharist is the celebration of Christ's full, perfect and sufficient sacrifice, offered once and for all for the whole world."[26] It is a memorial (*anamnesis*). It is not a mere calling to mind of a past event or of its significance, but the church's effectual proclamation of God's mighty acts.[27] Some would wish to link this dynamic view not with "a re-enactment of Christ's triumphant sacrifice,"[28]but with Christ's being present and bringing with him all the benefits of his once-for-all sacrifice for us.

64.   The term sacrifice is not used so readily by Methodists as by Roman Catholics when speaking of the eucharist. The language of sacrifice is more prominent in the hymns of Charles Wesley than in the prayers of the various Methodist communion services. This reflects in some measure the origins of the communion services: the traditional order which is dependent on the service in the *Book of Common Prayer* (written at a time when sacrifice was a term of controversy) and recent ones which have arisen in the context of the liturgical movement where sacrificial language has been less prominent because of the re-discovery of other related themes. In all this it is important to recognise that in both our churches our belief is not completely reflected in our traditional language or in our practice and piety.

65.   When Methodists use sacrificial language it refers first to the sacrifice of Christ once-for-all, second to our pleading of that sacrifice here and now, third to our offering of the sacrifice of praise and thanksgiving, and fourth to our sacrifice of ourselves in union with Christ who offered himself to the Father.

66.   Roman Catholics can happily accept all these senses of the term, but they are also accustomed to speak of the sacrifice of the Mass as something which the church offers in all ages of her history. They see the eucharist not as another sacrifice adding something to Christ's once-for-all sacrifice, not as a repetition of it, but as making present in a sacramental way the same sacrifice. For some Methodists such language would imply that Christ is still being sacrificed. Methodists prefer to say that Christ has offered one sacrifice for sins and now lives to make intercession for us, so that we in union with him can offer ourselves to the Father, making his sacrificial death our only plea.

67.   We have here a larger measure of agreement than we had expected. The obstacle to further agreement is at least in part the difference of language in our separate traditions.

EUCHARISTIC SHARING

68.   The Denver Report calls for further study of the relation between eucharistic union and ecclesiastical fellowship.[29] About intercommunion it says, "In Methodism any Christian who can conscientiously accept the invitation is welcomed to the Lord's table."[30] Certainly Methodists welcome to the Lord's table baptised communicant members of other communions who desire to come to it. But this does not mean that Methodism historically accepted or now universally accepts the method whereby an open invitation is given to all who love the Lord Jesus Christ (irrespective of church membership), although such an invitation is often given. To receive the communion is the duty and privilege of full members of the Methodist Church. The question how far this should be extended to children who have not yet been received into full membership or confirmed is at present being considered. Nor would Methodists think it fitting for Christians to receive communion in churches of any denomination at random, for communion with Christ is linked with membership of a local church.

69.   The present Roman Catholic discipline permits the access to the sacraments when in danger of death or in serious spiritual need of the eucharist, if "the separated brother has no access to a minister of his own Communion and spontaneously asks a Catholic priest for the sacraments — so long as he declares a faith in these sacraments in harmony with (*consentaneam*) that of the Church and is rightly disposed."[31] In other cases the judge of this need must be the diocesan bishop or the Episcopal Conference.

70.   The phrase "a faith in harmony with that of the Church" has been officially explained by this sentence: "This faith is not limited to a mere affirmation of the 'real presence' in the Eucharist, but implies the doctrine of the Eucharist as taught in the Catholic Church."[32] Whatever is required in exceptional cases would also be required for more general eucharistic sharing. A Roman Catholic in similar need may not ask for those sacraments except from a minister who has been validly ordained in the eyes of the Roman Catholic Church.[33]

71.   It is because of the central place which the eucharist has in Roman Catholic doctrine and practice that Roman Catholics require a comparison of the eucharistic doctrines held in the two churches. We are aware of some difficulty here. Roman Catholic doctrines have been expressed in detailed formulations; but it is not always easy to discern the essential doctrines in the historically conditioned and sometimes replaceable formulations in which they have been handed down. Methodist doctrine has received little official formulation and exists rather as an undefined tradition. Methodists do not celebrate the eucharist as frequently as Roman Catholics, although in many places the service is now regaining a central place.

72.   In this sacrament Roman Catholics and Methodists alike intend to do what Christ instituted and what the church does. Moreover we have in common our acceptance of the Christian faith as expressed in the Bible and in the historic creeds, and in particular a large measure of agreement about the meaning of the eucharist. We both acknowledge that our words cannot adequately express the joy and wonder that we experience in our celebration of the eucharist.

CONCLUSION

73.   In the eucharist we proclaim the Lord's death until he comes. We bring closer the day when God will be "all in all" (I Cor. 15:28). The eucharist makes God's kingdom to come in the world, in our churches, in ourselves. It builds up the church as the community of reconciliation dedicated to the service and salvation of mankind.

74.   The considerable degree of consensus reached in this statement does not conceal differences of approach. We hope that further developments in eucharistic worship and doctrine in both churches in the next few years will reveal an even greater resemblance and thus bring closer the union for which we all pray.

VII

MINISTRY

75.   The history of our work since Denver in this field follows very much the same pattern as with the eucharist. The Anglican/Roman Catholic Agreed Statement on the Doctrine of Ministry, entitled "Ministry and Ordination," was completed at Canterbury in 1973.[34] Again the English Roman Catholic/Methodist Commission generously accepted our invitation to examine the Canterbury Statement together with section VI of the Denver Report, and draw up a fresh statement. This they were able to let us have in time for our Bristol meeting and with such emendations as we there made it is embodied in the present report.

The Ministry: A Joint Roman Catholic-Methodist Statement

76.   The discussion of eucharist inevitably involves a discussion of ministry, and the Denver Report recorded a number of areas of agreement on this theme, together with certain problems for further study.[35] Since then the subject has also been treated by the Anglican/Roman Catholic International Commission in its report, •*Ministry and Ordination.* We take up some of these questions afresh in what follows.

OUR COMMON UNDERSTANDING

77.   Despite obvious outward differences we have in large measure a common understanding of ministry.

The fundamental ministry is Christ's own ministry, whose goal is to reconcile all people to God and to each other and to bring them into a new community in which they can grow together to their full freedom as children of God. This ministry was focused in Christ's life and death and resurrection. It did not end with his life on earth, but by the power of the Spirit continues now in and through his church. Christ still chooses and equips people for his ministry, just as he did in the beginning.

78.   In both our churches we affirm that sharing in Christ's ministry is a gift, for it depends entirely on God's initiative in calling and enabling and not on human choice and capacity. It is moreover a ministry exercised from within the church, which itself tests and confirms the call, prays for the gift of the Spirit, and sets apart the person called for this ministry.

79.   The person called by God and ordained by the church is commissioned to a lifelong ministry. It is a ministry to the church and to the world. In both directions it is the ministry of Christ himself, whose representative the minister is.

80.   The ordained minister, although his task may be different from that of others, does not work in isolation, but in cooperation with other ministries given to the church. Indeed all members of the church by their Christian vocation have a gift from God of ministry. They exercise this within the church and also in their life, their work, their family and all their relationships; and the Spirit bestows on them the gifts which are necessary for the fulfilment of this ministry. The nature of every Christian ministry is to serve and its goal is to build up in love.

Apostolic Ministry

81.   The ministry of Jesus Christ in the power of the Holy Spirit is continued in the power of the same Spirit in and by the ministry of the whole people of God. Within the ministry of the whole church we speak here primarily of the special ministry of those who are ordained, for whom both Methodists and Roman Catholics use the term minister. (For Methodists it is the usual term.)

82.   The ordained ministry is given to the church by God, and the apostles were the first "ministers of the gospel". They were commissioned by Christ himself, and each ordained minister in his turn receives through the church at his ordination the commission of Christ. Thus this ministry has existed from New Testament times until now.

83.   Though the words bishop, presbyter and deacon are to be found in the New Testament, the New Testament nowhere speaks of a three-fold ministry of bishop, presbyter and deacon. Gradually the three-fold ministry of bishop, presbyter and deacon developed. The details are obscure, but that it did develop in the sub-apostolic age is certain, and by the end of the second century the process of development was virtually complete through the church at large.

84.   We all agree that the church's apostolicity involves continuous

faithfulness in doctrine, ministry, sacrament and life to the teaching of the New Testament. In considering the ordained ministry of another church we use this faithfulness as our criterion, but we differ in the account we give of apostolic succession.

85.   For Roman Catholics the graded three-fold ministry is derived from the teaching of the New Testament through the living tradition of the church. True succession in ministry is guaranteed only by episcopal laying-on of hands in historical succession and authentic transmission of the faith within the apostolic college.

86.   Methodists hold that the New Testament does not lay down any one form of ministry as binding for all times and places, and therefore the single form of ministry which British Methodists and other non-episcopal churches have is at least as consonant with the presbyter-bishops of the New Testament as the three-fold ministry is. Methodists have no difficulty in accepting as true ministries those which emerged at the Reformation and in the eighteenth century, so long as they are faithful to New Testament ministry. They accept, however, the appropriateness of the three-fold ministry of other churches or for a united church. British Methodists affirmed it in the Churches of South India and North India and in the Anglican-Methodist Scheme of Union. The United Methodist Church of the U.S.A. and most of the churches which stem from it indeed have the three-fold ministry.[36]

87.   Moreover Methodists, both British and American, preserve a form of ministerial succession in practice and can regard a succession of ordination from the earliest times as a valuable *symbol* of the church's continuity with the church of the New Testament, though they would not use it as a *criterion*.

88.   Roman Catholics and Methodists agree that *episcope* (pastoral care and oversight) belongs essentially to the ordained ministry. Such *episcope* is exercised in different ways in their churches, but in each case it is carefully ordered with the purpose of the building-up and discipline of the faithful, the training of the young, the maintenance of the unity and peace of the church, and in the planning and direction of mission and evangelism.

89.   The ministerial structures of the two churches differ, but in both of them the collegial and individual aspect of the ordained ministry are closely related. In the Roman Catholic Church with its three-fold ministry the bishop exercises the fullness of the ordained ministry of word, sacrament and pastoral care. He alone has the power of ordaining and the overall responsibility of teaching and governing, but he is related to the whole church as a member of the college of bishops, of which the Pope is head, and as pastor of his own people shares the ministry with presbyters and deacons.

90.   Similarly in American Methodism, which also has a three-fold ministry, membership in the annual conference (as an ordained elder) is

primary, and all ministers have full and equal ministerial status. The bishop, as a member of the Council of Bishops, has responsibility for general oversight of the life of the church and possesses the power to ordain, but in this and all other matters he acts in conjunction with the conference.

91. In British Methodism, which has only one order of ministry and thus especially expresses the brotherhood of the ministry, each minister, equally with all his fellow-ministers, possesses the fullness of ministry; such functions as in many churches are exercised by bishops, belong to the conference, which in part delegates them to the President of the Conference, the chairmen of the districts and the superintendents of the circuits.

Priesthood

92. Our churches have used the word priesthood in different ways and this throws light on the difference of emphasis in our understanding of the Christian Ministry. Methodists have used it most naturally of the priesthood of the whole church, Roman Catholics of the priesthood of the ordained ministry.

93. This difference of emphasis obscures a great deal that is common in our thinking about priesthood. The New Testament uses the word priest of Christ, but never of ordained ministers. Moreover when the Letter to the Hebrews (e.g. 7:26) speaks of Christ as the high priest (*archiereus*) it describes him as accomplishing for mankind something which the priesthood of the old convenant failed to accomplish and to which no human priesthood can add anything. In that sense Christ's priesthood is the end of all human priesthood.

94. The New Testament also speaks of the church as a priesthood (e.g. I Peter 2:5) and of all members of the Christian community as priests (e.g. Rev. 1:6). Christians offer the sacrifice of praise and thanksgiving and the sacrifice of their lives (Hebrews 13:15-16) and they proclaim what God himself has done (I Peter 2:9).

95. Within the New Testament priestly language is also used of the exercise of a particular ministry, as when Paul describes his preaching as a priestly service (Romans 15:16). But the few such references do not use the word priest (*hiereus*) of an individual ordained minister.

96. By the end of the second century the term priest (*hiereus*) came to be used of ministers, although it was used first of bishops rather than presbyters. Gradually the ministry exercised was described more and more as a priesthood. In particular the eucharist was referred to as a sacrifice which the priest offered.

97. We both see the central act of the ordained ministry as presiding at the eucharist in which the ministry of word, sacrament and pastoral care is perfected. Roman Catholics affirm that in the way the ordained minister represents Christ to the body of the faithful he is a priest in a sense in which other Christians are not. The Second Vatican Council stated,

however, that "though they differ from one another in essence and not only in degree, the common priesthood of the faithful and the ministerial or hierarchical priesthood are nonetheless interrelated."[37] Each of them in its own special way is a participation in the one priesthood of Christ.

Ordination

98.   Roman Catholics and Methodists agree that by ordination a new and permanent relationship with Christ and his church is established. The ordained minister is called and enabled by the Holy Spirit to be the representative person who focuses in his ministry the manifold ministries of the whole church. He is a sign of the gospel and of the oneness of Christ's church, both to the church and to the world; an ambassador of Christ who bids men to be reconciled to God and declares to them the forgiveness of sins; a priest who embodies the priesthood of all believers in which he shares, and by his ministry serves and sustains it.

99.   Roman Catholics affirm that orders are indelible. Through the sacrament of orders, the ordained minister is sealed by the Holy Spirit and configured to Christ the Priest; he receives a permanent gift which empowers him to preach the word of God with authority, to preside at the eucharist and to absolve sinners in the name of the church. In the Roman Catholic Church only those who are ordained to the priesthood are entitled to preside at the eucharist.

100.   Methodists do not normally speak of the indelibility of ordination. But in the Methodist Church, if a minister resigns from the exercise of his ministry in full connexion[38] with the conference, or is suspended or dismissed from it, and is later authorised to resume it, his ordination is not repeated, and his orders are in this sense irremovable.

101.   For Methodists also the rule is that it is ordained ministers who preside at the eucharist. "The eucharist, which sacramentally expresses the whole gospel, is the representative act of the whole Church, and it is fitting that the representative person should preside."[39] But this does not imply that a eucharist is not valid unless an ordained minister presides, and the rule is therefore held to admit exceptions, when the conference recognises a situation in which members of the church are in danger of being deprived of the eucharist, because there are no ordained ministers in their neighborhood, and consequently grants a dispensation to a layman (in a particular area for a definite period of time) to preside at the eucharist. This is of rare occurrence, and it is a practice which is constantly under review.

102.   The Roman Catholic Church, in keeping with her traditional practice, does not ordain women to the priesthood. Methodists can find no theological objection to the ordination of women. They hold that God has manifestly called women as well as men to the ministry of word and sacraments; therefore they ordain them.

Conclusion

103.   We have elsewhere welcomed *An Agreed Statement on Eucharistic Doctrine* by the Anglican/Roman Catholic International Commission, and we are delighted now to welcome the statement on *Ministry and Ordination*. With much of it we are in agreement, as will be seen by what we ourselves have written. We especially appreciate the fine exposition of scripture and the way in which the ministry is set in the context of Christ's ministry and the ministry of the whole church. However, the place given to scripture and the understanding of the ministry lead Methodists to question the close parallel made between the formation of the canon of scripture and the emergence of the threefold ministry, [40]and to seek clarification of the statement that the Christian ministry "belongs to another realm of the gifts of the Spirit".[41]

104.   Our conversations together and our joint statement indicate a number of differences between Methodists and Roman Catholics. Some of them are differences simply of form or emphasis or language. Thus we both affirm the need for oversight, but we embody it in different forms. We both speak of ministry as apostolic, but we do it with a different emphasis. We both use the term ministry, but Roman Catholics commonly use the term priesthood. It remains to be seen whether at those points where the differences seem to be substantial they are indeed so. The crucial examples are the threefold ministry and the apostolic succession. Methodists are not in principle opposed to the ministry's being in the threefold form or in the historical succession. But they do not consider either of these to be necessary for the church or for the ministry. (In fact all Methodists preserve a form of ministerial succession and most Methodists have a threefold form of ministry.)

105.   We live in a time when members of both our churches have grown in mutual understanding and regard and in common witness and service. We rejoice in this. We rejoice equally in the growing number of ways in which ministers have been able to work together in the proclamation of the gospel, in the care of Christian people, and in the struggle to create a more just and compassionate society. It is our hope that the call from God to serve in the ministry, which has been tested and confirmed by our churches in their separation, may find its fulfilment as they minister together both in the church and in the world.

VIII

AUTHORITY

106.   Section VII of the Denver Report began with these words, "Problems connected with authority have exercised the Commission from the beginning of our conversations, and have cropped up during our discussions of other themes, e.g. ministry, eucharist. We do not feel that our direct discussions on this theme have been more than exploratory

. . . discussions on this subject will be a necessary item on any future agenda of Roman Catholic/Methodist conversations."[42]

107.   Since Denver we have not been oblivious of this necessity, but unfortunately this field is the one in which we suffered most delay in enlisting the kind of cooperation on which our general plan of work depended.[43] It is perhaps understandable that no one should be eager to embark lightly on so difficult a subject, but in the end it was yet again the English Joint Commission that came to the rescue. By the time they did so, it was too late to have any reasonable expectation of material in a form suitable to be included here, though what we have seen (especially a paper on "Authority in Doctrine," by the Rev. Rupert Davies) suggests that yet another valuable contribution to the dialogue is in prospect. This paper and section VII of the Denver Report both justify the hope that Roman Catholic/Methodist discussion has a distinctive contribution to make to a crucial subject – a distinctiveness which will not be compromised if attention is given to parallel discussions elsewhere. Examples of these are the discussions in progress in the Anglican/Roman Catholic International Commission and the national Lutheran/Roman Catholic dialogue in the U.S.A. It seems clear that the next stage of our conversations will have to take this subject as a principal one on its agenda.

IX

CHURCH UNION NEGOTIATIONS

108.   At Reuti in 1973 the Commission voted to invite Dr. Gerard Moede (then at Geneva) to write for it a survey of Methodist participation in church union negotiations and in united churches throughout the world, and to add his reflections on what implications this involvement holds (whether of theology or of policy) for Methodist/Roman Catholic dialogue, with special reference to mutual recognition of ministry.

109.   The important and substantial paper furnished by Dr. Moede was discussed at length at the Venice meeting of 1974. Discussion, however, was general, focusing mainly on the merits and demerits of existing unions and plans and at length gravitating towards the more limited topic of the advantages and disadvantages of World Confessional organizations. In the time available for discussion there was no question of justice being done to the many questions raised by the paper, especially those about the implications of our own dialogue. The paper remains as a compelling reminder of unfinished business and it is difficult to see how another five-year period of dialogue would carry conviction if it failed to grapple with these issues.

110.   In this connection it is appropriate to record that at the British Methodist Conference of 1975 a motion was proposed and passed with acclamation, "that those appointed by the Methodist Conference to the British Methodist/Roman Catholic conversations be asked – provided the

competent Roman Catholic authorities agree — to explore the conditions on which communion might be established between the Methodist Church and the Roman Catholic Church."

* * *

111. At the first of this second series of conversations, at Rome in December 1972, we agreed that, besides the specific subjects of theological discussion dealt with in sections II-VII of the Denver Report, and again taken up here in the foregoing paragraphs, there were matters mentioned in section VIII of the Denver Report, and especially in Para. 121, which demanded our attention. This paragraph spoke of "the responsibility we feel for serious planning of the education of our churches at lay, ministerial and local levels." The "we" here refers to the Commission, but the responsibility is one which extends further and the Commission's role can only be a stimulating one.

112. Since the Secretariat for Promoting Christian Unity has produced a section of its *Directorium* dealing with Ecumenical Education, we felt that a beginning might be made by eliciting reactions to this from Methodists involved in ministerial training and other forms of religious education. Members of the staff of Queen's College, Birmingham, England, an ecumenical college containing many Methodists, responded on behalf of British Methodism. The question still remains of primary importance, and there are many places where cooperation on the lines suggested by the Vatican document is in progress. Perhaps it may be hoped that at the Dublin Conference those present who have experience of such cooperation will give an account of it and so interest and encourage others.

113. Another aspect of ecumenical education and of Roman Catholic/ Methodist cooperation which we discussed briefly at our first meeting was that of the ecumenical aspects of religious use of the public communications media, and we owe thanks to Fr. Agnellus Andrew of UNDA for reflections and information on this.

114. Number 3 of our "Call to Joint Action" of 1973 read as follows: "Churches often publish statements on moral questions. Some of these should be studied together to make explicit their common content. Then the area of agreement can be further explored and a joint witness made to these moral principles."

115. It was our intention to promote a beginning here by arranging for a joint comparative study of the "Social Principles of the United Methodist Church," adopted by the 1972 General Conference in Atlanta, Georgia, and the statement, *Moral Questions* (London: C.T.S., 1971), put out by the Episcopal Conference of England and Wales, but several attempts in different places to get this done were unsuccessful. The feeling behind this section of the "Call to Action" was that such "denominational" statements often represent a lost ecumenical opportunity — a chance missed of giving a witness in this crucial field which would be all the stronger as a joint witness.

116.   Obviously this is no less true now than it was four years ago. Not all such opportunities are neglected, but we would strongly exhort our church leaders to consider always the possibility of joining their voices when such utterances are called for. We have offered above, for example (see Para. 45), a summary of a Methodist statement on euthanasia which the *Catholic Medical Quarterly* (January 1975) was able to print.

117.   As we have explained earlier, the second series of our conversations has had a different method and scope from the first; it was more experimental and even involved some act of confidence that the affinities, common concerns and hopes to which the Denver Report had pointed are widely shared in our communities. Hence it is right that some form of balance sheet should be offered as a result of our experience. It would be idle to deny that the general picture presented by our experience is an uneven one — this is clear enough from what has been said above. What is remarkable is that wherever Roman Catholic/Methodist discussion and cooperation take place at all, the available evidence suggests that the experience is a positive one. We hear nothing of tensions, frustrations and flagging interest, but much of growth in understanding and sympathy.

118.   The conclusion to be drawn from this by those who have not had the experience and who still hesitate is simple. Those who have made a start best know that there is still a long road to travel, but that is not a reason for failing to start, nor yet for fainting by the way. We should always be ready for further experiment, for extending our contacts and joint concerns.[44]

119.   Neither John Wesley and his followers nor the great apostolic figures of Catholic history were marked by a readiness for discouragement or an unwillingness to swim against the tide. It is our privilege to live in an age when we clearly see the search for unity as integral to the whole witness to Christ, and though that vision is not proof against doubts and discouragement we should not betray the spirit of resolution and confidence which, in Christ, we have inherited from his great servants.

PARTICIPANTS

Catholics:
Bishop Michael Bowen, Brighton, England
Msgr. Charles Moeller, Rome
Reverend T.F. Stransky, C.S.P., New York, U.S.A.
Reverend Michael Hurley, S.J., Dublin, Ireland
Msgr. W.A. Purdy, Rome

Methodists:
Bishop William R. Cannon, Atlanta, Georgia, U.S.A.
Bishop Prince A. Taylor, Jr., Princeton, New Jersey, U.S.A.

Reverend A. Raymond George, Bristol, England
Dr. José Miguez Bonino, Buenos Aires, Argentina
Dr. Lee F. Tuttle, Lake Junaluska, North Carolina, U.S.A.

Notes

1. Lee F. Tuttle, ed.: *Proceedings of the Twelfth World Methodist Conference,* Denver, Colorado, August 18-26, 1971 (Nashville & New York: Abingdon), pp. 46-49 (Paras. 34-50).
2. *Proceedings*, pp. 35-7.
3. Dr. Robert Nelson, "Salvation: Illusion, Puzzle or Joy?"; Fr. T. Stransky, "A Report on the Bangkok Conference"; Mons. Charles Moeller, "Reflections on Bangkok"; Bishop F. W. Schäfer, "Possible Themes for Dialogue Emerging from Bangkok and Mexico City".
4. Mons. C. Moeller, "Jesus Christ Frees and Unites"; Fr. Michael Hurley, S. J., "Prevenient Grace and Salvation Today: A Note on John Wesley"; Dr. J. Miguez Bonino, "The Wesleyan Tradition of Conversion in Relation to Salvation Today".
5. Methodists have characteristically spoken of assurance in this connection, but this should not be seen as a form of certainty which removes the need for hope. Assurance, itself a gift of the Holy Spirit, was no guarantee of perseverance, nor even a necessary accompaniment of saving faith.
6. *Proceedings*, p. 49 (Para. 47).
7. *Ibid.*, pp. 66-68. Cf. also Section II, Para. 49, p. 49; Section II, Para. 68, p. 53, and Section IV, Para. 78a, p. 55.
8. *Ibid.*, Paras. 6-7, p. 41.
9. *Ibid.*, Paras. 51-68, pp. 49-53.
10. Cf. *ibid.*, Para. 51, p. 49.
11. *Ibid.*, Paras. 62-7, pp. 52-3.
12. *Ibid.*, Para. 68, p. 53.
13. *Ibid.*, pp. 266-76.
14. Cf. *infra*, Paras. 76-105.
15. *Proceedings*, Paras. 70-71, pp. 53-4.
16. *Ibid.*, Para. 74, p. 54.
17. Cf. *infra*, Para. 116.
18. This Commission, described for convenience here and elsewhere as "English," was set up on the Roman Catholic side by the Ecumenical Commission of England and Wales and on the Methodist side by the Methodist Conference of Great Britain.
19. *Proceedings*, Para. 83, pp. 56-7.
20. Windsor, September 1971, *An Agreed Statement on Eucharistic Doctrine* (London: SPCK, 1972), Para. 7, p. 7. Hereafter cited as Windsor.
21. *Ibid.*, Para. 6, p. 6.
22. *Constitution on the Sacred Liturgy*, Section 7.
23. *Ibid.*, Para. 7, p. 7.
24. The Windsor Statement has as its footnote to Para. 6: "The word *transubstantiation* is commonly used in the Roman Catholic Church to indicate that God acting in the eucharist effects a change in the inner reality of the elements. The term should be seen as affirming the *fact* of Christ's presence and of the mysterious and radical change which takes place. In contemporary Roman

Catholic theology it is not understood as explaining *how* the change takes place."

25. Windsor, Para. 6, p. 6.
26. *Proceedings*, Para. 83, pp. 56-7.
27. Windsor, Para. 5, p. 6.
28. *Proceedings*, Para. 83, pp. 56-7.
29. *Ibid.*, Para. 85, p. 58.
30. *Ibid.*, Para. 84, p. 58.
31. The Secretariat for Promoting Christian Unity: *The Ecumenical Directory I*, 55; cf. *Instruction Concerning Cases When Other Christians May Be Admitted to Eucharistic Communion in the Catholic Church*, 1972, 4b.
32. The Secretariat for Promoting Christian Unity: *A Note about Certain Interpretations of the "Instruction Concerning Particular Cases when other Christians may be Admitted to Eucharistic Communion in the Catholic Church*," October 17, 1973, 7.
33. Cf. *Ecumenical Directory I*, 55.
34. *Ministry and Ordination: A Statement on the Doctrine of the Ministry Agreed by the Anglican-Roman Catholic International Commission* (London: SPCK, 1973). Hereafter cited as *Ministry and Ordination*.
35. *Proceedings*, Paras. 87-98, pp. 58-60.
36. By American Methodism we refer both to the United Methodist Church of the United States of America and to the churches historically related to it. By British Methodism we refer both to the British Methodist Church and to the churches derived from it, as well as to the Methodist Church in Ireland.
37. *Dogmatic Constitution on the Church*, 2.10.
38. A Methodist minister is said to be "in full connexion with the conference" or "a member of the annual conference" when he is in good standing as a minister and has the rights, privileges and responsibilities, and duties which that involves.
39. "Statement on Ordination," British Methodist Conference, 1974, Para. 16. Cf. "The central act of worship, the Eucharist, is the memorial of that reconciliation and nourishes the church's life for the fulfilment of its mission. Hence it is right that he who has oversight in the church and is the focus of its unity should preside at the celebration of the eucharist." (*Ministry and Ordination*, Para. 12, p. 8.)
40. *Ministry and Ordination*, Para. 6, p. 5.
41. *Ibid.*, Para 13, p. 9.
42. *Proceedings*, Para. 99, p. 60.
43. Professor Norman Young, to whom the Commission has been indebted for generous help in several fields, did supply us at our 1973 meeting with an interesting reflection on the question from the background of Australian dialogue.
44. It is most encouraging, for example, to hear, as this report is being prepared, that a joint committee for study and collaboration has been set up between the Catholic Conference of Bishops of Latin America (CELAM) and the Council of Evangelical Methodist Churches of Latin America (CIEMAL) and has already held its first meeting at Cochabamba, Bolivia. One of its avowed aims is collaboration with our international Commission.
   Another encouraging result of the Commission's "Call to Action" is the lively book of essays by English Catholics and Methodists, edited by Brian Frost and Leo Pyle, *Dissent and Descent* (London: Epworth Press, 1975).

HONOLULU REPORT, 1981

Prefatory Note

1. The successive Joint Commissions between the Roman Catholic Church and the World Methodist Council have hitherto presented reports only at five-yearly intervals, on the occasion of the meetings of the World Methodist Council in 1971 and 1976. The present Commission (1977-81), feeling that such infrequent reports are insufficient to sustain the interest of our Churches in its work, has sought to make its work public as soon as it was ready, so that it might benefit from the comments and criticisms of theologians in both Churches. Hence the earlier parts of this report will be already familiar in substance to many readers (cf. below).

In these earlier interim publications the Commission invited theologians of both Churches to send their comments on the texts, and such comments as were received have been used in revising the texts for this quinquennial publication.

2. Planning the work of the quinquennium at Bad Soden in 1977, the Commission took as general theme a study of the Holy Spirit in the hope that it would shed fresh light on various questions which have challenged both our traditions and do so even more urgently today, but which our separation has hitherto left us to approach in different ways.

3. At the next meeting in Rome in January 1979 we were able to summarize the fundamentals of our shared doctrine in a paper which we felt free to entitle "Towards an Agreed Statement on the Holy Spirit" (World Methodist Council, P.O. Box 518, Lake Junaluska, NC, and "One in Christ" Vol. XV (1979) n⁰ 3, pp. 274-81). See §§ 7-22).

4. At Epworth-by-the-Sea in January 1979 we went on to examine, in the light of this agreement, questions already broached in earlier discussions since 1967; the resulting report (see below §§ 23-28) was published as "The Holy Spirit, Christian Experience and Authority" (World Methodist Council, as above, 1979, and "One in Christ" XVI (1980) n⁰ 3, pp. 225-233).

5. The last meeting of the quinquennium, at Rome, December 1980, continued to examine the theme of Authority particularly in its relation to conscience 'in the practical sphere of Christian moral decisions' (see below §§ 39-47). One particular field of these decisions, Christian marriage, was chosen for closer scrutiny, with the emphasis on marriage as a Christian vocation (§§ 48-56) and witness.

6. We have tried to maintain a concern which was evident in the earlier reports of Denver and Dublin, to speak together to men and women of our time. Hence we were led at the outset to point to "encouraging signs of the activity of the Holy Spirit" in the Church today. These signs—a quest for prayer, a care for human need and suffering, a passion for justice for all the oppressed, a groping hunger for truth now clearly unsatisfied by the achievements and claims of science and technology—are evident not only among Christians but among many others as well. The signs are widely recognised and offer what we believe an opportunity and a challenge to that "broader common witness" among Christians which Pope Paul VI called for in *"Evangelii Nuntiandi."*

It is in the conviction that such common witness is both manifested and strengthened by dialogue in search of wider agreement and increasing convergence that we offer the present report.

I. TOWARD AN AGREED STATEMENT ON THE HOLY SPIRIT

Introduction: "Why an agreed statement on the Holy Spirit?"

7. Methodists and Catholics repeatedly discover a notable rapport when they speak of spirituality, the life of the **Spirit**. In view of the signs discernible in the world today, of which we have just spoken, it seems right and good that Catholics and Methodists (themselves seeking to respond to the prompting of the Spirit bringing them together) should speak with one voice regarding this fundamental doctrine, and in the hope that this voice would be echoed by our brothers and sisters in many other Churches. The doctrine of the Person of the Holy Spirit has never been a point of division between us; and our discussions have shown that differing traditional emphases and forms of expression are complementary and mutually enriching, rather than divisive or a cause of dissension.

Finally, we are aware that the doctrine of the Holy Spirit underlies much of the "ecumenical agenda" still to be considered by our Churches (cf. sections II and III).

A. GOD THE HOLY SPIRIT

The Holy Spirit in the Godhead

8. The Holy Spirit is God. He is fully and perfectly divine, just as are the Father and the Son, possessing as they do all the divine attributes, so that he is all-wise, knows everything, is everywhere present, is all-powerful and eternal. There never was a time when he was not, and there will never be a time when he will cease to be.

9. The testimony of the Church is that God is one, yet he is also three. The unity of God lies in his nature. Though these three Persons have the

same nature, they are not one and the same Person. The Holy Spirit is the Lord and Life-Giver, proceeding from the Father and the Son, as the Western Tradition states it, or through the Son, as the Eastern Tradition states it, to be adored and glorified with them, and active with them in the salvation of people. He is not simply a mode of the Godhead; he is a Person, just as are the Father and Son, distinct from each though one with both.

10. That which differentiates the three as Persons is their relations to each other in the Godhead. The Father is the source and fountainhead; the Son is eternally begotten of him and is related to him as Son to Father; the Holy Spirit is related to the Father and the Son, proceeding from the Father and the Son (or from the Father through the Son).
It is by their relationship that the Divine Persons are distinguished. Within the Godhead the Son and the Spirit proceed from the unoriginated Father. One approach in Western theology links the procession of the Son with the intellect—He is the Word—and the procession of the Spirit with the will—He is Love, the personal Love of Father and Son.

11. The Biblical witness shows that in their operations each Person plays a special part. Though the Triune God has always been at work and involved in the lives of people since creation, it is primarily through the missions of the Son in the Incarnation and of the Spirit after the resurrection in the foundation and life of the Church that we come to know that the one God is Trinity and are led into some understanding of the work of the three Persons through God's saving acts in history. The Spirit is God's Gift of Himself to His people. He is Lord and Giver of Life. He is the love of God reaching out to humankind for its transformation and salvation.
Hence it is on the work of the Spirit that this statement will concentrate. Although ultimately the Spirit is to be adored rather than explored, Christian tradition has always sought to understand him better in order to love him and respond more fittingly to his many gifts.

B. THE WORK OF THE SPIRIT

The Holy Spirit discloses the meaning of Creation

12. Creation and salvation, which is "new creation", are closely linked. Scripture sees salvation history as a marvel of creation; God's work of creation, especially of humankind, is related to his Word and to his "breath of life", the Creator Spirit. Throughout the Old Testament the Spirit and the Word of God never cease to act together. In the New Testament the Word of God made flesh by the action of the Spirit does nothing without the spirit and the consummation of his work is the gift of the Spirit.

The Holy Spirit at work in justification and regeneration

13. The Holy Spirit was active and creative at the conception of Jesus (Mt. 1,18-20; Lk. 1,35), at his baptism (Mk. 1,9,11; Mt. 3,13-17; Lk. 3,12-13), and during his entire public ministry (Mk. 3,22-30; 9,29; Mt. 12,25-32; Lk. 11,20; 4,1-14; 10,21).
A new stage in the work of the Spirit, namely the founding of the Church, was begun through Christ's death, resurrection and the giving of the spirit to the disciples.
Today from every side we hear the question once posed by Paul. "Wretched man that I am! Who will deliver me from this body of death?" (Rom. 7,24). With or without their knowing it, the questioners are asking about justification: how may a sinner find a gracious God? how may a meaningless life be given meaning?
The Holy Spirit is present and active within us throughout the entire experience of conversion which begins with an awareness of God's goodness and an experience of shame and guilt, proceeds to sorrow and repentance, and ends in gratitude for the possession of a new life given us through God's mercy in Jesus Christ.
Justification is not an isolated forensic episode, but is part of a process which finds its consummation in regeneration and sanctification, the participation of human life in the divine.

14. Here, of course, the key concept is "pre-venience", a concept emphasized by both the Council of Trent and John Wesley. Always it is the Spirit's special office to maintain the divine initiative that precedes all human action and reaction. The Holy Spirit is God himself, present and active in human hearts and wills, "nearer to us than breathing, closer than hands or feet". This is why, when some wrongly denied the Church's latent sense of the Spirit's prevenience, the Church's positive response was rightly to reaffirm the splendid title: Lord and Giver of Life.
The Council of Trent teaches that the beginning of justification in adults takes place by means of the Lord's prevenient grace which moves us to conversion, enabling us freely to choose to follow the inspiration God gives us when he touches our hearts with the light of the Holy Spirit. "When Scripture says, 'Turn to me, and I turn to you' (Zech. 1,3), we are reminded of our freedom. When we answer, 'Turn us, Lord, to you and we shall be turned' (Lam. 5,21), we confess that we are prevented (moved first) by grace" (Session 6: Decree on Justification, Ch. 5, DS 1525).

15. In justification God through the atoning work of Christ restores a sinner to a right relationship with himself. In such a restoration, both the initiative, the agency and the consummation is the ministry of the Holy Spirit as he brings Christ to us and leads us to him. When a sinner is led to Christ and receives him, he is re-born and given the power to turn

away from a life curved back upon itself toward a "new life", opened out to love of God and neighbor.

Thus the tragic malignancies of sin may be healed; thus the deformed self may be formed, reformed and fulfilled. Blind eyes may be opened; atrophied wills renewed; minds bemused by idols of pride, avarice and greed may be liberated so as to judge by other norms. Thus a new future, for self and society, may be opened up to permanent and constructive "revolution". This is our reconciliation to God who was in Christ reconciling us to himself. And this is justification: to be regarded and treated as righteous, for Christ's sake; and yet also to be put in the way of becoming righteous. All of this is done by the initiatives of the Father's redeeming mercy, manifested in the Son's atoning grace, through the Holy Spirit's activity within our hearts.

16. "The Spirit himself is bearing witness with our spirit that we are children of God" (Rom. 8,16). We receive the Spirit of adoption, who dwells in Christians, pouring God's love into our hearts, enabling us to say "Abba" and in the Our Father to pray for forgiveness, conscious of weakness but fully confident of God's merciful love for us in Christ. Moreover, when we do not know how to pray, it is the Spirit who intercedes for us (Rom. 8,26).

17. According to the Fourth Gospel, the ultimate purpose of the mission of Jesus was to give the gift of the Holy Spirit to His disciples (Jn. 20,22-23). The Holy Spirit brings about the forgiveness of sins because it is His role to teach us, the disciples of Jesus, all things necessary for our salvation and bring to our remembrance all that Jesus said (Jn. 14,26). Because He is the Spirit of Truth, He bears witness to Jesus and enables us to be witnesses in our turn (15,26-27). He guides us into all the truth, declares the things that are to come, and so glorifies Jesus (16,13-14). By revealing to us the sonship of Jesus and the meaning of His mission, the Holy Spirit by the very fact shows the wrongness of the fundamental sin: lack of faith in Jesus (Jn 16,8-11).

18. The Holy Spirit sanctifies the regenerate Christian. Sanctification is a process that leads to perfect love. Life in the Spirit is human life, lived out in faith, hope and love, to its utmost in consonance with God's gracious purposes in and for his children. As Wesley put it, the end of human existence is the recovery and the surpassing of the perfection in which that existence was first conceived and created:

". . . Hence (in the end of creation) will arise an unmixed state of holiness and happiness far superior to that which Adam enjoyed in paradise . . . And to crown all, there will be a deep and intimate and uninterrupted union with God—a constant communion with the Father and His Son Jesus Christ through the Holy Spirit, a continual enjoyment of the Three-One God, of all the creatures in him" (*The New Creation*, § 18).

The Holy Spirit and the Christian Community

19. The chief mark of the post-Easter Church is that God gives to it the Spirit and thus creates the community of the New Covenant. The risen and exalted Lord takes possession of the world through his body, the Church, into which members are baptized in the Spirit. Our obedience is a sign of Christ's Lordship as we show in our lives his dying and his rising. His Spirit of power and love makes obedience possible by breaking the slavery of sin and giving freedom. Yet disobedience remains and only the daily offering of our bodies as a living sacrifice can display the triumph of his grace. By the Spirit we drink the cup of Christ and share his life.
By grace we are saved through faith, not because of works (cf. Eph. 2,8-9). Baptism, which is celebrated within the believing community, is the outward sign and means of grace and of faith.

20. The Holy Spirit gives to us a variety of spiritual gifts (charismata) (cf. I Cor. 12,4) which equip the different members of the body for ministry: these are not confined to such gifts as prophecy or speaking with tongues. In the Charismatic Movement or neo-Pentecostalism many have come to a new experience of life in the Spirit: but they must remember that the Spirit's work is not easily distinguished from the actions of the free human beings through whom he works: not all human works are the work of the Spirit. Guided by the Spirit's gift of discernment (I Cor. 12,10) we must develop criteria to distinguish those that are. The fruit of the Spirit is "love, goodness, faithfulness, gentleness, self-control" (Gal. 5,22-23). And these are the evidence of true faith.

21. The Spirit guides the development of the Church. In every age, as the Paraclete, he reminds us of all that Jesus said, leads us into all truth, and enables us to bear witness to salvation in Christ.
The Holy Spirit inspires Christians as they seek to obey Christ's commission to make disciples of all nations.
At the last God will triumph over sin and death and in fulfillment of his pledge of the Spirit bring all who love him to unending glory.

The Holy Spirit transforms the human community into the Kingdom of God.

22. God inaugurated his Kingdom in Christ.
The coming of this Kingdom involves the transformation of the human community now marred by sin with its resultant oppression and poverty into a community of justice, love and peace.

The Holy Spirit, applying the finished work of Christ, wills to accomplish this social and political transformation in and through people, especially in and through those who acknowledge the risen Christ as the Lord of history. And therefore we are to pray for, work toward, and hope for the attainment of this goal.

The present work of the Holy Spirit is the first fruits of his transformation (Rom. 8,23). Though we have no grounds for thinking that this transformation will be complete in this world, we nevertheless believe that all Christians must strive for it in order to bear witness to God's promise to complete this transformation in the world to come.

II. THE HOLY SPIRIT, CHRISTIAN EXPERIENCE AND AUTHORITY

23. Still bearing in mind the signs of the work of the Spirit which we believe to be discernible today (cf. above para.6) we pass from general agreements on the Holy Spirit to considering Christian experience (seeing it as the Spirit's guiding and ordering work in the Church).

A. CHRISTIAN EXPERIENCE

Christian experience is a rich field largely unexplored at least in ecumenical dialogue.

We agree that "Life in the Spirit is human life lived out ... to its utmost in consonance with God's gracious purpose" (cf. above para. 18). It is faith's awareness of the Holy Spirit's initiative within the human heart, stimulating and guiding the believer to yet more faith and hope and love. Such awareness sees both the world and history as interpersonal, as lying within God's care and providence. This awareness is focused in God's self-disclosure in Jesus Christ and directed toward life together in the Church, in which the Holy Spirit presides, indwelling, inspiring and conforming Christians to the mind that was in Christ (Phil. 2,5).

24. Christian religious experience includes the assurance of God's unmerited mercy in Christ, the inner witness of the Spirit that we are indeed children of God, pardoned and reconciled to the Father (Romans 8,12-17). The same Spirit also guides the faithful to a knowledge of all the truth as it is in Christ Jesus, and to an ever more faithful obedience to God's righteous rule within the human community at large. Despite our inability to manifest it perfectly, the fruit of the Spirit (Gal. 5,22-23) is ever a potent factor in drawing others into Christian fellowship.

25. Both Catholics and Methodists have found in John Wesley's Christian experience and his comments on "experimental religion" an edifying instance of that to which we are pointing. After a full dozen years of faithful ministry in Christ's name and to the needy (in Oxford, in Lincolnshire

and Georgia) Wesley's heart was "strangely warmed" and he came into an "assurance" that God had taken away his sins and had saved him from the law of sin and death (cf. Journal, May 24, 1978).[1] Significantly, it was this deeply personal experience that led Wesley into a yet more effective ministry, still more deeply grounded in his awareness that it was the Holy Spirit who enabled him to communicate to others the gospel of salvation by faith and holiness in heart and life. Thus, the doctrine of the "witness of the Spirit" (i.e. the hinge of any idea of Christian experience) looms large in Wesley's teaching early and late (Discourse 1, 1748, and Discourse II, 1764). It must be acknowledged that later Methodist theologians have tended to be more "rationalistic" or more "pragmatic". However, we have found new meanings in the evident similarities between Wesley and the mainstream of Catholic spirituality. This convergence could have significant implications for our own growing spiritual awareness of "oneness in Christ" and for the future of the cause of Christian unity. Thus we have agreed that a reclamation of our complex heritage by both sides would benefit our respective communities and also enhance our present experience of unity in the Spirit.

27. In the Post-Reformation Roman Catholic tradition generally, it has been the saints and spiritual masters, rather than the scholastic theologians, who have stressed the centrality of Christian experience. In this matter, however, Vatican II appears as a turning point. The Council documents speak frequently of the transforming activities of the Holy Spirit, in persons, in the Church, in the world. They stress the task of discerning "the signs of the times" and of the Spirit's leading in these shadowed, changing times. It is not an exaggeration to say that these post-conciliar years have witnessed a rediscovery within the Catholic fold of Christian faith as "experience", understood afresh as intimacy with Christ in prayer and as liberating presence in persons and communities. The most evident signs of this "new spirit" include the rise of various centres of spirituality, houses of prayer, the charismatic renewal, cursillos and marriage-encounter movements, Bible study groups, new ministries, more active roles for women in the church, new efforts in the promotion of justice, new missionary ventures. These "signs" might quite properly remind Methodists of how their early "class meetings" could look if they, too, were updated. We are able, therefore, to affirm together the crucial importance of "heart religion" since we agree that Christianity is a communion of believers, a "fellowship with the Father and with his Son Jesus Christ" (I John 1, 1–3; for the Spirit's role in this cf. 3, 24; 4, 13). We form a mystical body whose Head is Christ (Eph. 4). Our common aim is to live together, in the Spirit, that Christ may be formed in us, our hope of glory, to the end that the Father's righteous will may be done on earth as it is in Heaven. The Holy Spirit is the prime artisan of our Christian experience, since it is he who "completes the work of Christ by placing himself as the innermost reality in each human being" (P. Evdokimov, in "Panagion et Panagia",

BSFEM, 27, 1970, p.61). It is the Holy Spirit who enables us to pray "Lord Jesus" and "Abba, Father"; it is he who fashions us in the image of Jesus; it is he who calls us into obedience to the Father's righteous rule on earth and beyond all this to our very first duty of glorifying God and enjoying him forever.

28. Together, then, we affirm that the Christian experience toward which we aspire as one includes mystery and clarity, feeling and reason, individual conscience and acknowledged authority, charisms and sacraments, spiritual exercises and service, individual and communal "discernments of spirits", local community and worldwide mission, fidelity to the past and openness to the present and future. We are agreed that Christian experience requires for its development the disciplines of prayer and devotion, the truth accessible in Holy Scriptures, the nourishment of the sacraments, the encouragement that comes from God's abundant gifts of grace and wisdom, for witness and service in the world.

29. Further, since it is in our totality as human persons that God joins us to himself, we are agreed that our affective states are also subject to the Spirit's absolute "prevenience". As we seek to be instructed by the Scriptures and by the spiritual treasures of the Christian tradition, our "spiritual senses" are developed to greater and greater keenness. In the Spirit, we see the Lord, hear his voice, taste his sweetness, breathe the fragrance of his presence, experience the healing power and the gift of new life of him who dwells in our hearts and speaks to us through the witness and need of others. At the same time, this experience is open to the rule of reason and to all responsible uses of practical knowledge. "Knowledge and vital piety" belong together, as correctives to imbalances from either side. By the same token, there must be careful balancing between the voice of individual conscience and the voice of legitimate external authority, in church or society—by the constant acknowledgement that both conscience and all external authorities are regulated by the Word of God, by the faith of the Church and by the shared experience of the Christian faithful.

30. Catholics and Methodists agree that progress in purification from sin and its effects as well as growth in holiness, namely love of God and neighbor, requires the development of our God-given powers of spiritual discernment in individual and social experience. We rejoice in our mutual discoveries of significant resources in our respective traditions which aid such development, such as the *Sermons* and spiritual directives of John Wesley and, say, the *Spiritual Exercises* of St. Ignatius Loyola. We are convinced that as we recover and reclaim this rich mutual heritage for ourselves, we might grow closer to each other on a deeper level.

31. We also rejoice to recognize the emergence of new communities of fellow Christians who are seeking to support each other in their Christian

witness and service—as what St. Ignatius spoke of as "friends in the Lord"—. These experiences in community demand of all who share in this unfeigned fidelity in faith, voluntary moral discipline and sacrificial service. They call us all to a livelier concern for more apt understanding of Holy Scriptures as we are guided by the same Spirit who inspired them. Equally, we acknowledge ourselves as under the imperatives of love that follow from the summons to seek first the Kingdom of God and his righteousness, in our lives and in his world. The Holy Spirit is God's first gift to those who believe and to all who confess Jesus Christ as Lord to the glory of the Father. Out of these shared convictions, we call upon all our sisters and brothers in Christ to join in more ardent pursuit of these higher levels of Christian experience and more effective ways of expressing our faith, hope and love in and to the world for which Christ died. In this way we shall be drawn into an actual communion in Christ and, as we may hope, more readily thereafter into *communio in sacris,* full sacramental fellowship.

32. Our respective liturgical traditions give expression to this common faith:

"Almightly God, to whom all hearts are open, all desires known, and from whom no secrets are hid: cleanse the thoughts of our hearts by the inspiration of the Holy Spirit, that we may perfectly love thee and worthily magnify thy holy Name; through Christ our Lord"
(Methodist Service of Holy Communion: and Roman Missal, Votive Mass of the Holy Spirit).
"Father all-powerful, and ever living God, we do well, always and everywhere, to give you thanks, in you we live and move and have our being. Each day you show us a Father's love; your Holy Spirit, within us, gives us on earth the hope of unending joy. Your gift of the Spirit who raised Jesus from the dead is the foretaste and promise of the Paschal Feast of heaven . . ."
(Roman Missal, Preface VI for Sundays in Ordinary Time).

B. THE HOLY SPIRIT AND AUTHORITY IN THE CHURCH

33. To men and women sealed by the Spirit in baptism, gathered in the Church, in the communion of Christ's gift of himself, Christ's authority is mediated through the Spirit, who is Love, and hence all authority that flows from this source is part of God's good gift. Whether it be the personal authority of holiness or the charism of episcope conferred by the Spirit on the ordained ministry, whether it be teaching or disciplinary, authority implies that what is propounded, commanded or recommended ought to be accepted on the ground that it comes from this source.

34. There is no disagreement that the Church has authority to teach. In the Church, the revelation of God in Christ comes to us through Scripture, and to maintain God's people in the truth is the loving work of the Spirit in the Church. But this maintenance is not a matter of mere repetition of formulae. The Spirit moves the Church to constant reflection on the Scriptures which he himself inspired and on their traditional interpretation, so that she may speak with undiminished authority to men in different times and places, in different social and cultural settings, facing new and difficult problems. This is not of course to question the abiding importance of credal statements and such Conciliar pronouncements as the Chalcedonian definition. The enduring validity of these does not restrict the power of the Spirit to speak in new ways to the Church, whose living voice never speaks in isolation from its living past. It stands under the living word of God. The old oppositions of Scripture and Tradition have given way to an understanding which we share, that Scripture in witness to the living tradition from which it arose has a normative role for the total tradition of the Church as it lives and is guided still by the Spirit of truth.

35. Ours is not the only dialogue in which special difficulties have been voiced, and persist, in the matter of papal claims and the character of dogmatic definitions (Paul VI's address to S.P.C.U. plenary 1968). We should take notice of the progress of other dialogues, but we believe that emotions surrounding such relatively modern terms as infallibility and irreformability can be diminished if they are looked at in the light of our shared doctrine concerning the Holy Spirit. The papal authority, no less than any other within the Church, is a manifestation of the continuing presence of the Spirit of Love in the Church or it is nothing. Indeed it should in its exercise be pre-eminently such a manifestation. It was declared at Vatican I to be "for the building up and not the casting down on the church"— whether of the local Church or the communion of local Churches.

36. This primary aspect has been obscured by the emotions and polemics surrounding such terms as infallibility and universal and immediate jurisdiction. As with other dogmas, the terms which express the dogma of 1870 belong to their time, and must be understood in the context of that time and of the debates of that era. The truth behind them is capable of fuller understanding in new settings by all concerned. Already Vatican II's Constitution of the Church, *Lumen Gentium,* and other documents have done something to adjust an imbalance left by the unfinished business of Vatican I.

The terms referred to are not to be explained away: from different standpoints we are agreed that this would be neither useful nor honest. Yet they are not claims about human qualities or glorifications of an office. They are to be understood in the light of the total conception and the total responsibility of teaching and disciplinary office in the Church—a pastoral office mirroring the constant presence and solicitude of the Spirit within the Church, leading into truth and disciplining in love. Thus, and thus only, whatever its forms and nomenclature, can any authority be understood and legitimized.

However the claims implied in such terms are circumscribed and clarified, it is unlikely that Methodists in the foreseeable future will feel comfortable with them. But Methodist awareness of the papacy has enlarged and greatly altered in recent times, and the general idea of a universal service of unity within the Church, a primacy of charity mirroring the presence and work in the Church of the Spirit who is love, may well be a basis for increased understanding and convergence.

37. We have said above that the personal authority of holiness (para.33) also shows the Spirit present and at work. This points to the question of a relationship which we discussed as long ago as Denver (1971)—that of authority and conscience. This has often been seen less as a relationship than as a Protestant/Catholic antithesis. If what we have agreed so far is true, this view can only be a distortion. That authority is a service of the Gospel, that the assent of faith is free or nothing, that the one witnesses to the other, no Catholic will deny: that Christian conscience is formed within the life of the Church, which is life in the Spirit, no Methodist will dispute. More questions on this relationship must arise in our next phase of work, on practical, ethical and moral judgements, but these agreed principles will apply.

38. We have agreed that:

"The coming of this Kingdom involves the transformation of the human community now marred by sin with its resultant oppression and poverty into a community of justice, love and peace" (cf. above para. 22).

We are not under the illusion that the signs of the activity of the Holy Spirit we started by pointing to are signs to be found everywhere. There is much cause for disquiet, in the impatience and contempt, not for tyrannical and arbitrary authority but for the fundamental authority which alone makes ordered life possible. The contempt for human life, for diplomatic immunity, for our natural inheritance, are saddening signs of the times. What we said above about the criteria by which alone authority can be understood or legitimized clearly applies, for Christians, to all authority ecclesiastical or secular. Hence, it is that we see concern for the poor and the oppressed and for the conservation of God's gifts as one test by which all authority is to be judged. All arbitrary and absolute authority, denying the respect due to human beings and to creation, is unchristian.

III. CHRISTIAN MORAL DECISIONS

Introduction

39. The Christian vocation is heard in the teaching of Christ, the Saviour, who instructed his disciples to "be perfect therefore as your heavenly Father is perfect" (Mt. 5,48). The perfection of God is his love, for God is love (I Jn. 4,8,12). The Christian is aware that discipleship of Jesus means imitation of him whose love was so great that he did not hesitate to lay down his life for all (Jn. 15,13). The Church announces the totality of the mystery of Christ. It echoes his call to us to be converted and to follow along his way, stressing in all things the primacy of charity. The Church is the heir of divine revelation and proclaims Christ and his message to further his mission and to summon men and women to respond in faith, hope and love.

40. The Church is also called "God's people" (I Peter 2,9-10). It is within the setting of the Christian fellowship that one hears the call of Christ and is moved to respond with the fullness of one's being. The call is never ending and the response should be constant and willing. Through the power of the presence of the Holy Spirit, God's gift to his people, the Church accepts responsibility for taking part in the formation of the individual conscience, always aware that it is the secret core and sanctuary where each of us enjoys an intimacy with God. The Christian derives much benefit from the riches of the Church, i.e. the Scriptures, the community, worship and teaching, all of which have their effect in order that each person may bring forth much fruit.

41. The Christian likewise is called to live in the setting of creation, and enjoys the society of men and women. Here the Church stands as a student and teacher. It learns from human developments and is enriched by advances in empirical sciences and behavioral studies. It thus becomes aware of human problems and difficulties and is prepared to bring its own insights and sensitivity to the search for solutions. It is strongly aware of the presence of evil which seeks to challenge the Kingdom of God. It, therefore, does not hesitate to identify and confront what is evil in order to preserve and affirm what is good.
The Church is likewise aware of a person's propensity to sin and failures. It supports every effort to answer the call to perfection. The Church acts in mercy and kindness but when challenged in matters of morality is compelled in the Spirit to speak.

42. The Lord has called us to repent and believe that the Good News and therefore this call to conversion should manifest itself in the activity of the Christian. We have said earlier that "We acknowledge ourselves as under

the imperatives of love that follow from the summons to seek first the Kingdom of God and *his* righteousness, in our lives and in his world" and to pursue "more effective ways of expressing our faith, hope and love in and to the world for which Christ died" (cf. above, § 31).

We acknowledge that belief and behavior, faith and works, should not be separated. Therefore issues of ethics and morality, which involve the relation between conscience and authority, are not peripheral to but at the heart of the faithful hearing of the Gospel.

43. Whether we see conscience as a separate faculty or as the mobilizing of all our faculties to discern the good and shun evil, we agree that the human capacity we call conscience is the gift of God and is of vital significance for the moral life.

Conscience does not act as an independent source of moral information. Since people have the responsibility of fostering, protecting and following their conscience, it needs to be formed and informed and must therefore be open to guidance from authority.

Therefore in moral decision-making, as in coming to terms with doctrinal formulations, the Christian is one who stands under authority. The normative authority is Scripture interpreted in the light of Tradition (the living voice of the Church), Reason and Experience (cf. above, § 34).

44. People have both the responsibility to see that their conscience is open to authoritative guidance and the right freely and faithfully to follow that conscience. Thus we agree that no one is to be forced to act in a manner contrary to conscience, or to be restrained from acting according to conscience, "as long as the just requirements of public order are observed" (Vatican II, *Declaration on Religious Freedom,* n.2) and the rights of others are not infringed.

We are agreed that "freedom of conscience" does not mean "make up your mind on moral matters with no reference to any other authority than your own sense of right and wrong." There may come a point when the Church is compelled to say, "If you persist in exercising your freedom of conscience in this way you put yourself outside the Church."

45. We agree in asserting the importance of natural law which God himself enables us to perceive. In this perception the supernatural gift of prevenient grace plays a major part. "No man is entirely destitute of what is vulgarly called *natural conscience.* But this is not natural: it is more properly termed *preventing grace. . .* Everyone, unless he be one of the small number whose conscience is seared with a hot iron, feels more or less uneasy when he acts contrary to the light of his own conscience" (J. Wesley, Works, VI 485). The natural law which is thus discerned stems from the generous provision of the Creator God.

What is revealed in Jesus Christ, our Incarnate Redeemer, is God's hidden purpose already being worked out through the whole of his creation; the "ethics of revelation" do not negate but are consistent with the created order within which God brings human nature to its fulfillment. ("Our human nature is the work of your hands made still more wonderful by your work of redemption", Collect of Christmas Day, Roman Breviary). Therefore moral theologies based on natural law and those that appeal more directly to an "ethic of revelation" need not be in conflict. Consequently the moral judgements the Christian makes, as a Christian, are not in fulfillment of an imposed divine imperative alien to his own well-being but are a response to the will of God to enhance and fulfill all that is genuinely human. While we can distinguish between the duties one has as a member of the Church and as a member of the human community, these should be seen as harmonious, with conscience providing guidance in both spheres. We recognize that in both our Churches official statements and actions are frequently assigned greater authority than they are entitled to. Conflict about what weight to give to such statements and actions can thereby arise within the individual conscience, and between Christians.

46. We have already indicated (above, §§ 27 and 34) that we are in agreement that the Church must always be subject to the headship of the Incarnate Lord and that the Holy Spirit makes Christ present to us, so mediating his authority to us in love through Word and Sacraments; these in turn are witnessed to by the worshipping community and by Creeds and Confessions. Only then do we come to the point of divergence, which must not be allowed to obscure this agreement. Within this context, what persons or bodies in the Church can give guidance on moral issues and with what authority?

47. In both our Churches we have various procedures for offering guidance on moral issues, and this Commission recognizes the need for closer study and comparison of these procedures. In neither Church does the following out of these procedures always match the ideal, for each Church recognizes "how great a distance lies between the message she offers and the human failings of those to whom the Gospel is entrusted" (Vatican II: Church in the Modern World, 43).
In both our Churches we are under ecclesiastical authority, but we recognize a difference in that some pronouncements of the Catholic Church are seen as requiring a higher degree of conscientious assent from Catholics than the majority of pronouncements of the responsible bodies of Methodism require of Methodists.
Where there are differences between us on what decisions should be made and what actions taken on particular moral and ethical issues, we need to look not just at these differences but at what gives rise to them, in each case enquiring whether they reflect only social and historical conditions or fundamental divisions over issues of conscience and authority.

CHRISTIAN MARRIAGE

48. Both the Denver and the Dublin reports contain sections on "Christian Home and Family". We wish to reaffirm what was said in these reports, particularly the general picture of Christian marriage presented in Denver, § 71, and the call to common witness "to the centrality of marriage in God's purpose for the human community" so strongly voiced in the Dublin report, § 39.
Our discussions have led us further in our agreement about the sacramental nature of marriage and its implications for the wider community.

49. In particular we are able to affirm that it is not only the wedding but the whole marriage that is sacramental. The relationship, the continual, lived out, total giving and sharing of the spouses is a genuine sign of God's love for us, Christ's love for us, Christ's love for the Church.
While Catholics speak of marriage as a sacrament and Methodists do not, we would both affirm, in the words of the introduction to the 1979 "Service of Christian Marriage" of the United Methodist Church: "Christian marriage is the sign of a lifelong covenant between a man and a woman. They fulfil each other, and their love gives birth to new life *in* each and *through* each. This union of love is possible only because Christ is the bond of unity. . . The marriage of a baptised couple is a covenant between equals that celebrates their unity in Jesus Christ. They make a little family within the household of God; a 'little church' in the Body of Christ. . . The Protestant reformers of the sixteenth century were unwilling to call marriage a sacrament because they did not regard matrimony as a necessary means of grace for salvation. Though not necessary for salvation, certainly marriage is a means of grace, thus, sacramental in character. It is a covenant grounded in God's love. A Chrisitian marriage is both a plea for and an expression of daily grace" (p.14). So too the Introduction to the 1969 Rite of Marriage of the Roman Catholic Church teaches: "Married Christians, in virtue of the sacrament of matrimony, signify and share in the mystery of that unity and fruitful love which exists between Christ and his Church; they help each other to attain the holiness in their married life and in the rearing and education of their children and they have their own special gift among the people of God" (§ 1).

50. Marriage is sacramental in nature because it is the living and life-giving union in which the covenantal love of God is made real. This is the point of Ephesians 5,21-34, where marriage is related to "a great mystery; but that I mean in reference to Christ and the Church" (5,32).
The text is actually speaking of two mysteries, both hidden from the beginning: the mystery of marriage and the mystery of Christ and his Church. It points out that Christian marriage is inserted into the sphere of redemption and that married love is sanctifying in all its spiritual and physical expressions.

The Old Testament image of marriage as a covenant describing God's relationship with Israel illustrates the richness and power of imagery. The covenant tradition in Hosea is really a multiplicity of images which extends into images of marriage, of land, and of fatherhood. The story is an intricate, often puzzling blend of the bonded and the broken, and by reflecting on their own daily experience in the light of it married couples might greatly enrich their lives.

The significance of the man-woman relationship of life and love in relationship to Christ and to the Church is proclaimed in the medieval use of Sarum, the preferred rite of the English Churches prior to the Reformation (dependent in turn on the Gregorian Sacramentary), a text now used in the revised Roman Rite of Marriage.

That marriage is a sign of Christ's covenant with the Church, precisely because as a social institution it is perceived as a covenant, is clearly stated in the nuptial blessing of the Sarum use: "O God, you consecrated the union of marriage by a mystery so profound as to prefigure in the marriage covenant the sacrament of Christ and the Church. O God, you join woman and man and give to their alliance, the first to be established by you, that blessing which enriches it, and which alone was not forfeited in punishment for original sin by the curse of the Deluge".

The mystery is not only in the "mysterious" union of Christ and his Church but also in human marriage itself. Thus, marriage is a natural sign of a holy mystery precisely because the relationship, conjugal and parental, is what Christ takes up and sanctifies.

51. The richness of this vision of Christian marriage can be explored endlessly. It speaks of the reciprocal illumination between the natural and the supernatural, between the world of creation and the world of redemption, between the secular and the sacred. The good gift of the creator becomes also a personal gift of the Saviour. This vision shows that the sacramentality of marriage is not to be limited to the marriage ceremony, since the entire fabric of the marriage lived out by the couple is what constitutes its ecclesial witness.

52. When we assert that the sacramentality of marriages springs from the whole of the marriage, several themes can be noted in particular as belonging to the sacramentality and spirituality of the marriage:

—The couple's daily love for each other, not only with its joys but also with its pains, sufferings and uncertainties over so many years, reflects the covenant love of God for us. The couple's sexual sharing should itself be understood as sacramental.

—The couple's love for their children not only in bearing them, but even more so in the years of love and care for them, proclaims or sacramentalizes God's love for all of us.

—The couple's reaching out in concern to the larger community is also very much a part of the sacramental witness of marriage.
The demands of a marriage as it develops are themselves a source of spiritual enrichment.

53. For the Christian marriage demands commitment, fidelity and permanence. However unpopular this may be today, the Church must proclaim it because it is the will of God and revealed in Scripture and expressed in the liturgy.
The commitment of the spouses to love for each other is rooted in their love for God (cf. Mt. 22,33-40) and His love for them. Their communion is made possible by the God who loves them first (cf. I John 4,17).
Fidelity counters the deepest and most pervasive temptation of marriage, that of withdrawing into a self-centered and 'privatized' life. Marital fidelity is not purely negative, a mere safeguard; it is a self-giving that creates a community of love and life and a deeper mutual trust in which there can be greater freedom and openness to others. But such faithfulness is anchored in God who makes faithful marriage possible.

54. We all subscribe to this teaching on Christ's will for matrimonial permanence and fidelity and this despite our different approaches to the problems of matrimonial nullity and of marital breakdown. We believe that further dialogue on these topics may well reveal closer unity of understanding, since we are all alarmed at the trivialization of marriage and the increase of divorce in the societies from which we come.

55. The bond of Christian marital union, between man and woman is holy by its nature. Through their commitment to marital partnership the spouses pledge themselves to love and serve one another in Christ. Marriage likewise is ordered to the procreation and education of children. The marital union thus grows into the unit of the family. Here the marriage partners are associated with the creation work of God who both blessed and charged man and woman at the beginning "Be fruitful and multiply" (Gen. 1,18). Human intimacy and human responsibility thus deepen and mature as all the family members grow in wisdom, age and grace before God and men and with one another.

56. Married couples need to discover and affirm the beauty and the treasure of Christian marriage. Because marriage is a sacramental covenant it is a living, prophetic sign to all people. The love and life of a married couple is a particular visible and credible expression of the universal "loving kindness and fidelity" of the Father of our Lord Jesus Christ. In this way the spouses and their children should be open to the wider community in which other people become their neighbors in Christ.

A blessing at the end of the Rite of Marriage of the Roman Catholic Church concludes:

"May you always bear witness to the love of God in this world, so that the afflicted and the needy will find in you a generous friend, and welcome you into the joys of heaven".

And the Introduction to the Marriage Service of the United Methodist Church reminds us that

"the purpose of Christian marriage is not only to fulfill the needs of domestic intimacy, but also to enable the family to accept duties and responsibilities in the Christian community for society at large . . . The family . . . is a 'domestic Church' " (p. 15).

The Future

57. A feeling which emerged from our last meeting (agreed to be one of the best we have had) and from reflection on the past quinquennium as a whole is that any further stage of our dialogue should concentrate more intensive study on such problems or differences as have recurred and seemed most obstinate in the past three quinquennia. This greater concentration was we believe already beginning during the past five years.

In the belief that time will be saved if a programme is already set out for the consideration of our Churches in this report, we unanimously submit the following themes and suggestions for procedure:

Theme for quinquennium: THE NATURE OF THE CHURCH.

Year 1. The Doctrine of the Church
Year 2. The Church as Institution (Structures and Polity)
Year 3. The Doctrine of the Primacy
Year 4. The Church in the Modern World (cf. Denver report: etc.).

Detailed programme for the first year: DOCTRINE OF THE CHURCH (Feb. 1982): There would be four papers:

a) General paper on Sacrament and Sign (the Sacramental idea—a philosophical and theological paper)
b) The Church as Sacrament: how God works through his Church
c) The Word and the Church
d) Universal and Local: the Communities and the Church (NOTE: this to be a doctrinal paper).

Methodists would be responsible for papers (a) and (c), Catholics for (b) and (d).

Each paper would be matched by a response prepared by a designated member of the other team; the paper would be sent to them well in advance of the meeting to ensure this.

58. Our experience strongly underlines the advantage of having papers available to all members in advance and we propose as a principle that writers of papers should aim to get them to the secretaries two months before the meeting. A short bibliography is also useful. Finally we would hope that both the WMC and the Catholic authorities would endorse the importance of the dialogue and ask that those taking part give it high priority among their engagements.

59. We submit these recommendations in a spirit of thankfulness to God for what has been achieved, of confidence that continued dialogue of a more concentrated kind on central issues will continue to bear fruit, and of hope that this and earlier reports will be more widely studied in our Churches and lead to a steady increase in that cooperation between Catholics and Methodists which is already encouragingly evident in many places.

60. What we have shared and said together about the Holy Spirit enhances our confidence about the future of our relations. We are all alike under the judgement of God, but all alike confident of the presence and power of his Spirit, which is Love. That Spirit brought us into dialogue; has produced fruits of that dialgoue; while we continue joyfully to accept this authority and prompting we cannot presume to set limits to what he may yet work in us. While we continue to work at our problems we are challenged to neglect no opportunity of witnessing in common to what God does for us and offers to all persons. Such witness we can be sure will already carry its own authority.

Jan. 31, 1981

NOTE: The World Methodist Council, meeting in Honolulu, Hawaii (1981) expressed its opinion that baptism might more satisfactorily be stated to be *an* outward sign and means both of grace and of faith rather than *the* outward sign. (See paragraph 19).

PARTICIPANTS

Methodists
Rt. Revd. Bishop William R. Cannon, Bishop of the Raleigh Area, United Methodist Church (Co-Chairman)

Rt. Revd. Bishop James M. Ault, Bishop of the Pittsburgh Area, The United Methodist Church
Revd. Dr. James Cone, Union Theological Seminary
Dr. Kwesi Dickson, Legon University, Accra, Ghana
Revd. Dr. Ira Gallaway, First United Methodist Church, Peoria, Illinois
Revd. A. Raymond George, Wesley College, Bristol, England
Revd. Prof. Eric Osborne, Queen's College, Melbourne, Australia
Dr. Norman Young, Queen's College, Melbourne, Australia
Dr. Albert Outler, Perkins School of Theology, Dallas, Texas
Revd. Dr. Joe Hale, General Secretary of the World Methodist Council (Secretary).

Catholics
Rt. Revd. Francis Stafford, Auxiliary Bishop of Baltimore (Co-Chairman)
Rt. Revd. Monsignor Charles Moeller, Secretary of Secretariat for Promoting Christian Unity
Revd. Edward Malatesta, S.J., Jesuit School of Theology, Berkeley
Revd. Cuthbert Rand, Ushaw College, Durham, England
Rt. Revd. Mgr. Richard Stewart, Secretariat for Promoting Christian Unity
Rt. Revd. Mgr. Jorge Mejia, Secretariat for Promoting Christian Unity
Revd. Jerome Vereb, C.P., Secretariat for Promoting Christian Unity
Rt. Revd. Mgr. William Purdy. Secretariat for Promoting Christian Unity (Secretary).

Note

1. "About a quarter before nine, while he (the reader of Luther's Preface to Romans) was describing the change which God works in the heart through faith in Christ, I felt my heart strangely warmed. I felt I did trust in Christ, Christ alone, for salvation; and an assurance was given me that he had taken away my sins, even mine, and saved me from sin and death" (cf. Dublin report, note 6 to no. 12, which recalls that Methodists do not see "assurance" as "a form of certainty which removed the need for hope").

OLD CATHOLIC-ORTHODOX CONVERSATIONS

Doctrine of God 1975
Christology 1975 and 1977
Ecclesiology 1977, 1979, and 1981

Historical Introduction:

Similarly to the dialogue between the Old Catholics and the Anglicans, conversations between the Old Catholic Church and the Orthodox started in the years right after 1870. At the very first Congress of the Old Catholics in Munich in 1871, where Orthodox theologians were among the guests, the hope for a reunion with the Orthodox Church was expressed. At the Union Conferences in Bonn, which took place in 1874 and 1875 under Döllinger's responsibility but without the official authorisation of the churches, Orthodox, like Anglicans, were partners of the Old Catholics.

After this first movement, however, there came a period of stagnation and, at times, even of critical and controversial reaction on the part of some of the Greek and Russian theologians. Only after the foundation of the "International Old Catholic Bishops' Conference" in 1889 which solidified the internal communion of the Old Catholic fellowship, discussions with the Russian Church were resumed between the Commissions of St. Petersburg and Rotterdam. These commissions then met regularly between 1884 and 1913 and came to concrete results on several theological problems which needed clarification.

The First World War interrupted these conversations. The beginning of the movement of "Faith and Order" and its first conferences offered the Old Catholics an opportunity to resume and intensify the contacts, particularly with representatives of the Ecumenical Patriarchate. At the same time, though independent from those contacts, the rapprochement of the Anglicans and the Orthodox as well as the contacts between the Anglicans and the Old Catholics took on significance for the Orthodox/Old Catholic relationships. In this connection, an official meeting was called in Bonn, in October 1931. But the time had not yet come to enter into full intercommunion although the desire for such intercommunion was strong on both sides. Then came the outbreak of the Second World War. Therefore the agreements with regard to teaching and order of the Ancient Church remained without effect for some time to come.

It was only at the beginning of the sixties that contacts were taken up again in connection with the ecumenical initiative of the Patriarch Athenagoras. These contacts soon led to a phase of official discussions between Old Catholics and Pan-Orthodoxy. The First Pan-Orthodox Conference (Rhodes 1961) recommended an intensification of Old Catholic/Orthodox relations. The Third Conference (1964) formally decided to resume the dialogue with the Old Catholics as well as with the Anglicans and set up an Orthodox preparatory commission which started functioning in 1966 at the meeting in Belgrade.

Finally, in July 1973, the Joint Orthodox/Old Catholic Commission — which had been suggested already in April 1962 on the occasion of the visit of the President and Secretary of the Old Catholic Bishops' Conference to the Ecumenical Patriarch—met in Penteli near Athens to decide upon their common task. Together they planned the scope, methods and schedules of the official dialogue. Six main theological subjects, subdivided in various sections, were to be treated in these dialogues: 1. Doctrine of God; 2. Christology; 3. Ecclesiology; 4. Soteriology; 5. Doctrine of the Sacraments and 6. Eschatology.

On the basis of the recommendations made in Penteli, it was decided to take the following methodical steps: firstly, preliminary drafts were to be elaborated—independently, though after consultation—by Orthodox and Old Catholic theological experts; secondly, common drafts were to be worked out by both commissions or by a jointly appointed sub-commission; finally, the divergences which would appear were to be dealt with in the plenary sessions of the Theological Commission in order to work out common texts which then would be presented to the respective church authorities.

After dealing with all six issues foreseen by the Penteli programme, the overall result is to be officially submitted to the leading representatives of both church communions for announcement of the completion of the dialogue and for decision concerning further proceedings in view of establishing full communion.

Three plenary sessions of the Theological Commission have taken place since Penteli: Chambésy 1975, Chambésy 1977 and Bonn 1979, where three common statements on the Doctrine of God, three common statements on Christology and the first three texts on Ecclesiology were received.

(The original version of all texts is in German. They are published in: "Internationale Kirchliche Zeitschrift", 1976, 1978 and 1979.)

DOCTRINE OF GOD
Agreed Statement, Chambésy 1975

I./1 DIVINE REVELATION AND ITS TRANSMISSION

(1) The Triune God—Father, Son, and Holy Spirit—created the world and 'has not left himself without witness' (*Acts* 14:17), but revealed and continues to reveal himself in many and various ways in the world and in history.

(2) 1. God reveals himself in his works, for 'ever since the creation of the world his invisible nature, namely his invisible power and divinity, has been clearly perceived in the things that have been made' (*Rom.* 1:20) and this especially in the human beings who were created in his image and likeness, who 'show that what the law requires is written on their hearts' (*Rom.* 2:15).

(3)   2. Human beings were disobedient to the divine commandment and sinned, and their likeness to God became distorted and obscured, and they were unable to know the true God, 'became futile in their thinking and their senseless minds were darkened'; they therefore 'worshiped and served the creature rather than the Creator' (*Rom.* 1:21, 25)

But God the All Merciful, 'who desires all human beings to be saved and to come to the knowledge of the truth' (*1 Tim.* 2:4) chose to reveal himself to the world in a direct and personal way. God revealed himself, therefore, directly and effectively 'of old to the fathers by the prophets' (*Heb.* 1:1) and this in the people of Israel. This revelation of God, although real, was nevertheless partial and educational in character: 'the law was our custodian until Christ came' (*Gal.* 3:24).

(4)   3. 'But when the time had fully come, God sent forth his Son' (*Gal.* 4:4). 'And the Word became flesh and dwelt among us' (*John* 1:14). In Jesus Christ there took place the whole and perfect revelation of God: 'in him the whole fulness of the deity dwells bodily' (*Col.* 2:9). Only in Jesus Christ is salvation possible: 'and there is salvation in no one else' (*Acts* 4:12). In Jesus Christ, the Triune God, whose essence is inaccessible and incomprehensible to us, revealed himself in his salvific energies and, indeed, in his whole plenitude: 'We say that we do indeed know our God from his energies, . . . but his essence remains beyond our reach' (Basil the Great, Letter 234, 1).

(5)   4.   This supernatural revelation in Christ is communicated in the tradition of the holy apostles, which was handed on in written form in the Scriptures inspired by God and in oral form by the living voice of the Church. The oral tradition is preserved, on the one hand, in the Creed and other definitions and canons of the seven ecumenical councils and local synods, in the writings of the holy fathers and in the holy liturgy and generally in the Church's liturgical practice, and, on the other hand, finds expression in the continued official teaching of the Church.

(6)   5. Scripture and tradition are not different expressions of the divine revelation but distinct ways of expressing one and the same apostolic tradition. Nor does any question arise, therefore, of the precedence of one over the other: 'both have the same force in relation to true religion' (Basil the Great, On the Holy Spirit, 27:2). 'Scripture is understood within the tradition, but the tradition preserves its purity and the criterion of its truth through Scripture and from the content of Scripture' (Inter-Orthodox Preparatory Commission for the Holy and Great Synod, 16th to 28th July 1971, Chambésy 1973, p. 110). The apostolic tradition is preserved and handed on unadulterated by the Church in the Holy Spirit.

In the view of the Joint Orthodox-Old Catholic Theological Commission, the above text on 'Divine Revelation and Its Transmission' reproduces the doctrine of the Orthodox and Old Catholic Churches.

I/2 THE CANON OF HOLY SCRIPTURE

(7)   Holy Scripture consists of the books of the Old and New Testaments which have been accepted by the Church into the canon established by it and in use in it. They are:

(8)   a) In the Old Testament the twenty-two — according to a different reckoning the thirty-nine — books of the Hebrew canon, together with another ten books, the so-called 'Anagignoskomena', i.e., books 'read' or 'worth reading', which were later known in the West as 'deuterocanonic'; a total of forty-nine books.

The first-mentioned thirty-nine books are 'canonical': Genesis, Exodus, Leviticus, Numbers, Deuteronomy, Joshua, Judges, Ruth, 1 and 2 Samuel, 1 and 2 Kings, 1 and 2 Chronicles, Ezra (Greek 2 Esra, Vulgate and Slavic 1 Esra), Nehemiah, Esther, Psalms, Job, Sayings of Solomon, Ecclesiastes, Song of Solomon, Isaiah, Jeremiah, Lamentations of Jeremiah, Ezekiel, Daniel, Obadiah, Joel, Jonah, Amos, Hosea, Micah, Nahum, Zephaniah, Habakkuk, Haggai, Zechariah, Malachi.

The additional ten books, the Anagignoskomena, are: Judith, Greek: 1 Esra (Vulgate: 3 Esra, Slavic: 2 Esra), 1, 2 and 3 Maccabees, Tobias, Jesus Sirach, Wisdom of Solomon, Baruch and the Letter of Jeremiah.

(9)   The 'canonical' books are distinguished by the special authority constantly accorded to them by the Church; but the Church also values highly the Anagignoskomena which have long been part of its canon of Holy Scripture.*

(10)   b) The canonical books of the New Testament number twenty-seven in all, namely: the four gospels of Matthew, Mark, Luke and John; the Acts of the Apostles; the letters of Paul: Romans, 1 and 2 Corinthians, Galatians, Ephesians, Philippians, Colossians, 1 and 2 Thessalonians, 1 and 2 Timothy, Titus, Philemon and Hebrews; the Catholic Epistles: James, 1 and 2 Peter, 1, 2 and 3 John, Jude; and the Revelation of John.

In the view of the Joint Orthodox-Old Catholic Theological Commission, the above text on 'The Canon of Holy Scripture' reproduces the doctrine of the Orthodox and Old Catholic Churches.

---

* With respect to the books in Greek 1 Esra (Vulgate 3 Esra, Slavic 2 Esra) and 3 Maccabees, the Old Catholic Commission adds the following qualification: Although these books are not rejected by their Church, they are not included in the Old Catholic lists of the biblical books, which derive from an old Latin tradition. The International Conference of Old Catholic bishops still has to declare its position on this point.

I/3   THE HOLY TRINITY

(11)   We believe and confess One God in three hypostases, Father, Son and Holy Spirit. The Father, who 'loved' the Son 'before the foundation of the world' (*John* 17:24), revealed himself through him in the Holy Spirit in order that this love might be in his disciples (*John* 17:26) through the communion of the Holy Spirit who has been 'sent into our hearts' (*Gal.* 4:6). This revelation is an ineffable and inexplicable mystery, a mystery of love, 'for God is love' (*1 John* 4:8).

(12)   1. On the basis of this revelation we believe that the God who is by nature one is triune in the hypostases or persons. Father, Son and Holy Spirit denote the three modes of being, without beginning and eternal, of the three persons and their interrelationships; these persons are indivisibly bound up with one another and united in one divine nature. Thus 'we worship the unity in the trinity and the trinity in the unity, in their paradoxical differentiation and unity' (Gregory of Nazianzus, PG 35, 1221).

(13)   2. We interpret this unity, on the one hand and above all, in terms of the unity and identity of the divine nature, and on the other hand in terms of the unity and identity of the properties, energies and will and when we understand the Son and the Holy Spirit to derive from the Father as their one origin and ground (*aition*), we are careful to preserve the unity without confusion. The three divine persons are united in the one God, bound together yet without confusion, on the one hand because they are of one nature, on the other hand because they interpenetrate each other without confusion. Therefore 'from the unity of nature and the mutual penetration of the hypostases and from the identity of their will and work, their power and might and movement, we know that God is one and undivided; for truly one is God: God (Father) and the Word and his Spirit' (John of Damascus, PG 94, 825), to the eternal exclusion of any separation or division of nature, any subordination of the three persons on the pretext of precedence or eminence.

(14)   3. But we interpret the trinity on the one hand in terms of the difference between the three persons, on the other hand, in terms of the diversity of their processions. Thus the three divine persons are distinct from each other without being divided; each has the fulness of divinity, and the one divine nature remains, of course, undivided and unseparated, so that 'the divinity is undivided in the distinct (hypostases)' (*ameristos en memerismenois* — Gregory of Nazianzus PG 36, 149). The Father is distinct from the other persons inasmuch as from his nature and from all eternity he begets the Son and sends forth the Holy Spirit. The Son is distinct from the other persons inasmuch as he is begotten of his Father; the Holy Spirit inasmuch as he proceeds from the Father. Thus the Father is unbegotten, without ground (*anaitios*) and without origin, but at the same time is the one origin and the one root and spring of the Son and the Holy Spirit' (Basil the Great, PG 31, 609). He alone is their ground (*aitios*) who from eternity begets the Son and sends forth the Holy Spirit. As for

the Son, he is begotten of the Father; the Holy Spirit is sent forth or proceeds from the Father. The Father, therefore is without ground (*anaitios*) and himself the ground (*autoaitios*), whereas the Son and the Holy Spirit have their ground in the Father, the Son because he is begotten, the Spirit because he is sent forth, and indeed in both cases, without beginning and eternally, undivided and unseparated. Accordingly the mysterious and ineffable but nevertheless real distinction between the three hypostases or persons of the Holy Trinity consists exclusively in these their three incommunicable properties, namely, in the unbegottenness of the Father, the begottenness of the Son, and in the procession of the Holy Spirit. 'The three holy hypostases are distinct exclusively in these hypostatic properties, not in nature, but by the distinctive feature of each hypostasis, and thus separated they remain inseparable' since they 'do not denote the nature but the mutual relationship and mode of being' (John of Damascus, PG 94, 824, 837).

(15) 4. On the Holy Spirit in particular, it is taught in Holy Scripture (*John* 15:26), in the Niceno-Constantinopolitan Creed of the 2nd Ecumenical Council, and in the ancient Church generally, that he proceeds from the Father, the source and origin of divinity. His eternal procession from the Father is here to be distinguished from his temporal revelation and sending into the world, which takes place through the Son. When therefore we understand the procession of the Holy Spirit in the sense of his eternal being and procession without beginning, we confess the procession from the Father alone, and not also from the Son. But when we understand it in the sense of the temporal procession of the Holy Spirit, then we confess the procession from the Father through the Son or even from both Father and Son.

(16.) Accordingly we believe in the Holy Spirit 'who proceeds from the Father . . . and is communicated to the whole creation through the Son . . . We do not say that the Spirit is from the Son . . . (But) we confess that he is revealed and communicated to us through the Son . . . (He is) the Holy Spirit of God the Father, since it is indeed from the Father that he proceeds, but he is also called (Spirit) of the Son because he is indeed revealed and communicated to the creation through the Son, but does not derive his being from the Son' (John of Damascus, PG 94, 821.832.833. [849]; 96, 605).

(17) In this sense the Doctrinal Letter of the International Conference of Old Catholic Bishops in 1969 states: 'We entirely reject the addition of the *filioque* adopted in the West in the eleventh century without recognition by an ecumenical council. The ground for this rejection is not merely the uncanonical form of this addition, though this in itself represented an offence against love as the bond of unity. But above all we repudiate any theological doctrine which makes the Son joint author of the Spirit.' In a similar sense, the special statement of the same Bishops' Conference in the same year, 'On the Filioque Question', also emphasizes 'that there is only one principle and one source in the most holy Trinity, namely, the Father'.

In the view of the Joint Orthodox-Old Catholic Theological Commission, the above text on 'The Holy Trinity' reproduces the doctrine of the Orthodox and Old Catholic Churches.

Chambésy, Geneva, Orthodox Centre of the Ecumenical Patriarchate
August 20-28, 1975

Signatures of all members of the Joint Commission present.

CHRISTOLOGY
Agreed Statement, Chambésy 1975 and 1977

II/1   THE INCARNATION OF THE WORD OF GOD

(1)   1. We believe in Jesus Christ, the only Son and the only Word of God 'who for us human beings and for our salvation came down from heaven and was incarnate of the Holy Spirit of the Virgin Mary and became a human being' (Niceno-Constantinopolitan Creed). In the incarnation the eternal and timeless God entered time and history as a human being 'in order to unite the human race once again in himself as its head' (Cyril of Alexandria, PG 76, 17).

Jesus Christ has two natures: he is perfect God who has everything the Father has, except his unbegottenness; but at the same time he is also perfectly human 'with a rational soul and body', like us in every respect except our sin.

As human being Jesus Christ stands out from all other human beings by his supernatural birth and sinlessness, since his incarnation took place through the Holy Spirit and from the Virgin Mary, and he was also free from original sin and from all personal sin.

(2)   2. Concerning the two natures of Christ, the divine and the human, we confess what the Church teaches on the basis of Holy Scripture and Holy Tradition: namely, that the two natures, the divine and the human, have been hypostatically united in Christ, and this indeed in the hypostasis or person of God the Word, 'without confusion without change, without division, without separation' (4th Ecumenical Council).

(3)   Jesus Christ is God-man, the one divine person in two natures, the divine and the human, with two wills and two operations (*energeiai*). But since the person of Jesus Christ unites the two natures and it is this person which wills and operates accordingly, we can therefore call the operations of the Lord divine-human. 'He does what the human being does not just in a human manner, for he is not only human but also divine; and he does what God does not just in a divine manner, for he is not only divine but also human' (John of Damascus, PG 94, 1060). Through the 'mutual interpenetration' or 'mutual indwelling' of the two natures, not only is the duality of the natures, wills and operations preserved but also the unity of the person.

(4)   3. The hypostatic union has certain consequences for the dogma of the Holy Trinity:

a)   Although the whole divine nature was united with the human nature in Jesus Christ, the whole Holy Trinity did not become incarnate but only the second person of the Trinity.

b)   The incarnation does not bring about any alteration or change in the unalterable and unchangeable God.

(5)   4. The hypostatic union results in:

a)   The exchange or mutual communication of the properties. In the hypostatic union, the two natures, the divine and the human, communicate to each other their properties, by penetrating each other and indwelling in each other.

b)   The divinisation (*theosis*) of the human nature of Christ. It abides, of course, 'within the limits proper to it and within its kind' (6th Ecumenical Council).

c)   The sinlessness of Christ.

d)   The worship of Christ even in respect of his human nature. We owe worship to the divine-human person of the Lord.

e)   The Virgin Mary is truly God-bearer and Mother of God.

(6)   5. The incarnation of the eternal Word of God, which took place out of love for humanity, is an inaccessible and inconceivable mystery, to be appropriated in faith . . .

In the view of the Mixed Orthodox-Old Catholic Commission, the above text on 'The Incarnation of the Word of God' represents the doctrine of the Orthodox and Old Catholic Churches.

II/2   THE HYPOSTATIC UNION

(7)   Concerning the hypostatic union of the two natures, the teaching of the Church is:

1. The divine nature was united with the human nature hypostatically, i.e., in the hypostasis or person of God the Word. In his incarnation he assumed not human nature in general, but an inidividual human nature. This did not exist previously; it was 'without hypostasis of its own nor did it have any prior individuality . . . but the Word of God itself became hypostasis to the flesh' (John of Damascus, PG 94 1024. 985). Consequently, the Lord did not assume a human hypostasis but a human nature, and this indeed is human nature in its entirety. The individual human nature assumed was a true and complete one 'with rational soul and body' (4th Ecumenical Council). It did not exist previously in an individual independent of the one person of Jesus Christ, nor had it previously been created, but its existence began in the moment of the divine incarnation 'of the Holy Spirit of the Virgin Mary', in the unity of the person or hypostasis of the Word of God. It therefore never had any other hypostasis than that only of the Son of God.

(8)   2. Jesus Christ is therefore the one person 'in two natures', the divine

and the human, but not 'from two natures'. The 4th Ecumenical Council teaches us to confess ' . . . one and the same Christ, Son, Lord, Only-begotten, recognized in two natures, without confusion, without change, without division, without separation; the distinction of natures being in no way annulled by the union, but rather the characteristics of each nature being preserved and coming together to form one person and subsistance (hypostasis). The hypostatic union of the two natures in Christ, which took place 'in the moment of the conception, without confusion or separation', remains forever indivisible and indissoluble. The human nature remains forever inseparably united with the divine nature. The God-man is therefore 'Jesus Christ, the same yesterday, and today and forever' (*Heb.* 13:8).

(9)   3. Since there are two natures, the divine and the human, in Jesus Christ, there are also in him two freely operating wills, appertaining to the natures, the divine and the human; two operations (*energeiai*) appertaining to the natures, the divine and the human, as well as two free wills (*autexousia*) appertaining to the natures, the divine and the human; the wisdom and the knowledge, too, are both divine and human. Because the Lord is equal in nature to God the Father, he wills and operates in freedom as God; because he is also equal in nature to us human beings, he wills and operates in freedom also as a human being. 'Willing and operating' he possesses of course 'not divided but united; he wills and works in each of the two natures, of course, in communion with the other'. We therefore understand the two wills not as contrary or as striving against each other, but each as willing in harmony the same thing each according to its own mode. Certainly the weak human will follows the strong divine will and subordinates itself to that will, for both wills and operations 'acted in unity' and 'cooperated for the salvation of the human race' (6th Ecumenical Council). Put in general terms: 'Since the hypostasis of Christ is one and Christ is one, he is one who wills in accordance with both natures: as God on the basis of good pleasure, as human being in obedience' (John of Damascus, PG 95, 160).

(10)   The Church teaches therefore what the fathers of the 6th Ecumenical Council also defined: 'We adhere firmly in every way to the "without confusion" and "without division" and proclaim in short: Since we believe that one of the Holy Trinity, after the incarnation of our Lord Jesus Christ, is our true God, we affirm that his two natures are shown in his one hypostasis . . . The distinction of natures in the one hypostasis is seen in the fact that each nature wills and operates what is its own in communion with the other. Accordingly, we also praise the wills and operations appertaining to the two natures, which cooperate for the salvation of the human race.' Even after the union 'his divinized human will was not annihilated but continued all the stronger'.

   In the view of the Joint Orthodox-Old Catholic Theological Commission the above text on 'The Hypostatic Union' reproduces the doctrine of the Orthodox and Old Catholic Churches.

Chambésy, Geneva, Orthodox Centre of the Ecumenical Patriarchate
August 20-28, 1975
Signatures of all members of the Joint Commision present.

II/3 THE MOTHER OF GOD

(11)   The Church believes that the divine and human natures are hypostatically united in Jesus Christ. It accordingly believes also that the Blessed Virgin Mary gave birth not to a human being merely but to the God-man (the divine-human being) Jesus Christ and that she is therefore truly Mother of God as the 3rd Ecumenical Council defined and the 5th Ecumenical Council confirmed. According to St. John of Damascus, the name 'Mother of God' 'embraces the whole mystery of the divine dispensation' (i.e., plan of salvation) (*de fide orth*. 3.12. PG 94, 1029).

(12)   1. In the Virgin Mary, the Son of God assumed human nature in its entirety, body and soul, in virtue of the divine omnipotence, for the power of the Most High overshadowed her and the Holy Spirit came upon her (Luke 1:35). In this way the Word was made flesh (John 1:14). By the true and real motherhood of the Virgin Mary, the Redeemer was united with the human race.

(13)   There is an intrinsic connection between the truth of the one Christ and the truth of the divine motherhood of Mary. ' . . . for a union of two natures took place; therefore we confess one Christ, one Son, one Lord. According to this understanding of the unconfused union, we confess the Holy Virgin to be *'theotokos'* because God the Word was made flesh and lived as a human being and from the very conception united to himself the temple taken from her' (3rd Ecumenical Council, Formula of Union, Mansi 5.592). ' . . . we teach with one voice that the Son (of God) and our Lord, Jesus Christ, is to be confessed as one and the same person . . . begotten of his Father before the worlds according to his Godhead but in these last days born for us and for our salvation of the Virgin Mary, the Mother of God, according to his humanity' (4th Ecumenical Council, Definition of Faith, Mansi 7.116).

(14)   2. Venerating the Virgin Mary as Mother of God, whose pregnancy is called by St. Ignatius of Antioch 'a mystery to be cried aloud' (ad Eph. 19:1), the Church also glorifies her perpetual virginity. The Mother of God is ever-Virgin, since, while remaining a maiden, she bore Christ in an ineffable and inexplicable manner. In their address to the Emperor Marcian, the fathers of the 4th Ecumenical Council declared: ' . . . the fathers . . . have expounded the meaning of faith for all and proclaimed accurately the blessing of the incarnation: how the mystery of the plan of salvation was prepared from on high and from the maternal womb, how the Virgin was named Mother of God for the sake of him who granted her virginity even after her pregnancy and kept her body sealed in a glorious manner, and how she is truly called Mother because of the flesh of the

Lord of all things, which came from her and which she gave to him' (Allocutio ad Marc. Imp. Mansi 7.461B). And in its decision the 7th Ecumenical Council declared: 'We confess that he who was incarnate of the immaculate Mother of God and Ever-Virgin Mary has two natures' (Definitio, Mansi 13.377A). As St. Augustine says: 'He was born of the Holy Spirit and the Virgin Mary. And even the birth as human being is itself lowly and lofty. Why lowly? Because as human being he is born of a human being. Why lofty? Because he was born of a virgin. A virgin conceived, a virgin gave birth, and after the birth she remained a virgin' (de symb. ad cat. 1.3, 6. PL 40.630). (Cf. also St. Sophronius, Patriarch of Jerusalem, General Epistle, PG 87.3164, 3176, Mansi 9.476, 485; St. John of Damascus, de fid. orth. 4,14. PG 94. 1161; St. Maximus the Confessor, ambig. PG 91, 1276A etc.).

(15)   3. Accordingly the Church venerates in a very special way the Virgin Mother of God, though 'not as divine but as Mother of God according to the flesh' (St. John of Damascus, de imag. 2,5. PG 94,1357). If, because of the redemption in Christ and its blessings, the Church glorifies God above all and offers him the worship of true adoration due to the divine nature alone, at the same time it venerates the Mother of God as chosen vessel of the work of salvation, as she who accepted the word of God in faith, humility and obedience, as gateway through which God entered the world. It calls her the Blessed One, the first of the saints and the pure handmaid of the Lord, and thereby ascribes to her a relative sinlessness by grace, from the time the Holy Spirit descended upon her, for our Saviour Jesus Christ alone is sinless by nature and absolutely.

(16)   The Church does not recognize the recent dogmas of an immaculate conception and bodily assumption of the Mother of God. But it celebrates the entry of the Mother of God into eternal life and solemnly observes the festival of her dormition.

(17)   4. The Church venerates the Mother of God also in her role as intercessor for human beings before God, which is hers in particular because of her outstanding place in the work of salvation. But it distinguishes between the intercession of the Mother of God and the quite unique mediatorship of Jesus Christ: 'For there is one mediator between God and humanity — the man Jesus Christ' (1 Tim. 2:5). 'O Merciful One, show your love to humankind; accept the Mother of God who bore you, who intercedes for us, and save your helpless people, O our Saviour' (Saturday Vespers, Tone 8, Theotokion). ' . . . O God . . . grant us all to share the life of your Son in fellowship with the Virgin Mary, the Blessed Mother of our Lord and God . . . and of all your saints. Look upon their life and death and answer their intercessions for your Church on earth' (Divine Liturgy of the Old Catholic Church of Switzerland).

(18)   Although the Mother of God is also called 'mediatrix' (*mesitria*) in the hymns of the Church, this is never anywhere in the sense of co-mediatrix or co-redemptrix but only in the sense of intercessor.

In the view of the Joint Orthodox-Old Catholic Theological Commission, the above text on the 'Mother of God' reproduces the doctrine of the Orthodox and Old Catholic Churches.

Chambésy, Geneva, Orthodox Centre of the Ecumenical Patriarchate,

August 23-30, 1977

Signatures of all members of the Joint Commission present.

ECCLESIOLOGY
Agreed Statement, Chambésy 1977, Bonn 1979 and Zagorsk 1981

III/1
THE NATURE AND MARKS OF THE CHURCH

(1)   By its very nature the church is intimately related to the mystery of the Triune God who reveals himself in Christ and the Holy Spirit (cf. Eph. 5:32). It is 'the treasure house of God's ineffable mysteries' (St. John Chrysostomos, Ep. 1 ad Cor. hom. 16,3. PG 61, 134).

(2)   No explicit and complete definition of the term 'Church' is to be found in Scripture and Tradition. What we find are many images and symbols from which in an indirect way the nature of the Church can be known.

(3)   According to the Scriptures, the Church is 'the body of Christ' (Rom. 12:4f.; 1 Cor. 12:13, 27), 'the people of God' (1 Pet. 2:10), the 'household' or 'temple' of God (1 Tim. 3:15; Eph. 2:19; 1 Cor. 3:16f.), the 'royal priesthood' (1 Pet. 2:9), the bride of Christ (cf. Mk. 2:20; Mt. 25:1ff.; Rev. 21:2), God's 'vineyard' (Isa. 5:7).

(4)   Tradition also provides descriptions in which one or other aspect of the Church is emphasized: it is episcopal in structure, it has a priestly and charismatic character, it is a communion of believers, it is composed of all the true believers of all the ages, it is the human race united in the God-man.

(5)   The Church, therefore, by its very nature is no mere human fellowship, no passing phenomenon of human history. It is rooted in God's eternal decision and plan for the benefit of the world and the human race. In the Old Testament it was prefigured in Israel and announced in advance by the prophets to be the coming people of God of the new covenant in which God would establish his final and universal sovereignty on earth (Isa. 2:2; Jer. 31:31). In the fulness of time it became a reality in the incarnation of the Word of God, through the proclamation of the Gospel, the choice of the twelve apostles, the institution of the Lord's Supper, Christ's death on the cross and his resurrection, as well as through the sending of the Holy Spirit at Pentecost for the sanctification of the Church and the equipment of the apostles for their work.

(6)   Thus the Church founded by the Lord on earth is the body of Christ, with Christ as its Head, a divine-human organism; a community which can be described and perceived and, at the same time, an inward and spiritual relationship between its members and its divine founder and among themselves. As the pilgrim people of God, the Church lives on earth in expectation of its coming Lord until the fulfilment of the kingdom of God. It exists and lives both in heaven, in those already made perfect who there celebrate the victory, and on earth in believers who fight the good fight of faith (cf. 2 Tim. 4:6). In one aspect the Church is invisible and heavenly, in the other it is earthly and visible, a community and organism with a pastoral and priestly ministry, which is structurally linked with the apostles, with abiding dogmatic and ethical principles and a constant ordered worship, a body in which clergy and laity are differentiated.

(7)   In the Church, the new life in Christ is a reality in the Holy Spirit; in it the grace and divine life of the Head is given to all members of the Body for their sanctification and salvation.

The Church established by the Lord on earth cannot, therefore, be merely something inward, an invisible fellowship or an ideal and indefinable Church of which the individual churches are only imperfect images. Such a conception of the nature of the Church is in contradiction to the spirit of Scripture and Tradition; it destroys the real content of revelation and the historical character of the Church.

(8)   Dogmatic expression is given of the nature of the Church in the Niceno-Constantinopolitan Creed, as confirmed by the 4th Ecumenical Council in Chalcedon. In this creed the confession of faith in the Triune God is followed by the confession of faith in 'the one, holy, catholic and apostolic Church'.

(9)   The Church is 'one', for just as Christ the Head of the Church is one, so too there is also *one* body animated by the Holy Spirit, in which Christ as Head and believers as members are united. In this body all the local churches are united to one another by the unity of faith, worship and order. The unity of faith and worship represents the bond which binds believers with the redeemer and with one another, in love and peace and finds expression in the confession of the same faith and in celebration of the same liturgy, insofar as it rests on dogma. The unity of order takes the form of the exercise of leadership on the basis of the same principles and the recognition by believers of *one* ministry and *one* authority in accordance with the canonical rules, namely the episcopate which has a conciliar structure.

(10)   If the members of the Church perceive the truths of faith in various ways, this does not destroy or diminish the unity of faith; nor does this happen if the Church sometimes exercises patience towards people who depart from the unity of faith and order, and does not exclude them from the body of the Church, for pastoral considerations and in the exercise of 'economy'.

(11)   Although the Church, the body of Christ, has many members, therefore, these nevertheless all constitute *one* body and are united in an indivisible unity. The Lord prayed for this unity and, in doing so, pointed at the unity of Father and Son (John 17:21), as the ground of the unity of believers is the image of the unity of the Triune God. 'For Father, Son and Holy Spirit have *one* will. Thus it is his will also that we, too, should be one, when he says: That they *all may be one* as You and I are *one* (St. John Chrysost. in John hom. 78,3. PG 59, 425).

(12)   The Church is '*holy*' since Christ its head is holy and gave himself for it 'that he might sanctify it . . . that the Church might be presented before him in splendour, without spot or wrinkle or any such thing, that it might be holy and without blemish' (Eph. 5:25-27). Christ made the Church the 'household of God' (1 Tim. 3:15; Heb. 3:6); he gave it fellowship and share in his holiness and grace and in his divine life; he who sanctified the people through his own blood' (Heb. 13:12). Christians are therefore also called saints (Acts 9:13).

(13)   The fact that members of the Church sin does not nullify the holiness of the Church. The fathers were agreed in condemning those who because of immoderate and ascetic tendencies took the view that the Church is a community made up exclusively of completely sanctified members.

(14)   The Church is '*catholic*', since Christ its head is the Lord of all things. It is predestined to extend to the whole creation, over all peoples and through all ages (Mt. 28:20; Mk. 16:15; Acts 1:8). This is the external quantitative meaning of catholicity.

(15)   The Church is called '*Catholic*' in the inner qualitative sense of the word because although it is scattered over the whole earth, it is always and everywhere the same. It is '*catholic*', because it has the 'sound doctrine' (Tit. 2:1; cf. 1 Tim. 6:20), continues in the original tradition of the apostles and truly continues and preserves 'that which has been believed everywhere, always and by all' (Vincent of Lerins, Commonit. II, 3 PL 50, 640). The Church is '*Catholic*' therefore in the sense that it is the orthodox, authentic and true Church.

(16)   According to St. Cyril of Jerusalem, 'the Church is called catholic because it extends over all the world from one end of the earth to the other; and because it teaches universally and completely one and all those doctrines which ought to come to the knowledge of humankind, concerning things both visible and invisible, heavenly and earthly; and because it brings into subjection to godliness the entire human race, governors and governed, learned and unlearned; and because while it deals exhaustively with and heals every kind of sin of soul and body, it also possesses in itself every form of virtue which can be named, in deeds and words and in every kind of spiritual gift' (Cyr. Hier. Cat. 18,23. PG 33, 1044).

(17)   The Church is '*apostolic*', since its divine founder was the first 'apostle' (Heb. 3:1; cf. Gal. 4:4), and because it is built upon 'the foundation of

the apostles and prophets, Christ Jesus himself being the chief corner-stone' (Eph. 2:20).

(18)   The mission of Jesus has a wider context: the Son is sent into the world by the Father, and he himself sends the disciples (cf. John 20:21) to whom he says: 'He who hears you, hears me' (Lk. 10:16). After their death the mission of the Church is continued, the inheritance of truth entrusted by the Lord to the apostles is preserved and passed on in the spiritual life, in the celebration of the sacraments and in doctrine. The apostolic doctrine preserved by the Church is the inner aspect of its apostolicity. Its other element is the unbroken series and succession of pastors and teachers of the Church, starting from the apostles, which is the outward mark and also the pledge of the truth of the Church. These two elements of apostolicity, the inner and the outer, support and condition one another; if either one or the other is lacking the essential apostolicity and fullness of truth of the Church are impaired.

(19)   The four dogmatic marks of the Church mutually interpenetrate each other in indissoluble unity and point to the indestructibility and infallibility of the Church, the 'pillar and ground of the truth' (1 Tim. 3:15).

In the view of the Joint Orthodox-Old Catholic Theological Commission, the above text on 'The Nature and Marks of the Church' reproduces the doctrine of the Orthodox and Old Catholic Churches.

Chambésy, Geneva, Orthodox Centre of the Ecumenical Patriarchate, August 23-30, 1977.

Signatures of all members of the Joint Commission present.

III/2

THE UNITY OF THE CHURCH AND THE LOCAL CHURCHES

(20)   1. The Church is the one indivisible Body of Christ in which the believers, as members of this Body, are united with Christ as its Head and with one another. The supreme expression and the perennial source of this unity is the sacrament of the Eucharist, communion with the body and blood of Christ: 'Because there is *one* loaf, we, many as we are, are *one* body; for it is of *one* loaf of which we all partake' (1 Cor. 10:17 NEB).

(21)   2. The one Church on earth exists in the many local Churches whose life is centred on the celebration of the holy Eucharist in the communion with the lawful bishop and his priests. 'Let all follow the bishop as Jesus Christ did the Father, and the priest as you would the Apostles . . . Let that Eucharist be held valid which is offered by the bishop or by one to whom the bishop has committed this charge' (Ignatius of Antioch, *Smyrn.* S. 1 PG 5,582; tr. *The Fathers of the Church,* Catholic University of America Press, Washington, D.C. 1947, vol. 1 p. 121).

(22) 3. The spread of the Christian faith to different lands and among many peoples and the consequent rise of a multitude of local Churches did not abolish the unity of the Church nor does their existence now do so, so long as the local Churches maintain pure and undefiled in the harmonious disposition of all, the faith transmitted to them from the Lord through the Apostles. Unity in faith is the supreme principle of the Catholic Church: 'The Church . . . has received from the apostles and their disciples the faith . . . in one God, the Father Almighty . . . and in one Christ Jesus, the Son of God . . . and in the Holy Spirit . . . The Church, having received this preaching . . . although scattered throughout the whole world, yet, as if occupying but (of doctrine) just as if it had but one soul, and one and the same heart, and it proclaims them, and teaches them, and hands them down, with perfect harmony, as if it possessed only one mouth' (Irenaeus, *Adv. Haer.* 1:10, 1-2; *Ante-Nicene Fathers*, tr. Roberts and Donaldson, Eerdmans, Grand Rapids, Michigan, vol. 1 p. 330; Pg. 7, 549.552).

(23) 4. As a fellowship of believers united around the bishop and the priests and as the Body of Christ, each local Church is the manifestation of the whole Christ in one particular place. It represents the sacramental reality of the whole Church in its own locality. For it is in no divided form, that the life, that has been given to the Church by God the Father through the presence of Christ in the Holy Spirit, is given to the local Churches; each local Church, on the contrary, has that life in its fulness. Thus, for all the differences in custom and usage, the life of the local Churches is in essence one and the same: 'There is one body and one Spirit, . . . one Lord, one faith, one baptism; one God and Father of all . . . ' (Eph.4:4-6). There are not many bodies but the one Body of Christ, undivided and whole, in each place. This unity of life in the local Churches reflects the unity of the Holy Trinity itself.

(24) 5. The local Churches recognize in one another the same reality and they affirm their essential identity, above all, by the unity of their liturgical and sacramental life, their unity in the basic principles of canonical order and of church government, as well as by the unity of the episcopate. Authentic expression has been given to these basic principles in the canons of the Seven Ecumenical Synods and the acknowledged local Synods or they are attested in the Church Fathers. Since the Church in this present time still awaits deliverance from all evil and must therefore pray God so to deliver it, to make it perfect in His love and bring it together from the ends of the earth into His kingdom (Didache 10,5; 9,4), the local Churches must devotedly maintain the essential unity given to them, and constantly struggle against the forces of sin and division.

(25) 6. In the course of history, the local Churches have established larger groupings in defined geographical areas, with one of the bishops placed at the summit as the prime bishop. They affirm and practice their fellowship by the common reception of the eucharistic gifts by their members, by the exchange of visits between their leaders and represen-

tatives, by the interchange of messages of greeting, as well as by mutual aid and intercession, as well as in other ways in accordance with the distinctive gifts received by each. Each is careful to observe the rule forbidding intervention or meddling in the domestic affairs of the others.

(26) 7. On matters of faith and other common concerns, i.e., where issues arise which concern them all and exceed the competence of each individual Church, the local Churches take counsel together and make common decisions, faithfully observing in such Synods the order of honour and rank canonically established in the Church. They do so, above all, in Ecumenical Synods, which are the supreme authority in the Church, the instrument and the voice through which the Catholic Church speaks, in which there is a constant effort to preserve and strengthen its unity in love.

In the view of the Mixed Orthodox-Old Catholic Commission, the above text on 'The Unity of the Church and the Local Churches' represents the doctrine of the Orthodox and Old Catholic Churches.

III/3   THE BOUNDARIES OF THE CHURCH

(27) 1. The love of God and His purpose of salvation are unlimited and embrace all human beings of all times in the whole of creation, for it is His will 'that all should find salvation and come to know the truth' (1 Tim. 2:4). In accordance with the divine plan of salvation, it is in and through the Church founded by God and not at a distance from it and independently of it that humanity comes to partake of salvation, for in the Church is found the divine truth, to it the Saviour has entrusted the means of achieving beatitude; the Church is the sure way to salvation and eternal life. Salvation is offered to believers in the Church by the Holy Spirit which abides always in it. This is why Irenaeus also says: '*Ubi ecclesia, ibi et Spiritus Dei, et ubi Spiritus Dei, illic ecclesia et omnis gratia*' ('For where the Church is, there is the Spirit of God, and where the Spirit of God is, there is the Church and every kind of grace', Iren. *adv. Haer.* III,24; *Ante-Nicene Fathers*, vol. 1, p. 458).

(28) 2. Because of sin, not everyone accepts the saving grace of God and comes to the fellowship of the Church. But not all those who do come to the Church confess the divine truth as revealed by Jesus Christ in the fulness of time. Journeying through history, the Church of Christ has become divided into many Churches which disagreed with each other because the faith and doctrines handed down from the apostles were debased. This led among other things to the false and unacceptable theory that the true visible Church, the Church of the age of the apostles and church fathers, no longer exists today but that each of the individual Churches retains only a portion, greater or less, of the true Church and that none of them, therefore, can be regarded as a genuine and essentially complete representation of the true Church. Up to our time the teachings

of the Christian Churches and Confessions differ in some respects, not just in unessentials but even in fundamental points of Christian doctrine.

(29) 3. But from the day it was founded right down to our own days, the true Church, the one, holy, catholic and apostolic Church, has gone on existing without any discontinuity wherever the true faith, worship and order of the ancient undivided Church are preserved unimpaired as they are reflected and formulated in the definitions and canons of the Seven Ecumenical Synods and the acknowledged local Synods, and in the church fathers.

(30) 4. Our Mixed Commission gives heresy and schism the appropriate significance and regards communities which continue in heresy and schism as in no sense workshops of salvation parallel to the true visible Church. It nevertheless believes that the question of the Church's boundaries can be seen in a larger light. Since it is impossible to set limits to God's power whose will it is that all should find salvation and come to know the truth and since further the Gospel clearly speaks of salvation by faith in the unique Son of God, — 'He who puts his faith in the Son has hold of eternal life, but he who disobeys the Son shall not see that life' (John 3:36) — it can be considered as not excluded that the divine omnipotence and grace are present and operative wherever the departure from the fulness of truth in the one Church is not complete and does not go to the lengths of a complete estrangement from the truth, wherever 'God Himself is not called in question', wherever the source of 'life, the Trinity, is sincerely proclaimed and the mystery of the divine economy in the incarnation is acknowledged' (Petrus III, Patriarch of Alexandria, Letter to Michael Kerularios, PG 120, 798-800).

(31) 5. On this view of the question of the Church's boundaries, where the unity of the Church as the Body of Christ is understood in a wider sense, all who believe in Christ are called to seek lovingly, sincerely and patiently to enter into dialogue with one another, and to pray unceasingly for the restoration of the Church's unity in faith and full fellowship so that the Lord God may lead all to know the truth and to attain the fulness of unity.

In the view of the Mixed Orthodox-Old Catholic Commission, the above text on 'The Boundaries of the Church' represents the doctrine of the Orthodox and Old Catholic Churches.

Bonn, Greek-Orthodox Metropoly

August 20-24, 1979

Signatures of all members of the Joint Commission present.

PARTICIPANTS

Participants of the Meeting in the Orthodox Centre in Chambésy
(20-28th August 1975)

ORTHODOX MEMBERS

Ecumenical Patriarchate:
Irenaios, Metropolitan of Germany, Chairman
Professor Emmanuel Photiadis
Patriarchate of Alexandria:
Parthenios, Metropolitan of Carthage
Nikodemos, Metropolitan of Central Africa
Patriarchate of Jerusalem:
Kornelios Rodussakis, Archimandrite
Professor Chrysostomos Zaphiris, Archimandrite
Patriarchate of Moscow:
Philaret, Metropolitan of Berlin
Nikolaj Gundjajev, Archpriest
Patriarchate of Romania:
Professor Isidor Todoran, Priest
Professor Stefan Alexe, Priest
Patriarchate of Bulgaria:
Professor Ilja Tsonevski
Church of Cyprus:
Chrysostomos Chrysanthos, Metropolitan of Limasol
Professor Andreas Mitsidis
Church of Greece:
Professor Johannes Karmiris
Professor Johannes Kalogirou
Professor Megas Pharantos
Church of Finland:
Johannes Seppälä, Priest

OLD CATHOLIC MEMBERS

Church of Switzerland:
Léon Gauthier, Bishop, Chairman
Professor Herwig Aldenhoven, Priest
Church of Holland:
Professor Petrus Johannes Maan, Canon
Church of Germany:
Josef Brinkhues, Bishop
Professor Werner Küppers, Priest

Church of Poland (representing the Polish-National Catholic Church of the United States of America and Canada)
Tadeusz R. Majewski, Bishop
Wiktor Wysoczanski, Priest
Church of Austria:
Dr. Günter Dolezal, Priest

Participants of the Meeting in the Orthodox Centre in Chambésy
(23-30th August 1977)
ORTHODOX MEMBERS
Ecumenical Patriarchate:
Irenaios, Metropolitan of Germany, Chairman
Professor Emmanuel Photiadis
Patriarchate of Alexandria:
Parthenios, Metropolitan of Carthage
Patriarchate of Jerusalem:
Kornelios, Metropolitan of Sebastia
Chrysostomos, Metropolitan of Gardikion
Patriarchate of Moscow:
Philaret, Metropolitan of Berlin
Nikolaj Gundjajev, Archpriest
Patriarchate of Serbia:
Professor Dimitrije Dimitrijevic, Priest
Patriarchate of Romania:
Professor Stefan Alexe, Priest
Patriarchate of Bulgaria:
Professor Ilja Tsonevski
Church of Cyprus:
Professor Andreas Mitsidis
Church of Greece:
Professor Johannes Kalogirou
Professor Megas Pharantos

OLD CATHOLIC MEMBERS
Church of Switzerland:
Léon Gauthier, Bishop, Chairman
Professor Herwig Aldenhoven, Priest
Church of Holland:
Professor Petrus Johannes Maan, Canon
Martien Parmentier, Priest
Church of Germany:
Professor Werner Küppers, Priest
Professor Christian Oeyen, Priest

Church of Austria:
Dr. Günter Dolezal, Priest
Church of Poland:
Tadeusz Majewski, Bishop
Maksymilian Rode, Bishop
(these also represented the Polish-National Catholic Church in the USA and Canada)
Orthodox consultants or interpreters
Dr. Theodoros Nikolaou
Grigorij Skobej
Old Catholic consultants or interpreters
Professor Peter Amiet, Priest
Urs von Arx, Priest
Dieter Prinz, Priest

Participants of the Meeting in the Greek-Orthodox Metropoly of Germany in Bonn-Beuel (20-24th August 1979)

ORTHODOX MEMBERS
Ecumenical Patriarchate:
Irenaios, Metropolitan of Germany, Chairman
Professor Emmanuel Photiadis
Patriarchate of Alexandria:
Parthenios, Metropolitan of Carthage
Patriarchate of Jerusalem:
Kornelios, Metropolitan of Sebaste
Chrysostomos, Metropolitan of Persisterion
Patriarchate of Moscow
Philaret, Metropolitan of Minsk and White Russia
Nikolaj Gundjajev, Archpriest
Patriarchate of Romania:
Professor Stefan Alexe, Priest
Patriarchate of Bulgaria:
Professor Ilja Tsonevski
Church of Cyprus:
Varnavas, Bishop of Salamina
Dr. Benediktos Englesakis
Church of Greece:
Professor Johannes Karmiris
Professor Johannes Kalogirou

OLD CATHOLIC MEMBERS
Church of Switzerland:
Léon Gauthier, Bishop, Chairman
Professor Herwig Aldenhoven, Priest
Church of Holland:
Professor Petrus Johannes Maan, Priest
Church of Germany:
Professor Werner Küppers, Priest
Church of Austria:
Dr. Günter Dolezal, Priest
Church of Poland:
Tadeusz Majewski, Bishop
Professor Maksymilian Rode, Bishop
Church of USA and Canada'
Dr. Wiktor Wysoczanski, Priest
Orthodox consultants or interpreters:
Augustinos, Bishop of Elaia
Vasilios, Bishop of Aristi
Professor Theodoros Nikolaou
Dr. Grigorij Skobej
Old Catholic consultants or interpreters:
Professor Peter Amiet, Priest
Koenraad Ouwens, Priest

ECCLESIOLOGY, 1981

I

(1) The source and confirmation of the authority of the Church as the God-Man union is the power, received from the Father, and the authority of the Lord and her Head, Jesus Christ (Mt. 28. 18; Lk. 10. 16). The Lord manifested this power and authority, connected with the Redemption, during His earthly life, and after His Resurrection invested the Apostles with them, and through the Apostles—the bishops and the entire Church (Mt. 28, 19-20; Jn. 20. 21)

The Lord, Who promised the Church that He would be with her *always, even unto the end of the world* (Mt. 28. 20), also sent her *another Comforter—the Spirit of truth* (Jn. 14. 16-17; 15. 26; 16.13), to be with her always and to instruct her on all the truths. For this reason the Church is defined as the Church of the living God, the pillar and ground of the truth (1 Tim. 3. 15).

(2) The Church manifests her power and authority in the Name of Jesus Christ, through the power and action of the Comforter Who lives in her. That is why she accomplishes her work authoritatively, not through outside compulsion, but by means of the spiritual forces which suffuse her in all of her members and which are *love, joy, peace, longsuffering, gentleness, goodness, faith, meekness, temperance* (Gal. 5. 22-23).

(3) This manifestation of the Church's authority leads her members to an inner readiness to accept the Divine Truth authoritatively advanced by the Church and to obediently assimilate it in the *liberty wherewith Christ hath made us free* (Gal. 5. 1). The Truth is perceived through the Holy Spirit, for the Truth makes us free (Jn. 8. 32), because *where the Spirit of the Lord is, there is liberty* (2 Cor. 3. 17).

II

(1) The authority of the Church, the bearer of which is the entire Church as the Body of Christ, was historically manifested through the acts and decisions by which Holy Scripture and Holy Tradition were protected from any distortion and falsification by heretics; the canonical books of Holy Scripture were separated from spurious ones, and its canon was defined; the living tradition of faith was preserved, interpreted and handed down; the Creed was formulated, completed and disseminated; questions of the priesthood and government, the order of service and of Church life were defined.

(2) The interpretation of Holy Scripture is a constant concern of the Church. Holy Scripture is not higher than the Church: it originated in her, and, as the Church lives in the light of the witness of Divine Revelation so, too, is Holy Scripture weighed and interpreted in union with the Tradition living in the Church and the decisions regarding the Faith formulated by the Church. Therefore, a true teaching is only that which,

while being higher than problems depending on time and linguistic expressions, accords essentially with Holy Scripture and Holy Tradition. In manifesting her authority in dogmatic decisions, the Church always draws on both, i.e., Holy Scripture and Holy Tradition, while preserving the witness of both and deepening her comprehension of them.

(3) Of particular significance for the Church is the singleminded teaching of her Fathers and Teachers. Apostolic Tradition is preserved and explained in their works of which Holy Scripture is a divinely inspired written monument. The Church perceives this singlemindedness of the Fathers as authoritative witness to the Truth (Vincent of Lérins, *Commonitorium,* 3 and 28 and the entire patristic tradition).

III

The following are the individual bearers and manifestors of authority in the Church:

(1) The bishop, who heads the Local Church canonically in Apostolic Succession. The place and work of a bishop in the sphere of authority was elucidated by St. Ignatius of Antioch, who pointed out that one who obeys the bishop accepts the authority of God, because the authority of God is represented and borne by the bishop (Epistle to the Magnesians, 3, 1, 2; 6, 1; to the Trallians, 2, 1), who always acts in conjunction with the presbyters ordained by him. "Thus as the Lord did nothing without the Father (being united with him), either by Himself or by means of His Apostles so you must do nothing without the bishop and the presbyters." (Epistle to the Magnesians, 7, 1, cf. Mt. 4. 1; Epistle to the Trallians, 3, 1; to the Smyrnaeans, 8, 1).

Through the power, authority and grace of his dignity the bishop preserves the purity of the dogmatic teaching of the Church and maintains her order; he is the celebrator of the Sacraments, and, through his preaching, leads the flock entrusted to him along the salvific path of the Gospel grace. In his Church, the bishop acts in union and harmony with the presbyters and the people, who follow him as their Gospel shepherd. According to St. Cyprian [of Carthage] "the Church is made up of the people, united to their priest, flock cleaving to its shepherd. Hence you should know that the bishop is in the Church, and the Church in the bishop" (Epistle 66.8).

(2) The councils of the Church and predominantly the ecumenical. At the councils, every bishop represents his Church by virtue of his episcopal dignity; the decisions of the councils deserve authority and have it, inasmuch as the Church, represented by the assembled bishops, agrees with them (cf. Acts 15).

IV

(1) The authority of the Church is also connected with the common confession of faith of the Church. This is a unanimous, general awareness and faith of the clergy and people, a broader witness of the entire Church

Plenitude which shares in the responsibility for the preservation of the Truth handed down and for the integrity and purity of the Teaching. A common confession of the Church also comprises the definitive criterion for recognition of the Ecumenical Councils as such, and their Fathers as the true interpreters of the Faith of the Church which they rightly represent.

(2) This common confession is expressed in different ways. Its manifestors are the confessors of and martyrs for the Faith, theologians and mystics, Holy Fathers, charismatics, and in general all those who received the Gifts of the Holy Spirit in Baptism and Confirmation and who are called in equal measure to bear witness to the Gospel in the world, as well as to divine services and other forms of ecclesiastical life.

(3) It should be pointed out in conclusion that authority at all stages and in all forms of its manifestation presupposes the spirit of truth, love, wisdom from humility, and freedom. It is only in this way that the authority of the Church and authority within the Church is manifested for the benefit of her life and service in the world, inasmuch as the Lord of the Church, to Whom all power and authority were given in Heaven and on earth, manifested this power among men *as he that serveth* (Lk. 22. 27; Jn. 13. 14-17). It is for this reason that the authority of the Church, wholly directed as it is at creating the Body of Christ and its growth in love (Eph. 4. 11-16), should bear the nature of service.

The above-mentioned regarding the authority of the Church and authority within the Church comprises, as was determined by our Mixed Orthodox-Old Catholic Theological Commission on Dialogue, the teaching of both the Orthodox and Old Catholic Churches.

THE INFALLIBILITY OF THE CHURCH

The true God (Jn. 3. 33; 17.3; Rom. 3. 4; 1 Thess. 1. 9) sent His Son, Who is the Truth (Jn. 14. 6) "for us men, and for our salvation", which is realized in the Church He founded. The Son thus sends to her from the Father the Comforter, the Spirit of Truth, which proceeds from the Father, that He may be with her for all time and instruct her in all truths (Jn. 14. 15-17). That is why the Church participates in God's truth, faithfulness and infallibility. The Holy Spirit bears witness to Christ; therefore the Church, too, receiving and passing on the Apostolic Tradition, bears witness to her Lord and His teaching, being illumined by the Comforter (Jn. 15. 26-27), Who teaches her everything and reminds her of everything which Christ said (Jn. 14. 26; 15. 26).

The Church, despite the human infirmity of her members, preserves the Revealed Truth, the *good thing* entrusted to her (2 Tim. 1. 14) in purity and undefiled, because Christ is with her until the end of ages (Mt. 28. 20) so that *the gates of hell* should not *prevail against it* (Mt. 16. 18). For this reason the Church is called *the house of God, the pillar and ground of the truth* (1 Tim. 3. 15) and can correctly pass on to her members the Faith handed down to her and truthfully give witness to it before the world. The infallibility of the Church proceeds from her Lord and the Holy Spirit. The Church is within Christ, and He acts through her by means of the Spirit Who is sent into the hearts of the faithful (Gal. 4. 6). This essential infallibility is not destroyed by the sins or transgressions of the members (Rom. 3. 3-4).

The Church is infallible only as a whole; infallibility does not apply to individual members, be they bishops, patriarchs or popes, not to the clergy alone, the people alone, or separate Local Churches. Inasmuch as the Church is a community of the faithful all of whom *hath learned of the Father* (Jn. 6. 45), infallibility applies to the Church's integrity. All together, the clergy and the people, comprise, as members, the Body of Christ and are thus *the fullness of him that filleth all in all* (Eph. 1. 23). For this reason the totality of the fruitful, who *have an unction from the Holy One,* know the truth correctly and live by it (1 Jn. 2. 20, 27), is not amiss when it professes unanimously their common Faith, from bishops to any one of the faithful people.

That is why the Ecumenical Council alone is the supreme organ of the Church in the infallible proclamation of her Faith. Below it, like the mouth of the entire Church, stand the Local Councils, the bishops and all the individual members of the Church, just as in the apostolic times the Council of Apostles did, at which the Apostles along with the presbyters of the entire Local Church of Jerusalem authoritatively expressed the will of the whole Church, and received more authority than the authority of any single Apostle (Acts 15). The Ecumenical Council, inspired by the Holy Spirit in its proclamations, is infallible as a result of accord with the entire Catholic Church. Not a single council would be an Ecumenical Council without this accord.

The Church formulates dogmatic decisions when there is a threat to sound teaching or she needs a special interpretation or witness to thwart heresies and schisms or to preserve Church unity. Naturally, infallibility applies only to the saving truth of the Faith.

Holy Scripture, which witnesses to the Incarnate Eternal Word of God, is fundamentally inspired by the Holy Spirit, Who is the Spirit of Christ. For this reason the leadership of the Church through the Holy Spirit is always viewed in conformity with Holy Scripture and with the Apostolic teaching handed down, and is always related to one or the other (Jn. 16. 13). Hence the continuation, based on them, of the Faith which is preserved in the Church, includes existence in the fullness of this Faith, according to the witness of the Church all through the centuries.

The above-mentioned points with respect to Church infallibility, comprise, as determined by our Mixed Orthodox-Old Catholic Theological Commission on Dialogue, the teaching of both the Orthodox and Old Catholic Churches.

CHURCH COUNCILS

The Church, as the Body of Christ, is the temple of the Holy Spirit, whose members were baptized into the One Body, and therefore all partake of the New Life and come to know the Truth in the Holy Spirit.

The early ecclesiastical episcopal and conciliar system comprises the expression of Church life as the community of all members in the unity of the body of Christ. For this reason the bishops, who, as the representatives of the Head of the Church, i.e., Christ, lead the conciliar and Eucharistic gathering, are bound with the entire people of God as members of the One Body (St. Ignatius Theophoros. *To the Smyrnaeans,* 8. 2).

The conciliar nature as the basis of Church order manifests itself in the diversity of the New Life in Christ through the Holy Spirit (I Cor. 12, 1-31). For this reason the Church, as the people called by God, redeemed by Christ and illumined by the Holy Spirit, may be called the Great Council which reflects the oneness in the Triune God of the Father, of the Son, and of the Holy Spirit.

This basic nature of the Church acquires a precise form particularly during representative conferences of bishops of the Local Churches at their councils during discussions and adoption of decisions which are eventually subject to adoption or rejection by the entire Church.

This conciliar life of the Church receives its highest expression at an Ecumenical Council, which is convened to adopt binding decisions on matters of Faith and Church Order concerning the entire Church, through the bishops as representatives of the society of all the Local Churches. The Ecumenical Councils serve as the highest organ of the Church for wiping out heresies, formulating dogmatic teachings, forming and consolidating Church life, and preserving Church unity which rests on the true Faith.

Seven councils are recognized as ecumenical *per se:* the councils of Nicaea (325), of Constantinople (381), of Ephesus (431), of Chalcedon (451), of Constantinople (553 and 680), and of Nicaea (787). A common Creed and recognition of the One, Holy, Catholic and Apostolic Church were formulated at them, and the unity of the Local Churches in the One Holy Body of Chrsit manifested itself. For this reason the Ecumenical Councils are not higher than the Church as a whole, but are within her. Thus the ecumenism of any council and acceptance of its decisions are not conditioned by its convening alone. More precisely, it becomes ecumenical by virtue of its subsequent free recognition by the Plenitude of the Church.

By their participation in the full life of the Church, her members— the clergy and laity—effect their unity in the Body of Christ. The infallibility of the Church is expressed in this unity and integrity. In conformity with this Ecumenical Councils may also recognize the decisions of the Local Councils as adopted through the inspiration of the Holy Spirit. Incidentally, it was the Local Councils that prepared the content of the decisions of the Ecumenical Councils and contributed to the adoption of these conciliar decisions.

Conciliar decisions are divided into definitions of faith and rules. Of these, the definitions touching upon dogma based on Revelation, receive absolute authority and are constantly binding for the entire Church. Consequently, they are not subject to change or abolition, i.e., to anything that would alter their content. Nevertheless, the Church can effect their hermeneutic revelation through modern phraseology in accordance with emergent circumstances and needs for clarification and witness to the Faith. The rules of the Local as well as Ecumenical Councils, if they do not apply to questions of the Faith, are theoretically subject to substitution or addition by means of new rules of respective later councils.

In general, the Churches, both Orthodox and Old Catholic, believe that their councils have the right, if need be, to enact laws and apply them within their own bounds.

The above-mentioned points concerning the Church Councils comprise, as was determined by our Mixed Orthodox-Old Catholic Theological Commission on Dialogue, the teaching of both the Orthodox and Old Catholic Churches.

THE NEED FOR APOSTOLIC SUCCESSION

(1) Apostolic succession here is taken to mean the transmission, through the canonical imposition of hands, of the grace of the priesthood, as well as the continuation and preservation in purity of the Teaching and Faith passed on by the Apostles. In the continuous succession of the bishops from the Apostles the former comprises the foundation of Apostolic Succession, while the latter constitutes an essential sign of it. Deviation from Apostolic Teaching destroys Apostolic succession, and anti-canonical ordination by unauthorized persons violates it.

Clearly, Apostolic succession in a broader sense is something essential for the life of the Church and imperative for her continuation of the redemptive work of the Lord thanks to the reliable transmission of the sanctifying and saving grace. As Jesus Christ was sent by the Father so, too, did He send the Apostles, gathering the people of God through them and founding and nurturing His Church.

(2) The Apostles, as eyewitnesses of the Risen Christ and leaders of the newly-founded Church, do not and cannot have successors. However, they have successors in the entire apostolic work of gathering the Church at any time and setting her in order through the preaching of the Word of God, through their leading position and their activity in the liturgical life, and through celebrating the Sacraments, the Holy Eucharist in particular.

Although the New Testament speaks of the many gifts and services of the faithful, there can be no doubt about the uniqueness and inimitability of the basic significance of the apostolic calling and work (Acts 1. 21, 22; 1 Cor. 12. 28; Eph. 2. 20; Rev. 21. 14).

(3) The Church receives her life from Christ, Who is present in her and acts through the Holy Spirit. Christ is the Lord of the Church, who talks with her, loves her and is heard by her. This union of Christ and the Church is understood not as something abstract, but as a concrete reality and experience through persons called by Christ. As this was effected in the times of the Apostles so, too, should it be effected in our day in all ages, because the order of the Church is essentially the same as the one given by Christ.

As a society of believers which cannot exist without this order, the Church must remain in continuous temporal contact with her origins and with the Church of the preceding and future generations. For this reason the vocation of the priesthood in Apostolic Succession is not something new, something unrelated to the origins of the Church; it is the repetition and continual transmission of that which has existed in the Church from the very beginning. The imposition of hands with a prayer in communion with the entire Church is the only mystic means of transmitting the grace of the priesthood indicated in Holy Scripture and Tradition [For details see the texts on the Sacraments which the commission will be working on in the future].

(4) The necessity of observing uninterrupted Apostolic Succession as both continuation of Apostolic Teaching and the transmission of the priesthood and grace, and the mission by the canonical imposition of hands comprises the common teaching of the Fathers of the Church.

(5) The Orthodox Easter Church emphasized particularly the necessity of Apostolic Succession just as in the early day so today in the above-mentioned sense, making this question fundamental to any endeavour to restore Christian unity. The Old Catholic Church also adheres firmly to this view regarding the necessity.

The above-mentioned points concerning Apostolic Succession comprises, as was established at our Mixed Orthodox-Old Catholic Theological Commission on Dialogue, the doctrine of both the Orthodox and Old Catholic Churches.

Zagorsk/Moscow, September 20, 1981

PARTICIPANTS

Inter-Orthodox Commission:
Metropolitan Damaskinos of Tranoupolis
Prof. Dr. Theodoros Zisis
Metropolitan Parthenios of Carthage
Archbishop Cornelios of Sebasteia
Metropolitan Filaret of Minsk and Byelorussia
Archpriest Prof. Nikolai Gundyaev

Hieromonk Savva Milosevic
Bishop Adrian of the Romanian Orthodox Archdiocese of Central and
  Western Europe
Father Prof. Stefan Alexe
Prof. Dr. Ilija Tsonevsky
Bishop Barnabas of Salamis
Hierodeacon Pavlos
Prof Dr. Ioannis Kalogirou
Prof. Dr. Vlasios Fidas
Archbishop Ioann of Chkondidi and Tsager
Bishop Anania of Akhaltsikhe
Archpriest Dr. Serafim Zelezniakowicz
Bishop Alexi of Joensuu
Hieromonk Ambrosius (Jasklainen)

Old Catholic Commission:
Bishop Léon Gauthier of the Christian Catholic Church of Switzerland
Prof. Ernst Hammerschmidt
Father Peter Maan
Prof. Martin Parmentier
Prof. Christian Oeyen
Prof. Dr. Herwig Aldenhoven
The Rev. Dr. Günter Dolezal
Bishop Tadeusz Majewski
Bishop Dr. Maksymilian Rode
The Rev. Wiktor Wysoczanski

Note

For details on the Fourth Meeting of the Mixed Theological Commission on Orthodox-Old Catholic Dialogue, Zagorsk—Moscow, September 15-21, 1981, see
JMP No. 12, 1981, p. 52.

PENTECOSTAL-ROMAN CATHOLIC CONVERSATION

Report 1976

Final Report

of the Dialogue between the Secretariat for Promoting Christian Unity of the Roman Catholic Church and Leaders of Some Pentecostal Churches and Participants in the Charismatic Movement within Protestant and Anglican Churches, 1976

Introduction

1. The series of talks described as the Roman Catholic/Pentecostal dialogue had its beginning in the contacts made by individual members of the Pentecostal Churches with the Vatican Secretariat for Promoting Christian Unity in 1969 and 1970. With the assistance of Rev. David du Plessis, an international Pentecostal leader, noted figure among Pentecostals and a guest at the Second Vatican Council, and Fr. Kilian McDonnell, O.S.B., Director of the Institute for Ecumenical and Cultural Research, Collegeville, U.S.A., the initial impulse was clarified and concrete proposals began to emerge.

2. In 1970 the first of two exploratory meetings was held to see if a serious theological discussion between Roman Catholics and Pentecostals on the international level would be possible. The first gathering was largely an occasion for beginning to know one another. At the second meeting in 1971 each side put "hard" questions to the other, a more purposeful conversation resulted, and it became clear that it would be possible to undertake discussions of a more systematic kind.

3. Therefore, later in 1971, a small steering committee with members from both sides worked out a program of topics which could be treated at meetings over a five-year period.

4. The dialogue has a special character. The bilateral conversations which the Roman Catholic Church undertakes with many world communions (e.g. the Anglican Communion, the Lutheran World Federation etc.) are prepared to consider problems concerning church structures and ecclesiology and have organic unity as a goal or at least envisage some kind of eventual structural unity. This dialogue has not. Before it began it was made clear that its immediate scope was not "to concern itself with the problems of imminent structural union", although of course its object was Christians coming closer together in prayer and common witness. Its purpose has been that "prayer, spirituality and theological reflection be a shared concern at the international level in the form of a dialogue between the Secretariat for Promoting Christian Unity of the Roman Catholic Church and leaders of some Pentecostal Churches and participants in the charismatic movements within Protestant and Anglican Churches".

5. The dialogue has sought "to explore the life and spiritual experience of Christians and the Churches", "to give special attention to the meaning for the Church of fullness of life in the Holy Spirit", attending to "both the experiential and theological dimensions" of that life. "Through such dialogue" those who participate "hope to share in the reality of the mystery of Christ and the Church, to build a united testimony, to indicate in what manner the sharing of truth makes it possible . . . to grow together".

6. Certain areas of doctrinal agreement have been looked at with a view to eliminating mutual misunderstandings. At the same time, there has been no attempt to minimize points of real divergence. One of these, for example, is the importance given to faith and to experience, and their relation in Christian life.

7. The dialogue has been between the Roman Catholic Church and some Pentecostal Churches. Here, too, there have been special features. On the Roman Catholic side, it has had the usual authorization given by the Secretariat for Promoting Christian Unity to such meetings on an international scale and the participants were appointed officially by the Secretariat. The Pentecostal participants were either appointed officially by their individual Churches (and in several cases are leaders of these Churches), or else came with some kind of approbation of their Churches. Therefore, it has been a dialogue with some Pentecostal Churches and with delegates of others. These are Churches which came into being over the last fifty or sixty years when some Protestant churches expelled those who made speaking in tongues and other charismatic manifestations an integral part of their spirituality.

8. In addition, there were participants in the charismatic movement who were invited by the Pentecostals. They belong to Anglican or Protestant Churches which already have bilateral dialogues in progress with the Roman Catholic Church. Therefore, it is as participants in the charismatic movement and not primarily as members of their own Churches that they share in the dialogue.

9. It was also pointed out in the beginning that "this dialogue is not directly concerned with the domestic pastoral question of the relationship of the charismatic movement among Catholics to the Catholic Church. The dialogue may help indirectly to clarify this relationship but this is not the direct concern of our deliberations".[1]

10. At the first meeting of the dialogue in Horgen, Switzerland, June 1972, an exegetical approach was taken in order to study "baptism in the Holy Spirit" in the New Testament, its relation to repentance and the process of sanctification and the relation of the charismata to it. At Rome in June, 1973 the second meeting was devoted to the historic background of the Pentecostal movement, the relation of baptism in the Holy Spirit to the rites of Christian initiation, and the role of the Holy Spirit and the gifts of the Spirit in the mystical tradition. The third meeting, held at Schloss Craheim, West Germany, June 1974, focused on the theology of Christian

initiation, the nature of sacramental activity, infant and adult baptism. At the fourth meeting held in Venice, May 1975, the areas of public worship (especially eucharistic celebration), the human dimension in the exercise of the spiritual gifts, and discerning of spirits were the main concern. In Rome, May 1976 the final session was devoted to the topic of prayer and praise.

Baptism in the Holy Spirit

11.   In the New Testament the expression "to baptize in the Holy Spirit" (Mk 1, 8) is used to express, in contrast to the baptism of John, (Jn 1, 33) the baptism by Jesus who gives the Spirit to the new eschatological people of God, the Church (Acts 1, 5). All men are called to enter into this community through faith in Christ who makes them disciples through baptism and sharers of his Spirit (Acts 2, 38, 39).

12.   In the Pentecostal movement "being baptized in the Spirit", "being filled with the Holy Spirit", and "receiving the Holy Spirit" are understood as occurring in a decisive experience distinct from conversion whereby the Holy Spirit manifests himself, empowers and transforms one's life, and enlightens one as to the whole reality of the Christian mystery (Acts 2, 4; 8, 17; 10, 44; 19, 6).

13.   It is the Spirit of Christ which makes a Christian (1 Cor 12, 13) and that life is "Christian" inasmuch as it is under the Spirit and is characterized by openness to his transforming power. The Spirit is sovereignly free, distributing his gifts to whomsoever he wills, whenever and howsoever he wills (1 Cor 12, 11; Jn 3, 7, 8). There is also the human responsibility to seek after what God has promised (1 Cor 14, 1). This full life in the Spirit is growth in Christ (Eph 4, 15, 16) which must be purified continually. On the other hand, due to one's unfaithfulness to the promptings of the Spirit (Gal 6, 7-9; 1 Jn 3, 24) this growth can be arrested. But also new ways open up and new crises occur which could be milestones of progress in the Christian life (2 Cor 3, 17, 18; 2 Cor 4, 8-11).

14.   The participants are conscious that during the nineteen centuries other terms have been used to express this experience called "baptism in the Holy Spirit". It is one used today by the Pentecostal movement. Other expressions are "being filled with the Holy Spirit", "receiving the Holy Spirit". These expressions should not be used to exclude traditional understandings of the experience of and faith in the reality of Christian initiation.

15.   The Holy Spirit gratuitously manifests himself in signs and charisms for the common good (Mk 16, 17-18), working in and through but going beyond the believer's natural ability. There is a great variety of ministries in which the Spirit manifests himself. Without minimizing the importance of these experiences or denying the fruitfulness of these gifts for the Church, the participants wished to lay stronger stress on faith, hope and charity as sure guides in responding to God (1 Cor 13, 13-14, 1; 1 Thess 1,

3-5). Precisely out of respect for the Spirit and his gifts it is necessary to discern between true gifts and their counterfeits (1 Thess 5, 22; 1 Jn 4, 1-4). In this discernment process the spiritual authority in the church has its own specific ministry (1 Jn 4, 6; Acts 20, 28-31; 1 Cor 14, 37, 38) because it has special concern for the common good, the unity of the Church and her mission in the world (Rom 15, 17-19; Acts 1,8).

Christian Initiation and the Gifts

16.   From the earliest non-canonical texts of the Church there is witness to the celebration of Christian initiation (baptism, laying on of hands/chrismation, eucharist), as clearly expressing the request for and the actual reception of the Holy Spirit. The Holy Spirit dwells in all Christians (Rom 8,9), and not just in those "baptized in the Holy Spirit". The difference between a committed Christian without such a Pentecostal experience and one with such an experience is generally not only a matter of theological focus, but also that of expanded openness and expectancy with regard to the Holy Spirit and his gifts. Because the Holy Spirit apportions as he wills in freedom and sovereignty, the religious experiences of persons can differ. He blows where he wills (Jn 3,8). Though the Holy Spirit never ceased manifesting himself throughout the entire history of the church, the manner of the manifestations has differed according to the times and cultures. However, in the Pentecostal movement, the manifestation of tongues has had, and continues to have, particular importance.

17.   During times of spiritual renewal when charismatic elements are more manifest, tensions can arise because of prejudice, lack of mutual understanding and communication. Also, at such times as this the discerning of spirits is more necessary than ever. This necessity should not lead to discernment being misused so as to exclude charismatic manifestations. The true exercise of the charisms takes place in love and leads to a greater fidelity to Christ and his church. The presence of charismatic gifts is not a sign of spiritual maturity and those who lack experience of such gifts are not considered to be inferior Christians. Love is the context in which all gifts are rightly exercised, love being of a more definitive and primary order than the spiritual gifts (*1 Cor* 13). In varying degrees all the charisms are ministries directed to the building up of the community and witness in mission. For this reason mystical experiences, which are more generally directed toward personal communion with God, are distinguished from charismatic experiences which, while including personal communion with God, are directed more to ministerial service.

The Giving of the Spirit and Christian Initiation

18.   The Holy Spirit, being the agent of regeneration, is given in Christian initiation, not as a commodity but as he who unifies us with Christ and the Father in a personal relationship. Being a Christian includes the reception of grace through the Holy Spirit for one's own sanctification as well as

gifts to be ministered to others. In some manner all ministry is a demonstration of the power of the Spirit. It was not agreed whether there is a further imparting of the Spirit with a view to charismatic ministry, or whether baptism in the Holy Spirit is, rather, a kind of release of a certain aspect of the Spirit already given. An inconclusive discussion occurred on the question as to how many impartings of the Spirit there were. Within classical Pentecostalism some hold that through regeneration the Holy Spirit comes *into* us, and that later in the baptism in the Spirit the Spirit comes *upon* us and begins to flow from us. Finally, charisms are not personal achievements but are sovereign manifestations of the Holy Spirit.

Baptism

19.   Baptism involves a passing over from the kingdom of darkness to Christ's kingdom of light, and always includes a communal dimension of being baptized into the one Body of Christ. The implications of this concord were not developed.

20.   In regard to baptism, the New Testament reflects the missionary situation of the apostolic generation of the Church and does not clearly indicate what may have happened in the second and following generation of believers.

21.   In that missionary situation Christian initiation involved a constellation normally including proclamation of the Gospel, faith repentance, baptism in water, the receiving of the Spirit. There was disagreement as to the relationship of these items, and the order in which they may or should occur. In both the Pentecostal and Roman Catholic tradition laying on of hands may be used to express the giving of the Spirit. Immersion is the ideal form which most aptly expresses the significance of baptism. Some, however, regard immersion as essential, others do not.

22.   In discussing infant baptism, certain convergences were noted:

   a) Sacraments are in no sense magical and are effective only in relationship to faith.

23.   *b)* God's gift precedes and makes possible human receiving. Even though there was disagreement on the application of this principle, there was accord on the assertion that God's grace operates in advance of our conscious awareness.

24.   *c)* Where paedobaptism is not practiced and the children of believing parents are presented and dedicated to God, the children are thus brought into the care of the Christian community and enjoy the special protection of the Lord.

25.   *d)* Where paedobaptism is practiced it is fully meaningful only in the context of the faith of the parents and the community. The parents must undertake to nurture the child in the Christian life, in the expectation that, when he or she grows up, the child will personally live and affirm faith in Christ.

26.   Representatives of the charismatic movement in the historic churches expressed different views on baptism. Some agreed substantially with the Roman Catholic, others with the classical Pentecostal view.

27.   Attention was drawn to the pastoral problem of persons baptised in infancy seeking a new experience of baptism by immersion later in life. It was stated that in a few traditions rites have been devised, involving immersion in water in order to afford such an experience. The Roman Catholics felt there were already sufficient opportunities within the existing liturgy for reaffirming one's baptism. Rebaptism in the strict sense of the word is unacceptable to all. Those participants who reject paedobaptism, however, explained that they do not consider as rebaptism the baptism of a believing adult who has received infant baptism. This serious ecumenical problem requires future study.

Scripture, Tradition and Developments

28.   The church is always subject to sacred Scriptures. There was, however, considerable disagreement as to the role of tradition in interpretation of Scripture.

29.   The Pentecostal and charismatic movements have brought to the understanding of Scripture a new relevance and freshness to confirm the conviction that Scripture has a special message, vital to each generation. Moreover, these movements challenge the exegetes to take a new look at the Sacred Text in the light of the new questions and expectations the movements bring to Scripture.

30.   It was agreed that every church has history, and is inevitably affected by its past. Some developments in that past are good, some are questionable; some are enduring, some are only temporary. A discernment must be made on these developments by the churches.

31.   The dialogue considered that in the context of the charismatic movement in the historic churches there was justification for new groups and communities within the churches. Though such movements have a legitimate prophetic character, their ultimate purpose is to strengthen the church, and to participate fully in her life. Therefore, the charismatic movement is not in competition with the churches, nor is it separate from them. Further, it should recognize the church authorities. In a word the charismatic renewal is a renewal in the Body of Christ, the Church, and is therefore in and of the Church.

Public Worship

32.   Public worship should safeguard a whole composite of elements: spontaneity, freedom, discipline, objectivity. On the Roman Catholic side, it was noted that the new revised liturgy allows for more opportunities for spontaneous prayer and singing at the Eucharist and in the rites of penance. The Pentecostal tradition has come to accept a measure of structure in worship and recognizes the development in its own history toward some liturgy.

33.   In the Roman Catholic context the phrase *ex opere operato* was discussed in relation to the celebration of the sacraments. The disquiet of some participants was removed by the explanation of the Roman Catholic doctrine of grace which stresses that the living faith of the recipient of a sacrament is of fundamental importance.

Public Worship and the Gifts

34.   Corporate worship is a focal expression of the worshipper's daily life as he or she speaks to God and to other members of the community in songs of praise and words of thanksgiving (Eph 5, 19-20; 1 Cor 14, 26). Our Lord is present in the members of his body, manifesting himself in worship by means of a variety of charismatic expressions. He is also present by the power of his Spirit in the Eucharist. The participants recognized that there was a growing understanding of the unity which exists between the formal structure of the eucharistic celebration and the spontaneity of the charismatic gifts. This unity was exemplified by the Pauline relationship between chapters eleven to fourteen of I Corinthians.

The Human Aspect

35.   There exists both a divine and human aspect to all genuinely charismatic phenomena. So far as concerns the human aspect, the phenomena can rightly be subject to psychological, linguistic, sociological, anthropological and other investigation which can provide some understanding of the diverse manifestations of the Holy Spirit, but the spiritual aspect of charismatic phenomena ultimately escapes a purely scientific examination. While there is no essential conflict between science and faith, nevertheless, science has inherent limitations, particularly with regard to the dimensions of faith and spiritual experience.

36.   A survey of the scientific literature on speaking in tongues was presented. Another presentation outlined a Jungian psychological evaluation of the phenomenology of the Holy Spirit. However neither of these topics was developed adequately in discussion and they await more extended consideration. This could be done in the context of a future treatment of the place of speaking in tongues as an essential factor in the Pentecostal experience.

37.   The relationship between science and the exercise of the spiritual gifts, including that of healing, was discussed. Classical Pentecostals, as well as other participants, believe that through the ministry of divine healing can come restoration to sound health. Full agreement was not reached in this matter in view of the importance of the therapeutic disciplines and the participants recommended further in-depth study.

Discernment of spirits

38.   The New Testament witnesses to the charism of the discerning of spirits (1 Cor 12,10), and also to a form of discernment through the testing of the spirits (1 Jn 4,1), and the proving of the will of God (Rom 12,2),

each exercised in the power of the Spirit. There are different aspects of discernment of spirits which allow for human experience, wisdom and reason as a consequence of growth in the Spirit, while other aspects imply an immediate communication of the Spirit for discernment in a specific situation.

39.   Discernment is essential to authentic ministry. The Pentecostal tradition lays stress on the discerning of spirits in order to find "the mind of the Spirit" for ministry and public worship. It is also understood as a diagnostic gift which leads to the further manifestation of other charismata for the edification of the Body of Christ and the work of the Gospel. The operation of this gift in dependence upon the Spirit develops both in the believer and community a growth in a mature sensitivity to the Spirit.

40.   Normally, but not absolutely, expectancy is a requisite for the manifestations of the Spirit through human acts on the part of the believer and the community, that is, an openness which nevertheless respects the sovereignty of the Spirit in the distribution of his gifts. Because of human frailty, group pressure and other factors, it is possible for the believer to be mistaken or misled in his awareness of the Spirit's intention and influence in the believer's acts. It is for this reason that criteria are essential to confirm and authenticate the genuine operation of the Spirit of truth (1Jn 4, 1-6). These criteria must be based upon the scriptural foundation of the Incarnation, the Lordship of Christ and the building up of his church. The important element of community criteria involves the common wisdom of a group of believers, walking and living in the Spirit, when, led by those exercising the ministry of discernment, a mature discipline results and the group is capable of discerning the mind of God.

41.   The Roman Catholic tradition understands such community discernment to be exercised by the whole church of which her leaders receive a special charism for this purpose. All traditions find a confirmatory individual criterion in the extent to which the believer is influenced in his daily life by the Spirit of Christ who produces love, joy, peace: the plenitude of the fruit of the Spirit (Gal 5,22).

Prayer and Praise

42.   The relationship between the objective and the subjective aspect of Christian life was raised. Prayer has two main forms: praise and petition. Both have an objective and a subjective aspect.

In the prayer of praise the essential aspect is worship itself, the adoration of the Father in the Spirit and in the truth of Christ (cf. Jn 4, 23-24). One of the expressions of this prayer of praise is the gift of tongues, with joy, enthusiasm, etc.

In the prayer of petition, the believer has always to distinguish between God the Giver, and the gift of God.

43.   Also discussed was the relationship between the word of God and

our experience of the Spirit. The Bible must always be a control and a guide in the Christian experience; but on the other hand, the spiritual experience itself constantly invites us to read the Bible spiritually, in order that it become living water in our Christian life.

44.   We recognize multiple aspects of the total Christian experience which embraces the presence of God (joy, enthusiasm, consolation, etc.), and also the experience of our own sin and the experience of the absence of God, with Christ dying on the Cross (Mk 15, 34; Phil 3, 10); desolation, aridity and the acceptance of our personal death in Christ as an integral part of the authentic Christian life and also of the true praise of God.

Topics for Further Discussion

45.   In the course of conversations a number of areas were touched on which are recommended for further study. Among them were the following:

a)   Speaking in tongues as a characteristic aspect of the experience in the Pentecostal movement.

b)   The subjective dispositions relative to the baptism in the Holy Spirit.

c)   The relationship between the faith of the individual and the faith of the community in terms of content.

d)   The relationship between faith and experience.

e)   The psychological dimension of charismatic experience.

f)   An examination of the charismata of healing and the casting out of demons.

g)   The relationship between the sacraments and conscious personal response of God.

h)   The nature of the sacramental event and, in this context, the nature of the church.

i)   The problem of interpreting Scripture.

j)   The ministries and the ministry gifts: their purpose and operation.

k)   The social implications of spiritual renewal.

Character of the Final Report

46.   The character of the final report compiled by the Steering Committee which has served the dialogue does not represent the official position of the classical Pentecostal denominations of the charismatic movement in the historic Protestant churches, or of the Roman Catholic Church. Rather it represents the content of the discussions. Though the conclusions are the result of serious study and dialogue by responsible persons, it does not commit any of the churches or traditions to the theological positions here expressed, but is submitted to them for suitable use and reaction.

It has been the consensus of all participants that the dialogue has been an occasion of mutual enrichment and understanding and offers the promise of a continuing relationship.

PARTICIPANTS

MEMBERS OF THE COMMISSION:

Pentecostals:

Dr. David J. du Plessis, Oakland, Cal., U.S.A. (co-chairman)
Dr. Allan Hamilton, Portland, Ore., U.S.A.
Reverend Clement Le Cossec, Le Mans, France
Dr. John L. Meares, Washington, D.C., U.S.A.
Reverend Justus T. du Plessis, Lyndhurst, Rep. of South Africa
Reverend Carton Spencer, Lima, N.Y., U.S.A.

Charismatics:

Reverend Arnold Bittlinger (Lutheran), Wetzhausen, FRG
Reverend Michael Harper (Anglican), Hounslow, England
Dr. J. Rodman Williams (Presbyterian), Anaheim, Cal., U.S.A.

Roman Catholics:

Father Kilian McDonnell, O.S.B., Collegeville, Minn., U.S.A.
(co-chairman)
Father Pierre Duprey, Rome
Father Jean Leclercq, O.S.B., Clervaux, Luxembourg
Father Joseph Lecuyer, Rome
Father Heribert Mühlen, Paderborn, FRG
Father Ignace de la Potterie, S.J., Rome

SECRETARIES:

Pentecostal:

Reverend W. Robert McAlister, Rio de Janeiro, Brazil

Catholic:

Msgr. Basil Meeking, Rome

Note

1. This quotation and all others used above are from the "Report of Steering Committee Meeting, Rome, 25-26 October, 1971".

REFORMED-ROMAN CATHOLIC CONVERSATIONS

*The Presence of Christ
in Church and World*

*Final Report of the Dialogue between the World
Alliance of Reformed Churches and the Secretariat
for Promoting Christian Unity, 1977*

THE PRESENCE OF CHRIST IN CHURCH AND WORLD
Final Report

INTRODUCTION

(1) "The Presence of Christ in Church and World" is the topic treated in the series of dialogues between representatives of the World Alliance of Reformed Churches and the Secretariat for Promoting Christian Unity of the Roman Catholic Church.

(2) The choice of that topic and the enabling process for such a series at the international level go back to informal conversations among participants from both bodies who were present at the Uppsala Assembly of the World Council of Churches. These proved sufficiently promising for the Executive Committee of the World Alliance of Reformed Churches to meet in June, 1968, to "explore elements in the new situation that may make the initiation of Reformed/Roman Catholic dialogue wise at this time." The Decree on Ecumenism of Vatican II made it clear that readiness for such dialogue existed also on the Roman Catholic side. As a result, two preliminary meetings between staff of the World Alliance of Reformed Churches and the Secretariat for Promoting Christian Unity were held, one in Geneva in November of 1968, and one in Vogelenzang (Holland) in April of 1969. These two preliminary meetings affirmed the desirability and feasibility of proceeding with official Reformed/Roman Catholic conversations on a world level.

(3) In doing so, neither body wished to detract from the importance of similar, more-or-less official conversations which had been going on for some time at the national level in Holland, France, Switzerland, the United States and other countries. Such national discussions have the advantage of being able to focus on problems common to the Church in the local situation. Since they are undertaken with the aim of being responsible to their respective official sponsors and of engaging them in the issues, these national dialogues deal with matters of considerable consequence, such as the significance of the mutual recognition of Baptism. Still, there are limitations which restrict the full significance of national talks. In many countries and areas dialogues are not occurring nor are likely to occur soon — areas, for example, where Christians are persecuted or where either Reformed or Roman Catholics are a restricted minority, or in areas where both find themselves in a society which severely discourages reconciling conversations among Christian bodies. Even where there are national dialogues, they often are conducted independently of other conversations going on between the same bodies in other contexts, which leads to much unnecessary duplication. Moreover, because of the world-wide implications of some of the issues under discussion, and because of the need to influence the centres of universal authority and coordination, it

was felt that the international dialogues were called for as ways of exploring new avenues in Reformed/Roman Catholic relations and of making wider use of the results already being obtained at the national level. It is therefore understood that the dialogues at various levels are complementary.

(4) In deciding to proceed with these official conversations at the international level, both Roman Catholic and Reformed officials were mindful of the utility of bilateral consultations with other partners then underway. These would not be duplicated, though, since there are tensions which are peculiar to the relations between these two traditions. Both parties were convinced that by addressing the other in these bi-lateral consultations they would be exercising a responsibility each feels for the other and which both feel would be mutually enriching. Both parties were strongly motivated by the need to keep the discussions in the broader perspective of how these would advance their common concern to manifest the relevance of Christ in the world today.

(5) The Geneva meeting in November of 1968 chose for the session in Vogelenzang the theme "The Presence of Christ in Church and World" " . . . because it seemed to have a bearing not only on the ultimate salvation of man but also on his life and happiness here and now. It was also expected that the discussion on the presence of Christ in Church and World, especially the meaning of his saving humanity, would tend to bring to light the differences between the two communions and that an honest appraisal of these differences could help the two traditions to overcome them and discover together what they must do in order to become more credible in the eyes of the world" (Joint Report, Vogelenzang, April 17–19, 1969).

(6) The expectations for this theme were borne out. Its discussions at Vogelenzang uncovered a need to attend to three traditional problems related to the central one of understanding the Lordship of Christ today: Christology, ecclesiology, and the attitude of the Christian in the world. Though the problems are traditional ones, the Church confronts them in a new form today: the historical conditions which shaped their earlier formulations have radically changed, developments in the secular world cry for urgent attention, and the findings of the historical sciences and biblical exegesis demand new perspectives on inherited positions. So fruitful and demanding were the results of the initial exploration of this theme that it was mandated as the theme for the subsequent official conversations which began in Rome in April of 1970. The subtopics of the series were: "Christ's Relationship to the Church" (Rome, Spring, 1970), "The Teaching Authority of the Church" (Cartigny, Switzerland, Spring, 1971), "The Presence of Christ in the World" (Bièvres, France, Winter, 1972), "The Eucharist" (Woudschoten-Zeist, the Netherlands, Winter, 1974), and "The Ministry" (Rome, March 1975). (For details of themes, sub-themes, authors and participants see Appendix.)

(7) Each delegation to these meetings was comprised of five permanent members, a staff person from each sponsoring office, and one consultant from each communion, appointed for his special expertise in the subject

under consideration at a given session. The names of the regular teams, the special consultants and the staff persons involved are listed at the end of this report.

(8)   Each meeting lasted five days and followed a regular pattern. Four position papers, two from each team, circulated in advance. Each of these papers was discussed in plenary, and subcommittees were appointed to bring to the plenary a report which summarized the initial discussion of these position papers. The whole consultation then went through these reports, discussed again the issues which were raised by them, and then came to a common statement which summarized the findings of that particular session.

(9)   The initial step in the conversations was a matter, on many issues of listening carefully to one another in order to discern what lies behind the different terminologies to which we have grown accustomed. It was not the purpose of these sessions consciously to work toward specific recommendations on the topics assigned them. Rather, the task was to locate the present convergences, continuing tensions, and open questions which emerged from the process just described. The several reports on each session were therefore more descriptive than prescriptive. The discussions were based on position papers which deliberately sought to break new ground on the topic under consideration; while the discussions were notably marked by theological perspectives which transcended predictable confessional alignments, it was understood that whatever concrete recommendation might arise from the final report would simply be the result of this process of critical inquiry and discussion.

(10)   After each meeting, a press release, the wording of which was agreed to by both delegations, was issued, but it was decided that it was best to wait until the final report, covering the whole series, was ready before publishing in any detail the results on the several discussions. At the conclusion of the fifth session, a committee was appointed to prepare a draft of the final report which was referred again to the permanent members of the conversations, who met in Rome, 21-26 March 1977, and agreed on the final report, which with recommendations went to the World Alliance of Reformed Churches and the Secretariat for Promoting Christian Unity.

(11)   The final report, presented here, deliberately refrained from any attempt at a synthesis and offers instead the agreed revision of the five separate reports with which each session was invariably concluded. The official report in its final form represents the common mind of those engaged in the various steps of its formulation and acceptance. It cannot, however, reproduce all the diversity of styles, plurality of theological method, heat of conviction and novelty of insight which went into the position papers and their discussion.

(12)   It will be seen that during its working sessions the Commission's method was determined, among other things, by the desire in the case of

each separate theme to produce a survey of the degree of agreement, disagreement and unresolved issues. But as we see it, the value of these discussions does not lie only in their necessarily provisional 'results'. What the authors of the report hope, rather, is that the readers may let themselves be drawn into the inner dynamic of the movement which gripped us from our very first meetings and never ceased to do so. The way was long and difficult and sometimes it seemed to be leading nowhere. Even though the following pages occasionally may still reveal certain inconsistencies, obstacles, reactions and surprises, we felt it impossible to eliminate these realistic features completely. But the intercessions of many, our prayers together in the name of Jesus, deepening trust, brotherly patience, scholarly seriousness, will to persist, to continue to listen to each other, not infrequently also a touch of hilarity—these things were all part and parcel of the experience which was given us with our discoveries and which can be only imperfectly reflected in the record of our discussions.

CHRIST'S RELATIONSHIP TO THE CHURCH

Response to Christ's Unifying Action

(13)   The starting point of these discussions was the recognition that, in Jesus Christ, God has made joint cause with sinful humanity and aims at the renewal of the world. Therefore all those who are connected with the name of Jesus Christ have the joint task of bearing witness to this Gospel.

The Riches of Christ and the Wealth of Witnesses

(14)   Since in Christ "the complete being of the Godhead dwells embodied" (*Col.* 2:9), there is necessarily a wealth of witnesses—which is what we actually find in the New Testament—in order that something at least of "the unfathomable riches of Christ" (*Eph.* 3:8) may be passed on. Thus the mission and task of Jesus, which are authoritative for the Church of every age and culture, including our own today, are reflected in a witness which has been characterised by choice and variety since the apostolic beginnings.

Some of the Norms of the Church, according to the New Testament

(15)   Norms for the belief and practice of the Church are not simply to be found in insolated proof-texts or in clearly discernible primitive patterns, but in the New Testament considered as a whole and as testimony to the divine purpose and mission for Israel, for the Church and for all humanity. In this respect, New Testament theology reckons with the content of the promise contained in the history of God's covenantal dealings with his people in the Old Testament.

(16)   There was complete agreement in presenting ecclesiology from a clear christological and pneumatological perspective in which the Church is the object of declared faith and cannot be completely embraced by a historical and sociological description.

There was an agreement in presenting the Church as the "body of Christ" (*cf. 1 Cor.* 12,12 f. 27; *Eph.* 5,30). The Apostle Paul's description of the Church as the body of Christ presupposes knowledge of the death, resurrection and exaltation of the Lord. The Church exists therefore as the body of Christ essentially by the Holy Spirit, just as does the exalted Lord. Stress was laid, however, on the complementary character of other images, particularly that of the bride (*cf. Eph.* 5, 25-32), which warn us against any absolute identification.

(17) Theological language is largely metaphorical because the metaphor is an indispensable way by which to understand and speak about realities which otherwise cannot be understood and expressed. A caveat was entered against any suggestion that theological language is to be understood exclusively as metaphorical language. The illegitimacy of any absolute identification is shown by other passages which interpret the body of Christ as a picture for the Church united in Christ's name (*Rom.* 12:5). It came as a surprise to us to observe that the decisions we are faced with today did not always correspond to our confessional boundaries.

The constantly different form

(18) Apart from the essential characteristics just presented which are *de rigueur* for every period and culture, the Church assumes different forms depending on the historical heritage it carries with it and the social and cultural situation in which it is set and in which it grows. Traces of a certain development are already discernible in the New Testament. It was fully agreed that the essential characteristics of the one Church assume concrete form in a variety of patterns already in the New Testament. It is correct to consult the Bible for theologies of the nature of the Church which will serve as starting points for inferring the broad outlines of a Church constitution and for examining whether the present ecclesiastical structures correspond to it. This applies, for example, to the meaning of "local church". In New Testament times a local district was a quite restricted geographical area, while in a highly technological society what is meant by local is considerably broader. But both Roman Catholic and Reformed agreed that the Church Catholic is really represented and exists in the local Church.

(19) When it comes to the correct use of the New Testament in material for contemporary doctrines of the Church and ministry, it was further recognized that difficulties are not to be easily overcome by taking only some parts of the New Testament as normative while relegating other parts to a secondary position. Christ discloses himself under the conditions of historical relativity. Theology must undertake the difficult task of seeking the normative within the relative, and of applying what is thereby found to the concrete realization of the Church in different historical situations.

(20) Theology, whether Reformed or Roman Catholic, cannot rest content with a gap between exegetical research and Church doctrine. No long-range progress in any ecumenical dialogue can be expected which does not

deal with that gap. With respect, however, to such a question as that of the relation between, on the one hand, the results of historical criticism on the direct role of Jesus Christ in the origin of the Church and, on the other hand, the acceptance of such a role by believers, it was not agreed by all that the problem is only one of a gap between exegetical research and Church doctrine. Some maintained that, in this case, we have to do rather with a distinction between using the New Testament as historical source and accepting the New Testament as witness. This does not mean that for the faithful the quest for the historical Jesus is made superfluous by a preoccupation with a supposedly different Christ of faith; it means only that the New Testament witness itself comprises a plurality of witnesses and various interpretations of the one Christ event.

In the service of Christ for the world

(21)   In the community of Christians all the members are personally bound to Christ and therefore under obligation to serve Him. Office-bearers (see chapter on "Ministry" below) are also members of the body who at one and the same time serve the Lord and the community in order to fulfil their mission in the world.

(22)   The Church does not keep aloof from the world. On the contrary, it is part of the world. As such it attests the efficacy of its Lord's word and work. At the same time it is an anticipatory announcement of what Jesus has destined for all men. In this sense the Church exists wholly for the world and even in its weakness is the salt of the earth (*cf. Mt* 5,13).

(23)   We were all agreed that the ethical decisions which necessarily follow from the Gospel of the Kingdom of God and the believing acceptance of this Gospel extend also to the realm of politics. In both confessions there were those who inclined to place greater emphasis on the need for a certain caution and those who stressed the need to derive concrete political decisions from the New Testament message and the possibility of doing so.

THE TEACHING AUTHORITY OF THE CHURCH

(24)   We are agreed that the Church has its authority to the extent that it listens to the Word Christ speaks to it ever afresh.

In the history of the Church, the difference between Catholics and Reformed has always focussed on the alternative: "Scripture and Tradition" and "Scripture only". Catholics stressed the need for and the authority of the Church's teaching office in the interpretation of Scripture, whereas the Reformed declared that Scripture interprets itself and, as God's Word, must be strictly distinguished from all human tradition, desiring in this way to do justice not only to the doctrine of justification but also to the total witness of the Old and New Testaments.

Holy Scripture

(25)   Both on the Catholic and on the Reformed side today, the problem is no longer presented in terms of the battle lines of post-Tridentine polemic.

Historical researches have shown not only how the New Testament writings are themselves already the outcome of and witness to traditions, but also how the canonisation of the New Testament was part of the development of tradition.

Since the Second Vatican Council, Catholic teaching has stressed the very close connection between Scripture and Tradition: "springing from the same divine source, both so to speak coalesce and press towards the same goal" (*Dei Verbum,* 9). Scripture and Tradition thus constitute "the one holy treasure of the Word of God bequeathed to the Church" (*Dei Verbum,* 10) with a special dignity attaching to the Scriptures because in them the apostolic preaching has been given especially clear expression (*cf. Dei Verbum,* 8).

In the light of these facts, the customary distinction between Scripture and Tradition as two different sources which operate as norms either alternatively or in parallel has become impossible.

(26)   We are agreed that as *creatura Verbi* the Church together with its Tradition stands under the living Word of God and that the preacher and teacher of the Word is to be viewed as servant of the Word (*cf. Lk* 1,2) and must teach only what the Holy Spirit permits him to hear in the Scriptures. This hearing and teaching take place in a living combination with the faith, life and, above all, the worship of the community of Christ.

We are agreed that the development of doctrine and the production of confessions of faith is a dynamic process. In this process the Word of God proves its own creative, critical and judging power. Through the Word, therefore, the Holy Spirit guides the Church to reflection, conversion and reform.

(27)   Since we approach our dealings with the Scriptures from our own particular tradition, in each case, we tend to hear God's Word in different ways: we understand even central affirmations from different standpoints and emphasise them in different ways.

Since Scripture is clothed in the language and concepts of the ancient world and is related only indirectly to our modern problems, all churches must perforce go beyond the immediate letter of Scripture.

In addition there is the internal diversity of Holy Scripture with which we are more closely familiar today.

For all these reasons the Church is compelled and obliged constantly to reinterpret the biblical message.

(28)   In this area of interpretation different forms of tradition have been developed, the legitimation of one's own particular practice occasionally providing one of the motivating elements. On the whole the Reformed

sought a direct support for their doctrine in the apostolic witness of Scripture, whereas the Roman Catholic Church perceived the apostolic witness more strongly in the life of faith of the whole Church, in the measure that it constantly strove in the course of the centuries to apprehend the fullness of the divine truth (*cf. Dei Verbum,* 8).

This difference in attitude may rest on a difference in pneumatology: Catholic thought is primarily sustained by confidence in the *continuing* presence of the Spirit as a *constantly renewed* gift of the ascended Lord.

(29) In the Reformed Churches, the so-called "Scripture principle", i.e. the confidence that the Word of God constantly creates the understanding of itself afresh, postulates in the life of the Church a carefully maintained relationship between the theologically trained servant of the Word and the theologically informed, responsible total community.

(30) The Catholic Church stresses within the community the special service of those who with the aid of the Holy Spirit accept pastoral responsibility and must also make provision, therefore, for the right interpretation and proclamation of the Word of God.

Canon

(31) The conviction of the Church is that it hears the voice of the living Lord which also speaks today out of the writings of the apostles and prophets. Since it is the same Holy Spirit who inspired the authors of the sacred books and who enlightens the Church's readers today, the Church has the promise of hearing God's Word from the Bible even today and tomorrow.

(32) The Scriptures were accepted by the ancient Church because these writings attested the living tradition of the Gospel (summed up in the so-called *regula fidei*) because they were written by the apostles as eyewitnesses or by their disciples, handed down by the Church which itself has an apostolic origin. In accordance with both the Catholic and the Reformed tradition, the Church played its part in the process whereby the canon was formed, even if we cannot define this part more precisely.

In the light of this common understanding, the traditional controversy as to whether canonisation was the decision of a "possessing" Church or the receiving recognition of an "obeying" Church is out of date.

(33) The ancient Church took the view that the different voices speaking in the Canon can and should come to expression side by side in the Church, since despite their differences, they all point to the same centre, namely to salvation in Jesus Christ.

The apostolic witness has primary significance therefore. It remains a continuing task of both Churches to explicate and to ensure respect for the not merely historical but also theological precedence of the apostolic period.

Confessions

(34) Raising the question whether the establishment of the confession of

faith is for the Church a creative activity or an advance in its perception of the fulness already given, we noted once again that the dialogue was made more difficult by questions of terminology, since the term "confession of faith" occupies a different position in our two traditions and we recognised the importance of remembering the different functions which confessions of faith can have in the Church and in society.

(35)   We tried, nevertheless, to bring out certain points of convergence and to identify, too, the different and opposing positions.

For its witness in the world, the Church must always express its faith by confessions in which it interprets the Word of God in the language of today, a task which is never completed. Such a confession of faith is always the expression of an experience of salvation as lived in the Church at a given moment of its history.

(36)   The history of Christian doctrine presents us with a process of constant interpretative efforts with discontinuous stages of restructuring, each of which represents the Church's effort to reformulate its faith in a particular age and cultural environment. But this discontinuity of structuring is not opposed to a homogeneity of meaning: the transcendence of this meaning is thus emphasized in relation to these formulations. In consequence none of the proposed formulations is definitive in the sense that there will never be any need for a new interpretation in a new social and cultural situation. The more so since the inexhaustible riches of the revelation deposited in Scripture constantly compel us to return to the foundation event to discover again and again in it new aspects unsuspected by previous generations.

(37)   For the Catholics, the affirmations of the past are normative as guides for subsequent reformulations. For the Reformed, they have a real positive value which is nevertheless subordinate to the authority of Scripture.

So far as instruction is concerned, for the Reformed it is the community as a whole which is responsible and which delegates qualified people; whereas for the Catholics there is a distinctive responsibility of the pastoral ministry: the latter is rooted in the believing community but does not derive its authority from an act of delegation on the part of the latter.

(38)   Practice, however, often differs somewhat from theoretical affirmations, either because these are illegitimately hardened or because in fact compensatory elements play a part. Among the Reformed there are people, whether or not invested with official authority, who in fact play a considerable role. Among the Catholics stress is laid on the importance of the "sense of the faith", common to the whole of the believers, by which they discern the Word of God and adhere to it (*cf. Lumen Gentium,* 12), and which finds concrete expression in, among other things, the actual "reception", constantly renewed, of councils and the decisions of the teaching authority.

Infallibility

(39)   Whereas the Reformed note that the expression "the infallibility of the Church" is almost never used in their tradition, Catholics note for their part that this word is relatively a recent one in theological terminology and seems hardly a happy term because of the maximising interpretations to which it often gives rise. As for the theology of infallibility, apart from the fact that too often there has been a tendency to reduce the question of the infallibility of the Church to the particular problem of the infallibility of the Pope, and even to a certain manner of exercising this latter, it should be stated that it has been developed into a one-sidedly juridical problem which makes it all the more irreconcilable with Reformed thinking. We are nevertheless able to formulate a certain viewpoint in common.

(40)   The promise made by God to the Church is this: God remains faithful to his covenant and, despite the weaknesses and errors of Christians, he makes his Word heard in the Church.

(41)   Catholics hold that God's faithfulness to his Church necessarily means that when the People of God unanimously declares that a doctrine has been revealed by God and therefore demands the assent of faith, it cannot fall into error. And in particular that those who have been specially charged with the teaching mission are protected by a special charisma when it is a matter of presenting the revealed message. "The bishops taken in isolation do not enjoy the prerogative of infallibility; yet, even though dispersed throughout the world and conserving the bond and communion between them and with the successor of Peter, when in their authentic teaching concerning questions of faith and morals they declare with full agreement that it is necessary to support unhesitatingly such and such a point of doctrine, they then announce infallibly the teaching of Christ. This is all the more evident when, assembled in an ecumenical council, they teach and decide on questions of faith and morals for the whole Church; and their definitions must be adhered to in the obedience of faith" (*Lumen Gentium*, 25).

This is equally the case when the bishop of Rome, in the rare cases specified by Vatican I, expresses himself *ex cathedra*. Nevertheless, what has just been said does not imply that all the expressions chosen are necessarily the best available nor again that the ecclesial authorities enjoy this charisma in a permanent manner or that they cannot be mistaken in a certain number of affirmations on which they do not commit themselves fundamentally.

(42)   The Reformed rejection of any infallibility which is accorded to men derives from a repugnance to bind God and the Church in this way, in view of the sovereignty of Christ over the Church and of the liberty of the Spirit, a repugnance strengthened by the experience of frequent errors and resistances to the Word on the part of the Church. In addition there is a fear lest confidence in the infallibility of a formulation should distort the personal character of faith in the living Christ; further, the fact that many

Reformed take the resistance of man to the Spirit of God so seriously today that any assertion of the infallibility of the Church becomes impossible. Apart from that, for Reformed sensibility, any claim to infallibility in the modern world represents an obstacle to the credibility of the proclamation.

The misgivings concerning the idea of ecclesiastical infallibility do not detract from the decisive though subordinate weight given in the Reformed tradition to the ancient Ecumenical Councils in the transmission and interpretation of the Gospel. For the Reformed, however, what alone is infallible, properly speaking, is God's fidelity to his covenant, whereby he corrects and preserves his Church by the Spirit until the consummation of his reign.

THE PRESENCE OF CHRIST IN THE WORLD

Creation and Redemption

(43)   God is present in the world as its Creator, Sustainer, Lord of history who rules all things as Loving Father. Frequently in the history of Christian thought and today the point of departure for speaking of Christ's presence in the world is ecclesiological: Christ is present in the Church and through his Lordship over the Church, he exercises his Lordship over the world. This position leads to the conclusions that Christ's presence is limited to the presence the Church mediates, that he acts only in the Church, that his Lordship over the world operates only through the Church's mission, and that when the world and the Church are in conflict, Christ is always on the side of the Church. Of course the Church is the beloved Bride of Christ for whom he gave himself (*cf. Eph.* 5:25 ff.). Nevertheless, and for this reason above all, judgement begins at the house of God (*cf. 1 Pet.* 4:17).

(44)   Though it is true that there is a presence of Christ in the Church which places her in special relationship to the world, an "ecclesiological monopoly" on the presence of Christ and the conclusions which follow from it are exegetically untenable. The presence of Christ in the world is a consequence of the continuity of God's action in creation and redemption. This continuity of God's acting in creation and redemption is found in the covenant he made in the Old Testament with Israel and renewed and transformed in the New Testament with all humanity. The continuity laid emphasis on the political and social implications of the saving work of Christ as well as on faith as a personal engagement. In the New Testament "the new creation" (*cf. 2 Cor.* 5,17) is seen as the restoration and completion of the purposes of the Creator. Christ is the redeemer of the whole world, in him God has reconciled the world to himself (2 Cor. 5.19). The universal dimensions of the Lordship of the one Christ (*cf. Eph.* 1,21 ff.), to which Holy Scripture witnesses, speak pointedly today to a world deeply fragmented and in search of its unity.

(45) It is through the Spirit that Christ is at work in creation and redemption. As the presence in the world of the risen Lord, the Spirit affirms and manifests the resurrection and effects the new creation. Christ who is Lord of all and active in creation points to God the Father who, in the Spirit, leads and guides history where there is no unplanned development.

(46) The Father is the absolutely primary principle for he is "source, guide and goal of all that is" (*Rom.* 11:36; *cf. 1 Cor.* 8:6). The reason why we have been elected and predestinated in Christ is to "cause his glory to be praised" (*Eph.* 1.12,6). The purpose of the mystery of Christ himself is to make known to the rulers and authorities the infinite wisdom of God (*Eph.* 3:10). After the Fall, mankind became more and more alienated from the one God. One of the fruits of the messianic era will be that every knee shall bow to God (*Isa.* 45:23), that all the peoples will worship him (*Ps.* 22:30). This is what the Gospel of John means when it says: "This is my Father's glory, that you may bear fruit in plenty and so be my disciples" (*Jn.* 15:8).

(47) In response to the revelation of this triune God, Christians affirm that the purposefulness of history is the framework in which the diverse realities of all human activities are to be understood. On this ground we can also recognize that the process of secularisation, with its rejection of every clerical and theological qualification, has given all aspects of life an autonomy whose validity theology has come to recognize and this has stimulated us to seek for new ways of expressing Christ's involvement in the world. This remains true even if we do not agree with the rejection of transcendence which has often accompanied this process and even if we detect here the secularism which results from it as well as the adherence to various religions or pseudo-religions.

(48) We are agreed that there is a presence of the Spirit of Christ in the world. How and where can we recognize this effective presence? This problem presents us with a series of questions which arise today for all churches. These questions may be formulated as follows:

We look for his presence in the plan or purpose which God is realizing through all the complexities of history.

We look for his presence as Lord of history in those movements of the human spirit which, with or without the assistance of the Church, are achieving the ends of his Kingdom.

We look for his presence in those values and standards which owe their origin to the Gospel, but now have become embedded in public conscience and institutions.

(49) But in these questions we keep before us the following convictions:
— In the Cross Christ identifies himself with men in their sin (*cf. Isa.* 53, 4f.11f.; *Jn* 1,29; *2 Cor* 5,21) and need in order that they might be identified with him in the new victorious life of his resurrection (*cf. Rom* 6,4f.; *Col* 3,1-4). The first identification remains true and effective even

where it is not recognized. Christ is present in the poor and helpless who cry for liberation.

— The challenge of the world to the Church and its appeal for help may be at the same time a challenge and appeal from Christ, who in this way judges his Church, demands obedience and calls it to reformation.

— The Christian who looks back on his own life will say that Christ was active in it, leading him to repentance, conversion, and faith, even before he was aware or made any conscious response. We are therefore bound to claim, that Christ is similarly active in the lives of others for whom faith lies still in the future.

(50)   The Christian who recognizes the presence and activity of Christ in these forms will rejoice in them and be willing to cooperate with them. This is not to say that either the salvation of the individual or the transformation of society is complete unless the work of Christ is brought to conscious recognition through the power of the Spirit to interpret and convince. People can be liberated from the demonic dangers of absolute autonomy only by a firm recognition of the creatureliness and transience of the world they are trying to transform. To bring this world under the rule of God does not mean that in it we are to have our abiding city (*cf. Hebr* 13,14). There is no dichotomy between the Christians' personal response to the Christ they find in the Church and their corporate response along with others, Christian and non-Christian alike, to the Christ who confronts them with the world. To participate in the divine life by grace is to participate in God's love for the world which he has created and which, with the help of responsible and responsive people, he is re-creating.

Church and World

(51)   The Creator of the world does not want mankind to destroy itself through lack of liberty, peace and justice (*cf. Ezek* 18,32). Rather, through the revelation of his will, he leads mankind onto the road of salvation and in Jesus Christ offers it the gift of final redemption from all ungodly ties and participation in his divine life and thus in his freedom.

This movement towards freedom already begins with the election of the old people of the covenant, a people that he continually calls back to serve him freely.

(52)   In Jesus Christ there takes place the final reconcilation and with it also the call to the whole of the world (*cf. 2 Cor.* 5, 18-21). The Church that Christ has sent into the world has to carry this message of liberation (*cf. Lk* 4, 18 f.; *Jn* 8, 31-36; *Rom* 6, 18-22) among the peoples of the world, and with it also the call to that freedom which is God's gift to people in grace, all with a view to the perfection in which God will ultimately construct peace and liberty (*Cf.* Rom 8, 19-21). This statement already makes it clear that the fundamental relationship between the Church and the world lies in Jesus Christ who at one and the same time is the Head of the Church and the Lord of the world (*cf. Hebr* 1,2 f.; *Revel* 17, 14; 19, 15 f.).

(53) The Church professes that Christ himself is the carrier of the message of the rule of God and the liberation of mankind. If the Church goes out into the world, if it brings the Gospel to men and endeavours to realize more justice, more conciliation and more peace, then in doing so it is only following its Lord into domains that, unbeknown to men, already belong to him and where he is already anonymously at work.

(54) The Church was founded by Christ to share in the life which comes from the Father and it is sent to lead the world to Jesus Christ, to its full maturity for the glory and praise of the Father. It is therefore called to be the visible witness and sign of the liberating will of God, of the redemption granted in Jesus Christ, and of the kingdom of peace that is to come. The Church carries out this task by what it does and what it says, but also simply by being what it is, since it belongs to the nature of the Church to proclaim the word of judgement and grace, and to serve Christ in the poor, the oppressed and the desperate. (*Mt* 25, 31-40) More particularly, however, it comes together for the purpose of adoration and prayer, to receive ever new instruction and consolation and to celebrate the presence of Christ in the sacrament; around this centre, and with the multiplicity of the gifts granted by the Spirit (*cf. 1 Cor* 12, 4-11,28-30; *Rom* 12, 6-8; *Eph.* 4,11) it lives as a *koinonia* of those who need and help each other. We consequently believe in a special presence of Christ in the Church by which it is placed in a quite special position in relation to the world and we believe that the Church stands under the special aid of the Holy Spirit, above all in its ministry of preaching and sacraments. (*cf. Jn* 14,16.25f.; 15,26; 16,7-14)

(55) The Church can therefore correspond to its calling if its structure and its life are fashioned by love and freedom. Accordingly the Church does not seek to win human beings for a secular programme of salvation by propagandistic methods but to convert them to Christ and in this way to serve them. In its proclamation of the Gospel there is at the same time a powerful creative cultural dynamic.

(56) As a *communio* structured in this way the Church contradicts the structures of the various sectors of the life of modern secular society: opposing exploitation, oppression, manipulation, intellectual and political pressures of all kinds. The renewal of Christian congregations as authentic life forms will also influence the wider social and political context.

(57) In addition, the Christian commitment of alert and responsible Christians has often been organized in political parties, professional associations, trade unions and suchlike, with or without guidance from the official church authorities.

There is today a certain crisis in these activities. The solution of specific problems facing them today requires much expertise. In addition it sometimes happens that the claim of certain parties and interest groups to represent a Christian position is an obstacle to the Christian witness to all human beings. The decision on this question in each case may differ according to country and circumstance; but for us there is no specific confessional difference here.

(58) The official church authorities, who are often regarded as representatives of their communities, have to pay careful attention to whether and in what respects they are obliged by their Lord to speak a prophetic and pastoral word to the general public. Such an obligation will arise especially when no one else speaks up against certain injustices or abuses.

(59) Along the road which the Church at any given time takes through the world in the solidarity with human beings commanded by Christ, it must not tie itself down to a programme of its own but always remain open for ever new directives of the Holy Spirit promised to it. The Holy Spirit strengthens it in spite of all imperfectness and provisionality of social, even Christian, fashioning of life in fidelity to its redeemer and in obedience to the creator and upholder of the world. The Spirit is himself the pledge (*cf. Eph* 1,14; *2 Cor* 1,22) that its hope in the consummation of the recreation of the world will not be disappointed. (*cf. Rom* 8, 11,19-21; *2 Petr* 3,13).

The Church as the Effective Sign of Christ's Presence in the World

(60) The Church exposes its fundamental orientations and controlling loyalties by the way it lives, no matter what it says to the contrary. When the Church turns inward on itself and clings to outdated structures, it gives the impression that Christ is its exclusive possession rather than its Lord who goes before and leads. When the Church is truly a pilgrim people on the way through the world (*cf. Hebr* 13,14; *Phil* 3,20; *Gal* 4,26; *1 Petr* 2,11), it bears witness that Christ is the Lord over the world as well as the Church. The Church is a worshipping community whose prayers are inseparable from its prophetic and diaconal service. In worship and witness the Church celebrates the central fact of Christ's unity with his people. Being united to Christ in his death and resurrection, the Church is empowered with the Spirit to walk in newness of life and so to be a converted and converting presence in Christ's world. By living as a new people persuaded of God's acceptance in Christ, the Church is a persuasive sign of God's love for all his creation and of his liberating purpose for all men.

(61) In a world undergoing a profound transformation, the Church cannot become set in immobility on the plea that it is immutable, but must above all be listening to the Word of God in which it will discern, beyond all "conservatism" and all "progressivism", the transformations required of it precisely in virtue of its fidelity to this Word.

(62) First, the localness and the catholicity of the Church are to be kept in perspective. It is only by participating in the local community that we share in the life of the universal Church, but the local community without universality (in particular the small basic communities but likewise the local Churches at regional level) runs the risk of becoming a ghetto or of being arbitrarily dominated by individuals.

(63) Second, practical changes must take account of the great variety of

situations confronting the Churches and these changes presuppose both a de-centralization of the Church and a larger participation on all levels, quite especially on what is commonly (and perhaps misleadingly) called the laity.

Participation is essential because it springs from the very nature of the Christian vocation and also because a great many fields are quite inaccessible to the Church except through its lay members who live and work in them. Moreover this participation is important because the Church's effective witness depends in very large measure on expertise of the laity in diverse fields, expertise which the clergy do not have, have not had, but too often have presumed to have. However their participation in the life of the church is not merely to be seen in terms of their professional expertise. They also have the specific spiritual ministry, which they exercise through all activities including their technical competence. The church in all its members is ministerial.

(64) Third, the Church must take great care not to act too prematurely today, as it too often did in the past, to suppress disturbingly novel expressions of spiritual life and spontaneous forms of community, on the ground that they are merely expressions of the human spirit and not also expressions of the Holy Spirit.

(65) Fourth, the Church's faithful mutation is to be seen as consistent with the Church's historical character. This means that apostolic continuity, perhaps quite diversely defined, is integral to the Church's identity through change. It also means that when the Church has been obediently changeable, it has always taken into account the diverse socio-political and cultural contexts in which Christ's presence was known and confessed. Here arises the question of what belongs to the 'establishment' of the Church and of what emerges from the structures which Christ intended for His Church.

(66) In incorporating these and other characteristics of change we discussed how they will bear upon the new manifestation of the unity of the Church which is now emerging. The slogan "unity in necessary things" has been accepted but we have not yet specified what is necessary. An "ecumenism of convergence" with its focus on what is necessary will not demand uniformity nor the death of pluralism.

THE EUCHARIST

The Biblical Basis

(67) Reflection on the celebration of the Eucharist must start from the biblical sources, i.e.:
from the celebration of the Lord's Supper in the primitive Church,
from the celebration of the Last Supper of Jesus,
from the Old Testament background, particularly, the Jewish Passover.

(68)   When the Christian community assembled with glad and generous hearts (*Acts* 2:46) it celebrated the memorial of the death and resurrection of Jesus, experienced his presence as the exalted Lord in his Spirit and looked forward longingly to his return in glory. It thus regarded itself as the pilgrim People of God.

(69)   The traditional words of Jesus at the Last Supper, despite the differences in their transmission, recall that his acceptance of death "for many" inaugurates the new covenant of God with his People. The fulfilment of the old covenant does not mean the rejection of Israel (*cf. Rom* 11,1 f. 28 f.) but on the contrary the continuation of God's promises which are operative in the new gift of salvation in virtue of the reconciling fruits of the death of Jesus.

(70)   If this background is taken seriously, new possibilities of mitigating the traditional confessional quarrels emerge from the understanding of the New Testament accounts of the institution: for example,

In the words of institution the emphasis is on the fact of the personal presence of the living Lord in the event of the memorial and fellowship meal, not on the question as to how this real presence, (the word "is") comes about and is to be explained. The eating and drinking and the memorial character of the passover meal, with which the New Testament links Jesus' last meal, proclaim the beginning of the new covenant.

When Christ gives the apostles the commission "Do this in remembrance of me" the word "remembrance" means more than merely a mental act of "recalling".

The term "body" means the whole person of Jesus, the saving presence of which is experienced in the meal.

(71)   Reflection on the biblical sources along these lines can also help to relativise certain traditional alternatives (influenced by a dualistic anthropology and cosmology) which encumber the dialogue between the confessions (as for example, realism/symbolism, sacramentalism/inwardness, substance/form, subject/object). In relation to an objectification which tends to rigidity, the original biblical way of thinking helps us to a more profound understanding of the character of the Eucharist as an event.

(72)   The glorified body of the Lord with which the New Testament community had fellowship in the Supper is to be understood in accordance with the description of the risen Jesus Christ as the second Adam, who is both a body determined by the Spirit (*soma pneumatikon 1 Cor* 15:44) and a life creating Spirit (*pneuma zoopoioun 1 Cor* 15:45).

(73)   The concept of *koinonia* stresses not only fellowship with the exalted Lord Jesus Christ, but beyond this and precisely because of this also the fellowship of all who partake of the meal and are called together into the community of the Lord (*1 Cor* 10:17).

(74)   Reflection on the Supper of the primitive Christian community must not contemplate the past in retrospect and seek to restore it; on the con-

trary, it must liberate us for a new priestly ministry (*1 Pet* 2:9), which the Church has to perform in relation to the world of today.

The Paschal Mystery of Christ and the Eucharist

(75) Christ sends us into the world with the message of a new life and a new common life in fellowship with him. In our speaking and acting he bears witness to himself. His Gospel gathers, protects and maintains the *koinonia* of his disciples as a sign and beginning of his kingdom. He himself constantly calls this community to the memorial of his death; he himself comes into its midst as the living One through his word and causes this word to take shape in the celebration of the Supper in which he deepens and seals (*cf. Jn* 15,4f.; 6,56 f.; *1 Cor* 10,16) his fellowship with us and in which the new life of fellowship of Christendom is represented to the world (*1 Jn* 1:3). The presidence of the commissioned church office-bearer is there to show the assembled community that it does not have disposal itself over the Eucharist but simply carries out obediently what Christ has commissioned the Church to do.

(76) The fellowship and witness of the Church depend on its being filled by God with his Spirit (*cf. Lk* 24, 49; *Acts* 1,8; *Tit* 3,6).

The way of the disciples through the world since his return to the Father has been characterised by his hiddenness (*cf.* 1 *Jn* 3, 1 f.; 1 *Cor* 4, 9-13; *Jn* 15, 18-2). They await his return (*cf.* Phil 3,20 f.; Col 3,4; 1 *Jn* 2,28) and remain dependent on his promise never to leave them or forsake them (*cf. Jn* 14,18 f.; *Mt* 28,20). In the eucharistic meal they again and again experience his keeping of his promise.

This free, gracious presence of the Lord takes place in the Holy Spirit (*cf.* 1 *Cor* 2,10-13; *Jn* 14,16-20; 16,13-15), i.e., he himself lays the foundation for it, creates in itself and in us the means by which he imprints his presence in us, pours out on us his gifts and equips us to serve him.

So the Lord himself comes to us in his Spirit (*cf. Rom* 8,9; *Jn* 7,38 f.) through his word, attests himself in the holy signs and, giving his Church spiritual food and drink, accompanies it towards the future of the Kingdom in which the counsel of God finds its fulfilment.

(77) The whole saving work of God has its basis, centre and goal in the person of the glorified Christ.

Christ himself did not seek his own glory but the glory of him who sent him (*cf. Jn* 8:50; 7:18). Similarly he said: "It is meat and drink for me to do the will of him who sent me until I have finished his work" (*Jn* 4:34).

(78) The One who is exalted to God's right hand lived among us and died among us. He shared our spatial and temporal existence; despite our sin he was our fellow human being. In his exaltation, he remains what he was: the obedient son (*cf. Hebr* 5,8 f.; *Phil* 2,8) and our brother. In solidarity with the glorified One we live in the reality which he opened up to us by his life and death.

(79) This is experienced, confessed and portrayed by the Christian com-

munity in its celebration of the Supper with him. United with Christ by the
Holy Spirit, incorporated in him by baptism (*cf. 1 Cor* 12,12f.), it constantly receives anew his humanity in which he lived, died and was
glorified for us, as the real bond with God himself (*cf. Jn* 6,57).

(80) In his person, his life, his death and his resurrection, Christ has
established the new covenant.

In him person and work cannot be separated. What he did, derives its
saving power from what he is. He is our salvation because of what he did:

Christ the mediator (*cf. 1 Tim* 2,5; *Hebr* 8,6; 9,15) is no hybrid. He is
himself personally the mediation. In him and through him God's self-
offering to us as human beings is accomplished; in him and through him
humanity's surrender to God.

The sacrifice brought by Jesus Christ is his obedient life and death (*cf.
Hebr* 10,5-10; *Phil* 2,8). His once-for-all self-offering under Pontius
Pilate is continued by him for ever in the presence of the Father in virtue
of his resurrection. In this way he is our sole advocate in heaven (*cf. Hebr*
9,11 f.24; 10,13 f. 19-21; 7,24 f.; 1 *Jn 2,1; Rom* 8,34). He sends us his Spirit
so that we weak human beings, too, may call upon the Father and can also
make intercession for the world (*cf. Gal* 4,5; *Rom* 8,15 f.26).

(81) In its joyful prayer of thanksgiving, "in the Eucharist", when the
Church of Christ remembers his reconciling death for our sins and for the
sins of the whole world, Christ himself is present, who "gave himself up on
our behalf as an offering and sacrifice whose fragrance is pleasing to God"
(*Eph* 5:2). Sanctified by his Spirit, the Church, through, with and in God's
Son, Jesus Christ, offers itself to the Father. It thereby becomes a living
sacrifice of thanksgiving, through which God is publicly praised (*cf. Rom*
12,1; *1 Petr* 2,5).

The validity, strength and effect of the Supper are rooted in the cross
of the Lord and in his living presence in the Holy Spirit. Far from bypass-
ing us, they are fulfilled in our faith, love and service.

The witness, celebration and fruits of the Eucharist are crystallisa-
tions of the Church's proclamation and fellowship. They are therefore sustained by every movement in which the eternal Father for Christ's sake and
through him, accepts and recreates the lost world in the Holy Spirit.

The Presence of Christ in the Lord's Supper

(82) As often as we come together in the Church to obey our Lord's command to "do this in *anamnesis* of me", he is in our midst. This is the
presence of the Son of God who for us men and for our salvation became
man and was made flesh. Through the offering of his body we have been
sanctified and are made partakers of God. This is the great mystery
(*Sacramentum*) of Christ, in which he has incorporated himself into our
humanity, and in partaking of which the Church is built up as the Body of
Christ. This is the same mystery dispensed to us in the eucharistic celebration, for when we bless the cup it is the communion of the blood of Christ,

and when we break the bread it is the communion of the body of Christ (*1 Cor.* 10,16). The realisation of this presence of Christ to us and of our union and incorporation with him is the proper work of the Holy Spirit, which takes place in the eucharistic celebration as the Church calls upon the Father to send down his Holy Spirit to sanctify both the worshipping people and the bread and wine. How Christ is present in the Eucharist, we may apprehend to a certain extent by looking at the work of the same Holy Spirit, *e.g.*, in the birth of Jesus of the Virgin Mary and in his resurrection in body from the grave — although as acts of God they are explicable only from the side of God and not from the side of man.

(83) It is in this light that we may understand something of the specific presence of Jesus Christ in the Eucharist, which is at once sacramental and personal. He comes to us clothed in his Gospel and saving passion, so that our partaking of him is communion in his body and blood (*John* 6, 47-56; *1 Cor.* 10, 17). This presence is sacramental in that it is the concrete form which the mystery of Christ takes in the eucharistic communion of his body and blood. It is also personal presence because Jesus Christ in his own person is immediately present, giving himself in his reality both as true God and true Man. In the Eucharist he communicates himself to us in the whole reality of his divinity and humanity — body, mind and will, and at the same time he remains the Son who is in the Father as the Father is in him.

(84) The Reformed and Roman Catholics are convinced of the centrality of this common christological confession. The specific mode of Christ's real presence in the Eucharist is thus to be interpreted as the presence of the Son who is both consubstantial with us in our human and bodily existence while being eternally consubstantial with the Father and the Holy Spirit in the Godhead (*John* 17, 21-23). It is important to see that Calvin's Christology was mainly inspired by the theology of St. Cyril of Alexandria and of St. Athanasius. It would be easy to be misled by the term "extra Calvinisticum" which arose out of early 17th century polemics among Protestants; and even the Calvinist teaching then was that after the incarnation the eternal Word, fully joined to the humanity in the hypostatic union, was nevertheless not restricted to, or contained within the flesh, but existed *"etiam* extra carnem". This doctrine, that the logos is at the same time incarnate and present in the whole world, is not a Calvinist speciality, but is common to the Christology of pre-Chalcedonian as well as post-Chalcedonian orthodoxy, East and West. What clearly matters is the fully trinitarian context which is guarded by this doctrine and the Christological presuppositions on which there are no fundamental disagreements between Roman Catholic and Reformed traditions.

(85) We celebrate the Eucharist with confidence because in Jesus Christ we have the new and living way which he has opened for us through his flesh (*Heb.* 10, 19-20). He is both Apostle from God and our High Priest (*cf. Heb.* 3,1) who has consecrated us together with him into one, so that in his self-offering to the Father through the eternal Spirit (*cf. Heb.* 9,14),

he offers us also in himself and so through our union with him we share in that self-offering made on our behalf. It is the same Spirit who cries "Abba, Father" (*cf. Mk.* 14,36) in him who cries "Abba, Father" in us, as we in the Eucharist take the Lord's Prayer into our own mouth (*Rom.* 8, 15f., 26f.).

(86)   In this union of the Church on earth with the risen and ascended Christ, which he continues to sustain through its eucharistic communion with him, the Church is enabled by grace to participate in his reconciling mission to the world. Christ and his Church share in this in different ways. Christ vicariously as Mediator and Redeemer, the Church as the community of the redeemed to whom he has entrusted the ministry of reconciliation (*cf.* 2 *Cor.* 5, 18) and stewardship of the mysteries (*cf.* 1 *Cor.* 4.1). "As often as you eat this bread and drink this cup you proclaim the Lord's death till he comes" (*1 Cor.* 11, 26). Thus precisely because the mission of the Church is grounded in, and sustained through eucharistic communion with Christ, it is sent out by Christ into all nations and all ages in the service of the Gospel, in reliance upon his promise that he will be present to it always unto the end of the world (*cf. Mt.* 28, 18-20).

The Eucharist and the Church: Christ, the Church and the Eucharist

(87)   "This one accepts sinners and eats with them" (*Lk.* 15:2), is characteristic of Christ's work. The power and effect of his death and resurrection confront and confound the power of death and sin. The institution of the Eucharist constitutes the Church as the community of love where the power of his death and resurrection is mediated by the One intercessor between God and the sinner. For the time between his first and second coming, our Lord instituted the Eucharist as a sacrificial meal. Sinful men and women, rich and poor, religious and secular people, united at the Lord's table, are the first-fruits of that communion, peace and joy, which are promised to all who hunger and thirst for righteousness (*cf. Mt.* 5,6).

The Eucharist and the Renewal of the Church

(88)   The Eucharist is a source and criterion for the renewal of the Church. The Church's renewed understanding of the Eucharist may lead to a renewed way of celebrating the Eucharist, revealing the Church more clearly as essentially "the Eucharistic community".

The renewal of the Church through the Eucharist includes a continuous summons to church unity. The division of the churches at the precise point where the Church should reveal its true nature as the one, holy, catholic and apostolic Church calls urgently for ecumenical agreement on the meaning of the Eucharist and its relation to the Church.

At the same time the Eucharist requires and inspires the Church's sense of her vocation to bring the Gospel to the whole world in proclaiming the good news of God's salvation and exercising the work of reconciliation in its deeds. Since the Eucharist means "thanksgiving" the members of the Church will show forth a life that is inspired and sustained by this sense of gratitude. Renewal, unity and mission are inseparable characteristics of the Church as it receives in faith the gift of the Eucharist.

Eucharist, Liturgy and Dogma

(89) The Eucharist is an expression of the Church's faith. That faith is expressed in part in its liturgical life, according to the principle "lex orandi, lex credendi". It is an essential function of liturgy to hand on the Gospel in the formulations of its prayer, and also in the forms of ritual practice.

In the course of history certain formulae have been taken up in dogmatic and liturgical usage, primarily as protective devices to safeguard the faith against misinterpretation. These formulae have been usually developed from a context of controversy, from which the passage of time has tended to detach them. Such formulations need to be re-examined in order to see whether they are still adequate as safeguards against misunderstanding, or have themselves become sources of misunderstanding, especially in the ecumenical situation.

There is therefore a pastoral responsibility on the churches to see that such formulae contribute to the genuine communication of the Gospel to the contemporary world.

The Eucharist and Church Organization

(90) In the visible aspects of the Church, the Eucharist should reveal to the world the authentic reality of the Church. Similarly, the Eucharist should continually empower the Church to recall itself to the vision of that reality. The Eucharist thus enables the Church both to reveal its true nature to the world, and to shape itself in conformity to that same reality.

As a community of men and women living in the world, the Church organizes itself in varying ways in the course of history. This organization of the Church's way of life should not obscure the true face of the Church, but allow it to be seen in its true being. It is the Eucharist which is the source of continuing scrutiny of the organization and life of the Church.

In particular, the law of the Church should reflect Christ's law of love and freedom. The Church's law is not an absolute, but always serves a pilgrim people. One of the functions of that law is to promote the constant renewal of the Church in its preaching of the Gospel and in its service to mankind. The law of the Church must be in harmony with the law of the Kingdom, revealed in the Eucharist.

General Comment

(91) While we are aware of the serious discrepancy between our claims to common theological understanding and our actual practices, we gratefully acknowledge the way our investigations and discussions have resulted in a greater appreciation of the richness in our respective eucharistic doctrines and practices. We believe we have reached a common understanding of the

meaning and purpose and basic doctrine of the Eucharist, which is in agreement with the Word of God and the universal tradition of the Church. We also believe that the way is clearly opening out before us on which remaining misunderstandings and disagreements about the Lord's Supper can be cleared up. The terminology which arose in an earlier polemical context is not adequate for taking account of the extent of common theological understanding which exists in our respective churches. Thus we gratefully acknowledge that both traditions, Reformed and Roman Catholic, hold to the belief in the Real Presence of Christ in the Eucharist; and both hold at least that the Eucharist is, among other things:

(1) a memorial of the death and resurrection of the Lord;

(2) a source of loving communion with him in the power of the Spirit (hence the epiclesis in the liturgy), and

(3) a source of the eschatological hope for his coming again.

Lines of Investigation

(92) Our dialogue has convinced us of the urgent need to pursue the following questions:

— the constitutive elements of a eucharistic service, especially in view of its relation to certain forms of Christian fellowship, called in some countries "agape-celebrations";

— the use of the Eucharist today which grows out of a faithful reflection on the tradition and on the vast changes which typify life today;

— the urgent contemporary pastoral questions of mutual eucharistic hospitality.

Study of these questions should take into account:

— the rich connotations of memorial (anamnesis);

— the biblical and patristic "non-dualist" categories;

— the false antinomies which can be corrected by a study of such themes as "body, person, presence, spiritual";

— the question of the proper role of the ordained ministry in the celebration of the Eucharist.

ON MINISTRY

(93) The Church bases its life on the sending of Christ into the world and the sending of the Holy Spirit that men and women may be joined to Christ in his service; its authority is inseparable from its service in the world which is the object of God's creative and reconciling love. As servants of their servant Lord, ministers of the Church must serve the world with wisdom and patience. Without lively personal discipleship, there can be no credible exercise of office. At the same time, those who bear office in the Church must adhere to the promise that the Lord determines to build up his community even through imperfect servants. Our common effort at a deeper common understanding of the nature of ministry in the

Church has also to be motivated by concern for the service of the Church in the world.

Apostolicity

(94) The whole Church is apostolic. To be an apostle means to be sent, to have a particular mission. The notion of mission is essential for understanding the ministry of the Church. As Christ is sent by the Father, so the Church is sent by Christ. But this mission of the Church has not simply a Christological reference. The sending of Christ and the equipment of the Church in his service are also works of the Holy Spirit. The mission of the Holy Spirit belongs to the constitution of the Church and her ministry, not merely to their effective functioning. Too often, imbalances in theologies of the ministry are the result and sign of an insufficiently trinitarian theology. It is by the power of the Spirit that the Lord sustains his people in their apostolic vocation. This power manifests itself in a variety of ways which are *charismata* — gracious gifts of the one Spirit (*cf. I Cor* 12,4ff.). Guided by and instrumental to the work of God in this world, the Church has a charismatic character.

(95) The Church is apostolic because it lives the faith of the original apostles, continues the mission given by Christ to them, and remains in the service and way of life testified to by those apostles. The canonical scriptures are the normative expression of this apostolicity. It is within the normative expression of this apostolicity contained in the New Testament that a witness is given to the special ministry given by Christ to the Twelve, and to Peter within that circle of Twelve.

(96) The extension of Christ's ministry, including his priestly office, belongs to all members of his body (*cf. I Petr* 5,5-9). Each member contributes to that total ministry in a different fashion; there is a distribution of diverse gifts (*cf. I Cor* 12,4-11), and every baptized believer exercises his or her share in the total priesthood differently. This calling to the priesthood of all those who share in the body of Christ by baptism does not mean that there are no particular functions which are proper to the special ministry within the body of Christ.

Special Ministry

(97) Within apostolicity in general there is a special ministry to which the administration of Word and Sacrament is entrusted. That special ministry is one of the charismata for the exercise of particular services within the whole body. Ordination, or setting apart for the exercise of these special services, takes place within the context of the believing community. Hence, consultation with that community, profession of faith before that community, and liturgical participation by that community belong to the process of ordination. This is important to underline because we need to go beyond an understanding of ordination which suggests that those consecrated to the special ministry are given a *potestas* and derive a dignity from Christ without reference to the believing community.

(98)   The liturgical validation at the time of the act of ordination includes the invocation of the Holy Spirit ("epiclesis") with the laying on of hands by other ordained ministers. The invocation of the Holy Spirit is a reminder of the essential role which the doctrine of the Trinity must fulfil in any balanced understanding of the ministry. It gives proper weight both to Jesus Christ's historical and present action and to the continual operation of the Holy Spirit. The laying on of hands is an efficacious sign which initiates and confirms the believer in the ministry conferred. It is not the community which produces and authorizes the office but the living Christ who bestows it on the community and incorporates this office into its life.

(99)   The continuity of this special ministry of Word and Sacrament is integral to that dimension of Christ's sovereign and gracious presence which is mediated through the Church. The forgiveness of sins and call to repentance are the exercise of the power of the keys in the upbuilding of the Church. This power Christ entrusted to the apostles with the assurance of his continued presence to the end of the age. The apostolic continuity depends not only on Christ's original commission but also on his continual call and action.

Apostolic Succession

(100)   There are several senses of "apostolic succession"; but when it is taken in its usual meaning to refer to the continuity of the special ministry, clearly it occurs within the apostolicity which belongs to the whole church. Reformed and Roman Catholic both believe that there is an apostolic succession essential to the life of the Church, though we locate that succession differently (see below). We agree that no one assumes a special ministry solely on personal initiative, but enters into the continuous special ministry of Word and Sacrament through the calling of the community and the act of ordination by other ministers.

(101)   Apostolic succession consists at least in continuity of apostolic doctrine; but this is not in opposition to succession through continuity of ordained ministry. The continuity of right doctrine is guarded by the application of Holy Scripture and transmitted by the continuity of the teaching function of the special ministry. As with all aspects of the Church's ministry, so with the particular case of apostolic succession: it requires at once a historical continuity with the original apostles and a contemporary and graciously renewed action of the Holy Spirit. The Church lives by the continuity of the free gift of the Spirit according to Christ's promises, and this excludes a ritualistic conception of succession, the conception of mechanical continuity, a succession divorced from the historical community.

Episkopé and Collegiality

(102)   We agree that the basic structure of the Church and its ministry is collegial. When one is consecrated to the special ministry, one accepts the

discipline of being introduced into a collegial function which includes being subject to others in the Lord and drawing on the comfort and admonition of fellow ministers.

This "collegiality" is expressed on the Reformed side by the synodical polity, and, on the Roman Catholic side, by the episcopal college, the understanding of which is in process of further development. In the Reformed polity, the synod functions as a corporate episcopacy, exercising oversight of pastors and congregations. We consider it would be worthwhile to investigate in what ways the diverse functions of the Reformed office of elder could be further developed in a modern form and made fruitful in the life of the Church.

We agree that the collegial structure must be expressed in different ways in different times and we have to be sensitive to the pluriformity of charismata. This principle of collegiality is not to be limited to the level of the synods, and in the Roman Catholic Church not to the episcopal college, neither to clergy only, but to be realized at all levels of church life. The vision of "Sobornost" may be a help here.

Different Emphases within Both Traditions

(103)   There are theological positions on the ministry which cut across confessional loyalties; different emphases are present in both traditions and are not as sharply to be sorted out along denominational lines as has been commonly thought. Some emphasize the "over-againstness" of the Spirit and structure; some emphasize the Spirit's work to shape and animate structure. One position more or less deplores the restriction of apostolic succession, for example, to institutionalization by means of what it takes to be mere continuity of laying on of hands. Another position more or less rejoices in that institutionalization as another instance of Christ's mediating his gracious presence through earthen vessels. Some locate apostolic continuity almost entirely in the succession of apostolic proclamation, while others locate it in an unbroken continuity which also indispensably includes the laying on of hands.

(104)   Some Reformed see God's fidelity as known mainly through his overcoming the Church's infidelity, and in this case tradition is seen as much as betrayal as transmission. Others, including Reformed and Roman Catholic, take a more confident view of the way the Church is able, by God's fidelity, to sustain a faithful deliverance of that which was once received. Some see in an application of the analogy of the incarnation to ecclesiology a de-emphasis on the work of the Spirit and the Lordship of Christ over the Church. Others see incarnational analogies appropriately applied to the Church when set in a trinitarian context which provides for the dynamic of Christ's work through the Holy Spirit. This may mean that one point of convergence is that no one wishes to speak of the Church as "extension of Incarnation" but that real divergence occurs among us in the way we use incarnational language about the Church.

Different Emphases between the Two Traditions

(105)   The divergences which do exist between Roman Catholic and
Reformed doctrines of the ministry often arise less from conceptions
which are objectively different than from differences of mentality which
lead them to accentuate differently elements which are part of a common
tradition. In any event, there are differences of doctrine which lie behind
the varied ways ministerial office is dealt with in the Reformed and the
Roman Catholic perspectives. We are not to minimize the way the doctrinal differences have been shaped in part by particular cultural,
sociological, economic factors as well as different nuances of spirituality.

(106)   Both Roman Catholic and Reformed theology are particularly
aware of the importance of the structure of the Church for the fulfilment
of its commission. The Roman Catholic Church, in this regard, has derived a predominantly hierarchical ordering from the Lordship of Christ,
whereas, from the same Lordship of Christ, the Reformed Church has
decided for a predominantly presbyterial-synodical organization. Today
both sides are taking a fresh look at the sense of the Church as it appears
in images of the early Church.

(107)   There is a difference in the way each tradition approaches the question of how far and in what way the existence of the community of
believers and its union with Christ and especially the celebration of the
Eucharist necessitates an ordained office-bearer in the Church. In how far
does the institutional connection with the office of Peter and the office of
bishop belong to the regularly appointed ministry in the Church? For
Roman Catholics, connection with the Bishop of Rome plays a decisive
role in the experience of Catholicity. For the Reformed, catholicity is most
immediately experienced through membership in the individual community. When it comes to the relation between ministry and sacrament, the
Roman Catholics find that the Reformed minimize the extent to which
God, in his plan for salvation, has bound himself to the Church, the
ministry and the sacraments. The Reformed find that too often Roman
Catholic theology minimizes the way the Church, the ministry and the
sacraments remain bound to the freedom and the grace of the Holy Spirit.

Open Questions

(108)   As with our dialogue about the Eucharist so with our dialogue
about Ministry we have come to recognize some continuing questions
which we face in common. These questions confront both traditions and
we need each other in the future to come to an even fuller understanding
of Ministry.

How essential are the distinctions of rank within the ministry? What
theological significance is to be assigned to the distinction between bishop,
priest and deacon? Can it be said that in many cases the ordained pastor
exercises the episcopal office?

What closer definition can we give to the tension between office and
charisma?

How are we to define more closely the relation between office and priesthood which has traditionally been very differently understood in the different churches?

Does the distinctive feature of the office consist in the role of president, understanding this presidency not as a title of honour but rather as a ministry for the upbuilding of the Church: as leadership, proclamation, administration of the sacraments?

On the other hand, how do we view the tendency to make the task of leadership and administration independent of the actual exercise of preaching and administering the sacraments?

What place is there for a real theological understanding of the ministry between the Western emphasis on legal organization and the Eastern emphasis on the relationship to liturgy?

How are we to understand the principle of corporate leadership of the congregation as developed in the Reformed tradition, and how is the relation between pastors and elders to be ordered?

(109) What is the meaning of the laying on of hands: mission, transfer of a *potestas*, or incorporation into an *ordo*?

To what extent can the laying on of hands with an invocation of the Holy Spirit be described as a "sacrament"?

What conditions (in substance and in form) are to be envisaged for a mutual recognition of ministries?

What meaning is to be given to the term *defectus*? Can a ministry be called in question or be nullified as such by a formal *defectus* — or can the latter be compensated by reference to the faith of the Church?

To what extent can abuses in the Church's ministries be dealt with by institutional measures? Examples of abuses: false doctrine of the leader or the majority, triumphalism, mechanical conception of ordination, church personality cults, dominance of the structure. Possibilities of correction in the direction of the collegiality principle (reference of the one to the other — combination of the hierarchical with the synodal pattern).

(110) A particularly urgent question, it seems to us, is the extent to which our reflections concerning the ministry are determined by distinctive Western thought patterns and historical experiences. To what extent is our concern with the past a hindrance rather than a stimulation to the development of a new shape of ministry? How can we be faithful at the same time to insights of the Christian tradition and to new experiments of the people of God?

These questions aim at further clarifying the nature of the total ministry which belongs to the whole people of God, and of the special ministry within it. Such further clarification is necessary for the continual reform and edification of the Church as a fit instrument of Christ's service in the world.

* * *

(111)   Having thus reached the end of our conversation, we attach importance to the following statement:

Our discussions have opened up to us unexpected perspectives of
common insights and tasks which have been buried under conflicts which
lasted for many centuries. They have been carried on with a sense of
repentance for the divisions among Christians which belie the Church's
message of reconciliation in a torn world. A note of joy and thanksgiving
continues to dominate in view of the fact that Christ, the Lord of the
world and the Church, permits us to share in making manifest the unity
which he in fact effects by his Word and Spirit.

PARTICIPANTS

MEMBERS OF THE COMMISSION:

Reformed:

Professor Dr. David Willis, U.S.A. (co-chairman)
Professor Paul J. Achtemeier, U.S.A. (meetings 1975 and 1977)
Professor John M. Barkekeley, Ireland (meeting 1972)
Professor Dr. Markus Barth, Switzerland (meeting 1974)
Professor Dr. A. Bronkhorst, Netherlands (meetings 1972 and 1974)
Professor Dr. George B. Caird, England (meetings 1970-1972)
Professor Dr. Gottfried Locher, Switzerland (meetings 1971-1975)
Professor Dr. Amadeo Molnar, Czechoslovakia (meetings 1970, 1971
and 1975)
Professor Dr. G.C. van Niftrik, Netherlands (meeting 1970)
Professor Dr. Jacques de Senarclens, Switzerland (meeting 1970)
Professor Dr. W.C. van Unnik, Netherlands (meetings 1971, 1974 and
1975)

Catholics:

Professor Dr. Kilian McDonnell, O.S.B., U.S.A. (co-chairman)
Professor Dr. Roger Aubert, Belgium
Professor Dr. Josel Ernst, FRG
Dr. Josef Hoffman, France
Professor Dr. J.F. Lescrauwaet, M.S.C., Netherlands

MEMBERS EX OFFICIO:

Reformed

Dr. Raymond V. Kearns, U.S.A. (representing Dr. Marcel Pradervand,
meeting 1970)
Rev. Dr. Edmond Perret, Switzerland (meetings 1971-1975)

Catholics:

Rev. Jérôme Hamer, O.P., Rome (meetings 1970-1972)
Msgr. Charles Moeller, Rome (meetings 1974 and 1975)

CONSULTANTS:

Reformed:
Professor Dr. Christian Maurer, Switzerland (meeting 1970)
Professor Dr. Eduard Schweizer, Switzerland (meeting 1971)
Professor Jacques Ellul, France (meeting 1972)
Professor Dr. Thomas Torrance, Scotland (meeting 1974)
Professor Willy A. Roeroe, Indonesia (meeting 1974)
Professor Dr. Martin Anton Schmidt, Switzerland (meeting 1975)
Reverend Francis Dankwa, Ghana (meeting 1975)

Catholics:
Professor Dr. Aelred Cody, O.S.B., Italy (meeting 1970)
Professor Dr. Jean Pierre Jossua, O.P., France (meeting 1971)
Professor Dr. René Coste, France (meeting 1972)
Reverend James Quinn, S.J., Scotland (meeting 1975)
Fr. Yves-M. Congar, O.P., France (meeting 1975)

SECRETARIES:

Reformed:
Reverend Richmond Smith, Switzerland

Catholics:
Reverend Dr. August Hasler, Rome (meetings 1970 and 1971)
Reverend Olaf Wand, A.A., Rome (meeting 1972)
Reverend Pierre M. de Contenson, O.P., Rome (meetings 1974 and 1975)
Reverend Stiepan Schmidt, S.J., Rome (meeting 1977)

WORLD COUNCIL OF CHURCHES OBSERVERS:

Professor Dr. Vilmos Vajta, France (meetings 1970–1972 and 1975)
Professor Dr. J.B. Boerdenaker, Holland (meeting 1974)

COMMISSION ON FAITH AND ORDER

Baptism
Eucharist
Ministry

Report of the Faith and Order Commission,
World Council of Churches, Lima, Peru 1982

The World Council of Churches is "a fellowship of churches which confess the Lord Jesus Christ as God and Saviour according to the scriptures and therefore seek to fulfil together their common calling to the glory of the one God, Father, Son and Holy Spirit" (Constitution).

The World Council is here clearly defined. It is not a universal authority controlling what Christians should believe and do. After only three decades, however, it has already become a remarkable community of some three hundred members. These churches represent a rich diversity of cultural backgrounds and traditions, worship in dozens of languages, and live under every kind of political system. Yet they are all committed to close collaboration in Christian witness and service. At the same time, they are also striving together to realize the goal of visible Church unity.

To assist the churches towards this goal, the Faith and Order Commission of the World Council provides theological support for the efforts the churches are making towards unity. Indeed the Commission has been charged by the Council members to keep always before them their accepted obligation to work towards manifesting more visibly God's gift of Church unity.

So it is that the stated aim of the Commission is "to proclaim the oneness of the Church of Jesus Christ and to call the churches to the goal of visible unity in one faith and one eucharistic fellowship, expressed in worship and common life in Christ, in order that the world might believe" (By-Laws).

If the divided churches are to achieve the visible unity they seek, one of the essential prerequisites is that they should be in basic agreement on baptism, eucharist and ministry. Naturally, therefore, the Faith and Order Commission has devoted a good deal of attention to overcoming doctrinal division on these three. During the last fifty years, most of its conferences have had one or another of these subjects at the centre of discussion.

The three statements are the fruit of a 50-year process of study stretching back to the first Faith and Order Conference at Lausanne in 1927. The material has been discussed and revised by the Faith and Order Commission at Accra (1974), Bangalore (1978) and Lima (1982). Between the Plenary Commission meetings, a steering group on Baptism, Eucharist and Ministry has worked further on the drafting, especially after September 1979 under the presidency of Frère Max Thurian of the Taizé Community.

The ecumenical documents also reflect ongoing consultation and collaboration between the Commission members (approved by the churches) and with the local churches themselves. The World Council's Fifth Assembly (Nairobi 1975) authorized the distribution for the churches' study of an earlier draft text (Faith and Order Paper No. 73). Most significantly, over a hundred churches from virtually every geographical area and ecclesiastical tradition returned detailed comments. These were carefully analyzed at a 1977 consultation in Crêt-Bérard (Faith and Order Paper No. 84).

Meanwhile particularly difficult problems were also analyzed at special ecumenical consultations held on the themes of infant and believers' baptism in Louisville, 1978 (Faith and Order Paper No. 97), on episkopé (oversight) and the episcopate in Geneva, 1979 (Faith and Order Paper No. 102). The draft text was also reviewed by representatives of Orthodox Churches in Chambésy, 1979. In conclusion, the Faith and Order Commission was again authorized by the World Council's Central Committee (Dresden, 1981) to transmit its finally revised document (the "Lima text" of 1982) to the churches, along with the request for their official response as a vital step in the ecumenical process of reception.

This work has not been achieved by the Faith and Order Commission alone. Baptism, eucharist and ministry have been investigated in many ecumenical dialogues. The two main types of interchurch conversations, the bilateral and the multilateral, have proved to be complementary and mutually beneficial. This is clearly demonstrated in the three reports of the Forum on Bilateral Conversations: "Concepts of Unity" (1978), "Consensus on Agreed Statements" (1979), and "Authority and Reception" (1980), subsequently published in Faith and Order Paper No. 107. Consequently, the Faith and Order Commission in its own multilateral consideration of the three themes has tried to build as much as possible on the specific findings of the bilateral conversations. Indeed, one of the tasks of the Commission is to evaluate the net result of all these particular efforts for the ecumenical movement as a whole.

Also important for the development of this text has been the witness of local churches which have already gone through the process of uniting across confessional division. It is important to acknowledge that the search for local church union and the search for universal consensus are intimately linked.

Perhaps even more influential than the official studies are the changes which are taking place within the life of the churches themselves. We live in a crucial moment in the history of humankind. As the churches grow into unity, they are asking how their understandings and practices of baptism, eucharist and ministry relate to their mission in and for the renewal of human community as they seek to promote justice, peace and reconciliation. Therefore our understanding of these cannot be divorced from the redemptive and liberating mission of Christ through the churches in the modern world.

Indeed, as a result of biblical and patristic studies, together with the liturgical revival and the need for common witness, an ecumenical fellowship has come into being which often cuts across confessional boundaries and within which former differences are now seen in a new light. Hence, although the language of the text is still largely classical in reconciling historical controversies, the driving force is frequently contextual and contemporary. This spirit will likely stimulate many reformulations of the text into the varied language(s) of our time.

Where have these efforts brought us? As demonstrated in the Lima text, we have already achieved a remarkable degree of agreement. Certainly we have not yet fully reached "consensus" (*consentire*), understood here as that experience of life and articulation of faith necessary to realize and maintain the Church's visible unity. Such consensus is rooted in all communion built on Jesus Christ and the witness of the apostles. As a gift of the Spirit it is realized as a communal experience before it can be articulated by common efforts into words. Full consensus can only be proclaimed after the churches reach the point of living and acting together in unity.

On the way towards their goal of visible unity, however, the churches will have to pass through various stages. They have been blessed anew through listening to each other and jointly returning to the primary sources, namely "the Tradition of the Gospel testified in Scripture, transmitted in and by the Church through the power of the Holy Spirit" (Faith and Order World Conference, 1963).

In leaving behind the hostilities of the past, the churches have begun to discover many promising convergences in their shared convictions and perspectives. These convergences give assurance that despite much diversity in theological expression the churches have much in common in their understanding of the faith. The resultant text aims to become part of a faithful and sufficient reflection of the common Christian Tradition on essential elements of Christian communion. In the process of growing together in mutual trust, the churches must develop these doctrinal convergences step by step, until they are finally able to declare together that they are living in communion with one another in continuity with the apostles and the teachings of the universal Church.

This Lima text represents the significant theological convergence which Faith and Order has discerned and formulated. Those who know how widely the churches have differed in doctrine and practice on baptism, eucharist and ministry, will appreciate the importance of the large measure of agreement registered here. Virtually all the confessional traditions are included in the Commission's membership. That theologians of such widely different traditions should be able to speak so harmoniously about baptism, eucharist and ministry is unprecedented in the modern ecumenical movement. Particularly noteworthy is the fact that the Commission also includes among its full members theologians of the Roman Catholic and other churches which do not belong to the World Council of Churches itself.

In the course of critical evaluation the primary purpose of this ecumenical text must be kept in mind. Readers should not expect to find a complete theological treatment of baptism, eucharist and ministry. That would be neither appropriate nor desirable here. The agreed text purposely concentrates on those aspects of the theme that have been directly or indirectly related to the problems of mutual recognition leading to unity. The main text demonstrates the major area of theological convergence; the added commentaries either indicate historical differences that have been overcome or identify disputed issues still in need of further research and reconciliation.

In the light of all these developments, the Faith and Order Commission now presents this Lima text (1982) to the churches. We do so with deep conviction, for we have become increasingly aware of our unity in the body of Christ. We have found reason to rejoice in the rediscovery of the richness of our common inheritance in the Gospel. We believe that the Holy Spirit has led us to this time, a *kairos* of the ecumenical movement when sadly divided churches have been enabled to arrive at substantial theological agreements. We believe that many significant advances are possible if in our churches we are sufficiently courageous and imaginative to embrace God's gift of Church unity.

As concrete evidence of their ecumenical commitment, the churches are being asked to enable the widest possible involvement of the whole people of God at all levels of church life in the spiritual process of receiving this text. Specific suggestions relating to its use in the worship, witness and study of men and women in the churches are included as an appendix to this document.

The Faith and Order Commission now respectfully invites all churches to prepare an official response to this text at the highest appropriate level of authority, whether it be a council, synod, conference, assembly or other body. In support of this process of reception, the Commission would be pleased to know as precisely as possible

— *the extent to which your church can recognize in this text the faith of the Church through the ages;*
— *the consequences your church can draw from this text for its relations and dialogues with other churches, particularly with those churches which also recognize the text as an expression of the apostolic faith;*
— *the guidance your church can take from this text for its worship, educational, ethical, and spiritual life and witness;*
— *the suggestions your church can make for the ongoing work of Faith and Order as it relates the material of this text on Baptism, Eucharist and Ministry to its long-range research project "Towards the Common Expression of the Apostolic Faith Today".*

It is our intention to compare all the official replies received, to publish the results, and to analyze the ecumenical implications for the churches at a future World Conference on Faith and Order.

William H. Lazareth
Director of the
Secretariat on
Faith and Order

Nikos Nissiotis
Moderator of the
Commission on
Faith and Order

Baptism

I. THE INSTITUTION OF BAPTISM

1. Christian baptism is rooted in the ministry of Jesus of Nazareth, in his death and in his resurrection. It is incorporation into Christ, who is the crucified and risen Lord; it is entry into the New Covenant between God and God's people. Baptism is a gift of God, and is administered in the name of the Father, the Son, and the Holy Spirit. St Matthew records that the risen Lord, when sending his disciples into the world, commanded them to baptize (Matt. 28:18–20). The universal practice of baptism by the apostolic Church from its earliest days is attested in letters of the New Testament, the Acts of the Apostles, and the writings of the Fathers. The churches today continue this practice as a rite of commitment to the Lord who bestows his grace upon his people.

II. THE MEANING OF BAPTISM

2. Baptism is the sign of new life through Jesus Christ. It unites the one baptized with Christ and with his people. The New Testament scriptures and the liturgy of the Church unfold the meaning of baptism in various images which express the riches of Christ and the gifts of his salvation. These images are sometimes linked with the symbolic uses of water in the Old Testament. Baptism is participation in Christ's death and resurrection (Rom. 6:3–5; Col. 2:12); a washing away of sin (I Cor. 6:11); a new birth (John 3:5); an enlightenment by Christ (Eph. 5:14); a reclothing in Christ (Gal. 3:27); a renewal by the Spirit (Titus 3:5); the experience of salvation from the flood (I Peter 3:20–21); an exodus from bondage (I Cor. 10:1–2) and a liberation into a new humanity in which barriers of division whether of sex or race or social status are transcended (Gal. 3:27–28; I Cor. 12:13). The images are many but the reality is one.

A. Participation in Christ's Death and Resurrection

3. Baptism means participating in the life, death and resurrection of Jesus Christ. Jesus went down into the river Jordan and was baptized in solidarity with sinners in order to fulfil all righteousness (Matt. 3:15). This baptism led Jesus along the way of the Suffering Servant, made manifest in his sufferings, death and resurrection (Mark 10:38–40, 45). By baptism, Christians are immersed in the liberating death of Christ where their sins are buried, where the "old Adam" is crucified with Christ, and where the power of sin is broken. Thus those baptized are no longer slaves to sin, but free. Fully identified with the death of Christ, they are buried with him and are raised here and now to a new life in the power of the resurrection of Jesus

Christ, confident that they will also ultimately be one with him in a resurrection like his (Rom. 6:3–11; Col. 2:13, 3:1; Eph. 2:5–6).

B. CONVERSION, PARDONING AND CLEANSING

4. The baptism which makes Christians partakers of the mystery of Christ's death and resurrection implies confession of sin and conversion of heart. The baptism administered by John was itself a baptism of repentance for the forgiveness of sins (Mark 1:4). The New Testament underlines the ethical implications of baptism by representing it as an ablution which washes the body with pure water, a cleansing of the heart of all sin, and an act of justification (Heb. 10:22; I Peter 3:21; Acts 22:16; I Cor. 6:11). Thus those baptized are pardoned, cleansed and sanctified by Christ, and are given as part of their baptismal experience a new ethical orientation under the guidance of the Holy Spirit.

C. THE GIFT OF THE SPIRIT

5. The Holy Spirit is at work in the lives of people before, in and after their baptism. It is the same Spirit who revealed Jesus as the Son (Mark 1:10–11) and who empowered and united the disciples at Pentecost (Acts 2). God bestows upon all baptized persons the anointing and the promise of the Holy Spirit, marks them with a seal and implants in their hearts the first instalment of their inheritance as sons and daughters of God. The Holy Spirit nurtures the life of faith in their hearts until the final deliverance when they will enter into its full possession, to the praise of the glory of God (II Cor. 1:21–22; Eph. 1:13–14).

D. INCORPORATION INTO THE BODY OF CHRIST

6. Administered in obedience to our Lord, baptism is a sign and seal of our common discipleship. Through baptism, Christians are brought into union with Christ, with each other and with the Church of every time and place. Our common baptism, which unites us to Christ in faith, is thus a basic bond of unity. We are one people and are called to confess and serve one Lord in each place and in all the world. The union with Christ which we share through baptism has important implications for Christian unity. "There is . . . one baptism, one God and Father of us all . . ." (Eph. 4:4–6). When baptismal unity is realized in one holy, catholic, apostolic Church, a genuine Christian witness can be made to the healing and reconciling love of God. Therefore, our one baptism into Christ constitutes a call to the churches to overcome their divisions and visibly manifest their fellowship.

E. THE SIGN OF THE KINGDOM

7. Baptism initiates the reality of the new life given in the midst of the present world. It gives participation in the community of the Holy Spirit. It is a sign of the Kingdom of God and of the life of the world to come.

Through the gifts of faith, hope and love, baptism has a dynamic which embraces the whole of life, extends to all nations, and anticipates the day when every tongue will confess that Jesus Christ is Lord to the glory of God the Father.

III. BAPTISM AND FAITH

8. Baptism is both God's gift and our human response to that gift. It looks towards a growth into the measure of the stature of the fullness of Christ (Eph. 4:13). The necessity of faith for the reception of the salvation embodied and set forth in baptism is acknowledged by all churches. Personal commitment is necessary for responsible membership in the body of Christ.

9. Baptism is related not only to momentary experience, but to life-long growth into Christ. Those baptized are called upon to reflect the glory of the Lord as they are transformed by the power of the Holy Spirit, into his likeness, with ever increasing splendour (II Cor. 3:18). The life of the Christian is necessarily one of continuing struggle yet also of continuing experience of grace. In this new relationship, the baptized live for the sake of Christ, of his Church and of the world which he loves, while they wait in hope for the manifestation of God's new creation and for the time when God will be all in all (Rom. 8:18–24; I Cor. 15:22–28, 49–57).

10. As they grow in the Christian life of faith, baptized believers demonstrate that humanity can be regenerated and liberated. They have a common responsibility, here and now, to bear witness together to the Gospel of Christ, the Liberator of all human beings. The context of this common witness is the Church and the world. Within a fellowship of witness and service, Christians discover the full significance of the one baptism as the gift of God to all God's people. Likewise, they acknowledge that baptism, as a baptism into Christ's death, has ethical implications which not only call for personal sanctification, but also motivate Christians to strive for the realization of the will of God in all realms of life (Rom. 6:9ff; Gal. 3:27–28; I Peter 2:21–4:6).

IV. BAPTISMAL PRACTICE

A. BAPTISM OF BELIEVERS AND INFANTS

11. While the possibility that infant baptism was also practised in the apostolic age cannot be excluded, baptism upon personal profession of faith is the most clearly attested pattern in the New Testament documents.

In the course of history, the practice of baptism has developed in a variety of forms. Some churches baptize infants brought by parents or guardians who are ready, in and with the Church, to bring up the children in the Christian faith. Other churches practise exclusively the baptism of believers who are able to make a personal confession of faith. Some of these churches encourage infants or children to be presented and blessed in a service which usually involves thanksgiving for the gift of the child and also the commitment of the mother and father to Christian parenthood.

All churches baptize believers coming from other religions or from unbelief who accept the Christian faith and participate in catechetical instruction.

12. Both the baptism of believers and the baptism of infants take place in the Church as the community of faith. When one who can answer for himself or herself is baptized, a personal confession of faith will be an integral part of the baptismal service. When an infant is baptized, the personal response will be offered at a later moment in life. In both cases, the baptized person will have to grow in the understanding of faith. For those baptized upon their own confession of faith, there is always the constant requirement of a continuing growth of personal response in faith. In the case of infants, personal confession is expected later, and Christian nurture is directed to the eliciting of this confession. All baptism is rooted in and declares Christ's faithfulness unto death. It has its setting within the life and faith of the Church and, through the witness of the whole Church, points to the faithfulness of God, the ground of all life in faith. At every baptism the whole congregation reaffirms its faith in God and pledges itself to provide an environment of witness and service. Baptism should, therefore, always be celebrated and developed in the setting of the Christian community.

13. Baptism is an unrepeatable act. Any practice which might be interpreted as "re-baptism" must be avoided.

B. BAPTISM—CHRISMATION—CONFIRMATION

14. In God's work of salvation, the paschal mystery of Christ's death and resurrection is inseparably linked with the pentecostal gift of the Holy Spirit. Similarly, participation in Christ's death and resurrection is inseparably linked with the receiving of the Spirit. Baptism in its full meaning signifies and effects both.

Christians differ in their understanding as to where the sign of the gift of the Spirit is to be found. Different actions have become associated with the giving of the Spirit. For some it is the water rite itself. For others, it is the anointing with chrism and/or the imposition of hands, which many churches call confirmation. For still others it is all three, as they see the Spirit operative throughout the rite. All agree that Christian baptism is in water and the Holy Spirit.

C. TOWARDS MUTUAL RECOGNITION OF BAPTISM

15. Churches are increasingly recognizing one another's baptism as the one baptism into Christ when Jesus Christ has been confessed as Lord by the candidate or, in the case of infant baptism, when confession has been made

by the church (parents, guardians, godparents and congregation) and affirmed later by personal faith and commitment. Mutual recognition of baptism is acknowledged as an important sign and means of expressing the baptismal unity given in Christ. Wherever possible, mutual recognition should be expressed explicitly by the churches.

16. In order to overcome their differences, believer baptists and those who practise infant baptism should reconsider certain aspects of their practices. The first may seek to express more visibly the fact that children are placed under the protection of God's grace. The latter must guard themselves against the practice of apparently indiscriminate baptism and take more seriously their responsibility for the nurture of baptized children to mature commitment to Christ.

V. THE CELEBRATION OF BAPTISM

17. Baptism is administered with water in the name of the Father, the Son and the Holy Spirit.

18. In the celebration of baptism the symbolic dimension of water should be taken seriously and not minimalized. The act of immersion can vividly express the reality that in baptism the Christian participates in the death, burial and resurrection of Christ.

19. As was the case in the early centuries, the gift of the Spirit in baptism may be signified in additional ways; for example, by the sign of the laying on of hands, and by anointing or chrismation. The very sign of the cross recalls the promised gift of the Holy Spirit who is the instalment and pledge of what is yet to come when God has fully redeemed those whom he has made his own (Eph. 1:13–14). The recovery of such vivid signs may be expected to enrich the liturgy.

20. Within any comprehensive order of baptism at least the following elements should find a place: the proclamation of the scriptures referring to baptism; an invocation of the Holy Spirit; a renunciation of evil; a profession of faith in Christ and the Holy Trinity; the use of water; a declaration that the persons baptized have acquired a new identity as sons and daughters of God, and as members of the Church, called to be witnesses of the Gospel. Some churches consider that Christian initiation is not complete without the sealing of the baptized with the gift of the Holy Spirit and participation in holy communion.

21. It is appropriate to explain in the context of the baptismal service the meaning of baptism as it appears from scriptures (i.e. the participation in Christ's death and resurrection, conversion, pardoning and cleansing, gift of the Spirit, incorporation into the body of Christ and sign of the Kingdom).

22. Baptism is normally administered by an ordained minister, though in certain circumstances others are allowed to baptize.

23. Since baptism is intimately connected with the corporate life and worship of the Church, it should normally be administered during public worship, so that the members of the congregation may be reminded of their own baptism and may welcome into their fellowship those who are baptized and whom they are committed to nurture in the Christian faith. The sacrament is appropriate to great festival occasions such as Easter, Pentecost and Epiphany, as was the practice in the early Church.

Eucharist

I. THE INSTITUTION OF THE EUCHARIST

1. The Church receives the eucharist as a gift from the Lord. St Paul wrote: "I have received from the Lord what I also delivered to you, that the Lord Jesus on the night when he was betrayed took bread, and when he had given thanks, he broke it, and said: 'This is my body, which is for you. Do this in remembrance (*anamnesis*) of me.' In the same way also the cup, after supper, saying: 'This cup is the new covenant in my blood. Do this, as often as you drink it, in remembrance of me.'" (I Cor. 11:23–25; cf. Matt. 26:26–29; Mark 14:22–25; Luke 22:14–20).

The meals which Jesus is recorded as sharing during his earthly ministry proclaim and enact the nearness of the Kingdom, of which the feeding of the multitudes is a sign. In his last meal, the fellowship of the Kingdom was connected with the imminence of Jesus' suffering. After his resurrection, the Lord made his presence known to his disciples in the breaking of the bread. Thus the eucharist continues these meals of Jesus during his earthly life and after his resurrection, always as a sign of the Kingdom. Christians see the eucharist prefigured in the Passover memorial of Israel's deliverance from the land of bondage and in the meal of the Covenant on Mount Sinai (Ex. 24). It is the new paschal meal of the Church, the meal of the New Covenant, which Christ gave to his disciples as the *anamnesis* of his death and resurrection, as the anticipation of the Supper of the Lamb (Rev. 19:9). Christ commanded his disciples thus to remember and encounter him in this sacramental meal, as the continuing people of God, until his return. The last meal celebrated by Jesus was a liturgical meal employing symbolic words and actions. Consequently the eucharist is a sacramental meal which by visible signs communicates to us God's love in Jesus Christ, the love by which Jesus loved his own "to the end" (John 13:1). It has acquired many names: for example, the Lord's Supper, the breaking of bread, the holy communion, the divine liturgy, the mass. Its celebration continues as the central act of the Church's worship.

II. THE MEANING OF THE EUCHARIST

2. The eucharist is essentially the sacrament of the gift which God makes to us in Christ through the power of the Holy Spirit. Every Christian receives this gift of salvation through communion in the body and blood of Christ. In the eucharistic meal, in the eating and drinking of the bread and wine, Christ grants communion with himself. God himself acts, giving life to the body of Christ and renewing each member. In accordance with Christ's promise, each baptized member of the body of Christ receives in the eucharist the assurance of the forgiveness of sins (Matt. 26:28) and the pledge of eternal life (John 6:51–58). Although the eucharist is essentially one complete act, it will be considered here under the following aspects: thanksgiving to the Father, memorial of Christ, invocation of the Spirit, communion of the faithful, meal of the Kingdom.

A. THE EUCHARIST AS THANKSGIVING TO THE FATHER

3. The eucharist, which always includes both word and sacrament, is a proclamation and a celebration of the work of God. It is the great thanksgiving to the Father for everything accomplished in creation, redemption and sanctification, for everything accomplished by God now in the Church and in the world in spite of the sins of human beings, for everything that God will accomplish in bringing the Kingdom to fulfillment. Thus the eucharist is the benediction (*berakah*) by which the Church expresses its thankfulness for all God's benefits.

4. The eucharist is the great sacrifice of praise by which the Church speaks on behalf of the whole creation. For the world which God has reconciled is present at every eucharist: in the bread and wine, in the persons of the faithful, and in the prayers they offer for themselves and for all people. Christ unites the faithful with himself and includes their prayers within his own intercession so that the faithful are transfigured and their prayers accepted. This sacrifice of praise is possible only through Christ, with him and in him. The bread and wine, fruits of the earth and of human labour, are presented to the Father in faith and thanksgiving. The eucharist thus signifies what the world is to become: an offering and hymn of praise to the Creator, a universal communion in the body of Christ, a kingdom of justice, love and peace in the Holy Spirit.

B. THE EUCHARIST AS ANAMNESIS OR MEMORIAL OF CHRIST

5. The eucharist is the memorial of the crucified and risen Christ, i.e. the living and effective sign of his sacrifice, accomplished once and for all on the cross and still operative on behalf of all humankind. The biblical idea of

memorial as applied to the eucharist refers to this present efficacy of God's work when it is celebrated by God's people in a liturgy.

6. Christ himself with all that he has accomplished for us and for all creation (in his incarnation, servanthood, ministry, teaching, suffering, sacrifice, resurrection, ascension and sending of the Spirit) is present in this *anamnesis*, granting us communion with himself. The eucharist is also the foretaste of his *parousia* and of the final kingdom.

7. The *anamnesis* in which Christ acts through the joyful celebration of his Church is thus both representation and anticipation. It is not only a calling to mind of what is past and of its significance. It is the Church's effective proclamation of God's mighty acts and promises.

8. Representation and anticipation are expressed in thanksgiving and intercession. The Church, gratefully recalling God's mighty acts of redemption, beseeches God to give the benefits of these acts to every human being. In thanksgiving and intercession, the Church is united with the Son, its great High Priest and Intercessor (Rom. 8:34; Heb. 7:25). The eucharist is the sacrament of the unique sacrifice of Christ, who ever lives to make intercession for us. It is the memorial of all that God has done for the salvation of the world. What it was God's will to accomplish in the incarnation, life, death, resurrection and ascension of Christ, God does not repeat. These events are unique and can neither be repeated nor prolonged. In the memorial of the eucharist, however, the Church offers its intercession in communion with Christ, our great High Priest.

9. The *anamnesis* of Christ is the basis and source of all Christian prayer. So our prayer relies upon and is united with the continual intercession of the risen Lord. In the eucharist, Christ empowers us to live with him, to suffer with him and to pray through him as justified sinners, joyfully and freely fulfilling his will.

10. In Christ we offer ourselves as a living and holy sacrifice in our daily lives (Rom. 12:1; I Peter 2:5); this spiritual worship, acceptable to God, is nourished in the eucharist, in which we are sanctified and reconciled in love, in order to be servants of reconciliation in the world.

11. United to our Lord and in communion with all saints and martyrs, we are renewed in the covenant sealed by the blood of Christ.

12. Since the *anamnesis* of Christ is the very content of the preached Word as it is of the eucharistic meal, each reinforces the other. The celebration of the eucharist properly includes the proclamation of the Word.

13. The words and acts of Christ at the institution of the eucharist stand at the heart of the celebration; the eucharistic meal is the sacrament of the body and blood of Christ, the sacrament of his real presence. Christ fulfills in a variety of ways his promise to be always with his own even to the end of the world. But Christ's mode of presence in the eucharist is unique. Jesus

said over the bread and wine of the eucharist: "This is my body . . . this is my blood . . ." What Christ declared is true, and this truth is fulfilled every time the eucharist is celebrated. The Church confesses Christ's real, living and active presence in the eucharist. While Christ's real presence in the eucharist does not depend on the faith of the individual, all agree that to discern the body and blood of Christ, faith is required.

C. THE EUCHARIST AS INVOCATION OF THE SPIRIT

14. The Spirit makes the crucified and risen Christ really present to us in the eucharistic meal, fulfilling the promise contained in the words of institution. The presence of Christ is clearly the centre of the eucharist, and the promise contained in the words of institution is therefore fundamental to the celebration. Yet it is the Father who is the primary origin and final fulfilment of the eucharistic event. The incarnate Son of God by and in whom it is accomplished is its living centre. The Holy Spirit is the immeasurable strength of love which makes it possible and continues to make it effective. The bond between the eucharistic celebration and the mystery of the Triune God reveals the role of the Holy Spirit as that of the One who makes the historical words of Jesus present and alive. Being assured by Jesus' promise in the words of institution that it will be answered, the Church prays to the Father for the gift of the Holy Spirit in order that the eucharistic event may be a reality: the real presence of the crucified and risen Christ giving his life for all humanity.

15. It is in virtue of the living word of Christ and by the power of the Holy Spirit that the bread and wine become the sacramental signs for Christ's body and blood. They remain so for the purpose of communion.

16. The whole action of the eucharist has an "epikletic" character because it depends upon the work of the Holy Spirit. In the words of the liturgy, this aspect of the eucharist finds varied expression.

17. The Church, as the community of the new covenant, confidently invokes the Spirit, in order that it may be sanctified and renewed, led into all justice, truth and unity, and empowered to fulfil its mission in the world.

18. The Holy Spirit through the eucharist gives a foretaste of the Kingdom of God: the Church receives the life of the new creation and the assurance of the Lord's return.

D. THE EUCHARIST AS COMMUNION OF THE FAITHFUL

19. The eucharistic communion with Christ who nourishes the life of the Church is at the same time communion within the body of Christ which is the Church. The sharing in one bread and the common cup in a given place demonstrates and effects the oneness of the sharers with Christ and with their fellow sharers in all times and places. It is in the eucharist that the

community of God's people is fully manifested. Eucharistic celebrations always have to do with the whole Church, and the whole Church is involved in each local eucharistic celebration. In so far as a church claims to be a manifestation of the whole Church, it will take care to order its own life in ways which take seriously the interests and concerns of other churches.

20. The eucharist embraces all aspects of life. It is a representative act of thanksgiving and offering on behalf of the whole world. The eucharistic celebration demands reconciliation and sharing among all those regarded as brothers and sisters in the one family of God and is a constant challenge in the search for appropriate relationships in social, economic and political life (Matt. 5:23f; I Cor. 10:16f; I Cor. 11:20–22; Gal. 3:28). All kinds of injustice, racism, separation and lack of freedom are radically challenged when we share in the body and blood of Christ. Through the eucharist the all-renewing grace of God penetrates and restores human personality and dignity. The eucharist involves the believer in the central event of the world's history. As participants in the eucharist, therefore, we prove inconsistent if we are not actively participating in this ongoing restoration of the world's situation and the human condition. The eucharist shows us that our behaviour is inconsistent in face of the reconciling presence of God in human history: we are placed under continual judgment by the persistence of unjust relationships of all kinds in our society, the manifold divisions on account of human pride, material interest and power politics and, above all, the obstinacy of unjustifiable confessional oppositions within the body of Christ.

21. Solidarity in the eucharistic communion of the body of Christ and responsible care of Christians for one another and the world find specific expression in the liturgies: in the mutual forgiveness of sins; the sign of peace; intercession for all; the eating and drinking together; the taking of the elements to the sick and those in prison or the celebration of the eucharist with them. All these manifestations of love in the eucharist are directly related to Christ's own testimony as a servant, in whose servanthood Christians themselves participate. As God in Christ has entered into the human situation, so eucharistic liturgy is near to the concrete and particular situations of men and women. In the early Church the ministry of deacons and deaconesses gave expression in a special way to this aspect of the eucharist. The place of such ministry between the table and the needy properly testifies to the redeeming presence of Christ in the world.

E. THE EUCHARIST AS MEAL OF THE KINGDOM

22. The eucharist opens up the vision of the divine rule which has been promised as the final renewal of creation, and is a foretaste of it. Signs of this renewal are present in the world wherever the grace of God is manifest and human beings work for justice, love and peace. The eucharist is the feast at which the Church gives thanks to God for these signs and joyfully

celebrates and anticipates the coming of the Kingdom in Christ (I Cor. 11:26; Matt. 26:29).

23. The world, to which renewal is promised, is present in the whole eucharistic celebration. The world is present in the thanksgiving to the Father, where the Church speaks on behalf of the whole creation; in the memorial of Christ, where the Church, united with its great High Priest and Intercessor, prays for the world; in the prayer for the gift of the Holy Spirit, where the Church asks for sanctification and new creation.

24. Reconciled in the eucharist, the members of the body of Christ are called to be servants of reconciliation among men and women and witnesses of the joy of resurrection. As Jesus went out to publicans and sinners and had table-fellowship with them during his earthly ministry, so Christians are called in the eucharist to be in solidarity with the outcast and to become signs of the love of Christ who lived and sacrificed himself for all and now gives himself in the eucharist.

25. The very celebration of the eucharist is an instance of the Church's participation in God's mission to the world. This participation takes every-day form in the proclamation of the Gospel, service of the neighbour, and faithful presence in the world.

26. As it is entirely the gift of God, the eucharist brings into the present age a new reality which transforms Christians into the image of Christ and therefore makes them his effective witnesses. The eucharist is precious food for missionaries, bread and wine for pilgrims on their apostolic journey. The eucharistic community is nourished and strengthened for confessing by word and action the Lord Jesus Christ who gave his life for the salvation of the world. As it becomes one people, sharing the meal of the one Lord, the eucharistic assembly must be concerned for gathering also those who are at present beyond its visible limits, because Christ invited to his feast all for whom he died. Insofar as Christians cannot unite in full fellowship around the same table to eat the same loaf and drink from the same cup, their missionary witness is weakened at both the individual and the corporate levels.

III. THE CELEBRATION OF THE EUCHARIST

27. The eucharistic liturgy is essentially a single whole, consisting histori-cally of the following elements in varying sequence and of diverse impor-tance:

- hymns of praise;
- act of repentance;
- declaration of pardon;
- proclamation of the Word of God, in various forms;

- confession of faith (creed);
- intercession for the whole Church and for the world;
- preparation of the bread and wine;
- thanksgiving to the Father for the marvels of creation, redemption and sanctification (deriving from the Jewish tradition of the *berakah*);
- the words of Christ's institution of the sacrament according to the New Testament tradition;
- the *anamnesis* or memorial of the great acts of redemption, passion, death, resurrection, ascension and Pentecost, which brought the Church into being;
- the invocation of the Holy Spirit (*epiklesis*) on the community, and the elements of bread and wine (either before the words of institution or after the memorial, or both; or some other reference to the Holy Spirit which adequately expresses the "epikletic" character of the eucharist);
- consecration of the faithful to God;
- reference to the communion of saints;
- prayer for the return of the Lord and the definitive manifestation of his Kingdom;
- the Amen of the whole community;
- the Lord's prayer;
- sign of reconciliation and peace;
- the breaking of the bread;
- eating and drinking in communion with Christ and with each member of the Church;
- final act of praise;
- blessing and sending.

28. The best way towards unity in eucharistic celebration and communion is the renewal of the eucharist itself in the different churches in regard to teaching and liturgy. The churches should test their liturgies in the light of the eucharistic agreement now in the process of attainment.

The liturgical reform movement has brought the churches closer together in the manner of celebrating the Lord's Supper. However, a certain liturgical diversity compatible with our common eucharistic faith is recognized as a healthy and enriching fact. The affirmation of a common eucharistic faith does not imply uniformity in either liturgy or practice.

29. In the celebration of the eucharist, Christ gathers, teaches and nourishes the Church. It is Christ who invites to the meal and who presides at it. He is the shepherd who leads the people of God, the prophet who announces the Word of God, the priest who celebrates the mystery of God. In most churches, this presidency is signified by an ordained minister. The one who presides at the eucharistic celebration in the name of Christ makes clear that the rite is not the assemblies' own creation or possession; the eucharist is received as a gift from Christ living in his Church. The minister of the eucharist is the ambassador who represents the divine initiative and ex-

presses the connection of the local community with other local communities in the universal Church.

30. Christian faith is deepened by the celebration of the Lord's Supper. Hence the eucharist should be celebrated frequently. Many differences of theology, liturgy and practice are connected with the varying frequency with which the Holy Communion is celebrated.

31. As the eucharist celebrates the resurrection of Christ, it is appropriate that it should take place at least every Sunday. As it is the new sacramental meal of the people of God, every Christian should be encouraged to receive communion frequently.

32. Some churches stress that Christ's presence in the consecrated elements continues after the celebration. Others place the main emphasis on the act of celebration itself and on the consumption of the elements in the act of communion. The way in which the elements are treated requires special attention. Regarding the practice of reserving the elements, each church should respect the practices and piety of the others. Given the diversity in practice among the churches and at the same time taking note of the present situation in the convergence process, it is worthwhile to suggest:

• that, on the one hand, it be remembered, especially in sermons and instruction, that the primary intention of reserving the elements is their distribution among the sick and those who are absent, and
• on the other hand, it be recognized that the best way of showing respect for the elements served in the eucharistic celebration is by their consumption, without excluding their use for communion of the sick.

33. The increased mutual understanding expressed in the present statement may allow some churches to attain a greater measure of eucharistic communion among themselves and so bring closer the day when Christ's divided people will be visibly reunited around the Lord's Table.

Ministry

I. THE CALLING OF THE WHOLE PEOPLE OF GOD

1. In a broken world God calls the whole of humanity to become God's people. For this purpose God chose Israel and then spoke in a unique and decisive way in Jesus Christ, God's Son. Jesus made his own the nature, condition and cause of the whole human race, giving himself as a sacrifice for all. Jesus' life of service, his death and resurrection, are the foundation of

a new community which is built up continually by the good news of the Gospel and the gifts of the sacraments. The Holy Spirit unites in a single body those who follow Jesus Christ and sends them as witnesses into the world. Belonging to the Church means living in communion with God through Jesus Christ in the Holy Spirit.

2. The life of the Church is based on Christ's victory over the powers of evil and death, accomplished once for all. Christ offers forgiveness, invites to repentance and delivers from destruction. Through Christ, people are enabled to turn in praise to God and in service to their neighbours. In Christ they find the source of new life in freedom, mutual forgiveness and love. Through Christ their hearts and minds are directed to the consummation of the Kingdom where Christ's victory will become manifest and all things made new. God's purpose is that, in Jesus Christ, all people should share in this fellowship.

3. The Church lives through the liberating and renewing power of the Holy Spirit. That the Holy Spirit was upon Jesus is evidenced in his baptism, and after the resurrection that same Spirit was given to those who believed in the Risen Lord in order to recreate them as the body of Christ. The Spirit calls people to faith, sanctifies them through many gifts, gives them strength to witness to the Gospel, and empowers them to serve in hope and love. The Spirit keeps the Church in the truth and guides it despite the frailty of its members.

4. The Church is called to proclaim and prefigure the Kingdom of God. It accomplishes this by announcing the Gospel to the world and by its very existence as the body of Christ. In Jesus the Kingdom of God came among us. He offered salvation to sinners. He preached good news to the poor, release to the captives, recovery of sight to the blind, liberation to the oppressed (Luke 4:18). Christ established a new access to the Father. Living in this communion with God, all members of the Church are called to confess their faith and to give account of their hope. They are to identify with the joys and sufferings of all people as they seek to witness in caring love. The members of Christ's body are to struggle with the oppressed towards that freedom and dignity promised with the coming of the Kingdom. This mission needs to be carried out in varying political, social and cultural contexts. In order to fulfil this mission faithfully, they will seek relevant forms of witness and service in each situation. In so doing they bring to the world a foretaste of the joy and glory of God's Kingdom.

5. The Holy Spirit bestows on the community diverse and complementary gifts. These are for the common good of the whole people and are manifested in acts of service within the community and to the world. They may be gifts of communicating the Gospel in word and deed, gifts of healing, gifts of praying, gifts of teaching and learning, gifts of serving, gifts of guiding and following, gifts of inspiration and vision. All members are called to

discover, with the help of the community, the gifts they have received and to use them for the building up of the Church and for the service of the world to which the Church is sent.

6. Though the churches are agreed in their general understanding of the calling of the people of God, they differ in their understanding of how the life of the Church is to be ordered. In particular, there are differences concerning the place and forms of the ordained ministry. As they engage in the effort to overcome these differences, the churches need to work from the perspective of the calling of the whole people of God. A common answer needs to be found to the following question: How, according to the will of God and under the guidance of the Holy Spirit, is the life of the Church to be understood and ordered, so that the Gospel may be spread and the community built up in love?

II. THE CHURCH AND THE ORDAINED MINISTRY

7. Differences in terminology are part of the matter under debate. In order to avoid confusion in the discussions on the ordained ministry in the Church, it is necessary to delineate clearly how various terms are used in the following paragraphs.

a) The word *charism* denotes the gifts bestowed by the Holy Spirit on any member of the body of Christ for the building up of the community and the fulfilment of its calling.

b) The word *ministry* in its broadest sense denotes the service to which the whole people of God is called, whether as individuals, as a local community, or as the universal Church. Ministry or ministries can also denote the particular institutional forms which this service may take.

c) The term *ordained ministry* refers to persons who have received a charism and whom the church appoints for service by ordination through the invocation of the Spirit and the laying on of hands.

d) Many churches use the word *priest* to denote certain ordained ministers. Because this usage is not universal, this document will discuss the substantive questions in paragraph 17.

A. THE ORDAINED MINISTRY

8. In order to fulfil its mission, the Church needs persons who are publicly and continually responsible for pointing to its fundamental dependence on Jesus Christ, and thereby provide, within a multiplicity of gifts, a focus of its unity. The ministry of such persons, who since very early times have been ordained, is constitutive for the life and witness of the Church.

9. The Church has never been without persons holding specific authority and responsibility. Jesus chose and sent the disciples to be witnesses to the

Kingdom (Matt. 10:1–8). The Twelve were promised that they would "sit on thrones judging the tribes of Israel" (Luke 22:30). A particular role is attributed to the Twelve within the communities of the first generation. They are witnesses of the Lord's life and resurrection (Acts 1:21–26). They lead the community in prayer, teaching, the breaking of bread, proclamation and service (Acts 2:42–47; 6:2–6, etc.) The very existence of the Twelve and other apostles shows that, from the beginning, there were differentiated roles in the community.

10. Jesus called the Twelve to be representatives of the renewed Israel. At that moment they represent the whole people of God and at the same time exercise a special role in the midst of that community. After the resurrection they are among the leaders of the community. It can be said that the apostles prefigure both the Church as a whole and the persons within it who are entrusted with the specific authority and responsibility. The role of the apostles as witnesses to the resurrection of Christ is unique and unrepeatable. There is therefore a difference between the apostles and the ordained ministers whose ministries are founded on theirs.

11. As Christ chose and sent the apostles, Christ continues through the Holy Spirit to choose and call persons into the ordained ministry. As heralds and ambassadors, ordained ministers are representatives of Jesus Christ to the community, and proclaim his message of reconciliation. As leaders and teachers they call the community to submit to the authority of Jesus Christ, the teacher and prophet, in whom law and prophets were fulfilled. As pastors, under Jesus Christ the chief shepherd, they assemble and guide the dispersed people of God, in anticipation of the coming Kingdom.

12. All members of the believing community, ordained and lay, are interrelated. On the one hand, the community needs ordained ministers. Their presence reminds the community of the divine initiative, and of the dependence of the Church on Jesus Christ, who is the source of its mission and the foundation of its unity. They serve to build up the community in Christ and to strengthen its witness. In them the Church seeks an example of holiness and loving concern. On the other hand, the ordained ministry has no existence apart from the community. Ordained ministers can fulfil their calling only in and for the community. They cannot dispense with the recognition, the support and the encouragement of the community.

13. The chief responsibility of the ordained ministry is to assemble and build up the body of Christ by proclaiming and teaching the Word of God, by celebrating the sacraments, and by guiding the life of the community in its worship, its mission and its caring ministry.

14. It is especially in the eucharistic celebration that the ordained ministry is the visible focus of the deep and all-embracing communion between Christ and the members of his body. In the celebration of the eucharist,

Christ gathers, teaches and nourishes the Church. It is Christ who invites to the meal and who presides at it. In most churches this presidency is signified and represented by an ordained minister.

B. Ordained Ministry and Authority

15. The authority of the ordained minister is rooted in Jesus Christ, who has received it from the Father (Matt. 28:18), and who confers it by the Holy Spirit through the act of ordination. This act takes place within a community which accords public recognition to a particular person. Because Jesus came as one who serves (Mark 10:45; Luke 22:27), to be set apart means to be consecrated to service. Since ordination is essentially a setting apart with prayer for the gift of the Holy Spirit, the authority of the ordained ministry is not to be understood as the possession of the ordained person but as a gift for the continuing edification of the body in and for which the minister has been ordained. Authority has the character of responsibility before God and is exercised with the cooperation of the whole community.

16. Therefore, ordained ministers must not be autocrats or impersonal functionaries. Although called to exercise wise and loving leadership on the basis of the Word of God, they are bound to the faithful in interdependence and reciprocity. Only when they seek the response and acknowledgment of the community can their authority be protected from the distortions of isolation and domination. They manifest and exercise the authority of Christ in the way Christ himself revealed God's authority to the world, by committing their life to the community. Christ's authority is unique. "He spoke as one who has authority (*exousia*), not as the scribes" (Matt. 7:29). This authority is an authority governed by love for the "sheep who have no shepherd" (Matt. 9:36). It is confirmed by his life of service and, supremely, by his death and resurrection. Authority in the Church can only be authentic as it seeks to conform to this model.

C. Ordained Ministry and Priesthood

17. Jesus Christ is the unique priest of the new covenant. Christ's life was given as a sacrifice for all. Derivatively, the Church as a whole can be described as a priesthood. All members are called to offer their being "as a living sacrifice" and to intercede for the Church and the salvation of the world. Ordained ministers are related, as are all Christians, both to the priesthood of Christ, and to the priesthood of the Church. But they may appropriately be called priests because they fulfil a particular priestly service by strengthening and building up the royal and prophetic priesthood of the faithful through word and sacraments, through their prayers of intercession, and through their pastoral guidance of the community.

D. The Ministry of Men and Women in the Church

18. Where Christ is present, human barriers are being broken. The Church is called to convey to the world the image of a new humanity. There is in Christ no male or female (Gal. 3:28). Both women and men must discover together their contributions to the service of Christ in the Church. The Church must discover the ministry which can be provided by women as well as that which can be provided by men. A deeper understanding of the comprehensiveness of ministry which reflects the interdependence of men and women needs to be more widely manifested in the life of the Church.

Though they agree on this need, the churches draw different conclusions as to the admission of women to the ordained ministry. An increasing number of churches have decided that there is no biblical or theological reason against ordaining women, and many of them have subsequently proceeded to do so. Yet many churches hold that the tradition of the Church in this regard must not be changed.

III. THE FORMS OF THE ORDAINED MINISTRY

A. Bishops, Presbyters and Deacons

19. The New Testament does not describe a single pattern of ministry which might serve as a blueprint or continuing norm for all future ministry in the Church. In the New Testament there appears rather a variety of forms which existed at different places and times. As the Holy Spirit continued to lead the Church in life, worship and mission, certain elements from this early variety were further developed and became settled into a more universal pattern of ministry. During the second and third centuries, a threefold pattern of bishop, presbyter and deacon became established as the pattern of ordained ministry throughout the Church. In succeeding centuries, the ministry by bishop, presbyter and deacon underwent considerable changes in its practical exercise. At some points of crisis in the history of the Church, the continuing functions of ministry were in some places and communities distributed according to structures other than the predominant threefold pattern. Sometimes appeal was made to the New Testament in justification of these other patterns. In other cases, the restructuring of ministry was held to lie within the competence of the Church as it adapted to changed circumstances.

20. It is important to be aware of the changes the threefold ministry has undergone in the history of the Church. In the earliest instances, where threefold ministry is mentioned, the reference is to the local eucharistic community. The bishop was the leader of the community. He was ordained and installed to proclaim the Word and preside over the celebration of the eucharist. He was surrounded by a college of presbyters and by deacons who

assisted in his tasks. In this context the bishop's ministry was a focus of unity within the whole community.

21. Soon, however, the functions were modified. Bishops began increasingly to exercise *episkopé* over several local communities at the same time. In the first generation, apostles had exercised *episkopé* in the wider Church. Later Timothy and Titus are recorded to have fulfilled a function of *episkopé* in a given area. Later again this apostolic task is carried out in a new way by the bishops. They provide a focus for unity in life and witness within areas comprising several eucharistic communities. As a consequence, presbyters and deacons are assigned new roles. The presbyters become the leaders of the local eucharistic community, and as assistants of the bishops, deacons receive responsibilities in the larger area.

22. Although there is no single New Testament pattern, although the Spirit has many times led the Church to adapt its ministries to contextual needs, and although other forms of the ordained ministry have been blessed with the gifts of the Holy Spirit, nevertheless the threefold ministry of bishop, presbyter and deacon may serve today as an expression of the unity we seek and also as a means for achieving it. Historically, it is true to say, the threefold ministry became the generally accepted pattern in the Church of the early centuries and is still retained today by many churches. In the fulfilment of their mission and service the churches need people who in different ways express and perform the tasks of the ordained ministry in its diaconal, presbyteral and episcopal aspects and functions.

23. The Church as the body of Christ and the eschatological people of God is constituted by the Holy Spirit through a diversity of gifts or ministries. Among these gifts a ministry of *episkopé* is necessary to express and safeguard the unity of the body. Every church needs this ministry of unity in some form in order to be the Church of God, the one body of Christ, a sign of the unity of all in the Kingdom.

24. The threefold pattern stands evidently in need of reform. In some churches the collegial dimension of leadership in the eucharistic community has suffered diminution. In others, the function of deacons has been reduced to an assistant role in the celebration of the liturgy: they have ceased to fulfill any function with regard to the diaconal witness of the Church. In general, the relation of the presbyterate to the episcopal ministry has been discussed throughout the centuries, and the degree of the presbyter's participation in the episcopal ministry is still for many an unresolved question of far-reaching ecumenical importance. In some cases, churches which have not formally kept the threefold form have, in fact, maintained certain of its original patterns.

25. The traditional threefold pattern thus raises questions for all the churches. Churches maintaining the threefold pattern will need to ask how

its potential can be fully developed for the most effective witness of the Church in this world. In this task churches not having the threefold pattern should also participate. They will further need to ask themselves whether the threefold pattern as developed does not have a powerful claim to be accepted by them.

B. Guiding Principles for the Exercise of the Ordained Ministry in the Church

26. Three considerations are important in this respect. The ordained ministry should be exercised in a personal, collegial and communal way. It should be *personal* because the presence of Christ among his people can most effectively be pointed to by the person ordained to proclaim the Gospel and to call the community to serve the Lord in unity of life and witness. It should also be *collegial,* for there is need for a college of ordained ministers sharing in the common task of representing the concerns of the community. Finally, the intimate relationship between the ordained ministry and the community should find expression in a *communal* dimension where the exercise of the ordained ministry is rooted in the life of the community and requires the community's effective participation in the discovery of God's will and the guidance of the Spirit.

27. The ordained ministry needs to be constitutionally or canonically ordered and exercised in the Church in such a way that each of these three dimensions can find adequate expression. At the level of the local eucharistic community there is need for an ordained minister acting within a collegial body. Strong emphasis should be placed on the active participation of all members in the life and the decision-making of the community. At the regional level there is again need for an ordained minister exercising a service of unity. The collegial and communal dimensions will find expression in regular representative synodal gatherings.

C. Functions of Bishops, Presbyters and Deacons

28. What can then be said about the functions and even the titles of bishops, presbyters and deacons? A uniform answer to this question is not required for the mutual recognition of the ordained ministry. The following considerations on functions are, however, offered in a tentative way.

29. *Bishops* preach the Word, preside at the sacraments, and administer discipline in such a way as to be representative pastoral ministers of oversight, continuity and unity in the Church. They have pastoral oversight of the area to which they are called. They serve the apostolicity and unity of the Church's teaching, worship and sacramental life. They have responsibility for leadership in the Church's mission. They relate the Christian community in their area to the wider Church, and the universal Church to their community. They, in communion with the presbyters and deacons and the

whole community, are responsible for the orderly transfer of ministerial authority in the Church.

30. *Presbyters* serve as pastoral ministers of Word and sacraments in a local eucharistic community. They are preachers and teachers of the faith, exercise pastoral care, and bear responsibility for the discipline of the congregation to the end that the world may believe and that the entire membership of the Church may be renewed, strengthened and equipped in ministry. Presbyters have particular responsibility for the preparation of members for Christian life and ministry.

31. *Deacons* represent to the Church its calling as servant in the world. By struggling in Christ's name with the myriad needs of societies and persons, deacons exemplify the interdependence of worship and service in the Church's life. They exercise responsibility in the worship of the congregation: for example by reading the scriptures, preaching and leading the people in prayer. They help in the teaching of the congregation. They exercise a ministry of love within the community. They fulfil certain administrative tasks and may be elected to responsibilities for governance.

D. VARIETY OF CHARISMS

32. The community which lives in the power of the Spirit will be characterized by a variety of charisms. The Spirit is the giver of diverse gifts which enrich the life of the community. In order to enhance their effectiveness, the community will recognize publicly certain of these charisms. While some serve permanent needs in the life of the community, others will be temporary. Men and women in the communities of religious orders fulfil a service which is of particular importance for the life of the Church. The ordained ministry, which is itself a charism, must not become a hindrance for the variety of these charisms. On the contrary, it will help the community to discover the gifts bestowed on it by the Holy Spirit and will equip members of the body to serve in a variety of ways.

33. In the history of the Church there have been times when the truth of the Gospel could only be preserved through prophetic and charismatic leaders. Often new impulses could find their way into the life of the Church only in unusual ways. At times reforms required a special ministry. The ordained ministers and the whole community will need to be attentive to the challenge of such special ministries.

IV. SUCCESSION IN THE APOSTOLIC TRADITION

A. APOSTOLIC TRADITION IN THE CHURCH

34. In the Creed, the Church confesses itself to be apostolic. The Church lives in continuity with the apostles and their proclamation. The same Lord who sent the apostles continues to be present in the Church. The Spirit

keeps the Church in the apostolic tradition until the fulfilment of history in the Kingdom of God. Apostolic tradition in the Church means continuity in the permanent characteristics of the Church of the apostles: witness to the apostolic faith, proclamation and fresh interpretation of the Gospel, celebration of baptism and the eucharist, the transmission of ministerial responsibilities, communion in prayer, love, joy and suffering, service to the sick and the needy, unity among the local churches and sharing the gifts which the Lord has given to each.

B. SUCCESSION OF THE APOSTOLIC MINISTRY

35. The primary manifestation of apostolic succession is to be found in the apostolic tradition of the Church as a whole. The succession is an expression of the permanence and, therefore, of the continuity of Christ's own mission in which the Church participates. Within the Church the ordained ministry has a particular task of preserving and actualizing the apostolic faith. The orderly transmission of the ordained ministry is therefore a powerful expression of the continuity of the Church throughout history; it also underlines the calling of the ordained minister as guardian of the faith. Where churches see little importance in orderly transmission, they should ask themselves whether they have not to change their conception of continuity in the apostolic tradition. On the other hand, where the ordained ministry does not adequately serve the proclamation of the apostolic faith, churches must ask themselves whether their ministerial structures are not in need of reform.

36. Under the particular historical circumstances of the growing Church in the early centuries, the succession of bishops became one of the ways, together with the transmission of the Gospel and the life of the community, in which the apostolic tradition of the Church was expressed. This succession was understood as serving, symbolizing and guarding the continuity of the apostolic faith and communion.

37. In churches which practise the succession through the episcopate, it is increasingly recognized that a continuity in apostolic faith, worship and mission has been preserved in churches which have not retained the form of historic episcopate. This recognition finds additional support in the fact that the reality and function of the episcopal ministry have been preserved in many of these churches, with or without the title "bishop". Ordination, for example, is always done in them by persons in whom the Church recognizes the authority to transmit the ministerial commission.

38. These considerations do not diminish the importance of the episcopal ministry. On the contrary, they enable churches which have not retained the episcopate to appreciate the episcopal succession as a sign, though not a guarantee, of the continuity and unity of the Church. Today churches, including those engaged in union negotiations, are expressing willingness to accept episcopal succession as a sign of the apostolicity of the life of the

whole Church. Yet, at the same time, they cannot accept any suggestion that the ministry exercised in their own tradition should be invalid until the moment that it enters into an existing line of episcopal succession. Their acceptance of the episcopal succession will best further the unity of the whole Church if it is part of a wider process by which the episcopal churches themselves also regain their lost unity.

V. ORDINATION

A. THE MEANING OF ORDINATION

39. The Church ordains certain of its members for the ministry in the name of Christ by the invocation of the Spirit and the laying on of hands (I Tim. 4:14; II Tim. 1:6); in so doing it seeks to continue the mission of the apostles and to remain faithful to their teaching. The act of ordination by those who are appointed for this ministry attests the bond of the Church with Jesus Christ and the apostolic witness, recalling that it is the risen Lord who is the true ordainer and bestows the gift. In ordaining, the Church, under the inspiration of the Holy Spirit, provides for the faithful proclamation of the Gospel and humble service in the name of Christ. The laying on of hands is the sign of the gift of the Spirit, rendering visible the fact that the ministry was instituted in the revelation accomplished in Christ, and reminding the Church to look to him as the source of its commission. This ordination, however, can have different intentions according to the specific tasks of bishops, presbyters and deacons as indicated in the liturgies of ordination.

40. Properly speaking, then, ordination denotes an action by God and the community by which the ordained are strengthened by the Spirit for their task and are upheld by the acknowledgment and prayers of the congregation.

B. THE ACT OF ORDINATION

41. A long and early Christian tradition places ordination in the context of worship and especially of the eucharist. Such a place for the service of ordination preserves the understanding of ordination as an act of the whole community, and not of a certain order within it or of the individual ordained. The act of ordination by the laying on of hands of those appointed to do so is at one and the same time invocation of the Holy Spirit (*epiklesis*); sacramental sign; acknowledgment of gifts and commitment.

42. (a) Ordination is an invocation to God that the new minister be given the power of the Holy Spirit in the new relation which is established between this minister and the local Christian community and, by intention, the Church universal. The otherness of God's initiative, of which the ordained ministry is a sign, is here acknowledged in the act of ordination itself. "The Spirit blows where it wills" (John 3:3): the invocation of the

Spirit implies the absolute dependence on God for the outcome of the Church's prayer. This means that the Spirit may set new forces in motion and open new possibilities "far more abundantly than all that we ask or think" (Eph. 3:20).

43. (b) Ordination is a sign of the granting of this prayer by the Lord who gives the gift of the ordained ministry. Although the outcome of the Church's *epiklesis* depends on the freedom of God, the Church ordains in confidence that God, being faithful to his promise in Christ, enters sacramentally into contingent, historical forms of human relationship and uses them for his purpose. Ordination is a sign performed in faith that the spiritual relationship signified is present in, with and through the words spoken, the gestures made and the forms employed.

44. (c) Ordination is an acknowledgment by the Church of the gifts of the Spirit in the one ordained, and a commitment by both the Church and the ordinand to the new relationship. By receiving the new minister in the act of ordination, the congregation acknowledges the minister's gifts and commits itself to be open towards these gifts. Likewise those ordained offer their gifts to the Church and commit themselves to the burden and opportunity of new authority and responsibility. At the same time, they enter into a collegial relationship with other ordained ministers.

C. The Conditions for Ordination

45. People are called in differing ways to the ordained ministry. There is a personal awareness of a call from the Lord to dedicate oneself to the ordained ministry. This call may be discerned through personal prayer and reflection, as well as through suggestion, example, encouragement, guidance coming from family, friends, the congregation, teachers, and other church authorities. This call must be authenticated by the Church's recognition of the gifts and graces of the particular person, both natural and spiritually given, needed for the ministry to be performed. God can use people both celibate and married for the ordained ministry.

46. Ordained persons may be professional ministers in the sense that they receive their salaries from the church. The church may also ordain people who remain in other occupations or employment.

47. Candidates for the ordained ministry need appropriate preparation through study of scripture and theology, prayer and spirituality, and through acquaintance with the social and human realities of the contemporary world. In some situations, this preparation may take a form other than that of prolonged academic study. The period of training will be one in which the candidate's call is tested, fostered and confirmed, or its understanding modified.

48. Initial commitment to ordained ministry ought normally to be made without reserve or time limit. Yet leave of absence from service is not

incompatible with ordination. Resumption of ordained ministry requires the assent of the Church, but no re-ordination. In recognition of the God-given charism of ministry, ordination to any one of the particular ordained ministries is never repeated.

49. The discipline with regard to the conditions for ordination in one church need not be seen as universally applicable and used as grounds for not recognizing ministry in others.

50. Churches which refuse to consider candidates for the ordained ministry on the ground of handicap or because they belong, for example, to one particular race or sociological group should re-evaluate their practices. This re-evaluation is particularly important today in view of the multitude of experiments in new forms of ministry with which the churches are approaching the modern world.

VI. TOWARDS THE MUTUAL RECOGNITION OF THE ORDAINED MINISTRIES

51. In order to advance towards the mutual recognition of ministries, deliberate efforts are required. All churches need to examine the forms of ordained ministry and the degree to which the churches are faithful to its original intentions. Churches must be prepared to renew their understanding and their practice of the ordained ministry.

52. Among the issues that need to be worked on as churches move towards mutual recognition of ministries, that of apostolic succession is of particular importance. Churches in ecumenical conversations can recognize their respective ordained ministries if they are mutually assured of their intention to transmit the ministry of Word and sacrament in continuity with apostolic times. The act of transmission should be performed in accordance with the apostolic tradition, which includes the invocation of the Spirit and the laying on of hands.

53. In order to achieve mutual recognition, different steps are required of different churches. For example:

a) Churches which have preserved the episcopal succession are asked to recognize both the apostolic content of the ordained ministry which exists in churches which have not maintained such succession and also the existence in these churches of a ministry of *episkopé* in various forms.

b) Churches without the episcopal succession, and living in faithful continuity with the apostolic faith and mission, have a ministry of Word and sacrament, as is evident from the belief, practice, and life of those churches. These churches are asked to realize that the continuity with the Church of the apostles finds profound expression in the successive laying on of hands by bishops and that, though they may not lack the continuity of the apostolic tradition, this sign will strengthen and deepen that continuity. They may need to recover the sign of the episcopal succession.

54. Some churches ordain both men and women, others ordain only men. Differences on this issue raise obstacles to the mutual recognition of ministries. But those obstacles must not be regarded as substantive hindrance for further efforts towards mutual recognition. Openness to each other holds the possibility that the Spirit may well speak to one church through the insights of another. Ecumenical consideration, therefore, should encourage, not restrain, the facing of this question.

55. The mutual recognition of churches and their ministries implies decision by the appropriate authorities and a liturgical act from which point unity would be publicly manifest. Several forms of such public act have been proposed: mutual laying on of hands, eucharistic concelebration, solemn worship without a particular rite of recognition, the reading of a text of union during the course of a celebration. No one liturgical form would be absolutely required, but in any case it would be necessary to proclaim the accomplishment of mutual recognition publicly. The common celebration of the eucharist would certainly be the place for such an act.

Commentaries

Numbers of the commentaries refer to paragraph numbers of the documents.

Baptism

6. The inability of the churches mutually to recognize their various practices of baptism as sharing in the one baptism, and their actual dividedness in spite of mutual baptismal recognition, have given dramatic visibility to the broken witness of the Church. The readiness of the churches in some places and times to allow differences of sex, race, or social status to divide the body of Christ has further called into question genuine baptismal unity of the Christian community (Gal. 3:27–28) and has seriously compromised its witness. The need to recover baptismal unity is at the heart of the ecumenical task as it is central for the realization of genuine partnership within the Christian communities.

12. When the expressions "infant baptism" and "believers' baptism" are used, it is necessary to keep in mind that the real distinction is between those who baptize people at any age and those who baptize only those able to make a confession of faith for themselves. The differences between infant and believers' baptism become less sharp when it is recognized that

both forms of baptism embody God's own initiative in Christ and express a response of faith made within the believing community.

The practice of infant baptism emphasizes the corporate faith and the faith which the child shares with its parents. The infant is born into a broken world and shares in its brokenness. Through baptism, the promise and claim of the Gospel are laid upon the child. The personal faith of the recipient of baptism and faithful participation in the life of the Church are essential for the full fruit of baptism.

The practice of believers' baptism emphasizes the explicit confession of the person who responds to the grace of God in and through the community of faith and who seeks baptism.

Both forms of baptism require a similar and responsible attitude towards Christian nurture. A rediscovery of the continuing character of Christian nurture may facilitate the mutual acceptance of different initiation practices.

In some churches which unite both infant-baptist and believer-baptist traditions, it has been possible to regard as equivalent alternatives for entry into the Church both a pattern whereby baptism in infancy is followed by later profession of faith and a pattern whereby believers' baptism follows upon a presentation and blessing in infancy. This example invites other churches to decide whether they, too, could not recognize equivalent alternatives in their reciprocal relationships and in church union negotiations.

13. Churches which have insisted on a particular form of baptism or which have had serious questions about the authenticity of other churches' sacraments and ministries have at times required persons coming from other church traditions to be baptized before being received into full communicant membership. As the churches come to fuller mutual understanding and acceptance of one another and enter into closer relationships in witness and service, they will want to refrain from any practice which might call into question the sacramental integrity of other churches or which might diminish the unrepeatability of the sacrament of baptism.

14. (a) Within some traditions it is explained that as baptism conforms us to Christ crucified, buried and risen, so through chrismation Christians receive the gift of the pentecostal Spirit from the anointed Son.

(b) If baptism, as incorporation into the body of Christ, points by its very nature to the eucharistic sharing of Christ's body and blood, the question arises as to how a further and separate rite can be interposed between baptism and admission to communion. Those churches which baptize children but refuse them a share in the eucharist before such a rite may wish to ponder whether they have fully appreciated and accepted the consequences of baptism.

(c) Baptism needs to be constantly reaffirmed. The most obvious form of such reaffirmation is the celebration of the eucharist. The renewal of baptismal vows may also take place during such occasions as the annual celebration of the paschal mystery or during the baptism of others.

18. As seen in some theological traditions, the use of water, with all its positive associations with life and blessing, signifies the continuity between the old and the new creation, thus revealing the significance of baptism not only for human beings but also for the whole cosmos. At the same time, the use of water represents a purification of creation, a dying to that which is negative and destructive in the world: those who are baptized into the body of Christ are made partakers of a renewed existence.

21. Recent discussion indicates that more attention should be given to misunderstandings encouraged by the socio-cultural context in which baptism takes place.

(a) In some parts of the world, the giving of a name in the baptismal liturgy has led to confusion between baptism and customs surrounding name-giving. This confusion is especially harmful if, in cultures predominantly not Christian, the baptized are required to assume Christian names not rooted in their cultural tradition. In making regulations for baptism, churches should be careful to keep the emphasis on the true Christian significance of baptism and to avoid unnecessarily alienating the baptized from their local culture through the imposition of foreign names. A name which is inherited from one's original culture roots the baptized in that culture, and at the same time manifests the universality of baptism, incorporation into the one Church, holy, catholic and apostolic, which stretches over all the nations of the earth.

(b) In many large European and North American majority churches infant baptism is often practised in an apparently indiscriminate way. This contributes to the reluctance of churches which practise believers' baptism to acknowledge the validity of infant baptism; this fact should lead to more critical reflection on the meaning of baptism within those majority churches themselves.

(c) Some African churches practise baptism of the Holy Spirit without water, through the laying on of hands, while recognizing other churches' baptism. A study is required concerning this practice and its relation to baptism with water.

Eucharist

8. It is in the light of the significance of the eucharist as intercession that references to the eucharist in Catholic theology as "propitiatory sacrifice" may be understood. The understanding is that there is only one expiation, that of the unique sacrifice of the cross, made actual in the eucharist and presented before the Father in the intercession of Christ and of the Church for all humanity.

In the light of the biblical conception of memorial, all churches might want to review the old controversies about "sacrifice" and deepen their understanding of the reasons why other traditions than their own have either used or rejected this term.

13. Many churches believe that by the words of Jesus and by the power of the Holy Spirit, the bread and wine of the eucharist become, in a real though mysterious manner, the body and blood of the risen Christ, i.e., of the living Christ present in all his fullness. Under the signs of bread and wine, the deepest reality is the total being of Christ who comes to us in order to feed us and transform our entire being. Some other churches, while affirming a real presence of Christ at the eucharist, do not link that presence so definitely with the signs of bread and wine. The decision remains for the churches whether this difference can be accommodated within the convergence formulated in the text itself.

14. This is not to spiritualize the eucharistic presence of Christ but to affirm the indissoluble union between the Son and the Spirit. This union makes it clear that the eucharist is not a magical or mechanical action but a prayer addressed to the Father, one which emphasizes the Church's utter dependence. There is an intrinsic relationship between the words of institution, Christ's promise, and the *epiklesis,* the invocation of the Spirit, in the Liturgy. The *epiklesis* in relation to the words of institution is located differently in various liturgical traditions. In the early liturgies the whole "prayer action" was thought of as bringing about the reality promised by Christ. The invocation of the Spirit was made both on the community and on the elements of bread and wine. Recovery of such an understanding may help us overcome our difficulties concerning a special moment of consecration.

15. In the history of the Church there have been various attempts to understand the mystery of the real and unique presence of Christ in the eucharist. Some are content merely to affirm this presence without seeking to explain it. Others consider it necessary to assert a change wrought by the Holy Spirit and Christ's words, in consequence of which there is no longer just ordinary bread and wine but the body and blood of Christ. Others again have developed an explanation of the real presence which, though not claiming to exhaust the significance of the mystery, seeks to protect it from damaging interpretations.

19. Since the earliest days, baptism has been understood as the sacrament by which believers are incorporated into the body of Christ and are endowed with the Holy Spirit. As long as the right of the baptized believers and their ministers to participate in and preside over eucharistic celebration in one church is called into question by those who preside over and are members of other eucharistic congregations, the catholicity of the eucharist is less manifest. There is discussion in many churches today about the inclusion of baptized children as communicants at the Lord's Supper.

28. Since New Testament days, the Church has attached the greatest importance to the continued use of the elements of bread and wine which Jesus used at the Last Supper. In certain parts of the world, where bread and wine are not customary or obtainable, it is now sometimes held that local food and drink serve better to anchor the eucharist in everyday life. Further study is required concerning the question of which features of the Lord's Supper were unchangeably instituted by Jesus, and which features remain within the Church's competence to decide.

Ministry

9. In the New Testament the term "apostle" is variously employed. It is used for the Twelve but also for a wider circle of disciples. It is applied to Paul and to others as they are sent out by the risen Christ to proclaim the Gospel. The roles of the apostles cover both foundation and mission.

11. The basic reality of an ordained ministry was present from the beginning (cf. para. 8). The actual forms of ordination and of the ordained ministry, however, have evolved in complex historical developments (cf. para. 19). The churches, therefore, need to avoid attributing their particular forms of the ordained ministry directly to the will and institution of Jesus Christ.

13. These tasks are not exercised by the ordained ministry in an exclusive way. Since the ordained ministry and the community are inextricably related, all members participate in fulfilling these functions. In fact, every charism serves to assemble and build up the body of Christ. Any member of the body may share in proclaiming and teaching the Word of God, may contribute to the sacramental life of that body. The ordained ministry fulfils these functions in a representative way, providing the focus for the unity of the life and witness of the community.

14. The New Testament says very little about the ordering of the eucharist. There is no explicit evidence about who presided at the eucharist. Very soon however it is clear that an ordained ministry presides over the celebration. If the ordained ministry is to provide a focus for the unity of the life and witness of the Church, it is appropriate that an ordained minister should be given this task. It is intimately related to the task of guiding the community, i.e. supervising its life (*episkopé*) and strengthening its vigilance in relation to the truth of the apostolic message and the coming of the Kingdom.

16. Here two dangers must be avoided. Authority cannot be exercised without regard for the community. The apostles paid heed to the experience and the judgment of the faithful. On the other hand, the authority of ordained ministers must not be so reduced as to make them dependent on the common opinion of the community. Their authority lies in their responsibility to express the will of God in the community.

17. The New Testament never uses the term "priesthood" or "priest" (*hiereus*) to designate the ordained ministry or the ordained minister. In the New Testament, the term is reserved, on the one hand, for the unique priesthood of Jesus Christ and, on the other hand, for the royal and prophetic priesthood of all baptized. The priesthood of Christ and the priesthood of the baptized have in their respective ways the function of sacrifice and intercession. As Christ has offered himself, Christians offer their whole being "as a living sacrifice". As Christ intercedes before the Father, Christians intercede for the Church and the salvation of the world. Nevertheless, the differences between these two kinds of priesthood cannot be overlooked. While Christ offered himself as a unique sacrifice once and for all for the salvation of the world, believers need to receive continually as a gift of God that which Christ has done for them.

In the early Church the terms "priesthood" and "priest" came to be used to designate the ordained ministry and minister as presiding at the eucharist. They underline the fact that the ordained ministry is related to the priestly reality of Jesus Christ and the whole community. When the terms are used in connection with the ordained ministry, their meaning differs in appropriate ways from the sacrificial priesthood of the Old Testament, from the unique redemptive priesthood of Christ and from the corporate priesthood of the people of God. St. Paul could call his ministry "a priestly service of the gospel of God, so that the offering of the Gentiles may be acceptable by the Holy Spirit" (Rom. 15:16).

18. Those churches which practise the ordination of women do so because of their understanding of the Gospel and of the ministry. It rests for them on the deeply held theological conviction that the ordained ministry of the Church lacks fullness when it is limited to one sex. This theological conviction has been reinforced by their experience during the years in which they have included women in their ordained ministries. They have found that women's gifts are as wide and varied as men's and that their ministry is as fully blessed by the Holy Spirit as the ministry of men. None has found reason to reconsider its decision.

Those churches which do not practise the ordination of women consider that the force of nineteen centuries of tradition against the ordination of women must not be set aside. They believe that such a tradition cannot be dismissed as a lack of respect for the participation of women in the Church. They believe that there are theological issues concerning the nature of humanity and concerning Christology which lie at the heart of their convictions and understanding of the role of women in the Church.

The discussion of these practical and theological questions within the various churches and Christian traditions should be complemented by joint study and reflection within the ecumenical fellowship of all churches.

21. The earliest Church knew both the travelling ministry of such missionaries as Paul and the local ministry of leadership in places where the Gospel was received. At local level, organizational patterns appear to have varied according to circumstances. The Acts of the Apostles mention for Jerusalem the Twelve and the Seven, and later James and the elders; and for Antioch, prophets and teachers (Acts 6:1–6; 15:13–22; 13:1). The letters to Corinth speak of apostles, prophets and teachers (1 Cor. 12:28); so too does the letter to the Romans, which also speaks of deacons or assistants (Rom. 16:1). In Philippi, the secular terms *episkopoi* and *diakonoi* were together used for Christian ministers (Phil. 1:1). Several of these ministries are ascribed to both women and men. While some were appointed by the laying on of hands, there is no indication of this procedure in other cases.

Whatever their names, the purpose of these ministries was to proclaim the Word of God, to transmit and safeguard the original content of the Gospel, to feed and strengthen the faith, discipline and service of the Christian communities, and to protect and foster unity within and among them. These have been the constant duties of ministry throughout the developments and crises of Christian history.

26. These three aspects need to be kept together. In various churches, one or another has been over-emphasized at the expense of the others. In some churches, the personal dimension of the ordained ministry tends to diminish the collegial and communal dimensions. In other churches, the collegial or communal dimension takes so much importance that the ordained ministry loses its personal dimension. Each church needs to ask itself in what way its exercise of the ordained ministry has suffered in the course of history.

An appreciation of these three dimensions lies behind a recommendation made by the first World Conference on Faith and Order at Lausanne in 1927: "In view of (i) the place which the episocpate, the council of presbyters and the congregation of the faithful, respectively, had in the constitution of the early Church, and (ii) the fact that episcopal, presbyteral and congregational systems of government are each today, and have been for centuries, accepted by great communions in Christendom, and (iii) the fact that episcopal, presbyteral and congregational systems are each believed by many to be essential to the good order of the Church, we therefore recognize that these several elements must all, under conditions which require further study, have an appropriate place in the order of life of a reunited Church . . . ."

31. In many churches there is today considerable uncertainty about the need, the rationale, the status and the functions of deacons. In what sense can the diaconate be considered part of the ordained ministry? What is it that distinguishes it from other ministries in the Church (catechists, musicians, etc.)? Why should deacons be ordained while these other ministries do not receive ordination? If they are ordained, do they receive ordination in the full sense of the word or is their ordination only the first step towards ordination as presbyters? Today, there is a strong tendency in many churches to restore the diaconate as an ordained ministry with its own dignity and meant to be exercised for life. As the churches move closer together there may be united in this office ministries now existing in a variety of forms and under a variety of names. Differences in ordering the diaconal ministry should not be regarded as a hindrance for the mutual recognition of the ordained ministries.

34. The apostles, as witnesses of the life and resurrection of Christ and sent by him, are the original transmitters of the Gospel, of the tradition of the saving words and acts of Jesus Christ which constitute the life of the Church. This apostolic tradition continues through history and links the Church to its origins in Christ and in the college of the apostles. Within this apostolic tradition is an apostolic succession of the ministry which serves the continuity of the Church in its life in Christ and its faithfulness to the words and acts of Jesus transmitted by the apostles. The ministers appointed by the apostles, and then the *episkopoi* of the churches, were the first guardians of this transmission of the apostolic tradition; they testified to the apostolic succession of the ministry which was continued through the bishops of the early Church in collegial communion with the presbyters and deacons within the Christian community. A distinction should be made, therefore, between the apostolic tradition of the whole Church and the succession of the apostolic ministry.

36. In the early Church the bond between the episcopate and the apostolic community was understood in two ways. Clement of Rome linked the mission of the bishop with the sending of Christ by the Father and the sending of the apostles by Christ (Cor. 42:44). This made the bishop a successor of the apostles, ensuring the permanence of the apostolic mission in the Church. Clement is primarily interested in the means whereby the *historical* continuity of Christ's presence is ensured in the Church thanks to the apostolic succession. For Ignatius of Antioch (Magn. 6:1, 3:1–2; Trall. 3:1), it is Christ surrounded by the Twelve who is permanently in the Church in the person of the bishop surrounded by the presbyters. Ignatius regards the Christian community assembled around the bishop in the midst of presbyters and deacons as the *actual* manifestation in the Spirit of the apostolic community. The sign of apostolic succession thus not only points to historical continuity; it also manifests an actual spiritual reality.

39. It is clear that churches have different practices of ordination, and that it would be wrong to single out one of those as exclusively valid. On the other hand, if churches are willing to recognize each other in the sign of apostolic succession, as described above, it would follow that the old tradition, according to which it is the bishop who ordains, with the participation of the community, will be recognized and respected as well.

40. The original New Testament terms for ordination tend to be simple and descriptive. The fact of appointment is recorded. The laying on of hands is described. Prayer is made for the Spirit. Different traditions have built different interpretations on the basis of these data.

It is evident that there is a certain difference between the unspoken cultural setting of the Greek *cheirotonein* and that of the Latin *ordo* or *ordinare.* The New Testament use of the former term borrows its basic secular meaning of "appointment" (Acts 14:23; II Cor. 8:19), which is, in turn, derived from the original meaning of extending the hand, either to designate a person or to cast a vote. Some scholars see in *cheirotonein* a reference to the act of laying on of hands, in view of the literal description of the action in such seemingly parallel instances as Acts 6:6, 8:17, 13:3, 19:6; I Tim, 4:14; II Tim. 1:6. *Ordo* and *ordinare,* on the other hand, are terms derived from Roman law where they convey the notion of the special status of a group distinct from the plebs, as in the term *ordo clarissimus* for the Roman senate. The starting point of any conceptual construction using these terms will strongly influence what is taken for granted in both the thought and action which result.

Index of Joint Statements

P—RC Pentecostal-Roman Catholic: Final Report 1976
R—RC Reformed-Roman Catholic: The Presence of Christ . . . 1977

---

*Paragraph numbers found in parenthesis in the text have been added for convenience in indexing this volume and are not part of the original text.

Index

$14.9

GROWTH IN AGREEMENT

The last fifteen years have witnessed significant progress in the theological consensus of the world's Christian communities. Although still separated along denominational lines existing since the Reformation, the principal Christian churches have engaged in ongoing discussions in an effort to understand and reconcile their differences.

This book is a collection of reports that have resulted from bilateral talks between churches on a world level. All of the talks have been official encounters by authorized representatives of the churches, and nearly all the dialogues focused on doctrinal matters. In the long run, however, this process has pointed beyond mere doctrinal consensus and toward the living fellowship of Christians.

All persons actively engaged in the Christian ecumenical dialogue or who are interested in its progress will find this a valuable resource book.

Harding Meyer, a prominent Lutheran theologian, has for many years been associated with the Institute for Ecumenical Research in Strasbourg, France. **Lukas Vischer** is the former director of the Department of Faith and Order of the World Council of Churches and is presently director of the Protestant Office for Ecumenism in Berne, Switzerland.

This book is being published jointly by Paulist Press and the World Council of Churches.

Paulist Press
0-8091-2497-1

and

World Council of Churches
2-8254-0679-1